VISIONS OF POLITICS

The second of three volumes of essays by Quentin Skinner, one of the world's leading intellectual historians. This collection includes some of his most important essays on the political thought of the Italian Renaissance, each of which has been carefully revised for publication in this form. All of Professor Skinner's work is characterised by philosophical power, limpid clarity and elegance of exposition. These essays, many of which are now recognised classics, provide a fascinating and convenient digest of the development of his thought.

QUENTIN SKINNER is Regius Professor of Modern History in the University of Cambridge and a Fellow of Christ's College. He has been the recipient of several honorary degrees, and is a Fellow of numerous academic bodies including the British Academy, the American Academy and the Academia Europea. His work has been translated into nineteen languages, and his many publications include *The Foundations of Modern Political Thought* (two volumes, Cambridge, 1978), *Machiavelli* (Oxford, 1981), *Reason and Rhetoric in the Philosophy of Hobbes* (Cambridge, 1996) and *Liberty before Liberalism* (Cambridge, 1998).

VISIONS OF POLITICS

Volume 2: Renaissance Virtues

QUENTIN SKINNER

Regius Professor of Modern History, University of Cambridge

CAMBRIDGE
UNIVERSITY PRESS

University Printing House, Cambridge CB2 8BS, United Kingdom

One Liberty Plaza, 20th Floor, New York, NY 10006, USA

477 Williamstown Road, Port Melbourne, VIC 3207, Australia

4843/24, 2nd Floor, Ansari Road, Daryaganj, Delhi - 110002, India

79 Anson Road, #06-04/06, Singapore 079906

Cambridge University Press is part of the University of Cambridge.

It furthers the University's mission by disseminating knowledge in the pursuit of education, learning and research at the highest international levels of excellence.

www.cambridge.org
Information on this title: www.cambridge.org/9780521589253

© in this collection Quentin Skinner 2002

This publication is in copyright. Subject to statutory exception and to the provisions of relevant collective licensing agreements, no reproduction of any part may take place without the written permission of Cambridge University Press.

First published 2002
7th printing 2015

A catalogue record for this publication is available from the British Library

ISBN 978-0-521-58106-6 Hardback
ISBN 978-0-521-58925-3 Paperback

Cambridge University Press has no responsibility for the persistence or accuracy of URLs for external or third-party internet websites referred to in this publication, and does not guarantee that any content on such websites is, or will remain, accurate or appropriate.

Contents

VOLUME 2
RENAISSANCE VIRTUES

List of plates	*page* vii
General preface	ix
Full contents: Volumes 1–3	xii
Acknowledgements	xiv
Conventions	xvii

1	Introduction: The reality of the Renaissance	1
2	The rediscovery of republican values	10
3	Ambrogio Lorenzetti and the portrayal of virtuous government	39
4	Ambrogio Lorenzetti on the power and glory of republics	93
5	Republican virtues in an age of princes	118
6	Machiavelli on *virtù* and the maintenance of liberty	160
7	The idea of negative liberty: Machiavellian and modern perspectives	186
8	Thomas More's *Utopia* and the virtue of true nobility	213
9	Humanism, scholasticism and popular sovereignty	245
10	Moral ambiguity and the Renaissance art of eloquence	264
11	John Milton and the politics of slavery	286
12	Classical liberty, Renaissance translation and the English civil war	308

| 13 | Augustan party politics and Renaissance constitutional thought | 344 |
| 14 | From the state of princes to the person of the state | 368 |

Bibliographies 414
Index 451

Plates

The plates are between pages 204 and 205

1 *The city and countryside under tyranny* (western wall)
2 *The rule of tyranny* (western wall)
3 *The rule of virtuous government* (northern wall)
4 *Justice and Concord* (detail of Plate 3)
5 *The effects of virtuous government in the city* (eastern wall)
6 *The effects of virtuous government in the countryside* (eastern wall)
7 *The effects of tyranny in the city* (western wall)
8 *Siena as Supreme Judge of the Sienese* (detail of Plate 3)
   (Plates 1–8: Ambrogio Lorenzetti, *Buon governo*, fresco cycle, Sala dei Nove, Palazzo Pubblico, Siena)
9 Giotto, *The Last Judgement,* fresco (western wall, Cappella degli Scrovegni, Padua)
10 *Dancers in the city* (detail of Plate 5)
11 Giotto, *Justice,* fresco (southern wall, Cappella degli Scrovegni, Padua)
12 Andrea di Bonaiuto, *Allegory of the Church,* fresco (Cappellone degli Spagnoli, Santa Maria Novella, Florence)

General preface

Several of the chapters in these volumes are appearing in print for the first time. But most of them have been published before (although generally in a very different form) either as articles in journals or as contributions to collective works. Revising them for republication, I have attempted to tread two slightly divergent paths at the same time. On the one hand, I have mostly allowed my original contentions and conclusions to stand without significant change. Where I no longer entirely endorse what I originally wrote, I usually indicate my dissent by adding an explanatory footnote rather than by altering the text. I have assumed that, if these essays are worth re-issuing, this can only be because they continue to be discussed in the scholarly literature. But if that is so, then one ought not to start moving the targets.

On the other hand, I have not hesitated to improve the presentation of my arguments wherever possible. I have corrected numerous mistranscriptions and factual mistakes. I have overhauled as well as standardised my system of references. I have inserted additional illustrations to strengthen and extend a number of specific points. I have updated my discussions of the secondary literature, removing allusions to yesterday's controversies and relating my conclusions to the latest research. I have tried to make use of the most up-to-date editions, with the result that in many cases I have changed the editions I previously used. I have replied to critics wherever this has seemed appropriate, sometimes qualifying and sometimes elaborating my earlier judgements. Finally, I have tinkered very extensively with my prose, particularly in the earliest essays republished here. I have toned down the noisy polemics I used to enjoy; simplified the long sentences, long paragraphs and stylistic curlicues I used to affect; taken greater pains to make use of gender-neutral language wherever possible; and above all tried to eliminate overlaps between chapters and repetitions within them.

I need to explain the basis on which I have selected the essays for inclusion in these volumes. I have chosen and grouped them – and in many cases supplied them with new titles – with two main goals in mind. One has been to give each volume its own thematic unity; the other has been to integrate the volumes in such a way as to form a larger whole.

The chapters in volume 1, *Regarding Method*, are all offered as contributions to the articulation and defence of one particular view about the reading and interpretation of historical texts. I argue that, if we are to write the history of ideas in a properly historical style, we need to situate the texts we study within such intellectual contexts and frameworks of discourse as enable us to recognise what their authors were *doing* in writing them. To speak more fashionably, I emphasise the performativity of texts and the need to treat them intertextually. My aspiration is not of course to perform the impossible task of getting inside the heads of long-dead thinkers; it is simply to use the ordinary techniques of historical enquiry to grasp their concepts, to follow their distinctions, to recover their beliefs and, so far as possible, to see things their way.

The other volumes are both concerned with leading themes in early-modern European political thought. In volume 2, *Renaissance Virtues*, I focus on the fortunes of republicanism as a theory of freedom and government. I follow the re-emergence and development from the thirteenth to the sixteenth century of a theory according to which the fostering of a virtuous and educated citizenry provides the key to upholding the liberty of states and individuals alike. My concluding volume, *Hobbes and Civil Science*, examines the evolution and character of Thomas Hobbes's political thought, concentrating in particular on his theory of the state. I consider his views about the power of sovereigns, about the duties and liberties of subjects and about the grounds and limits of political obedience. I attempt in turn to relate these issues to Hobbes's changing views about the nature of civil science and its place in his more general scheme of the sciences.

While stressing the unity of each volume, I am anxious at the same time to underline the interrelations between them. I have attempted in the first place to bring out a general connection between volumes 2 and 3. As we turn from Renaissance theories of civic virtue to Hobbes's civil science, we turn at the same time from the ideal of republican self-government to its greatest philosophical adversary. Although I am mainly concerned in volume 3 with the development of Hobbes's thought, much of what he has to say about freedom and political obligation can also be read as a critical commentary on the vision of politics outlined in volume 2. The linkage in which I am chiefly interested, however, is the one I seek to trace between the philosophical argument of volume 1 and the historical materials presented in volumes 2 and 3. To put the point as simply as possible, I see the relationship as one of theory and practice. In volume 1 I preach the virtues of a particular approach; in the rest of the book I try to practise what I preach.

As I intimate in my general title, *Visions of Politics*, my overarching historical interest lies in comparing two contrasting views we have inherited in the modern West about the nature of our common life. One speaks of sovereignty as a property of the people, the other sees it as the possession of the state. One gives centrality to the figure of the virtuous citizen, the other to the sovereign as representative of the state. One assigns priority to the duties of citizens, the other to their rights. It hardly needs stressing that the question of how to reconcile these divergent perspectives remains a central problem in contemporary political thought. My highest hope is that, by excavating the history of these rival theories, I may be able to contribute something of more than purely historical interest to these current debates.

Full Contents: Volumes 1–3

VOLUME 1: REGARDING METHOD

1	Introduction: Seeing things their way	*page* 1
2	The practice of history and the cult of the fact	8
3	Interpretation, rationality and truth	27
4	Meaning and understanding in the history of ideas	57
5	Motives, intentions and interpretation	90
6	Interpretation and the understanding of speech acts	103
7	'Social meaning' and the explanation of social action	128
8	Moral principles and social change	145
9	The idea of a cultural lexicon	158
10	Retrospect: Studying rhetoric and conceptual change	175

VOLUME 2: RENAISSANCE VIRTUES

1	Introduction: The reality of the Renaissance	1
2	The rediscovery of republican values	10
3	Ambrogio Lorenzetti and the portrayal of virtuous government	39
4	Ambrogio Lorenzetti on the power and glory of republics	93
5	Republican virtues in an age of princes	118
6	Machiavelli on *virtù* and the maintenance of liberty	160

7	The idea of negative liberty: Machiavellian and modern perspectives	186
8	Thomas More's *Utopia* and the virtue of true nobility	213
9	Humanism, scholasticism and popular sovereignty	245
10	Moral ambiguity and the Renaissance art of eloquence	264
11	John Milton and the politics of slavery	286
12	Classical liberty, Renaissance translation and the English civil war	308
13	Augustan party politics and Renaissance constitutional thought	344
14	From the state of princes to the person of the state	368

VOLUME 3: HOBBES AND CIVIL SCIENCE

1	Introduction: Hobbes's life in philosophy	1
2	Hobbes and the *studia humanitatis*	38
3	Hobbes's changing conception of a civil science	66
4	Hobbes on rhetoric and the construction of morality	87
5	Hobbes and the classical theory of laughter	142
6	Hobbes and the purely artificial person of the state	177
7	Hobbes on the proper signification of liberty	209
8	History and ideology in the English revolution	238
9	The context of Hobbes's theory of political obligation	264
10	Conquest and consent: Hobbes and the engagement controversy	287
11	Hobbes and his disciples in France and England	308
12	Hobbes and the politics of the early Royal Society	324

Acknowledgements

I remain deeply obliged to the large number of colleagues who supplied me with detailed comments on the original versions of the chapters in these volumes, and I am very glad of the chance to renew my thanks to them here. This is also the moment to single out a number of friends who have given me especially unstinting support and encouragement in my work over the years. I list them with the deepest gratitude: John Dunn, Clifford Geertz, Raymond Geuss, Fred Inglis, Susan James, John Pocock, John Thompson, Jim Tully. My debt to them can only be described – in the words of Roget's indispensable *Thesaurus* – as immense, enormous, vast, stonking and mega.

I also owe my warmest thanks to those friends who have helped to give the individual volumes in this book their present shape. For advice about the argument in volume 1 I am particularly grateful to Jonathan Lear, Kari Palonen, Richard Rorty and the late Martin Hollis. For numerous discussions about the themes of volume 2 I am similarly indebted to Philip Pettit and Maurizio Viroli. As will be evident from my argument there, I also learned a great deal from chairing the European Science Foundation workshop 'Republicanism: A Shared European Heritage'. Special thanks to Martin van Gelderen and Iain Hampsher-Monk for many instructive and enjoyable conversations, and for helping to make our meetings such a success.[1] For advice about volume 3 I owe an overwhelming debt to Kinch Hoekstra, Noel Malcolm and Karl Schuhmann, all of whom have shown a heartwarming readiness to place at my disposal their astounding knowledge of early-modern philosophy. A number of my recent PhD students have likewise helped me by commenting on individual chapters or on my project as a whole. My thanks to David Armitage, Geoffrey Baldwin, Annabel Brett, Hannah Dawson, Angus

---

[1] The papers read and discussed at our meetings have now been published in two volumes: Martin van Gelderen and Quentin Skinner (eds.), *Republicanism: A Shared European Heritage* (Cambridge University Press, 2002).

Gowland, Eric Nelson, Jürgen Overhoff, Jonathan Parkin and Richard Serjeantson.

As well as receiving so much assistance from individual scholars, I owe at least as great an obligation to the institutions that have sustained me throughout the long period in which I have been working on the materials presented here. The Faculty of History in the University of Cambridge has provided me with an ideal working environment throughout my academic career, and I have benefited immeasurably from my association with Christ's College and Gonville and Caius College. I never cease to learn from my colleagues and from the many brilliant students who pass through the Faculty, and I owe a particular debt to the University for its exceptionally generous policy about sabbatical leave. This is the first piece of work I have completed while holding my current post as a Leverhulme Major Research Fellow. I hope that other publications will follow, but in the meantime I already owe the Leverhulme Trust my warmest thanks for its support.

I need to reserve a special word of appreciation for the owners and custodians of the paintings and manuscripts I have examined. I am indebted to the Marquis of Lansdowne for permission to consult the Petty Papers at Bowood, and to the Duke of Devonshire and the Trustees of the Chatsworth settlement for allowing me to make extensive use of the Hardwick and Hobbes manuscripts at Chatsworth. I am similarly grateful for the courtesy and expertise I have encountered in the manuscript reading rooms of the Bibliothèque Nationale, the British Library, the Cambridge University Library, the Bodleian Library and the Library of St John's College Oxford. I am likewise grateful for the friendly helpfulness of the custodians of the Cappella degli Scrovegni in Padua and the Palazzo Pubblico in Siena.

For permission to reproduce photographs my thanks are due to Alinari (Florence), the Warburg Institute (University of London) and Dost Kitavebi (Ankara). For permission to make use of material that originally appeared in their pages I am grateful to the following journals and publishers: Blackwells and Co., The British Academy, *Comparative Studies in Society and History*, *Essays in Criticism*, Europa Publications, *The Finnish Yearbook of Political Thought*, *The Historical Journal*, *History and Theory*, *History of Political Thought*, *The Journal of Political Philosophy*, *The Journal of the Warburg and Courtauld Institutes*, Macmillan and Co., *New Literary History*, *Politics*, *Prose Studies*, The Royal Historical Society, Stanford University Press and The University of Pennsylvania Press.

I have benefited from an extraordinary amount of patient and resourceful assistance in the final stages of preparing these volumes for the Press. Richard Thompson amended the quotations in several articles in which I had originally modernised the spelling of early-modern texts. Alice Bell devoted an entire summer to checking transcriptions and references with wonderful meticulousness. Anne Dunbar-Nobes undertook the enormous labour of assembling the bibliographies, rewriting them in author-date style, reformatting all the footnotes and checking them against the bibliographies to ensure an exact match.

While these volumes have been going through the Press I have received a great deal more in the way of technical help. Anne Dunbar-Nobes agreed to serve as copy-editor of the book, and saw it into production with superb professionalism as well as much good cheer. Philip Riley, who has for many years acted as proofreader of my work, generously agreed to perform that task yet again, and duly brought to bear his matchless skills, patience and imperturbability.

I cannot speak with sufficient admiration of my friends at Cambridge University Press. One of my greatest pieces of professional good fortune has been that, throughout my academic career, Jeremy Mynott has watched over the publication of my books with infallible editorial judgement. Richard Fisher has likewise been a pillar of support over the years, and has edited the present work with characteristic enthusiasm, imagination and unfaltering efficiency. My heartfelt thanks to them both, and to their very able assistants, for so much goodwill and expertise.

I cannot end without acknowledging that, if it were not for Susan James and our children Olivia and Marcus, I could not hope to manage at all.

The reprinting of these volumes has provided me with a welcome opportunity to weed out some small inaccuracies. I am very grateful to Richard Westerman for helping me to recheck the text.

Conventions

Abbreviations. The following abbreviations are used in the footnotes:
BL: British Library
BN: Bibliothèque Nationale
DNB: Dictionary of National Biography
OED: Oxford English Dictionary

Bibliographies. These are simply checklists of the primary sources I have actually quoted and the secondary authorities on which I have relied. They make no pretence of being systematic guides to the ever-burgeoning literature on the themes I discuss. In the bibliographies of printed primary sources I list anonymous works by title. Where a work was published anonymously but its author's name is known, I place the name in square brackets. In the case of anonymous works where the attribution remains in doubt, I add a bracketed question-mark after the conjectured name. The bibliographies of secondary sources give all references to journal numbers in arabic form.

Classical names and titles. I refer to ancient Greek and Roman writers in their most familiar single-name form, both in the text and in the bibliographies. Greek titles have been transliterated, but all other titles are given in their original language.

Dates. Although I follow my sources in dating by the Christian era (CE and BCE), I have had to make some decisions about the different systems of dating prevalent in the early-modern period. The Julian Calendar ('Old Style') remained in use in Britain, whereas the Gregorian ('New Style') – ten days ahead of the Julian – was employed in continental Europe from 1582. When quoting from sources written or published on the Continent I use the Gregorian style, but when quoting from

British sources I prefer the Julian. For example, I give Hobbes's date of birth as 5 April rather than 15 April 1588, even though the latter date is technically correct from our point of view, given that the Gregorian calendar was adopted in Britain in the eighteenth century. A further peculiarity of early-modern British dating is that the year was generally taken to start on 25 March. I have preferred to follow the continental practice of treating the year as beginning on 1 January. For example, I treat Hobbes's translation of Thucydides – entered in the Stationers' register with a date of 18 March 1628 – as entered in 1629.

Gender. Sometimes it is clear that, when the writers I am discussing say 'he', they do *not* mean 'he or she', and in such cases I have of course followed their usage rather than tampered with their sense. But in general I have tried to maintain gender-neutral language as far as possible. To this end, I have taken full advantage of the fact that, in the British version of the English language, it is permissible for pronouns and possessives after *each, every, anyone*, etc. to take a plural and hence a gender-neutral form (as in 'to each their need, from each their power').

References. Although I basically follow the author-date system, I have made two modifications to it. One has been rendered necessary by the fact that I quote from a number of primary sources (for example, collections of Parliamentary debates) that are unattributable to any one author. As with anonymous works, I refer to these texts by their titles rather than the names of their modern editors and list them in the bibliographies of primary sources. My other modification is that, in passages where I continuously quote from one particular work, I give references so far as possible in the body of the text rather than in footnotes. Except when citing from classical sources, I generally give references in arabic numerals to chapters from individual texts and to parts of multi-volume works.

Transcriptions. My rule has been to preserve original spelling, capitalisation, italicisation and punctuation so far as possible. However, I normalise the long 's', remove diphthongs, expand contractions, correct obvious typographical errors and change 'u' to 'v' and 'i' to 'j' in accordance with modern orthography. When quoting in Latin I use 'v' as well as 'u', change 'j' to 'i', expand contractions and omit diacritical marks. Sometimes I change a lower-case initial letter to an upper, or vice versa, when fitting quotations around my own prose.

Translations. When quoting from classical sources, and from early-modern sources in languages other than English, all translations are my own except where specifically noted. I make extensive use of the editions published in the Loeb Classical Library, all of which contain facing-page versions in English. But because these renderings are often very free I have preferred to make my own translations even in these instances. I must stress, however, that I remain grateful for the availability of these editions, and have generally been guided by them in making my own translations, even to the extent of adopting turns of phrase.

I

Introduction: The reality of the Renaissance

As the title of this volume intimates, I see considerable virtue in continuing to speak about the era of the Renaissance. This commitment needs defending, however, since the concept of the Renaissance has in recent times fallen into disrepute, and a number of reasons have been given for avoiding it. One is simply that the term is too vague to be of much use. A second doubt has stemmed from the post-modern critique of meta-narratives and the teleological forms of historical writing to which they give rise. But the most widespread suspicion has arisen from the fact that the metaphor embodied in speaking of the Renaissance – the metaphor of revival and more specifically of rebirth – is so clearly an honorific one. The difficulty here is that, as soon as we reflect on the contours of early-modern European history, it becomes embarrassingly obvious that a majority of the population would have been surprised to learn about a rebirth or a recovery of anything that added any value to their lives. The most prevalent objection to employing the term is thus that it marginalises and devalues those for whom the Renaissance never happened.[1]

These are serious objections, but there is no escaping the fact that, in the period covered by the chapters that follow, there was *something* that, for *some* people, was undoubtedly reborn and restored. This is by no means to imply that we can point to a determinate moment at which (to invoke the other traditional metaphor) the dark ages ended and a new light began to dawn. There remains a marked tendency among intellectual historians to think in these terms, and to speak of 'a decisive break' and a 'rapid transformation' of Italian cultural life around the year 1400, after which we can see that 'the threshold between the Medieval and the Renaissance has been crossed'.[2] As I argue in chapter 2, however,

[1] As Kelly 1999 classically argues, this category included most women. Cf. my discussion in chapter 5, section II below.
[2] Baron 1966, pp. 8, 449; Pocock 1975, p. 52.

no such moment of sudden transition can be observed in the history of moral or political thought. If there was a rebirth, it was a protracted and difficult one.

If we are looking for origins, we probably need to direct our gaze as far back as the twelfth century, the period in which the Italian universities emerged as centres for the teaching of Roman law. As a preliminary to studying Justinian's *Codex*, students were introduced to the *Ars rhetorica*, and thus to the idea that successful forensic oratory will often depend at least as much on persuasive delivery as on legal proof. Towards the end of the thirteenth century, the teaching of rhetoric began to be approached in a new way, evidently under the influence of the methods of instruction prevailing in the French cathedral schools. No longer were the manuals of ancient rhetoric examined simply as sources of practical rules; they were also used as guides to the acquisition of a better Latin style. Out of this renewed interest in the language of ancient Rome arose the first glimmerings of the humanist movement.[3] A growing number of *literati* – most of them originally trained as lawyers – began not merely to study the classics but to reacquaint themselves with the full range of the *studia humanitatis*.[4] There was a humanist circle at Arezzo in the early fourteenth century, and a further group centring on the poet and historian Albertino Mussato at Padua shortly afterwards. These were among the earliest writers to reimmerse themselves in Roman poetry, especially Horace and Virgil; in the Roman historians, especially Livy and Sallust; and in the writings of such moralists as Juvenal, Seneca and, above all, Cicero, whom they turned into the best-known and most widely cited author of classical antiquity.

Once the language and literature of ancient Rome became the objects of so much fascination, the humanists began to busy themselves about the recovery of ancient manuscripts, the editing of texts, the establishment of attributions and so forth. But some of them – above all Petrarch and his disciples – continued to pursue the broader ambition of reviving the Roman syllabus of the *studia humanitatis*, thereby giving wider currency to the study of ancient rhetoric, poetry, history and moral philosophy. This was the rebirth of which the humanists of the *quattrocento* liked to speak. Leonardo Bruni, in the *Dialogus* he addressed to Pier Paolo Vergerio in 1401, singles out Petrarch as 'the man who restored the *studia humanitatis* at a time when they had become extinct'.[5] A generation later,

---

[3] On the early humanists as teachers of the rhetorical arts see Kristeller 1962.
[4] For the Paduan background see Billanovich 1981 and Siraisi 1973, pp. 43–58.
[5] Bruni 1952, p. 94: 'hic vir studia humanitatis, quae iam extincta erant, reparavit'.

we find Lorenzo Valla proclaiming in the Preface to his *Elegantiarum Latinae Linguae* that 'whereas good letters had almost died out, they are now revived and reborn in our own time'.[6]

I have little to say in the chapters that follow about the revival of classical poetry, since my principal focus of attention is on the rebirth and development of the other three elements in the *studia humanitatis*: rhetoric, history and moral philosophy. I turn to the place of classical rhetoric in Renaissance moral theory in the course of chapter 10, but I am concerned in several earlier chapters with the pivotal place occupied by the *Ars rhetorica* in the evolution of humanist political thought. As I show in chapter 2, the *dictatores* or teachers of rhetoric in the Italian law-schools were at the same time the originators of a genre of advice-books for the guidance of city magistrates, a genre that had a remarkably enduring impact on Renaissance thought. I trace the emergence of this pre-humanist literature in chapter 2, while in the first half of chapter 3 I examine in greater detail its leading themes. By the early decades of the fourteenth century we already find the *dictatores* engaged in polemics against the rival scholastic tradition of political philosophy. Coluccio Salutati was to summarise the quarrel at the end of the century when he declared that, whereas the dialectical methods of the schoolmen merely 'prove in order to teach', the humanists recognise the need for a moral theory with the power 'to persuade in order to guide'.[7] One of the distinguishing features of humanism came to be the belief that wisdom must never be disjoined from eloquence. We must always seek to teach and persuade at the same time.[8]

I am also much concerned with the role of history in Renaissance political theory, and thus with the next major element in the *studia humanitatis*. As early as the mid-thirteenth century, we already find the *dictatores* espousing a Ciceronian view of history as the light of truth and the best guide to acting prudently in public life. They particularly liked to draw their lessons from the histories of Sallust, their favourite authority on the rise and fall of republican regimes. As we shall see when we come to John Milton's political writings in chapter 11, Sallust retained his popularity throughout the Renaissance, and remains the ancient historian whom Milton quotes most frequently. Meanwhile the Italian humanists devoted themselves from an early stage to writing the history of their

---

[6] Valla 1543, *Praefatio*, p. 4: 'ac pene cum literis ipsis demortuae fuerint, aut hoc tempore excitentur ac reviviscant'.
[7] Emerton 1925, p. 358.
[8] For two classic discussions of this point see Gray 1963 and Seigel 1968.

own times in an increasingly classical style. We already find Albertino Mussato in his *De Gestis Italicorum* meditating in the style of Sallust on the fall of the Paduan commune, while the vicissitudes of the Florentine republic later gave rise to a sequence of remarkable histories from the pens of Leonardo Bruni, Poggio Bracciolini and, last and most influentially, Niccolò Machiavelli in his *Istorie Fiorentine* of the 1520s.

Of all the elements in the *studia humanitatis*, however, the one on which I principally concentrate is the final and culminating element, the study of ancient moral and political philosophy. With the investigation of this theme, we reach the point at which it becomes not merely convenient but inescapable to speak of the distinctive contribution of Renaissance humanism to the history of moral and political thought.

The context out of which the political theory of the humanists initially arose was that of the city-republics of the *Regnum Italicum*.[9] These communities began to evolve their distinctive political systems as early as the closing decades of the eleventh century. It was then that a number of Italian cities took it upon themselves, in defiance of papal as well as imperial suzerainty, to appoint their own 'consuls' and invest them with supreme authority. This happened at Pisa in 1085 (the earliest recorded instance), at Milan, Genoa and Arezzo before 1100, and at Bologna, Padua, Florence, Siena and elsewhere by the 1140s.[10] During the second half of the twelfth century a further important development took place. The consular system was gradually replaced by a form of government centred on ruling councils chaired by officials known as *podestà*, so called because they were granted supreme power or *potestas* in executive as well as judicial affairs. Such a system was in place at Parma and Padua by the 1170s, at Milan and Piacenza by the 1180s, and at Florence, Pisa, Siena and Arezzo by the end of the century.[11] By the opening years of the thirteenth century, many of the richest communes of Lombardy and Tuscany had thus acquired the *de facto* status of independent republics, with written constitutions guaranteeing their elective and self-governing arrangements.

Soon afterwards the *dictatores* began to produce their advice-books for the leaders of these communities, the earliest surviving example being the anonymous *Oculus Pastoralis* of c.1220. I examine this genre from various angles in chapters 2, 3 and 4, paying as much attention to the visual as to the literary representation of the city-republics and their

---

[9] This was the name generally given to that area of modern Italy, extending south as far as Rome, which had originally formed part of Charlemagne's *Imperium*.
[10] Waley 1988, p. 35; Jones 1997, pp. 130–51.   [11] Waley 1988, pp. 42, 196, 201, 205, 207.

distinctive forms of government. I focus in particular on the greatest surviving attempt to convey their ideals in visual terms, the so-called *Buon governo* frescoes painted by Ambrogio Lorenzetti in the Palazzo Pubblico of Siena in the late 1330s. I argue in chapter 3 that Lorenzetti presents us with a typically pre-humanist analysis of virtuous rule, while in chapter 4 I explore the connections he draws between the upholding of civic virtue and the attainment of glory and greatness, the highest goals for cities and citizens alike.

The revival of classical republicanism was a relatively short-lived spectacle in early Renaissance Italy. The central tenet of the *dictatores* was that, if you wish to live in peace and rise to glory, you must cleave to an elective system of government. By the end of the thirteenth century, however, this cardinal assumption was beginning to be widely questioned, not least because it seemed to many observers that self-government had simply proved to be a recipe for endless and debilitating civil strife. If peace and glory are your goals, they instead began to urge, it will always be safer to entrust your community to the strong government of a single *signore* or hereditary prince. These sentiments served at once to legitimise and encourage the widespread shift during this period *dal' commune al principato*, from traditional systems of elective government to the acceptance of princely rule. Such changes took place at Mantua and Verona in the 1270s, at Pisa, Piacenza and Parma by the end of the 1280s and at Ravenna, Rimini and elsewhere before the end of the century.[12]

I follow this transition in chapter 5, showing how the genre of advice-books for city magistrates mutated into the so-called mirror-for-princes literature of the high Renaissance. I sketch the evolution of this latter genre in the fifteenth century, and go on to claim that it supplies us with the context we need in order to make sense of Niccolò Machiavelli's *Il Principe* of 1513. I argue that Machiavelli's text is best viewed as a further contribution to the mirror-for-princes genre, but at the same time as a satirical attack on its fundamental assumption that princely virtue is the key to glory and greatness.

The transition from elective to hereditary systems of government in the *Regnum Italicum* was by no means universal nor uncontested. Florence and Venice clung onto their status as independent city-republics throughout the fourteenth and fifteenth centuries, and in the course of that period engendered a new political literature in which the values of self-government were eloquently carried over into the age of princes.

---

[12] Waley 1988, pp. 165–72.

I turn in chapter 5 to show how the humanists of *quattrocento* Florence revived the classical ideal of the 'free state' or *vivere libero* and restated it in the highest rhetorical style. I end by arguing that this background of Florentine 'civic humanism' provides us with the context that enables us to grasp what Machiavelli is doing in his *Discorsi*, his commentary on the early books of Livy's history of Rome. While the *Discorsi* are largely given over to a passionate, almost nostalgic restatement of the great tradition of Florentine republicanism, Machiavelli at the same time reiterates and develops his earlier attack on the humanist ideal of civic virtue and its role in public life.

If we reflect on the political literature surveyed in the first half of this volume, we can readily isolate a number of elements that go to make up the distinctive contribution of Renaissance humanism to early-modern political thought.[13] The most important concept revived by the humanists was the classical idea of the *civitas libera* or 'free state'. Freedom in the case of a political body, the humanists argue, means the same as in the case of a natural one. A body politic, like a natural body, is free if and only if it is moved to act by its own will. But to speak of a political body as moved by its own will is to speak of its being moved by the general will of its citizen-body as a whole. It follows that, when we speak of living in a free state, what we mean is that we are living in a self-governing community, one in which the will of its citizens is recognised as the basis of law and government.

Closely associated with this ideal of the *civitas libera* in the minds of the humanists is the category of the *civis* or citizen, whose standing they like to contrast with that of the *subditus* or subject. As these terms imply, the humanists think of citizens as prescribing laws to themselves, while *subditi* are merely subject to laws imposed on them by kingly overlords. The significance of citizenship for the humanists is in turn connected with two further values of which they endlessly speak. One is the importance of living a life of *negotium*, of active participation in civic affairs, and not of *otium* or contemplative withdrawal, the value extolled in Aristotelian and scholastic thought. An early and pointed expression of this commitment can be found in a letter written by Pier Paolo Vergerio in 1394. He imagines himself as Cicero, responding to Petrarch's expressions of disgust in his *Vita Solitaria* at the fact that Cicero had devoted so much of his time to public affairs. 'It has always seemed to me', Cicero is made to retort, 'that the man who surpasses all others in his nature and way of

---

[13] For an interesting attempt to isolate a more extensive set of values said to be definitive of Renaissance thought see Burke 1974, pp. 245–7.

life is the one who bestows his talents on the government of the *respublica* and in working for the benefit of everyone.'[14] The life of *negotium*, the life of those who willingly commit themselves to furthering the goals of their community, is the one that deserves the highest praise.[15]

If we all have a duty as citizens to serve the public good, we need to know what talents we must cultivate if we are to pursue the life of *negotium* to the best effect. This brings the writers I am considering to the core value of which they speak, that of *virtus* or civic virtue. It is by means of *virtus*, they all agree, that good citizens can alone hope to sustain their city in war and peace, thereby bringing glory to their community as well as to themselves. As I show in chapter 8, a further note of hostility to scholasticism becomes audible at this point, since the schoolmen generally insist that lineage and wealth are no less necessary than virtue for the effective practice of citizenship. By contrast, the humanists make it one of their slogans that *virtus vera nobilitas est*, that virtue alone enables us to play our part as citizens of true nobility and worth.

One further concept that sounds throughout the political writings of the humanists is that of *libertas*, the term they use to describe the freedom of individual citizens as well as of communities. Chapters 2 and 5 trace the emergence of a neo-Roman understanding of this value, showing that it was treated as a property of citizens by contrast with slaves, and was consequently defined in terms of independence and absence of arbitrary domination by others. Among humanists of the high Renaissance, I argue that the fullest and most influential restatement of this classical vision was furnished by Machiavelli in his *Discorsi*. Having outlined in chapter 5 the intellectual context out of which his views arose, I turn in chapters 6 and 7 to scrutinise his theory of *libertà* itself. In chapter 6 I focus on his concept of *corruzione*, and hence on his analysis of how citizens are prone to undermine the conditions of their own freedom. In chapter 7 I turn to his distinctive vision of civic *virtù*, and hence to his complementary analysis of the qualities we need to cultivate if we are to uphold the *vivere libero* and our own *libertà* at the same time.

So far I have spoken of the first half of this volume, in which I concentrate on the humanist political theories of the Italian Renaissance. In the second half I trace the fortunes of these theories in northern Europe, and especially in early-modern England. I begin with the initial reception of humanist values in the opening years of the sixteenth century.

---

[14] Vergerio 1934, pp. 439–40: 'ita semper visum est praestare omnibus vel genere vel vita quisquis ad administrandam rempublicam impertiendosque saluti omnium labores se accommodasset'.
[15] See Vergerio 1934, p. 439 on *negotium* and p. 444 on fleeing *solitudo*.

Chapter 8 considers Sir Thomas More's *Utopia* of 1516, which I take to be one of the earliest and most original attempts to introduce a classical understanding of civic virtue and self-government into English political thought. In chapter 9 I turn away from humanist theories of freedom and citizenship to the contrasting understanding of these concepts espoused by the schoolmen of the early sixteenth century. I concentrate on the figures of Jacques Almain and John Mair, for whom the securing of liberty was connected not with the cultivation of civic virtue but with the maintenance of natural rights. Arguing in contractarian terms wholly foreign to humanism, they envisage civil associations essentially as devices for ensuring that the rights we possess in the pre-political state of nature are more effectively upheld. I argue in chapters 6 and 7 that, because of the powerful hold still exercised by this analysis over modern political philosophy, several features of the rival neo-Roman theory have been misleadingly dismissed as confused. One of my aims in this group of chapters is to contrast these two models of freedom, and at the same time to rescue the neo-Roman model from a number of misunderstandings propagated by its scholastic critics and their modern counterparts.

I turn in chapters 10, 11 and 12 to consider the fortunes of humanist political theory in early-modern England. Chapter 10 looks at the reception of classical rhetoric in Tudor England and the subsequent growth of hostility to the humanist ideal of a union between reason and eloquence. Chapters 11 and 12 follow the rise and temporary triumph in English political theory of the neo-Roman understanding of political liberty. I illustrate the neglected but enormously powerful impact of this theory in helping to destabilise the Stuart monarchy, and later in helping to legitimise the 'free state' briefly established after the execution of Charles I in 1649.

With chapter 13 I move from the seventeenth to the early eighteenth century. I investigate the process by which the distinctive preoccupations of Renaissance humanism, above all as articulated in the political theory of Machiavelli, were adopted and developed by the so-called neo-Harringtonian opponents of the later Stuart monarchy.[16] I also show how it came about that, in the early decades of the eighteenth century, these neo-classical ideals were pressed into service as part of Lord Bolingbroke's campaign to unseat the whig oligarchy. What emerges is the remarkable extent to which the spirit of Machiavelli's *Discorsi* haunts the party politics of Augustan England.

[16] For the coinage of the term see Pocock 1975, pp. 423–61.

I bring this volume to a close with a chapter on the acquisition of the concept of the state as the master noun of our political discourse. According to the humanist vision of politics, the most basic aim of any ruler, as Machiavelli expressed it, must always be *mantenere lo stato*, to maintain his state or standing as a prince.[17] This eventually yielded place to the much more abstract idea that there is an independent apparatus, that of the state, which every ruler has a duty to maintain. This is the momentous transition I attempt to outline in chapter 14. I conclude with the figure of Thomas Hobbes, the earliest and greatest philosopher to argue with complete self-consciousness that the person standing at the heart of politics is not the person of the ruler but the purely artificial person of the state.

Mention of Hobbes brings me, finally, to the connections between this volume and volume 3 of the present work. Hobbes is the most formidable enemy of the values I take to be definitive of Renaissance political thought. His theory of the covenant collapses any distinction between subjects and citizens. His claim that in covenanting we specifically give up our right to govern ourselves undermines the need for an active and virtuous citizenship. His theory of freedom repudiates the claim that anyone living in conditions of domination and dependence must have been deprived of their liberty. His theory of state sovereignty challenges the fundamental humanist contention that sovereignty in a free state must remain the possession of the citizen-body as a whole.

What swings into view at this juncture is one of the deepest divisions in modern European political thought. On one side stands the neo-Roman theory of freedom and self-government, the theory most influentially formulated by the humanists of the Renaissance. On the other side stands the modern theory of the state as the bearer of uncontrollable sovereignty, the theory developed by the defenders of absolutism in the seventeenth century and definitively articulated in the philosophy of Hobbes. Having devoted the present volume to the first of these visions of politics, my principal aim in volume 3 will be to show how Hobbes attempted to obliterate and replace it.

---

[17] Machiavelli 1960, pp. 16, 25–6, 73–4, 80.

2

The rediscovery of republican values

I

The Italian city-republics first began to develop their distinctive political systems as early as the closing decades of the eleventh century. It was then that a number of northern communes took it upon themselves, in defiance of papal as well as imperial suzerainty, to appoint their own 'consuls' and invest them with supreme judicial authority. This happened at Pisa in 1085 (the earliest recorded instance), at Milan, Genoa and Arezzo before 1100, and at Bologna, Padua, Florence, Lucca, Siena and elsewhere by the 1140s.[1] During the second half of the twelfth century a further important development took place. The consular system was gradually replaced by a form of government centred on ruling councils chaired by officials known as *podestà*, so called because they were granted supreme power or *potestas* in executive as well as judicial affairs. Such a system was in place at Padua by the 1170s, at Milan by the 1180s, and at Florence, Pisa, Siena and Arezzo by the end of the century.[2]

By the opening years of the *duecento*, many of the richest communes of Lombardy and Tuscany had thus acquired the status of independent city-republics, with written constitutions guaranteeing their elective and self-governing arrangements.[3] For all their self-confidence, however, these urban communities remained deeply anomalous within the legal structures of thirteenth-century Europe. Technically they were mere vassals of the Holy Roman Empire, which vigorously pursued its claims over

---

This chapter is partly derived from the opening sections of my contribution entitled 'Political Philosophy' in *The Cambridge History of Renaissance Philosophy*, ed. Charles B. Schmitt and Quentin Skinner (Cambridge, 1988), pp. 387–452, and partly from my essay 'Machiavelli's *Discorsi* and the Pre-humanist Origins of Republican Ideas' in *Machiavelli and Republicanism*, ed. Gisela Bock, Quentin Skinner and Maurizio Viroli (Cambridge, 1990), pp. 121–41.

[1] Waley 1988, pp. 32, 35; Jones 1997, pp. 130–51.
[2] For excellent outlines of the system see Waley 1988, pp. 32–68 and Artifoni 1986, pp. 688–93.
[3] For a valuable survey of the socio-economic foundations of the communes and their views about citizenship see Coleman 2000, pp. 199–228.

northern Italy (the so-called *Regnum Italicum*) throughout the late twelfth and early thirteenth centuries. Frederick Barbarossa mounted five invasions between 1154 and 1190, while Frederick II continued the fight from 1237 until his death in 1250. By this time, moreover, the emperors were able to support their traditional demands by invoking the authority of Roman law, the study of which had become a leading academic discipline in the course of the twelfth century, initially under the inspiration of Irnerius and his followers at the University of Bologna. To these early Glossators it seemed incontestable that the *Codex* of Justinian viewed the *Imperator* as sole *princeps* and 'lord of the whole world'. Equating this figure with the Holy Roman Emperor, they concluded that, despite the *de facto* independence of so many of the Italian cities, they must be altogether subject *de iure* to the imperial power. As the Bolognese Glossator Lothair explained in a judgement solicited by the emperor Henry IV, if the *Imperator* is the sole *dominus mundi*, he must at the same time be the sole bearer of *imperium*, the one authority capable of making laws and commanding obedience.[4]

Even more anomalous than the *de facto* independence of the cities was their republicanism, the fact that they placed their highest executive and judicial functions in the hands of salaried officials elected for strictly limited periods of time. The basic assumption of most writers on statecraft at this period was that all government must be viewed as a God-given form of lordship. As John of Salisbury had put it in his *Policraticus* of 1159, all rulers constitute 'a kind of image on earth of the divine majesty'. They not only stand above the laws but 'can be said to partake in a large measure of divine virtue themselves'.[5] From these assumptions it was widely agreed to follow that hereditary monarchy must be not merely the best but the only conceivable form of legitimate rule. This is taken for granted by John of Salisbury and such followers as Helinandus of Froidmont,[6] who opens his *De Bono Regimine Principis* of c.1200 with the assertion that kings are directly chosen for us by God himself.[7] Gerald of Wales asserts in similar vein in his *De Principis Instructione* of c.1217 that 'the establishment of a princely form of power is actually a matter of necessity among men, no less than it is among the

---

[4] Gilmore 1941, pp. 15–19.
[5] Salisbury 1909, vol. 1, p. 236: 'in terris quaedam divinae maiestatis imago...magnum quid divinae virtutis declaratur inesse principibus'. For the date of the *Policraticus* see Nederman 1990, pp. xviii–xix.
[6] The twelve chapters of Helinandus's *De Bono Regimine Principis* are largely taken, often word for word, from Book IV of John of Salisbury's *Policraticus*.
[7] Helinandus of Froidmont 1855, p. 755, quoting and glossing Deuteronomy 17.15.

birds, the bees and the rest of brute creation'.[8] Finally, it was universally accepted – in line with the inescapable authority of St Augustine – that God's purpose in ordaining such princely powers must have been, as John of Salisbury adds, 'to repress the wicked, to reward the good' and so to uphold the law of God on earth.[9]

Given these assumptions, the city-republics of the *Regnum Italicum* stood in urgent need of a civic ideology capable of legitimising their anomalous legal position and of vindicating their systems of elective self-government.[10] According to many recent commentators, however, the earliest communes initially failed to rise to this challenge, and consequently lacked any means of conceptualising their freedom and political independence. These intellectual developments, we are told, had to await the recovery and dissemination of Aristotle's moral and political theory in the latter part of the thirteenth century. J. G. A. Pocock, for example, has contended that it was 'the politics of the polis' that came to be 'cardinal to the constitutional theory of Italian cities'.[11] Nicolai Rubinstein has likewise argued that Aristotle's *Politics* 'provided a unique key to the new world of urban politics', and that 'no such guide had existed before the rediscovery' of his texts.[12]

Some scholars have gone even further, insisting that we cannot speak even at this juncture of a distinctive ideology of self-governing republicanism. Hans Baron in particular has maintained that such an ideology was formulated for the first time – in an explosive and deeply influential moment of creativity – in Florence at the start of the fifteenth century.[13] Only then did the humanists begin to argue that the values of political liberty and participative citizenship need to be sustained by an elective system of republican rule. Only at that juncture, therefore, can we begin to speak of what Baron described as 'the new philosophy of political engagement' characteristic of the early Renaissance.[14] Florence, on this interpretation, was 'unique among the cities of Medieval Europe in giving rise to such a developed set of ideas appropriate to urban life'.[15]

---

[8] Wales 1891, p. 8: 'nec solum in apibus, avibus et brutis animalibus, verum in hominibus principalis potestas est necessaria'. For the date of composition see Berges 1938, p. 294.

[9] Salisbury 1909, vol. 1, pp. 236–7: 'instituta est ad vindictam malefactorum, laudem vero bonorum'.

[10] For a survey of the development of city-state culture, and for a number of comparative perspectives, see Hansen 2000.

[11] Pocock 1975, p. 74.   [12] Rubinstein 1982, p. 153.

[13] On this allegedly 'new ideology' and 'new outlook' see Baron 1966, pp. 29, 49, 121. For references to other scholars who have put forward similar views see Skinner 1978a, pp. 27, 79 and notes. For an effective critique see Grafton 1991, pp. 15–20.

[14] Baron 1966, p. 439; cf. Witt 1971, p. 173.

[15] Holmes 1973, p. 113; cf. also Holmes 1973, pp. 111, 112.

The rediscovery of republican values

No one doubts that the revival of Aristotelianism and the rise of Florentine humanism were of vital importance for the evolution of republican thought.[16] But it is misleading to suggest that it was only with the emergence of these intellectual movements that an ideology of self-governing republicanism began to be formulated in the communes of the *Regnum Italicum*. We are still too much in thrall to Jacob Burckhardt's vision of the Renaissance, still too ready to suppose that there must be one particular moment at which we can hope to contemplate the dawn of humanism and the recovery of classical values, including the values of republican self-government.[17] As I shall try to suggest in what follows, the reassertion of these values and their accompanying practices was a long and incremental process, one that stretches back to the era in which the communes were originally founded.[18] More specifically, I want to argue, the recovery and adaptation of Aristotle's texts largely served to confirm and underpin two earlier traditions of thought in which the distinctive arrangements of the early communes had already been very effectively celebrated and legitimised.

II

The authority chiefly invoked by the city-republics in their earliest attempts to defend their way of life was the Codex of Roman law. By the end of the twelfth century, a number of Glossators were beginning to reinterpret the passages on public law in Justinian's *Digest* in such a way as to support rather than to question the autonomy of the cities and their elective forms of government.[19] The first of the leading Glossators to expound the law of Rome in this fashion was Lothair's great opponent Azo, a native of Bologna and a celebrated teacher of civil law at the university in the opening years of the thirteenth century.

Glossing the concepts of *iurisdictio* and *merum imperium* in his *Summa Super Codicem*, Azo wrote in such a way as to vindicate the sovereignty of all communities possessing *de facto* independence. 'We must begin',

---

[16] On the former theme see Ullmann 1977 and the valuable series of essays collected in Davis 1984. For the impact of Aristotelian studies on civic activity see Coleman 1998. On the latter see the classic accounts in Baron 1966 and Pocock 1975. For an attempt to survey both strands of thought see Skinner 1978a, pp. 49–112 and Skinner 1978b, pp. 113–84.

[17] See, for example, Baron 1966, pp. 8, 105, 449 and Pocock 1975, p. 52, both of whom see a 'decisive break' and a crossing of the threshold between the medieval and the Renaissance around the year 1400.

[18] A similar point is made in Sapegno 1984, pp. 949–60 and in Nederman 1991, 1992 and 1995, a valuable series of revisionist articles.

[19] Mochi Onory 1951 discusses the analogous reinterpretation of the Decretals undertaken by a number of canonists in the same period.

he announces in his section *De Iurisdictione*, 'by considering the meaning of the term *iurisdictio* itself.' 'It is a power', he goes on, 'publicly established as a matter of necessity, of stating that which is lawful and right and establishing that which is equitable.'[20] So far this was orthodox doctrine. But as soon as Azo turns to ask who can lawfully possess such power, and hence exercise *merum imperium*, he announces a radical new departure. 'I admit', he writes, 'that the very highest *iurisdictio* rests with the *princeps* alone.'[21] However, it cannot be doubted 'that any magistrate in a city has the power to establish new law'.[22] 'So my position', he concludes – in a direct allusion to his debate with Lothair – 'is that it must be lawful for *merum imperium* to be wielded by these other higher powers as well.'[23]

If we turn to Azo's *Quaestiones* we find him defending the sovereignty of independent kingdoms in the same terms. He states his position most clearly in commenting on the dispute between King John of England and Philip Augustus of France, in the course of which the latter had been criticised for ceding certain rights of vassalage. Azo remarks that the first observation to be made in defence of the French king is that 'because it is evident nowadays that every ruler possesses the same power within his own territory as the emperor, it follows that it must have been for the king to act in this matter just as he pleased'.[24] A proposition with momentous consequences for the defence of national autonomy against the legal pretensions of the Holy Roman Empire is thus announced as if it were already accepted in practice as the merest commonplace.

From the point of view of the Italian city-republics, however, Azo's greatest contribution was that he also defended a doctrine of popular sovereignty. For this aspect of his argument he relied on a distinctive analysis of the term *universitas*, the central concept in the Roman law theory of corporations. The earliest Glossators had originally invoked this theory to furnish an account of the place within cities or kingdoms of such lesser institutions as guilds, monasteries and the new phenomenon of universities. But by the end of the twelfth century – especially in the writings of Azo's teacher Bassianus – they had also begun to use the

---

[20] Azo 1966a, III. 13, p. 67: 'videamus ergo in primis quid sit iurisdictio . . . [est] potestas de publico introducta cum necessitate iuris dicendi et aequitatis statuendae'.
[21] Azo 1966a, III. 13, p. 68: 'plenissimam iurisdictionem soli principi competere dico'.
[22] Azo 1966a, III. 13, p. 68: 'quilibet magistratus in sua civitate ius novum statuere potest'.
[23] Azo 1966a, III. 13, p. 69: 'sed merum imperium etiam aliis sublimioribus potestatibus competere dico'. On the significance of this contention see Calasso 1957, pp. 83–123.
[24] Azo 1888, pp. 86–7: 'quilibet hodie videtur eandem potestatem habere in sua terra, quam imperator, ergo potuit facere quod sibi placet'.

term to denote any collectivity possessing its own juridical standing.²⁵ As a result, they came to speak of entire bodies of citizens as instances of *universitates*, as political bodies and hence as legal *personae* capable of speaking with a single voice and of acting with a unified will in the disposition of their affairs. It was this application of the term that Azo went on to put to such revolutionary use.

First he argued that the consent of the whole people considered as an *universitas* is always necessary if the highest powers of *imperium* and thus of *iurisdictio* are to be lawfully instituted. He derived this conclusion from his interpretation of the *Lex regia* mentioned in Book I of the *Digest*. According to this enactment, 'what pleases the emperor has the force of law, the reason being that, by way of the *Lex regia*, which has been passed concerning his authority, the people confer upon him, and place in his hands, their own entire authority and power'.²⁶

Glossing this alleged decree in his *Lectura Super Codicem*, Azo concludes that 'the power of the emperor to make law' arose lawfully because 'it was assigned to him by the people' in whose hands it must originally have reposed.²⁷ So far this too was orthodox teaching among the Glossators, who must unquestionably be regarded as a leading source of the doctrine – later so central to contractarian as well as scholastic political theory – that all legitimate political authority must derive from an act of consent.²⁸ Azo parts company with his teachers, however, when he goes on to argue that, even after the establishment of a prince with full *imperium* and *iurisdictio*, 'the power to make laws, if it was a power that the people possessed before that time, is one that they will continue to possess afterwards'.²⁹ As Azo himself observes, the accepted interpretation of the *Lex regia* had always been that 'although the Roman people at one time possessed the power to make laws, they no longer possess it, having transferred all their authority to the emperor by means of the *Lex regia* itself'.³⁰ This had been Irnerius's view, subsequently endorsed by such distinguished Bolognese Glossators as Rogerius and Placentinus. But Azo

---

²⁵ Michaud-Quantin 1970, p. 28; cf. Black 1984, pp. 44–53.
²⁶ *Digest* 1985, I. 4. 1, vol. 1, p. 14: 'Quod principi placuit, legis habet vigorem: utpote cum lege regia, quae de imperio eius lata est, populus ei et in eum omne suum imperium et potestatem conferat.'
²⁷ Azo 1966b, I. XIV. 11, p. 44: 'potestas [imperatoris] legis condendae ... in eum transtulit populus'.
²⁸ Tierney 1982, pp. 29–53.
²⁹ Azo 1966b, I. XIV. 11, p. 44: 'potestas legis condendae ... si populus ante habebat, et adhunc habebit'.
³⁰ Azo 1966b, I. XIV. 11, p. 44: 'populus Romanus non habet potestatem legis condendae, quod olim habebat: sed lege regia in eum transtulit populus omne ius quod habebat'.

denies this reading outright. 'My own view', he retorts, 'is that the people never transferred this power except in such a way that they were at the same time able to retain it themselves.'[31] We can see how this is possible, he adds, once we introduce the idea of the *populus* considered as an *universitas*. 'For it is not the people who are excluded by the *Lex regia* from the power to make laws, but merely the individuals who make up the body of the people. They are indeed excluded, but not the people considered as an *universitas*.'[32]

If the people transfer and yet retain the power to make laws, who is the true possessor of that power in the last resort? Azo is fully aware of the local relevance as well as the momentous implications of the question. He answers at a later stage in his *Lectura* by introducing a distinction between a ruler's relationship to his subjects *ut singulis* and *ut universis*, a distinction destined to be endlessly cited in subsequent legal debates about the concept of *merum imperium*. Azo presents his solution in the course of glossing the title *Longa Consuetudo*, the title concerned with the relations between custom and law. He begins by considering the standard objection to the contention that, in the exemplary instance of the Roman people, the right to make laws was never yielded up. Even if they initially retained it, the objection runs, 'it must by now have lapsed through loss of use, with the result that today it is lodged entirely in the emperor's hands'.[33] Azo first counters by repeating his earlier contention that the people 'never transferred this power at all except in such a way that they were able at the same time to retain it'.[34] But he now adds the crucial corollary that, 'from this it follows that, although the emperor is of greater power than any individual member of the populace, he is not of greater power than the populace as a whole'.[35] The emperor's unquestionable authority to legislate is thus rendered compatible with an unqualified defence of the *populus sive universitas* as the ultimate bearer of sovereignty.

As Azo recognised, this doctrine carried with it two further and even more radical implications, both of which he underlines in glossing the title *De Legibus* in his *Summa Super Codicem*. Although we habitually speak of rulers as the bearers of *iurisdictio*, strictly speaking 'we should speak of

---

[31] Azo 1966b, I. XIV. 11, p. 44: 'vel dic quod non transtulit ita quin sibi retineret'.
[32] Azo 1966b, I. XIV. 11, p. 44: 'hic non excluditur populus, sed singuli de populo... ideo singuli excluduntur, non universitas sive populus'.
[33] Azo 1966b, VIII. LIII. 2, p. 671: 'abrogandae per desuetudinem, hodie est omnis potestas et omne ius in imperatorem'.
[34] Azo 1966b, VIII. LIII. 2, p. 671: 'sed nec est ita translata quin sibi retinuerit'.
[35] Azo 1966b, VIII. LIII. 2, p. 671: 'unde non est major potestatis imperator quam totus populus, sed quam quilibet de populo'.

the right to exercise that power as being transferred to them only in the sense of being conceded, because the people will not in the least have abdicated the power themselves'.³⁶ The true status of rulers is merely that of *rectores*, officials whose authority is assigned to them not in the form of a donation but merely as a matter of administrative convenience. The other implication is that the people must retain the capacity to depose their rulers and resume the exercise of their sovereignty should their *rectores* fail at any time to discharge their duties satisfactorily. This in fact happened, as Azo remarks, at more than one moment in the history of the Roman people, 'for even after they had transferred their power to make laws, they were nevertheless able to revoke that transfer at a later stage'.³⁷

Azo's way of defending the people's authority to set up and set down their own chosen forms of government remained an important element in the ideology of the Italian city-republics throughout their later history. Hugolinus and his pupils at Bologna continued to explore the implications of Azo's argument in the later thirteenth century, while a number of canonists followed Huguccio of Pisa's lead in deploying a parallel theory to elucidate the relationship between the pope and the *universitas* of the church.³⁸ During the early decades of the fourteenth century Bartolus of Sassoferrato reformulated the defence of the city-republics in still more radical terms with his doctrine of *sibi princeps*, the doctrine that each independent *civitas* may be regarded as 'a *princeps* unto itself' and hence as the bearer of its own sovereignty.³⁹ While these later developments are well known, however, the point on which I have sought to insist is that we already find a legal defence of the independent and sovereign status of the Italian city-republics fully articulated in the opening decades of the thirteenth century.

III

By the time of Azo's death in c.1230, a yet further body of ancient texts was beginning to be pressed into service to defend the independence of the Italian city-republics and their elective forms of government. A number of writers began to invoke the authority of the moralists and

---

³⁶ Azo 1966a, I. 14, p. 9: 'potestas... dicitur enim translata id est concessa, non quod populus omnino a se abdicaverit'.
³⁷ Azo 1966a, I. 14, p. 9: 'nam et olim transtulerat, sed tamen postea revocavit'.
³⁸ Tierney 1955, pp. 132–53.
³⁹ Skinner 1978a, pp. 53–65. For later *de facto* arguments about the sovereignty of the city-republics see Canning 1987, pp. 93–131 and Ryan 2000.

historians who had celebrated the virtues of the ancient Roman republic in the period just before it was swallowed up into the principate. The authorities on whom they chiefly relied were Sallust and Cicero, later the favourite political writers of many leading humanists of the *quattrocento*.[40] So extensive, indeed, was the reliance of the earliest spokesmen for the communes on these sources that it would not be inappropriate to describe them as the originators of a humanist literature – or at least a recognisably pre-humanist literature – on the problems of city government.[41]

We need to consider two closely related bodies of texts produced by these pre-humanist commentators.[42] First there were the numerous treatises on the *Ars dictaminis* issued by those who acted as *dictatores* or teachers of rhetoric in the law-schools of the *Regnum Italicum*.[43] These treatises generally comprised a set of model speeches and letters, often preceded by a theoretical discussion of the rhetorical arts.[44] A small number of these writings survive from as early as the beginning of the twelfth century. Hugh of Bologna's *Rationes Dictandi*, for instance, appears to have been produced around the year 1120.[45] For the most part, however, the earliest surviving examples date from the opening decades of the thirteenth century, by which time the genre had become well established, not to say highly repetitious in content.[46] Among the leading examples from this era are Raniero da Perugia's *Ars Notaria* of c.1215,[47] Thomas of Capua's *Ars Dictandi* of c.1230,[48] Boncompagno da Signa's *Rhetorica Novissima* of 1235[49] and Guido Faba's numerous writings of the same period,[50] including his *Dictamina Rhetorica* of 1226–8,[51] his *Epistole* of

[40] The importance of Sallust's histories in this context has not perhaps been sufficiently emphasised. But for two excellent studies see Smalley 1971, pp. 165–75, and (for a discussion centring specifically on Italy) Rubinstein 1957, pp. 165–83.
[41] On the humanistic character of these writings see Nederman 1992.
[42] Artifoni has provided the fullest recent discussion of these writers in a fine series of articles. See Artifoni 1986, 1994a, 1994b and 1997. On the later history of rhetoric and its connections with political theory in the Renaissance see Kahn 1985 and Skinner 1996.
[43] On these writers the classic studies remain Kristeller 1961 and Kristeller 1965. See also Kristeller 1988. But for a different approach see Witt 1982, pp. 1–35. For an excellent survey, citing many of the writers I discuss, see also Artifoni 1986.
[44] Murphy 1974, pp. 218–20 refers to Hugh of Bologna's pioneering distinction between the introductory theoretical treatise (the *Ars*) and the ensuing model examples (the *Dictamina*).
[45] Murphy 1974; for an edition see Bologna 1863, pp. 53–94.
[46] For a survey of the literature of this period see Murphy 1974, pp. 194–265.
[47] Monaci 1905 discusses Raniero's *Dictamina* and republishes some fragments. For the suggested date of composition see Bertoni 1947, p. 253.
[48] For an edition and the suggested date of composition see Capua 1929.
[49] Signa 1892; for the date of composition see Gaudenzi 1895, p. 112.
[50] For a full list of Faba's rhetorical writings see Pini 1956, pp. 42–3 and notes.
[51] Faba 1892; for the date see Gaudenzi 1895, p. 133.

1239–41[52] and his *Parlamenti ed Epistole* of 1242–3.[53] We should also note that, by the end of the thirteenth century, a number of similar treatises had begun to appear in the *volgare*.[54] Matteo de' Libri's vernacular *Arringhe* dates from c.1275,[55] Giovanni da Vignano's *Flore de Parlare* from c.1290,[56] Filippo Ceffi's *Dicerie* from c.1330.[57]

The other body of writings to be considered are the pre-humanist treatises on city government designed specifically for the guidance of *podestà* and other magistrates. This genre was originally an offshoot of the *Ars dictaminis*, with most of the early treatises still containing model letters and speeches in addition to general advice on how to manage city affairs.[58] The earliest surviving work of this description is the anonymous *Oculus Pastoralis*, which has usually been dated to the 1220s.[59] This was followed by Orfino da Lodi's *De Sapientia Potestatis*, an advice-book composed in leonine verse during the 1240s.[60] The next such work to survive – by far the fullest and most important – was Giovanni da Viterbo's *Liber de Regimine Civitatum*, probably completed in the course of the 1250s.[61] This was in turn followed – and to some degree plagiarised[62] – by Brunetto Latini in his *Livres dou trésor* of 1266, a widely used encyclopedia that concludes with a section entitled 'On the government of cities'.[63]

These writers are all committed to the view that the best form of constitution for a *commune* or *civitas* must be republican as opposed to monarchical in character. If a city is to have any prospect of attaining its highest goals, it is indispensable that its administration should remain in the hands of elected officials whose conduct can in turn be regulated by the people and their established customs and laws. To understand how this conclusion was reached, we need to begin by asking what

---

[52] Faba 1893; for the date see Gaudenzi 1895, p. 145.
[53] Faba 1889; for the date see Gaudenzi 1895, p. 145.
[54] As Castellani 1955, pp. 5–75 shows, however, Faba had pioneered the production of vernacular *Dictamina* a generation earlier.
[55] Libri 1974; for the date see Kristeller 1951, p. 285n.
[56] Vignano 1974; for the date see Frati 1913, p. 265.
[57] Ceffi 1942; for the date see Giannardi 1942, pp. 5, 19.
[58] For this connection between rhetoric and politics – between the *rhetor* and the *rector* – see Artifoni 1986.
[59] *Oculus* 1966. Franceschi 1966, p. 3 suggests 1222 as the date of composition; Sorbelli 1944, p. 74 suggests 1242.
[60] Lodi 1869; for the date see Sorbelli 1944, p. 61.
[61] Viterbo 1901; for the suggested date of composition see Folena 1959, p. 97. But Hertter 1910, pp. 52–3 suggests 1228, while Sorbelli 1944, pp. 94–6 suggests 1263.
[62] Najemy 1994a provides the best consideration of the evidence.
[63] Latini 1948. See Sorbelli 1944, pp. 99–104, Carmody 1948, pp. xiii–xx, xxii–xxxii and Najemy 1994a for details about the dating and sources of the *Trésor*.

these writers had in mind when they spoke about the goals or ends of communities, and in particular about the highest goal to which a city can aspire.

The goal they emphasise above all is that of attaining greatness – greatness of standing, greatness of power, greatness of wealth. This preoccupation is in part expressed in a distinctive literature devoted to celebrating the *magnalia* or signs of greatness in cities. By far the most celebrated contribution to this genre, Leonardo Bruni's *Laudatio Florentinae Urbis*, is a much later work, composed in 1403–4 in the highest humanist style.[64] But there are several examples dating from the period in which the pre-humanist ideology of the city-republics was first articulated. One of the earliest is the anonymous poem in praise of the city of Lodi, *De Laude Civitatis Laudae*, probably written in the 1250s.[65] Perhaps the best known are Bonvesin della Riva's panegyric on Milan, *De Magnalibus Mediolani* of 1288, and the *Liber de Laudibus Civitatis Ticinensis*, an anonymous panegyric on Pavia of c.1320.[66]

The same preoccupation with glory and greatness suffuses the pre-humanist treatises on city government. The main inspiration for their claim that these are the highest ends of civic life derives from the Roman historians and moralists, most notably from Sallust. Not only do they draw on his account in the *Bellum Catilinae* of how the Roman republic grew to greatness – how the *respublica crevit*[67] – but they also like to quote the passage from the *Bellum Iugurthinum* in which the king of Numidia congratulates Jugurtha on the honour and glory won by his deeds, while adjuring him at the same time to remember how small communities succeed in rising to greatness – how *parvae res crescunt*.[68]

All the pre-humanist writers speak in similar terms. The *Oculus Pastoralis*, which opens with a set of model speeches designed for incoming *podestà*, particularly advises such officials to promise that their government will serve 'to increase both glory and honour', thereby ensuring 'that the city grows to greatness'.[69] The model speeches included in Giovanni da Viterbo's *Liber de Regimine Civitatum* likewise emphasise the value of 'increase', as well as the importance of ensuring

---

[64] Bruni 1968. Baron 1966, pp. 191–224 gives a classic analysis of this text. But he marks too sharp a break with pre-humanist discussions, especially when he speaks (pp. xvii and 202–4) of 'a new ideal of "greatness"' in the *Laudatio*. For a contrasting appraisal see Seigel 1966, pp. 3–48.
[65] *De Laude* 1872. For the suggested date of composition see Hyde 1965, p. 340.
[66] See Riva 1974 and *Liber de Laudibus* 1903.   [67] Sallust 1931a, X. 1, p. 16.
[68] Sallust 1931b, X. 6, p. 148.
[69] See *Oculus* 1966, pp. 25, 27 on conducing 'ad incrementum et gloriam et honorem' and on the hope that 'excrescit civitas'.

that cities are able to grow and flourish.[70] By the end of the thirteenth century we find the same ideas beginning to be expressed in the vernacular. Matteo de' Libri advises both ambassadors and *podestà* to promise that they will ensure increase and growth,[71] while Giovanni da Vignano's model speech for outgoing *podestà* bids them express the hope that the city they have been administering 'will at all times grow and increase', above all in prosperity.[72]

At the same time, the vernacular writers begin to invoke a new concept to describe their vision of the proper ends of civic life. They speak of *grandezza*, using a term evidently coined to supply the lack, in classical Latin, of an expression at once denoting grandeur and magnitude. We already find Guido Faba speaking in this fashion in his *Parlamenti ed Epistole* of the early 1240s. In his model speech intended for the use of newly elected *podestà*, Faba advises them to promise 'to do whatever may be necessary for the maintenance of the standing and *grandeça* of the commune, and for the increase of the honour and glory of those friendly to it'.[73] Shortly afterwards the same terminology recurs in one of the vernacular passages in Giovanni da Viterbo's *Liber de Regimine Civitatum*. An incoming *podestà*, he advises, should vow to uphold 'the honour and *grandecça* and welfare' of the city given into his charge.[74] By the next generation, we find the same terminology in standard use among the writers of vernacular *Dictamina*. Matteo de' Libri instructs outgoing magistrates to proclaim that they have in fact succeeded in upholding the city's '*grandeça*, honour, good standing and repose'.[75] Giovanni da Vignano echoes the same sentiments in virtually the same phraseology, urging ambassadors and magistrates alike to speak of their city's 'exaltation, *grandeça* and honour',[76] of its 'good standing, *grandeça* and repose',[77] and at the same time of 'the honour, *grandeça*, unity and repose' of all its citizens.[78]

---

[70] See Viterbo 1901, p. 231, col. 2 on the importance of ensuring that 'civitates crescunt'. Cf. also Viterbo 1901, p. 232, col. 1 on the value of 'incrementum' and of 'maximum incrementum'.
[71] See Libri 1974, pp. 10, 70 on the duty to bring 'acresimento de ben en meglo' and to assure 'bon stato, gradeça et acresemento'.
[72] See Vignano 1974, p. 286 for the wish 'che questa terra sempre acresca'.
[73] See Faba 1889, p. 156 on the need 'de fare quelle cose . . . che pertegnano ad statum et a grandeça di questo communo, et ad adacresemento de gloria e d'onore de tuti quilli c'ameno questa citade'.
[74] See Viterbo 1901, p. 234, col. 2 on the need to act 'ad honore et grandecça, et utilitate de questu communu', and cf. Viterbo 1901, p. 231, col. 1 on the need to promote 'granneça'.
[75] Libri 1974, p. 99: 'grandeça, honori, bon stato e bon reposo'. For further references to *grandezza* see Libri 1974, pp. 12, 28, 53, 69–70, 93, 110, 112, 114.
[76] Vignano 1974, p. 237: 'exaltamento, grandeça et honore'.
[77] Vignano 1974, p. 259: 'bom stato, grandeça e reposo'.
[78] Vignano 1974, p. 251: 'honore, grandeça e unita e reposo'. For similar formulae see Vignano 1974, pp. 237, 239, 245, 251, 286–7.

What policies need to be pursued if civic *grandezza* is to be attained? The pre-humanist writers are at first content to reiterate the familiar Augustinian assumption that no community can hope to flourish unless it lives in perfect peace. The *Oculus*, for example, contains a model speech for chief magistrates to deliver in the face of warring factions, warning them that 'only through quiet and tranquillity and peace can a city grow great'.[79] Brunetto Latini similarly lays it down in his chapter on the virtue of concord that 'peace brings very great good, while war lays it waste'.[80] The same arguments are subsequently reiterated by the writers of vernacular *Dictamina*. Matteo de' Libri strongly associates the rule of those who enable their communities 'to live in total tranquillity' with the attainment of 'honour and good standing'.[81] Filippo Ceffi writes even more emphatically, offering repeated assurances that if a city 'can manage to maintain itself in a good and peaceable state', this will always conduce 'to your honour and your *grandezza*'.[82]

During the early part of the fourteenth century, however, a number of writers began to voice a certain anxiety about such unqualified celebrations of peace.[83] Sallust was again their main authority at this stage. As he had emphasised at the start of the *Bellum Catilinae*, it was during the period when Rome had been forced to wage continual wars against savage neighbouring peoples, and subsequently against the invading Carthaginians, that the republic had grown to greatness. By contrast, it was when this period was followed by an era of peace and plenty that Roman *virtus* began to decline. The fruits of peace proved to be avarice and self-interest, and with the resulting loss of civic virtue the free and self-governing republic eventually collapsed.[84]

With traditional systems of communal government everywhere falling prey to the rise of *signori* in the early fourteenth century,[85] a number of the pre-humanist political writers began to express similar doubts. Albertino Mussato, for example, prefaces his history of the collapse of civic liberty in his native Padua with an explanation taken almost word for word from Sallust's account.[86] The same theme later assumed an even greater

[79] *Oculus* 1966, p. 27: 'Per quietam autem tranquilitatem et pacem ipsius excrescit civitas.'
[80] Latini 1948, p. 292: 'pais fait maint bien et guerre le gaste'.
[81] Libri 1974, p. 79 stresses the connection between being able 'permanere in gran tranquillitate' and the capacity 'aquistar honor et bon stato'.
[82] See Ceffi 1942, p. 27 for the claim that, if your city 'possa mantenersi in buono e pacifico stato', this will conduce 'a vostro onore e grandezza'. For other formulae to the same effect cf. Ceffi 1942, pp. 36, 47, 61.
[83] On the contrast between peace and liberty see Valeri 1942.
[84] Sallust 1931a, VI–XIII, pp. 10–22.   [85] For a classic survey of this transition see Ercole 1929.
[86] This is pointed out in Rubinstein 1957, p. 172 and note.

prominence in *quattrocento* humanist histories designed to celebrate the virtues of republican liberty.[87] The fear that long periods of peace may lead to enervation and decadence is forcefully expressed, for example, in Poggio Bracciolini's *Historiae Florentini Populi*. A love of peace, he implies in a passage closely modelled on Sallust, may sometimes pose a threat to liberty.[88] If freedom and self-government are to be upheld against the encroachments of tyranny, it may sometimes be necessary to fight for liberty instead of insisting on peace at any price.

There was one aspect of this debate, however, on which all the pre-humanist writers were agreed. Even if it may sometimes prove necessary to wage war on others in the name of liberty and *grandezza*, the preservation of peace within one's own city must never be jeopardised. The avoidance of internal division and discord is regarded by everyone as an indispensable condition of civic greatness. Once again, it is Sallust who is most often quoted to this effect. The passage invariably cited is the speech from the *Bellum Iugurthinum* in which the king of Numantia addresses Jugurtha and his other two heirs:

I bequeath to all three of you a kingdom that will prove strong if you conduct yourself well, but weak if you behave badly. For it is by way of concord that small communities rise to greatness; it is as a result of discord that even the greatest communities fall into collapse.[89]

These sentiments had already become proverbial when Sallust voiced them, but his authority had the effect of turning them into one of the most widely quoted *dicta* on politics throughout the era of the Renaissance.[90]

The negative aspect of Sallust's admonition was strongly echoed in the pre-humanist treatises. 'It is due to the fact that all cities nowadays are divided within themselves', Giovanni da Viterbo declares, 'that the good effect of government is no longer felt.'[91] Brunetto Latini makes the same observation in the course of advising magistrates on what to do if they find themselves in charge of a city 'at war with itself'. 'You must point out how concord brings greatness to cities and enriches their citizens, while

---

[87] See the discussion of Poggio's republicanism in Oppel 1974, pp. 221–65.
[88] Bracciolini 1964–9b, vol. 2, p. 299. Cf. Oppel 1974, pp. 223–4.
[89] Sallust 1931b, X. 7, p. 148: 'Equidem ego vobis regnum trado firmum, si boni eritis, sin mali, imbecillum. Nam concordia parvae res crescunt, discordia maxumae dilabuntur.' The passage is strongly echoed by a number of the pre-humanist writers. See, for example, Lodi 1869, p. 57 and *De Laude* 1872, p. 372.
[90] The last sentence is quoted as proverbial in Seneca 1917–25, XCIV. 46, p. 40.
[91] Viterbo 1901, p. 221, cols. 1–2: 'Nam cum civitates omnes hodie sunt divise...cesset bonus effectus regiminis.'

war destroys them; and you must recall how Rome and other great cities ruined themselves by internal strife.'[92] Matteo de' Libri offers precisely the same advice in a model speech designed for captains of city militias to declaim in order to stiffen the resolve of ruling magistrates to deal with internal faction fights. 'Think of Florence and Siena, and of how they have destroyed themselves by internal war; think of Rimini, and of many other places throughout this country, and of how internal hatred has ruined them.'[93]

More optimistically, many of these writers also take up the positive aspect of Sallust's argument. 'Cities that are ruled and maintained in a state of peace', Giovanni da Viterbo proclaims, 'are able to grow, to become great, and to receive the greatest possible increase.'[94] Brunetto Latini underlines the argument, referring his readers directly to Sallust for the judgement that, just as discord destroys the greatest undertakings, so 'small things, through concord, are able to grow great'.[95] Matteo de' Libri, in a model speech designed for *capitani* to deliver if civic discord impends, similarly advises them to remind the parties involved that 'concord and unity cause everything to advance and grow great'.[96]

One of the problems that most preoccupies these writers is accordingly that of understanding how civic concord can best be preserved. The authority to whom they invariably turn at this juncture is Cicero, for whom the ideal of a *concordia ordinum* had been of overriding importance. Cicero had laid it down in a much-cited passage from Book I of his *De Officiis* that 'anyone who looks after the interests of only one part of a citizen body, while neglecting the rest, introduces into the government of a city the most pernicious element of all, namely sedition and discord'.[97] He inferred that the key to preserving civic concord must therefore be to give precedence to the ideal of the common good – the *bonum commune* or *communes utilitates* – over any considerations of selfish or factional advantage.

---

[92] Latini 1948, p. 404: 'die comment concorde essauce les viles et enrichist les borgois, et guerre les destruit; et ramentevoir Romme et les autres bonnes viles ki por la guerre dedans sont decheues et mal alees'.

[93] Libri 1974, p. 147: 'Pensative de Florencia, de Sena, commo son gite per la guerra dentru... Pensative de Rimino, comm' è conço per l'odio dentro, e de multe terre de quella contrata.'

[94] Viterbo 1901, p. 231, col. 2: 'civitates reguntur et tenentur pacifice, crescunt, ditantur et maximum recipiunt incrementum'.

[95] Latini 1948, p. 292: 'Salustes dist, par concorde croissent les petites choses et par discorde se destruisent les grandismes.'

[96] Libri 1974, p. 18: 'la concordia et l'unitate acrese et avança tuti bene'.

[97] Cicero 1913, I. XXV. 85, p. 86: 'Qui autem parti civium consulunt, partem neglegunt, rem perniciosissimam in civitatem inducunt, seditionem atque discordiam'.

Cicero summarises his conclusions in the form of two basic precepts for the guidance of magistrates, both of which he claims to have taken from Plato:

> First, they must look after the welfare of every citizen to such a degree that, in everything they do, they make this their highest priority, without any consideration for their own advantage. And secondly, they must look after the welfare of the whole body politic, never allowing themselves to care only for one part of the citizens while betraying the rest.[98]

Both these suggestions were eagerly seized upon by the pre-humanist writers on city government. We already find the author of the *Oculus Pastoralis* including in the model speech for incoming *podestà* a demand that all magistrates should treat it as their duty 'to promote the welfare of the whole community', thereby guaranteeing it 'honour, exaltation and benefit, and a happy state'.[99] Giovanni da Viterbo quotes the entire passage in which Cicero had explained the connections between the avoidance of discord and the promotion of the common good,[100] while Brunetto Latini repeats in his chapter 'Of Concord' that, if this virtuous condition is to be attained, 'we must follow nature and place the common good above all other values'.[101]

This still leaves the question of how to ensure in practice that the common good is followed, and thus that no member of the community is ever neglected or unfairly subordinated to anyone else. Here again the pre-humanist writers remain in complete agreement with their Roman authorities. These results can only be brought about, they declare, if our magistrates uphold the dictates of justice in all their public acts. They define the ideal of justice, in accordance with the teachings of Roman law, as the principle of giving to each their due, *ius suum cuique*. But to ensure that everyone receives their due, they argue, is the same as ensuring that no one's interests are excluded or unfairly subjected to those of anyone else. The ideal of justice is accordingly seen as the bedrock. To act justly is the one and only means of promoting the common good, without which there can be no hope of preserving concord and hence of attaining greatness.

---

[98] Cicero 1913, I. XXV. 85, p. 86: 'Unum, ut utilitatem civium sic tueantur, ut, quaecumque agunt, ad eam referant obliti commodorum suorum, alterum, ut totum corpus rei publicae curent, ne, dum partem aliquam tuentur, reliquas deserant.'

[99] See *Oculus* 1966, p. 26 on the need to act 'pro utilitate communitatis istius' in order to bring it 'ad honorem, exaltationem et comodum ac felicem statum'.

[100] Viterbo 1901, p. 265, col. 2.

[101] Latini 1948, p. 291: 'devons nous ensivre nature et metre avant tout le commun profit'. For further references to the ideal of the common good see Latini 1948, pp. 405, 415, 417. Cf. the references to the 'bene comune' in Ceffi 1942, pp. 46, 57.

Once again, Sallust provides one of the main inspirations for this argument. As he had put it with characteristic succinctness in his *Bellum Catilinae*, it was 'by acting with justice as well as with industry that the Roman republic grew to greatness'.[102] But the pre-humanist writers are even more indebted at this juncture to a similar passage from the start of Cicero's *De Officiis*. When introducing the topic of justice, Cicero had begun by declaring that it constitutes the primary means 'by which the community of men and women and, as it were, their common unity, is preserved'.[103]

These sentiments are frequently transcribed by the pre-humanist writers almost word for word. Giovanni da Viterbo begins his treatise by laying it down that the prime duty of chief magistrates is 'to render to each person their due, in order that the city may be governed in justice and equity'.[104] The importance of this principle, as one of his model speeches later explains, stems from the fact that 'when cities are ruled by these bonds of justice, they grow to greatness, become enriched and receive the greatest possible increase'.[105] Brunetto Latini likewise argues at the start of his chapter on the government of cities that 'justice ought to be so well established in the heart of every *signor* that he assigns to everyone his right'.[106] The reason, he too explains, is that 'a city which is governed according to right and truth, such that everyone has what he ought to have, will certainly grow and multiply, both in people and in wealth, and will endure for ever in a good state of peace, to its honour and that of its friends'.[107]

By the time we come to the writers of vernacular *Dictamina* at the end of the century, we find these connections between justice, the common good and the attainment of greatness presented almost as a litany. 'He who loves justice', as Matteo de' Libri proclaims 'loves a constant and perpetual will to give to each his right; and he who loves to give to each his right loves tranquillity and repose, by means of which countries rise to

---

[102] Sallust 1931a, X. 1, p. 16: 'labore atque iustitia res publica crevit'.
[103] Cicero 1913, I. VII. 20, p. 20: 'qua societas hominum inter ipsos et vitae quasi communitatis continetur'. Cf. also the claim in Cicero 1949, II. LIII. 160, p. 328 that it is *iustitia* which serves to maintain the *communes utilitates*.
[104] Viterbo 1901, p. 220, col. 1: 'ius suum cuilibet reddatur, et regatur civitas in iustitia et equitate'.
[105] Viterbo 1901, p. 231, col. 2: 'Per haec enim frena [iustitia et equalitas] civitates reguntur... crescunt, ditantur et maximum recipiunt incrementum.'
[106] Latini 1948, p. 392: 'Justice doit estre si establement fermee dedens le cuer au signor, k'il doinst a chascun son droit.'
[107] Latini 1948, p. 403: 'La cités ki est governee selonc droit et selonc verité, si ke chascuns ait ce k'il doit avoir... certes, ele croist et mouteplie des gens et d'avoir et dure tousjours en bone pais a l'onour de lui et de ses amis.'

the highest *grandeça*.'[108] Giovanni da Vignano writes in virtually identical terms, thereby furnishing yet a further summary of the ideology I have been anatomising. The essence of good government is to act justly; to act justly is to give to each their due; to give to each their due is the key to maintaining civic concord; and 'it is by means of all these things', Giovanni concludes, 'that countries are able to rise to *grandeça*'.[109]

With this injunction to love justice and treat it as the foundation of civic greatness, we reach the heart of the ideology articulated by the early *dictatores*. But there still remained one question of the highest practical importance. Under what system of government have we the best hope of ensuring that our leading magistrates do in fact obey the dictates of justice, so that all these benefits flow from their rule?

It is at this point that the *dictatores* respond with their celebration of the system of government most familiar to them, the system based on ruling councils chaired by elected magistrates. If justice is to be upheld and civic greatness attained, they all agree, government by hereditary princes or *signori* must at all costs be avoided; some form of elective and self-governing system must always be maintained.

Once again, the authorities most often invoked in support of this basic commitment are the apologists of the Roman republic in its final phase. The vehement anti-Caesarism of Cicero's *De Officiis* naturally made it a key text.[110] But the most frequently quoted argument against hereditary rule was yet again taken from Sallust's *Bellum Catilinae*. The danger with kingship, Sallust had warned, is that 'to kings, good men are objects of even greater suspicion than the wicked'.[111] The reason is that 'to kings, the good qualities of others are invariably seen as a threat'.[112] This explains why 'it was only when the city of Rome managed to become liberated from its kings that it was able, in such a short space of time, to rise to such greatness'.[113] Only when everyone is permitted to contend for honour, without fear of exciting envy or enmity from their rulers, can the heights of civic glory be scaled.

Among the pre-humanist writers, it is Brunetto Latini who reiterates this argument with the strongest emphasis. His chapter 'Of Signories'

---

[108] Libri 1974, p. 34: 'quel k'ama iustitia ama constante e perpetua voluntate de dare soa raxone a çascuno; e ki ama soa raxone a çascuno, ama tranquilitate e reposo, per le qual cose le terre montano in grand grandeça'.
[109] Vignano 1974, p. 296: 'per le qua' cose fare le terre montano in grandeça'.
[110] For the denunciation of Julius Caesar as a tyrant see Cicero 1913, II. VII. 23, p. 190.
[111] Sallust 1931a, VII. 3, p. 12: 'Nam regibus boni quam mali suspectiores sunt.'
[112] Sallust 1931a, VII. 3, p. 12: 'semperque eis [viz. regibus] aliena virtus formidulosa est'.
[113] Sallust 1931a, VII. 3, pp. 12–14: 'Sed civitas...adepta libertate quantum brevi creverit.'

opens with the briskest possible statement of the case. 'There are three types of government, one being rule by kings, the second rule by leading men, the third rule by communes themselves. And of these, the third is far better than the rest.'[114] At the start of his chapter 'On the Government of Cities' he proceeds to give his grounds for this conclusion. Where kings and princes enjoy ultimate control, as in France and in most other countries, they consider only their own interests, 'selling offices and assigning them to those who pay most for them, with little consideration for the good or benefit of the townsfolk'.[115] But where the citizens themselves retain control, as in Italy, 'they are able to elect, as *podestà* or *signore*, those who will act most profitably for the common good of the city and all their subjects'.[116]

The pre-humanist writers assign no distinctive name to the form of government they most admire. They are content to describe it as one of the types of *regimen* or *reggimento* by which a *civitas* or *commune* can lawfully be ruled.[117] When they are more specific, they merely add that the *regimen* in question can be described as one in which power remains in the hands of the commune itself.[118] Save for one or two remarks in Giovanni da Viterbo,[119] and later in Albertino Mussato,[120] there is no sign of the later disposition to use the term *res publica* to distinguish such elective forms of government from hereditary monarchies. Still less is there any hint of the suggestion canvassed by Cicero in *De Officiis* to the effect that self-governing regimes are the only forms of *res publicae* truly worthy of the name.[121]

There is one point, however, at which a number of these writers make use of a concept that was later to be central to the political vocabulary of *quattrocento* republicanism. As we have seen, they treat it as a distinctive virtue of elective systems that they guarantee the equality of all

---

[114] Latini 1948, p. 211: 'Seignouries sont de iii manieres, l'une est des rois, la seconde est des bons, la tierce est des communes, laquele est la trés millour entre ces autres.'
[115] Latini 1948, p. 392 claims that, in France and other kingdoms, rulers 'vendent les provostés et les baillent a ciaus ki plus l'achatent (poi gardent sa bonté ne le proufit des borgois)'.
[116] Latini 1948, p. 392: 'en Ytaile ... li communité des viles eslisent lor poesté et lor signour tel comme il quident qu'il soit plus proufitable au commun preu de la vile et de tous lor subtés'.
[117] See, for example, Faba 1892, p. 66; Viterbo 1901, p. 222, col. 1; Ceffi 1942, p. 45.
[118] See, for example, Latini 1948, pp. 211, 392.
[119] Viterbo 1901, p. 255, col. 2; p. 262, col. 1; and p. 272, col. 1 uses the term *res publica* to describe self-governing cities.
[120] Mussato 1727, col. 722: 'Formam publicam tenendam in civitate, ne figura reipublicae adeo usque deleta sit, quin faciem effigiemque habere censeatur.'
[121] Cicero 1913, II. VIII. 29, p. 196. This passage, implying that Rome was only a true *res publica* under its traditional constitution, is crucial to understanding the process by which the term *res publica* eventually ceased to be used to refer to any type of body politic, and instead came to be used specifically to describe elective systems of government such as Cicero had in mind.

The rediscovery of republican values

citizens before the law. No one's interests are excluded, no one is unfairly subordinated to anyone else. But this, they maintain, is in effect to advance a thesis about political liberty, a value they equate not with holding particular privileges from higher authorities but with a state of civic independence.[122] The inference they draw is that only under elective regimes can individuals hope to follow a free way of life, unconstrained by any unjust dependence or servitude. As a result – following a usage established by Cicero[123] – they begin to describe such regimes as 'free governments', commending them as the only means to ensure that every citizen is permitted to live 'in a free state'.[124]

We already encounter an intimation of this development at the start of Giovanni da Viterbo's *Liber de Regimine Civitatum*, where he argues that the term *civitas* itself derives from the phrase *civium libertas*.[125] A further hint can be found in Bonvesin della Riva's panegyric on Milan, in which the chapter in praise of the city's traditional form of communal government is entitled 'The Commendation of Milan by Reason of its Liberty'.[126] A generation later, we find Albertino Mussato underscoring the contrast with the servitude to be expected under hereditary *signori* in the course of recounting the fall of the Paduan commune. Mussato repeatedly equates the attempt by his fellow-citizens to uphold their *res publica* against the challenge of the Della Scala family with the attempt 'to fight in defence of the liberty of one's native community'.[127]

It is in Filippo Ceffi's *Dicerie*, however, that the upholding of liberty is most emphatically connected with elective forms of government. In his model speech for citizens to use when receiving a new *podestà*, Ceffi characterises such magistrates as the preservers of liberty.[128] In a later speech designed for a similar occasion, he advises citizens to remind the incoming *podestà* of their expectation that every citizen 'will be able to live both safely and in a state of liberty' under his rule.[129] Most striking of all is his model speech designed for citizens to use in the event of

---

[122] For the contrasting understanding of freedom in terms of privileges see Harding 1980.
[123] See, for example, his distinction between living under tyranny and living 'in libera civitate' in Cicero 1913, II. VII. 23–4, p. 190. Cf. also Cicero 1913, II. XXII. 78–9, p. 254 on the liberty of citizens.
[124] It is thus an exaggeration to claim, as does Witt 1971, p. 175, that 'a republican concept of *libertas*' only re-emerges in 'the early years of the Quattrocento'. But cf. Witt 1971, pp. 186–8 for an interesting discussion of some earlier accounts.
[125] Viterbo 1901, p. 215, col. 2: 'Civitas autem dicitur civium libertas.' Cf. also Viterbo 1901, p. 271, col. 1 on the connection between liberty and self-government.
[126] Riva 1974, p. 166: 'De commendatione Mediolani ratione libertatis.'
[127] See, for example, Mussato 1727, p. 658: 'pro patria libertate decertant'.
[128] Ceffi 1942, pp. 32, 35.
[129] Ceffi 1942, p. 41: 'che noi possiamo iscampare e vivere liberamente sotto la vostra segnoria'.

having to capitulate to a *signore*. Here Ceffi explicitly equates such a change of government with the forfeiture of liberty. What he advises the leaders of a commune to say in this predicament is that 'due to the harshness of war, we find ourselves obliged to hand over our liberty and our system of justice, which have been in our possession for many years'.[130] We already hear the claim that was later to sound so strongly in early-modern republicanism, the claim that it is possible to live freely only in a free state.

IV

The texts I have been considering were mostly in circulation by the middle years of the thirteenth century. A few years later, William of Moerbeke's pioneering translation of Aristotle's *Politics* also began to circulate in the *Regnum Italicum*. Starting from that point of origin, there rapidly arose a new intellectual movement of even greater significance for the defence of the Italian city-republics and their distinctive way of life.[131] Although Aristotle's *Politics* was first seriously studied at the University of Paris, it soon became obvious that its central doctrines were of special relevance to the *Regnum Italicum*, particularly his emphasis on city-states as the appropriate units of political analysis and his special enthusiasm for elective systems of ruling and being ruled.[132] So it is not surprising to find that, in the half-century after Moerbeke's translation became available, most of the influential adaptations of Aristotle's ideas came from Italian writers on the newly named subject of 'political science'.[133]

The first and greatest of these scholastic commentators was St Thomas Aquinas, scion of a noble Neapolitan family,[134] who composed his unfinished *De Regno*[135] as well as beginning his *Summa Theologiae* in the course of the 1260s. He in turn exercised an overwhelming influence over a

---

[130] Ceffi 1942, p. 61: 'per asprezza di guerra, siano condotti a donare nostra libertade e giustizia, la quale abbiamo posseduta per molti anni'. As Rubinstein 1952 shows, the assumption that the preservation of liberty requires the maintenance of a self-governing republic became a commonplace of political rhetoric in Florence in the later fourteenth century.

[131] This scholastic background to Renaissance political theory is especially well discussed in Rubinstein 1982, pp. 153–200.

[132] Aristotle 1996, I. 2, 1253^a, pp. 13–14 and III. 1, 1275^a, pp. 61–2.

[133] For the background to this development see Nederman 1991. Latini 1948, p. 391 already speaks of 'politique' as 'la plus haute science'.

[134] For the significance of Aquinas's Italian background see Catto 1976.

[135] In the edition I am using, Aquinas's text is printed (together with Ptolemy of Lucca's continuation) in the form of a single text under Aquinas's title. However, to avoid confusion with Ptolemy's work I have preferred to cite Aquinas's treatise under its alternative title, *De Regno*.

number of other Italian members of the Dominican Order, many of whom attended his lectures at Paris as well as studying his commentaries. These included Remigio de' Girolami, a native of Florence and the author of the Thomist tracts *De Bono Pacis* and *De Bono Communi*;[136] Ptolemy of Lucca, whose *De Regimine Principum* was long assumed to be the work of Aquinas himself; and Henry of Rimini, author of a major treatise of moral and political theory, largely Thomist in inspiration, entitled *Tractatus de Quatuor Virtutibus Cardinalibus*. By the end of the thirteenth century the path from Italy to Paris and back again was being trodden by philosophers and theologians of all persuasions, including the two most famous writers on politics of early fourteenth-century Italy. One of these was Giles of Rome, whose *De Regimine Principum* remained one of the most widely cited contributions to its genre for many generations.[137] The other was Marsilius of Padua, the author of perhaps the greatest work of political Aristotelianism, the *Defensor Pacis* of 1324.

Aristotle gave these writers a new confidence as well as a new armoury of concepts with which to challenge the orthodox Augustinian assumption that all governments are imposed by God's ordinance as a remedy for human sinfulness. Generally they begin by affirming that 'to live a social and political life together', as Aquinas puts it, 'is altogether natural to mankind'[138] and that 'living in a city is living in a perfect community, one that is capable of supplying all the necessities of life'.[139]

When they turn to consider the purposes served by such *communicationes politicae*, they generally offer a purely Aristotelian — and hence a strongly positive — account of the values that such communities are able to promote. 'First among these', in Aquinas's words, 'is the preservation of the unity of peace',[140] a sentiment strongly echoed by Remigio and Marsilius in the titles of their treatises.[141] As well as maintaining peace on earth, however, there is an even greater blessing that well-ordered political societies can bring. By preventing strife, they are able to supply us with a

---

[136] On Remigio see Minio-Paluello 1956.
[137] For a study see Blythe 1992, pp. 60–76.
[138] Aquinas 1973, I. 1, p. 257: 'naturale autem est homini ut sit animal sociale et politicum, in multitudine vivens'.
[139] Aquinas 1973, I. 2, p. 259: 'in civitate vero, quae est perfecta communitas, quantum ad omnia necessaria vitae'.
[140] Aquinas 1973, I. 3, p. 259 says that the duty 'ut pacem unitatis procuret' is the one 'ad quod maxime rector multitudinis intendere debet'. See also Rimini 1472, II. 3, fo. 28ʳ: 'finis enim qui intenditur in regimine civitatis est pax'. See too Rome 1607, III. II. 3, p. 456: 'pax et unitas civium debent esse finaliter intenta a legislatore'.
[141] Remigio 1959, p. 124 begins with the claim that 'summum bonum multitudinis et finis eius est pax'. Marsilius 1928, I. I. 4, p. 3 likewise begins by claiming that 'pacis seu tranquillitatis fructus optimi [sunt] ... propter quod pacem optare, non habentes quaerere'.

framework of security within which we can hope to pursue our chosen ends and thereby attain a life of happiness. As Marsilius explains – quoting directly from the *Politics* – the highest goal of any political community is 'that of enabling us not merely to live together, but to live the good life in the manner most appropriate to mankind'.[142]

The authority of Aristotle's *Politics* also enables these writers to mount a new challenge to the belief that all properly constituted political societies must take the form of hereditary and God-given lordships. Aristotle had devoted much of Book 3 of the *Politics* to considering the relationship between different styles of *regimen* and the goals of public life. Far from concluding that monarchical rule is indispensable, he had argued that three different kinds of government are all capable of realising the supreme goal of enabling us 'to live together and to live well'. These he had listed as monarchy, aristocracy and what William of Moerbeke was to translate (or rather, transliterate) as *politia*, 'the case where the body of the people acts in the name of the common good'.[143] In Book 2, moreover, Aristotle had even thrown out the further remark – fully explored in Book 4 – that 'there are some experts who maintain that the very best form of polity will be one in which there is a mixture of all these various different forms of government'.[144]

Confronted with these novel typologies, the schoolmen at first continued to insist that a virtuous monarchy must still be regarded as the best form of rule. This remained Aquinas's view, both in *De Regno* and the *Summa*, and in this judgement he was followed without hesitation by such early disciples as Henry of Rimini and Giles of Rome.[145] Even in these theorists, however, we already find the terms of the debate entirely transformed by the impact of Aristotle's arguments. The reasons now given for preferring a *regimen regni* are no longer connected with the suggestion that God ordains kingly power as a natural form of lordship. Instead the rule of princes is defended on the naturalistic and explicitly Aristotelian grounds that, as Aquinas puts it in *De Regno*, 'experience

---

[142] Marsilius 1928, I. IV. 3, p. 12 states that the 'causa finalis civitatis' is that of enabling us 'vivere autem ipsum et bene vivere conveniens hominibus'. Cf. Aquinas 1973, I. 15, p. 274: 'ad hoc enim homines congregantur ut simul bene vivant'.
[143] Aristotle 1872, III. IV (1279^a), p. 179: 'quando autem multitudo ad commune conferens vivit'.
[144] Aristotle 1872, II. III (1265^b), p. 92: 'quidam quidem igitur dicunt, quod oportet optimam politiam ex omnibus esse civibus mixtam'.
[145] Aquinas 1973, I. 4, p. 260: 'sicut autem regimen regis est optimum'. Cf. Aquinas 1952, I^a. II^{ae}, Qu. 105, art. 1, ad. 2, p. 503: 'dicendum quod regnum est optimum regimen populi'. See also Rimini 1472, II. 12, fo. 36^r: 'regimen regni, in quo unus principatus est cum virtute ... est optimus inter omnes principandi modos'. See too Rome 1607, III. II. 3, p. 456: 'regnum est optimus principatus'.

shows that those provinces or cities which live under the rule of a single king are above all able to rejoice in peace, flourish in justice and delight in abundance of wealth'.[146]

The precise form of monarchical government defended by Aquinas and his followers is also far removed from the traditional image of hereditary lordship. They argue for a system of elective monarchy in which there are strong elements of aristocratic and popular control. Aquinas presents the classic statement of this commitment in the course of his long analysis of the concept of law in the *Summa Theologiae*. He begins by reiterating that the best form of government is monarchy, the next best aristocracy. This, he claims, is one of the two major points that Aristotle makes about the good ordering of political societies. But Aristotle's other point is that 'the only way to ensure peace among the people is for everyone to play some part in the business of government'.[147] Putting these two contentions together – in a chain of reasoning not to be found in Aristotle – Aquinas goes on to commend a very specific form of limited rule:

It follows from this that the best form of government, whether of a kingdom or a city-state, must therefore be one in which a single individual is placed in command of everyone else and rules them virtuously, but in which there are others under him who are also capable of governing virtuously, and in which all the citizens are involved in public affairs, not merely as electors of their rulers but as potential members of the government themselves.[148]

The best type of polity, in short, is said to be a 'well-mixed' or *bene commixta* form of monarchy, one in which the virtues of all the pure types of *regimen* are combined while their shortcomings are balanced out.

We need finally to note that several of these early Thomists show a new and remarkable willingness to criticise the institution of monarchy itself. They generally do so, moreover, from the perspective of the very different arrangements prevailing in the Italian city-republics. Aquinas himself concedes in *De Regno* that 'men living under a monarchy are often

---

[146] Aquinas 1973, I. 3, p. 260: 'hoc etiam experimentis apparet. nam provinciae vel civitates quae sunt sub uno rege reguntur, pace gaudent, iustitia florent et affluentia rerum laetantur'. Cf. Rome 1607, III. II. 3, p. 456: 'hanc autem unitatem et concordiam magis efficere potest ... si dominetur unus princeps'.

[147] Aquinas 1952, I^a. II^{ae}, Qu. 105, art. 1, resp., p. 502: 'Quorum unum est ut omnes aliquam partem habeant in principatu: per hoc enim conservator pax populi.'

[148] Aquinas 1952, I^a. II^{ae}, Qu. 105, art. 1, resp., p. 502: 'Unde optima ordinatio principum est in aliqua civitate vel regno, in qua unus praeficitur secundum virtutem qui omnibus praesit; et sub ipso sunt aliqui principantes secundum virtutem; et tamen talis principatus ad omnes pertinet, tum quia ex omnibus eligi possunt, tum quia etiam ab omnibus eliguntur.'

slower to exert themselves on behalf of the common good', and that 'in consequence of this, as we see from experience, a single city governed by an annually elected *rector* is sometimes capable of achieving more than any king, even if he is ruler of three or four cities'.[149] Henry of Rimini goes even further. Although he begins by defending monarchy as the best form of government, he not only follows Aquinas almost word for word in arguing that the best *species regni* is an elective form of mixed monarchy,[150] but he proceeds to add the wholly novel suggestion that 'if we consider all the polities of Christendom at the present time, the one that appears to approximate most closely to this ideal of a *regimen mixtum* is the government of the people of Venice'.[151] The Venetian system, he goes on to explain, is based on a *Dux* who is elected for life and supported by 'about four hundred nobles and gentlemen who take part in public debates', as well as by 'an advisory body of forty leading citizens known as the *conciliarii*'.[152] The presence of the *Dux* means that 'this can properly be called a monarchical form of government'. But the addition of the *conciliarii* 'make it resemble a *regimen optimatum*', while the fact that they are elected 'by the nobles and by many honourable citizens' supplies 'an element of a popular regime' and allows us to conclude that 'all three forms of government are represented'.[153]

To this analysis Henry added the immensely influential claim that this unique constitution serves to explain why 'the people of Venice flourish in so much peace and security'. This is why 'no one oppresses anyone else' and why 'you seldom if ever hear of murders or even the shedding of human blood' in Venice.[154] From this moment we can date the unfolding of one of the most potent myths of early-modern political theory: the

---

[149] Aquinas 1973, I. 5, p. 262: 'Plerumque namque contigit, ut homines sub rege viventes, segnius ad bonum commune nitantur ... unde experimento videtur quod una civitas per annuos rectores administrata, plus potest interdum quam rex aliquis, si haberet tres vel quattuor civitates.'

[150] Rimini 1472, II. 15, fo. 37^r thinks that 'principatus mixtus ex tribus est optimus', provided that 'principes eliguntur'.

[151] Rimini 1472, II. 15, fo. 37^r: 'inter politias nostris temporibus in populo Christiano fuerunt politia gentis Venetorum ad hoc regimen mixtum videtur appropinquare'.

[152] Rimini 1472, II. 16, fo. 37^v: 'in ipsa namque circiter quadrigenti tam ex nobilibus quam etiam ex honorabili populo ad consilia publica admittuntur', with the *Dux* 'praedictus a maioribus quadraginta quos conciliarios vocant'.

[153] Rimini 1472, II. 16, fo. 38^r: Because of the presence of the *Dux*, 'regimen regni dici potest'. Because of the *maiores*, 'regimen optimatum', while the fact that 'non solum maiores nobiles sed etiam de populo honorabili' are involved in the election of the *Dux* means there is also 'aliud de politia populi'. We may therefore say that 'ex tribus regiminibus aliquid participat'.

[154] Rimini 1472, II. 16, fo. 38^r: 'Venetorum gens tanta pace et securitate fruitur ... nullius alterius oppressor ... omnia homicidia vel humani sanguis effusiones aut nunquam aut raro ibi audiuntur.'

myth of Venice as the *serenissima*, together with the attribution of this condition to her distinctive form of elective government.[155]

Once Aristotle's authority began to be invoked to criticise prevailing conceptions of monarchy, it proved a short step to the repudiation of the belief that monarchy in any form deserves to be accounted the best type of government. This step was duly taken by a number of Italian schoolmen in the early decades of the fourteenth century. They arrived at a vision of politics in which the self-governing arrangements of the city-republics were not merely defended as legally viable forms of government, but were celebrated as nothing less than the best means of bringing about the highest ends of public life.[156]

Ptolemy of Lucca warmly embraces this conclusion in the final book of his *De Regimine Principum*.[157] He begins by setting out the three forms of government agreed by Aristotle to be based on right reason. These are said to be monarchy, aristocracy and 'the rule of the many, a form of regime known as a polity (from the Greek word *polis*) because of being especially well suited to cities, as we see above all in various parts of Italy'.[158] Later in his discussion, however, Ptolemy drastically alters Aristotle's typology, claiming that the fundamental distinction is between 'polities' on the one hand and 'despotic' forms of government on the other, 'with monarchy being included under the heading of despotism'.[159] This prepares us for his novel and dramatic conclusion that 'wherever you encounter a people confident of their own intelligence, you will never find them being ruled except by such a "political" form of government'. This in turn explains, he ingenuously adds, 'why it is that this form of political authority flourishes above all in Italy'.[160]

A similar commitment lies at the heart of Marsilius of Padua's *Defensor Pacis*. It is true that in Book 1 chapter 8 he assures us that 'it forms no part of my present purpose to decide which of the well-tempered

---

[155] Fasoli 1958 shows that the celebration of Venice as *serenissima* was well established by this time. But Robey and Law 1975 point out that Henry of Rimini seems to have been the first writer to attribute this achievement to Venice's political arrangements.
[156] For the suggestion that this context best serves to explain Marsilius's preoccupations in the *Defensor Pacis* see Rubinstein 1965.
[157] For a study see Blythe 1992, pp. 92–117.
[158] Ptolemy 1973, IV. 1, p. 325: 'Si autem per multos...tale regimen politiam appellant, a *polis*...quia hoc regimen proprie ad civitates pertinet, ut in partibus Italiae maxime videmus.'
[159] Ptolemy 1973, IV. 8, p. 336 compares the *regimen politicum* with the *regimen despoticum*, 'includendo in despotico etiam regale'.
[160] Ptolemy 1973, IV. 8, p. 336: 'Qui autem...in confidentia suae intelligentiae sunt, tales regi non possunt nisi principatu politico...tale autem dominium maxime in Italia viget.' For further discussion see Davis 1984.

forms of government is the best'.[161] But in chapter 12 he introduces a categorical distinction between the location of the sovereign power to enact laws and the purely administrative duty of ensuring that they are duly carried out. Marsilius concedes that the *pars principans* – the executive and administrative functions of government – can equally well be discharged by a popular or an aristocratic assembly, and even allows in chapter 9 that 'a better method might conceivably be to institute an elective form of monarchy'.[162] But the commitment he wishes above all to emphasise – 'in line with the truth as well as with Aristotle's doctrine in the *Politics*' – is that 'the legislator, that is to say the primary and proper source of the authority to make laws, must be equated with the people, the *universitas* of the citizens as a whole'.[163]

Marsilius places only one restriction on this otherwise unqualified doctrine of popular sovereignty. The powers of the legislator, he adds, can alternatively be confined to the weightier part (*valentior pars*) of the citizen-body, 'taking into consideration the quality as well as the quantity of the persons involved'.[164] But in essence his conclusion is that, if peace and the means to live the good life are to be preserved, the body of the people must remain sovereign at all times. They must ensure that the *pars principans* is elected (chapter 9); that our magistrates are granted a minimum of discretion to vary the laws (chapter 11); and that they are capable of being removed from office by the electorate at any time (chapter 18).

As we have seen, Ptolemy of Lucca had already arrived at a similar conclusion. But whereas he had merely asserted it, Marsilius offers a careful argument in favour of equating the *legislator humanus* with the *universitas civium*.[165] His strategy is to examine the causes of discord within communities, thereby isolating the main enemies of peace that need to be overcome. One such enemy is said to be faction and the formation of political splinter groups. The danger here is that 'if the law is enacted merely by one or a few citizens, they will consult their own good rather

---

[161] Marsilius 1928, I. VIII. 4, p. 29: 'quis autem bene temperatorum principatuum sit optimus... non habet praesentem speculationem'.

[162] Marsilius 1928, I. IX. 5, p. 33: 'fortasse perfectior est regalis monarchia... vel instituitur per electionem'.

[163] Marsilius 1928, I. XII. 3, p. 49: 'nos autem dicamus secundum veritatem atque consilium Aristotelis III *Politicae* capitulo 6°, legislatorem seu causam legis effectivam primam et propriam esse populum seu civium universitatem'.

[164] Marsilius 1928, I. XII. 3, p. 49: 'valentiorem inquam partem considerata quantitate personarum et qualitate in communitate'.

[165] But for a critique of this comparison between Ptolemy and Marsilius see Blythe 2000.

than attending to the good of the community as a whole'.[166] But the gravest cause of discord arises when the powers of jurisdiction within a community are in any way divided. This can easily happen when there is no clear judicial hierarchy, as was often the case in the Italian city-republics. 'For in such circumstances a citizen may appear before a given judge, ignoring the others, and may be able to obtain an acquittal, only to find himself convicted for contempt by the judges he has ignored.'[167] Even worse, however, are the divisions that arise from a source of discord unknown even to Aristotle, a source Marsilius isolates in chapter 19 of Book 1 and discusses with a boldness that won him instant excommunication and lasting notoriety. This further source, he declares, is the papacy, 'whose lust for power, based on the so-called *plenitudo potestatis* allegedly handed down by Christ, makes it the leading cause of intranquillity and strife in all cities and kingdoms everywhere'.[168]

It is Marsilius's central contention that, once these enemies of peace are identified, we can see that our only hope of vanquishing them lies in placing all power in the hands of the people. Chapters 12 and 17 of Book 1 argue that, if we are to forestall the development of factional or divided jurisdictions, the people must serve as the sole judicial as well as executive authority within their own community. The whole of Book 2 goes on to add that, if the lusts of the papacy are to be bridled, the people must at the same time strip the church of all coercive powers of *iurisdictio*, transferring them to 'the faithful human legislator' within each individual polity. The effect of taking these steps will not only be to restore peace; it will also return the church to the condition that Christ originally intended, the condition in which the sole function of the priesthood is to preach and practise the Christian faith.

V

The rediscovery of the Aristotelian corpus undoubtedly gave the political writers of early *trecento* Italy a new impetus in defending their traditional systems of government. They were able to mount a yet more authoritative

---

[166] Marsilius 1928, I. XII. 5, p. 51: 'si per unum aut paucos quosdam proprium magis quam commune attendentes commodum, lex ipsa feratur'.
[167] Marsilius 1928, I. XVII. 3, p. 91: 'quod si tamen appareat coram uno, reliquis spretis, et ab illo fortassis absolvatur a culpa et poena civili, a reliquis tamen damnabitur propter contumaciam'.
[168] Marsilius 1928, I. XIX. 12, p. 108: 'affectio principatus, quem sibi deberi asserunt ex eisdem (ut dicunt) per Christum tradita plenitudine potestatis, causa est singularis illa quam intranquillitatis seu discordiae civitatis aut regni factivam diximus'.

challenge to the belief that government should be viewed as a God-given form of lordship, and they were able to insist with a new assurance that the best type of government need not be a form of lordship at all. The point I have sought to emphasise, however, is that these values had already been inculcated by Azo and his pupils in their commentaries on the *Codex*, as well as by the pre-humanist spokesmen for the communes in their numerous treatises on the duties of city magistrates. Although they had no access to Greek philosophy, these writers were able to recover from the legal and moral philosophy of ancient Rome an eloquent and powerful defence of civic freedom, self-government and popular sovereignty. While the recovery of the Aristotelian corpus was undoubtedly of great importance, it was by no means as crucial as some scholars have supposed to the construction of a full-scale defence of republican self-government. As I have tried to show, the articulation of a civic ideology suited to the defence of the communes can in fact be traced to a period scarcely later than the formation of the communes themselves.

3

Ambrogio Lorenzetti and the portrayal of virtuous government

I

Between the early thirteenth and mid-fourteenth centuries, the city-republics of the *Regnum Italicum* engendered a distinctive political literature concerned with the ideals and methods of republican self-government. As we saw in chapter 2, several of the most eminent philosophers of the age took part in the argument, including St Thomas Aquinas and Marsilius of Padua. But it was an artist, Ambrogio Lorenzetti of Siena, who made the most memorable contribution to the debate. This took the form of the celebrated cycle of frescoes he painted between 1337 and 1339[1] in the Sala dei Nove of the Palazzo Pubblico in Siena.[2] Although it is obvious that these paintings do not constitute a text of political theory in the conventional sense, it is equally obvious even to the casual observer that they are basically intended to convey a series of political messages. It is with the question of how to read and interpret those messages that I shall principally be concerned.

I wish in particular to re-examine the central section of the frescoes, the section that occupies the middle level of the northern wall (see Plate 3). As the verses inscribed beneath this part of the painting explain, the

---

This chapter is a revised version of an article that originally appeared under the title 'Ambrogio Lorenzetti: The Artist as Political Philosopher' in the *Proceedings of the British Academy*, 72 (1987), pp. 1–56.

[1] See Bowsky 1981, pp. 287–8 for the commission and cf. Rowley 1958, vol. 1, pp. 130–1, for lists of payments. These suggest that the work was mainly undertaken between April 1338 and May 1339. There have been three major modern restorations of the cycle. The first was undertaken in the early 1950s, while the other two date from the 1980s, the more recent having been completed in 1988. My original description of the paintings was written before the two most recent restorations, but I have specifically noted all relevant points at which they have had the effect of changing what can now be seen.

[2] The paintings are generally known as the *Buon Governo* frescoes or as the 'allegory of good government'. But I have preferred to avoid these descriptions. The proposed title is definitely not original, and strictly speaking the paintings are not allegories.

painting itself is intended to represent that form of government which we are bound to establish if we are induced to act exclusively by the dictates of the holy virtue of justice.[3] The question I should like to re-open is what exact theory of government, what ideal of social and political life, is being held up for our admiration in this spectacular way.

One particular answer has come to enjoy the status of an orthodoxy among recent students of Lorenzetti's masterpiece. The work is said to be 'inspired both by Aristotelian and by Thomist ideas',[4] and to have 'its roots in scholasticism'.[5] More precisely, it is said to be 'largely based on Aristotelian philosophy in contemporary adaptation', specifically the adaptation by St Thomas Aquinas.[6] The painting is, in short, a work of 'Thomistic Aristotelianism'.[7] While it basically confronts us with 'an Aristotelian allegory of Good Government in principle',[8] this is mediated by 'contemporary scholastic and juristic interpretation', and above all by the doctrines of Aquinas's *Summa Theologiae*.

These arguments, long accepted by art historians and historians of ideas alike,[9] have recently been applied as a means of identifying the mysterious regal figure who dominates this middle section of the frescoes. To explain his significance, it is claimed, we need to focus on Aquinas's restatement of 'the Aristotelian concept of the common good as the basis and criterion of good government'.[10] The figure is in fact 'a personification of the *bonum commune* in the Thomistic-Aristotelian sense'.[11] The final message of the painting is thus that 'the common good must be

---

[3] My latest transcription (post-1988 restoration) of the opening of the verses on the simulated tablet reads as follows: 'QUESTA SANTA VIRTU [La Giustizia] LADOVE REGGE. INDUCE ADUNITA LIANIMI / MOLTI. EQUESTI ACCIO RICCOLTI. UN BEN COMUN PERLOR SIGROR SIFANNO.' Before the restoration of the early 1980s the penultimate word appeared as 'signor'. This seems much preferable, as the word 'sigror' makes no sense in any language. Note that in this and in all subsequent transcriptions I have expanded all contractions marked on the inscriptions themselves. It is perhaps worth adding that, along the base of each section of the frescoes, there is also a running set of verses. These are partly reproduced in Starn and Partridge 1992, Appendix 1, pp. 261–6. Starn and Partridge make much of the fact that the written and the visual evidence are sometimes out of line with each other. But there is no reason to assume that these verses formed part of the original design of the frescoes. Since their provenance and even their dating remain unclear, it seems best not to invoke them to interpret (or to deconstruct) Lorenzetti's iconographical scheme.

[4] Smart 1978, p. 104.   [5] Borsook 1980, p. 36.   [6] Rubinstein 1958, p. 184.
[7] Bowsky 1981, p. 290.   [8] Baxandall 1985, p. 32.
[9] For the former, see Feldges-Henning 1972, p. 146 and Southard 1978, pp. 64, 276. For the latter, see Zdekauer 1913, p. 405 and Larner 1971, p. 85.
[10] See Rubinstein 1958, p. 184. For the same claim see also Dowdall 1923, p. 113.
[11] Oertel 1968, p. 363.

raised to the position of the ruler' if the blessings of good government are to be enjoyed.[12]

My excuse for returning to these issues is a doubt I have come to feel about whether the context of scholastic political philosophy offers a helpful or even a relevant guide to explicating Lorenzetti's work. I have come to feel that there is almost nothing in this middle section of the frescoes that presupposes any acquaintance with either Aristotle's or Aquinas's thought. To suppose otherwise, I shall argue, has caused the iconography of this central section of the frescoes to be largely misconstrued and, more specifically, has caused the mysterious regal figure to be misidentified. I shall argue instead that this aspect of Lorenzetti's cycle is best interpreted as a contribution to the pre-humanist political culture I began to examine in chapter 2. My principal suggestion in what follows will thus be that, if we turn back to these pre-humanist writers, and to the Roman authorities on whom they relied, we shall find ourselves better equipped to approach and perhaps to explicate some of the more cryptic messages encoded in Lorenzetti's masterpiece.

II

I need to begin by singling out three elements from the pre-humanist culture I examined in chapter 2 that appear to have a close bearing on Lorenzetti's work. We need in the first place to consider a number of official documents, in particular the surviving written constitutions of the city-republics. Among these, the most relevant for my present purposes are the *Breves* of Siena assembled in 1250, the Latin constitution of the city drawn up in 1262 and the more extended *volgare* version of 1309–10. We also need to re-examine two further sources of evidence I have already mentioned in chapter 2. First there are the various treatises on the *Ars dictaminis*, especially those composed by *dictatores* like Guido Faba with clearly defined moral and political commitments.[13] But of still greater importance are the specialised treatises on city-government that first began to circulate in the early decades of the *duecento*. As I have already noted, these include the anonymous *Oculus Pastoralis* of the 1220s, Orfino da Lodi's *De Sapientia Potestatis* of the early 1240s and the two major contributions from the middle years of the century, Giovanni da Viterbo's

---

[12] Rubinstein 1958, p. 185. For more recent endorsements see Tuve 1963, p. 290; Feldges-Henning 1972, p. 145; Borsook 1980, p. 35; Bowsky 1981, p. 288; Frugoni 1983, pp. 136, 150, 157.
[13] On Faba as a spokesman for the communes see Wieruszowski 1971, pp. 367-8 and note.

Liber de Regimine Civitatum of c.1250 and Brunetto Latini's encyclopaedic *Li Livres dou trésor* of 1266.[14]

None of these writers had any direct acquaintance with the works of Aristotle. Orfino da Lodi, Giovanni da Viterbo, Guido Faba and the author of the *Oculus* all completed their treatises before the earliest Latin version of the full *Nicomachean Ethics* started to circulate in the early 1250s,[15] and considerably before William of Moerbeke issued the first Latin translation of the *Politics* a decade later.[16] Even Brunetto Latini, writing in the 1260s, still had access only to the brief and inaccurate paraphrase of the *Ethics* translated from the Arabic by Hermannus Alemannus in 1243–4.[17] Still more striking is the fact that, among the writers of *dictamina* and similar compilations in the next generation, the doctrines of Aristotle and his modern disciples appear to have had virtually no impact. When, for example, Geremia da Montagnone assembled his *Compendium Moralium Notabilium* between 1295 and his death in c.1320,[18] he showed a full awareness of the Aristotelian texts, but made no attempt to integrate them with, or use them to displace, the more traditional authorities he continued to cite. Finally, if we turn to the moral and political assumptions embodied in such products of the *Ars dictaminis* as Matteo de' Libri's *Arringhe* of c.1275, or Giovanni da Vignano's *Flore de Parlare* of c.1290, or Filippo Ceffi's *Dicerie* of c.1330, we encounter in every case an exclusive reliance on the traditional authorities, with no mention or even awareness of the Aristotelian texts.

The authorities on whom these writers continue to rely are the moralists not of ancient Greece but of Rome. All the tracts I have cited were overwhelmingly indebted to a small selection of texts from the late Roman republic and early principate that had never ceased to be studied and quoted throughout the middle ages. Among these, a few works by Sallust, Seneca, and especially Cicero stand out, above all Cicero's youthful *De Inventione* and his *De Officiis*. It is clear that most of the Italian writers on city government knew these texts at first-hand, while some of them seem to have known *De Officiis* almost by heart.[19]

---

[14] For these works and their dates of composition see above, chapter 2, section III.
[15] On this translation (almost certainly the work of Robert Grosseteste) and its dating see Grabmann 1916, pp. 220–37.
[16] Grabmann 1946, pp. 111–13.
[17] For Latini's use of this translation see Marchesi 1904, pp. 116–17. On the translation and its dating see Grabmann 1916, pp. 204–14, 219–20, who answers doubts about the attribution expressed in Marchesi 1904, pp. 106–9.
[18] Ullman 1973, p. 81.
[19] For these claims see Wieruszowski 1971, pp. 602–4, 610–19, and Alessio 1979, pp. 123–69.

The writers I am considering were yet more deeply indebted to a number of *Florilegia* and moral treatises derived from these Roman sources.[20] They knew about Seneca's theory of the virtues from the *Formula Vitae Honestae*, a tract of remarkably wide circulation that was generally believed to be by Seneca himself,[21] although Geremia da Montagnone was aware that it came from the early Christian era[22] and some fourteenth-century copyists correctly attribute it to Bishop Martin of Braga.[23] Similarly, they knew about Cicero's *De Officiis* both from the anonymous *Moralium Dogma Philosophorum* of the mid-twelfth century[24] and from the massive *Summa Virtutum et Vitiorum* compiled by Guillaume Perrault a century later,[25] both of whom treat Cicero's text as their veritable Bible in matters of moral and political philosophy.

If we now turn to examine these pre-humanist treatises, we are bound to be struck in the first place by their wide measure of agreement about the most precious value in civic life. They all accept that the goal of good government must be the preservation of peace on earth. The aspiration that everyone must foster is that of living in a state of concord and tranquillity with everyone else.

It is sometimes claimed that this vision of concord and peace was first formulated by Aquinas and his disciples at the end of the thirteenth century.[26] As we saw in chapter 2, however, the same values were no less central to early thirteenth-century writers on city government. The *Oculus* opens with a model speech to be delivered by chief magistrates on assuming office. They are instructed to assure the populace that they will bring glory to the city, and will do so 'by bringing peace, tranquillity and perfect love to you all'.[27] Orfino da Lodi similarly lays it down at the start of his section entitled 'Lessons for a chief magistrate' that they must 'fear God and uphold the laws in order to bind the community to

---

[20] Tuve 1963, pp. 268–70, 276–88 rightly distinguishes the Ciceronian and Senecan strands and cautions against overemphasising the alleged influence of Aristotle.
[21] Nearly 150 MSS survive from the fourteenth and fifteenth centuries alone. For this fact, and for the attribution to Seneca, see Braga 1950, p. 204.
[22] Montagnone 1505, Sig. A, 2^b places the *Formula* chronologically between the works of Priscian and Ambrose. As Braga 1950, p. 6 notes, Martin died in 579.
[23] See, for example, BL Add. MSS 22041, a fourteenth-century copy of the *Formula*, which begins (fo. 324r): 'Incipit libellus... [a] Martino episcopo'.
[24] Williams 1957 claims (pp. 737–8) that the tract must have been composed between 1145 and 1170 and offers good reasons (pp. 742–6) for doubting the usual attribution to Guillaume de Conches. I have treated the work as anonymous, although the edition I use still assumes the work to be by Conches.
[25] Dondaine 1948, pp. 186–7 argues that the treatise was written between 1236 and 1249.
[26] See for example Rubinstein 1958, pp. 186–7.
[27] *Oculus* 1966, p. 25: 'portantes inter vos pacem tranquilam et amorem perfectum'.

peace'.²⁸ Giovanni da Viterbo organises his entire treatise around the distinction between war and peace, arguing at the beginning of his section on war that 'the *podestà* or *rector* of a city must seek to avoid conflict by every means in his power', since his duty is 'to ensure in every possible way that the city he is governing remains in peace, quietness and tranquillity'.²⁹

The same ideal, expressed in more formal language, recurs no less prominently in the official documents of the period. The 1309 Constitution of Siena places the utmost emphasis on the point. The rubrics concerning the duties of the *Nove Signori* – the merchant oligarchy who ruled the city from 1287 to 1355 – repeatedly insist that their principal obligation is 'to conserve the city in perpetual peace and pure justice'.³⁰ They themselves must be 'lovers of peace and justice'³¹ and a special rubric reminds them that they are granted their 'licence and unrestrained power and authority' for the specific purpose of ensuring that 'the city and the commune and the people of Siena are reduced to a condition of true and rightful and trustworthy peace and unity, both individually and as a community'.³²

It is true that Aquinas and his disciples endorse the same commitment. But there is one point at which their treatment of peace stands in marked contrast with that of the pre-humanist writers on city government. Aquinas thinks of *pax* essentially as a state of concord with others and of peace with oneself.³³ By contrast, the pre-humanist writers continue to invoke the essentially Roman belief – which finds no place in Aquinas's analysis – that where there is peace there must also have been a triumph over discord, a victory over the forces of dissension and war that constantly threaten to destroy our common life.

Prudentius's *Psychomachia*, composed in the late fourth century and immensely popular throughout the middle ages, had bequeathed a compelling account of peace as a triumphant force 'who puts her enemies to flight, drives away war', and thereby serves as 'the fulfilment of the

---

²⁸ Lodi 1869, p. 52, 'Doctrina potestatis': 'Primo Deum timeat, servet mandataque legis... Ut patriam paci iungat.'
²⁹ Viterbo 1901, p. 270: 'nam potestas sive rector civitatis, in quantum potest, vitare debet guerram... cum ad officium eius pertineat curare modis omnibus, quibus potest ut pacatam, pacificam et tranquillam retineat civitatem, quam regit'.
³⁰ Lisini 1903, vol. 2, p. 488: 'che essa città... in pace perpetua et pura giustitia si conservi'.
³¹ Lisini 1903, vol. 2, p. 488: 'amatori et di pace et di giustitia'.
³² Lisini 1903, vol. 2, p. 498: 'Li Nove... abiano licentia et libera podestà et balia et pieno officio di reducere la città... a vera et dritta et leale pace et unità, communalmente et singularmente.'
³³ Aquinas 1962, IIᵃ. IIᵃᵉ, Qu. 29, art. 1, resp., p. 158.

labour of virtue'.³⁴ Geremia da Montagnone quotes this passage in his *Compendium*,³⁵ while Orfino da Lodi similarly speaks of peace as the victorious outcome of 'the battle and flight of discord'.³⁶ Giovanni da Viterbo's summary of the duties of magistrates invokes the same tradition of thought:

> It is the duty of every chief magistrate who is good and serious to ensure that the community he is ruling remains in peace and quiet. This he will be able to achieve without difficulty as long as he acts conscientiously to free the community of evil men and ensure that he conquers them. For it is crucial that the sacrilegious and the thieves, the deceivers and those who exhibit *furor*, should all be conquered.³⁷

As so often, Giovanni provides the fullest and most down-to-earth summary of the standard pre-humanist arguments.

Peace being the central value of civic life, the question that chiefly preoccupies these writers is how to ensure that her numerous enemies are duly destroyed. Among her foes the most obvious is said to be *guerra* or war. But the most insidious – to which the pre-humanist writers devote far more attention – is generally described as *discordia* or civic disunity. As we saw in chapter 2, they all quote Sallust's judgement in his *Bellum Iugurthinum* to the effect that this is the force that causes even the greatest undertakings to collapse.³⁸ And they all reiterate the distinctions drawn by Sallust and other Roman moralists in considering the different forms that civic discord can take.

One of these is said to be pure lawlessness, a failing that these writers associate in particular with the mob. The *Oculus* inveighs against the characteristic *furor* of the multitude,³⁹ while Orfino da Lodi similarly denounces 'the supreme *furor* of those who ignore the sacred character of the laws'.⁴⁰ Filippo Ceffi's *Dicerie* contains a model speech to be delivered in the face of such *furiosa gente*,⁴¹ while Guido Faba's invective against

---

³⁴ Prudentius 1949–53, lines 631–2, vol. 1, p. 322: 'Pax inde fugatis/hostibus alma abigit bellum'. Prudentius 1949–53, line 769, vol. 1, p. 332: 'pax plenum Virtutis opus'. Cf. the account, based on Prudentius, in Giamboni 1968, pp. 91–2.
³⁵ Montagnone 1505, fo. 46b.
³⁶ See the section 'De pugna et fuga discordiae' in Lodi 1869, p. 50.
³⁷ Viterbo 1901, p. 247: 'Congruit bono presidi et gravi curare ut pacata et quieta sit provincia quam regit; quod non difficile optinebit, si sollicite agat, ut malis hominibus provincia careat, eosque conquirat: nam et sacrilegos et latrones, plagiarios et fures, conquirere debet.'
³⁸ Sallust, 1931b, X. 6, p. 148. There is an allusion to this passage in *Oculus* 1966, p. 61. We also find it quoted in Conches 1929, p. 27; in Perrault 1618, vol. 2, p. 282; and in Latini 1948, p. 292.
³⁹ See *Oculus* 1966, p. 65 on the 'furor populi'. The phrase recurs in Mussato 1900, p. 33.
⁴⁰ Lodi 1869, p. 76: 'Supremus furor est sacras contempnere leges.'
⁴¹ Ceffi 1942, p. 57. Cf. Libri 1974, p. 146.

the unruly Florentines for starting fires and using stones as projectiles serves as a reminder to city magistrates of the form that such *dissensio* is likely to take.[42] A similar warning appears in the *Breves* of Siena, which charge the city police to exercise particular vigilance 'in the case of *fures*, malefactors and those who throw stones at houses or the civic buildings of Siena'.[43]

The other and even graver form of *discordia* is said to be faction, whose baleful effects these writers lament in tones of increasing despair. As Giovanni da Viterbo complains, 'there is scarcely a city to be found anywhere nowadays that is not divided against itself'.[44] Brunetto Latini opens his chapter on the government of cities with an even stronger invective against *divisio*:

Wars and hatreds have so much increased among Italians of the present time that division is found within every city, together with so much enmity between different parties of townspeople as to make it certain that anyone who acquires the love of one group will be visited with the malevolence of the other.[45]

Latini may already be registering a fear that the city-republics of the *Regnum Italicum* will be unable to survive unless they set their warring houses in order.

How are these enemies of civic tranquillity to be overcome? The pre-humanist writers answer with a single voice. The only way to bring about the triumph of peace is to ensure that no one is able to pursue their own ambitions at the expense of the public good. Everyone must somehow be induced to place the *bonum commune*, the *communes utilitates*, above all calculations of individual or factional advantage.

It has often been claimed that this argument only re-enters Western political theory with the reworking of Aristotelian categories by Aquinas and his disciples.[46] But in fact the same assumptions, taken not from Greek sources but from Cicero and Seneca, can already be found in virtually all the pre-humanist writers on city government. The source on which they chiefly liked to draw is Cicero's celebration of the ideal of the *bonum commune* at the start of *De Officiis*:

---

[42] Faba 1893, p. 375.
[43] *Breves Officialium*, p. 75: 'a furibus et malefactoribus et proicientibus lapides supra domos vel domum civium senensium'.
[44] Viterbo 1901, pp. 244–5: 'vix enim aliqua reperitur hodie civitas, que inter se non sit divisa'.
[45] Latini 1948, p. 394: '[La] guerre et haine est si muteplice entre les ytaliens au tans d'ore ... k'il a devision en trestoutes les viles et enemistié entre les .ii. parties des borgois, certes, kiconques aquiert l'amour des uns il li covient avoir la malevoeillance de l'autre.'
[46] For a representative example see Ullmann 1975, pp. 176–80.

We are not born simply for ourselves, for our country and friends are both able to claim a share in us. People are born for the sake of other people in order that they can mutually benefit one another. We ought therefore to follow Nature's lead and place the *communes utilitates* at the heart of our concerns.[47]

More succinctly, and scarcely less influentially, Seneca underlines the same point, arguing in his *Epistulae* that 'the common good and the wise man's good are the same',[48] and adding in *De Clementia* that 'man is clearly a social animal born for the common good'.[49]

Later in Book 1 of *De Officiis* Cicero had applied these considerations specifically to 'those who aim to take charge of public affairs'.[50] They must 'care for the good of the whole citizen body to such a degree that, in everything they do, they devote themselves solely to that end'.[51] They must 'look after the entire body-politic, never caring only for one part of it while deserting the rest'.[52] They must remember that 'anyone who considers only one part of the citizenry, while neglecting the rest, will be introducing sedition and *discordia* into the city, the most pernicious danger of all'.[53]

Partly through the intermediary of *Moralium Dogma Philosophorum*, in which the above passages from Cicero are all transcribed,[54] these doctrines came to pervade the pre-humanist literature on city government. The *Oculus* includes a model speech to be delivered by an incoming *podestà* in which he promises that all his actions will aim 'to promote the welfare of the community as a whole'.[55] Giovanni da Viterbo concludes his chapter on the benefits that a *podestà* should bring by quoting the entire passage from *De Officiis* on the duties of those who take charge of civic affairs.[56] But the most extensive discussion of the common good – largely based on the *Dogma* and Giovanni's use of it – can be found in Brunetto Latini's *Li Livres dou trésor*. He too quotes Cicero on

---

[47] Cicero 1913, I. VII. 22, p. 22: 'non nobis solum nati sumus ortusque nostri partem patria vindicat, partem amici... homines autem hominum causa esse generatos, ut ipsi inter se aliis alii prodesse possent, in hoc naturam debemus ducem sequi, communes utilitates in medium afferre'.
[48] Seneca 1917–25, vol. 2, LXXXV. 36, p. 306: 'Commune bonum est sapientis'.
[49] Seneca 1928–35, vol. 1, I. III. 2, p. 364: 'hominem sociale animal communi bono genitum videri'.
[50] Cicero 1913, I. XXV. 85, p. 86 on those 'qui rei publicae praefuturi sunt'.
[51] Cicero 1913, I. XXV. 85, p. 86: 'utilitatem civium sic tueantur, ut, quaecumque agunt, ad eam referant'.
[52] Cicero 1913, I. XXV. 85, p. 86: 'totum corpus rei publicae curent, ne, dum partem aliquam tuentur, reliquas deserant'.
[53] Cicero 1913, I. XXV. 85, p. 86: 'Qui autem parti civium consulunt, partem neglegunt, rem perniciosissimam in civitatem inducunt, seditionem atque discordiam.'
[54] Conches 1929, pp. 27, 30, 36.
[55] See *Oculus* 1966, p. 26 on the need to act 'pro utilitate communitatis istius'.
[56] Viterbo 1901, p. 268.

the need to take Nature as our guide and 'to place the common good above everything else'.[57] 'Each one of us', he adds, 'must do everything in our power on behalf of the common good of our city and fatherland.'[58] He also follows Cicero in laying special emphasis on the need for chief magistrates to take this lesson to heart. The elected *sires* of a city must be prepared 'to work night and day for the common good of the city and all its citizens'.[59] They must 'guard the common good in peace and honesty',[60] ensuring that all their decisions, especially those taken in their capacity as judges, 'are such as will further the common good'.[61]

Cicero was again the source for the account these writers give of how to prevent the pursuit of selfish or factional advantage from undermining the pursuit of the common good. The key to avoiding such divisiveness, Book 2 of *De Officiis* had argued, lies in recognising the need to uphold 'the two *fundamenta* of public life, the first being *concordia*, the second *aequitas*'.[62]

To live in *concordia* is to acknowledge that no man is an island, and thus that we need to act together in a *coniunctio ordinum* if the ideal of the common good is to be upheld.[63] Cicero had invoked a favourite metaphor to convey this thought, claiming that the social bonds created by the giving and receiving of benefits serve to link or tie us together in a voluntary but unified group.[64] *De Finibus* refers lovingly to these twin 'bonds of concord', while warning that they will always be broken if people simply follow their own good.[65] *De Republica* similarly speaks of *concordia* as 'the best and lightest rope of safety in society', a passage well known to later generations as a result of its inclusion by St Augustine in Book 2 of *De Civitate Dei*.[66] The same image of a double *vinculum concordiae* is also implicit in the oft-quoted passage from *De Officiis* in which Cicero

---

[57] Latini 1948, p. 291: 'por ce devons nous ensivre nature et metre avant tout le commun profit'.
[58] Latini 1948, p. 284: 'on doit faire tot son pooir por le commun profit de son païs et de sa vile'.
[59] Latini 1948, p. 392: 'Li sires... veillier dejour et de nuit au commun proufit de la vile et de tous homes.'
[60] Latini 1948, p. 253: 'garde le comun bien en pais et en honesteté'.
[61] Latini 1948, p. 408 on the duty to act 'por le bien dou commun'. Cf. also Latini 1948, pp. 405, 415, 418.
[62] Cicero 1913, II. XX. 78, p. 254: 'fundamenta rei publicae, concordiam primum,... deinde aequitatem'.
[63] See Cicero 1913, III. XXII. 88, p. 362 on the need for an 'ordinum coniunctio ad salutem rei publicae'.
[64] The same image recurs in Seneca's *De Beneficiis*. See Seneca 1928–35, vol. 3, VI. XLI. 2, p. 448.
[65] Cicero 1931, II. XXXV. 117, p. 208 speaks of two 'vincla concordiae', these being *beneficium* and *gratia*.
[66] See Augustine 1957–72, XII. XXII, vol. 4, p. 110 and XXII. XXX, vol. 7, p. 376 for references to the *vinculum concordiae*.

speaks once more about acts of giving and receiving as 'linking each individual in society together with everyone else'.[67]

According to Cicero, the second *fundamentum* of civic peace is the virtue of *aequitas*. Among Roman legal and political theorists, this term had been applied in two distinguishable ways. It was used on the one hand to express the concept of legal equity, the principle that the law sometimes needs to be supplemented or corrected by recourse to natural justice. This was the idea lying behind the passages from Ulpian on the concept of *naturalis aequitas* included in the *Digest*,[68] and this was how the concept was subsequently understood by scholastic philosophers as well as commentators on the civil law. When Aquinas, for example, speaks of *aequitas* in the *Summa*, he defines it simply as 'that quality which pertains to moderating the letter of the law'.[69]

The term was also used, however, to refer more broadly to the idea of fairness between individuals, in contrast to malice, treachery or the infliction of harm. This wider understanding was due above all to Cicero, and especially to his analysis in *De Officiis*.[70] As in the case of the *vinculum concordiae*, the concept is obviously a metaphorical one. To describe something in Latin as *aequus* is simply to use a synonym for *planus*, and is thus to describe it as flat or level or smooth. So when Cicero speaks of the need for arrangements between citizens to be *aequus*, his use of the image underlines his demand that – as *De Officiis* puts it – 'private individuals must live on level terms, on a fair and equal footing, with their fellow citizens'.[71] As a later passage adds, such a willingness to smooth out our differences is the only means of ensuring 'that the interests of all citizens are considered on level terms rather than being handled in a divisive way'.[72]

The pre-humanist writers adopt exactly the same viewpoint. They fully agree about the fundamental importance of *concordia*, a concept they connect more closely with peace than is usual in the writings of

---

[67] See Cicero 1913, I. VII. 22, p. 24 on how giving and receiving serve 'devincere hominum inter homines societatem'.

[68] See, for example, *Digest*, IV. IV. 1, vol. 1, p. 125; XI. VII. 14. 10, vol. 1, p. 352; XII. IV. 3. 7, vol. 1, p. 374.

[69] Aquinas 1962, II^a. II^{ae}, Qu. 120, art. 2, ad. 3, p. 548: 'pertinet aliquid moderari, scilicet observantiam verborum legis'.

[70] See Cicero 1913, III. X. 43, p. 310, where *aequitas* is related to fairness. Cf. Cicero 1913, I. XIX. 62, p. 64, where it is contrasted with malice or treachery, and Cicero 1913, I. IX .30, p. 30 where the contrast is with the infliction of harm.

[71] Cicero 1913, I. XXXIV. 124, p. 126: 'Privatum autem oportet aequo et pari cum civibus iure vivere.'

[72] Cicero 1913, II. XXIII. 83, p. 258: 'commoda civium non divellere atque omnis aequitate eadem continere'.

Aquinas and his followers.⁷³ They also make frequent allusion to the image of giving and receiving as the twin bonds of the *vinculum concordiae*. The author of the *Dogma* – who quotes but also adapts Cicero's analysis – appears to have served as an important intermediary at this as at many other points. He explains that the obligations of concord include 'that of binding men together in society by a reciprocity of duties, giving and receiving alternately'.⁷⁴ He accordingly defines concord as 'the virtue that spontaneously binds together citizens and compatriots who live together under the same law and in the same place'.⁷⁵ Brunetto Latini reiterates the image, speaking of concord as 'a virtue that ties together under one law and in one place all those who are of one city or one country'.⁷⁶ Finally, a number of later writers of *dictamina*, such as Matteo de' Libri and Giovanni da Vignano, extend the metaphor, using it as a means of proclaiming the value of leagues between cities. An ambassador seeking to form such an alliance, they both suggest, ought always to point out in its favour that 'a rope is much stronger when it is redoubled'.⁷⁷

These writers also accept that this wider notion of *aequitas* is fundamental to the preservation of social life. In their treatises on city government they usually focus on the narrower concept of legal equity, arguing that city magistrates must be prepared, in Giovanni da Viterbo's phrase, 'to be lovers of equity as well as strict justice'.⁷⁸ But in their moral treatises they often find a prominent place for the Ciceronian image of *aequitas* as a principle of fair and level dealing between citizens. Guillaume Perrault, for example, considers the ideal in some detail in analysing the concept of justice. If justice consists in rendering to each their due, we ought to ask what is due to whom. To superiors, he suggests, what is due is obedience; to inferiors, what is due is discipline; but 'with respect to those who are our equals, what is due is *aequitas*'.⁷⁹ He proceeds to define the virtue as 'a love of equality in every case where equality of treatment

---

⁷³ For the linking of peace and concord see *Oculus* 1966, p. 61; Viterbo 1901, pp. 230–1; Latini 1948, p. 215; Vignano 1974, p. 256.
⁷⁴ Conches 1929, p. 27: 'Concordia...devincire hominum inter homines societatem mutatione officiorum, dando accipiendo.' Brescia 1507, fo. 57ʳ similarly speaks of 'concordia...vinciens [cives]'.
⁷⁵ Conches 1929, p. 27: 'Concordia est virtus concives et compatriotas in eodem iure et cohabitatione spontanee vinciens.'
⁷⁶ Latini 1948, p. 291: 'Concorde est une vertus ki lie en .i. droit et en une habitation ceaus d'une cité et d'un païs.' Cf. also Giamboni 1968, p. 65.
⁷⁷ Libri 1974, p. 92: 'la fune, quando ella è reduplicata, plù forte è'. See also *Oculus* 1966, p. 39; Viterbo 1901, p. 225; Vignano 1974, pp. 280–1.
⁷⁸ Viterbo 1901, p. 252: 'sint aequitatis et iustitiae amatores'. Cf. also *Oculus* 1966, p. 36; Lodi 1869, p. 54; Libri 1974, p. 160.
⁷⁹ Perrault 1618, vol. 1, p. 295: 'dicendum est de aequitate quae est respectu paris'.

is appropriate',[80] to which he adds that 'this virtue is indispensable to all who live together in any form of social life'.[81]

There remains the question of what will induce us, prone as we are to follow our own selfish interests, to act together in a spirit of equity and concord to promote the common good. Again these writers answer with a single voice. There can be no prospect of our attaining these goals unless we submit to the dictates of justice and allow them to regulate our lives. As Cicero had declared in *De Inventione*, it is only if the requirements of justice are followed that the common good can be conserved.[82] Without justice, as he had added in *De Republica* in a passage made famous by St Augustine, there can be no prospect of holding the bond of concord in place.[83]

There are two *topoi* which these writers like to quote to encapsulate this argument. One states that justice represents the ultimate bond of human society. Cicero had laid it down that legal justice 'binds human society together',[84] but it seems to have been due to the influence of Martin of Braga's *Formula Vitae Honestae* that the idea of *iustitia* as the ultimate *vinculum societatis humanae* came to be widely taken up.[85] Guillaume Perrault lays great emphasis on Martin's phrase,[86] as does Giovanni da Viterbo,[87] while the section on justice in Geremia da Montagnone's *Compendium* includes the entire passage from the *Formula* in which it had occurred.[88]

The other *topos* states that, if the common good is to be promoted, it is indispensable that our rulers should be lovers of justice. *Diligite iustitiam qui iudicatis terram*: 'Love justice, you who judge the earth'. This injunction, the opening of the apocryphal Book of Wisdom, resounds throughout the pre-humanist literature on city government.[89] Guillaume Perrault quotes it at the start of his section on justice,[90] and it is quoted twice more in the *Oculus*,[91] twice more by Giovanni da Viterbo[92] and twice more in Brunetto Latini's *Trésor*.[93] Even more significantly, there is a visual tradition of inscribing the motto on Tuscan wall-paintings of the period. We find it on the scroll held by the Virgin in Simone Martini's *Maestà*, the great fresco he painted in 1315 in the Council chamber adjoining the

---

[80] Perrault 1618, vol. 1, p. 295: 'Et est aequitas amor aequalitatis in his in quibus debet esse aequalitas.'
[81] Perrault 1618, vol. 1, p. 295: 'Virtus aequitatis valde necessaria est his qui sunt in aliqua societate.'
[82] Cicero 1949, II. LIII. 160, p. 328: 'Iustitia est habitus animi communi utilitate conservata.'
[83] Augustine 1957–72, II. XXI, vol. 1, p. 218: 'concordia, artissimum atque optimum omni in re publica vinculum incolumitatis'.
[84] Cicero 1928, I. XV. 42, p. 344: 'ius, quo devincta est hominum societas'.
[85] Braga 1950, p. 246: 'iustitia ... [est] vinculum societatis humanae'.
[86] Perrault 1618, vol. 1, p. 154.   [87] Viterbo 1901, p. 254.   [88] Montagnone 1505, fo. 24b.
[89] On the theme of *sapientia Salomonis* see Artifoni 1997.   [90] Perrault 1618, vol. 1, p. 244.
[91] *Oculus* 1966, pp. 36, 66.   [92] Viterbo 1901, pp. 246, 257.   [93] Latini 1948, pp. 273, 414.

Sala dei Nove in the Palazzo Pubblico in Siena.[94] We see it once more on the scroll held by the infant Jesus in Lippo Memmi's *Maestà* of 1317 on the southern wall of the Sala di Dante in the Palazzo Communale in San Gimignano.

For all the importance these writers attach to the idea of justice, however, most of them remain content to analyse the concept in relatively simple terms. Some confine themselves to citing the familiar definition from the *Digest*, according to which the virtue consists of rendering to each their due, *ius suum cuique tribuens*. A few, however, feel prompted to ask what is involved in the application of that principle. One influential answer had been given by the author of *Moralium Dogma Philosophorum*. He divides the general idea of justice into severity and liberality, claiming that severity is what is due to the pestiferous, while those who act beneficially are owed a liberal tribute or reward.[95] Both Guillaume Perrault and Giovanni da Viterbo take up the same argument. Perrault opens his discussion of penal justice by explaining that it is simply a matter of rendering to malefactors what they deserve.[96] Giovanni similarly devotes one of his model speeches designed for the use of chief magistrates to insisting that the sword of justice 'is for returning evil with evil, not evil with good in the manner of the New Testament'.[97]

It is in Brunetto Latini's *Trésor*, however, that we find the most ambitious attempt to spell out the implications of the idea that justice consists essentially in desert. The authority on whom he mainly relies is Averroes in his somewhat idiosyncratic paraphrase of *Nicomachean Ethics*, a source he in turn adapts and paraphrases to suit his own purposes. Like Aristotle, Latini begins – in Book 2 chapter 28 – by considering the general idea of legal justice. But whereas Aristotle's next theme had been the nature of just distribution, neither Averroes nor Latini makes any mention of that issue. They instead switch directly to Aristotle's next topic, the question of rectification. Here Latini argues that the just man is essentially an *ygailleour*, a rectifier of unequal states of affairs.[98] A *sire* who imposes justice in this sense will 'find himself obliged to equalise states of affairs that are not equal'. This means, Latini explains, that 'it will fall to him to kill some, to wound others, to send others into exile'.[99] This is because

---

[94] The inscription reads: '[D]iligi/te iusti/tiam q/iudica/tis ter/ram.'
[95] Conches 1929, pp. 12–13. See also Mussato 1900, p. 48.   [96] Perrault 1618, vol. 1, p. 242.
[97] Viterbo 1901, p. 235: 'non reddendo eisdem secundum novum testamentum bonum pro malo sed malum pro malo'.
[98] Latini 1948, p. 198: 'L'ome juste est ygailleour.'
[99] Latini 1948, p. 198: 'li sires de la justice s'efforce d'ygaillier les choses ki ne sont ygaus, donc il li covient l'un ocire, l'autre navrer, l'autre chacier en exil'.

his basic duty is 'to offer satisfaction in the case of harms that have been received, in such a way that his subjects are able to live in a rightful state of equality'.[100]

Latini later returns to the issue in Book 2 chapter 38, in which he clarifies his earlier argument by further explaining the sense in which the just man may be said to equalise things. 'He does so in two ways: one is by handing out money and dignities; the other is by saving and paying back those who have received harm.'[101] By these means, Latini concludes, 'those who rectify acts and things between men serve as upholders of the law, guarding and doing justice both to those who do harm and to those who suffer it'.[102]

After his initial discussion of punitive justice in Book 2 chapter 28, Latini turns to consider a different question about *ygaillance*. This arises from the fact that 'citizens and people living together in cities engage in mutual exchanges with each other'.[103] So we need a further principle of equalisation to cover these *entreservices*. For we need to ensure that (to cite Latini's own examples) metal-workers can hope to exchange their wares with cordwainers or with carpenters in accordance with the precepts of justice.[104] This further point is also taken up in Book 2 chapter 38, where Latini repeats that there are principles of justice involved not merely in rewarding and punishing, but also 'in giving and receiving and exchanging'. 'For drapers give cloth for other things', while 'metal-workers give what they make in metal for other things', and all such *entreservices* ought to be regulated according to the requirements of justice.[105]

These discussions, however, still leave unanswered the most important practical question about justice. What will induce us, self-interested as we are, to accept the intrusion of so many legal regulations into our daily lives? According to scholastic and contractarian theories of government, the answer is relatively straightforward. We are capable of intuiting the principles of justice, and of recognising that we shall ultimately be

---

[100] Latini 1948, pp. 198–9: 'fere satisfation des torsfés quant il avienent, issi que ses subtés vivent en bone fermeté d'ygaillance'.
[101] Latini 1948, p. 204: 'c'est en ii. manieres, l'une est departir pecune et dignité, l'autre est sauver et apoier ceus ki ont recheu tort'.
[102] Latini 1948, p. 204: 'Et cil ki saine et sauve les fais et les choses ki entre les homes sont est cil ki fist la loi, et esgarde et fet justice entre ciaus ki font les torsfés et ciaus ki les reçoivent.'
[103] Latini 1948, p. 199: 'Li citein, et cil ki habitent ensamble en une vile, s'entreservent li uns as autres.'
[104] Latini 1948, p. 199.
[105] Latini 1948, p. 205: 'Justice ... ne puet estre sans doner et prendre et changier; car li drapiers done drap pour autre chose dont il a mestier, et li fevres done son fier por autre chose.'

following our own best interests if we establish a regulated form of social life based on imposing those principles in the form of positive laws. It follows that, as long as we are rational, we are bound to consent to the setting up of a form of magistracy that will have the effect of imposing the rule of law equally upon everyone. This is essentially the doctrine that Aquinas and his disciples derive from the Aristotelian thesis of natural sociability, a thesis they supplement with the contention that our capacity to intuit the rules of justice derives from their being at the same time the laws of God.

According to another and strongly contrasting tradition of thought, however, we are not innately social or political animals at all. This doctrine, stoic and anti-Aristotelian in origin, stems in its most influential version from the moral and rhetorical writings of Cicero and Seneca. Cicero's *De Inventione* opens with a classic statement of the case:

> There was a time when men wandered about in the fields in the manner of wild beasts. They conducted their affairs without the least guidance of reason but instead relied largely on bodily strength. There was no divine religion and the understanding of social duty was in no way cultivated. No one recognised the value inherent in an equitable code of law.[106]

Cicero goes on to insist that we should not think of our forefathers as having willingly abandoned this primitive way of life. Rather 'they began by crying out against any changes because of their novelty', preferring to continue in their pre-political and anti-social ways.[107]

From these assumptions Cicero infers that, since we now live under the rule of law, 'some great and wise man' must at some juncture have succeeded in persuading us to forswear our original and brutish way of life.[108] The shift to our present social and political arrangements cannot therefore be seen as the fruit of our own decision, rationally and voluntarily made. No such shift would ever have taken place in the absence of an heroic figure who is held up for our admiration throughout this tradition of thought: the figure of the wise and eloquent lawgiver. It must have been due to such a *vir sapiens*, Cicero insists, that men were at first persuaded 'to keep faith, follow the rules of justice and work for the common

---

[106] Cicero 1949, I. I. 2, p. 4: 'Nam fuit quoddam tempus cum in agris homines passim bestiarum modo vagabantur... nec ratione animi quicquam, sed pleraque viribus corporis administrabant; nondum divinae religionis, non humani offici ratio colebatur... non, ius aequabile quid utilitas haberet, acceperat.'

[107] Cicero 1949, I. II. 2, p. 6: 'primo propter insolentiam reclamantes'.

[108] Cicero 1949, I. II. 2, p. 4: 'quidam magnus videlicet vir et sapiens'.

good'.¹⁰⁹ It must have been due to his combination of *eloquentia* with *sapientia* that he managed to impose these rules upon reluctant and barbarous men, 'inducing them to submit without violence to the dictates of justice'.¹¹⁰

The quality of *sapientia* is accordingly hailed by Cicero as 'the mother of all good things'¹¹¹ and 'the leader of all the virtues'.¹¹² By *sapientia* we are able to acquire 'a knowledge of things at once human and divine, including a knowledge of the relations between men and the gods, and of human society itself'.¹¹³ Seneca in his *Epistulae* later adopts essentially the same viewpoint, adding that *sapientia* ought above all to act 'as our mistress and ruler',¹¹⁴ since 'it is wisdom which disposes us to peace and calls mankind to concord'.¹¹⁵

If we turn to the pre-humanist writers on city government, we find exactly the same arguments taken up. Orfino da Lodi and Giovanni da Viterbo both lay particular stress on the importance of *sapientia*,¹¹⁶ but it is Brunetto Latini who quotes and follows the Ciceronian analysis with the greatest fidelity. The idea of wisdom as the quality that ought above all to preside over our common life is central to his section entitled 'The precepts of the vices and virtues'. His chapter on 'What Cicero says about the virtues' claims that 'the hearts of wise men resemble celestial paradise',¹¹⁷ while a later chapter adds that 'without sense and wisdom we are unable to live aright, either in relation to God or to the world'.¹¹⁸ He ends his discussion by quoting the injunction from the Book of Proverbs to the effect that we must 'purchase wisdom at the expense of all other possessions' for 'it is more precious than any treasure' and 'nothing can be compared with it'.¹¹⁹

Latini also stresses, however, that most men lack the wisdom that alone enables them to accept the dictates of justice. Left to themselves, 'men

---

¹⁰⁹ Cicero 1949, I. II. 2, p. 6: 'ut fidem colere et iustitiam retinere... [et laborare] communis commodi causa'.
¹¹⁰ Cicero 1949, I. II. 2, p. 4: 'commotus oratione... ad ius voluisset sine vi descendere'.
¹¹¹ Cicero 1928, I. XXII. 58, p. 362: 'mater omnium bonarum rerum sit sapientia'.
¹¹² Cicero 1913, I. XLIII. 153, p. 156: 'Princepsque omnium virtutum illa sapientia.'
¹¹³ Cicero 1913, I. XLIII. 153, p. 156: 'rerum est divinarum et humanarum scientia, in qua continetur deorum et hominum communitas et societas inter ipsos'.
¹¹⁴ Seneca 1917–25, vol. 2, LXXXV. 32, p. 304: 'Sapientia domina rectrixque est.'
¹¹⁵ Seneca 1917–25, vol. 2, XC. 26–7, p. 414: 'sapientia... paci favet et genus humanum ad concordiam vocat'.
¹¹⁶ See Lodi 1869, pp. 74, 75, 90 and Viterbo 1901, pp. 217, 220, 245–6, 276, 278.
¹¹⁷ Latini 1948, p. 228 on 'li cuers des sages': 'tele ame estre resamblable au paradis celestiel'.
¹¹⁸ Latini 1948, p. 231: 'sans sens et sans sapience ne poroit nus bien vivre, ne a Dieu ne au monde'.
¹¹⁹ Latini 1948, p. 232: 'por toutes tes possessions achate sapience, ki est plus precieuse ke nul trezors... et nule chose amee ne puet estre comparee a lui'.

would willingly hold on to the freedom given them by nature, and would have no wish to bow their necks to the yoke of *signories*'.[120] Going beyond these allusions to the *De Inventione*, he adds that this can actually be proved historically. 'For at the beginning of this age, when there was neither king nor emperor on earth, justice was unknown, and the people of that time lived in the matter of beasts', subsisting 'without law and without any form of communal life'.[121]

It follows, for Latini no less than for Cicero, that those who live under the rule of law must at some stage have been induced to accept the dictates of justice by the wisdom of a great lawgiver. At first, Latini imagines, 'evil actions multiplied and malefactors remained unpunished'.[122] But 'later there arose an outstanding leader who, by means of his wisdom, assembled men together and ordained that they should live together, maintaining human company and establishing the rules of justice and rightfulness'.[123] Already we are in the presence of the belief, later so crucial to Italian humanism, that the eloquent orator is at the same time the ideal citizen, the *vir vere civilis*.

With this vision of the relations between wisdom and justice, we arrive at the heart of the moral assumptions embodied in the pre-humanist literature on city government. The hope by which these writers are animated is that, if our rulers are inspired by wisdom, and therefore love justice, their enactments will succeed in binding us together in concord and equity in such a way as to bring about the common good and, in consequence, the triumph of peace.

III

While the pre-humanist writers I have been considering owe an overwhelming debt to the moral philosophy of ancient Rome, it was not their principal ambition to analyse the very abstract concepts on which I have so far concentrated. Indeed, they commonly discuss them in a far less systematic manner than my paraphrase has probably implied. They

---

[120] Latini 1948, p. 272: 'Li home gardaissent volentiers la franchise que nature lor avoit donnee: et n'eussent mie mis lor cos au joug des signories.'

[121] Latini 1948, pp. 271–2: 'car au comencement dou siecle, quant il n'avoit en tiere ne roi ne empereor, ne justice n'estoit conneue, les gens de lors vivoient en guise de bestes ... sans loi et sans communité'.

[122] Latini 1948, p. 272: 'les males oevres mouteplioient perilleusement et li maufetour n'estoient chastoiet'.

[123] Latini 1948, p. 272: 'Lors furent aucun preudome ki par lor sens assamblerent et ordenerent les gens a abiter ensamble et a garder humaine compaignie et establirent justice et droiture.'

Lorenzetti and the portrayal of virtuous government

were chiefly preoccupied by two questions of a related but far more practical character. One was what specific form of government we ought to institute if we wish to maximise our chances of enjoying the blessings of peace. The other was what qualities we ought to be looking for in those who rule over us, and thus what our ideal should be of truly virtuous government. By way of rounding off my account of this pre-humanist literature, these are issues I need finally to address.

Turning first to the question of forms of government, it is striking to find that on this issue the scholastic writers of the period speak with several different voices. Aristotle had distinguished in *Politics* four different types of lawful regime: monarchy, aristocracy, democracy and that form of mixed government which seeks to combine the values of each pure type while avoiding their weaknesses.[124] Confronted with this classification, the scholastic writers of the *Regnum Italicum* respond in a variety of ways. Some, like Giles of Rome, insist on the superiority of monarchical regimes.[125] Others, like Henry of Rimini and Ptolemy of Lucca, defend the virtues of elective government.[126] Still others suggest that the true spirit of Aristotle's typology will only be captured if we recognise that the best form of government may vary with varying circumstances.

By contrast, the pre-humanist writers are convinced that one type of regime is indisputably to be preferred.[127] As we saw in chapter 2, Brunetto Latini offers the crispest summary of the common viewpoint. 'There are three forms of government', he declares at the start of his chapter on *Signories*, 'the first being rule by kings, the second rule by the nobles, the third rule by the *commune* itself.' And among these, he adds, 'the third is better than the others'.[128] Later he explains in more detail what he means by speaking of communes as the possessors of *signorie*. The form of government he has in mind is 'that which is peculiar to Italy', where the citizens elect their own magistrates, permit them to hold power 'only for a single year' and bind them to act 'in whatever way seems most beneficial to the common good of the city and all their subjects'.[129]

Discussing this type of regime, the earliest treatises on city government usually address themselves specifically to the figure of the chief

---

[124] Aristotle 1996, 1279 a–b and 1293b–1295a, pp. 70–2, 102–7.   [125] Rome 1607, p. 456.
[126] Rimini 1472, II. 14, fos. 37a–b; Ptolemy 1973, pp. 323, 336.
[127] There is one interesting exception: Pseudo-Apuleius 1981, p. 20 insists on the necessity of a monarchical regime.
[128] Latini 1948, p. 211: 'Seignouries sont de iii manieres, l'une est des rois, la seconde est des bons, la tierce est des communes, laquele est la trés millour entre ces autres.'
[129] Latini 1948, p. 392: '[en Ytaile] il sont par annees... tel comme il quident qu'il soit plus proufitables au commun preu de la vile et de tous lor subtés'.

magistrate, an official whose position they designate in a variety of ways. The *Oculus* speaks of the *rector*, and sometimes of the *potestas*,[130] while the vernacular writers of *dictamina* sometimes speak of the *signore* and sometimes of the *podestà*, two terms they generally use interchangeably.[131] Later writers, however, normally assume that power will be vested not with an individual *podestà* but rather with a *signoria* – with a body of *priores* or *signori* acting together as a ruling group. Giovanni da Viterbo, for example, while offering his advice 'to the *potestas* or *rector* or *preses*', makes it clear that he thinks of such magistrates principally as the chairmen of executive councils. Supreme authority he accordingly takes to be lodged mainly with those councils themselves, in line with the Roman law maxim – beloved of all these writers – to the effect that *quod omnes tangit, ab omnibus comprobatur*, 'what touches all must be approved by all'.[132]

These assumptions echo the actual constitutions of the city-republics, which normally assigned supreme political authority to a *signoria* or group of *priores*. In the case of Siena, the Constitution of 1262 gives untrammelled power 'to propose anything that seems to promote the good and pacific state of the people and commune of Siena' to the secret council of the *Viginti Quattuor*, the Twenty-four Priors.[133] The vernacular version of the Constitution issued in 1309–10 likewise addresses itself mainly to the ruling council of the *Nove*, who are invariably described as *signori* of the city and are said to be invested 'with a plenitude of *podestà* and complete authority'.[134]

This plenitude of *podestà* was generally conceived in all-embracing terms. The *Nove*, for example, were given effective control of Siena's main council, as well as constituting an inner council of their own for most executive purposes.[135] Sometimes the holders of such positions were also assumed to be invested with the highest legal authority, including the *ius gladii* or right of judicial execution over citizens.[136] Furthermore, their writ was assumed to run not merely within the city but throughout the *contado*, a point on which the Constitution of 1309 lays particular emphasis. The *Nove* are required to appoint governors to all fortified places within Sienese territory, the aim being to ensure that local *signori* remain faithful to the city and are able at the same time to deal

---

[130] *Oculus* 1966, pp. 23, 25 *et passim*.
[131] See, for example, Faba 1889, pp. 159–60 and Ceffi 1942, pp. 47–8.
[132] Viterbo 1901, pp. 218, 221, 260.
[133] *Il Constituto del Comune di Siena 1262*, p. 72 on the 'consilium secretum' of the Priores XXIIII, 'in quo ... proponant id, quod videbitur ... pro bono et pacifico statu populi et comunis Senarum'.
[134] See Lisini 1903, vol. 2, p. 488 on the *Nove Signori* and their 'pienitudine di podestà et balìa'.
[135] Bowsky 1981, pp. 85–103.   [136] See *Oculus* 1966, pp. 26, 35 and Latini 1948, pp. 413, 417, 420.

with anyone suspected of being a rebel or traitor to the commune.[137] Finally, the *Nove* were able to call on a considerable measure of armed support. They maintained one body of police under their own command; they revived the post of *capitano del popolo* and placed him in charge of another; and by an ordinance of 1302 they appear to have recruited a further force of *contadini* to keep the peace in the surrounding countryside.[138]

Reflecting on the nature of these powers, the pre-humanist writers often describe them in elaborately symbolic terms. City magistrates are instructed to deliver their judgements 'from a throne of glory';[139] to carry a sceptre 'in their strong right hand, with extended arm';[140] and to ensure that the sceptre itself 'is not like a reed, but strong and made of wood, like a shepherd's staff'.[141] Drawing on a familiar set of classical images, Giovanni da Viterbo adds that our leading magistrates constitute the 'heads' of the body politic, while we as citizens form the limbs or 'members' of such bodies, living 'under' our heads and in obedience to their commands.[142] Brunetto Latini proposes a more Biblical set of metaphors to convey a similar thought. He speaks of our *sires* as 'shields and guards of our community',[143] and warns that 'their shoulders must never be feeble', because 'anyone who accepts a *signorie*' must recognise 'that he is submitting his shoulders to a great charge'.[144]

For all the plenitude of power assigned to such *signori*, however, these writers remain insistent that their authority can never be lawfully exercised except in the manner characterised by the *Oculus* as *rectoralis*.[145] City magistrates are always addressed as mere officials, never as *domini* or lords, and much emphasis is placed on the limited character of their rule. They can only hold office for brief and statutory periods of time. They can only be elected with the consent of the citizen-body as a whole. While in office, they can only exercise authority in accordance with the existing laws and customs of the commune.[146] The effect, as Giovanni da Viterbo summarises, is that the laws themselves rule, in accordance

---

[137] Lisini 1903, vol. 1, p. 99; vol. 2, pp. 502–3, 506–7. Cf. *Breves Officialium*, pp. 31, 102–4.
[138] Bowsky 1981, pp. 36–42, 120, 129.
[139] On the 'solium gloriae' see Viterbo, 1901, p. 233 and cf. Latini 1948, p. 406.
[140] Viterbo 1901, p. 247: 'manu forti et brachio extenso'.
[141] *Oculus* 1966, p. 63: 'non arundineum, sed ligneum et fortem, simillem baculo pastorali'.
[142] Viterbo 1901, pp. 222, 231, 234, 249, 260–1. Cf. also Vignano 1974, pp. 285, 296.
[143] Latini 1948, p. 408: 'soit il chiés et gardeour dou commun'.
[144] Latini 1948, pp. 398–9: a good sire 'n'a pas les espaules fiebles', since 'il sousmet ses espaules a si grant charge'.
[145] *Oculus* 1966, pp. 23–4.
[146] See for example the discussion of the powers of the *Nove* in Bowsky 1981, pp. 54–84.

with the precept that 'those who preside over the affairs of *res publicae* must themselves be analogous to the laws'.[147]

This contrasting perspective is likewise expressed in elaborately metaphorical terms. One favourite image pictures our rulers as tied or bound by their obligation to execute justice and procure the common good. Orfino da Lodi speaks of *rectores* as 'tied by the law'.[148] Guido Faba advises in one of his model speeches that an incoming *podestà* should acknowledge that 'I am bound to serve you at all times'.[149] Giovanni da Viterbo, thinking more of ruling *signorie* than of individual *rectores*, similarly claims that 'a *podestà* is tied to accept whatever the city council has decreed'.[150] The same image recurs still more frequently in official documents. The *Breves* of Siena begins by describing each official as 'held' to the performance of his duties and 'tied by his own special brief'.[151] The Sienese Constitution of 1309–10 likewise states in virtually every rubric concerning the *Nove* that 'they ought and are bound' to act as the constitution prescribes.[152] As a result, the final guise in which these writers portray their rulers is as bondsmen or slaves to the public good. Orfino da Lodi says of city *rectores* that they 'serve the public'[153] while Giovanni da Viterbo speaks of every elected official as a public servant.[154] Brunetto Latini similarly concludes his chapter on city government by advising *sires* at the end of their *signorie* that 'you should offer yourselves and all your power in the service of the city for the whole of your life'.[155]

This apparently paradoxical vision of our rulers as at once masters and servants is further clarified by means of an especially revealing image drawn from Cicero's *De Officiis*. Cicero had declared in Book I that 'it is the particular duty of our magistrates to recognise that *se gerere personam civitatis*' – that they represent or 'bear in their own person' the *persona* of the city itself. To this he had added that 'they must also remember that all their powers are committed to them in trust'.[156] The importance of this

---

[147] Viterbo 1901, p. 238: 'hii, qui praesunt rei publicae, legum similes sint'.
[148] Lodi 1869, p. 55: 'Rector... lege tenetur.'
[149] Faba 1889, p. 157: 'omne tempo sono obligato a li vostro servisii'.
[150] Viterbo 1901, p. 261: 'quod consilium decrevit, potestas observare tenetur'. See also Libri 1974, p. 72.
[151] *Breves Officialium*, p. 7: 'alligatur Statuto... suo Breve speciali ligetur'.
[152] Lisini 1903, vol. 2, p. 498 states that the *Nove* 'sieno tenuti et debiano', a formula that recurs at pp. 499, 500, 501 *et passim*.
[153] Lodi 1869, p. 55: 'Rector... rem publicam servet.'
[154] Viterbo 1901, pp. 222, 234, 259, 272.
[155] Latini 1948, p. 422: 'offrir toi et tout ton pooir en lor service en tote ta vie'.
[156] Cicero 1913, I. XXXIV. 124, p. 126: 'Est igitur proprium munus magistratus intellegere se gerere personam civitatis debereque... ea fidei suae commissa meminisse.'

passage can hardly be overestimated. The author of the *Dogma* quotes it in its entirety at the start of his section on 'the duties of those engaged in public affairs'.[157] Giovanni da Viterbo quotes it again at the end of one of his principal chapters on the duties of magistrates.[158] Both writers are able in consequence to articulate one of the most central but elusive concepts in this tradition of thought: the concept of representation, the idea that the powers of our rulers are nothing other than an expression of, a way of representing, the powers of the community over which they preside.

I turn finally to consider the other major and closely related question raised by the pre-humanist writers on city government. What range of virtues and other qualities are required on the part of our chief magistrates if they are to succeed in promoting the common good and in consequence the cause of peace?

The ideal magistrate is said to be distinguished by his possession of all the virtues 'that go to make a perfect man'.[159] These attributes are in turn agreed to fall into two categories. First come the so-called 'contemplative' or 'theological' virtues, a group of qualities seldom examined in much detail, although always mentioned with deep reverence. Generally they are content to follow St Paul's teaching in I Corinthians 13, where he had laid it down that there are three theological virtues, faith, hope and charity, and that the greatest of these is charity. Brunetto Latini, for example, simply summarises the conventional wisdom when he states that the gift of charity accompanies faith and hope, and is in itself 'the bond of perfection and queen of all the other virtues'.[160]

The other category of virtues – the object of their main and sometimes their sole attention – they describe in a variety of ways. Some follow their Roman authorities in calling them the qualities of the active as opposed to the contemplative life.[161] Some prefer the term originally coined by St Ambrose, who had spoken of them as the 'cardinal' virtues.[162] But others make clearer the connection between these attributes and the arts of government by adopting Macrobius's suggestion[163] that we should

---

[157] Conches 1929, p. 47.   [158] Viterbo 1901, p. 268.
[159] The claim that the virtues 'perfectum te facient virum' occurs in Braga 1950, p. 247.
[160] Latini 1948, p. 310: 'ele est dame et roine de toutes vertus et liiens de la perfection'.
[161] Latini 1948, pp. 230, 308.
[162] But this usage was mainly confined to scholastic philosophers. See, for example, Aquinas 1952, I^a. II^{ae}, Qu. 61, art. 1, resp., p. 267, quoting and agreeing with St Ambrose. See also Rome 1607, p. 58.
[163] Macrobius 1893, I. VIII. 5, pp. 517–18.

think of them as the 'political' virtues,[164] 'the qualities that are most of all needed by those involved in government'.[165]

Among these qualities, the greatest in order of importance is invariably said to be prudence. One influential source of this judgement was Martin of Braga, who had argued in his *Formula* that 'there are four species of virtue' and that 'among these the first is prudence'.[166] Giovanni da Viterbo, for example, simply transcribes Martin's account at the start of his own section on the qualities of magistrates.[167] A second source of the same judgement was Cicero's *De Officiis*, especially as expounded and elaborated by such moralists as the author of the *Dogma* and Guillaume Perrault. If we turn, for example, to Brunetto Latini's section on the virtues and vices, we find him drawing heavily on both these authorities. He opens his general chapter on moral virtue by quoting Perrault's assertion that 'anyone who well considers the truth will find that prudence is the foundation of all the other virtues'.[168] He begins his own analysis of prudence by citing the *Dogma* to the effect that this is the virtue 'which goes before all the others'.[169] And he brings his discussion to a close by referring to Perrault's further claim that 'prudence, which is the first of the virtues, is also the queen and ruler of all the rest'.[170]

Beyond this point, however, there is no agreement; rather we need to distinguish between two contrasting lines of thought. According to the dominant tradition, largely inherited from Cicero, there are three further cardinal virtues. They are justice, fortitude and temperance, with justice being viewed as by far the most important. Cicero had put forward these contentions in *De Inventione*[171] as well as in Book 1 of *De Officiis*. The latter analysis focuses first on *iustitia*, then on the virtue of those who act *magno animo et fortiter* and finally on *temperantia*. The discussion is prefaced by the claim that these are the qualities needed to preserve the community of mankind, and that among these social virtues 'the

---

[164] See, for example, Faba 1956, p. 128.
[165] Conches 1929, p. 79: 'Primae [virtutes] sunt politicae... conveniunt illis qui regunt rempublicam.'
[166] Braga 1950, p. 237: 'Quattuor virtutum species [sunt]... harum prima est prudentia.'
[167] Viterbo 1901, p. 252.
[168] Latini 1948, p. 230: 'ki bien consire la verité, il trovera que prudence est le fondement des unes et des autres [vertus]'. Cf. Perrault 1618, vol. 1, pp. 157, 176.
[169] Latini 1948, p. 231: '[Prudence] vait par devant les autres vertus.' Cf. Conches 1929, p. 8.
[170] Latini 1948, p. 248: 'prudence, ki est li premiere des autres, et ki est dame et ordeneresse'. Cf. Perrault 1618, vol. 1, p. 155.
[171] Cicero 1949, II. LIII. 159, p. 326: 'virtus... habet igitur partes quattuor: prudentiam, iustitiam, fortitudinem, temperantiam'.

Lorenzetti and the portrayal of virtuous government 63

greatest glory lies in justice, on the basis of which alone men are called good'.[172]

This classification, which appears again in Cicero's *Tusculanae Disputationes*,[173] was in turn adopted by Macrobius in his immensely influential commentary on Cicero's *Somnium Scipionis*.[174] From there it seems to have passed into general currency.[175] It recurs, for example, in most of the moral treatises of Ciceronian inspiration that were later quarried by the pre-humanist writers on city government. The author of the *Dogma* lists the three principal virtues of social life with evident attention to their order of priority as justice, fortitude and temperance;[176] so does Guillaume Perrault in his *Summa*;[177] so does Guido Faba in his *Summa de Viciis et Virtutibus*.[178] Finally, the same classification recurs yet again in the writings of Aquinas and his immediate followers. Aquinas himself maintains in the *Summa* that the three cardinal virtues of social life are justice, fortitude and temperance, and quotes Aristotle as his authority for the further claim that 'if we are speaking of legal justice, then it is manifest that this virtue is more excellent than any of the other moral virtues'.[179] Giles of Rome repeats the classification in his *De Regimine Principum*;[180] so does Henry of Rimini in his *De Quattuor Virtutibus Cardinalibus*.[181]

By contrast with this orthodoxy, a rival way of thinking about the virtues arose out of Senecan roots. One striking difference between this tradition and the Ciceronian one is that justice, instead of taking precedence over the other social virtues, is placed last on the list. This is the ordering that Seneca himself adopts in his discussion of 'perfect virtue' in his *Epistulae*, in the course of which he enumerates the four leading virtues as temperance, fortitude, prudence and, finally, justice.[182] Martin of Braga – who may have had access to a lost Senecan tract[183] – later proposes the same ordering in his *Formula*, adding the explicit

---

[172] Cicero 1913, I. VII. 20, p. 20: 'iustitia, in qua virtutis est splendor maximus, ex qua viri boni nominantur'.
[173] Cicero 1927, III. XVII. 36–7, p. 270.   [174] Macrobius 1893, I. VIII. 7, p. 518.
[175] See Lottin 1942–60, vol. 3, pp. 154, 156, and Tuve 1966, pp. 59–60. It is thus misleading to claim (as does Wieruszowski 1971, p. 488n.) that the conception of justice as highest among the political virtues is a specifically Aristotelian one.
[176] Conches 1929, p. 7.
[177] Perrault 1618, vol. 1, p. 152 cites Macrobius. But cf. Perrault 1618, vol. 1, p. 176.
[178] Faba 1956, p. 129.
[179] Aquinas 1962, II^a. II^{ae}, Qu. 58, art. 12, resp., p. 289: 'si loquamur de iustitia legali, manifestum est quod ipsa est praeclarior inter omnes virtutes morales'.
[180] Rome 1607, pp. 58, 71–82.   [181] Rimini 1472, II. 1, fo. 25a; III. 1, fo. 60b; IV. 1, fo. 97a.
[182] Seneca 1917–25, vol. 3, CXX. 11, p. 388: 'conprehendimus temperantiam, fortitudinem, prudentiam, iustitiam'.
[183] Tuve 1966, p. 206.

claim that justice ought to be considered after the other virtues.[184] With the *Formula* as an intermediary, the same analysis subsequently resurfaces in several of the pre-humanist treatises on city government. Giovanni da Viterbo, for example, simply transcribes his chapter on justice from Martin's account.[185] Brunetto Latini likewise adopts the Senecan classification, while making it even clearer that his relegation of justice to last place is no mere accident. After prudence, he declares, we should speak 'first of temperance and fortitude rather than of justice, because these two qualities serve to address the heart of man to works of justice'.[186] It follows, he later repeats, that 'justice comes after all the other virtues'.[187]

The other distinctive feature of the Senecan tradition lies in the prominence it assigns to the virtue of magnanimity. The Latin term *magnanimitas* had been coined by Cicero, who had used it to render the Greek ideal of the 'high souled' man.[188] But the concept cannot be said to figure very prominently in his moral thought. In *De Officiis* he mentions it only once, in a passage of some obscurity, where he appears to connect or perhaps to equate it with fortitude.[189] In *De Inventione* he never mentions it at all, in spite of the fact that his analysis of fortitude in that work includes a highly influential attempt to itemise its various *partes* or elements.[190]

Seeking to reconcile Cicero's various pronouncements, Macrobius originated the suggestion that the right way to think about magnanimity must be to regard it as one of the subordinate elements of fortitude.[191] Thereafter this classification came to be widely accepted. The author of the *Dogma*, for example, treats magnanimity together with constancy as the two eyes of fortitude,[192] an image reiterated by Guido Faba in his *Summa de Viciis et Virtutibus*.[193] Guillaume Perrault, following Macrobius even more closely, maintains that the general idea of fortitude can be divided into six elements, and that these can be itemised as magnanimity, faith, security, patience, constancy, and magnificence.[194] Finally, Aquinas and his immediate disciples – for all their basically Aristotelian allegiances – treat the concept of magnanimity in much the same way. When Aquinas discusses the cardinal virtues in the *Summa*, he explicitly asks 'whether magnanimity is a part of fortitude'. Citing Macrobius

---

[184] Braga 1950, pp. 237, 246.   [185] Viterbo 1901, pp. 252, 253–4.
[186] Latini 1948, p. 248: 'premierement d'atemprance et de force que de justice, por çou ke l'un et l'autre est por adrecier le corage de l'home as oevres de justice'.
[187] Latini 1948, p. 271: 'Justice vient aprés toutes les autres vertus.'   [188] Gauthier 1951, pp. 168–9.
[189] Cicero 1913, I. XLIII. 152, pp. 154–6.   [190] Cicero 1949, II. LIV. 163, p. 330.
[191] Macrobius 1893, I. VIII. 7, p. 518.   [192] Conches 1929, p. 79.
[193] Faba 1956, p. 129.   [194] Perrault 1618, vol. 1, pp. 210–42.

as his leading authority, he answers that 'magnanimity is indeed to be understood as a part of fortitude', and adds that the right way to conceive of it is 'as a secondary element joined to fortitude as the principal quality'.[195]

Within the Senecan tradition, by contrast, the virtue of magnanimity occupies an absolutely central place.[196] Seneca in his *Epistulae* originally fixed the familiar application of the term to describe those who hold themselves aloof from small-minded resentments and jealousies. 'The quality of magnanimity', as he puts it, 'cannot stand out unless we learn to view with disdain the petty concerns that preoccupy the ordinary run of men.'[197] He accordingly thinks of it as a virtue particularly suited to those who have charge of public affairs. 'Although magnanimity graces all who possess it, good fortune gives it greater opportunities, and it shows to better advantage in the judgment-seat than in lower places.'[198] He proceeds to draw the moral in a highly rhetorical passage in the *Epistulae*:

If we could look into the soul of a good man, we should find it shining here with justice, there with fortitude, here with temperance and prudence too! But in addition, and arising out of all these virtues, we should find the virtue of magnanimity, the very greatest of all these qualities.[199]

Seneca is prepared to argue, in short, that magnanimity is not merely a leading virtue of social life but is arguably the most important of all.

If we turn to the moral theories of Aquinas and his disciples we find these arguments considered and deliberately set aside.[200] But if we turn to the pre-humanist writers on city government we find the same arguments strongly endorsed. As before, Martin of Braga's *Formula* seems to have served as a crucial intermediary in the transmission of these

---

[195] Aquinas 1962, II^a. II^{ae}, Qu. 129. art. 5, p. 582: 'Utrum magnanimitas sit pars fortitudinis.' Resp., p. 583: 'Magnanimitas ponitur pars fortitudinis, quia adiungitur ei sicut secundaria principali.' So too Rimini 1472, III. 4, fo. 69a.

[196] Gauthier 1951, p. 157, arguably makes insufficient distinction between these strands of thought. For a valuable corrective see Tuve 1963.

[197] Seneca 1917–25, vol. 2, LXXIV. 13, p. 120: 'magnanimitas... non potest eminere, nisi omnia velut minuta contempsit, quae pro maximis volgus optat'.

[198] Seneca 1928–35, vol. 1, I. V. 3, p. 370: 'Decet magnanimitas quemlibet mortalem... tamen magnanimitas in bona fortuna laxiorem locum habet meliusque in tribunali quam in plano conspicitur.'

[199] Seneca 1917–25, vol 3, CXV. 3, p. 320: 'Si nobis animum boni viri liceret inspicere... videremus, hinc iustitia, illinc fortitudine, hinc temperantia prudentiaque lucentibus!... et ex istis magnanimitas eminentissima'.

[200] See, for example, Aquinas 1962, II^a. II^{ae}, Qu. 129, art. 5, 1, p. 582, where he cites (and goes on to reject) the arguments of Cicero and Seneca.

values.[201] The *Formula* consistently speaks of magnanimity not as one of the subordinate elements of fortitude, but rather as a synonym for fortitude itself.[202] Giovanni da Viterbo and Brunetto Latini adopt the same viewpoint, and both initiate their discussions of magnanimity by quoting Martin's observation to the effect that 'this virtue is also known as fortitude'.[203]

Turning to analyse the concept, they continue to make clear their essentially Senecan allegiances. In particular, they agree that magnanimity is a quality mainly to be associated with those of great fortune and public importance. Giovanni da Viterbo starts by arguing that an ideal magistrate should be endowed with discretion and magnanimity above all else, and later cites the entire passage in which Seneca had argued that magnanimity is an attribute peculiarly suited to those who sit in judgement on others.[204] Speaking even more fulsomely, Brunetto Latini adds that magnanimity 'is the virtue that gives a man boldness and a sure heart, and grants him the courage he needs in order to undertake great things'.[205]

Latini ends by committing himself to the view that magnanimity is perhaps the most splendid of all the virtues. His special emphasis on the point derives from the fact that he takes his argument at this juncture not only from Martin's *Formula*, but also from Averroes's paraphrase of *Nicomachean Ethics*. Drawing on this novel source, he is able to include a further chapter celebrating the virtue in even more ringing terms. He opens with the familiar claim that 'the magnanimous are those who devote themselves to great affairs'.[206] But he adds a number of distinctive details, arguing that the magnanimous man is distinguished not merely by his unwillingness to concern himself with petty things, but also by his sense 'that it is a nobler thing to give than to receive'.[207] This generosity of spirit means that 'when such a man receives, he sets himself to make a return', and that 'he is negligent about small expenses'.[208] 'To speak the truth', Latini concludes, 'he who is magnanimous is the greatest and

---

[201] Gauthier 1951, p. 240. [202] Braga 1950, pp. 237, 241, 248.
[203] Viterbo 1901, p. 253: 'Magnanimitas vero, quae et fortitudo dicitur.' Cf. Latini 1948, pp. 260–1 and Pseudo-Apuleius 1981, p. 22.
[204] Viterbo 1901, pp. 220, 274.
[205] Latini 1948, p. 261: 'ceste vertu done a home seur cuer et hardement et li fait avoir grant corage entour les hautes choses'.
[206] Latini 1948, p. 193: 'Magnanimes est celui ki est atornés a grandismes afferes.'
[207] Latini 1948, p. 194: 'que plus noble chose est doner ke reçoivre'.
[208] Latini 1948, p. 194: 'Et quant il recoit, il se porchace dou rendre et dou contrechangier. Et est negligens en petit despens.'

most honourable of men.' This being so, 'we may say that magnanimity is the crown and brightest of the virtues, for there is no virtue to equal it'.[209]

Summarising the constitutional theory I have been describing, we might say that it embodies two simple if strenuous demands. The first is that, if we wish to live in peace, we must institute a form of government based on the rule of elected *signori* who are tied or bound to conduct themselves entirely according to the laws and customs of their community. The other is that these *signori* must in turn be capable, all passion spent,[210] of discharging the duties of their office in a perfectly virtuous way. As Giovanni da Vignano concludes, it is only by having such magistrates that a city can hope to remain 'in tranquillity and a good state'. Our ambition must therefore be to find a chief magistrate through whom (*per lo quale*) we can hope to attain these ends.[211] We need a magistrate, as Matteo de' Libri repeats, 'through whom (*per cui*) we can and ought to remain in a state of great tranquillity and repose'.[212]

According to the Sienese Constitution of 1309–10, these ideal requirements have actually been realised in practice. The opening rubric on the duties of the *Nove* begins by declaring that the goal of good government should be to ensure 'that this city and all its people, its *contado* and all its jurisdictions, are conserved in perpetual peace and pure justice'.[213] If these goals are to be achieved, the rubric continues, it is essential 'that the city should be governed by (*per*) men who are lovers of peace and justice'.[214] And this is why, it goes on to proclaim, 'it is hereby enacted and ordained that the office of the *Nove signori*, defenders and governors of the commune and people of the city and jurisdictions of Siena, both are and ought to be established in perpetuity within the city of Siena, for the preservation of its good and peaceable state'.[215]

---

[209] Latini 1948, 'Et a la verité dire, celui ki est magnanimes est li plus grans hom et li plus honorables ki soit . . . Donques est magnanimités courone et clartés de toutes vertus, car ele n'est se par vertu non.'
[210] This is stressed in *Breves Officialium*, p. 7; *Il Costituto de Comune di Siena 1262*, p. 25; Viterbo 1901, p. 260. The source appears to be Sallust 1931a, LI. 1, p. 88.
[211] Vignano 1974, p. 270: 'per lo quale lo nostro comune posa e dibia durare e ponsare in tranquilità e bom stato'.
[212] Libri 1974, p. 79: 'per cui possa et dibia permanere in gran tranquillitate e reposo'.
[213] Lisini 1903, vol. 2, p. 488: 'Che essa città et popolo tutto, et lo contado et giurisditione d'essa in pace perpetua et pura giustitia si conservi.'
[214] Lisini 1903, vol. 2, p. 488: 'che essa citta sia governata per huomini amatori et di pace et di giustitia'.
[215] Lisini 1903, vol. 2, p. 488: 'statuto et ordinato e', che l'officio de' signori Nove difenditori et governatori del comune et del popolo de la città et giurisditione di Siena sia et essere debia imperpetuo ne la citta di Siena, per governatione del buono et pacifico stato de la citta'.

IV

I now want to return to Ambrogio Lorenzetti, and to my initial suggestion that the central section of his frescoes in the Sala dei Nove (Plate 3) can best be interpreted as a further statement of the pre-humanist civic ideology I have tried to delineate.

As we have seen, the most precious value in civic life according to the writers I have been considering is the preservation of peace. Moreover, they inherited from their Roman authorities a distinctive idiom for expressing the idea that certain values ought particularly to be cherished. Such values, it was said, ought to be *in medio*, in our midst; they ought indeed to be actively brought forth *in medium*, into the centre of things. Cicero, for example, had declared in *De Officiis* that our highest duty must be to act in such a way that *communes utilitates in medium afferre* – in such a way that the ideal of the common good is placed at the heart of our common life.[216] Seneca had similarly spoken in his *Epistulae* of 'that fortunate time when the benefits of nature lay open *in medio*' – in such a way as to be possessed by all.[217] One way of expressing the central principle of the ideology I have been examining would thus be to say that it asks us to place the ideal of peace *in medio*, thereby ensuring that this is the value cherished and enjoyed above all.

Lorenzetti illustrates this exact conception of peace. The figure inscribed with the *titulus* PAX is literally placed *in medio*, in the midst of the entire composition. Lorenzetti's cycle is distributed over three walls of the Sala dei Nove, with the figure of Peace appearing on the central wall. This wall is in turn divided into three levels, with the symbolic depiction of virtuous government in the middle, a set of medallion paintings above, and a large Giottesque dado beneath. This middle painting is in turn organised into three sections, with cherubim figures at the top, various groups of citizens at the bottom, and the figure of Peace, together with the virtues, in the middle.[218] The figure of Peace is thus seated at the centre of the middle section of the middle painting of the cycle as a whole. Far more eloquently than any of the literary sources, Lorenzetti proclaims that peace is indeed the value that deserves to be placed *in medio*, at the heart of our common life.

So far this could equally well be described as a Thomist representation of peace. As we have seen, however, there is one point at which Aquinas's

---

[216] Cicero 1913, I. VII. 22, p. 22. [217] Seneca 1917–25, vol. 2, XC. 36, p. 422.
[218] Feldges-Henning 1972, p. 146.

analysis contrasts sharply with that of the pre-humanist writers on city government, and at this point Lorenzetti's portrayal strongly recalls the pre-humanist as opposed to the Thomist account. The figure of Peace is shown leaning back on her right elbow, pressing against a large cushion which in turn presses down upon a full suit of armour and holds it in place. Her right foot rests in triumph on a large black helmet, while the hem of her garment partly covers a shield lying alongside it. Peace is depicted, in short, not simply as 'an absence of discord', in Thomist phrase. She is represented as a victorious force, her repose the outcome of a battle won against her darkest enemies.[219]

Describing these enemies, the pre-humanist writers isolated two in particular: external *Guerra* and internal *Discordia*, the latter being a product partly of factious *Divisio* and partly of the *Furor* of the masses. If we turn to the left or 'sinister' side of Lorenzetti's frescoes, we encounter just these companions of tyranny and enemies of peace (Plate 2). They are seated upon the left hand – again the 'sinister' side – of the demonic central figure, behind whose head a *titulus* in silver lettering reads TYRAMMIDES.[220] On Tyranny's extreme left hand[221] we see the helmeted figure of War, who is dressed in dark blue robes, with a gold-hilted sword upraised in his right hand and the word GUERRA inscribed in gold lettering on his shield.[222] Next to him sits a female figure marked [D]IVISIO, dressed in black and white, with golden hair falling loose and dishevelled in contrast with the carefully plaited hair on the figure of Peace. She is holding a carpenter's saw, using it to cut an object held in her left hand, an evident allusion to Sallust's dire warning that *Divisio* will always serve to tear a body politic to pieces.[223] Next to her and closest to the figure of Tyranny stands a black hybrid beast marked FVROR. This we are surely intended to recognise as a representation of the brutish multitude, especially as we see it armed with a stone in just the manner that the *Breves* of Siena had warned the city police to expect from the mob. The whole ensemble brings home to us the horrors

---

[219] Frugoni 1983, p. 164.
[220] This *titulus* has only been legible since the first of the two restorations undertaken in the 1980s. As Donato 2001 rightly stresses, the figure should be understood as a representation not of a tyrant but rather of tyranny.
[221] Note that, when I speak of 'his' or 'her' left and right, I am speaking from the point of view of the figures in the painting; when I speak of 'our' or 'the' right or left, I am referring to the spectator's point of view.
[222] This barbarism was used (in preference to *bellum*) by all the pre-humanist writers on city government.
[223] Sallust 1931b, XLI. 5, p. 222.

attendant on what Bonvesin della Riva had described in *De Magnalibus Mediolani* as 'tyrampnidis dominatio', the enslaving power of tyrannical government.²²⁴

How can we hope to overcome these enemies of Peace? We can hope to do so, the pre-humanist writers maintain, only if we live together in *concordia* and *aequitas* in such a way as to promote the common good. If we now focus on the central section of Lorenzetti's frescoes, we find ourselves confronting a magnificent representation of these further arguments, together with an attempt to provide visual equivalents for the whole range of metaphors in which they were habitually expressed.

We see, most prominently, a representation of the Ciceronian claim that *concordia* constitutes one of the two *fundamenta* of public life. Beneath the mysterious regal figure, and upon his 'good' side, we see a group of twenty-four citizens holding a double rope – one strand red, the other grey – handed to them by a seated female figure marked CONCORDIA. The allusion is clearly to the *vinculum concordiae*, the double bond of concord mentioned in several of the pre-humanist treatises on city government. Moreover, the citizens are shown holding the rope rather than being held by it, an evident reference to the further claim that any such agreement to act together as a political unity must always be voluntary in character.

We also see a representation of *aequitas*, the quality Cicero had described as the other *fundamentum* of civic peace. The figure of Concord holds across her knees a large *runcina* or carpenter's plane. Now a plane is an implement specifically designed to level out roughnesses and produce a smooth surface.²²⁵ So the appearance of a *runcina*, especially in such close association with *concordia*, must surely be intended to symbolise the Ciceronian vision of *aequitas*.²²⁶ We are being reminded that we must smooth out our differences as citizens rather than accentuate any divisions between us if we are to enjoy the blessings of peace. Lorenzetti underlines the allusion by means of two further visual effects. The contrasting figure of *Divisio* is also shown holding a carpenter's tool, the saw with which she divides the object held in her left hand. And the citizens processing together in concord are all exactly uniform in height, each

---

²²⁴ Riva 1974, p. 24.
²²⁵ For *runcinae* as instruments used to level rough surfaces (*levigare*) see, for example, Arnobius 1953, pp. 324–5.
²²⁶ Such commentators as have mentioned the plane have generally assumed that it forms part of the symbolism of *concordia*. See, for example, Oertel 1968, p. 235; Feldges-Henning 1972, p. 145; Frugoni 1983, p. 146. But cf. Rubinstein 1958, p. 186n.

'on level terms' with everyone else in just the manner prescribed by the ideal of *aequitas* in Cicero's account.

This still leaves the question of how we can hope to act together in concord and equity to promote the common good. According to the pre-humanist writers, we can never hope to do so unless we are persuaded by the wisdom of a great lawgiver to submit ourselves to the dictates of justice. This further contention, the heart of the ideology I have been examining, we again find closely reflected in Lorenzetti's visual argument.

At the top of the picture Lorenzetti shows Wisdom in the guise of a winged cherubim figure. The *titulus* above her head identifies her as SA[PI]ENTIA; the scales of justice hang down from her right hand. This depiction of Wisdom giving rise to justice has usually been treated as a straightforward allusion to Aquinas's *Summa Theologiae*.[227] But in fact the provenance of Lorenzetti's imagery is far from straightforward. One problem is that he seems to contradict rather than to illustrate Aquinas's beliefs about the place of divine wisdom in human affairs. Aquinas maintains that the only way to participate in divine wisdom is by speculative reason. But he thinks of human law as the outcome not of speculative but of practical reasoning. So he never thinks of legal justice as a direct product of wisdom. He always claims that just laws arise 'as an outcome of man's natural capacity to participate by way of practical reasoning in the eternal law'.[228]

A further problem is that Lorenzetti's portrayal of Wisdom hardly seems to accord with the assumptions of the neo-Ciceronian ideology he usually follows with such fidelity. As we have seen, Cicero had conceived of our ability to live under the rules of justice as a legacy we owe to the wisdom of great lawgivers. But Lorenzetti displays Wisdom not as a human attribute but rather as a heavenly power. Although his depiction of the relationship between wisdom and justice is obviously closer to the Ciceronian than the Thomist account, he treats his authorities at this juncture with an unusual degree of licence. It may be that he found himself constrained by pictorial requirements, and specifically by his commitment to the three-tier organisation of his painting as a whole. But as we shall see, there are several other moments at which he departs from the programme suggested by the pre-humanist literature on city government. The right moral to draw is perhaps that these moments best

---

[227] Rubinstein 1958, p. 183.
[228] Aquinas 1952, I^a. II^{ae}, Qu. 91, art. 3, ad 1, p. 415: 'ex parte rationis practicae naturaliter homo participat legem aeternam'.

serve to remind us (should any reminder be needed) that Lorenzetti is at no point merely illustrating an existing ideology of civic life. He is at the same time contributing to that ideology, and in a uniquely spectacular way.

Beneath the figure of Wisdom Lorenzetti illustrates the idea of justice. To speak more accurately, what he illustrates is the idea of justice or fairness as the essence of the law, not justice or righteousness as a personal attribute. (He treats the latter as a separate concept – as do his sources – and illustrates it separately on the extreme right of the picture.)[229] Justice is represented in the guise of an enthroned female figure who surmounts both Concord and the procession of citizens, making the point that they must all live 'under' her sway if the common good is to be served. The figure is recognisable as Justice not merely by her pair of scales,[230] but also by the *titulus* in gold lettering around her head, which quotes the opening of the Book of Wisdom: DILIGITE [IVSTITIA]M Q[UI] IVDICATIS TE[RR]AM. The centrality of this ideal is underlined not merely by the size and placing of the figure herself, but also by the explanatory verses inscribed beneath the frescoes. At the foot of Tyranny's throne a figure marked IVSTI[TIA] lies prone, while the accompanying verses explain that 'where justice lies bound, no one ever joins together to promote the common good'.[231] By contrast, the verses beneath the central fresco assure us that, where the holy virtue of justice rules, 'she induces many minds to act in unity'.[232]

The provenance and meaning of Lorenzetti's image of justice have recently occasioned much debate. There is an obvious though not an exact visual precedent in Giotto's portrayal of IUSTICIA in the Cappella degli Scrovegni.[233] But this still leaves the problem of identifying the source of the visual tradition itself. The solution which has usually been proposed is that the whole tradition, including Lorenzetti's invocation of it, stems essentially from Aristotle's *Nicomachean Ethics*, perhaps mediated by various Thomist commentaries.[234] More recently, however, Chiara Frugoni has argued that this offers too simplified an account of

---

[229] This makes it misleading to claim that justice 'appears twice' in Lorenzetti's scheme, as is claimed in Rowley 1958, vol. 1, p. 101; in Oertel 1968, p. 235; and in Frugoni 1983, p. 161.
[230] On the scales of justice see *Oculus* 1966, p. 64; Faba 1889, p. 154; Viterbo 1901, pp. 226, 259.
[231] 'LADOVE STA LEGATA LA IUSTITIA. NESSUNO ALBE[N] COMUNE GIAMAY/ SACORDA.'
[232] As we have seen, the verses on the simulated tablet beneath the central section of the frescoes begin: 'QUESTA SANTA VIRTU [La Giustizia] LADOVE REGGE. INDUCE ADUNITA LIANIMI / MOLTI.'
[233] Pfeiffenberger 1966. I comment further on these parallels in chapter 4, section IV.
[234] Rubinstein 1958, pp. 182–4, 186–7.

Lorenzetti's sources, and has proposed instead that the Book of Wisdom needs in particular to be invoked if this central section of the frescoes is to be 'globally' explicated.[235]

There is I think nothing to be said in favour of the latter argument. One difficulty is that the Book of Wisdom seems powerless to explain so many of Lorenzetti's most prominent symbolic effects. It contains, for example, no celebration of the need for peace to be situated *in medio*, no mention of the *vinculum concordiae*, no reference to *concordia* and *aequitas* as the twin *fundamenta* of civic life. But the main objection is that there is no reason to single out this particular text as a direct inspiration for any feature of Lorenzetti's work. This applies even to the *titulus* surrounding the head of Justice. As we have seen, the injunction to love justice was a *topos* that could equally well have been taken from almost any of the pre-humanist treatises on city government.[236]

There might seem to be a much stronger case for concluding that Lorenzetti's portrayal must be taken either directly from Aristotle or else from various Thomist commentaries. The decisive evidence appears to be furnished by the *tituli* above the heads of the two angels who appear to right and left of the figure of Justice herself. The *titulus* on the left reads [DIS]TRIBVTIVA, the one on the right COMVTATIVA. These terms make no appearance in any of the pre-humanist treatises on city government. But the problem of how to formulate rules of justice in relation to distribution and exchange is central to Book 5 of *Nicomachean Ethics*. If we turn, moreover, to Grosseteste's original translation of the *Ethics*, we find him introducing the terms *iustum distributivum* and *iustum commutativum* to describe these precise aspects of justice.[237] And if we turn to Aquinas's *Summa Theologiae*, we find him adopting the same terminology in his own analysis of just distribution and exchange.[238] So it seems, as students of Lorenzetti's painting have generally concluded, that at this point we come upon 'perhaps the most obvious representation' of 'Thomistic-Aristotelian themes' in the whole cycle of frescoes.[239]

For all its plausibility, however, this thesis creates more puzzles than it solves. The most obvious is that, although the terms *distributiva* and

---

[235] Frugoni 1983, pp. 140, 160–1.
[236] If any part of the Old Testament helped to provide Lorenzetti with his inspiration, a stronger case could be made for the Book of Proverbs, 8.12–16 on wisdom as the source of the other virtues.
[237] Aristotle 1972, pp. 233, 236.
[238] Aquinas 1962, II^a. II^{ae}, Qu. 61, art. 1, resp., p. 299: 'duae sunt iustitiae species, scilicet commutativa et distributiva'.
[239] Rubinstein 1958, p. 182; Smart 1978, p. 105; Bowsky 1981, p. 289.

commutativa are unquestionably Aristotelian in origin, the theory of justice depicted by Lorenzetti is hardly Aristotelian at all. It is true that the activity represented under the heading COMVTATIVA, although far from unambiguous, might perhaps be interpreted as an exchange. The angel confronts two figures, and is usually said to be giving them various articles. Since they are both kneeling in the conventional posture of donors, however, it may well be they who are making the gifts. The figure on the left appears to be handing over two metal-tipped lances; the one on the right is holding out (and perhaps offering up) an object which, while it definitely looks cylindrical, cannot in the present condition of the painting be further identified.

Further puzzles arise in the case of the actions illustrated under the heading [DIS]TRIBVTIVA. Again we see an angel with two kneeling figures. The one on the right, who holds a palm of glory, is being crowned; the one on the left, whose weapon lies beside him, is being decapitated by the angel with a sword. The main difficulty here is that neither in the *Nicomachean Ethics*, nor in Aristotle's later analysis in the *Politics*, nor in any of Aquinas's comments on these texts is it ever suggested that Aristotle's concept of *iustum distributivum* is connected with the infliction of punishment. As Aristotle (in Grosseteste's version) emphasises in Book 5 of the *Ethics*, the problem with which he is alone concerned in asking what constitutes *iustitia* in relation to *distributionibus* is that of discovering a rule of fairness for the allocation of scarce and valued resources. The examples he offers of such *partibilia* are money and honours, and the thesis he defends is that the appropriate rule to follow must be to distribute them *secundum dignitatem* or according to worth.[240] At no point is the issue of punitive justice ever raised.

Chiara Frugoni has proposed a drastic solution to these difficulties. She suggests that the *titulus* [DIS]TRIBVTIVA belongs with the episode on the right, COMVTATIVA with the one on the left.[241] One problem with this hypothesis, however, is that it is wholly speculative. There is no independent evidence that these particular *tituli* were ever effaced, still less that they have come to be reversed. A further problem is that the episode on the right is not self-evidently an instance of distribution. Frugoni is obliged to assume that the two figures are both receiving gifts, which is doubtful in itself; that the lance or spear is a symbol of office, which is even more conjectural; and that the unidentifiable cylindrical object is a strong-box 'full of money', which seems quite unjustified.[242]

---

[240] Aristotle 1972, pp. 231–2. [241] Frugoni 1983, p. 138. [242] Frugoni 1983, p. 139.

The decisive objection to Frugoni's thesis, however, is that it leaves us with an unrecognisable portrayal of commutative justice. When Aristotle raises the issue of fairness in relation to exchange, he does so in the context of quoting the Pythagorean maxim that 'reciprocity is a straightforward instance of justice'.[243] He begins by observing that this looks questionable, since neither of the two forms of justice he has by then distinguished – distribution and rectification – can be said to involve pure reciprocity. But he concedes that such relationships nevertheless seem to 'hold people together' when it comes to questions of trade, barter, and exchange between citizens. So he feels it appropriate to examine the principles involved.[244]

Nothing in his ensuing examination, however, bears any resemblance to either of the episodes characterised by Frugoni as instances of commutative justice. As we have seen, one of these takes the form of a kneeling figure being crowned. Since the issue of commutative justice is held to arise only in exchanges between equals, however, neither Aristotle nor Aquinas ever suggests that it might be connected with the receiving of honours or rewards. The other alleged instance shows a kneeling figure being executed. But as Aristotle himself stresses, his sole aim in raising the question of fair exchanges is to establish whether pure reciprocity counts as a form of justice. The awarding of penalties for wrong-doing is obviously unconnected with this issue, and is mentioned at no point. Nor can this latter difficulty be met, as Frugoni postulates,[245] by pointing to the passage in Aquinas's commentary where he follows Aristotle in noting that 'two sorts of transactions' mark our common life, and that judges either punish or recompense in such cases. For in Aquinas, as in Aristotle, these observations are made in the course of considering the nature of rectificatory, not commutative, justice.[246]

Suppose, however, that we turn instead to the pre-humanist literature on city government as a possible guide to explaining Lorenzetti's depiction of justice. If we revert to these sources, and in particular to Brunetto Latini's distinctive analysis in the *Trésor*, most of the puzzles we have been considering can be resolved.

As we have seen, Latini argues that justice consists essentially in the rectifying of inequalities. Some arise from *entreservices*: the metalworker needs to be able to engage in fair exchanges with the draper,

---

[243] Aristotle 1972, p. 235: 'contrapassum esse simpliciter iustum'.
[244] Aristotle 1972, p. 236.   [245] Frugoni 1983, p. 139.
[246] Aristotle 1972, p. 233. The passage from Aquinas's commentary quoted in Frugoni 1983, p. 139 actually glosses 1131 a, 1–5.

the cordwainer, the carpenter. But others arise from social behaviour, requiring an *ygailleur* who can 'rectify' in two further ways: by punishing the wicked, especially by executing them or sending them into exile; and by rewarding the good, especially by handing out money and honours.

The two angels flanking Lorenzetti's figure of Justice seem to be engaged in precisely these forms of *ygaillance*. The one on the left appears to be acting as a rectifier in both the ways singled out in Latini's account. With his right hand he executes one kneeling figure, thereby punishing the wicked; with his left he crowns the other, thereby rewarding good conduct with honour. Meanwhile the angel on the right appears to be regulating *entreservices*. He receives from the two kneeling figures different items which they evidently wish to exchange in accordance with the mediating rules of justice. The figure on the right cannot be identified, but there is certainly a case for saying that the one on the left may be (as in Latini's example) a metal-worker, handing over spears or lances in the expectation of receiving commensurable articles in return. If this is so, it may well be that the figure on the right represents one of the other trades mentioned by Latini – that of draper, cordwainer, or carpenter. Since the object he is holding is definitely cylindrical, perhaps the best guess is that he is a draper with a bale of cloth,[247] a representative of one of Siena's most important industries.

It is worth recalling in conclusion the *topos* cited by so many of the pre-humanist writers to the effect that justice constitutes the ultimate bond of human society. For this is a further conception that Lorenzetti seems to illustrate. As we have seen, the double rope of concord held by the procession of citizens is handed to them by the figure of Concord. She in turn receives it, however, from the two angels of justice. The red cord originates as the girdle worn by the angel on the left, the grey as the girdle of the one on the right. Each cord passes through one of the pans in the scales of justice; both are then gathered by the figure of Concord, in whose left hand they are woven into a single rope. Justice is thus depicted as the source from which the double rope of concord ultimately derives, and hence as the ultimate bond of human society.

I now turn to the right-hand side of Lorenzetti's central painting, and so to the mysterious regal figure who dominates this section of the frescoes. As I began by observing, he is usually interpreted as a symbolic representation of the Thomist doctrine of the common good. He 'personifies the common good'; he is 'meant to represent the Common

---

[247] But in the light of the latest restoration of the frescoes I now feel less sure about this detail.

Good'.²⁴⁸ Lorenzetti's final message is thus that 'the common good must be raised to the position of the ruler' if we are to enjoy the blessings of peace.²⁴⁹

One difficulty with this interpretation is that it seems to involve a misunderstanding of Thomist doctrine. Aquinas never argues that the common good should be equated with the laws and those who enforce them. His thesis in the *Summa* is that 'all law is ordained to bring about the common good',²⁵⁰ and thus that 'legal justice is the particular virtue that looks to the common good'.²⁵¹ So he never suggests that the common good should be raised to the position of a ruler. Rather he insists that rulers have a duty to uphold the laws in such a way that they attain 'their own ultimate end, which consists in the realisation of the common good'.²⁵²

My main contention, however, is that there are good reasons for doubting whether this part of the frescoes has any connection with Thomist political ideas at all. As before, a more illuminating guide to Lorenzetti's visual effects can I think be found in the pre-humanist literature on city government.

As we have seen, the pre-humanist writers took the key to attaining the common good to lie in assigning a plenitude of power to an elected *signore* or *signoria*. Such powers were in turn held to include at least the following elements: full legal as well as legislative authority; full control of city and *contado* alike, including the right to command the allegiance of local feudatories; and full military as well as police backing for the implementation of these policies.

Lorenzetti faithfully mirrors all these aspects of civic government. First of all, he symbolises the authority of city magistrates over local feudatories. We see two noblemen in armour kneeling at the foot of the regal figure, offering him their castle in an evident act of homage. Next, he provides a strongly realistic portrayal of the legal powers of city magistrates. Below the regal figure, and upon his 'sinister' hand, we see a band of *fures* roped together under arrest, their enslaving bonds offering a strong contrast to the bonds of concord voluntarily held by the

---

[248] Rubinstein 1965, p. 55; Rubinstein 1958, p. 181. Cf. also White 1966, pp. 251–2.
[249] Rubinstein 1958, p. 185, a view endorsed in Tuve 1963, p. 290; Feldges-Henning 1972, p. 145; Borsook 1980, p. 35; Bowsky 1981, p. 288; Frugoni 1983, pp. 136, 150, 157.
[250] Aquinas 1952, I^a. II^{ae}, Qu. 90, art. 2, resp., p. 411: 'omnis lex ad bonum commune ordinatur'.
[251] Aquinas 1962, II^a. II^{ae}, Qu. 58, art. 6, resp., p. 285: 'iustitia legalis est specialis virtus ... quod respicit commune bonum'.
[252] Aquinas 1952, I^a. II^{ae}, Qu. 90, art. 2, ad. 3, p. 412: 'ad ultimum finem, qui est bonum commune'. For further instances see Michel 1932, pp. 243–4.

procession of worthy citizens on the other side. One of the *fures* has his head partly covered with a black cloth, a familiar device for representing someone convicted of a capital crime. Lorenzetti also hints at the various types of armed strength available for the enforcement of justice. We see one group of foot-soldiers standing behind the procession of citizens; they are all carrying lances, and one stares fixedly up at the regal figure above. A further group stands behind the two kneeling noblemen; again they are carrying lances, and again one of them looks up into the face of the regal figure. This latter group may perhaps be a representation of the special force of *contadini* apparently recruited by the Nove in 1302 to keep the peace in the Sienese countryside, a possibility suggested by their proximity to the two feudatories and by the fact that the device on their shields is a lion rampant, the emblem of the Sienese *popolo*. Lastly, behind this group and to the right we see four mounted lancers. They are helmeted, grim-faced, the two on the right are fully armoured, and one of them gazes up into the impassive face of the figure marked IVSTITIA.

Lorenzetti also portrays with remarkable fidelity the various images used to convey the majesty of public authority. The writers on city government liked to speak of the need for magistrates to deliver their judgements from a throne of glory. Lorenzetti duly shows the regal figure seated on a high and sumptuously covered throne. They liked to speak of magistrates as shields and defenders of their communities, carrying sceptres in their strong right hands. Lorenzetti duly shows the regal figure holding a golden staff in his right hand, a shield in his left. Some pre-humanist writers described the duties of government as a burden our magistrates carry on their shoulders. Around the shoulders of the regal figure Lorenzetti duly displays the letters C·S·C·V.[253] The initials are those of the *Commune Senarum, Civitas Virginis*, the community whose government is thus shown to weigh upon the regal figure as he bears its burdens on behalf of the people.[254] Most of the pre-humanist writers spoke in addition of our magistrates as set 'over' us while we are obliged

---

[253] The inscription now reads C·S·C·C·V. But the second 'C' is a later interpolation. Valle 1782–6, p. 220n. saw only C·S·C·V, as did Cavalcaselle and Crowe 1885, p. 210. For technical information about the interpolation see Rowley 1958, vol. 1, p. 99n. The lettering accompanying the similar figure portrayed on the Gabella cover for 1344 reads C·S·C·V. See Carli 1950, pp. 39–40 and pl. XV. It has become even clearer since the 1988 restoration that the second 'C' is an interpolation: the style of lettering is different and the gold is brighter than in the other letters.

[254] *Commune Senarum* (not *Civitas Senarum*, as Carli 1950, p. 39, suggests), this being the city's official designation. See *Il Costituto del Comune di Siena 1262*, p. 25. And *Civitas Virginis* (not *Civitatis Virginis*, as is ungrammatically suggested by Cavalcaselle and Crowe 1885, vol. 3, p. 210; Rowley 1958, vol. 1, p. 99; Feldges-Henning 1972, p. 145; and others). For Siena as the city of the Virgin see Bowsky 1981, p. 160.

to live 'under' their command. Lorenzetti duly displays the whole spectrum of citizens – the malefactors, the procession of worthies, the squads of foot-soldiers – as standing 'under' the regal figure and in several cases looking up at him as he sits enthroned 'over' the entire populace.

For all these elements of majesty, however, the writers on city government always insisted that true *signori* remain mere public servants, installed in office by the consent of the people to procure the common good. And as we have seen, they liked to express this contrasting perspective in a further set of metaphors. One favourite image spoke of such *signori* as tied or bound to rule according to the dictates of justice. Again Lorenzetti illustrates this exact conception, depicting the regal figure as bound by the double red and grey rope of concord originating with the figure of Justice. Commentators on the frescoes have generally claimed that the regal figure is simply holding the rope, which is being transferred or handed to him by the procession of citizens.[255] Closer inspection reveals, however, that the rope encircles his hand, while its ends hang down to the left – two indications that we are to think of it as knotted around his wrist. Symbolically the difference is of obvious significance. Although the regal figure holds a sceptre in the same hand, he is shown as bound or constrained to wield it according to the dictates of justice and the will of the citizens, in line with the maxim that 'What touches all must be approved by all.'

Lorenzetti even attempts in a number of ways to convey the idea that the powers of elected *signori* are simply an expression of, a way of representing, the powers of the community over which they preside. He shows the regal figure as grey-bearded, white-haired, and thus as *senex* or old – a possible allusion to Sena, the Latin name for the city of which he is head.[256] He is dressed in black and white, the heraldic colours of the commune of Siena. At his feet a she-wolf suckles a pair of twins, the ancient symbol of the Roman republic which the Sienese had adopted and emblazoned on the arms of their city in 1297.[257] And on his shield we can still faintly discern an image of the Virgin Mary, chosen by the Sienese as their special patron just before their victory over the Florentines at Montaperti in 1260.[258] The Virgin sits enthroned with the infant Jesus upon her left hand, and with two haloed supporters kneeling on either side of her. This strongly recalls the portrait of the Virgin to be seen

---

[255] Rowley 1958, vol. 1, p. 100; Rubinstein 1965, p. 55; Feldges-Henning 1972, p. 145; Frugoni 1983, p. 136. But cf. the excellent remarks in Southard 1978, p. 280.
[256] I owe this thought to Southard 1978, p. 60.
[257] See Larner 1971, p. 113, and cf. Southard 1978, pp. 47, 66.   [258] Southard 1978, p. 48.

on the left of the two central roundels beneath Simone Martini's *Maestà* in the adjoining council chamber of the *consiglio grande* in the Palazzo Pubblico. Around the edge of Simone's roundel can be read the motto of the Sienese republic, further emphasising the city's special indebtedness to the mother of God: SALVET VIRGO SENAM VET[EREM] QVAM SIGNAT AMENAM. If we turn back to Lorenzetti's fresco, we find around the edge of the shield held by the regal figure a faint and fragmentary version of what must certainly be the same motto: SALVE[T] VI[RG]O SE[NA]M [VETEREM] [QV]AM [SIGNAT AMENAM].

I conclude that the regal figure has been misidentified by those who have seen it as a personification of the common good. The figure is, rather, a symbolic representation of the type of *signore* or *signoria* that a city needs to elect if the dictates of justice are to be followed and the common good secured. To put the point more precisely in the language used by the pre-humanist writers, the figure constitutes a symbolic representation of the type of magistracy by means of which a body of citizens can alone hope to create or attain an ideal of the common good, and hence obtain the blessings of peace.[259]

It is arguable that Lorenzetti offers an even more exact and local allusion to the type of magistracy he wishes to commend. He does so by the unusual way in which he groups the virtues around the regal figure and relates them to the image of Peace. As we have seen, the writers on city government had inherited two rival traditions of thought about the virtues of public life. According to the more usual view, seven qualities are indispensable to good government: the three 'theological' virtues of faith, hope and charity, together with the four 'cardinal' virtues of prudence, justice, temperance and fortitude. According to the rival Senecan tradition, however, we ought rather to think of five civic virtues, since we ought to add the quality of magnanimity to the conventional list and indeed to give it pride of place.

Lorenzetti prefers to follow this latter and less orthodox scheme. He groups the figures marked FIDES, CARITAS and SPES around the head of the regal figure, puts those marked PRVDENTIA and MAGNANIMITAS in pride of place next to him, and flanks them with FORTITVDO, TENPERANTIA and IVSTITIA. And he situates the

---

[259] Some commentators have suggested that the figure symbolises the commune itself. See for example Wieruszowski 1971, p. 491; Rowley 1958, vol. 1, p. 99; Tuve 1963, p. 290; Larner 1971, p. 83; Southard 1978, pp. 60–1. I have sought to argue, however, that what is symbolised is not a social entity but a form of government, albeit one that in turn represents the commune. But for a fuller discussion of this issue, partly revising what is said here, see chapter 4 section III.

whole tableau of civic virtues on the same plane as the figure of Peace, the value whose triumph these qualities are said to secure.

As a result, Lorenzetti is able to contrive a further and very important symbolic effect. By adopting the scheme of five virtues and placing them in the company of Peace, he is able to surround the regal figure with a total of nine symmetrically disposed qualities. He is thus able firmly to associate the number nine with his representation of an ideally virtuous *signore*. It is perhaps not fanciful to see in this arrangement a celebration of the *Nove Signori* of Siena as an ideal *signoria*, especially as it was they who commissioned Lorenzetti to paint his frescoes for their own council chamber in the Palazzo Pubblico.[260] Given the setting of the paintings, they might even be held to carry the force of a continual reminder to the *Nove* of the civic values they were sworn to uphold.[261]

The idea that the *signoria* of a commune may be said to 'represent' the commune itself is one that appears elsewhere in Tuscan art of the early *trecento*. Perhaps the clearest exemplification of the idea can be found in one of the reliefs carved on the tomb of Bishop Guido Tarlati in the cathedral at Arezzo. Under an enthroned and venerable figure the explanatory legend reads COMM[UN]E IN SIGNORIA.[262] With his portrait of the *Nove* 'representing' the city, Lorenzetti offers a distinctively Sienese version of the same general theme.

Among those who have identified Lorenzetti's regal figure as the Common Good, however, it has always seemed an unanswerable argument that, as Nicolai Rubinstein observes, 'if we turn to the inscription at the bottom of the fresco, we find the explicit statement that the Ruler is meant to represent the Common Good'.[263] What the verse states is that, wherever the holy virtue of justice rules, many souls are able to act together in such a way that 'un ben comun perlor signor sifanno'.[264] This line has in turn been understood to say that they are able to act in such a way as to 'constitute the *ben comun* as their *signor*' [265] or to 'make up the common weal – *Ben Comun* – for their lord'.[266]

These renderings appear to me to embody a questionable understanding of the word *per* in the vital line. As we have seen, a number

---

[260] Bowsky 1981, pp. 100, 287–8.
[261] For a further exploration of the functions of Lorenzetti's cycle see White 2000, pp. 53–60.
[262] Wieruszowski 1971, pp. 489–90.   [263] Rubinstein 1958, p. 181.
[264] As explained in note 3 above, 'signor' is how the penultimate word appeared before the restoration of the early 1980s. It now appears as 'sigror', which makes no sense.
[265] Dowdall 1923, p. 113.
[266] Feldges-Henning 1972, p. 146. Rowley 1958, vol. 1, p. 127 (followed by Bowsky 1981, p. 289), instead suggests 'a common good for their master undertake'.

of pre-humanist treatises – to say nothing of the Sienese Constitution of 1309–10 – insist that the common good and the triumph of peace can only be brought about *per* – by means of, through the agency of – an elected *signore* or *signoria* dedicated to upholding the dictates of justice. The crucial word *per* in the verses accompanying Lorenzetti's fresco should I think be understood in the same way. What the verses state is that, where justice induces many souls to act together, they can hope to create or attain for themselves, through the agency of their *signore*, an ideal of the common good. They confirm that the regal figure in Lorenzetti's fresco is an ideally virtuous *signore*, a symbolic representation of the type of magistracy through which the common good can alone be attained.

V

I turn lastly to reconsider the other and more general claim which has usually been made about this section of Lorenzetti's frescoes: that the tableau of virtues surrounding the central figure can best be interpreted as an expression of scholastic ideas, and specifically of Aquinas's moral and political thought.[267]

There are certainly many elements in Lorenzetti's design that can readily be explicated in this way. Consider first the figures of Faith, Hope and Charity floating above the head of the regal figure, with Charity in pride of place. Aquinas singles out just these qualities as the major theological virtues,[268] and endorses St Paul's judgement that 'in the order of perfection charity takes precedence over faith and hope'.[269] Consider similarly the figure of Justice, who is shown with a crown in her left hand and a sword in her right. Aquinas makes use of both these images, assuring us that 'a crown of justice is laid up' for those who behave righteously,[270] and that 'our rulers, when they punish malefactors, are lawfully defending the community with the sword'.[271] Consider finally the figure of Prudence, whom we see on the left of the regal figure, garbed with particular richness, crowned as the noblest of the virtues and

---

[267] For this claim see Rubinstein 1958, pp. 186–7; Yates 1969, p. 101; Bowsky 1981, p. 288.
[268] Aquinas 1952, I^a. II^{ae}, Qu. 62, art. 3, resp., p. 274.
[269] Aquinas 1952, I^a. II^{ae}, Qu. 62, art. 4, resp., p. 275: 'ordine vero perfectionis, caritas praecedit fidem et spem'.
[270] Aquinas in the *Summa* twice quotes with approval St Paul's reference (2 Timothy 4.8) to the 'corona iustitiae' reserved for those who keep the faith. See Aquinas 1952, I^a. II^{ae}, Qu. 4, art. 3, p. 25 and Aquinas 1952, I^a. II^{ae}, Qu. 114. art. 3, p. 567.
[271] Aquinas 1962, II^a. II^{ae}, Qu. 40, art. 1, resp., p. 207: '[Principes] ... licite defendunt eam materiali gladio ... dum malefactores puniunt.'

pointing with her right hand to a *cartouche* inscribed PRETERIT PRESE FUTM.²⁷² Aquinas speaks in the *Summa* of prudence as 'nobler than all the other virtues'²⁷³ and goes on to explain that what distinguishes prudence is the ability to learn about things in the future (*futura*) by way of considering things in the present (*praesentibus*) as well as things in the past (*praeteritis*).²⁷⁴

Even in these instances, however, there is no reason to conclude that Lorenzetti must have drawn on Aquinas or any other scholastic authority. The pre-humanist writers on city government could equally well have supplied him with his inspiration for the disposition of all these figures. As we have seen, the belief that prudence should be regarded as queen or ruler of the virtues was one that most of the pre-humanist writers shared; so was the belief that faith, hope and charity constitute the leading theological virtues; so was the belief that the greatest of these is charity. The same point can be made about the symbols that Lorenzetti chooses to associate with these qualities. The crown of justice was originally a Biblical image, and was subsequently taken up by a number of pre-humanist writers on the virtues.²⁷⁵ The idea that justice carries a sword can similarly be traced to St Paul's contention that no ruler bears the sword in vain, a warning echoed in many of the pre-humanist treatises on city government.²⁷⁶ And the formula connecting prudence with an understanding of past, present and future can be found not merely in Cicero's *De Officiis*,²⁷⁷ but also in Martin of Braga's *Formula Vitae Honestae*,²⁷⁸ as a result of which the same *topos* recurs in practically all the pre-humanist treatises.²⁷⁹

Even more striking, however, is the extent to which Aquinas's analysis of the virtues remains powerless to explain a number of Lorenzetti's visual effects, whereas the pre-humanist writers appear to offer a systematic guide to this part of his pictorial scheme.

---

²⁷² A likely source of these abbreviations is Cicero 1913, I. IV. 11, p. 12, where Prudence is connected with a knowledge of *praeteritum praesens* and *futurum*. Frugoni 1983, p. 161 suggests the Book of Wisdom as the source. But this makes no mention of *praesens* and speaks not of *futurum* but *de futuris*.
²⁷³ Aquinas 1962, IIᵃ. IIᵃᵉ, Qu. 47, art. 6, ad. 3, p. 239: 'Prudentia sit nobilior virtutibus moralibus.'
²⁷⁴ Aquinas 1962, IIᵃ. IIᵃᵉ, Qu. 47, art. 1, resp., p. 235: 'Cognoscere autem futura ex praesentibus vel praeteritis . . . pertinet ad prudentiam.'
²⁷⁵ See 2 Timothy 4.8, cited, for example, by Perrault 1618, vol. 1, p. 244.
²⁷⁶ Romans 13.4. Cf. *Oculus* 1966, p. 63; Faba 1889, p. 154; Viterbo 1901, p. 235; Latini 1948, p. 397.
²⁷⁷ Cicero 1913, I. IV. 11, p. 12.
²⁷⁸ Braga 1950, p. 240. Cf. the discussion in Panofsky 1970, pp. 184–6.
²⁷⁹ Conches 1929, p. 9; Perrault 1618, vol. 1, p. 166; *Oculus* 1966, pp. 43, 63; Viterbo 1901, p. 252; Giamboni 1968, p. 57; Latini 1948, p. 233.

This applies most obviously to the arrangement of the individual virtues. Lorenzetti places Justice at a greater distance from the central figure than any of the other virtues. This hardly answers to Aquinas's sense that 'among the moral virtues justice is the one that excels all the rest'.[280] But it seems an apt illustration of the strongly contrasting view we encountered in several of the pre-humanist treatises: the view that, as Latini expresses it, 'justice comes after all the other virtues'. So too with the figure of Magnanimity, whom we see together with Prudence at the centre of Lorenzetti's scheme. Nothing in Aquinas's analysis suggests such an arrangement, since he endorses the conventional assumption that magnanimity is merely one of the subordinate elements of fortitude.[281] Again, however, the pre-humanist writers seem to provide the key. As we have seen, a number followed Seneca's lead in thinking of magnanimity as perhaps the most dominant and splendid of the virtues. This is certainly how we see her depicted: dominantly positioned, her garments a more brilliant white even than those of Peace herself. Brunetto Latini had gone on to add that magnanimity is 'negligent about small expenses' and thinks it 'a nobler thing to give than to receive'. Lorenzetti duly shows her dispensing coins from a large dish held in her lap. Latini had concluded that magnanimity represents 'the crown and the brightest of all the virtues'. We duly see Lorenzetti's figure holding out a crown in her right hand.

If we turn to the symbols associated with the rest of the political virtues, a similar argument can be mounted in almost every case. Consider first the motifs assigned to Justice and Prudence. Although these are the most conventional of Lorenzetti's figures, Prudence displays one highly unusual iconographical feature. Among Tuscan painters and sculptors of this period, Prudence is generally pictured with a book, a pair of dividers, or sometimes a snake. For example, Andrea Pisano's figure of Prudence on the campanile of the Duomo at Florence is shown grasping a snake by its tail, while Giotto's figure in the Cappella degli Scrovegni in Padua is shown with dividers and a book. Lorenzetti, by contrast, displays Prudence cradling in her left hand a small black lamp,[282] the three flames of which illuminate the three words inscribed on her *cartouche*.

---

[280] Aquinas 1962, II^a. II^{ae}, Qu. 58, art. 12, resp., p. 289: 'ipsa [iustitia legalis] est praeclarior inter omnes virtutes morales'.
[281] Aquinas 1962, II^a. II^{ae}, Qu. 129, art. 5, resp., p. 583: 'magnanimitas ponitur pars fortitudinis'.
[282] Since the 1988 restoration this is no longer the case. We still see the three flames, but the lamp is now virtually the same pale blue colour as Prudence's garment, a disturbing 'restoration'.

There is nothing in the Thomist sources to suggest this attribute. Aquinas himself observes that prudence 'is divided and numbered apart from the other virtues';[283] he notes that prudence is regarded as a special virtue of teachers;[284] and he repeats St Matthew's injunction that we must learn to be as prudent as serpents.[285] He confines himself, in short, to mentioning the three qualities implied by prudence's conventional iconography. If we turn, however, to the pre-humanist writers, and to the moral treatises on which they relied, we find an obvious source for Lorenzetti's imagery. The author of *Moralium Dogma Philosophorum* speaks of prudence as 'carrying a lamp to show the way to the other virtues'.[286] Guillaume Perrault similarly observes that prudence 'carries a light before the rest of the virtues'.[287] Brunetto Latini reiterates the same metaphor, remarking that prudence 'goes before the other virtues and carries a lamp to show them the way'.[288]

Consider next the figure marked TENPERANTIA. So far as I am aware, this was iconographically unique at the time when Lorenzetti painted it. Among Tuscan artists of the period, Temperance is usually depicted with a vessel in each hand. Often she is pictured in the act of pouring liquid from one vessel into the other, an evident allusion to the belief that wine should be tempered by water. This is how she appears on the campanile of the Duomo at Florence, and this is how Lorenzetti himself portrays her in his fresco of c.1326 in the church of San Francesco in Siena. A decade later, however, he presents her in a completely different guise. She holds in her right hand the base of a large *horarium* or sand-glass, bending her gaze upon it and pointing with the index finger of her left hand to show us that the sands have half run out.

Again, there is nothing in Thomist tradition to indicate such an iconography. Aquinas opens his rubric on temperance in the *Summa* with the etymological claim that 'the very name of this virtue signifies a power of moderating or tempering something'.[289] If we turn, however, to the

---

[283] Aquinas 1962, II^a. II^{ae}, Qu. 47, art. 5, contra, p. 237: '[Prudentia] condividitur et connumeratur aliis virtutibus'.
[284] Aquinas 1962, II^a. II^{ae}, Qu. 49, art. 3, 3, p. 250.
[285] Aquinas 1962, II^a. II^{ae}, Qu. 56, art. 1, 2, p. 275.
[286] Conches 1929, p. 8: 'ferens lucernam et aliis [virtutibus] monstrans viam'. The passage is cited in Tuve 1966, p. 285.
[287] Perrault 1618, vol. 1, p. 153: 'prudentia caeteris [virtutibus] lumen praefert'.
[288] Latini 1948, p. 231: 'ele vait par devant les autres vertus et porte la lumiere et moustre as autres la voie'.
[289] Aquinas 1962, II^a. II^{ae}, Qu. 141, art. 1, resp., p. 613: 'in ipso eius nomine importatur quaedam moderatio seu temperies'. So too Rimini 1472, IV. 2, fo. 99b.

pre-humanist writers on city government, we find them drawing on a rival etymological suggestion which seems to furnish the key to Lorenzetti's imagery: the suggestion that there is a special connection between temperance and the keeping of time.

As so often, Cicero's *De Officiis* seems to have provided the inspiration for this line of thought. Discussing the virtue of temperance in Book I, Cicero not only relates it to the notion of acting in a 'timely' way, but argues that temperate behaviour can be compared with the behaviour of time itself. 'We must take care never to move too slowly nor too quickly' and 'we must take even greater care to ensure that the movements of our soul remain in harmony with nature'.[290] The implication that there may be an etymological link between *tempus* and *temperantia* was later spelled out by no less an authority than Varro in his treatise on the Latin language. 'It is from the temperate movements of the sun and moon', he declares, 'that time itself is named.'[291] The view that temperance is essentially a quality of timeliness recurs in a number of moral treatises of Ciceronian inspiration, most obviously in *Moralium Dogma Philosophorum*. This not only quotes Cicero's commendation of measured behaviour in *De Officiis*, but adds a number of other Ciceronian passages to the same effect, including the contention from *De Inventione* that temperance is the quality that serves to restrain all importunate movements.[292]

By way of such intermediaries, the same view of temperance found its way into several of the pre-humanist treatises on city government. Brunetto Latini in particular draws on the *Dogma* for his views about the importance of timely behaviour, adding that temperance is a virtue with five subsidiary members, the principal being a quality of *mesure* 'that enables all our movements and all our affairs to be conducted faultlessly and without disgrace'.[293] Latini's is not only the fullest of these discussions, but is also the one that Lorenzetti's unprecedented portrayal of Temperance seems most closely to evoke.

Consider finally the figure marked FORTITUDO, whose iconography embodies a number of even more unconventional features. The virtue of Fortitude is almost always depicted by Tuscan artists of this period as a Herculean hero, draped with the skin of a lion and carrying

---

[290] Cicero 1913, I. XXXVI. 131, p. 132: 'Cavendum autem est, ne aut tarditatibus utamur... aut in festinationibus suscipiamus... sed multo etiam magis elaborandum est, ne animi motus a natura recedant.'
[291] Varro 1938, VI. II. 3, vol. 1, p. 174: 'ab eorum [i.e. sol et luna] tenore temperato tempus dictum'.
[292] Conches 1929, pp. 41–2. Cf. Cicero 1949, II. LIV. 164, p. 330.
[293] Latini 1948, p. 250, on 'mesure': 'tous nos movemens et tous nos afferes, fait estre sans defaute et sans outrage'.

a club. This image, which clearly owes much to Ovid and Virgil,[294] recurs very widely: in the Cappella degli Scrovegni, on the campanile of the Duomo at Florence, in Giovanni Pisano's carvings on the pulpit of the Duomo at Pisa. Lorenzetti, by contrast, portrays Fortitude in a completely different and still more belligerent pose. A black-robed female figure, wearing a cuirass underneath her robes, she is shown carrying a shield in her left hand and a golden staff in her right, and is closely accompanied by two soldiers on horseback, each of whom is helmeted and fully armoured.

There is nothing in the writings of Aquinas or his immediate disciples to hint at Lorenzetti's exceptionally aggressive characterisation. On the contrary, the main emphasis in Thomist discussions is usually placed on the idea of fortitude as a matter of courage to endure rather than courage to fight. As Aquinas himself puts it in the *Summa*, 'the chief sign of fortitude is more a willingness to sustain dangers and stand one's ground than a willingness to attack'.[295] Nor – with one exception – is there any warrant for Lorenzetti's warlike portrait among the pre-humanist writers on city government. The exception, however, is of great significance. Brunetto Latini defines fortitude in his *Trésor* as that virtue which 'serves as a shield and a defence to a man, as his armour and his staff, enabling him not only to defend himself but to attack those who deserve it'.[296] It is Latini's description – for which I know of no precedent – which appears once again to have supplied the inspiration for Lorenzetti's iconography.

Given that Lorenzetti seems to have drawn specifically on Brunetto Latini's text for his portraits of Magnanimity, Temperance and Fortitude, it is worth commenting on one further claim about the cardinal virtues that figures prominently in *Li Livres dou trésor*, but again appears to be without parallel in any earlier work. Latini tells us at the start of his encyclopaedia that 'the second part will treat of the virtues and vices, and will thus be concerned with precious stones that give men delight and virtue'.[297] It was a commonplace to speak, in the manner of Pliny, of gemstones as having special or even magical virtues or properties. But Latini reverses the usual argument, claiming not that precious stones possess virtues, but that virtues can be symbolised by precious stones.

---

[294] Ovid 1977–84, XV, line 284, vol. 2, p. 384; Virgil 1999–2000, VII, lines 666–9, vol. 2, p. 48.
[295] Aquinas 1962, II^a. II^{ae}, Qu. 123, art. 6, resp., p. 561: 'principalior actus est fortitudinis sustinere, id est immobiliter sistere in periculis, quam aggredi'. So too Rimini 1472, III. 3, fo. 64b.
[296] Latini 1948, p. 260: '[Force est] escus et deffense de l'ome, c'est son hauberc et son glave, car ele fet l'ome deffendre soi et offendre a ciaus k'il doit.'
[297] Latini 1948, p. 17: 'La seconde partie ki traite des vices et des viertus est de precieuses pieres, ki donent a home delit et vertu.'

Latini reverts to this suggestion – an obvious pun on the title of his encyclopaedia – at the opening of Book 2, where he begins with a rhetorical flourish that appears to be all his own:[298]

This second part of the *Trésor* will be concerned with precious stones, that is, with the virtues. This teaching will be on the four principal virtues. The first of these is prudence, which is signified by the carbuncle, which lights up the night and is more splendid than any other stone. The second is temperance, which is signified by the sapphire, which is the colour of the sky, and is the most gracious stone in the world. The third is fortitude, which is signified by the diamond, which is so strong that it can break and pierce all other stones and metals, while nothing can harm it. The fourth is justice, which is signified by the emerald, the most virtuous and beautiful object that the eye of man can behold.[299]

It is perhaps the strongest evidence of Lorenzetti's dependence specifically on Latini's authority that he follows this account with such remarkable fidelity in depicting the four virtues concerned. He associates Temperance with the colour of the sky, giving her a cloak and flowing skirt of cerulean blue. He associates Justice with the colour of emeralds, giving her a pale green tunic under her purplish-red cloak. He associates Fortitude with diamonds, showing a large diamond-shaped ornament etched at the centre of her cuirass. Finally, he not only shows Prudence as the first among the virtues, and hence in pride of place, but he also shows her wearing a robe whose hem is encrusted with dark-coloured stones. These, we can surely conclude, must be intended to represent carbuncles.

I began with the general claim that Lorenzetti's frescoes give expression to various Ciceronian and Senecan themes that were first revived and developed by the ideologists of the Italian city-republics in the early decades of the thirteenth century. I have now arrived at the more specific contention that one particular statement of this ideology can be shown to have provided the source for most of Lorenzetti's symbolic effects. Brunetto Latini, Dante's teacher, was plunged by Dante in the *Inferno* into the seventh circle of hell.[300] My main conclusion is that, if we wish

[298] Though the germ of the idea can be found in Conches 1929, p. 79.
[299] Latini 1948, p. 175: 'Et ce est la seconde partie dou tresor, ki doit estre de pieres precieuses, ce sont les vertus ... Cist ensegnemens sera sor les .iiii. principaus vertus. Dont la premiere est prudence, ki est segnefiee par le carboncle, ki alume la nuit et resplendist sour toutes pieres. La seconde est atemprance, ki est segnefiee par le saphir, ki porte celestial coulor, et est plus gracieuse que piere du monde. La tierce est force, ki est segnefiee par le diamant, ki est si fort k'il ront et perce toutes pieres et tous metaus, et por poi il n'est chose ki le puisse donter. La quarte vertu est justice, ki est segnefiee par l'esmeraude, ki est la plus vertuouse et la plus bele chose que oil d'ome puisse veoir.'
[300] Dante 1966, XV, line 30, p. 245: 'Siete voi qui, ser Brunetto?'

to understand Lorenzetti's masterpiece, this is a depth of oblivion from which we shall have to rescue him.[301]

VI

I have been considering Ambrogio Lorenzetti's frescoes mainly as the expression of an ideology, and I have been examining that ideology mainly as a way of explicating his frescoes. I wish to conclude by prising these two elements apart, asking whether there may be anything further to be learnt from my analysis about Lorenzetti's masterpiece, or about the historical significance of the ideology I have delineated.

In the case of the frescoes, I should like to think that various elements in the organisation and colour scheme of the central section can now be more fully explained by reference to the evidence I have presented. I should now like to add that the same evidence can also be deployed as a means of reconsidering a crucial question about the painting's state of repair, and hence its authenticity.

The question I have in mind is one that has preoccupied commentators ever since this part of the cycle was restored in the early 1950s. As Cesare Brandi definitively established at that time, the section portraying the virtues underwent extensive repair within about twenty years of its completion in the late 1330s. It appears to have been vandalised either in the course of the riots that accompanied Charles IV's visit to Siena in 1356, or perhaps during the uprising of 1368. Whatever the occasion of the violence, the resulting damage was such that the whole area to the right of the regal figure had to be repainted, including the major figures of Magnanimity, Temperance and Justice.[302]

The most serious question this raises is whether the later artist (Lorenzetti having died in c.1348) was able to reproduce the original colour-scheme and iconographical details, or whether the destruction was so extensive as to force him to improvise.

It is certainly evident that various changes must have been introduced. In the area to the right of the regal figure, the cloth covering the bench on which the virtues are seated has been repainted with an inverted pattern and a darker colour-scheme, predominantly brown rather than orange and red. The handling of the drapery on the right-hand figures is less complex than on the left, while their faces altogether lack the

---

[301] Since I wrote these words, however, he has been rescued in Holloway 1993, a fully documented biography. On Latini and Dante see also Ventura 1997.

[302] Brandi 1955, pp. 119–23.

characteristic angularity that Lorenzetti imparts to Peace, Prudence and especially Fortitude. Closer inspection also discloses some clumsiness in the restoration of the section immediately to the right of the crack that separates off the area of damage, a crack that follows the right-hand fold of the regal figure's cloak. The hem of the cloak itself has been repainted in a simpler style, while the crown held out by Magnanimity has been superimposed on another crown of similar design, part of which remains rather confusingly visible.

Brandi himself inferred that, although the later artist probably reproduced as much as possible of Lorenzetti's work, he certainly fell short of anything like a literal imitation of what had been lost.[303] Recent scholars have voiced similar doubts,[304] while White has positively asserted that various elements in Lorenzetti's design must have been altered, claiming in particular that the sand-glass held by Temperance cannot be ascribed to a period earlier than the late 1350s.[305]

It is I think arguable, however, that Lorenzetti's basic design, colour scheme and iconography were all preserved, at least in the case of the major figures of Magnanimity, Temperance and Justice. The grounds for this optimism are furnished by the fact that Latini's *Trésor* evidently supplied Lorenzetti with the programme for his entire group of political virtues. As we have seen, Latini's descriptions of Fortitude and Magnanimity, which are virtually without precedent, are followed by Lorenzetti with complete fidelity. His descriptions of Prudence and Temperance, which are likewise distinctive, are no less carefully reproduced. There is indeed only one point at which Latini offers a strong visual clue that Lorenzetti fails to pick up. Latini's suggestion – again without parallel in other texts – that the cardinal virtues can be associated with particular precious stones is only imperfectly realised. As we have seen, Lorenzetti adopts the suggestion in the case of Fortitude and Prudence on the left, but not in the case of Temperance and Justice on the right.

It seems to me very likely, however, that this is simply due to the loss of those details at the time when the section on the right was repainted. Although we do not see the emerald associated with Justice, we see a rectangular black patch in just the position where, in the case of Fortitude, her diamond-shaped ornament is displayed.[306] So too with Temperance, whose sapphire is likewise missing, but whose blue tunic under her cloak is similarly marked with a black patch that looks even more like an

---

[303] Brandi 1955, p. 120.   [304] Rowley 1958, vol. 1, p. 142; Borsook 1980, p. 37.
[305] White 1969, p. 208.
[306] This is no longer the case. With the 1988 restoration the black patch has been removed.

instance of overpainting or repair.³⁰⁷ It may be that these patches were introduced by the later artist as a means of referring to certain details of Lorenzetti's design that he found impossible to reconstruct. So the black patch on Temperance ought perhaps to show a sapphire, the one on Justice an emerald.

Even if this seems unduly speculative, we are still left with the following facts. Lorenzetti painted the figure of Fortitude, which is clearly inspired by Latini's *Trésor*. A later artist (probably Andrea Vanni)³⁰⁸ repainted Magnanimity and Temperance, both of which are no less clearly taken from the same source. The most plausible inference is surely this: that the entire ensemble of the virtues reflects Lorenzetti's dependence on Latini, and thus that the later artist was in fact able to follow Lorenzetti's designs, except in the case of the small details just mentioned.

This is a finding of particular significance in relation to the portrayal of Temperance. As we have seen, this includes the earliest known depiction of a clock in the annals of Western art. White has argued that this feature must be a later addition, and that the original painting probably showed Temperance with 'her traditional cup'.³⁰⁹ Given Latini's contention, however, that Temperance is essentially a quality of 'measure' and 'timeliness', there is every reason to believe that, here as elsewhere, it was Latini who provided the inspiration for Lorenzetti's iconography. So there is every reason to conclude that the sand-glass held by Temperance must have formed an original feature of the work. The first appearance of a clock in Western art can be ascribed to the 1330s after all.

I turn lastly to indicate what I take to be the historical significance of the ideology I have described. Hans Baron and others have influentially argued that the ideal of republican self-government was first fully articulated in Italian political theory only around the year 1400.³¹⁰ This thesis has been justly criticised, however, for failing to recognise the emergence of similar doctrines among civil lawyers and especially scholastic political philosophers over a century earlier.³¹¹ The 'rebirth of the citizen' and the earliest conceptualisations of 'the new world of urban politics' have thus come to be associated in particular with the recovery and dissemination of Aristotle's *Politics* and *Nicomachean Ethics* in the closing decades of the thirteenth century.³¹²

---

³⁰⁷ This too is no longer the case. With the 1988 restoration this patch has also been removed.
³⁰⁸ Bellosi 1974, pp. 52-4 and pls. 110-13.   ³⁰⁹ White 1969, p. 208.
³¹⁰ Baron 1966, pp. 3-78.   ³¹¹ See for example Davis 1984, p. 254.
³¹² Pocock 1975, pp. 3, 66, 74-5; Ullmann 1977, pp. 94-6, 134; Ullmann 1975, pp. 176-80; Rubinstein 1982, p. 153.

This latter view, however, no less than that of Baron's, overlooks the fact that the pre-humanist ideology I have been considering embodies an ideal of citizenship, and a vision of self-governing republicanism, that predate by at least a generation the earliest availability of the Aristotelian texts. A number of scholars have of course pointed to this aspect of pre-humanist culture.[313] But they have tended to add that, as soon as Aristotle became available in translation, his views completely won the day and 'transformed Italian political thought'.[314] As I have tried to show, however, the theories formulated by the *dictatores* not only preceded the so-called Aristotelian revolution but survived it virtually unchanged. The outcome was a distinctive view of citizenship that eventually broadened out into the so-called civic humanism of the Renaissance.[315] It was from these humble origins, far more than from the impact of Aristotelianism, that the classical republicanism of Machiavelli, Guicciardini and their contemporaries originally stemmed. The political theory of the Renaissance, at all phases of its history, owes a far deeper debt to Rome than to Greece.

[313] Ullmann 1977, pp. 101, 134; Rubinstein 1982, pp. 153–4.
[314] Ullmann 1977, p. 96; Rubinstein 1982, p. 155. But for an excellent corrective see Celli 1980, pp. 50–2.
[315] My argument can thus be viewed as a special case of the general thesis argued in Kristeller 1979 and Kristeller 1988 about the origins and character of humanism, a thesis to which I am deeply indebted.

4

Ambrogio Lorenzetti on the power and glory of republics

I

My principal concern in this chapter, as in chapter 3, is with the cycle of frescoes painted by Ambrogio Lorenzetti in the Palazzo Pubblico in Siena between 1337 and 1339. But whereas in chapter 3 I was mainly interested in Lorenzetti's ideal of virtuous government, and accordingly focused my attention on the central section of the painting, I now want to extend my analysis to take in the organisation of the cycle as a whole. After attempting (in section II) to follow the line of Lorenzetti's narrative, I turn to the two most notorious iconographical puzzles raised by his masterpiece. One of these relates to the mysterious regal figure who dominates the ensemble of the political virtues on the northern wall. I still believe, obstinately perhaps, that the interpretation of this figure I offered in chapter 3 is basically correct.[1] But I have come to see that there are additional complexities and ambiguities to be explored, and these I attempt to address in section III. The other question I want to consider is the significance of the group of dancers who occupy the heart of the cityscape on the eastern wall. Here I believe that some decisive information about these yet more mysterious figures can be gleaned if we turn again to the literary sources, and this is the suggestion I follow up in section IV.

II

The best way to view Lorenzetti's fresco-cycle in sequence is to stand in front of the one natural light source in the Sala dei Nove, the window in the southern wall. From this vantage point the sections we see to

---

This chapter is a revised version of an article that originally appeared under the title 'Ambrogio Lorenzetti's *Buon governo* Frescoes: Two Old Questions, Two New Answers' in *The Journal of the Warburg and Courtauld Institutes*, 62 (1999), pp. 1–28.

[1] I should note, however, that some details of my argument have been questioned in Donato 2001.

our left (or 'sinister') side illustrate the rule of tyranny and its ruinous effects on city and countryside alike (Plates 1–2). Having been commissioned by the *Nove* to celebrate the values of a republic, Lorenzetti opens his narrative by highlighting an argument usually accorded marginal significance by the predominantly monarchical political theory of his age.[2] The neo-Aristotelian writers of the early *trecento* had generally insisted that, as Giles of Rome unhesitatingly declares, 'kingship is the best form of government',[3] although they usually concede the danger that monarchy can degenerate into tyranny.[4] Lorenzetti, by contrast, begins by reminding us with the utmost emphasis of the appalling consequences that ensue when this exact form of political degeneration takes place.[5] At the centre of his tableau we see a representation of tyranny, a concept figured in the form of a cross-eyed ruler robed in black and with demonic horns and fangs. Behind his back we duly read, in silver lettering, the word TYRAMMIDES (Plate 2). Although enthroned in the manner of a king, Tyranny is shown wielding a dagger in place of a sceptre, while the chalice in his left hand is no doubt a poisoned one. His foot rests on a goat, symbol of *luxuria*,[6] while the figure of IVSTI[TIA] lies captive beneath his throne. Above him hover AVARITIA, SUP[ER]BIA and VANAGLORIA, 'the leading enemies of human life' according to the *Oculus Pastoralis*, the earliest of the advice-books for city magistrates circulating in Tuscany at this time.[7] The central and presiding spirit is that of SUP[ER]BIA, universally regarded by the moralists of Lorenzetti's age as 'the queen of all the vices'.[8] Ranged on either side of Tyranny are the elements of force and fraud that keep such unjust and enslaving governments in power. To our left we see the insidious vices of CRVDELITAS, PRODITIO and FRAVS; to our right the outright violence of FVROR, [D]IVISIO and GVERRA.

As in the case of a literary narrative, Lorenzetti's pictorial argument asks to be read from left to right. So far as I know, this approach has

---

[2] On the need to read Lorenzetti's cycle as a narrative, albeit one that articulates an argument, see Belting 1985, pp. 151–68.

[3] Rome 1607, III. II. III, p. 456: 'Quod regnum est optimus principatus'.

[4] Rome 1607, III. II. VII, p. 468: 'summe debent cavere Reges & Principes, ne eorum dominium in tyrannidem convertatur', the reason being that 'tyrannus est pessimus principatus'.

[5] Rowley 1958, vol. 1, pp. 104–5. The point is also well brought out in Starn and Partridge 1992, pp. 21–2, although I see no evidence for their further claim (p. 22) that Lorenzetti's tableau shows us 'impulses that republicans feared in themselves'.

[6] Katzenellenbogen 1939, p. 61. Cf. Alciato 1621, Emblem 72, p. 321.

[7] *Oculus* 1966, p. 52 claims that 'hostes vite hominis... sunt praecipue superbia, inanis gloria, avaricia' (to which the writer adds 'invidia').

[8] Faba 1956, p. 98: 'Superbia quippe regina est omnium vitiorum.' See also Brescia 1507, fo. 55^v.

not been systematically followed,⁹ but it serves to uncover a number of interconnections between the different parts of Lorenzetti's cycle. If these are to be appreciated, we next need to shift our attention to the northern wall (Plate 3). Directly facing us is a white-robed female figure, identified by her *titulus* as PAX, whose depiction embodies a series of contrasts with the figure of GVERRA or War on the western wall (Plate 2). War is seated on Tyranny's extreme left hand, and thus in the most sinister position of all. Peace is seated at the centre of the middle tier of the middle painting of the cycle, and thus at the heart of civic life.¹⁰ War is shown in a posture of alert, his shield at the ready and his sword upraised. Peace is shown in an answering posture of repose, reclining on a cushion with an olive branch in her hand.

Below the triumph of Peace and to our left we see another female figure, marked CONCORDIA, whose depiction likewise embodies a series of contrasts with the figures on Tyranny's left hand. The closest companion of Tyranny is the monster representing FVROR, the Fury of the brutish multitude. The next companion is [D]IVISIO, civil Division, who is represented in a still more disturbing way. Her expression is demented, her long hair is dishevelled, and she holds a carpenter's saw with which she appears to be lacerating herself.¹¹ The figure of Concord sits, by contrast, with a placid expression and with her long hair neatly plaited down her back (Plate 4). She too is holding a carpenter's tool, for she is balancing a large plane across her knees. She thereby indicates her willingness to overcome division and fury by making the rough places plain,¹² smoothing out inequities and establishing the Ciceronian ideal of *concordia* and *aequitas* as the twin foundations of civic life.¹³

Above the figure of Concord, a further and larger female figure sits enthroned. As we saw in chapter 3, her *titulus* makes it clear that she is a representation of the idea of Justice. Here Lorenzetti has contrived an even sharper contrast with his depiction of tyrannical government on the western wall. There Justice is shown tumbled to the ground, dressed

---

⁹ But the need for such a reading is well emphasised in Belting 1985, p. 159.
¹⁰ But see Gibbs 1999, pp. 11–16 for the suggestion that, due to the later *trecento* repairs, the figure of Peace may now be more central and prominent than Lorenzetti intended. This I doubt, for reasons I have given above in chapter 3 section V.
¹¹ Sallust 1931b, XLI. 5, p. 222 speaks of the time when the *res publica*, divided into two parties, was thereby *dilacerata*. The figure of Discordia in Prudentius's *Psychomachia* has a 'scissa palla', a torn robe. See Prudentius 1949–53, line 685, vol. 1, p. 326. As noted in chapter 3, however, the latest restoration of the frescoes suggests that in Lorenzetti's portrayal Discordia may merely be cutting an object held in her left hand.
¹² Isaiah 40.4 and Luke 3.5.   ¹³ For this theme see chapter 3 section II.

in a plain white shift, her feet shackled and her golden hair unkempt. The cords of her balance have been severed, its pans have been cast aside and one of the cords has been seized by a choleric figure who is also holding the rope with which she is bound. On the northern wall we instead see Justice raised to the level of Peace. She is wearing an archaic tablet-woven robe encrusted with precious stones and her golden hair is plaited elegantly around her head.[14] Her balance is held aloft by a cherubim figure marked SA[PI]ENTIA and one cord from each of its pans passes into the hand of Concord. She in turn entwines the cords to form a *vinculum concordiae*, which she hands to a procession of richly clad citizens who are standing equably next to her.[15]

To the right of Peace sits a huge and mysterious regal figure on his throne. This part of Lorenzetti's composition echoes yet more closely his depiction of tyrannical government on the western wall, where we see the figure of Tyranny enthroned at the heart of a symmetrical ensemble of vices. The northern wall shows an identically symmetrical group, but in this case an ensemble of virtues. On the same level as Peace sit four female figures representing the 'cardinal' virtues FORTITVDO, PRVDENTIA, TENPERANTIA and IVSTITIA. They are joined by a fifth and central figure marked MAGNANIMITAS, whose presence and prominence reflect (as we saw in chapter 3) a specifically Senecan understanding of the political virtues. Above them in the blue empyrean hover the cherubim figures of the 'theological' virtues, FIDES, CARITAS and SPES.

If we now turn – still reading Lorenzetti's narrative from left to right – to examine the eastern wall, we find ourselves confronting a representation of 'the effects of just government' in town and countryside (Plates 5 and 6). This is the explanation of the panorama that we find in the *volgare* verses inscribed on the dado of the northern wall. They inform us, again in Senecan vein, that we are looking at 'all the useful, necessary and delightful civil effects' that flow from the rule of justice and peace.[16] As Jack Greenstein has perceptively observed, there is a dual sense in which we are looking at a vision of peace. The city and countryside are not only peaceful, but the angle of vision from which they are designed to be

---

[14] Gibbs 1999, p. 12 notes that similar weaving is represented in Giotto's portrait of the Virgin Mary in the Cappella degli Scrovegni.
[15] For the history of the idea of the *vinculum concordia* see chapter 3 section II.
[16] 'QUESTA SANTA VIRTU LADOVE REGGE.... SEGUITA POI OGNI CIVILE / EFFETTO. UTILE NECESSARIO E DIDILETTO.' 'Wherever the holy virtue [of justice] rules ... this gives rise to every useful, necessary and delightful civil effect.' Seneca's *De Beneficiis* appears to be the source for this classification of *effetti*. See Seneca 1928–35, vol. 3, I. 11. 1, pp. 34–6, where he distinguishes *beneficia* into 'necessaria ... utilia ... delicatos'.

viewed appears to be that of Peace herself, who is shown gazing at the panorama as she reclines at the centre of the adjacent wall.[17] What she is surveying is the outcome of placing the value of peace at the heart of our common life.

The left-hand side of this panorama features the city of Siena itself, identifiable both by its new cathedral[18] and by its *Porta Romana*, which frames the cityscape to its right (Plate 5).[19] The heart of the composition is formed by a group of nine dancers who move with linked hands in front of a tenth who is singing and playing the tambourine. From the centrality of their position, the solemnity of their demeanour and the arresting fact that they are enlarged in scale beyond any other figures in the scene, they leave us with a strong impression that they must bear some corresponding symbolic significance.

Around them the life of *negotium* flourishes, especially in the quarters to the right of the central *piazza*: a number of 'useful and necessary' trades are being carried on, a new building is nearing completion, a doctor of law is addressing his students.[20] To the left there is more emphasis on the 'delightful' life of *otium*: under an arched entrance a group of men and children talk and play, while at the doorway of a neighbouring house two women watch a coroneted lady and her attendants riding serenely by. A comparison is suggested with the picture on the opposite wall of tyrannical government and its effects on city life (Plate 7). There we see no *otium cum dignitate*: on the contrary, we see a finely dressed lady being roughly seized by soldiers. Nor do we see any *negotium*: the shops are boarded up, and only the armourer is at work.

To the right of the *Porta Romana* we behold the *effetti* of just government on the Sienese *contado* (Plate 6). Somewhat in the manner of a Book of Hours,[21] the work of different seasons is simultaneously displayed: sowing and hoeing the crop, reaping and threshing it, carrying it to the mill, ploughing the land after the harvest. While mules and pack-horses approach the city, a lady in a sumptuous red habit rides forth from its open

---

[17] Greenstein 1988, esp. pp. 496–8. Greenstein adds (p. 498) that the figure of Peace is also the source from which the cityscape is lit. This I doubt, however, as I explain below.

[18] Although this detail was probably added in the course of the mid-*trecento* renovations. For these see chapter 3 section VI.

[19] What we see, however, is the life of the city idealised, not rendered mimetically as is perhaps too readily assumed in Kempers 1989, pp. 71–84 and in Kempers 1992, esp. pp. 135–41. By contrast, see Belting 1985, pp. 159–60 and Greenstein 1988, esp. p. 493.

[20] Feldges-Henning 1972, pp. 153–4 notes that the red gown suggests a teacher of civil law (or possibly medicine).

[21] This was originally pointed out in Pächt 1950, esp. pp. 40–3. See also Pearsall and Salter 1973, esp. pp. 181–2.

gates. She is accompanied by a pair of hounds, and one of the attendants following her has a hawk on his wrist. A further comparison is suggested with the effects of tyrannical government pictured on the opposite wall (Plate 1). There the city gate has a portcullis which has been raised just sufficiently to allow a white-haired man, also dressed in red, to ride out into the barren *contado* with its burning villages. He too is accompanied by two attendants, but has prudently allowed them to go ahead of him. Both carry shields, and one is brandishing a lance while the other wears a long sword. Above them hovers an armed and winged figure whose *titulus* states that she represents TIMOR, and whose *cartouche* warns that 'none shall pass along this road without fear of death'.[22] By contrast, the hunters leaving the peaceful city are unarmed and unafraid, ambling along beneath the level gaze of a corresponding figure whose *titulus* states that she represents SECVRITAS, and whose *cartouche* promises that 'everyone shall go forth freely without fear'.[23]

As in the peaceful city, so in the peaceful *contado* a comparison seems to be intended between the 'delightful' life of *otium* – here represented by the lady out hunting – and the 'useful and necessary' activities of those who labour in the fields. Moreover, this simple typology is presented as exhaustive. Although a single beggar sits by the road, no other signs of old age or destitution are visible.[24] Nor do we see any representation of the life of the literally thousands of monks, nuns, friars and parish clergy who were living in Siena at this time.[25] Lorenzetti's idealised city and its *contado* are sites of not merely a prosperous but a remarkably secular life.

III

I began by observing that Lorenzetti's cycle confronts even the most casual observer with two notorious puzzles. One concerns the identity and significance of the mysterious regal figure who sits enthroned on the northern wall, staring severely back at us from amid his accompanying

---

[22] The third and fourth lines of the *cartouche* held by TIMOR read: 'PER QVESTA VIA. / NON PASSA ALCVN SENÇA DUBBIO DIMORTE.'
[23] The first line of the *cartouche* held by SECVRITAS reads: 'SENÇA PAVRA OGNVOM FRANCO CAMINI.' Tuve 1963, p. 292 correctly notes that *Moralium Dogma Philosophorum* includes a dialogue between Timor and Securitas. See Conches 1929, pp. 32–6. Tuve assumes that Lorenzetti must have had this particular source in mind. But the *topos* can be found in many other *duecento* texts, including Perrault 1618, III. V, 5, vol. 1, p. 210 and Latini 1948, pp. 263–5.
[24] A point well made in Kempers 1992, p. 141.
[25] For the numbers of the religious in the city at this period see Bowsky 1981, p. 20.

ensemble of virtues (Plate 8). As I noted in chapter 3, he has generally been described as *Ben Comun*, a representation either of the Commune itself[26] or of the concept of the Common Good.[27] By far the most influential reading of this aspect of the frescoes, that of Nicolai Rubinstein, maintains that what we see is a depiction of 'the Aristotelian concept of the common good as the basis and criterion of good government', the implication being that 'the common good must be raised to the position of the ruler' if good government is to be upheld.[28]

I remain convinced that the contrasting hypothesis I advanced in chapter 3 is basically on the right track. I maintain that the regal figure ought instead to be seen as a depiction of the type of *signore* or *signoria* that a city needs to elect if the dictates of justice are to be followed and the common good secured. Perhaps the most crucial piece of evidence in favour of this hypothesis is that this appears to be what we are told in the verses inscribed on the simulated tablet beneath this section of the frescoes. My suggested translation of the relevant lines reads as follows:

> Wherever this holy virtue of Justice rules
> She induces many souls to unity
> And those brought together in this way
> Create through[29] their *signor*[30] a common good for themselves.[31]

What confronts us, in short, is not a representation of the Common Good but rather of the type of *signor* (or *signoria*) best suited to bringing it about.

Reconsidering what I say in chapter 3, however, I now feel that I failed to indicate sufficiently clearly that Lorenzetti's image of the *signor*, if not ambiguous, is certainly bi-valent. It now seems to me that two

---

[26] For this reading see Rowley 1958, vol. 1, p. 99; Feldges-Henning 1972, p. 145; Leuchovius 1982, p. 30; Carli 1983, p. 40; Greenstein 1988, p. 492; Frugoni 1991, pp. 66, 68; Alexander 1996, p. 148.

[27] For the classic statement see Rubinstein 1958, esp. pp. 184–5. See also Borsook 1980, p. 35; Bowsky 1981, p. 288; Starn and Partridge 1992, pp. 50, 51, 56. Smart 1978, p. 105 suggests that what we see is a representation of the Common Good *and* the Sienese Commune.

[28] Rubinstein 1958, pp. 184, 185. See also Rubinstein 1997 for a restatement and elaboration of the argument.

[29] Rubinstein's interpretation requires that the word 'per' in the second line be translated as 'for' or 'as'; my interpretation requires that it be translated as 'through' or 'by means of'. Both meanings were current in the *trecento*, as is pointed out in Rubinstein 1997, p. 789. But in Latin the basic meaning of 'per' is 'through' or 'by means of', and this seems to have remained the basic meaning in the relevant *volgare* texts. See, for example, Libri 1974, p. 79; Vignano 1974, p. 270.

[30] As noted in chapter 3 note 3, this is how the word appeared before the restoration of the early 1980s. It now appears as 'sigror', which makes no sense.

[31] 'QUESTA SANTA VIRTU [La Giustizia] LADOVE REGGE. INDUCE ADUNITA LIANIMI / MOLTI. EQUESTI ACCIO RICCOLTI. UN BEN COMUN PERLOR SIGROR SIFANNO.'

distinct representations are embodied within it. I also failed to make clear that one of these representations is of the city itself. Many features of the enthroned figure indicate that he 'is' Siena. Around his shoulders are displayed the letters C·S·C·V[32] – *Commune Senarum, Civitas Virginis*.[33] He is dressed in black and white, then as now the heraldic colours of the Sienese commune. At his feet a she-wolf suckles a pair of twins, at once a visual contrast with the goat at the feet of Tyranny and a symbolic reminder of the ancient Roman republic whose insignia the Sienese had adopted in 1297.[34] On his shield can still be faintly discerned an image of the Virgin Mary, chosen by the Sienese as their special patron on the eve of their victory over the Florentines at Montaperti in 1260.[35] Perhaps most significantly of all, the regal figure is portrayed as grey-bearded, white-haired, and thus as *persona sena* – as an old person, but at the same time as Sena, the Latin name for Siena.[36]

While he represents the city, however, the regal figure is also the representation of a ruler, and more specifically a supreme judge. As I emphasise in chapter 3, a number of details make this reading inescapable. He is sitting enthroned on a seat of judgement. He is wearing a richly brocaded and jewel-encrusted robe of an almost imperial kind. He is holding a sceptre, the symbol of supreme authority, together with a shield to defend his people. Furthermore, his legal authority is shown to extend 'over' everybody, including even the fractious and independent nobility. At his feet a pair of nobles, identifiable by their armour and flowing hair, offer up their castles in an evident act of homage. The verses on the simulated tablet below confirm that 'everyone grants him taxes, tributes and lordships of lands'.[37]

What is less obvious, and what I originally failed to note, is the daring with which Lorenzetti has presented us not merely with an image of a supreme judge, but at the same time with a secularised image of the Last Judgement.[38] To see that this is so, we need only recall the apocalyptic vision of the Last Judgement painted by Giotto above the entrance to the Cappella degli Scrovegni in Padua in 1305 (Plate 9).[39]

---

[32] The inscription now reads C·S·C·C·V. As explained in chapter 3 section IV, however, the second 'C' appears to be a later interpolation.
[33] For Siena as the city of the Virgin see Bowsky 1981, pp. 160, 288.
[34] Larner 1971, p. 113.   [35] Bowsky 1981, pp. 274–5.   [36] Southard 1978, p. 60.
[37] 'ALLUI SIDANNO. CENSI TRIBUTI ESIGNORIE / DITERRE.'
[38] A point excellently made in Leuchovius 1982, pp. 32–3.
[39] Harrison 1995, p. 87 argues for 1308 as the earliest date by which the cycle could have been completed. But Padre Bellinati has pointed out that the consecration crosses in the Cappella are painted over the frescoes, the implication being that the frescoes must have been completed before the documented consecration date of 25 March 1305.

Not only is this the most celebrated portrayal of the scene from the period immediately preceding the completion of Lorenzetti's frescoes, but it appears that Lorenzetti must have known of it. As we shall see, he seems to have made a close study of Giotto's *grisaille* portrait of IUSTICIA (Plate 11) from the same cycle, since he incorporated several features into his own design. While examining this section of Giotto's frescoes, he could scarcely have failed to register the presence of the vast painting of the Last Judgement on the adjoining wall. Even if he merely glanced at it, he would have seen that the heart of the composition is formed by an enthroned central figure flanked by angels, elders and saints. He would also have seen that those who have won salvation are standing serenely in a line below the enthroned figure and to his right, while to his left the bound and naked figures of the damned are dragged down into a pit to be bestially tormented.

Whether or not Giotto was his source, Lorenzetti provides us with a secularised version of all these motifs. Below the enthroned figure and to his right we see the richly clad citizens standing amicably in pairs. There are twenty-four of them, a number that appears to carry a dual significance.[40] Twenty-four Elders, according to the Book of Revelation, sit with the Lord in the Court of Heaven.[41] But twenty-four was also (according to one way of counting) the total number of the Sienese *concistoro* or *signoria* at this time.[42] Lorenzetti's magistrates are loosely holding the *vinculum concordiae*, thereby emphasising that (as Albertano of Brescia had put it) 'concord is the virtue that, in a spontaneous way, binds together citizens and compatriots who live together in one place'.[43] The citizens are all of the same height, any differences of standing between them having evidently been smoothed away by Concord in obedience to the Ciceronian injunction that 'citizens should live together on equal

---

[40] Possibly even a triple significance if one recalls the 'ventiquattro seniori, a due a due' whom Dante encounters in the *Purgatorio*. See Dante 1967a, XXIX, line 83, p. 505, and cf. Rubinstein 1997, p. 783 and note.

[41] See Revelation 4.4 and cf. the valuable discussion in Leuchovius 1982, pp. 31, 34.

[42] Kempers 1992, p. 137 sees the *Nove* themselves, together with the *podestà*, the *maggior sindaco*, the *capitano del popolo*, three consuls of the merchant guild, four *provvisori* of the *Biccherna*, three collectors of the *Gabella* tax and two *camerarii*, a total of twenty-four. While Bowsky 1981, p. 23 stresses that the *Concistoro* (i.e., the full Sienese *signoria*) comprised only twenty officials, Rubinstein 1997 adds the four *Esecutori delle Gabelle*, thereby bringing the total back to twenty-four. Bowsky 1981, p. 289 also notes the fact that Siena was ruled between 1236 and 1271 by twenty-four *Priori*. As he adds, however, it is unclear why the Guelf *Nove* should have wished the Ghibelline regime of the *Viginti Quattuor* to be recalled. The twenty-four citizens remain something of a mystery.

[43] Brescia 1507, fo. 57ʳ: 'Concordia est virtus cives et compatriotas cohabitatione spontanea vinciens.'

and level terms'.[44] The leaders of the procession look up in supplication to the figure of the judge in just the manner of those who, at the Last Judgement, have duly been saved. Meanwhile, below this figure and to his left or 'sinister' side we see a contrasting group of reprobates.[45] They are divided from the elect (and elected) citizens by a large *cassone*, and are roped together with a *vinculum* that binds them coercively rather than being voluntarily held. One of them has his eyes covered with a black cloth, a sign that he has been convicted of a capital crime. Just as in the Last Judgement, the supreme judge on high has separated the sheep from the goats.

What Lorenzetti has done is thus to fuse an image of Siena with an image of a supreme ruler or judge. More exactly, what he offers us is an image of Siena *as* a supreme ruler or judge. While this is not incompatible with what I say in chapter 3, I failed to register the precision with which Lorenzetti illustrates the pivotal contention of the numerous treatises on city government circulating in early *trecento* Tuscany. As Brunetto Latini summarises in *Li Livres dou trésor*, the contention is that 'the good of the people' requires that '*signorie* should be held by the commune itself'.[46] 'The best form of *seignourie*', Latini goes on, is attained 'when communities in cities elect as their *poesté* and *signour* those who are most profitable to the common good of the city and all their subjects'.[47] This I take to be the final message of the huge enthroned figure. Lorenzetti is likewise telling us that, if Siena is to enjoy the blessings of concord and peace, the Sienese must ensure that their *signoria* genuinely represents them. The supreme ruler or judge of Siena must be the Sienese themselves.

It is worth underlining the distinctive way in which this commitment prompts Lorenzetti to handle the familiar comparison between good and evil government. While tyranny was universally condemned as the worst type of regime, the best type was widely held to be some form of regulated monarchy. But this is not in the least the contrast figured by Lorenzetti on the northern and western walls. As in Latini's typology

[44] Cicero 1913, I. XXXIV. 124, p. 126: 'oportet aequo et pari cum civibus iure vivere'.
[45] If I am right that Lorenzetti is echoing the conventional design of representations of the Last Judgement, this would be a reason for doubting the conjectural reconstruction proposed in Gibbs 1999, p. 13 and figure 4, in which the procession of worthy citizens appears again at the right of the picture.
[46] See Latini 1948, p. 211 on 'le bien dou peuple', the need to maintain 'La signorie de la commune' and the claim that this constitutes the best form of government.
[47] Latini 1948, p. 392: 'que . . . li communité des viles eslisent lor poesté et lor signour tel comme il quident qu'il soit plus proufitables au commun preu de la vile et de tous lor subtés'. For the claim that this form of government is 'la millour', see Latini 1948, p. 211.

of *signories*, so in Lorenzetti's: the comparison is emphatically between tyranny as the worst regime and republican self-government as the best. The rule of kings is not even presented as a candidate for bringing about the necessary and delightful *effetti* on which Peace benignly bends her gaze.

Once the enthroned figure is identified, we can also see that Lorenzetti has positioned him in such a way as to contrive a further and yet more daring symbolic effect. His head and shoulders extend into the empyrean above and beyond the virtues, with his head attaining almost the same level as the cherubim figures of Faith and Hope. The *persona* representing the *civitas* is thus portrayed in such a way as to associate the authority of the city with heavenly powers. We are left with the final impression that the city has been invested with its own religious significance, and thus that our duty may be to contemplate its authority with something approaching religious awe.

IV

I now turn to the other major iconographical question posed by Lorenzetti's masterpiece. This concerns the identity and significance of the dancers at the heart of his cityscape (Plate 10). They are displayed in three sub-groups around the central and static figure who is singing and holding the tambourine. There are two to the immediate right of the central figure, both of them with their backs to us; three more on the right, each of whom is seen in profile; and a group of four further figures on the left. So we see a total of ten figures in the sequence 'one, two, three, four' – a sequence whose significance was much discussed by medieval commentators on Platonist and Pythagorean numerologies.[48]

Although these dancers have almost always been described as women,[49] or more specifically as maidens,[50] there are several reasons for concluding that Lorenzetti must have intended to represent a group of young men.[51] As we shall see, the contemporary texts in which we find the main clues to explaining this section of the frescoes all assume that

[48] 'Unus, duo, tres. Quartum...' are the opening words of the Latin version of Plato's *Timaeus*. For the original see Plato 1929, p. 16. For the Latin version, and for an accompanying commentary well known in Lorenzetti's time, see Conches 1965, pp. 71–2.
[49] Rowley 1958, vol. 1, p. 108; DeWald 1961, p. 159; Feldges-Henning 1972, p. 147; Eorsi 1978, pp. 85–9; Bowsky 1981, p. 290; Carli 1983, p. 43; Starn and Partridge 1992, p. 51; Frugoni 1991, p. 67.
[50] White 1967, p. 93; Smart 1978, p. 105; Greenstein 1988, p. 496; Tarr 1990, p. 388.
[51] See Bridgeman 1991. Rightly in my view, Bridgeman's argument is now coming to be accepted. See Waley 1991, pp. 141–2; Donato 1995, pp. 23–41 and p. 148; Norman 1995, vol. 2, p. 161.

those taking part in such public dances will be male. But in the meantime it is worth adding that, as Bridgeman has pointed out,[52] Lorenzetti's tall and flat-chested figures are pictured in such a way that no *trecento* observer could readily have taken them to be other than men. It would have been very unusual for a woman to wear her hair short and uncovered in the manner affected by all the members of the dancing group. Lorenzetti in effect makes this point himself in his depiction of the unambiguously female figures who appear elsewhere in his cycle.[53] All of them have long golden hair worn in one of two styles. Either it hangs plaited down their backs, as in the case of Concord (Plate 4) and the lady riding with her attendants in the street (Plate 5), or else it is plaited and coiled around the head, as in the case of Peace and Justice (Plates 3 and 4)[54] and also in the case of the lady setting forth to hunt (Plate 6). It would also have been unusual for a woman to dress in such a way as to reveal – as in the case of all the dancers – the ankles and lower part of the leg. Once more Lorenzetti in effect makes the point himself. If we look again at the lady setting forth to hunt, or at the lady riding in the street, or at the two women watching her, we find that all of them are wearing dresses that wholly cover the ankles and feet. By contrast, the male citizens holding the *vinculum concordiae* are all shown – like the dancers – with costumes that leave the feet, the ankles and, in one instance, the lower part of the leg revealed. And while the length of the citizens' hair is more difficult to determine, since they all have their heads covered, it is clear in several cases that they are wearing it short.

This is not to imply that it would have been out of the question for women to dance in the streets of *trecento* Siena. There are several recorded instances of just such dances taking place.[55] Nor is it even to imply that the representation of women dancing was unknown in Tuscan wall-paintings of the same period. Beneath the portrait entitled IUSTICIA in the Cappella degli Scrovegni we come upon a small *grisaille* composition – barely more than ten centimetres high – at the centre of which Giotto

---

[52] The rest of this paragraph draws on the persuasive argument put forward in Bridgeman 1991.
[53] It might be thought question-begging to insist that any of Lorenzetti's figures are *unambiguously* female. But it is crucial that, in Latin, the nouns describing the virtues, the vices and other such abstractions are always feminine in gender, as a result of which it was almost universally accepted (at least in the period with which I am dealing) that representations of such concepts had to be female. Hence it seems justifiable at least to speak of Lorenzetti's figures of Pax, Concordia, Iustitia, etc., as unambiguously female.
[54] Here, as throughout, I am referring to the large-scale figure of Justice as a legal principle (on the left of the painting), not to the smaller figure of Justice as a personal quality (on the extreme right).
[55] Walcy 1991, pp. 141–2 challenges the claim in Bridgeman 1991, p. 250 to the effect that the spectacle of young women dancing in the streets would have been 'shocking'.

has depicted three figures taking part in a dance (Plate 11). The one on the right stares into a large mirror held in both hands, while the one in the centre plays a tambourine[56] for the one on the left, who is dancing energetically with left arm and right leg upraised. This last figure is evidently male: his movements are unashamedly athletic, his hair is short and uncovered and his tunic reaches only to his lower leg. But the other two are no less clearly female: their pose is modest and statuesque, their plaited hair hangs down their backs and their voluminous dresses trail on the ground.

A further example can be seen in the fresco cycle painted in the late 1360s by Andrea di Bonaiuto in the Chapterhouse (the Cappellone degli Spagnoli) of Santa Maria Novella in Florence.[57] There are two connected groups of dancers in the section of the so-called Allegoria della Chiesa devoted to illustrating worldly pleasures (Plate 12).[58] One contains four figures, the other three; both are dancing with linked hands, while an eighth figure on the right is singing and playing the tambourine. All these figures are clearly female. They all have long golden hair; two of them are wearing it plaited and coiled around the head, while the rest are wearing it down the back, in three cases plaited, in two cases hanging loose and even dishevelled. And in spite of the fact that they are pictured as moving, their dresses in every case cover the ankles and in three cases the feet as well.[59]

If we now reflect on these *trecento* conventions governing the representation of women dancing, it becomes hard to escape the conclusion that Lorenzetti must have intended to represent dancing men. Had he wished to portray women, he would have been far more likely to show them with long hair and with dresses sweeping the ground in the manner of the female dancers painted by Giotto and Andrea di Bonaiuto. As it is, he shows them with short hair and with tunics revealing their ankles and feet in the manner of the unambiguously male figures in his

---

[56] Although the circle of the tambourine has been gouged out and the hand holding it has been effaced.

[57] Gardner 1979, p. 108 argues that this part of the cycle, sometimes known as The Church Triumphant, was painted between 1365 and 1368.

[58] Borsook 1980, p. 50 treats the four seated figures above the dancers, as well as the dancers themselves, as allegorical representations of Worldly Pleasure.

[59] It must be conceded, however, that the left-hand dancer in the group of three, like several of Lorenzetti's dancers, has her skirt split to the thigh. Bridgeman 1991, p. 246 implies that no respectable woman would dress in such a way, but this may be an overstatement. On the other hand, it may be important that Andrea's figures are taking part in a scene of worldly pleasure and vice: although they are female, they are not respectable, as their loose and almost dishevelled hair is probably intended to suggest. See Alexander 1996 for further reflections on what he describes (p. 150) as 'the dominant negative discourse on dancing' at this period.

procession of citizens (Plate 3). So there seems to have been a case of mistaken identity: the dancers are almost certainly male.[60]

Lorenzetti's solemnly gyrating youths present us with at least two iconographical puzzles that cry out to be solved. One is the remarkable fact that the space in which they are dancing constitutes the painted light-source of the cityscape as a whole. The observation that the city itself is the source of the light suffusing it was originally made in a classic study by John White.[61] More recently, however, a number of scholars have proposed a different interpretation of the way in which the pictorial light in this section of the frescoes is handled. We are to think of the city, it is suggested, as metaphorically illuminated by the enlightening gaze of one or other of the symbolic figures on the northern wall. Chiara Frugoni has proposed the figure of divine Wisdom as the source of the light.[62] Jack Greenstein has instead suggested that 'the Peaceful City is lit by the light of Peace's sight'.[63] Yet more ingeniously, Roger Tarr has argued that the 'supramundane' light is reflected on to the city from the figure of the Virgin on the shield held by the *Signore*, with the golden colour and circular shape of the shield being intended to suggest a 'surrogate sun'.[64]

There are several reasons for preferring White's original analysis. The decisive one is that, as we shall see, the literary evidence relating to the metaphorical significance of light in this period tells overwhelmingly in favour of White's reading of Lorenzetti's scene. But so does the balance of the pictorial evidence.[65] All the revisionist interpretations share the assumption that we are to think of the city as fictively lit from somewhere on the northern wall, and hence from an angle to the left of the cityscape. But this is not how the light within the city is actually shown. If we are to think of the light as falling from anywhere on the northern wall, the left-hand side of the building to the left of the central piazza would have to be brightly lit. But in fact it is in relative darkness, while the entrance facing the piazza is far brighter. The light is shown, in other words, as falling upon the building from its right, and thus from the direction of the piazza. The possibility that the piazza itself may be the source of the light is duly confirmed if we turn to the cobbler's shop at its right-hand edge. The front of the shop is in shadow while its side

---

[60] Here I invoke the title of Bridgeman 1991. [61] White 1967, p. 96.
[62] Frugoni 1983, p. 161. [63] Greenstein 1988, p. 498.
[64] Tarr 1990, esp. pp. 388–90, 392.
[65] Norman 1995, vol. 2, p. 161 and note 47 gives an excellent account of the pictorial evidence and its support for White's account.

is again more brightly lit. So the light in this instance is shown falling from the left, and thus from the direction of the piazza once more. The same pattern is repeated with only minor contradictions[66] across the whole cityscape: the sides of the towers and buildings to the right of the dancers in the piazza are more brightly lit than their façades, but so are the sides of the towers and buildings to their left. As White originally concluded, the only way to render this pattern coherent is to conceive of the glowing centre of the city itself as the source of the light.[67]

I turn to the other and even more obvious question raised by the dancing group. What should we make of the fact that the garments worn by the two central dancers at the front are so strangely ornamented? The costume of the figure on the right is in tatters, and is decorated – there is no escaping this fact – with worms. The similarly flowing costume of the figure on the left is decorated with four-winged insects – not flies, but some species of dragonfly or moth. Presumably the insects are in fact moths, for the garment is shown as moth-eaten, with many holes in it through which the wearer's black underclothing can be seen.

To understand these effects, as well as the symbolic meaning of the dance itself, we need to grasp the significance that Lorenzetti's contemporaries would have attached to the presence in his painting of moths and worms. These were jointly the symbols of *tristitia*, the vice of despondency or moroseness. This symbolism can ultimately be traced to a passage from the old Vulgate version of the Book of Proverbs (suppressed as an interpolation after the Clementine Edition of 1592).[68] There we are told that 'just as a moth destroys a garment, and woodworm destroys wood, so *tristitia* destroys the heart of man'.[69] The passage was influentially singled out by Cassian in his *De Institutis Coenobiorum*,[70] and was thereafter cited and glossed by many writers on the virtues and vices, including a number who were closely studied by the preachers and moralists of Lorenzetti's time. Albertano of Brescia quotes the verse in his chapter on *Tristitia* in his *De Amore et Dilectione* of 1238,[71] and the image gained further currency when Andrea da Grosseto translated Albertano's treatise

---

[66] White 1967, p. 96 conceded the 'minor contradictions', but noted that they are 'the fault of clumsy restoration'.
[67] White 1967, p. 96. [68] I owe this fact to Jill Kraye.
[69] Proverbs 25.20 (Old Vulgate version): 'sicut tinea vestimento, et vermis ligno, ita tristitia viri nocet cordi'.
[70] Cassian 1965, IX. 2, p. 370.
[71] Brescia 1507, fo. 59^r: 'nam ut Salomon ait sicut tinea vestimenta & vermis ligna corrodit. Ita tristicia nocet hominis cordi.'

into the *volgare* in 1268.[72] By that time the *Summae Virtutum ac Vitiorum* of Guillaume Perrault had also begun to circulate widely, and Perrault directs us to the same verse when discussing the closely associated vice of *acedia*:[73]

> He who suffers from *acedia* lives a tedious life, from whence arises a certain *tristitia*, which is just as if a worm is gnawing at his heart. Hence Proverbs 25 says that, just as a moth destroys a garment, and woodworm destroys wood, so *tristitia* destroys the heart.[74]

Perrault's assumption that *tristitia* is a consequence of *acedia* was contentious, since a number of his contemporaries (including St Thomas Aquinas) maintained that the two terms may be different names for the same vice.[75] But the association of *tristitia* with moths and worms was accepted by everyone, as was the view that, in the words of Guido Faba's *Summa de Viciis et Virtutibus*, the sin of *tristitia* is possibly the gravest evil that can afflict the human soul.[76]

It may seem incongruous to find these symbols of sloth and despondency at the centre of Lorenzetti's bright and bustling picture of civic life. But we can begin to resolve the paradox if we recall the influential tradition stemming from Prudentius's *Psychomachia*, with its insistence on pairing off the vices with competing virtues.[77] Among Lorenzetti's contemporaries, the specific quality generally singled out to do battle with *tristitia* was *gaudium* or joyfulness. The source of the contrast was again Biblical,[78] and it was taken up by all the leading moralists of *duecento* Italy.[79] Albertano of Brescia assures us that 'a heart which is *gaudens* or joyful makes for a flourishing life, while a spirit which is *tristis* or despondent dries up the bones'.[80] Guido Faba likewise warns us that

---

[72] For the discussion of *tristizia* see Grosseto 1873, IV. XXX, pp. 359–62.

[73] For the complex relations between *acedia* and *tristitia*, stemming from Cassian's preference for the first term and Gregory the Great's for the second, see Wenzell 1967, esp. pp. 23–8, 51–5, 171–4. See also, more generally, Bloomfield 1952.

[74] Perrault 1618, II. V. III, vol. 1, p. 130: 'Acediosus est in taedio vitae. Unde habet quandam tristitiam, quae ad modum vermis corrodit cor eius. Unde Prover. 25. Sicut tinea vestimento, & vermis ligno: sic tristitia nocet cordi.'

[75] Aquinas 1962, II^a. II^{ae}, Qu. 158. art. 6, 1, p. 692: 'tristitia est vitium capitale, quod dicitur acedia'.

[76] Faba 1956, p. 114: 'nullum malum gravius tristitia'.

[77] Prudentius's *Psychomachia* ends with the triumph of Faith and Concord over *Discordia*. See Prudentius 1949–53, lines 664–723, vol. 1, pp. 324–8.

[78] See, for example, John 16.20; 2 Corinthians 6.10; Philippians 2.28.

[79] We also find it reiterated by neo-Aristotelian writers of the early *trecento*. For example, Rome 1607, I. III. VIII, p. 179 warns that 'tristitia ... fuganda est' and proposes three remedies, each of which involves finding virtuous means *gaudere et delectare*.

[80] Brescia 1507, fo. 59^r: 'Animus gaudens floridam vitam facit: spiritus vero tristis exsicat ossa.'

'*tristitia* leads a man to his death', and that 'you ought therefore to make sure that you express *gaudium*, so that your days are not consumed by *tristitia*'.[81]

We can go further in explaining the presence of the moths and worms if we reflect that *gaudium* was not only held to be the means of keeping *tristitia* at bay, but was also regarded as the natural response to blessings and benefits, and above all to the benefit of *pax* or civil peace. One source of this argument was again Biblical: St Paul associates *pax* and *gaudium* in several of his Epistles,[82] while Cassian quotes these passages in listing *gaudium* and *pax* among the fruits of the Holy Spirit that enable *tristitia* to be overcome.[83] But the same connection had already been made by a number of Roman moralists on whom the *duecento* writers on city government rely most heavily. Seneca in particular had influentially defined a benefit in his *De Beneficiis* as 'a well-intentioned act that brings *gaudium* to its recipient',[84] and had added in his *Epistulae* that the two situations in which we most naturally experience *gaudium* are when contemplating the love of our children or the peaceful well-being of our native land.[85]

The suggestion that *gaudium* is the proper response to *pax* is strongly emphasised in the official correspondence that passed between Emperor Frederick Barbarossa and the Italian cities at the close of the twelfth century. In a letter to the citizens of Forlì the emperor assures them that they will be fully justified if they 'express *gaudium* in perpetuity at their state of security and *pax*'.[86] In a letter to the Archbishop of Ravenna he similarly declares that everyone ought now 'to give full expression to their *gaudium* and enjoy their liberty and *pax*'.[87] The same sentiments recur in many of the advice-books composed for city magistrates in *duecento* Italy. The *Oculus Pastoralis* suggests that the *podestà* or chief magistrate of a commune should plead with factious citizens by telling them that 'my soul will feel immense *gaudium*' if only they will agree 'to maintain *pax*

---

[81] Faba 1956, pp. 115–16: 'La tristitia conduce l'uomo a morte . . . gaudeas igitur ne tui dies in tristitia consumantur'.

[82] Romans 14.17 and 15.13; Galatians 5.22.

[83] See Cassian 1965, IX. 11, p. 378: 'Fructus autem Spiritus est caritas, gaudium, pax . . .' Cf. 2 Corinthians 7.10 and especially Galatians 5.22.

[84] Seneca 1928–35, vol. 3, I. 6. 1, p. 22: 'Quid est ergo beneficium? Benevola actio tribuens gaudium.' Cf. also Seneca 1928–35, vol. 3, II. XXXV. 4, p. 122, where Seneca explains that the proper way to receive a benefit is 'to accept it, embrace it and express *gaudium*' ('excipe beneficium, amplexare, gaudere').

[85] Seneca 1917–25, vol. 2, LXVI. 37, p. 24: 'Prima [bona] secundum naturae sunt: gaudere liberorum pietate, patriae incolumitate.'

[86] Barbarossa 1979–85, Letter 677, vol. 2, p. 194: 'pace et securitate perpetualiter gaudeant'.

[87] Barbarossa 1979–85, Letter 718, vol. 2, p. 253: 'plena gaudeant atque fruantur libertate et pace'.

among themselves'.[88] Matteo de' Libri likewise remarks in his *Arringhe* that, whenever justice is peacefully imposed, 'everyone feels *gaudium* at possessing that which is theirs by right'.[89]

As a number of these writers add, the reason why we ought to feel *gaudium* at the rule of justice is not merely because it brings *pax*; we ought also to rejoice because peace in turn brings the yet nobler blessings of *gloria e grandezza*, civic glory and greatness. As we saw in chapter 2, the authority always cited on this crucial theme of civic *grandezza* was Sallust. Speaking about the early Roman republic at the start of his *Bellum Catilinae*, Sallust had argued that 'it was through labour and the rule of justice that the republic originally grew to greatness'.[90] Speaking in more general vein in his *Bellum Iugurthinum*, he had added in an endlessly quoted passage that 'it is from living in concord that small cities rise to greatness, while it is from civil discord that even the greatest cities decline and fall'.[91]

Alluding to this vision of the fruits of peace, the *Oculus Pastoralis* suggests that an incoming *podestà* should assure the assembled citizenry that, 'if there is tranquil peace and perfect love among you', this will lead 'to the growth, the glory and the honour of this most noble city'.[92] The *podestà* is advised to bring his speech to an end by calling on the populace to reflect on their prosperity and express their *gaudium* and thanks for it.[93] Giovanni da Viterbo in his *De Regimine Civitatum* likewise counsels a new *podestà* to link the preservation of *pax* with feelings of *gaudium*, and to emphasise that a city living in peace can expect to attain exaltation and greatness.[94] Brunetto Latini in the concluding chapter of his *Li Livres dou trésor* repeats that 'a city governed according to right and truth' will not only 'live for ever in a condition of good peace' but will experience the further blessing of 'growing and multiplying both in population and in wealth'.[95]

---

[88] *Oculus* 1966, pp. 26–7: 'Si... memoria vestra retinuisset in mente, quod Christus in cantico voluit [Luke 2.14] cunctos videlicet homines inter se pacem habere... meus gauderet animus in immensum.'

[89] Libri 1974, p. 125: 'çascuno possa gaudere de quel k'èso drito'.

[90] Sallust 1931a, X. 1, p. 16: 'labore atque iustitia res publica crevit'.

[91] Sallust 1931b, X. 6, p. 148: 'Nam concordia parvae res crescunt, discordia maxumae dilabuntur.'

[92] *Oculus* 1966, p. 25: 'ad incrementum et gloriam ac honorem huius nobilissimae civitatis... [si] inter vos pacem tranquilam et amorem perfectum [est]'. See also *Oculus* 1966, p. 61 for an allusion to Sallust's *Bellum Iugurthinum*.

[93] *Oculus* 1966, p. 26.

[94] Viterbo 1901, vol. 3, p. 231, col 1: the *podestà* should proclaim 'huius civitatis pax et concordia exaltatio et bonus status, et vestris amicis gaudium et maximum incrementum'.

[95] Latini 1948, p. 403: 'la cités ki est governce selonc droit et selonc verité... croist et mouteplie des gens et d'avoir et dure tousjours en bone pais'. Cf. Latini 1948, p. 292, where Sallust's *Bellum Iugurthinum* is quoted on the value of peace.

The idea of the glory and greatness of cities is always conveyed by images of light. Here too the metaphor is rooted in classical antiquity: Cicero in particular had spoken of the city of Rome as 'a light to the whole world'.[96] Once more, however, the dominant source is Biblical: the Lord is hailed not merely as the king of glory but as the light of the world,[97] while St Matthew asserts that the righteous shine forth like the sun.[98] Drawing on the words of the Apostle, the *Oculus Pastoralis* declares that the glory of magnificent cities is such that 'they shine like the sun in the presence of all'.[99] To have a well-governed city, Orfino da Lodi agrees, is to have 'safety and quiet, law, peace and happy glory', and this in turn amounts to having 'a light without a candle', a means to enlighten the world with 'propriety and good customs, peace, light and law'.[100] Writing in praise of the city of Milan, Bonvesin de la Riva similarly boasts that 'the amplitude of the glory of Milan has shone forth across the whole of the globe'.[101] Brunetto Latini repeats the *topos* with no less emphasis. When good works are done 'in the government of a commune and in all its affairs', they may be said 'to shine forth throughout the world like the brightness of the sun'.[102]

According to several of these writers, there is a natural way of expressing the *gaudium* we feel at the rule of *iustitia* and the resulting attainment of *pax* and *gloria*. This consists of taking part in a *tripudium*, a solemnly festive dance in which (as the name implies) the dancers move in stately triple time. A number of Roman moralists had argued that the act of dancing the *tripudium* offers a good means of banishing *tristitia*. Seneca in particular tells us in *De Tranquillitate Animi* that even the warlike Scipio enjoyed dancing 'in the style of the *tripudium*, the manly style in which the heroes of olden times used to dance at the time of games and festive celebrations'.[103] This enabled him not merely to follow the rule that 'the mind should be given the means to relax', but also to hold at bay

---

[96] Cicero 1976, IV. 11, p. 148: '[video] hanc urbem, lucem orbis terrarum'.
[97] Psalms 24.7–8; John 1.9; John 8.12.   [98] Matthew 13.43.
[99] *Oculus* 1966, p. 25; 'refulgent sicut sol in conspectu cunctorum'.
[100] Lodi 1869, p. 44: 'salus atque quies, lex, pax et gloria felix. / Lux sine candelis...decor et mores, pax, lux, lex'.
[101] Riva 1974, p. 190: 'Mediolani glorie latitudo dilatate per orbem terrarum.' Cf. also Riva 1974, pp. 50, 122, 196.
[102] Latini 1948, p. 403: '[les] bonnes oeuvres... [du] governement dou commun et de toutes ces choses... resplendissent parmi le monde comme la clarté dou soleil'.
[103] Seneca 1928–35, vol. 2, XVII. 4, p. 280: 'ut antiqui illi viri solebant inter lusum ac festa tempora virilem in modum tripudiare'.

'the feelings of weariness and despondency in the soul' that are otherwise liable to overwhelm us.[104]

In later antiquity we find it said that dancing the *tripudium* not only puts *tristitia* to flight but also constitutes a natural means of expressing the *gaudium* or *laetitia* that enables *tristitia* to be overcome. This is what the panegyrist Mamertinus affirms in his 'Act of Thanks' to the Emperor Julian in the year 362. According to Mamertinus's account, when the Emperor saluted his consul and received him graciously, this was taken to be a special sign of his excellence. The consequence was that 'the whole multitude danced the *tripudium*, leaping unceasingly as unconfined *gaudia* overwhelmed them'.[105] Cassian goes even further, associating the *tripudium* not merely with *laetitia* but with images of glory and light. He tells the cautionary tale of a monk who imprudently hastened to have himself circumcised when shown a vision 'of the Jewish people with Moses, the patriarchs and the prophets dancing the *tripudium* with the greatest *laetitia* and shining with the most resplendent light'.[106]

These assumptions were taken up and developed by several of the writers of advice-books in *duecento* Italy. Giovanni da Viterbo proposes in his *De Regimine Civitatum* that, when a city wishes to exhibit loyalty to a superior power, its spokesmen should declare that the signs of goodwill exhibited by their superiors 'have not only given rise to feelings of *gaudium*, but have led to the dancing of the *tripudium*'.[107] Giovanni da Vignano similarly suggests that, when news reaches a city of a military victory – and hence a return to peace – the townsfolk should send an embassy to their allies with the following announcement:

The men of our commune share the joy you feel, and in demonstration of the great joyfulness of heart felt by the men of this city when news of your victory arrived, they all feasted, they all danced, they all sang, and they all caused the trumpets, the cymbals and the tambourines to resound throughout the whole city.[108]

---

[104] Seneca 1928–35, vol. 2, XVII. 5, p. 280: 'Danda est animis remissio... animorum hebetatio quaedam et languor'.

[105] Mamertinus 1964, p. 142: 'Tripudiabat crebris saltibus multitudo... gaudia effrena superaverant.' Cf. also Mamertinus 1964, p. 264: 'cuncta gaudio calere, cuncta plausibus tripudiare'.

[106] Cassian 1886, II. VIII, p. 47: 'ostendit... Iudaeorum plebem cum Moysi, patriarchis, prophetis summa tripudiantem laetitia et splendidissimo lumine coruscantem'.

[107] Viterbo 1901, p. 223, col 2: the outcome will be that 'gaudium et tripudium generarunt'.

[108] Vignano 1974, p. 271: 'le vostre alegreçe sonon participate a li homigni del nostro comune... e che in demostramento de grande alegreça de coro, quando la novela vene de vostra victoria a li homigni de quela tera, tuti... chi bargordando, chi balando, chi cantando, e tuti... façando sonare trombe, çalamele et tamburi per tuta la tera'.

There is a record of just such a celebration taking place at Padua on the occasion when the *podestà* delivered up thanks on behalf of the city 'because of the restoration of peace among the citizens in the year 1310'.[109] The *podestà*'s message begins by proclaiming that 'your letters of peace brought immense *gaudia* to our hearts and led to the festive dancing of the *tripudium* with high exultation among the whole populace of Padua'.[110]

For the most memorable invocation of a dance to suggest such feelings of *gaudium*, we need to return to Giotto's frescoes in the Cappella degli Scrovegni in Padua. Around the dado of the Cappella, in *psychomachia* style, Giotto depicts seven vices to the left (or 'sinister') side of the entrance, with seven opposing virtues facing them. The two central portraits are entitled IUSTICIA and INIUSTITIA.[111] The former holds a balance in front of her, each hand supporting a diminutive figure on each of the pans (Plate 11). Lorenzetti's portrait of Justice on the northern wall (Plate 4) closely follows the same scheme: he too shows two angelic figures – marked [DIST]RIBVTIVA and COMVTATIVA – hovering above the pans of a balance held by the figure of divine Wisdom and steadied by the hands of Justice. The other and still more striking way in which Lorenzetti echoes Giotto is by adopting several details from the small *grisaille* composition painted by Giotto on the base of Justice's throne (Plate 11). As well as the three dancing figures I have discussed, Giotto shows two pairs of riders advancing towards the centre of the picture from right and left. The riders on the left are accompanied by a pair of hounds, and the figure at the rear is carrying a hawk. (Lorenzetti virtually copies these details in his depiction of the hunters riding forth from the city gates.) The leading rider advancing from the right ambles along with no less confidence, holding an olive branch in his right hand. The moral implicit in the tranquil scene is duly spelled out in the Latin poem inscribed beneath it:

> Perfect justice
> Weighs all things with an equal balance:
> Crowning good men
> She wields a sword against the vices
> And all express *gaudium*.

---

[109] *Gratulatio* 1741, pp. 131–2, the speech of thanks given by the *podestà* of Padua 'ob restauratam inter cives concordiam, Anno 1310'.
[110] *Gratulatio* 1741, p. 131: 'Immensa cordibus nostris gaudia, et universo populo Paduano magnarum exsultationum festiva tripudia Literae vestrae placibiles attulerunt.'
[111] For further discussion of Giotto's allegories of justice see Frojmovič 1996.

> If she freely reigns
> Everyone accomplishes joyfully
> Whatever they desire.[112]

Once again, the image of a dance is used to convey the joy we naturally feel at the rule of justice and the resulting attainment of peace.

As I have already intimated, there is a further point to be made about these accounts of dancing the *tripudium* as an expression of *gaudium* and thankfulness. While two of Giotto's dancers are undoubtedly female, we find it explicitly stated in several of the texts we have been examining that the *tripudium* was normally performed by men. As we have seen, Seneca assures us that in ancient times the *tripudium* was not merely a male but a manly dance, a dance 'in the virile style'.[113] Giovanni da Vignano likewise makes it clear that the dancing of which he speaks was performed by 'the men of the city'; it was they who danced as an expression of their 'great joyfulness of heart'.[114] The literary evidence thus tends to confirm the view that Lorenzetti's dancers are almost certainly male. There remains the fact that they look far from masculine, at least to the untutored modern eye. But no less an authority than Dante is on hand to assure us that this is what we should expect. Lorenzetti clearly aimed to represent a group of people in the period of their youth, *la gioventute* or even *adolescenza*.[115] And as Dante explains in his account of the four ages of man in Book 4 of the *Convivio*, we should not expect to find the attributes of manhood in their fullest form in anyone under the age of thirty-five.[116]

---

[112] In the transcription below I have laid out the verses to emphasise the rhythm and rhyme-scheme, although in the Cappella they appear as two long lines. There is a fragmentary third line and space for a fourth, but either the fourth line has been effaced or the space was never used. With all contractions expanded, my transcription reads as follows:

> Equa lance cuncta librat
> perfecta iusticia:
> coronando bonos vibrat
> ensem contra vicia
> cuncta gaudet. libertate
> ipsa si regnaverit
> agit cum iocunditate
> quisque quod voluerit.

I have treated the tironian mark following 'gaudet' as equivalent to a full stop. To read it instead as 'et' (as previous transcriptions have done) is at once to introduce a redundancy and to spoil the metre.

[113] Seneca 1928–35, vol. 2, XVII. 4, p. 280: 'virilem in modum tripudiare'.
[114] Vignano 1974, p. 271: 'li homigni del nostro comune ... in demostramento de grande alegreça de coro ... balando'.
[115] Cf. Dante 1995, IV. XXIII. 13, vol. 2, p. 410.
[116] Dante 1995, IV. XXIII. 9, vol. 2, p. 409. See Alexander 1996, pp. 149–50 for suggestions about Lorenzetti's portrayal of uncertainties and conflicts in gender roles.

With these considerations in mind, I can now return to Lorenzetti's dancers and draw my argument to a close by suggesting some answers to the questions I raised at the outset. Why is the space in which they are dancing pictured as the source of light? By showing us the heart of the city as radiant and illuminating, Lorenzetti aims, I think, to convey a sense of Siena's *gloria e grandezza*, the glory and greatness that come from living peaceably under a just form of government. Why are the garments of the two central dancers decorated with moths and worms? The gnawing destructiveness proverbially associated with these creatures is there, I think, to remind us that all sublunary things are subject to decay, that the sin of *tristitia* is always liable to overwhelm us, and that we need to cultivate joyful feelings if such despondency is to be held at bay.[117] But at the same time, the glory of the city and its peaceful activities are there to remind us that there is a great deal to feel joyful about. What, finally, is the significance of the fact that this entire section of the frescoes is organised around the image of a dance? The young men performing the solemnly festive *tripudium* are expressing, I take it, their natural and almost dutiful feelings of *gaudium* as they contemplate the *pax* and *gloria* exhibited throughout the swelling scene.

This account of the dancers and their symbolic significance differs in one important respect from all the interpretations I have read of this aspect of Lorenzetti's cycle. It has generally been assumed that the dance must be the representation of a concept. Some commentators have taken it to symbolise the place of the theatrical arts in civic life.[118] Others have taken it to refer more generally to the presence of the muses.[119] But the consensus among recent commentators has been that the dance should be taken to symbolise civic harmony.[120]

It is of course true that Lorenzetti's cycle contains many representations of such abstract ideas. As we have seen, the 'cardinal' and 'theological' virtues are illustrated, as are Peace, Concord and Security and the contrasting figures of War, Division and Fear. But it is striking that in each of these cases the viewer is alerted by an accompanying *titulus* to the symbolic significance of the figure concerned. Nor is there any reason

[117] Viterbo 1901, p. 239 col 2 and p. 240, col 1, offers a series of cautionary verses on the need 'to live joyfully' ('vivere iocunde') and to ensure that *tristitia* is banished (the chapter is entitled 'De tristitia evitanda'). See also the similar discussion in *Oculus* 1966, pp. 54–7.
[118] Feldges-Henning 1972, p. 154 associates the dancers with *Theatrica*, one of the *Artes mechanicae*, an interpretation endorsed in Borsook 1980, p. 35.
[119] Feldges-Henning 1972, p. 155 adds the suggestion about the Muses, a suggestion elaborated by Eorsi 1978, pp. 85–9.
[120] Carli 1983, p. 43; Robinson 1986; Greenstein 1988, pp. 502–3; Frugoni 1991, p. 67; Starn and Partridge 1992, p. 52; Donato 1995, p. 148.

why Lorenzetti should not have followed the same practice in his depiction of the dance. If, for example, his aim had indeed been to symbolise civic harmony, one might have expected him to surround the group with a *titulus* inscribed *consensio civilis* or some such explanatory phrase.

By contrast with these current (and largely speculative) interpretations, I am led by the literary sources to conclude that Lorenzetti's basic aim must simply have been to represent the act of dancing the *tripudium* in the streets. But at the same time he undoubtedly deploys a number of pictorial devices – the central positioning of the dancers, their allegorical costumes, their enlarged scale – to suggest that the act of publicly performing the *tripudium* must itself be understood to carry some special significance. It seems to me, accordingly, that the right question to ask about the dancing group must be: what conventional meaning would Lorenzetti's contemporaries have been most likely to attach to the representation of the act of dancing in the streets? My suggestion, to repeat, is that the dancers would most probably have been taken to be banishing *tristitia* and expressing their dutiful joyfulness at the scenes of civic peace and glory surrounding them.[121]

One might still want to ask why there are *nine* dancers in the group. But one might equally well ask why there are nine figures in the ensemble of Wisdom, Justice and Concord on the northern wall. Or why there are nine figures in the group of virtues surrounding the enthroned central figure. Or why the contrasting figure of Tyranny on the western wall is surrounded by nine vices. One might also want to ask why there are nine crenellations on each side of the central roof of the Palazzo Pubblico. Or why there are nine segments in the brick pavement of the *piazza* below. The answer must, I think, be the same in every case: these are all allusions to the *Signori Nove*, the nine ruling officials of Siena, who commissioned and paid for Lorenzetti's frescoes, just as they commissioned and paid for the rebuilding of the Palazzo Pubblico and the pavement outside. Not unnaturally, they wanted their signature on everything, and their signature was the number nine.[122]

---

[121] Although Alexander 1996, pp. 147, 150, endorses the view that the dance symbolises 'the political harmony of the citizens', he adds (rightly in my view) that 'joy in the city' is also represented. But he goes on to argue that the juxtaposition of the dance with 'the marriage procession' suggests a specifically sexual harmony of the kind 'that leads to the positive outcome of reproduction'. It is far from clear, however, that the figures juxtaposed with the dancers do in fact represent a marriage procession. Nor can I find anything in the literary sources to support Alexander's speculation that the dance represents a sexual form of harmony.

[122] For these 'signatures' of the Nine, see Bowsky 1981, pp. 286–8; Starn and Partridge 1992, p. 17.

Perhaps we can even carry the argument a stage further by asking one final question about the dominant figure whom I earlier identified as a representation of Siena as its own supreme judge. Who, when these frescoes were painted, claimed to be the supreme judge of the Sienese in virtue of representing the people of Siena? Once again, the answer is of course the Nine. In portraying the city of Siena as judge of the Sienese, Lorenzetti is at the same time offering a representation of the power held by the Nine as elected representatives of the citizens as a whole. So the joy expressed by the nine dancers at the civic peace and glory surrounding them is in turn a celebration of the achievement of the Nine, the bringers of all these beneficial effects.

5

Republican virtues in an age of princes

I

When in chapter 2 I focused on the *Regnum Italicum* in the thirteenth century, I concentrated on two connected arguments that were central to the burgeoning republican literature of that formative period. One was the belief that our chief aspiration in public life should be to uphold civic peace and unity, thereby enabling our community to attain its highest goals of *gloria* and *grandezza*. The other was the connected belief that, if these goals are to be realised, it is indispensable that we should institute and uphold an elective system of republican government.

By the end of the thirteenth century these assumptions were beginning to be widely questioned, not least because it appeared to so many commentators that self-government had simply proved a recipe for endless civil strife.[1] If our aim is to live in peace and unity, it began to be urged, it will always be safer to entrust our community to the strong government of a single *signore* or hereditary prince.[2] These sentiments served at once to legitimise and encourage the widespread shift during this period *dal' commune al principato*, from traditional systems of elective government to the acceptance of the rule of princes. Such changes took place at Mantua and Verona in the 1270s, at Treviso, Pisa, Piacenza and Parma by the end of the 1280s and at Ravenna, Rimini and elsewhere before the end of the century.[3] Dante was therefore speaking with only mild

---

This chapter has been developed from the central sections of my contribution entitled 'Political Philosophy' in *The Cambridge History of Renaissance Philosophy*, ed. Charles B. Schmitt and Quentin Skinner (Cambridge, 1988), pp. 387–452.

[1] See Hyde 1972 for contemporary discussions of this claim. For a magisterial account of faction and the transition to the rule of *signori* see Jones 1997, pp. 548–83, 600–42.

[2] Ercole 1932, pp. 279–86, 306–11 showed that the *signori* generally assumed power with the consent of the relevant body of citizens. The point is still worth stressing, if only because of the influential contrast developed in Baron 1966 between republican 'liberty' and the 'tyranny' of princely regimes. For a helpful corrective see Robey 1973, pp. 4–10 and references there.

[3] Waley 1988, pp. 165–72.

hyperbole – although his phrasing was undoubtedly tendentious – when he observed in the *Purgatorio* that 'all the cities of Italy' had become 'full of tyrants'.[4]

This transition, however, was by no means universal nor uncontested. Florence and Venice managed to cling onto their status as independent city-republics throughout the fourteenth and fifteenth centuries, and in the course of that period they engendered a political literature in which the values and practices of republican regimes were powerfully carried over into the age of princes. The outcome was a debate of unparalleled historical significance about the rival merits of self-government and princely rule. It is with the nature and evolution of that debate that the present chapter will be concerned.

II

It was already clear before the end of the thirteenth century that the city-republics of the *Regnum Italicum* had fallen into a state of crisis. Giovanni da Vignano in his *Flore de Parlare* of c.1290 was only one of many who expressed despair at their deepening difficulties. 'Remember and think', he exhorts his readers, 'how Pisa, how Arezzo, how Florence, how Modena, how Milan' have already been 'broken and destroyed and undone by their internal divisions and quarrelling'.[5]

Reflecting on the implications of this crisis, the political writers of the early fourteenth century tended to respond in one of two ways. Some reverted to the age-old claim that the surest means of bringing concord to the *Regnum Italicum* would be to accept the overlordship of the Holy Roman Emperor after all. Dino Compagni supports this solution in his *Cronica* of Florence,[6] but the most eloquent statement of the Ghibelline case is undoubtedly the one put forward by Dante in his *De Monarchia*.[7] Dante begins with the familiar contention that our highest earthly ambition should be to live 'in the calm and tranquillity of peace, since universal peace is the finest of all the gifts that have been ordained for our happiness'.[8] He then devotes the whole of his opening Book to defending

---

[4] Dante 1967a, VI, lines 123–4, p. 100: 'Ché le città d'Italia tutte piene/son di tiranni.'
[5] Vignano 1974, p. 314: 'recordivi e pensati como Pixa, como Areço, como Fiorença, como Modena, como Millam... [sono] guaste e destructe e desfate per le divisiom e per le brighe'. See also Libri 1974, pp. 147–8 and Ceffi 1942, p. 36.
[6] Compagni 1939, p. 210.
[7] For the date of composition (between 1314 and Dante's death in 1321) see Shaw 1996, pp. xxxii–xxxiv.
[8] Dante 1965, I. IV. 2, p. 143: 'in quiete sive tranquillitate pacis... quod pax universalis est optimum eorum que ad nostram beatitudinem ordinantur'.

the suggestion that, if the disorders of Italy are ever to be resolved, complete trust must be placed in the emperor as the sole authority capable of ending the prevailing strife.

Among Italian political writers of the early fourteenth century, however, the most usual proposal was that the numerous local *signori* who had begun to seize power in the cities ought simply to be accepted with gratitude as bringers of a more stable and stronger form of government. With this development, the genre of advice-books for city magistrates that we examined in chapter 2 went into steep decline, and a new preoccupation with the virtues of princely government began to declare itself.[9] Padua emerged as one of the leading centres of this new political literature, just as it had earlier provided the context for Marsilius's great statement of the opposing case.[10] Ferreto de' Ferreti, a member of Albertino Mussato's early humanist circle, composed a verse panegyric *De Scaligorum Origine* soon after the accession of Cangrande Della Scala as *signore* of Padua in 1328. The principal hope he expresses in his eulogy is that Cangrande's descendants 'will continue to hold their sceptres for long years to come'.[11] Pier Paolo Vergerio, who lived in Padua between 1390 and 1405, wrote his *De Monarchia* during those years, addressing it to the Carrara lords who were ruling the city by that time.[12] Giovanni da Ravenna, Chancellor of Padua during the 1390s, further celebrated the Carrara family in his *Dragmalogia de Eligibili Vite Genere* of 1404.[13] And Petrarch, who spent the closing years of his life in the city, likewise dedicated his treatise *De Republica Optime Administranda* to Francesco da Carrara in 1373.[14]

According to all these writers, the highest aim of government should be to ensure that, as Petrarch puts it, 'each citizen can live their life in freedom and security, with no innocent blood being spilled'.[15] If this framework for living the good life is to be held in place, everyone in authority 'must be concerned above all else with public peace'.[16] But peace can never be secured under Italy's traditional systems of republican rule. Vergerio treats this as obvious, while Giovanni da Ravenna points to the history of ancient Rome as conclusive evidence of this general

---

[9] On this development see Cox 1999.
[10] On the end of the Paduan commune see Hyde 1966, esp. pp. 252–82.
[11] Ferreti 1920, III, p. 100: 'ut longos teneant sceptra per annos'.
[12] For the date and biographical details see Robey 1973, pp. 8–9, 20–1.
[13] For the date and biographical details see Kohl 1980, pp. 22–9.
[14] On this part of Petrarch's life see Wilkins 1959, pp. 141–314.
[15] Petrarch 1554b, p. 420: 'ut et cives...liberi fuerint ac securi, nec ullius sanguis innoxius fu[n]deretur'.
[16] Petrarch 1554b, p. 420: 'ante alios quietis publicae studiosus'.

truth.[17] The moral is said to be obvious, and all these writers duly point it out: if there is to be any prospect of peace, we must cleave to princely government. As Petrarch triumphantly assures the Carrara family, it is wholly due to their standing as hereditary *signori* that they have 'ruled for so many years over a flourishing community in serene tranquillity and constant peace'.[18]

To these familiar claims a more high-flown argument was sometimes added, an argument stemming from a fundamentally Augustinian vision of the well-lived life. Such a life, Petrarch[19] affirms, will be one of withdrawal from mundane affairs – a *vita solitaria*, as he describes it in the title of one of his most famous books. This alone affords us the leisure or *otium* needed for great literary labours, as well as the tranquillity needed for contemplation and prayer.[20] The same commitment underlies Giovanni da Ravenna's *Dragmalogia*, which culminates in a bitter denunciation of the evils and hypocrisies inevitable in politics and a heartfelt defence of the good life as one of rustic retreat. To both writers this suggests a further reason for concluding that, as Giovanni puts it, 'the rule of a single man is always to be preferred, even if the man in question is only of moderate worthiness'.[21] Where one man rules, 'the rest of us are left completely free of public business, and are able to pursue our own affairs'.[22] This is a highly desirable arrangement, indispensable for the completion of any important task, but 'it is one that has rarely existed under a government of the people, though often under the rule of a king'.[23]

These celebrations of princely rule brought with them a number of related changes in the political literature of the period. As we saw in chapter 2, those who had written in favour of the self-governing communes had always thought of peace and its preservation as necessary for the attainment of yet higher goals, the highest of these being the achievement of *gloria* and *grandezza* by the community as a whole. By contrast, the theorists of princely government lay all their emphasis on the glory and greatness of rulers themselves, thereby converting a traditional interest

---

[17] Ravenna 1980, p. 124: 'per reges Romanum fundatum est et vires cepit imperium. deinde, ubi regi superbo superbi cives parere contempserunt, populariter res acta est... quanto fluctu et turbine civitatis'.

[18] Petrarch 1554b, p. 420: 'per annos florentem patriam, serena tranquillitate et constanti pace tenueris'.

[19] See Petrarch 1554a.

[20] See Petrarch 1975, vol. 1, pp. 261–565 and cf. Petrarch 1975, vol. 1, pp. 567–809.

[21] Ravenna 1980, p. 106: 'unius vel mediocriter boni eligibilius esse regimen'.

[22] Ravenna 1980, p. 132: 'nam ubi unus dominatur, suo quisque negotio prorsus publici securus vacat.'

[23] Ravenna 1980, p. 118: 'quod monarcha dominante sepe, politia raro, contigisse'.

in the values of communities into a preoccupation with a series of purely personal qualities.

This preoccupation with princely glory stood in even starker contrast with the values that the scholastic philosophers of the period wished to see propagated.[24] 'It is altogether inappropriate', Giles of Rome retorted, 'for a holder of regal power to seek his own fulfilment either in the attainment of glory or even of fame.'[25] St Thomas Aquinas had earlier raised the same objection yet more forcefully in his *De Regno*. 'The desire for human glory', he had warned, 'destroys any magnanimity of character.' To which he had added that 'to hold out such a reward to princes is at the same time very harmful to the people, since the duty of a good man is to show contempt for glory and all such temporal goods'.[26]

Among the many contrasts between the schoolmen and the humanists, one of the most revealing is that the latter never exhibit any such guilt or anxiety about worldly glory and its pursuit. On the contrary, we find Petrarch declaring that his whole purpose in offering advice to Francesco da Carrara is 'to lead you to immediate fame and future glory in the best possible way'.[27] Petrarch accepts that rulers ought to cultivate those qualities 'which serve not merely as a means to glory but as ladders to heaven at the same time'.[28] But this concession represents his sole acknowledgment of the deeply rooted Christian suspicion of *gloria mundi* and those who aspire to it. The rest of his letter to Francesco is filled with exhortations to undertake such tasks 'as will bring you a share of glory that your ancestors never attained'.[29] You must never hesitate, he concludes, 'to lust after a form of greediness that is generous and beyond reproach: a greediness to obtain the outstanding attribute of fame'.[30]

By focusing on the figure of the prince, the humanists at the same time introduced a number of other changes into the political literature of the

---

[24] Marsilius of Padua perhaps constitutes a partial exception. See Marsilius 1928, I. XVI. 14, p. 81.
[25] Rome 1607, I. I. 9, p. 27: 'quod non decet regiam maiestatem, suam ponere felicitatem in gloria, vel in fama'.
[26] Aquinas 1973, I. 8, p. 265: 'Deinde humanae gloriae cupido animi magnitudinem aufert ... simul etiam est multitudini nocivum, si tale praemium statuatur principibus: pertinet enim ad boni viri officium ut contemnat gloriam, sicut alia temporalia bona.'
[27] Petrarch 1554b, p. 420: 'rem ... et famae tuae praesenti, et venturae gloriae saluberrimam feceris'.
[28] Petrarch 1554b, p. 423: 'haec sunt autem non ad gloriam modo, sed ad coelum scalae'.
[29] Petrarch 1554b, p. 426: 'arripe quaeso, et hanc gloriae partem, quam maiores tui omnes ... non viderunt'.
[30] Petrarch 1554b, p. 428: 'cupiditatem irreprehensibilem generosam ... praeclaram famae supellectilem concupisce'.

fourteenth century. Concentrating on the attributes that rulers need to cultivate, they began to lay an overriding emphasis on the ideal of *virtus generalis*, the quality regarded by the ancient Roman moralists as the key to glory and greatness. As Cicero had promised in his *Tusculanae Disputationes*, 'where there is a passion for *virtus*, the attainment of glory will necessarily follow, even if it is not your objective'.[31] Petrarch was to give renewed expression to this belief when he assured Francesco da Carrara that 'true *virtus* brings us glory even when it may not be desired'.[32] By the end of the fourteenth century this assumption had become firmly entrenched as the leading tenet – almost the defining characteristic – of humanist political thought. The image in which the ideal eventually became encapsulated was that of Hercules at the crossroads. Xenophon in his *Memorabilia* recounts the story of the youthful Hercules and his meeting with Virtue and Vice, each of whom offers to show him a pathway through life. The heroic Hercules naturally chooses the more rugged direction pointed out to him by the figure of Virtue, rightly seeing it as his route to glory and immortal fame.[33]

Placing all their emphasis on the *virtus* of the prince meant that the early humanists found little to say about two issues on which the schoolmen always supposed it vital to pronounce. The latter generally recognised that the peace and security of a community will often depend on a ruler's willingness to act with *vis* as well as *virtus*, with military power as well as moral force. As a result, Aquinas and his disciples were much preoccupied with the concept of the Just War, seeking to specify the nature of the conditions that make it morally justifiable to declare war and to wage it.[34] By contrast, the early humanists are apt to stigmatise any appeal to *vis* at the expense of *virtus* as a sign of mere bestiality, endorsing the Stoic and Ciceronian proposition that the *virtus* we must cherish is the eponymous characteristic of the *vir*, the man of truly manly as opposed to brutish or beastly qualities.[35] As a result, they not only place a question mark, if only implicitly, against the doctrine of the Just

---

[31] Cicero 1927, I. XXXVIII. 91, p. 108: 'cupiditate... virtutis, quam necessario gloria, etiam si tu id non agas, consequatur'.

[32] See Petrarch 1554b, p. 420 for the idea that 'vera virtus' brings glory 'eamque vel invitam'.

[33] Xenophon's version of the story became generally known – at least to those humanists who could read Greek – after the first printing of his collected works in 1516. For the earliest Latin version see Xenophon 1545. For an early example of an emblematic rendering of the story see Haechtanus 1579, Sig. N, 3^v.

[34] For the classic defence of justice both *ad bellum* and *in bello*, see Aquinas 1962, II^a. II^{ae}, Qu. 40, art. 1, pp. 206–7.

[35] Cicero 1927, II. XVIII. 43, p. 194: 'Appellata est enim ex viro virtus.' See also Cicero 1913, I. IX. 34, p. 36 and cf. Petrarch 1554b, p. 433 quoting Cicero 1913, I. XXII. 74, pp. 74–6.

War; they also exhibit much less interest in arguing systematically about the relations between warfare and government.

The other topic on which the manuals of the early humanists remain largely silent concerns the design of political institutions. The schoolmen were much preoccupied with the constitutional arrangements needed to ensure that the people obtain a genuine share in the making of laws, and that secular and ecclesiastical jurisdictions are both confined within their proper spheres. By contrast, few of the early humanists have anything of substance to say about these matters at all. Marsilius's hard questions about the relations between spiritual and temporal power largely disappear from sight until the Reformation revived them with a vengeance. The humanists are generally content to assume that a prince of true *virtus* will of course be a loyal son of the church. The same is true of the careful arrangements devised by the schoolmen and civil lawyers to prevent the enemies of peace from seizing control of the apparatus of government. These concerns scarcely find an echo in early humanist political thought. The basic assumption shared by Petrarch and his successors is that, so long as the ruler is a man of *virtus*, the goals of peace and security will be adequately secured.

If *virtus* is the all-important quality, what does it mean for a prince to possess it? Petrarch's *De Republica Optime Administranda* furnishes a typical and deeply influential answer. Such a ruler will be distinguished by a number of personal virtues, in particular the avoidance of pride and avarice, the gravest of all the vices. Above all, however, he will be recognisable by the justice of his rule. Petrarch accordingly devotes his principal attention to analysing the concept of justice, in the course of which he discloses, more clearly than at any other point, the overwhelming extent of his debt to Cicero, and especially to the doctrines of *De Officiis*.

When Cicero discusses justice in Book I of *De Officiis*, he initially defines it in juristic terms as a matter of rendering to each their due.[36] But his chief concern is with what it means to speak of receiving one's due, and in addressing that further question he divides his analysis into two halves. One is taken up with a discussion of generosity, a virtue he takes to be inseparably bound up with justice itself. His other contention is that justice is only secured when we avoid *iniuria*, the infliction of harm in a manner contrary to right.[37] Such harm can arise in one of two ways: either as the product of fraud, the failure to keep one's word; or else as

---

[36] Cicero 1913, I. V. 15, p. 16.   [37] Cicero 1913, I. XIII. 41, pp. 44.

the product of force, of cruel or brutal treatment.[38] It follows that the two corresponding and indispensable requirements of justice must be *fides*, the willingness to treat one's word as one's bond,[39] and *clementia*, the avoidance of cruelty and violence.[40] A leader who possesses these attributes will always be loved and admired; and the capacity to inspire love rather than fear is the key to princely glory and fame.[41]

Holding, as Cicero does, that the virtue of *iustitia* is enough in itself to entitle a *vir* to be regarded as a good man,[42] he in turn emphasises that any vices tending to undermine justice – above all the vices of force and fraud – must be stigmatised as beastly as opposed to manly qualities:

It is possible to behave unjustly in one of two ways. One is by acting with brute force, the other by acting fraudulently. Both are completely alien to humankind, fraud because it resembles the act of a fox, brute force because it resembles the act of a lion. But of the two, fraud is worthy of the greater contempt.[43]

Cicero's sternly minatory observations helped to give rise to a long-enduring construction of masculinity according to which the *vir virtutis*, the man of true manliness, will always be recognisable by his anxiety to avoid behaving in brutal or beastly ways.

Petrarch and his humanist successors follow this Ciceronian analysis almost word for word. Justice is indeed a matter of rendering to each their due, Petrarch agrees, and this requires not merely the observance of good faith but the exercise of clemency and generosity at all times. If we ask what motives a prince may be said to have for behaving with justice, Petrarch simply refers us to Cicero's account. We are told above all to read, mark and learn Cicero's crucial chain of reasoning – endlessly cited by later humanists – to the effect that justice is the sole guarantee of popular affection, while the love of the people is in turn the sole guarantee of governmental security and the prince's own glory and fame.[44]

If *virtus* is the eponymous quality of the *vir*, the man of true manliness, what becomes of women in this moral scheme of things?[45] Given that *virtus* is imagined not merely as a specifically masculine quality, but also as the indispensable means of attaining public glory and posthumous

---

[38] Cicero 1913, I. XIII. 41, pp. 44–6.   [39] Cicero 1913, I. VII. 23, p. 24.
[40] Cicero 1913, I. XI. 35, p. 36.   [41] Cicero 1913, II. VII. 23, p. 190.
[42] Cicero 1913, I. VII. 20, p. 20.
[43] Cicero 1913, I. XIII. 41, pp. 44–6: 'Cum autem duobus modis, id est vi aut fraude, fiat iniuria, fraus quasi vulpeculae, vis leonis videtur; utrumque homine alienissimum, sed fraus odio digna maiore.'
[44] Petrarch 1554b, pp. 421–4.
[45] The question is perhaps most influentially raised in Kelly 1999.

fame, one consequence is that women are excluded almost by definition from taking part in public or political life.[46] This is not to say that women in *quattrocento* Italy invariably succumbed to the power of this image. Some achieved fame as humanist writers, such as Laura Cerata and especially Isotta Nogarola.[47] Some even seized power as rulers in their own right, such as the formidable Caterina Sforza, whom Machiavelli mentions with great respect in his *Discorsi* and *Istorie Fiorentine*.[48] Nor did male humanists refuse to recognise that women might in a certain sense be capable of attaining *virtus* in a high degree. But the virtues typically assigned to women reflect the basic assumption that the proper arena for their talents should be private and domestic as opposed to public in character.[49] These assumptions can be seen at their clearest in a work such as Leon Battista Alberti's *Della Famiglia*, written in Florence in the 1430s. The men of the family are exhorted to seek *fama* and *gloria* by cultivating the qualities of manly *virtù* and deploying them *virilissime* in an honourable life of public service.[50] By contrast, the women are expected to be beautiful, good at bearing children and ready to devote themselves prudently and industriously to the management of domestic life.[51] The virtues they are required to cultivate centre on modesty, constancy, obedience and above all fidelity.[52] For a women to lose her virtue was simply to be unchaste. Although the humanists liked to boast that they spoke for humanity, the qualities they most of all valued and celebrated were associated in their own minds with only one half of humankind.[53]

III

Although the system of government by *signori* had spread through most of the *Regnum Italicum* by the end of the fourteenth century, there were two exceptions to this rule, both of the utmost significance. Florence and Venice succeeded in fighting off the threat of internal 'tyranny' as well as external conquest, and in the course of doing so became increasingly hostile to the *signori* and their usurpations of traditional liberties. As

---

[46] Grafton and Jardine 1986, esp. pp. 29–57.
[47] King 1980, pp. 71–5; Kristeller 1980, pp. 96–8. For examples of their writing see King and Rabil 1983, pp. 57–69, 78–86.
[48] Machiavelli 1960, III. 6, pp. 407–8; Machiavelli 1962, VIII. 34, pp. 571–2.
[49] For similar assumptions in fifteenth- and sixteenth-century England see Hull 1982.
[50] Alberti 1971, pp. 125–6, 154–83.   [51] Alberti 1971, pp. 132–4, 139–42, 266–95.
[52] For a classic analysis of this 'double standard' see Thomas 1959.
[53] For the impact of the Renaissance and Reformation on the status of women see Sommerville 1995.

a result, a new genre of political literature began to emerge in both these surviving republics in the early years of the fifteenth century. It was a genre devoted at once to celebrating their civic greatness in the highest humanist style, and at the same time to explaining it in terms of their uninterrupted loyalty to their long-established systems of 'free' government.

As we saw in chapter 2, Henry of Rimini had already sought to account for Venice's achievements by reference to her unique constitution in his treatise of c.1300 on the cardinal virtues. His analysis remained well known throughout the fourteenth century,[54] and it seems to have exercised a direct influence on Pier Paolo Vergerio, whose *De Republica Veneta* of c.1400 took a further step towards the definitive articulation of the myth of Venice.[55] Vergerio agrees with Henry that the Venetians have proved uniquely successful in combining civic greatness with the preservation of peace. The explanation, he further agrees, lies in the nature of their constitution. The city 'is ruled by an administration of her optimates, and is thus a form of polity which it is appropriate to call, in Greek terminology, an aristocracy, this being the mean between monarchical and popular forms of rule'.[56] However, the government of Venice is far more admirable than a conventional aristocracy, for it contains monarchical and popular elements as well, 'and is thus a mixture of all the praiseworthy forms of polities'.[57] It is because of this mixed constitution, Vergerio concludes, and in particular because of its *stretto* or strictly limited access to government, that the Venetians have been able to scale the heights of glory without endangering their free institutions or the cause of civic peace.[58]

By the middle of the fifteenth century, Vergerio's basic insight had been embroidered by a number of other humanists, most notably George of Trebizond in the Preface to his translation of Plato's *Laws* in the early 1450s.[59] Discussing the constitution of Sparta in Books 3 and 4 of the *Laws*, Plato had formulated the earliest theoretical defence of the mixed constitution as the best and stablest form of government. George takes up these remarks and applies them directly to Venice, claiming that the

[54] On this point see Robey 1973, pp. 8–9.
[55] For the date see Robey and Law 1975, p. 29. For a partial translation see Vergerio 1997.
[56] Vergerio 1975, pp. 38–9: 'Venetorum respublica optimatum administratione regitur, quod genus civilitatis greco vocabulo aristocratiam licet appellare, que inter regium popularemque principatum media est.'
[57] Vergerio 1975, p. 39: 'ex omni genere laudabilis politie simul commixta est'.
[58] For Vergerio's survey of the three elements in the Venetian constitution see Vergerio 1975, pp. 39–46. See also Gilbert 1977, p. 184.
[59] For a discussion see Monfasani 1990.

city's aristocratic and 'directed' republicanism constitutes a realisation of Plato's ideal in practice.[60] Dedicating his translation to the Doge, George duly received a handsome remuneration for this flattering explanation of his adopted city's pre-eminence in the art of government.[61]

By the end of the century the image of Venice as the *serenissima* had become definitively fixed. Domenico Morosini draws heavily on it in his *De Bene Instituta Republica* of c.1500, although he concedes that Venice's constitution stands in need of some reformation if the city's admirable peacefulness is to be sustained.[62] Gasparo Contarini provides a classic summary of the entire argument, together with much empirical detail, in his *De Magistratibus Venetorum*, a work largely written in the 1520s and posthumously published in 1543. His conclusion is unambiguously celebratory in tone:

> There has never been a polity capable of rivalling Venice in the suitability of its constitution and laws for living a good and happy life. The outcome of these arrangements is there for all to see in the long continuation of our city in this flourishing state. And when I reflect on this fact, I always find myself amazed at the wisdom of our ancestors, their industriousness, their excellent *virtus* and their incredible love of their country.[63]

No breath of criticism disturbs the placid surface of Contarini's analysis.

During the first half of the fifteenth century, a no less strident note of patriotism began to resound through the political writings of the Florentine humanists. The tone was set by Leonardo Bruni's *Laudatio Florentinae Urbis*,[64] a celebration of the city's glory and greatness that took its form from Aristides's oration in praise of Athens, but took its main political arguments from the historians and moral philosophers of republican Rome.[65] Bruni opens with a fulsome description of Florence's civic grandeur: the greatness of her wealth, the splendours of her architecture, the immensity of her power. The rest of the panegyric is given over to explaining how Florence has managed to acquire so many glories.

---

[60] Trebizond 1970.   [61] Monfasani 1976, pp. 102–3, 120–1, 145–6.
[62] Morosini 1969. For the date of composition see Cozzi 1970, pp. 408–9. Begun in 1497, the work remained uncompleted at Morosini's death in 1509.
[63] Contarini 1968, p. 263: 'nulla tamen fuit, quae institutione ac legibus ad bene beateque vivendum idonei s cum hac nostra conferri possit: quo effectum esse perspicimus, ut neque adeo diuturna ulla unquam perstiterit. quam rem cum mecum ipse considero, magnopere mirari soleo maiorum nostrorum sapientiam, industriam, excellentem animi virtutem atque adeo incredibilem erga patriam charitatem.' For the date of Contarini's treatise see Gilbert 1967, pp. 174–6.
[64] For the date see Baron 1968, pp. 111–23.
[65] For Bruni's use of Aristides see Baron 1968, pp. 155–9, 167–9. On Bruni's civic panegyrics see Hankins 2000.

Bruni concentrates on expounding a single and highly influential theme: Florence's greatness is held to be the fruit of her *libertas*, the outcome of her enjoyment of 'a free way of life'.

When Bruni describes Florence as a free city, what he means is that the community is free in the sense of not living in dependence on the goodwill of anyone else, and is consequently free to act according to its own civic will. His meaning becomes plain as soon as he asks what forces need to be held at bay if liberty is to be preserved. The most obvious is said to be the danger of foreign conquest. To speak of Florence as a free city is thus to say that her citizens have managed to fight off such external threats to their autonomy, especially and most recently the threat posed by Visconti Milan.[66] The other and more insidious danger is said to arise when a powerful individual or faction within a city reduces it to servitude by seizing power and ruling in their selfish interests instead of promoting the common good. To predicate freedom of a city is thus to say in addition that its citizens have managed to forestall any such internal threats to their independence of action.[67]

Two institutions above all have enabled the Florentines to maintain their free way of life. To stave off foreign conquest they have evolved a formidable military machine, constantly performing 'outstanding deeds of martial prowess' and 'more than once liberating the whole of Italy from the peril of servitude'.[68] To meet the threat of internal subversion, they have held fast to their mixed republican constitution, thereby protecting the well-being of their community and in consequence the liberty of each individual citizen at the same time.

This degree of emphasis on republican *libertas* constitutes a major development in humanist political thought. It is true that, as we saw in chapter 2, a number of pre-humanist writers on city government had already associated the ideal of *libertas* with the maintenance of self-governing regimes. It is also true that, in the generation before Bruni, a number of humanist writers – including Bruni's own mentor Coluccio Salutati – had argued that the laws of a community must aim at the common good if liberty is to be preserved. Salutati had been content to assume, however, that this desideratum can be realised under a prudent

---

[66] Bruni 1968, pp. 256–8.
[67] As Bruni explains in section 2 (Bruni 1968, p. 245), this is where Rome eventually failed. The city fell under the yoke of the Caesars, 'those diseases and destroyers of the republic, who overthrew the people's liberty' ('pestes atque exitia rei publice, libertatem sustulerant').
[68] Bruni 1968, pp. 254, 256: 'egregia rei militaris facinora... non semel ab hac una urbe totam Italiam a servitutis periculo fuisse liberatam'.

and law-abiding *signore* no less than under a republic.[69] By contrast, Bruni and his successors take from the Roman historians – especially Sallust and Livy – a much stricter account of the relations between liberty, the common good and the achievement of civic glory. Sallust had argued in his *Bellum Catilinae* that 'because good men are objects of even greater suspicion to kings than the wicked', the city of Rome 'was only able to rise so suddenly to her incredible level of greatness once she gained her liberty' with the expulsion of her kings.[70] It was this perspective that Bruni and his heirs adopted. They not only argued that, if greatness is to be achieved, liberty must be upheld. They also insisted that, if liberty is to be kept as safe as possible, it is indispensable to maintain a mixed form of republican government.

There is also a contrast to be drawn between Leonardo Bruni's republicanism and the similar enthusiasm for mixed constitutions displayed by the admirers of Venice. Pier Paolo Vergerio and his Venetian followers argue that, to protect civic peace as well as liberty, the government of a republic must always be narrow or *stretto* in its social base. Leonardo Bruni by contrast devotes the final section of his *Laudatio* to commending a far more inclusive or *largo* type of regime. 'It is because Florence has recognised that what concerns the body of the people ought not to be decided except by the will of that body itself that liberty flourishes and justice is conserved in the city in such an exceptionally scrupulous way.'[71]

Although Bruni stresses the importance of military and constitutional machinery, he only reaches the bedrock of his argument when he asks what animates these institutions and enables them to flourish. A good Ciceronian, he answers that the key lies in the possession of *virtus*. By means of this quality, he asserts at the start of section 2, the Romans maintained their liberty and rose to dominate the world. By means of the same quality, he adds in a carefully contrived parallel at the start of section 3, Florence promises to attain a comparable level of glory and greatness.[72]

As we have seen, the previous generation of humanists had likewise emphasised the centrality of *virtus*. But here too Bruni's argument differs in significant ways. Petrarch and his admirers had maintained that the best way of life for ordinary citizens will always be one of *otium*, of

---

[69] De Rosa 1980, p. 144.
[70] Sallust 1931a, VII. 2–3, pp. 12–14: 'nam regibus boni quam mali suspectiores sunt... civitas incredibile memoratu est adepta libertate quantum brevi creverit'.
[71] Bruni 1968, p. 260: 'quod enim ad multos attinet, id non aliter quam multorum sententia decerni... iudicavit. hoc modo et libertas viget et iustitia sanctissime in civitate servatur.'
[72] Bruni 1968, pp. 244, 248.

contemplation and withdrawal from public affairs. Among the humanists of Bruni's generation this commitment is decisively reversed. Adopting Cicero's slogan that 'what is praiseworthy about *virtus* is always to be seen in action',[73] they equate *otium* with the mere dereliction of duty and insist that the life of political involvement, the *vita activa* centring on public *negotium*, must always be preferred. Even before Bruni's commendation of the Florentines for adopting these values, Pier Paolo Vergerio had furnished a classic statement of the same point of view. He had done so in a letter composed in 1394 in the form of a response to Petrarch in the name of Cicero, in which Cicero is made to take Petrarch to task for celebrating the life of *otium* or contemplative withdrawal.[74] 'It has always seemed to me', Cicero retorts, 'that the man who surpasses all others in his nature and way of life is the one who bestows his efforts on the government of the body politic and in working for the benefit of all.'[75] This means that 'the most mature and valuable philosophy must be the one that dwells in cities, shuns solitude and concerns itself with the good of the community as a whole'.[76]

Discussing the nature of this essentially civic *virtus*, Bruni's treatment again differs from that of Petrarch and his disciples. As we have seen, they had generally confined themselves to considering the *virtus* of princes. By contrast, Bruni and his admirers insist that, if liberty is to be protected and civic greatness attained, it is essential that the quality of *virtus* should be cultivated by each and every citizen. A further contrast derives from the fact that the earlier humanists had usually remained faithful to the traditional image of the ruler as a just judge, and had therefore placed all their emphasis on the virtue of justice. By contrast, Bruni develops a more complex and authentically Ciceronian account. He agrees about the centrality of justice, and continues to link it with *beneficentia* and the avoidance of *iniuria*.[77] But he places no less emphasis on the other three 'cardinal' virtues. First he mentions prudence, although only to observe that this is so widely agreed to be a leading attribute of the Florentines as to require no further comment.[78] Next he turns to courage, one of the

[73] Cicero 1913, I. VI. 19, p. 20: 'virtutis enim laus omnis in actione consistit'.
[74] For this dating see Robey 1973, p. 6.
[75] Vergerio 1934, pp. 439–40: 'ita semper visum est praestare omnibus vel genere vel vita quisquis ad administrandam rempublicam impertiendosque saluti omnium labores se accommodasset'.
[76] Vergerio 1934, p. 444: 'enim michi matura semper et prestans philosophia visa est, que in urbibus habitat et solitudinem fugit, que cum sibi tum communibus studet commodis'.
[77] See Bruni 1968, pp. 251–3 on *beneficentia, liberalitas* and *fides*.
[78] Bruni 1968, p. 251: 'nam ut prudentiam pretermittam, que omnium iudicio huic uni civitati maxima conceditur'.

major themes of his section explaining Florence's military victories.[79] Finally he discusses temperance, the importance of which underlies the whole of the *Laudatio*'s concluding section on the constitution of Florence. If a city is to remain at liberty, her citizens must avoid all forms of disorderliness, thereby maintaining a 'well-tempered' government. Florence's constitution serves to enthrone precisely this virtue in the hearts of all her citizens, thereby producing 'an unparalleled orderliness, elegance and unity in all her affairs'.[80] On this rousing note Bruni brings his panegyric to a close.

The moral of Bruni's story is that, if the highest goals of our community are to be realised, we must serve it with the full range of the civic virtues. This in turn leads him to allude to two further themes of Roman republican thought. One is the question of what constitutes the *optimus status* or best state of a commonwealth. The other is the question of what qualities may be said to distinguish a truly noble or praiseworthy citizen, a citizen of *vera nobilitas* whose conduct deserves to be honoured and admired. Bruni only mentions these issues in passing, but they form the essence of a closely related genre of Florentine political writing that emerged in the course of the fifteenth century. Buonaccorso da Montemagno in his *Oratio de Vera Nobilitate* of 1428 was perhaps the first to write specifically about these themes, and his dialogue was in turn one of the earliest works of Italian humanism to be translated into English. Later the same topic was taken up by Poggio Bracciolini in his *De Nobilitate* of c.1440, by Bartolomeo Sacchi in his *De Vera Nobilitate* of c.1475 and by a number of leading humanists of the next generation. Among these later writers, by far the most original and influential was Sir Thomas More. As I shall seek to show in chapter 8, one way of reading More's *Utopia* of 1516 is as yet another meditation on the implications of the claim that *virtus* alone constitutes true nobility.

These were by no means the first writers to argue that *virtus vera nobilitas est*. The proposition had been defended by some of the most celebrated Roman poets and moralists – notably by Horace, Seneca and Juvenal – and had never been wholly lost to sight. Brunetto Latini revives it in his *Livres dou trésor* in the 1260s, declaring in his analysis of the virtues in Book 2 that '*vertus* alone, as Horace says, is the only true nobility,

---

[79] See Bruni 1968, p. 253 on the need for 'courage and contempt of dangers' ('magnitudo animorum periculorumque contemptio') if foreign aggression is to be forestalled.

[80] Bruni 1968, p. 258: 'nusquam tantus ordo rerum, nusquam tanta elegantia, nusquam tanta concinnitas'.

there being nothing noble at all about those who follow a dishonourable life'.[81] A generation later, we find the same commitment magnificently echoed by Dante (Latini's pupil) in his *Convivio*, in which the argument culminates in the proclamation that 'nothing is more manifest than that, wherever there is virtue, there too we find nobility'.[82]

With the rise of scholasticism, however, these assumptions were directly challenged. Aristotle had argued in the *Politics* that, because public service requires leisure and the means to sustain it, the most effective and praiseworthy citizens will be those who are rich as well as virtuous, and who owe their wealth to inheritance rather than their own acquisitive skills. As a result, the contention that *vera nobilitas* must be a matter of lineage and wealth together with virtue came to be characteristic of scholastic legal and political thought. Giles of Rome, for example, simply invokes Aristotle's authority in expounding 'the widely accepted view that nobility consists in nothing other than ancient wealth'.[83] Likewise, Bartolus of Sassoferrato offers an extended critique of Dante's contrasting argument in discussing the concept of nobility in his *Commentaria* on the Code.[84]

When the humanists insist, therefore, on the equation between *virtus* and *vera nobilitas*, they are once again mounting a direct attack on the values of scholastic thought. This can be seen most clearly in Poggio Bracciolini's *De Nobilitate*, the most distinguished of the many Florentine contributions to the debate. Poggio's book takes the form of a dialogue between Niccolò Niccoli and the elder Lorenzo de' Medici. Both of them wish to understand the qualities that enable good citizens to act in such a way as to serve their community and ensure its glory and greatness.[85] Lorenzo expounds the orthodox scholastic case, explaining that 'Aristotle, whose genius surpasses that of every philosopher' has 'rightly observed that anyone who wishes to attain nobility must possess the virtues in company with wealth'.[86] But Niccolò refuses to be impressed. 'I am well aware', he retorts, 'that Aristotle is held to be the greatest of the

---

[81] Latini 1948, p. 296: 'Mais de la droite nobilité dist Orasces qu' ele est vertus solement... Donques n'a en celui nule noblesce ki use vie deshonestes.'

[82] Dante 1995, IV. XIX. 4, vol. 2, p. 381: 'nulla n'e piu manifesta che nobilitade essere dove e vertude'.

[83] Rome 1607, I. IV. 5, p. 204: 'nobilitas secundum communem acceptionem hominum nihil est aliud quam antiquatae divitiae'.

[84] Bartolus 1588, vol. 6, pp. 114–17.   [85] Bracciolini 1964–9a, vol. 1, pp. 65–6.

[86] Bracciolini 1964–9a, vol 1, pp. 74, 77: 'Aristoteles... cuius acumen ingenii omnibus philosophis antecellit... recte enim sensit Aristoteles qui virtutes suffultas divitiis voluit nobilitatem praebere.'

philosophers', but the question is not what Aristotle says 'but what appears to be closest to the truth'.⁸⁷ If we want the truth, he sweeps on, we must turn instead to Seneca, Juvenal, 'our own Cicero' and above all to the Platonic sources of their thought. We shall then recognise that 'nobility is born of *virtus* alone'.⁸⁸ Whether we hope to attain glory for ourselves or for our community, as philosophers or as leaders of civic affairs, the indispensable quality we must cultivate is *virtus*, 'which alone confers nobility on those who possess it, making them worthy of dignity and praise'.⁸⁹

IV

Leonardo Bruni's vision in the *Laudatio* – a vision of the cardinal virtues as the key to liberty, and liberty as the key to civic greatness – exercised a profound influence over the development of Florentine political theory in the first half of the fifteenth century. Within a decade of the *Laudatio*'s appearance, we find Cino Rinuccini reiterating essentially the same arguments in his fiercely patriotic *Risponsiva* addressed to Antonio Loschi.⁹⁰ During the 1420s, the same scale of values recurs in the writings of Giannozzo Manetti and Donato Acciaiuoli,⁹¹ as well as in Leonardo Bruni's own *Oratio* of 1428.⁹² And in the course of the 1430s the same concern with the role of *virtù* in the maintenance of a *vivere libero* – now expressed in the vernacular – can be found in Leon Battista Alberti's *Della Famiglia*⁹³ and in the almost slavishly Ciceronian pages of Matteo Palmieri's *Della Vita Civile*.⁹⁴

As the century progressed, however, these preoccupations came to seem less and less relevant to the political realities of the *Regnum Italicum* as a whole. Except in Florence and Venice, the *signori* everywhere continued to extend and consolidate their hold, with the result that a majority of humanists came to view their role as political advisers in a rather different light. Increasingly they took their task, as Petrarch had earlier done, to be that of furnishing the new princes of *quattrocento* Italy with

---

⁸⁷ Bracciolini 1964–9a, vol. 1, p. 74: 'fateor (Nicolaus inquit) istum principem appellari Philosophorum, sed tamen nulla me cuiusvis impediet autoritas, quin quod mihi simile vero videatur et loquar et sentiam'.
⁸⁸ Bracciolini 1964–9a, vol. 1, p. 79: 'nobilitatem ex sola nasci virtute'.
⁸⁹ Bracciolini 1964–9a, vol. 1, p. 80: 'eosque solos esse nobiles quibus virtutum officia laudem subministrarunt et dignitatem'.
⁹⁰ Witt 1970. ⁹¹ Garin 1954, pp. 211–87. ⁹² Skinner 1978a, pp. 76–7, 79.
⁹³ Alberti 1971.
⁹⁴ On this generation see Skinner 1978a, pp. 69–84. For a partial translation of the *Vita Civile* see Palmieri 1997.

manuals of advice on how best to maintain their distinctive forms of personal government.[95]

Among the earliest recipients of such advice-books were the Visconti dukes of Milan. Uberto Decembrio addressed his *De Republica* to Duke Filippo Maria in the 1420s,[96] while his son Pier Candido continued in similar vein with his *Vita* of Filippo Maria and his *De Laudibus Mediolanensis Urbis Panegyricus* of c.1435. The former work figures the duke as an ideal prince whose modesty, piety and benevolence won him widespread honour and fame.[97] The latter takes the form of a direct reply to Leonardo Bruni's *Laudatio* and a vehement affirmation of the claim that the rule of the Visconti is 'admired by other princes, venerated by the nobility and adored by the people'.[98] Later in the century, such panegyrics and advice-books became legion, with many of the most celebrated humanists of the age contributing to the debate. Bartolomeo Sacchi (known as Platina) dedicated his *De Principe Viro* to the Duke of Mantua's heir in 1471,[99] while Francesco Patrizi of Siena addressed his *De Regno* to Alfonso of Aragon later in the 1470s.[100] Finally, a group of humanists from the kingdom of Naples issued similar treatises towards the end of the century,[101] including Giuniano Maio, Diomede Carafa, Antonio de Ferrariis and Giovanni Pontano, whose *De Principe* of 1468 is at once a typical and an outstanding example of the genre.[102]

For the most part these mirror-for-princes manuals are simply an outgrowth of the Ciceronian and Petrarchan traditions we have already examined. It is true that some new elements are added, largely in acknowledgement of the increasing stability and self-confidence of princely regimes. One important development arose in connection with the shift of political discussion away from the *piazza* and *palazzo pubblico* towards the more private spaces of the prince's court.[103] We begin to encounter a corresponding awareness of the need to offer counsel not merely to rulers but also – in Pontano's words – 'to those who are nowadays called

---

[95] As Kristeller 1965, pp. 20–68 stresses, the prominence of this genre reflected a general disposition in this period to present moral thinking in the form of advice-books.
[96] Baron 1966, pp. 425–7. [97] Decembrio 1731, pp. 986–1020.
[98] Decembrio 1958, p. 1013: 'te principes mirantur, nobiles verentur, populi concupiscunt'. For the date see Zaccaria 1956, p. 21.
[99] For the dedication see Sacchi 1608, pp. 11–16. For a partial translation see Sacchi 1997. On the relations between this treatise and Sacchi's *De Optimo Cive* see Rubinstein 1985.
[100] For the dedication see Patrizi 1594a, pp. 1–9.
[101] On Naples as a centre of humanism see Bentley 1987.
[102] On Maio see Ricciardi 1968 and for a partial translation of his *De Maiestate* see Maio 1997. For a translation of Pontano's *De Principe* see Pontano 1997.
[103] For a discussion of 'the politics of place' in the *trecento* see Milner 2000.

courtiers'.[104] As early as the 1470s Diomede Carafa produced just such an advice-book, *Dello Optimo Cortesano*, specifically addressed to these new and potentially influential figures in the political landscape.[105] Within a generation the new genre had given rise to a masterpiece, Baldassare Castiglione's *Il Libro del Cortegiano*, drafted in the early years of the new century and first published in 1528.[106]

We also find a related and much-expanded interest in the more ritualistic aspects of princely government. Giuniano Maio's treatise, dedicated to King Ferrante of Naples in 1492, is actually entitled *De Maiestate*, and ends with a chapter on how a ruler should present himself as a suitable figure of grandeur and magnificence.[107] The same is true of Giovanni Pontano's *De Principe*, which includes a detailed discussion of the Ciceronian ideal of *decorum*, offering advice on how a prince should dress, speak and generally comport himself in order to proclaim the majesty of his office to the best effect.[108] We are already close to Machiavelli's assurance in *Il Principe* that rulers can always hope to protect themselves against intrusive questioning if they learn to exploit *la maestà dello stato*, the majesty of their princely state.[109]

For the most part, however, the humanists of the later *quattrocento* sketch a portrait of the ideal prince that scarcely differs from the one offered by Petrarch and his disciples. Such a ruler must aim, as Pontano puts it, 'to uphold peace among his subjects and a well-balanced government'.[110] He must also aspire to the highest goals of princely leadership, remembering that 'fame and majesty go perfectly together' and accordingly seeking 'to rise to greater glory every day'.[111] Nor do these writers differ from the earlier humanists in describing the measures that a ruler needs to adopt if he is to succeed in overcoming the malignity of fortune and thereby scaling the heights of honour, glory and fame. The only sure method, they agree, is to cultivate the quality of *virtus* in the highest degree. This quality, as Pontano proclaims, is the most splendid thing in the world, 'far more splendid even than the sun', for the blind

---

[104] Pontano 1952, p. 1052: 'quique aulici hodie vocantur'.
[105] For the date of composition (1479) see Carafa 1971, p. 64.
[106] Castiglione 1981. On the drafts (1516, 1521) and the date of publication (1528) see Cox 1994, p. xx.
[107] Maio 1956, ch. 19, pp. 223–31. For a translation see Maio 1997. See also Sacchi 1608, I. 12, pp. 68–74 on the *maiestas* of the prince.
[108] Pontano 1952, pp. 1046–8.
[109] Machiavelli 1960, ch. 18, p. 74.
[110] Pontano 1952, p. 1046: 'ad quietem populorum et regni moderationem'.
[111] Pontano 1952, pp. 1060, 1062: 'cum fama maxime constet maiestas... teque in dies magis ad gloriam excites'.

cannot see the sun, 'whereas even they can recognise *virtus* as plainly as possible'.[112]

The account of *virtus* to be found in these writers is again a largely familiar one. The prince is counselled to cultivate various personal virtues, in particular those clustering around the ideal of temperance and centring on such attributes as modesty, continence and affability.[113] But the most important element of *virtus*, the one that (as Pontano states at the outset) 'makes everyone accept a prince's rule with a glad heart when he possesses it', is held to be justice.[114] This attribute Pontano treats in wholly Ciceronian terms. Good princes must always administer something more than strict justice, for they must recognise that 'there are two further qualities that ought above all to be cultivated by those who wish to rule, the first being liberality, the other, clemency'.[115] But they must ensure above all that justice is upheld, and thus that *fides* or good faith is maintained at all times. They must keep faith with God, treating justice in that context as equivalent to piety or righteousness. They must likewise keep their promises to their fellow-men, honouring their word as their bond even when dealing with their enemies.[116]

To summarise, Pontano remarks, we may say that the ideal prince must exercise 'justice, piety, liberality and clemency'. This will ensure him the love of his people; and by winning their love rather than making himself an object of fear he will also ensure his own glory and fame.[117] To put the moral the other way round – as Pontano also does – the goal of princely glory must be reached *virtute non vi*: by the *virtus* of the *vir*, the truly manly man, and never by means of *vis* or sheer brute force. The ideal prince will be a prince of peace, and Pontano ends by assuring us that 'when he is beloved of all, he will not even need to maintain an army, since everyone will want him to live for ever'.[118]

During the second half of the fifteenth century, we find something akin to this literature beginning to burgeon even in the previously

---

[112] Pontano 1952, p. 1044: 'multo ergo splendidior est virtus [quam solem] ... quam etiam caeci apertissime videant'.
[113] For example, Pontano 1952, pp. 1028–32; Maio 1956, pp. 51–60, 143–62 and 163–74; Sacchi 1608, II. X, pp. 141–50 (Contra Avaritiam), II. XIII, pp. 171–9 (De Modestia).
[114] Pontano 1952, p. 1024: 'iustitia enim in quo fuerit, eius imperium aequo omnes animo patiuntur'.
[115] Pontano 1952, p. 1026: 'qui imperare cupiunt, duo sibi proponere in primis debent: unum, ut liberales sint; alterum, ut clementes.'
[116] Pontano 1952, p. 1026: 'multa consideranda sunt, et illud maxime, quo nihil turpius sit quam fidem non servare; cuius tanta vis est, ut etiam hosti, si data sit, servare tamen eam oporteat'.
[117] Pontano 1952, p. 1024.
[118] Pontano 1952, p. 1040: 'quem enim quisque amat, eum si fieri possit vivere perpetuo expetit, nullique minus exercitu opus est'.

inhospitable atmosphere of Florence.[119] With the rise of the Medici to positions of informal but decisive control over the affairs of the republic, a gradual retreat can be observed from the earlier and more stridently republican traditions of Florentine political thought.[120] This is not to say that the republicans went down without a fight. After Cosimo de' Medici's death in 1464, energetic debates in the *Pratiche* bore witness to the continuing efforts of leading citizens to re-establish a more broadly based and genuinely elective form of regime.[121] The debate was renewed once more in 1479, the year before Lorenzo de' Medici set up his new ruling Council of Seventy drawn from the ranks of his own partisans. His increasingly 'tyrannical' policies were subjected to a violent attack by his own erstwhile supporter, Alamanno Rinuccini, whose *De Libertate* contains an eloquent restatement of the traditional Florentine ideal of 'free' government.[122]

For the most part, however, the humanists were content to serve the times, and began to explore new lines of argument designed to fortify and celebrate Florence's increasingly oligarchic regime. This change of outlook first found expression in the form of a growing enthusiasm for markedly *stretto* as opposed to *largo* styles of republican government. In particular, the humanists begin to write in praise of Venice, commending its Dogeship and the aristocratic bias of its constitution, and thereby initiating a powerful movement in favour of reforming Florence's nominally more populist arrangements along Venetian lines.

One of the earliest statements of this point of view can be found in Poggio Bracciolini's *In Laudem Rei Publicae Venetorum*.[123] This appeared in 1459, the year after Cosimo de' Medici succeeded in establishing a new and more restricted ruling council in addition to the much larger assemblies praised in Leonardo Bruni's *Laudatio*. The standpoint Poggio adopts is that of an unashamed oligarch. Suppose, he begins, you wish to maintain a polity 'in which the very best men have charge of civic affairs, in which they are in turn controlled by the laws, and are dedicated above all to the promotion of the public interest, with all private concerns being treated as of secondary importance'.[124] If that is your aim, then

---

[119] On this transition see Hankins 1996, esp. pp. 129–33.
[120] On this transition see Brown 2000.
[121] See Pampaloni 1961, and for the documents relating to the debates of 1465 see Pampaloni 1962. For an earlier instance of such opposition see Cavalcanti 1973.
[122] See Rinuccini 1957 and cf. Varese 1961, pp. 133–48.
[123] For a translation see Bracciolini 1997.
[124] Bracciolini 1964–9c, vol. 2, p. 925: 'apud quos soli optimates civitatem regunt, obtemperantes legibus intentique omnes ad publici status utilitatem, omni rei privatae cura posthabita'.

it is essential to establish an aristocratic form of government. 'And in my judgement', Poggio adds, 'such a government has never been established in practice in the best possible manner except among the people of Venice.'[125]

Poggio goes on to explain that the key to Venice's achievement lies in the fact that the city is ruled 'by many ancient and noble families, into whose hands the entire conduct of the government is placed'.[126] The constitution is such that 'no role is assigned to the body of the people; rather the system is one in which all public offices are entrusted exclusively to persons of outstanding capacities within the ranks of the nobility'.[127] This means that 'no internal discord mars the administration of the city's government, no dissension, no quarrels among the citizens'.[128] As a result, the Venetians have duly reaped the reward of civic glory. 'Not only have they succeeded in conserving their republic, they have also expanded their power by land and sea, day by day, to the point where their fame and *virtus* have become celebrated throughout the whole world.'[129]

Such expressions of admiration for Venice soon became widespread. Poggio's argument received strong endorsement, for example, from Francesco Patrizi's *De Institutione Reipublicae* in the 1460s,[130] as well as from his own son Gianfrancesco's later and very similar eulogy on Venice.[131] During the last quarter of the century, however, these developments were supplemented and even supplanted by an even more striking shift of political allegiances. After Lorenzo de' Medici's accession to power in 1469, a growing number of humanists responded by offering him their direct support. Turning their backs on the concept of the *vita activa civilis*, they reverted to the contention that monarchy must after all be accounted the best form of government, and that this consideration must be given its due weight even in Florence.

The intellectual resources from which the Florentines gained the confidence to repudiate their republican heritage were largely Platonic in

---

[125] Bracciolini 1964–9c, vol. 2, p. 925: 'talem profecto nunquam nisi apud Venetos fuisse verissime affirmarim'.

[126] Bracciolini 1964–9c, vol. 2, p. 929: 'sunt enim familiae perantiquae ac nobiles permultae, in quibus rei publicae gubernatio continetur'.

[127] Bracciolini 1964–9c, vol. 2, p. 929: 'nulli plebeo aditus... solae nobilitati et ex ea viris praestantioribus publica demandantur officia'.

[128] Bracciolini 1964–9c, vol. 2, p. 928: 'nullae inter ipsos administranda re publica discordiae, nulla dissensio, nullae civium contentiones'.

[129] Bracciolini 1964–9c, vol. 2, p. 937: 'Veneti eorum rem publicam non conservarunt solum, sed in dies eorum imperium terra marique auxerunt, ut per universum orbem illorum fama virtusque celebretur.'

[130] Patrizi 1594b, III. 2, pp. 117–19.

[131] For the younger Poggio's eulogy of Venice see Gilbert 1977, p. 493.

character. One of the ways in which Platonism contributed to the destabilising of republican values was by underlining the claim – also put forward in the closing pages of Aristotle's *Nicomachean Ethics* – that the highest and noblest way of life must be one of *otium* or contemplative leisure. Cristoforo Landino's *De Vera Nobilitate* constitutes one of the most revealing documents in this transformation of Florentine humanism. Composed in the 1480s and dedicated to Lorenzo de' Medici,[132] it is couched in the form of a dialogue between Aretophilus, the lover of virtue, and Philotimus, the admirer of the rich. At first they merely rehearse a familiar set of arguments about true nobility. Philotimus defends the position – which he describes as 'that of Aristotle, the prince of philosophers' – according to which 'nobility is a matter of *virtus* in conjunction with ancient lineage and wealth'.[133] Aretophilus retorts that 'the one and only source of true nobility lies in the possession of *virtus*', a quality he equates with the four cardinal virtues.[134] So far there is nothing in the discussion to which Bruni or Poggio could have taken exception. The tone suddenly alters, however, with the introduction of the topic of religious belief.[135] Marsilio Ficino's writings are cited with reverence, and a note of genuine Platonism begins to be audible.[136] The noblest and most praiseworthy way of life, we are now assured, consists in rising above the mundane obligations of the *vita activa* by ascending to the heights of philosophy and finally to the realms of beatitude. Both participants endorse this rejection of *negotium* in favour of the pure life of the mind, and Aretophilus summarises their almost mystical conclusion in tones of suitable intensity. 'This, this I say is the only true nobility: it consists solely in this one excellence of the mind, a form of excellence which is not naturally produced by our own faculties, but is due to the infinite wisdom of God omnipotent himself.'[137]

Landino's treatise gave expression to an outlook shared by growing numbers of humanists in the closing decades of the fifteenth century. We find the same Platonist elements, for example, in Antonio de Ferrariis's *Epistola de Nobilitate* in 1488. For the best-known example, however, we

---

[132] Liaci 1970, p. 17 shows that it must have been completed after 1485 but before 1487.
[133] Landino 1970, p. 47: 'princeps [philosophorum] Aristoteles in antiquitate generis et opibus virtute partis nobilitatem ponit'.
[134] Landino 1970, pp. 67–8: 'virtus enim ... quae vera sit, verae nobilitatis sola atque unica datrix est'. They then discuss *prudentia* (pp. 68–70), *fortitudo* (pp. 70–1), *temperantia* (pp. 71–3) and *iustitia* (pp. 73–4).
[135] For a discussion of Landino's *studia divinitatis* see Trinkaus 1970, vol. 2, pp. 712–21.
[136] Landino 1970, p. 77 cites Ficino 'in suo illo divinissimo *De religione christiana* libro'.
[137] Landino 1970, p. 101: 'haec, haec est, inquam, vera nobilitas, haec unica generositas eius animi, quem non natura ipsa de materiae facultate produxit, sed ipse omnipotens Deus, sapientissimus Deus'.

must turn to Giovanni Pico della Mirandola's *Oratio* of 1486 on the dignity of man, in which we encounter an authentically Platonist scorn for 'those whose whole life is dedicated to the pursuit of profit or ambition' in the public realm.[138] Pico's proudest boast is that 'I myself have given up all interest in private as well as public business in order to devote myself entirely to a life of contemplative *otium*', this being an indispensable condition of all the noblest human pursuits, above all the pursuit of truth.[139]

As well as furnishing a renewed defence of the *vita contemplativa*, Plato's authority enabled Lorenzo's humanist supporters to mount a more direct attack on the participative ideals of Florentine republicanism. This they accomplished by invoking the concept of the philosopher-king, a doctrine Landino ingeniously connects with a further defence of *otium* against the demands of active citizenship in Book 1 of his *Disputationes Camaldulenses* in the early 1470s. If the noblest way of life is one of contemplative retreat, as Landino again affirms, 'the best state of a commonwealth' must be the one in which the citizens feel confident in placing their affairs in the hands of a wise guardian, thereby freeing themselves to pursue their own higher ends. It follows that monarchy must be the best form of government, a monarchy in which a prudent and philosophical ruler – such as Lorenzo himself – carries the burdens of the *vita activa* on behalf of everyone else.[140]

If we turn finally to the treatise *De Legibus et Iudiciis* composed in 1483 by Lorenzo's own chancellor Bartolomeo Scala, we meet with an even more fulsome defence of the despotism of the wise.[141] Scala's treatise takes the form of a debate between himself and Bernardo Machiavelli, the father of Florence's most celebrated writer on statecraft. Scala contends that the nature of government is such that, 'with so many different problems arising from day to day, it is highly desirable to be able to resolve them with a free hand and wide-ranging powers'.[142] The best solution is therefore to recognise that 'it is far better to live under the guidance of a good man and a wise judge than under the kind of dictates that men impose upon themselves'.[143] He ends his speech by coupling his proposal with a dire warning. 'If you fail to put one person in charge of

[138] Pico 1942, p. 132: 'tota eorum vita sit vel in quaestu, vel in ambitione posita'.
[139] Pico 1942, p. 132: 'relicta omni privatarum et publicarum rerum cura, contemplandi ocio totum me tradiderim'.
[140] Landino 1952, pp. 729–31.
[141] Brown 1979, pp. 295–6, 311–14 stresses Scala's Platonism. For a translation see Scala 1997.
[142] Scala 1940, p. 269: 'tot sunt que quotidie emergunt earum diversitates, in quibus merito solutiorem facultatem liberiusque iudicium desideres'.
[143] Scala 1940, p. 269: 'vivi potuit melius ad boni viri bonique iudicis arbitrium ... quam eam sibi imposuisse homines necessitatem'.

the full range of public affairs, there is nothing in the whole list of things that men have learnt to fear and avoid that you will not have cause to dread, expect and contemplate.'[144]

Bernardo Machiavelli counters with a traditional defence of the rule of law, a defence later echoed by his famous son in his *Discorsi* on Livy's history of Rome. 'We see all too frequently', Bernardo replies, 'that evil desires are characteristic of those who serve as leaders of men and have control of affairs in their hands.'[145] The only safe course of action is therefore to place our trust in a structure of laws rather than in the wisdom of a prince, 'this being the only rational way to live our lives'.[146] But Scala repudiates this conclusion outright, thereby turning his back on the most distinctive contribution of Florentine humanism to the political literature of the age. Instead he holds out the image of the wise guardian, the *pater patriae*, as the perfect ruler of Florence, and offers the figure of Cosimo de' Medici as a complete realisation of this Platonic ideal within the recent history of Florentine public life.[147]

V

By the time of Lorenzo de' Medici's death in 1492, an observer might well have concluded that Florentine republicanism, both in theory and practice, was likewise about to expire. Within two years, however, the French invasion of Italy changed everything.[148] The Medici were forced into exile, and under the ascendancy of Savonarola the institutions of the Florentine republic were restored and augmented. The Medici regained power in 1512, but their position at that stage remained far from secure. In 1527 they were obliged to go into exile once more, and it was not until after their return in 1530 that they finally began to convert the Florentine republic into a Medicean principate. During the intervening period, the debate between their supporters and their republican opponents gave rise to a further and extensive literature about the best means of

---

[144] Scala 1940, p. 270: 'si ducem rerum omnium actionumque humanarum neglexeris... nihil est omnino eorum que timere et fugere merito homines consueverunt non formidandum, non expectandum, non ferendum'.
[145] Scala 1940, p. 277: 'quod tamen quia prevalente cupiditate fieri ab his frequentissime videmus, qua presunt hominibus, et habent rerum gubernacula in manibus'.
[146] Scala 1940, p. 277: 'id est unica recte vivendi ratione'.
[147] See Scala 1940 p. 259 on 'Cosimus Medices pater patriae noster sapientissimus civis'. Cf. also Brown 1979, pp. 295–6.
[148] On the re-establishment of the Florentine republic see Butters 1985. On Florentine humanism in the generation after 1492 see Godman 1998. For the constitutional discussions following the *coup* of 1512 see Albertini 1955.

governing Florence. It was a debate in which the venerable issues of liberty *versus* princely rule were yet again rehearsed, but on this occasion with an unexampled brilliance and depth that left an indelible mark on the history of modern political thought.

When the Medici were first restored in 1512, a number of writers at once concluded that Florence would be well advised to accept a framework of princely government. One such writer was Paolo Vettori, who addressed some *Ricordi* on the subject to Cardinal de' Medici at the end of 1512.[149] Another was Lodovico Alamanni, whose *Discorso* of 1516 frankly acknowledges the desirability of stabilising the government of Florence under the Medici, and advises them on how to tighten their grip over the city's affairs.[150] But by far the most prescient observer to adopt this perspective was Niccolò Machiavelli in *Il Principe*, the draft of which he completed at the end of 1513.[151]

Machiavelli's masterpiece was thus conceived as a contribution to a familiar and well-worked genre, that of humanist advice-books for princes on the proper ends of government and how best to attain them. If we turn to Machiavelli's specific suggestions, moreover, we find that these too are at first sight almost equally familiar. The prince's basic aim, we learn in a phrase that echoes throughout *Il Principe*, must be *mantenere lo stato*, to maintain his power and existing frame of government.[152] As well as keeping the peace, however, a true prince must at the same time seek 'to establish such a form of government as will bring honour to himself and benefit the whole body of his subjects'.[153] This explains why Machiavelli admires Ferdinand of Aragon above all other contemporary rulers. His actions have been so great that 'he has become, for fame and glory, the greatest king in all Christendom'.[154] By contrast, this is why he expresses such contempt for Agathocles of Sicily, in spite of his astonishing achievements. His criminal methods 'were such as to win him power but not glory', whereas a true prince will always put honour and glory above everything else.[155]

---

[149] Vettori 1955, pp. 345–7. For a translation see Vettori 1997.
[150] Alamanni 1955, pp. 362–71.
[151] Machiavelli discusses the drafting of his book in a letter to Francesco Vettori of 10 December 1513. See Machiavelli 1961, pp. 301–6 and for a subtle analysis see Najemy 1993, pp. 215–40.
[152] For the importance of a contented populace see Machiavelli 1960, ch. 19, pp. 75–6.
[153] See Machiavelli 1960, ch. 16, pp. 101–2 on the need 'di introdurvi forma che facessi onore a lui e bene alla università delli uomini'.
[154] Machiavelli 1960, ch. 21, p. 89, describes Ferdinand's actions as 'tutte grandissime', such that 'è diventato per fama et per gloria el primo re de' Christiani'.
[155] Machiavelli 1960, ch. 8, p. 42 says of Agathocles's violent methods that 'possono fare acquistare imperio, ma non gloria'.

Turning to the means by which a prince can hope to win power and glory, Machiavelli again discloses his essentially humanist allegiances.[156] He places an overwhelming emphasis on the need for rulers to cultivate the quality of *virtù*. The possession of *virtù* is indispensable in the first place if you wish *mantenere lo stato*, to maintain your princely state. As chapter 6 summarises, 'a new prince will always find it more or less easy to keep himself in power, depending on whether he possesses the qualities of a *virtuoso* in a greater or lesser degree'.[157] The possession of *virtù* is likewise said to be crucial to the yet higher end of achieving princely glory. As the concluding Exhortation to the Medici insists, it is only by being *prudente e virtuoso* that a new ruler can hope 'to act in such a way as to bring honour to himself' and thereby scale the heights of glory and fame.[158]

There are two moments, however, at which Machiavelli dramatically diverges from the normal assumptions of advice-books for princes. As we have seen, the early humanists had often drawn a strong contrast between *virtus* and *vis*, between manly qualities and brutal force. By contrast, Machiavelli treats the willingness to exercise sheer brute force as an absolutely indispensable feature of good princely government.[159] It is entirely due to the neglect of this factor, he insists, that the Italian princes of his own day have found themselves overwhelmed.[160] He even adds, in a moment of dramatic exaggeration, that 'a prince should have no other thought or object, nor should he occupy himself with anything else, than war and its laws and discipline'.[161] His closing Exhortation repeats the same advice. 'Before all else', he instructs the Medici, 'you must raise an army of your own, this being the one foundation for everything else you undertake.'[162]

But what of Cicero's contention in *De Officiis* that a good leader will be distinguished above all by his willing to avoid brute force? As we have seen, Cicero had bequeathed to the humanist the belief that *virtus* is the

---

[156] On the importance of *gloria* throughout Machiavelli's political works see Price 1977.
[157] Machiavelli 1960, ch. 6, p. 30: 'un nuovo principe si truova a mantenerli più o meno difficultà, secondo che più o meno è virtuoso'.
[158] Machiavelli 1960, ch. 26, p. 101 on whether the condition of Italy 'dessi occasione a uno prudente e virtuoso di introdurvi forma che facessi onore a lui'.
[159] A point well brought out in Gilbert 1965, p. 154.
[160] Machiavelli 1960, ch. 24, pp. 97–8.
[161] Machiavelli 1960, ch. 14, p. 62: 'Debbe adunque uno principe non avere altro obietto né altro pensiero, né prendere cosa alcuna per sua arte, fuora della guerra et ordini e disciplina di essa.'
[162] Machiavelli 1960, ch. 26, p. 104: 'è necessario, innanzi a tutte l'altre cose, come vero fondamento di ogni impresa, provvedersi d'arme proprie'.

eponymous quality of the *vir*, and thus that good leaders must always cultivate manly as opposed to beastly qualities, taking care above all to avoid the sheer brutality of the lion and the cunning guile of the fox. Machiavelli retorts that there are indeed two ways of acting, 'one of which is proper to humankind while the other is proper to beasts'.[163] But since we live in a dark world in which no one can be relied upon to behave decently, manliness will never be enough. The ancients understood statecraft much better when they figured the prince as a centaur, half man and half beast. Not only does Machiavelli warn us that 'for a prince it is necessary to have a good understanding of how to use beastly methods'.[164] He also ridicules Cicero's earnest imagery by adding that those who fare best will be those who learn 'to imitate both the fox and the lion'.[165] The moral is underlined in chapter 19, in which Machiavelli discusses one of his favourite historical characters, the Roman emperor Septimius Severus. We are first assured that 'in Severus there were outstanding qualities of *virtù*'.[166] To which Machiavelli adds that Septimius's greatness lay in the fact that 'he well knew how to adopt the character of the fox as well as the lion', as a result of which he was feared and respected by everyone.[167]

The other moment at which Machiavelli challenges the prevailing assumptions of humanism is in explaining what it means to say that *virtù* is indispensable to a ruler's attainment of his goals. He raises the question immediately after his three central chapters on military power, introducing the topic in chapter 15 in a passage specifically calling attention to his own originality. Although it is true, he observes, that many others have discussed how a *virtuoso* prince should behave, his own analysis 'will depart very radically from the rules drawn up by those who have already examined these issues'.[168]

Machiavelli's first departure occurs when he mentions the personal virtues and vices, as opposed to those which help or hinder a ruler in discharging his public role. As we have seen, most earlier humanists had

[163] Machiavelli 1960, ch. 18, p. 72: 'quel primo è proprio dello uomo, quel secondo delle bestie'.
[164] Machiavelli 1960, ch. 18, p. 72: 'Per tanto a uno principe è necessario sapere bene usare la bestia'.
[165] Machiavelli 1960, ch. 18, p. 72: 'pigliare la golpe et il leone'. On anti-Ciceronian satire in *Il Principe* see Colish 1978 and Skinner 1981, pp. 39–40.
[166] Machiavelli 1960, ch. 19, p. 80: 'in Severo fu tanta virtù'.
[167] Machiavelli 1960, ch. 19, p. 80: 'bene seppe usare la persona della golpe e del lione'.
[168] Machiavelli 1960, ch. 15, p. 65: 'partendomi, massime nel disputare questa materia, dalli ordini delli altri'. For the fullest recent analysis of the resulting theory of princely virtue see Diesner 1985.

addressed themselves to this topic in stern and even puritanical tones. They had called on good princes to exhibit an exemplary standard of personal morality, and in particular to cultivate such qualities as sobriety, continence and affability. For Machiavelli, by contrast, the only question is whether a lack of these amiable attributes is likely to have the effect of undermining a prince's government. If not, then a wise prince, he suggests, 'ought to guard himself against such vices if he can, but if he finds that he cannot, then he should continue to indulge in them without giving the matter another thought'.[169]

Far more radical is the way in which Machiavelli targets the assumption lying at the heart of the entire humanist tradition of advice-books for princes. As we have seen, they had always insisted that the key to maintaining one's state and rising to the heights of princely glory lies in following as strictly as possible the dictates of justice. Machiavelli begins by recalling the usual humanist analysis of the elements that go to make up this cardinal virtue. He considers in turn liberality (chapter 16), clemency (chapter 17), the associated need to be loved rather than feared (chapter 17) and finally the paramount need to keep faith and honour one's word (chapter 18). He acknowledges that 'it would be a most admirable thing if a ruler could display all these qualities'.[170] But he vehemently rejects the fundamental humanist belief that these are the qualities a ruler must be sure to cultivate if he wishes to attain his highest ends. On the contrary, Machiavelli retorts, we must face the fact that 'because there is such a great distance between how people live and how they ought to live, anyone who gives up doing what people in general do in favour of doing what they ought to do will find that he ruins rather than preserves himself'.[171]

Machiavelli's main advice to princes is to reconsider the traditional image of just government in the light of this melancholy truth. You will then be forced, he insists, to acknowledge a number of hard truths that humanists seek to evade. One is that princes will always have good reasons to avoid the supposed virtue of liberality.[172] A second is that 'you

---

[169] Machiavelli 1960, ch. 15, p. 66: 'guardarsi, si elli è possibile; ma, non possendo, vi si può con meno respetto lasciare andare'.

[170] Machiavelli 1960, ch. 15, p. 65: 'che sarebbe laudabilissima cosa uno principe trovarsi di tutte le soprascritte qualità'.

[171] Machiavelli 1960, ch. 15, p. 65: 'perché elli è tanto discosto da come si vive a come si doverrebbe vivere, che colui che lascia quello che si fa per quello che si doverebbe fare, impara più tosta la ruina che la preservazione sua'.

[172] Machiavelli 1960, ch. 16, p. 68.

cannot escape being called cruel', especially if you are a new prince.¹⁷³ A third is that, whatever Cicero may say to the contrary, 'it is much safer for a prince to be feared than to be loved'.¹⁷⁴ And finally, it is necessary to place a question-mark against the supposed virtue of *fides*, the virtue that princes had always been urged to treat as the foundation of justice and to cultivate above all. The problem with this advice, Machiavelli replies, is that 'we see from experience in our own times that those princes who have done great things have been those who have set little store by the keeping of faith'.¹⁷⁵ The qualities he is recommending, he confesses, may indeed be vices, 'but they are vices by which you are able to rule'.¹⁷⁶

The truly *virtuoso* prince can therefore be recognised, according to Machiavelli, neither by his willingness to follow the traditional requirements of good government at all times, nor by his readiness (as in the case of Agathocles) to discount those requirements altogether.¹⁷⁷ Rather a truly *virtuoso* prince will be characterised by an unerring sense of when to acknowledge the dictates of justice and when to ignore them. He will be guided, in short, by necessity rather than by justice. A wise prince 'never departs from the ways of good government as long as he is able to follow them, but he knows how to enter upon the paths of wickedness whenever this is dictated by necessity'.¹⁷⁸

What is revolutionary about Machiavelli's *Il Principe* is thus that it offers, in effect, a new analysis of what should count as *virtuoso* behaviour in a prince. Machiavelli agrees that the term denotes those qualities which enable a prince to overcome the vagaries of fortune and to rise to honour, glory and fame.¹⁷⁹ But he denies that the qualities in question can in turn be equated with the traditional list of the princely virtues. A prince of true *virtù* will rather be someone who, in the proverbial phrase, makes a virtue of necessity. He will be ready at all times 'to turn and turn about as the winds and variations of fortune dictate'.¹⁸⁰

---

[173] Machiavelli 1960, ch. 17, p. 69: 'al principe nuovo è impossibile fuggire el nome di crudele'.
[174] Machiavelli 1960, ch. 17, p. 69: 'è molto più sicuro essere temuto che amato'.
[175] Machiavelli 1960, ch. 18, p. 72: 'si vede per esperienza, ne' nostri tempi, quelli principi avere fatto gran cose che della fède hanno tenuto poco conto'.
[176] Machiavelli 1960, ch. 16, p. 67: 'vizii che lo fanno regnare'.
[177] See Machiavelli 1960, ch. 8, pp. 42, explaining why Agathocles, who acquired and held power by criminal methods ('per scelera') cannot be accounted a *virtuoso* prince.
[178] Machiavelli 1960, ch. 18, p. 74: 'non partirsi dal bene, potendo, ma sapere intrare nel male, necessitato'.
[179] For a discussion of Machiavelli's view of *fortuna* see Flanagan 1972, but for a critique of this way of relating *fortuna* to *virtù* see Newell 1987.
[180] Machiavelli 1960, ch. 18, pp. 73–4: 'E però bisogna che elli abbi uno animo disposto a volgersi secondo ch' e' venti e le variazioni della fortuna li comandono.'

148 Visions of Politics: Renaissance Virtues

VI

Although many Florentine political writers felt ready to endorse the rule of the Medici after 1512, the same period also witnessed the last and finest flowering of the city's earlier traditions of republican thought.[181] Among those who continued to urge the republican cause, the majority agreed that Florence ought now to settle for an aristocratic or *stretto* form of mixed constitution, the form that Poggio had earlier commended in his panegyric on Venice.[182] The continuation of this strand of thought – now deployed to question rather than support the Medicean government – can be seen in many treatises of the period, including Antonio Brucioli's *Dialoghi* of 1526 and Pietro Vergerio's *De Republica Veneta* of the same year.[183] The culmination of this line of argument may be said to come with Donato Giannotti's *Della Repubblica di Veneziani*, published in 1540, in which the long-standing admiration of Florentine political theorists for Venice as an ideal republic is most fully expressed.[184]

Of all the Florentine theorists who continued to take Venice as their model, by far the most important was Francesco Guicciardini. His numerous political writings between 1512 and 1530 are united by a desire to see a restoration of the Florentine republic, together with a reformation of its institutions along Venetian lines. The point is first made in his treatise *Del Modo di Ordinare il Governo Popolare* of 1512. There Guicciardini argues that the basic weakness of the *largo* constitution established in Florence after the removal of the Medici in 1494 arose from an exaggerated polarity between its monarchical and populist elements. His proposed solution is the introduction of a senate of some two hundred *ottimati*, an institution designed to restore the balance between the two extremes in the approved Venetian style.[185] The same argument is later developed at greater length in his *Dialogo del Reggimento di Firenze* of the early 1520s, in which the constitution of Venice is praised in even more fulsome terms.[186] It is 'the best and most beautiful form of government

[181] For a detailed survey of republican political writings in this period see Silvano 1985. On the connections between the Florentine crisis and Machiavelli's political works see Guarini 1990.
[182] Gilbert 1977, pp. 234–6, 495 shows that, during the period of *largo* republican government established in Florence after 1494, the claim that Venice's more *stretto* system offered a superior model was kept alive by a group of disgruntled *ottimati* led by Bernardo Rucellai, whose *De Bello Italico* includes a eulogy of the Venetian constitution.
[183] For a discussion of these and kindred works see Gilbert 1977, pp. 204–5.
[184] For this treatise, drafted in 1526–7, see Gilbert 1977, pp. 204–11 and Skinner 1978a, pp. 140–1, 155, 172.
[185] See Guicciardini 1932, pp. 218–59 and the classic discussion in Pocock 1975, pp. 219–71.
[186] According to Brown 1994, p. x, the *Dialogo* was begun in 1521 and completed in 1524.

that has ever been seen, not merely in our own times, but in any city of the ancient world, since the elements of every type of regime – that of the one, the few and the many – are all embodied within it'.[187]

Against this chorus of admiration, however, one powerful and dissentient voice was raised. The voice was that of Niccolò Machiavelli in his *Discorsi* on the first ten books of Livy's history of Rome.[188] Turning sharply away from his impulsive endorsement of princely government, Machiavelli proceeded to devote the years between 1515 and 1519[189] to the development of a passionate, almost nostalgic restatement of the republican case. The assumptions and vocabulary of the *Discorsi* look back not merely to the republicanism of Leonardo Bruni and his followers a century earlier.[190] They also look back to the ideology of the communes we examined in chapter 2, thereby offering a brilliant restatement of a number of age-old questions about the values of elective and self-governing systems of rule.[191]

Machiavelli is still concerned in the *Discorsi* with the preservation of security and the attainment of glory and greatness. But the ideal of *grandezza* he now holds out is no longer a matter of great deeds performed by individual princes. His primary concern is with the distinctively republican ideal of civic glory and *grandezza*, a topic on which he speaks with fervent emphasis. He initially announces this commitment in the opening chapter of Book 1. First he turns to consider those cities which were originally founded by their own citizens 'without having any particular prince to direct them'.[192] Among these, he observes, both Athens and Venice can be numbered, 'both of which managed to rise from these small beginnings to the *grandezza* they now enjoy'.[193] Next he considers the contrasting case of cities originally founded by princes. 'Due to the fact that such cities do not have free beginnings', he argues, 'it very seldom happens that they are able to rise to greatness.'[194] Not only does Machiavelli announce

---

[187] Guicciardini 1932, pp. 138–9: 'è il più bello ed el migliore governo non solo de' tempi nostri, ma ancora che forse avessi mai a' tempi antichi alcuna città, perche participa di tutte le spezie de' governi, di uno, di pochi e di molti'.
[188] See Gilbert 1977, p. 203 on Machiavelli's hostility to Venice and cf. Pocock 1975, p. 186 for the claim that Machiavelli's *Discorsi* 'are best interpreted as a systematic dissent from the Venetian paradigm'.
[189] For this dating see Baron 1961.
[190] A linkage luminously traced in Baron 1966, pp. 428–9.
[191] On Machiavelli's place in this tradition see Viroli 1992, pp. 11–177.
[192] Machiavelli 1960, I. 1, p. 126: 'sanza altro principe particulare che gli ordinasse'.
[193] Machiavelli 1960, I. 1, p. 126: 'talché ogni piccolo principio li poté fare venire a quella grandezza nella quale sono'.
[194] Machiavelli 1960, I. 1, p. 126: 'E per non avere queste cittadi la loro origine libera, rade volte occorre che le facciano progressi grandi.'

the theme of *grandezza* at the outset, but he also hints at a link between *grandezza* and *libertà*, thereby introducing what proves to be one of his principal themes.

Turning next to the case of ancient Rome, Machiavelli repeatedly makes it clear that for him the basic question is how the early republic managed to rise to such unparalleled heights. The question recurs throughout Book 1, in the course of which Machiavelli discusses the Roman republican constitution. He constantly asks himself what features of the constitution enabled the republic 'to come to its ultimate *grandezza*',[195] 'to arrive at the *grandezza* it acquired'.[196] The question recurs even more prominently in Book 2, in which Machiavelli analyses Rome's military policies. Here he primarily devotes himself to considering what techniques of warfare enabled the Romans 'to attain *grandezza*'[197] or, more imposingly, 'to help themselves on the way towards supreme *grandezza*'.[198] The theme remains no less pervasive in Book 3, the principal aim of which is 'to show how much the actions of individual men contributed to make Rome great and brought about in that city so many good effects'.[199]

When Machiavelli turns to ask how civic greatness is attained, he again reveals himself a true heir of the long-standing republican traditions of the *Regnum Italicum*. The clearest evidence of these allegiances can be seen in the crucial passage at the start of Book 2 in which he considers the root cause of civic glory and greatness. His argument takes the form of a paraphrase (though without acknowledgement) of the endlessly quoted passage from the start of Sallust's *Bellum Catilinae* in which Rome's greatness had been explained as a fruit of her free way of life. 'Experience shows', as Machiavelli claims in echoing the argument, 'that cities have never been able to increase either in power or in wealth except while they have been able to sustain themselves in a state of liberty.'[200] To which he adds with studied understatement that 'this makes it easy to understand how it comes about that all peoples feel so much affection for living such a free way of life'.[201]

---

[195] Machiavelli 1960, I. 20, p. 185: 'venire a quella sua ultima grandezza'.
[196] Machiavelli 1960, I. 6, p. 143: 'venire a quella grandezza dove ei pervenne'.
[197] See Machiavelli 1960, II. 13, p. 312, speaking of 'i modi necessari a venire a grandezza'.
[198] Machiavelli 1960, II. 6, p. 294: 'per facilitarsi la via a venire a una suprema grandezza'.
[199] Machiavelli 1960, III. 1, pp. 383–4: 'dimostrare a qualunque quanto le azioni degli uomini particulari facessono grande Roma e causassino in quella città molti buoni effetti'.
[200] Machiavelli 1960, II. 2, p. 280: 'Si vede per esperienza le cittadi non avere mai ampliato né di dominio né di ricchezza se non mentre sono state in libertà.'
[201] Machiavelli 1960, II. 2, p. 280: 'E facil cosa è conoscere donde nasca ne' popoli questa affezione del vivere libero.'

Explaining what he means by predicating liberty of entire communities, Machiavelli again discloses the closeness of his links with his republican heritage. As he makes plain in the opening chapters of Book 1, he means that the body politic in question enjoys the capacity to act in pursuit of its own chosen ends, its actions being 'under the control of its own will' and in consequence directed to seeking the benefit of its members as a whole.[202] For a body politic no less than a natural body, the life of liberty is a life not lived in subjection to the will of anyone else.

The next question to ask is what type of regime is best suited to upholding liberty and thereby bringing greatness. Machiavelli admits that there is no reason in principle why a good prince should not frame his laws in such a way as to reflect the general will (and so promote the common good) of a body politic as a whole.[203] But the truth is that 'most of the time, the things that benefit a prince harm his city, while the things that benefit the city harm the prince'.[204] It follows that, to ensure liberty and promote greatness, the wisest course of action will always be to maintain an elective and self-governing form of republican government. 'What brings greatness to cities is not individual benefits but the pursuit of the common good, and there can be no doubt that it is only in republics that this ideal of the common good is properly recognised.'[205]

As Machiavelli repeatedly affirms in Book 1, the reason why the highest praise must always be accorded to the founders of cities and states is that such lawgivers never fail to recognise that the common good must be placed above all other values. Romulus's greatness as the founder of Rome stemmed from the fact that 'everything he did was done for the common good and not for personal advantage'.[206] The same perception guided the leading citizens of Rome whose achievements are celebrated in Book 3. Fabius, Manlius, Camillus and the others are continually singled out for their willingness to help Rome along the path to glory by acting 'entirely in favour of the public' and by placing 'the public welfare' and 'the public benefit' above all other goods.[207]

---

[202] See Machiavelli 1960, I. 2, p. 129 for the opening distinction between cities living 'in servitù' and those 'governate per loro arbitrio'.

[203] See Machiavelli 1960, I. 9, p. 154 for the claim that Romulus's *ordini* had this effect.

[204] Machiavelli 1960, II. 2, p. 280: 'Il più delle volte quello che fa per lui [il principe] offende la città, e quello che fa per la città offende lui.'

[205] Machiavelli 1960, II. 2, p. 280: 'non il bene particulare ma il bene comune è quello che fa grandi le città. E sanza dubbio questo bene comune non e osservato se non nelle republiche.'

[206] Machiavelli 1960, I. 9, p. 154: 'quello che fece fusse per il bene comune e non per ambizione propria'.

[207] See Machiavelli 1960, III. 23, p. 452 on Manlius acting 'tutto...in favore del publico'; III. 30, p. 467 on Camillus acting 'ad utile publico'; III. 47, p. 502 on Fabius acting 'per beneficio publico'.

This analysis is corroborated by Machiavelli's account of what it means to be a corrupt citizen. To suffer from the fatal vice of *corruzione* is to place one's own ambitions or party advantage above the common good. It is one of Machiavelli's firmest beliefs that to act in this way is invariably lethal to the cause of civic liberty and greatness. As he explains early in Book 1, it is always private or factional forces 'that ruin a free way of life'.[208] The claim is underlined in the discussion of the Decemviri later in Book 1. 'It is when the people cannot agree to make a law in favour of liberty, but instead form parties that turn to support some particular leader, that tyranny at once rises up.'[209] The same moral is drawn from the account of the fall of the Roman republic in Book 3. 'Sulla and Marius managed to find troops willing to follow them in actions contrary to the common good, and it was by these means that Caesar was able to place his country in subjection.'[210]

The republican writers of the *quattrocento* had never doubted these sentiments. But they had never ceased to argue with each other about what particular type of republican regime is best adapted to staving off corruption and ensuring the pursuit of the common good. As we have seen, Leonardo Bruni's view and that of his followers had been that the ruling councils of such a republic should include both the *grandi* and the *popolo*. But the view prevailing among Machiavelli's contemporaries was that, in order to combine liberty with civic peace, the leading share in government should be confined to the most prominent citizens.

Here too Machiavelli reverts to the more traditional standpoint. He cites the fashionable belief that the act of placing any authority 'in the disorderly hands of the common people will always be a cause of infinite dissensions and scandals in a republic'.[211] He describes the *stretto* Venetian system, and mentions the widespread opinion that 'it is because of placing the government in the hands of the nobility' that the ideal of liberty 'has been given a longer life in Venice than it enjoyed in Rome'.[212] Alone of his contemporaries, however, he is adamant in responding that the Roman system is nevertheless to be preferred in any city aiming at glory

---

[208] Machiavelli 1960, I. 7, p. 147: 'forze private... che sono quelle che rovinano il vivere libero'.
[209] Machiavelli 1960, I. 40, p. 227: 'E quando e' non convengano a fare una legge in favore della libertà, ma gettasi qualcuna delle parti a favorire uno, allora è che subito la tirannide surge.'
[210] Machiavelli 1960, III. 25, p. 456: 'Silla a Mario peterono trovare soldati che contro al bene publico gli seguitassono; per questo Cesare potette occupare la patria.'
[211] Machiavelli 1960, I. 5, p. 139: 'una qualità di autorità dagli animi inquieti della plebe, che è cagione d'infinite dissensioni e scandoli [sic] in una republica'.
[212] Machiavelli 1960, I. 5, p. 139: '[appresso de' Viniziani], la è stata messa nelle mani de' Nobili', giving 'la libertà di... Vinegia [sic] più lunga vita che quelle di Roma'.

Republican virtues in an age of princes 153

and greatness. 'It is always reasonable to expect', he maintains, 'that when the common people are set up as guardians of their own liberty, they will take better care of it' than will the nobility.[213]

But what of the long-standing objection that such a *largo* form of republicanism will prove incapable of combining freedom with civic harmony? As we saw in chapter 2, the earliest protagonists of the communes denied that the city-republics were any less well-ordered than princely regimes, a contention so far from the truth that their systems of elective government soon became widely discredited. By contrast, Machiavelli meets the objection with an argument that astonished his contemporaries.[214] He freely admits that 'if you produce a numerous and well-armed populace in the name of attaining greatness of power, you are sure to find them unmanageable'.[215] But he insists that, unless you produce such a populace, you will have no hope of attaining civic greatness at all. He thereby commits himself to the apparently paradoxical conclusion that it was actually 'due to the disunion between the Plebs and the Senate', and the repeated turmoil to which this gave rise, that Rome 'managed to become a perfect republic'.[216]

Machiavelli resolves the paradox in Book I chapter 4. Those who condemn Rome's tumults 'are failing to recognise that there are two contrasting outlooks in every republic, that of the leading men and that of the ordinary citizens, and that all the laws made in favour of liberty are born of the disunity between them'.[217] As a result, these critics 'appear to me to be complaining about the very things that were the primary cause of Rome's maintaining her freedom'.[218] They are 'concentrating on the clamour and outcry that arose from her tumults' when they ought to be reflecting 'on the splendid consequences to which they gave rise'.[219] These consequences, as Machiavelli's chapter-heading explains, were that 'the disunion between the Plebs and the Senate in Rome enabled that

---

[213] Machiavelli 1960, I. 5, p. 139: 'i popolari preposti a guardia d'una libertà, e ragionevole ne abbiano più cura'.
[214] For a good example of their reaction see Guicciardini 1965, p. 68.
[215] Machiavelli 1960, I. 6, p. 144: 'Pertanto se tu vuoi fare uno populo numeroso ed armato, per poter fare un grande imperio, lo fai di qualità che tu non lo puoi dopo maneggiare a tuo modo.'
[216] Machiavelli 1960, I. 2, p. 135: it was 'per la disunione della Plebe e del Senato' that Rome 'feca una republica perfetta'.
[217] Machiavelli 1960, I. 4, p. 137: 'non considerino, come e' sono in ogni republica due umori diversi, quello del popolo et quello de' grandi; e come tutte le leggi che si fanno in favore della libertà, nascano dalla disunione loro'.
[218] Machiavelli 1960, I. 4, p. 137: 'mi pare che biasimino quelle cose che furono prima causa del tenere libera Roma'.
[219] Machiavelli 1960, I. 4, p. 137: 'che considerino più a romori ed alle grida che di tali tumulti nascevano, che a' buoni effetti che quelli partorivano'.

republic to become free and attain greatness'.[220] Machiavelli's solution, in short, is to accept that broadly-based republics will lack for serenity, while recognising that this is something to be endured rather than reformed. As he puts it in his favourite tone of studied understatement, Rome's continual domestic unrest was undoubtedly 'an inconvenience' but 'it was an inconvenience indispensable to the attainment of Roman greatness'.[221]

When Machiavelli turns to explain how a polity of this nature can best be sustained, he again reveals the closeness of his ties with traditional republican arguments. What is above all required is that the citizen-body should possess the quality of *virtù* in the highest degree. This quality, we subsequently learn, may be said to embody three principal elements. The citizens must be prudent in all matters of war and peace, knowing how to judge the best courses of action and follow them out.[222] They must be courageous in defence of their liberty, the form of virtue required to fight off 'external servitude'.[223] And they must remain 'well-ordered' in the disposition of their civic affairs, ensuring that the business of government is conducted *ordinariamente*, in an orderly and well-tempered style.[224]

For all the closeness of these links between the *Discorsi* and earlier traditions of republicanism, however, there can be no doubt that one of Machiavelli's principal aims is to question and subvert these inherited patterns of thought. The first moment at which this becomes evident – as in *Il Principe* – is when he asks himself what should count as truly *virtuoso* behaviour. As we have just observed, he agrees that the term *virtù* names those attributes that enable citizens to help uphold the liberty and greatness of their native community. He also agrees that these attributes overlap to a considerable degree with the traditional list of the cardinal virtues, including as they do the need for prudence, courage and temperance. As in *Il Principe*, however, he flatly repudiates the further assumption that the most important aspect of civic *virtù* is justice, the virtue that consists in avoiding both cruelty and the ignominy that attends the breaking of faith:

---

[220] Machiavelli 1960, I. 4, p. 136: 'Che la disunione della Plebe e del Senato romano fece libera e potente quella republica.'

[221] Machiavelli 1960, I. 6, p. 146: 'uno inconveniente necessario a pervenire alla romana grandezza'.

[222] For the indispensability of prudence in government see Machiavelli 1960, I. 49, pp. 241–4; in warfare see II. 10, II. 14 and II. 27, pp. 302, 314, 362.

[223] On courage as an attribute of great military commanders see Machiavelli 1960, III. 25, p. 458. On the need for courage in each individual soldier see III. 36–7, pp. 484, 487.

[224] See Machiavelli 1960, I. 7, I. 23–4, I. 49, pp. 146–9, 188–92, 241–4.

The point that deserves to be noted and carried into practice by any citizen who finds himself advising his community is this: whenever what is at issue is the basic security of the community, no consideration should be given to questions of justice or injustice, clemency or cruelty, praiseworthiness or ignominy; rather, setting every other feature of the situation aside, you must be prepared to follow whatever course of action will in fact save the life and preserve the liberty of the community as a whole.[225]

As in *Il Principe*, the touchstone is necessity: it will always prove necessary to be courageous, temperate and prudent; but it will sometimes prove necessary to be unjust.

This is one of the lessons that Romulus is praised for having fearlessly taken to heart. When you act to promote the common good, you always run the risk 'that this will sometimes turn out to the disadvantage of one or another private individual'.[226] It follows that, if the common good is genuinely your goal, you must be prepared to abandon the ideal of justice. This is what Romulus recognised when he killed his own brother in the name of securing the future of Rome. Cicero had reacted with horror to this event in *De Officiis*, denouncing Romulus for a crime in which 'he forgot both his piety and humanity'.[227] But Machiavelli retorts that Romulus did well to recognise that 'when the effect is good, as it was in his case, this will always serve to excuse whatever was done'.[228] Machiavelli prefers to reserve his condemnation for Piero Soderini, the leader of the Florentine republic during his own lifetime. Soderini failed to grasp that 'one must at no point allow an evil to continue out of regard for a good when the good can easily be overwhelmed by the evil'.[229] Refusing to do evil that good might come of it, he brought ruin on the republic as well as himself.

The other juncture at which Machiavelli differs profoundly from earlier traditions of republicanism is in considering how the elements of *virtù* can best be enshrined in civic life. Leonardo Bruni and his followers had

---

[225] Machiavelli 1960, III. 41, p. 495: 'La quale cosa merita di essere notata ed osservata da qualunque cittadino si truova a consigliare la patria sua: perché dove si delibera al tutto della salute della patria, non vi debbe cadere alcuna considerazione né di giusto né d'ingiusto, né di piatoso né di crudele, né di laudabile né d'ignominioso; anzi, posposto ogni altro rispetto, seguire al tutto quel partito che le salvi la vita e mantenghile la libertà.'
[226] Machiavelli 1960, II. 2, p. 280: 'quantunque e' torni in danno di questo o di quello privato'.
[227] Cicero 1913, III. X. 41, p. 308: 'Omisit hic et pietatem et humanitatem.'
[228] Machiavelli 1960, I. 9, pp. 153–4: 'quando sia buono [viz., lo effetto] come quello di Romolo, sempre lo scuserà'. For a discussion of the literature on Romulus's fratricide see Berns 2000, pp. 39–70.
[229] Machiavelli 1960, III. 3, p. 387: 'non si debbe mai lasciare scorrere un male rispetto ad uno bene, quando quel bene facilmente possa essere da quel male oppressato'.

tended to be optimistic, even complacent, at this point in the argument. Bruni had regarded it as obvious that the Florentines are by nature prudent, and can be relied upon to display courage in defence of their liberty and a sense of orderliness in the conduct of their affairs. Machiavelli, by contrast, is deeply pessimistic about human nature. He believes that 'all men are evil, and will always act out the wickedness in their hearts whenever they are given free scope'.[230] He also believes that Christianity has made things worse by encouraging people to behave selfishly, instructing them to concentrate on their own glory in the life hereafter instead of their city's glory and greatness here and now, 'an attitude which has weakened the world and left it a prey to wicked men'.[231] To this problem he sees only one solution. If evil and self-interested citizens are to act with *virtù* and serve the common good, they will have to be forced to do so by the coercive powers of the law. 'So we may say that, just as hunger and poverty make men industrious, it is the laws that make them good.'[232]

For Machiavelli, accordingly, there remains one further and profound question of statecraft, a question to which much of Book I of the *Discorsi* is addressed. By means of what specific *leggi e ordini* can we hope to offset our natural corruption and enforce the rule of *virtù* in public life?

First Machiavelli considers the nature of the constitutional laws required to ensure an orderly and well-tempered government. The solution he proposes looks at first glance familiar enough: he places all his faith in a mixed constitution with a bicameral legislature. Because of his pessimistic view of human nature, however, he is led to present his argument in a revolutionary way. His is not the Aristotelian ideal of combining the different social elements together in such a way as to produce the most harmonious mixture. On the contrary, he assumes that 'in every polity there will be two opposed outlooks, that of the people and that of the nobility', and that each of these groups will at all times seek to promote its own advantage unless restrained.[233] The course of wisdom is accordingly to take account of these ineradicable hatreds and devise a constitution that will turn these private vices into public benefits. This is

---

[230] According to Machiavelli 1960, I. 3, p. 135 a lawgiver must 'presupporre tutti gli uomini rei, e che li abbiano sempre a usare la malignità dello animo loro qualunque volta ne abbiano libera occasione'.

[231] Machiavelli 1960, II. 2, p. 282: 'Questo modo di vivere adunque pare che abbi renduto il mondo debole, e datolo un preda agli uomini scelerati.'

[232] Machiavelli 1960, I. III, p. 136: 'Però si dice che la fama e la povertà fa gli uomini industriosi, e le leggi gli fanno buoni.'

[233] Machiavelli 1960, I. 4, p. 137: 'sono in ogni republica due umori diversi, quello del popolo e quello de' grandi'.

what the Romans succeeded in doing when they gave the nobles control of the senate while assigning the tribunate to the plebs. Each faction was able to keep watch over the other and prevent it from legislating purely in its own interests. The result was that 'all the laws made in favour of liberty resulted from the discord between them'.[234] Due to the force of law, a community of unsurpassed *virtù* was forged out of a tense equilibrium set up between two basically corrupt and self-interested groups. This in turn had the effect of preserving a system of liberty which, in the absence of such *ordini*, the rival factions would have undermined.

Machiavelli next tackles the even harder question of how to persuade naturally self-interested citizens to act with courage in defence of their communal liberty, even at the risk of losing their own lives. The best way to conjure up this further element of *virtù*, he suggests, is to manipulate the *ordini* relating to religion, and above all to insist – as the Romans always did – on the absolute sanctity of oaths.[235] Among the many illustrations Machiavelli offers of how this policy worked, he particularly singles out the behaviour of the Roman people after their defeat by Hannibal at Cannae. 'Many citizens gathered together who, despairing of their native land, agreed to abandon Italy and go to Sicily. Hearing of this, Scipio went to find them and, with a drawn sword in his hand, forced them to swear an oath not to abandon their native land.'[236] Taking the oath did not of course abate the people's terror; but it made them more frightened of evading their duties than of performing them, since it made them fear above all to break their promise to the gods. The result was that, being forced to act with a courage they would never have commanded of themselves, they stood their ground, eventually defeated Hannibal and thereby secured, by their enforced *virtù*, the liberty they had been ready to give up.

VII

For all its theoretical distinction, the last phase of Florentine republicanism had no immediate practical effects. After 1530 the Medici went on their travels no more, and by 1569 the Florentine republic had mutated

---

[234] Machiavelli 1960, I. 4, p. 137: 'tutte le leggi che si fanno in favore della libertà, nascano dalla disunione loro'.

[235] But for a reappraisal of this apparently functional view of religion see Colish 1999, which includes an exceptionally full survey of the scholarly literature.

[236] Machiavelli 1960, I. 11, p. 160: 'molti cittadini si erano adunati insieme, e sbigottiti della patria si erano convenuti abbandonare la Italia e girsene in Sicilia; il che sentendo Scipione gli andò a trovare, e col ferro ignudo in mano li constrinse a giurare di non abbandonare la patria'.

into the Grand Duchy of Tuscany. This is not to say, however, that the celebration of mixed constitutions came to an end. Venice survived as a republic, and managed to keep alive the theory of republican liberty even in the age of the Counter Reformation and beyond.[237] Among the many writers who, in the wake of Gasparo Contarini's classic analysis, continued to expatiate on the glories of the *serenissima*, the most important was Paolo Paruta in his *Discorsi Politici* of 1599. Paruta discusses the republic of ancient Rome in the first of his two discourses, that of modern Venice in the second. He traces the process by which the Romans lost their freedom with the coming of the empire, a decline he contrasts in the opening chapter of his second book with the unparalleled success of his own native city in combining greatness with liberty. As with his predecessors, he finds the key to this achievement in the Venetian constitution, all the parts of which are said to be so well disposed that the common good is invariably served.[238]

By the time Paruta was writing, however, the preoccupations of Italian political theory had largely shifted to accommodate the rise of absolutism, with the result that the printing presses were virtually monopolised by the contrasting genre of advice-books for princes. For the most part, these latter-day contributions to an already vast literature content themselves with examining the same range of issues that earlier writers had debated in the heyday of humanism. In some respects, however, they are very much the products of their own age. They make a determined effort to come to terms with Machiavelli's arguments, in strong contrast with the howls of execration that initially greeted the publication of his works in northern Europe. Francesco Guicciardini at once picks up the suggestion that there may be reasons for political action which form no part of ordinary moral reasoning, and is one of the earliest theorists to speak explicitly of 'reasons of state'.[239] By the end of the century, we find the same phrase being used as the title of dozens of political treatises in which a Machiavellian conception of prudence is elevated to a high place among the political virtues, the most important being Giovanni Botero's *Ragione di Stato* of 1589.[240]

The other distinctive development of the same period is a melancholy one, and serves to mark the end of the active contribution of Italian

---

[237] For this theme see Bouwsma 1968.
[238] Paruta 1852, vol. 2, p. 228: 'in Venezia, la forma e l'ordine del governo civile è in ogni parte ben disposto'.
[239] See Church 1972, p. 46; Maffei 1964, pp. 712-20.
[240] On this literature see Meinecke 1957, pp. 65, 116. On the transition from the *vivere libero* to *ragione di stato* see Viroli 1992, pp. 178-200, 238-80.

humanism to the political literature of the Renaissance. It takes the form of an increasing, eventually overwhelming, pessimism about the capacity of even the highest *virtù* to overcome the malignity of fortune.[241] We already encounter this tone of anxiety in Machiavelli's *Discorsi*.[242] We hear it more loudly in Guicciardini's *Ricordi*,[243] while in the writings of such mid-century sceptics as Nicolò Franco and Francesco Doni we find it used to cast doubt on the possibility of effective citizenship.[244] By the time we come to a work like Traiano Boccalini's *Ragguagli di Parnaso* in 1613, we encounter a tone of blank despair. The entire age stands condemned as one in which *virtù* can scarcely be recognised, and even when recognised can no longer be pursued.[245]

[241] On the relations between fate, fortune and freedom see Poppi 1988.
[242] See Machiavelli 1960, II. 17, pp. 322–8, the notorious chapter on artillery.
[243] Guicciardini 1945, no. 30, p. 15 and no. 189, p. 61. On the still deeper pessimism of Guicciardini's later *Storia d'Italia* see Gilbert 1965, pp. 288, 299.
[244] Grendler 1969, pp. 75–96.
[245] See Boccalini 1948, I. 39, vol. 1, pp. 326–8 on Machiavelli as a cause of the prevailing corruption of the age.

6

Machiavelli on virtù *and the maintenance of liberty*

I

James Harrington, meditating on the idea of a free state in his *Commonwealth of Oceana* in 1656, begins by suggesting that the theory and practice of government can be divided into two distinct historical periods.[1] The first was initiated 'by God himself in the fabric of the commonwealth of Israel', and was 'afterward picked out of his footsteps in nature and unanimously followed by the Greeks and the Romans'. This gave rise to the era of 'ancient prudence', an era in which the concept of political authority was analysed in terms of civic liberty and equality. Later, however, there followed a long and melancholy decline into the age of modern prudence, an age inaugurated by Julius Caesar when he overthrew 'the liberty of Rome' and thereby 'opened up a pathway to the barbarians', who eventually 'deformed the whole face of the world' with their 'ill features of government'.

A determined effort has been made, Harrington goes on, to eradicate the features of ancient prudence from modern political thought. The leader of this destructive movement has been Thomas Hobbes, whose *Leviathan* Harrington treats as the greatest monument to gothic barbarism in the entire literature on the art of government. Fortunately, however, there has been one modern commentator who has shown himself a 'learned disciple' of the Roman theorists, and has managed to preserve the fabric of ancient prudence in the face of modern vandalism. This heroic figure is Niccolò Machiavelli, 'the only politician' of later ages, whose *Discorsi* on Livy's history constitute, according to Harrington, the one significant attempt by a modern political philosopher to retrieve and elaborate a classical theory of liberty.

This chapter is a much revised version of an article that originally appeared under the title 'Machiavelli on the Maintenance of Liberty' in *Politics*, 18 (1983), pp. 3–15.

[1] All quotations in the opening two paragraphs come from Harrington 1977, p. 161.

These observations from the opening of Harrington's *Oceana* seem well worth developing, and my principal aim in what follows will be to enlarge on them. First of all, it is I think correct to suggest that there is a danger – far greater now than when Harrington was writing – that we may have lost touch with one fruitful way of thinking about the concept of political liberty. It also remains plausible to suggest that this may be due in part to the continuing influence of Thomas Hobbes and other 'gothic' theorists of freedom and government. Not only did they succeed in discrediting the very different way of thinking about law and liberty characteristic of Renaissance political theory, but their impact has remained astonishingly pervasive. If we turn, for example, to such leading contemporary theorists as John Rawls, Robert Nozick and their endless disciples, we encounter a self-conscious attempt to revive and extend the same gothic vision of politics. The vision is one in which liberty is a natural right, the antonym of liberty is coercion, and the maximising of liberty is seen as the chief (perhaps the sole) duty of enlightened governments.[2]

There is also much to be said for Harrington's further suggestion as to how we might profit from reflecting on earlier and contrasting ways of thinking about these issues. As he proposes, we can hardly do better than focus on the political theory of the Renaissance, and in particular on Machiavelli's analysis of liberty in his *Discorsi*.[3] I have already attempted in chapter 5 to sketch the intellectual context out of which Machiavelli's *Discorsi* arose. As I tried to show, one of his principal aims was to restore, revise and develop a traditional defence of communal forms of 'free' government. I now wish in the present chapter and in chapter 7 to examine in greater detail Machiavelli's theory of freedom itself, and at the same time to contrast it with the very different and arguably more blinkered understanding of the concept to be found in contemporary liberal thought.[4]

II

If we ask how we can hope to maintain our freedom as members of civil associations, contemporary exponents of gothic politics tend to respond

[2] For John Rawls's characterisation of his own theory as one that 'generalises and carries to a higher level of abstraction the traditional conception of the social contract' see Rawls 1971, p. 3. For Robert Nozick's invocations of the same tradition, especially as represented by John Locke, see Nozick 1974, pp. 9, 10–12.
[3] This suggestion is also pursued in the valuable discussion in Ivison 1997, pp. 52–78.
[4] For a similar contrast between liberal and civic humanist conceptions of freedom, centring on Locke's presentation of the case, see Tully 1993, pp. 315–23.

by echoing and endorsing the classical assumption that the task is not merely one of paramount importance but also of exceptional difficulty. The deep gulf that separates gothic from classical and especially neo-Roman theories of government begins to appear only when we turn to their rival explanations of what makes it so difficult to ensure that freedom is safely preserved.

Contemporary exponents of the gothic approach are generally content to repeat the answer put forward by Hobbes in *Leviathan*. Consider, for example, the account given by John Rawls in *A Theory of Justice*. When Rawls asks what makes our liberty such a fragile commodity, he explicitly announces his agreement with what he calls 'Hobbes's thesis', the thesis that the ineliminable threat to our freedom arises from our natural selfishness. As rational egoists, Rawls concedes, all of us have 'an inclination to self-interest', a disposition to increase our freedom of action as far as possible, even at the expense of others.[5] But it is obvious that, if each of us seeks to act in this fashion, we shall soon find ourselves encroaching upon and interfering with the liberty of others. The fact of limited altruism is thus held to set the basic problem for the theory of justice.

For a neo-Roman theorist like Machiavelli, the problem is more complicated. He agrees that the majority of citizens in any polity can safely be assumed to have it as their fundamental desire to lead as free a way of life as possible. It is true, he admits, that among the *grandi* 'we instead see a great desire to dominate others'.[6] But among the generality of people we usually find that 'their sole desire is not to be dominated, as a result of which their principal wish is to live freely', pursuing their own ends so far as possible without insecurity or unnecessary interference.[7] They want, in particular, to be able to enjoy 'the common benefit of a free way of life'.[8] They want to live without fear, to bring up their family without anxiety for their honour or welfare, and to be in a position 'freely to possess their property without distrust'.[9] These are the benefits that enable us to recognise and rejoice in the fact that we 'have been born in freedom and not as slaves'.[10]

Machiavelli's further claim, however, is that there is no possibility of our being able to attain these ends unless we live in a community of

[5] Rawls 1971, pp. 3–5, 239–40.
[6] Machiavelli 1960, I. 5, p. 139: 'si vedrà in quelli [nobili] desiderio grande di dominare'.
[7] Machiavelli 1960, I. 5, p. 139: 'sol desiderio di non essere dominati, e per conseguente maggiore volontà di vivere liberi'.
[8] Machiavelli 1960, I. XVI, p. 174: 'quella comune utilità ... del vivere libero'.
[9] Machiavelli 1960, I. XVI, p. 174: 'di potere godere liberamente le cose sue sanza alcuno sospetto'.
[10] Machiavelli 1960, II. 2, p. 284: 'che nascono liberi e non schiavi'.

which it can already be said that it enjoys *uno vivere libero*, a free way of life. Our community must be based on free institutions in which all of us as citizens participate. It must be kept entirely free from subjection to the will of any particular individual or group. To cite Machiavelli's way of putting the point, it must be free from any *dependenza* or *servitù*, whether imposed by a conqueror in the form of 'external servitude'[11] or by a tyrant who arises from within the community's own political system.[12]

Machiavelli's basic claim is thus that, if we wish to prevent our government from falling into the hands of tyrannical individuals or groups, we must organise it in such a way that it remains in the hands of the citizen-body as a whole. It is only if everyone remains willing to place their talents at the disposal of the community that the *bene commune*, the common good or public interest, can be upheld and factional interests controlled. And it is only if this happens that the personal liberty of each individual citizen can in turn be secured.[13] In the classical oxymoron that Machiavelli is restating, freedom is a form of service, since devotion to public service is held to be a necessary condition of maintaining personal liberty. As we saw in chapter 2, it was Sallust who provided the moralists and historians of the Renaissance with their main authority for insisting on this general truth. As he had stressed in a much-quoted passage from the start of the *Bellum Catilinae*, if we wish to maximise our freedom to live without anxiety or interference, we must first turn ourselves into wholehearted servants of the public good.[14]

Machiavelli's way of summarising these claims is to say that *libertà*, both personal and public, can only be maintained if the citizen-body as a whole displays the quality of *virtù*. The possession of *virtù* is in turn equated with a willingness 'to follow to the uttermost whatever course of action' – whether conventionally virtuous or not – 'will in fact save the life and preserve the liberty of one's native land'.[15] But therein lies the rub. For the sad truth, as Machiavelli repeatedly insists, is that most of us are not naturally *virtuoso*. On the contrary, most citizens are corrupt, by which Machiavelli means that their basic inclination, if left

---

[11] Machiavelli 1960, II. 2, pp. 279–80.
[12] Machiavelli 1960, I. 16, pp. 173–6 and I. 35, pp. 212–13.
[13] Machiavelli 1960, III. 8, pp. 413–16 and III. 41, pp. 494–5. Cf. Cadoni 1962, pp. 479–80 and Skinner 1981, pp. 53–73. For a recent exposition stressing this aspect of Machiavelli's work see Talamo 1997, esp. 93–101.
[14] The passage almost invariably invoked is Sallust 1931a, VI. 5, p. 12 and X–XI, pp. 18–22.
[15] Machiavelli 1960, III. 41, p. 495: 'seguire al tutto quel partito che le salvi la vita e mantenghile la libertà [della patria]'. For a full analysis of Machiavelli's uses of the term *virtù* see Price 1973.

unchecked, will be to place their own private interests above the public good.¹⁶ There are two contrasting ways, Machiavelli goes on, in which this threat of *corruzione*, this negation of *virtù*, tends to arise. The ordinary run of citizens are prone to be *ozioso*, to be lazy or inactive, as a result of which they often fail to devote any energies to their civic obligations at all.¹⁷ Even more dangerous to liberty, however, is the tendency for leading citizens to be moved by *ambizione*, personal ambitiousness. This prompts them to pervert the free institutions of their community in such a way as to favour their own family or social group, whereas they ought as *virtuosi* citizens to be upholding the interests of the community as a whole.¹⁸

For Machiavelli, accordingly, the fundamental threat to freedom is not simply posed by the fact of human selfishness. The problem is rather that, in pursuing our self-interested desires, we are prone at the same time to be self-deceived. We are prone to entertain false beliefs about the best means of attaining our desired goals, including the goal of maintaining our liberty. If we are *oziosi*, we tend to think of a free way of life as one in which there are no calls on our time and we are able to act as we please. If we suffer from *ambizione*, we instead tend to think that the best way of getting what we want will be to reshape the institutions of our community to serve our own ends. To act in either of these ways is to forget that, whenever we corruptly permit or pursue such policies hostile to the common good, we begin to subvert the free institutions of our community, and hence our own personal liberty at the same time. The paradox with which we have to reckon, as Machiavelli repeatedly reminds us, is that 'the people, deceived by a false image of the good, very often will their own ruin'.¹⁹

For a neo-Roman theorist such as Machiavelli, the problem of how to maintain our freedom in the face of our limited altruism accordingly seems more complicated than it does to a modern gothic theorist of liberty. For the latter, the dilemma is resolved as soon as we discover a fair means of regulating the tendency of self-interested individuals to threaten the freedom of others. It is assumed, that is, that the fundamental problem in the theory of liberty – and indeed in the theory of the state – is simply that of devising the best means of adjudicating between

---

¹⁶ For Machiavelli's most extended discussion of *corruzione* see Machiavelli 1960, I. 17–18, pp. 177–83. For a fuller account of *corruzione* as the negation of *virtù* see Skinner 1978a, pp. 163–7, 178–9.
¹⁷ Machiavelli 1960, I. 1, pp. 128–9 and II. 2, pp. 282–3.
¹⁸ Machiavelli 1960, I. 33, pp. 206–9; I. 37, pp. 215–18; I. 40, pp. 224–9.
¹⁹ Machiavelli 1960, I. 53, p. 249: 'il popolo molte volte ingannato da una falsa immagine di bene desidera la rovina sua'.

competing rational egoists. The problem is solved when each person is able to enjoy an equal right to the most extensive system of basic liberties compatible with a like system of liberty for all.[20] For a neo-Roman theorist, by contrast, the further problem is that of finding some means of transmuting our natural but self-destructive tendency to *corruzione* into a *virtuoso* concern for the common good. If this transmutation is rendered impossible by our incorrigible *ozio* or *ambizione*, the problem then becomes that of devising some mechanism for preventing these inescapably corrupt motives from having their natural but self-destructive effects. The deepest secret of psychology and statecraft is to understand how these acts of alchemy can be performed.

Machiavelli begins by asking how these self-destructive tendencies arise. What causes us to behave corruptly? He answers with a recurrent visual metaphor: we are easily blinded to the nature of our own best interests. This impairment of moral vision is capable of afflicting even the most *virtuosi* citizens. Quintus Fabius, one of the Decemvirs in early republican Rome, 'was an outstanding man, but became blinded by a little *ambizione* and changed from being a man of good behaviour into the very worst'.[21] So too with Manlius Capitolinus, who began as a great leader of the early republic but 'fell into such blindness of mind as a result of his envy of Camillus that he tried to raise a revolt in Rome'.[22] The danger is even more likely to be incurred by the rank-and-file of citizens. The ordinary people are always prone 'to be blinded by an appearance of false good'.[23] As Julius Caesar cunningly discovered, 'it is possible to blind the multitude so completely that they fail even to notice the yoke they are placing around their own neck'.[24]

It is perhaps worth underlining the general shape of Machiavelli's argument at this juncture. It is often supposed that, if we say of someone that there is a reason for them to act in a certain way, even though they are not motivated so to act, we must be committing ourselves to one of two arguments. We must either be positing a 'higher self' with different and more rational motives,[25] or else implying that there are certain purposes

---

[20] Here I allude to the 'final statement' of John Rawls's 'first principle' of justice. See Rawls 1971, p. 302.
[21] Machiavelli 1960, I. XLII, p. 230: 'Quinto Fabio...uomo ottimo, accecato da uno poco d'ambizione...mutò i suoi buoni costumi in pessimi.'
[22] Machiavelli 1960, III. 8, p. 414: 'per la invidia che lui aveva...a Cammillo; e venne in tanta cecità di mente, che...si misse a fare tumulti in Roma'.
[23] Machiavelli 1960, III. 28, p. 464: 'essere accecato...da una spezie di falso bene'.
[24] Machiavelli 1960, I. 17, p. 178: 'potette accecare quella moltitudine ch'ella non conobbe il giogo che da se medesima si metteva in sul collo.'
[25] See, for example, Berlin 1969, pp. 132–4, 151 and note.

which it is objectively rational for all agents to pursue.[26] It is then held to follow that our only means of coming to see that there is indeed a reason for us to act which differs from any of our current motives will be by finding some means of attuning ourselves to these objective reasons or to our higher self.

It is arguable that, if there are determinate human needs, there must be objective reasons of this character. And it is certainly true that, in a theory of liberty such as Kant's — which bears certain resemblances to Machiavelli's — we find their existence powerfully defended.[27] As we shall see, however, Machiavelli's own view of the matter occupies a middle ground between the two poles of this long-standing argument. By contrast with the assumption of much later philosophers like David Hume that 'reason is and ought only to be the slave of the passions', Machiavelli contends that there can be genuine reasons for action which are unconnected with any of our present desires. But by contrast with Kant's criticism of Hume, Machiavelli shows that it is possible to defend this position without having recourse, even implicitly, to the idea of objective reasons or higher selves.

To understand how Machiavelli arrives at this position, we need to begin by asking why he believes that we are so readily blinded to our own true interests. He principally focuses on the fact that political leaders are often so corrupt and ambitious that they deliberately mislead the people about the right courses of action to follow in order to attain their desired ends. The success of Appius Claudius in putting himself forward as leader of the Decemvirs is offered as an exemplary instance of this general truth. His actions show that even a *virtuoso* people can be totally blinded and thus deceived by an unscrupulous leader into enslaving themselves.[28] But the most shameless case is said to be that of Julius Caesar, against whom we are warned not to be deceived by his glory or the flattery of later ages.[29] Caesar provides the best example of how 'the powerful have proposed laws not in favour of public liberty but for their own power, with the result that the people have either been deceived or forced to decree their own ruin'.[30]

What makes it so easy for corrupt leaders to deceive and betray the people? Machiavelli first points to the capacity of great men to dazzle us

---

[26] For this assumption see, for example, Hollis 1979, pp. 1–15.
[27] For a contemporary analysis of this character, partly indebted to Kant, see Nagel 1970, pp. 13–17. Cf. also the discussion of 'real interests' in Geuss 1981, pp. 45–54.
[28] Machiavelli 1960, I. 35, p. 213.   [29] Machiavelli 1960, I. 10, pp. 156–9.
[30] Machiavelli 1960, I. 18, p. 181: 'i potenti proponevano leggi, non per la comune libertà ma per la potenza loro, ... talché il popolo veniva o ingannato o sforzato a diliberare la sua rovina'.

with their greatness, thereby preventing us from seeing – until it is too late – that they may be misusing their gifts in order to seize power for themselves. The problem is outlined in general terms in the discussion of dangerous citizens in Book 1 chapter 33:

> When in a republic a young noble of exceptional *virtù* rises up, the citizens all begin to turn their eyes towards him and to agree without any suspicion to honour him. The result is that, if he has any spark of *ambizione*, this mixture of the favours of nature with his situation will quickly bring him to a position in which, when the citizens recognise the mistake they have made, there are almost no remedies left to them.[31]

Machiavelli cites several cases in which this happened in ancient Rome, including that of Horatius as well as Julius Caesar.[32] But his chief example comes from much closer at hand:

> Cosimo de' Medici, who initiated the *grandezza* of the house of Medici in our own city, attained such a reputation by virtue of his own prudence and the ignorance of the other citizens that he began to alarm the government, so much so that other citizens judged it dangerous to offend him and even more dangerous to let him continue.[33]

The insidious rise of the Medici and their destructive impact on the traditional institutions of the Florentine republic are never far from Machiavelli's mind.

The most effective means, however, for political leaders to dazzle and mislead the people is through the corrupt use of their wealth. Sometimes the *grandi* may be so rich that they can employ their fortunes not merely to purchase loyalty but even to build up private armies.[34] Less spectacularly, but scarcely less effectively, the rich are always in a position to prevent people from seeing that their liberty is in jeopardy by bribing them to look the other way. Bribery, Machiavelli thinks, is in fact the most frequent cause of corruption in public life. He offers many instances of this depressing truth throughout the *Discorsi*, as well as discussing the

---

[31] Machiavelli 1960, I. 33, p. 207: 'se in una republica si vede surgere uno giovane nobile, quale abbia in se virtù istraordinaria, tutti gli occhi de' cittadini si cominciono a voltare verso lui e concorrere sanza alcuno rispetto a onorarlo: in modo che se in quello è punto d'ambizione, accozzati i favori che gli dà la natura e questo accidente, viene subito in luogo che quando i cittadini si avveggono dello errore loro, hanno pochi rimedi'.
[32] Machiavelli 1960, I. 24, pp. 191–2 and I. 33, pp. 206–9.
[33] Machiavelli 1960, I. 33, p. 207: 'Cosimo de' Medici, dal quale la casa de' Medici in la nostra città ebbe il principio della sua grandezza, venne in tanta riputazione col favore che gli dette la sua prudenza e la ignoranza degli altri cittadini, che ei cominciò a fare paura allo stato, in modo che gli altri cittadini giudicavano l'offenderlo pericoloso, ed il lasciarlo stare cosí, pericolosissimo.'
[34] Machiavelli 1960, I. 55, pp. 254–8.

problem in general terms in several chapters of Book 1.[35] Among the many cases he discusses, one of the most instructive is said to be that of Spurius Cassius in early republican Rome:

> This Spurius, being *ambizioso* and wishing to seize unlawful authority in Rome, spoke to the people and offered them money taken from the grain imported by the government from Sicily. They utterly refused it, believing that Spurius wished to give them the price of their liberty. But if the people had been corrupt, they would not have refused this bribe, and would thereby have opened up the road to tyranny which they closed.[36]

A still more shocking example – shocking because it was successful even in a period of great civic *virtù* – is that of the Decemvirs under Appius Claudius. Returning to their positions of absolute authority for a second year, they began to create a party for themselves by condemning prominent citizens, confiscating their property and giving it away to young members of the nobility. Machiavelli refers us to Livy's solemn judgement on the inevitable outcome: 'corrupted by these bribes, the young men preferred licence for themselves instead of liberty for all' and thereby destroyed the freedom of the city and its citizens at the same time.[37]

The dilemma posed by the prevalence of *corruzione* can now be summarised. On the one hand, there are good reasons for all of us to subordinate our private ambitions to the common good. Nor are these reasons 'external' to the boundaries of our present selves.[38] We are certainly capable of reflecting on the relationship between our current motives and our desired ends with enough clearsightedness to perceive that any tendency to behave corruptly must be eradicated if we are to avoid behaving in self-destructive as well as anti-social ways. But on the other hand, the vices of *ambizione* and avarice are very deeply rooted in human nature. As a result, it will always be difficult, perhaps impossible, to recollect our own patterns of motivation with sufficient tranquillity to prevent ourselves from falling into self-deception, or from being blinded into acting against our own best interests.

---

[35] On 'bribery and corruption' see Machiavelli 1960, I. 35, pp. 212–13; I. 46, pp. 235–6; I. 52, pp. 246–7.

[36] Machiavelli 1960, III. 8, pp. 413–14: 'Il quale Spurio, essendo uomo ambizioso e volendo pigliare autorità istraordinaria in Roma... parlando egli al popolo, ed offerendo di darli quelli danari che si erano ritratti dei grani che il publico aveva fatti venire di Sicilia, al tutto gli recusò, parendo a quello che Spurio volessi dare loro il prezzo della loro libertà. Ma se tale popolo fusse stato corrotto non arebbe recusato detto prezzo, e gli arebbe aperta alla tirannide quella via che gli chiuse.'

[37] Machiavelli 1960, I. 40, p. 226, quoting Livy III. XXXVII. 8: 'Quibus donis iuventus corrumpebatur, et malebat licentiam suam quam omnium libertatem.'

[38] For this way of putting the point see Nagel 1970, p. 7 and note.

This being so, we are brought back to the questions that need above all to be answered if the value of liberty is to be upheld. How is such *corruzione* to be overcome? How can we hope to reform our naturally self-interested patterns of behaviour in such a way as to avoid undermining our own as well as other people's liberty? If such a change in human nature is impossible, what can be done? Can we nevertheless hope to evolve some mechanism for preventing our incorrigible corruption from having its destructive – and self-destructive – effects?

III

One of Machiavelli's beliefs is that the solution to the problem of *corruzione* lies to some extent outside the boundaries of statecraft. We can never hope to overcome the forces of corruption unless we happen to enjoy a large measure of good fortune. Just as he contends in *Il Principe* that all great leaders are to some degree indebted for their ascendancy to the favourable attentions of the goddess Fortuna, so he affirms in the *Discorsi* that no community has the least hope of avoiding *corruzione* – and hence of assuring its *libertà* – unless it happens to be blessed with two large and wholly gratuitous pieces of luck. He begins by arguing – in the opening chapters of Book 1 – that the first stroke of fortune any city needs to enjoy is that of starting life in the hands of a great founding father, a leader and lawgiver of outstanding *virtù* to whom as a daughter the community may be said to owe its birth.[39] Later he goes on to insist – this being the principal theme of Book 3 – that although this element of good fortune is necessary, it is by no means sufficient to enable a city to attain greatness. It is also necessary that the community should be lucky enough to acquire a succession of later leaders in whom the natural tendency of mankind towards *corruzione* is similarly and almost miraculously replaced by a *virtuoso* commitment to the promotion of the public good.

Machiavelli strongly disagrees, however, with those who argue that the rise to greatness of any city is entirely a matter of luck, and he opens Book 3 by castigating Plutarch for propagating this calumny in the case of ancient Rome.[40] Machiavelli replies that the process is, at least to some degree, susceptible to *ragione* and thus to the elaboration of rules. His remaining task is accordingly that of giving an account of such guidelines as he believes can be formulated for the defence of liberty against its enemies.

[39] On this *prima fortuna* see Machiavelli 1960, I. 2, pp. 129–35; on the city as a *figliuola* see I. 11, p. 260.
[40] Machiavelli 1960, III. 1, p. 275.

One possibility is that our natural tendency to behave corruptly can perhaps be successfully transcended.[41] Perhaps we can manage to reach out, if not to a higher self, at least to a heightened state of selfhood. Perhaps we can aspire to that condition which Machiavelli sometimes seems to attribute to the citizens of early republican Rome. 'The love of their country was more potent in the whole body of the citizens than any other consideration',[42] so that 'they remained enemies for four hundred years to the name of kings and lovers of the glory and the common good of their native land'.[43]

One way in which we can perhaps be raised to this condition of naturally *virtuoso* citizenship is by means of the right education. It is hardly surprising to find Machiavelli putting forward this suggestion, since he lived in – and wrote for – an intellectual community in which it was widely believed that, in Erasmus's phrase, 'people are not born but made'.[44] The political treatises of Machiavelli's humanist contemporaries were often couched – as in the case of Erasmus himself – in the form of pedagogic handbooks, outlining the type of instruction best suited to instilling in political leaders a *virtuoso* desire to serve the common good.[45] Nor does Machiavelli question the conventional wisdom at this point. He declares at the start of Book 2 that 'when I think how it could have arisen that people in ancient times were greater lovers of *libertà* than nowadays, I conclude that the cause must have been the difference between the education given in antiquity and in the present age'.[46] He returns to the argument at the end of Book 3, claiming that 'the feebleness of the men of the present age is caused by the feebleness of their education'[47] and reminding us that the impressions we receive in our tender years tend to regulate our behaviour for the rest of our lives.[48]

---

[41] This element in Machiavelli's argument seems to me underestimated even in the best discussions of his views about liberty. See, for example, Colish 1971, p. 347, who in discussing 'the means of instituting *libertà*' confines her attention to the coercive effects of law.
[42] Machiavelli 1960, III. 8, p. 415: 'in tutti loro considerarono poté più lo amore della patria che alcuno altro rispetto'.
[43] Machiavelli 1960, I. 58, p. 264: 'essere stato per quattrocento anni inimico del nome regio, e amatore della gloria e del ben commune della sua patria'.
[44] For this phrase and its place in Erasmus's views about education see Skinner 1978a, pp. 241–3.
[45] See Erasmus 1997, esp. pp. 9–16, 61–5.
[46] Machiavelli 1960, II. 2, p. 282: 'Pensando dunque donde possa nascere che in quegli tempi antichi i popoli fossero più amatori della libertà che in questi, credo nasca da . . . la diversità della educazione nostra dall' antica.'
[47] Machiavelli 1960, III. 27, p. 461: 'la debolezza de' presenti uomini [e] causata dalla debole educazione loro'.
[48] Machiavelli 1960, III. 46, p. 501. But for a fuller and partly contrasting analysis see Pocock 1975, pp. 195–6.

Despite his endorsement of these commonplaces, Machiavelli appears uncertain about the value of this particular argument. He has little to say about the relationship between education and the promotion of *virtù*, and nothing at all about the specific training that might be expected to provide the best preparation for a life of citizenship. He instead devotes far more of his attention to a second possibility, the possibility that a body of citizens may be capable of transcending their natural selfishness if they are inspired by the example of truly *virtuoso* leadership. The working out of this line of thought occupies much of Book 3 of the *Discorsi*, the chief aim of which, as Machiavelli explains at the outset, 'is to show everyone how far the actions of individual men brought greatness to Rome and caused in that city so many good effects'.[49]

One way in which great leaders are capable of inducing deeds of *virtù* among their followers is by the sheer force of their example. Machiavelli puts forward this suggestion at the start of Book 3, and he subsequently illustrates it at considerable length. The reason, he argues, why any type of civil association can always be reformed 'simply by the *virtù* of a single man' is that 'these figures enjoy such a reputation, and furnish such a great example, that good men want to imitate them, while the wicked are ashamed to live a different way of life'.[50] The austere and demanding figure of Manlius Torquatus provides the best exemplification of this general truth. He acted at all times for the benefit of the community, without any regard for personal ambition, and thereby demonstrated that it is possible to reanimate the ancient *virtù* of a republic simply by means of exemplary deeds.[51]

As before, however, Machiavelli seems unwilling to place much weight on this argument. As he makes clear, the arrival on the political scene of a truly *virtuoso* leader is always a gift of fortune, and accordingly constitutes an unreliable means of promoting *virtù* in the citizen body as a whole. He concedes that, if a republic were fortunate enough to produce a continuous supply of leaders of Manlius's quality, the effect would not merely be to keep it from falling into ruin but would actually make it everlasting.[52] But he also points out that, even under the Roman republic, the stream of such *virtuosi* leaders eventually dried up. There were no further examples after Marcus Regulus in the middle of the third century, after

---

[49] Machiavelli 1960, III, 1, pp. 383-4: 'dimostrare a qualunque quanto le azioni degli uomini particulari facessono grande Roma e causassino in quella città molti buoni effetti'.

[50] Machiavelli 1960, III. 1, p. 382: 'questo ritiramento delle republiche [e possibile] dalla semplice virtù d'un uomo... nondimanco sono di tale riputazione e di tanto esempio che gli uomini buoni disiderano imitarle, e gli cattivi si vergognano a tenere vita contraria a quelle'.

[51] Machiavelli 1960, III. 22, pp. 448-54.   [52] Machiavelli 1960, III. 22, p. 450.

which corruption began to increase.[53] Machiavelli's final word on the subject accordingly takes the form of a warning against treating the idea of an everlasting commonwealth with any seriousness. We must never forget – and the goddess Fortuna's caprice is there to remind us – that 'we can never establish a perpetual republic, since its ruin will come in a thousand unexpected ways'.[54]

There is one further possibility that Machiavelli explores in asking whether it is possible to inspire large bodies of people to rise above their ingrained selfishness. He considers whether it may be possible to do so by manipulating their religious beliefs. One of the first general claims he makes about Roman religion in the sequence of chapters he devotes to this topic in Book I is that King Numa, Romulus's immediate successor, understood perfectly how religion can be 'well used' in this way. In particular, he appreciated the value of exploiting popular superstitions about portents and auguries, as a result of which 'the religion introduced by Numa was one of the prime causes of the happy success of the city of Rome'.[55]

A portent or augury, Machiavelli goes on to explain, is an alleged sign that the gods desire you to perform a certain action and will reward you if you perform it. The aim must therefore be to exploit this belief. It is not important that the people's leaders should give any credence to these signs themselves. Rather, Machiavelli implies, they will be in a stronger position to manipulate such superstitions if they do not share them at all.[56] All that matters is that ordinary people – especially if called on to fight a battle – should go into action believing that the gods are on their side. This will inspire them to fight with a preternatural degree of *virtù*, and this will in turn be very likely to win them the day, simply because 'such confidence is the primary cause of every victory'.[57]

Once again, however, Machiavelli seems uncertain about the strength of this argument, or at least about its relevance in Christian societies. Although he mentions a number of cases in which the Romans were dramatically successful in the manipulation of auguries,[58] he concedes at the same time that Christianity is much less susceptible to being 'well used' in this way.[59] Striking a wryer note, he adds that in any case Numa

[53] Machiavelli 1960, III. 1, p. 382.
[54] Machiavelli 1960, III. 17, p. 439: 'è impossibile ordinare una republica perpetua, perché per mille inopinate vie si causa la sua rovina'.
[55] Machiavelli 1960, I. 11, p. 162: 'la religione introdotta da Numa fu intra le prime cagioni della felicità di quella città [di Roma]'.
[56] Machiavelli 1960, I. 12, p. 164.
[57] Machiavelli 1960, III. 33, p. 476: 'la quale cosa [sc. la confidenza] è prima cagione d'ogni vittoria'.
[58] Machiavelli 1960, I. 13, pp. 167–9.   [59] Machiavelli 1960, I. 12, pp. 163–6.

had an easier time of it. This was because 'those ages were filled with religion, and the people with whom he had to deal were coarse and ignorant, which made it very easy for him to follow out his designs, imposing on them any new arrangement he wanted'.[60]

As Machiavelli's tone throughout the above discussion suggests, he is pessimistic about the prospect of changing human nature, of transforming our natural selfishness into a willing and *virtuoso* concern for the common good. He prefers to take people as they are, and to recognise that in general they are corrupt. He puts the point with memorable vehemence at the beginning of Book 1 chapter 3:

> As everyone who has written about the *vivere civile* has shown, and as every work of history is full of examples to attest, it is necessary for anyone who establishes a *republica* and ordains its laws to presuppose that all men are wicked, and that they will always act according to the malignity in their hearts whenever they are given free scope.[61]

Given that this is the most realistic axiom from which to work, the problem of how to uphold our liberty in the face of our own egoism remains to be solved. If we cannot hope to transcend our selfish desires, it becomes a matter of even greater urgency to discover how to curb and bridle them, so that our self-interested behaviour can somehow be prevented from having its natural but self-destructive effects.

IV

Accepting, as he generally does, that we cannot be expected to forswear our foolish ways, Machiavelli's basic proposal about how to contain our natural tendency to *corruzione* appears at first sight a familiar one. He places all his trust in the coercive power of the law to act as a guardian of our liberty. It is obvious, he assumes, 'that it is possible to make men better and less *ambiziosi* by fear of punishment', and it is this consideration that enables the law to preserve our liberty.[62] 'It is always possible for lawgivers in republics or kingdoms to bridle human appetites by taking

---

[60] Machiavelli 1960, I. 11, p. 162: 'che l'essere quelli tempi pieni di religione, a quegli uomini con i quali egli aveva a travagliare grossi, gli dettono facilità grande a conseguire i disegni suoi, potendo imprimere in loro facilmente qualunque nuova forma'.
[61] Machiavelli 1960, I. 3, p. 135: 'Come dimostrano tutti coloro che ragionano del vivere civile, e come ne è piena di esempli ogni istoria, è necessario a chi dispone una republica ed ordinare leggi in quella, presuppore tutti gli uomini rei, e che li abbiano sempre a usare le malignità dello animo qualunque volta ne abbiano libera occasione.'
[62] Machiavelli 1960, I. 29, p. 200: 'mantenendosi per paura di punizione gli uomini migliori e meno ambiziosi'.

away any hope of breaking the law with impunity.'[63] The indispensable role of the law is thus to deter us from *corruzione* and impose on us the necessity of behaving as *virtuosi* citizens by making it less tempting to follow our natural tendency to pursue our own interests at the expense of the common good. 'Hence it is said', as Machiavelli rhetorically concludes, 'that hunger and poverty make men industrious, while the laws make them good.'[64] He summarises once again at the end of Book I in terms that remind us of Rousseau's profound admiration for the *Discorsi*. 'The people', he declares, 'must be chained by the laws' if a free way of life is to last for any length of time.[65]

The best illustration of the law's capacity to maximise public (and hence personal) liberty is said to be provided by the constitution of the republic of ancient Rome. When Machiavelli begins by asking himself at the start of Book I how Rome 'managed to prevent herself over so many centuries from becoming corrupt', he answers by pointing to 'the many necessities that were forced upon her by the laws made by Romulus, Numa and the rest'.[66] From the outset, the Romans recognised that 'no *republica* can ever hope to become perfect unless she provides for everything by means of her laws and furnishes a remedy for dealing with every possible accident'.[67] Perceiving the significance of this fact, the Romans 'always recognised the necessity of creating new *ordini* when new necessities arose in the handling of their city's affairs'.[68] This was what eventually brought them their unique success. By maintaining 'law and order' – the right *leggi e ordini* – they were able to preserve their city's freedom and independence; and by preserving their free way of life they were able to scale the highest peaks of *grandezza*.

But how can the law be used to protect our liberty? As Machiavelli makes clear in several discussions in Books 1 and 3, the most obvious way is by stopping other people from unfairly interfering with our freedom to pursue our own ends. To understand his specific programme for using the law to bring this about, we first need to recall what he

---

[63] Machiavelli 1960, I. 42, pp. 230–1: '[e possible per] i latori di leggi delle republiche o di' regni a frenare gli appetiti umani, e tòrre loro ogni speranza di potere *impune* errare'.

[64] Machiavelli 1960, I. 3, p. 136: 'Però si dice che la fame e la povertà fa gli uomini industriosi, e le leggi gli fanno buoni.'

[65] See Machiavelli 1960, I. 58, p. 265, speaking of 'un popolo incatenato da quelle [leggi]'.

[66] Machiavelli 1960, I. 1, p. 129: 'quante necessitadi le leggi fatte da Romolo, Numa e gli altri la costringessono, talmente che ... non la poterono per molti secoli corrompere'.

[67] Machiavelli 1960, I. 34, p. 211: 'Talché mai fia perfetta una republica se con le leggi sue non ha provisto a tutto, e ad ogni accidente posto il remedio.'

[68] Machiavelli 1960, I. 49, p. 241: 'sempre nel maneggiare quella città si scoprivono nuove necessità, ed era necessario creare nuovi ordini'.

takes to be the most dangerous methods a citizen can use to threaten or undermine the freedom of others. One method – employed by the Decemvirs and later perfected by Julius Caesar – is to engineer for oneself a position of supreme authority, either civil or (even better) military, and then use it to promote one's corrupt ambitions at the expense of the common good. Machiavelli's response is very simple: there must be laws to prevent such positions of command from ever being instituted, unless they are established for limited periods and with the sole purpose of dealing with the emergency that prompted them to be set up.[69] This is because there is no surer method of placing everyone's liberty at risk than by assigning supreme power to any one citizen. Rome, as always, is offered as the most instructive example. As the chapter heading of Book 3 chapter 24 proclaims, it was 'the prolongation of supreme military commands that turned Rome into a slave'.[70]

The other means by which leading citizens can hope to undermine *libertà* is, as we have seen, by the corrupt use of their wealth. If they are very rich, they may be able to equip enough military retainers to threaten the liberty of an entire city. Even if they are only somewhat richer than average, they can always try to buy themselves unfair advantages by the judicious payment of bribes. Machiavelli's solution to the first of these problems is chillingly dramatic. 'Anyone who wishes to create a republic where there are many such feudal lords has no hope of doing so unless they are completely wiped out at the start.'[71] Machiavelli is unspecific about how this is to be done, and about the nature of the legislation needed to prevent any later recrudescence of such feudal arrangements. But he is emphatic in claiming that 'those republics in which a genuinely political and uncorrupted way of life is maintained never permit any of their citizens to enjoy the status or live in the fashion of such feudatories'.[72] He even adds with obvious approval that truly *virtuosi* republics 'put such people to death as the beginners of corruption and the cause of every scandal in government'.[73]

This still leaves the problem of bribery and corruption, to which Machiavelli responds with the same devastating simplicity. As he declares

---

[69] Machiavelli 1960, I. 34, pp. 209–12.
[70] Machiavelli 1960, III. 24, p. 455: 'La prolungazione degl' imperii fece serva Roma.'
[71] Machiavelli 1960, I. 55, p. 257: 'colui che vuole fare dove sono assai gentiluomini una republica, non la può fare se prima non gli spegne tutti'.
[72] Machiavelli 1960, I. 55, p. 256: 'quelle republiche dove si è mantenuto il vivere politico ed incorrotto, non supportono che alcuno loro cittadino né sia né viva a uso di gentiluomo'.
[73] Machiavelli 1960, I. 55, p. 256: 'come principii di corruttele e cagione d'ogni scandolo, gli ammazzono'.

when discussing the Roman agrarian law in Book I, 'those republics which have been well-ordered have always ensured that the public treasury remains rich while the citizens remain poor'.[74] Again, he does not specify the nature of the *ordini* required to preserve such a condition of virtuous austerity. But on the need for such *ordini* he has absolutely no doubts, as he makes clear in one of his most self-consciously rhetorical passages:

> I could demonstrate with a long oration how much better are the fruits of poverty than of riches, and how the first has honoured cities, provinces and whole regions while the second has ruined them, were it not that these considerations have already been made celebrated on many other occasions by other men.[75]

The point is one to which he frequently returns. We have to recognise that, 'because *corruzione* and lack of concern for a life of liberty spring from inequality',[76] it follows that 'the most useful thing a free city can do for itself is to keep its citizens poor'.[77]

We need to note in conclusion that, as well as these specific suggestions, Machiavelli has a more all-embracing proposal to make about how to use the law to prevent our freedom from being undermined. He argues in Book I chapter 5 that what is most of all needed is a special magistracy charged with the specific duty of upholding the freedom of citizens against anyone trying to interfere with them. He maintains that 'those who have shown the greatest prudence in setting up republics have taken it to be one of the most essential things they need to establish that there should be constituted just such a *Guardia della libertà*'.[78] He even goes so far as to add that 'depending on how well this arrangement is established, the *vivere libero* in question will last for a longer or a shorter time'.[79]

---

[74] Machiavelli 1960, I. 37, p. 216: 'le republiche bene ordinate hanno a tenere ricco il publico e gli loro cittadini poveri'.

[75] Machiavelli 1960, III. 25, p. 459: 'Potrebbesi con un lungo parlare mostrare quanto migliori frutti produca la povertà che la ricchezza, e come l'una ha onorato le città, le provincie, le sètte, e l'altra le ha rovinate, se questa materia non fusse stata molte volte da altri uomini celebrata.'

[76] Machiavelli 1960, I. 17, p. 179: 'perché tale corruzione e poca attitudine alla vita libera nasce da una inequalità'.

[77] Machiavelli 1960, III. 25, p. 457: 'la più utile cosa che si ordini in uno vivere libero è che si mantenghino i cittadini poveri'. The moral is several times repeated. See also Machiavelli 1960, II. 19, p. 334 and III. 16, p. 437.

[78] Machiavelli 1960, I. 5, pp. 138–9: 'Quelli che prudentemente hanno constituita una republica, in tra le più necessarie cose ordinate de loro è stato constituire una guardia alla libertà.'

[79] Machiavelli 1960, I. 5, p. 139: 'secondo che questa è bene collocata, dura più o meno quel vivere libero'.

V

So far, Machiavelli's analysis of the relationship between law and liberty is founded on familiar premises. As we have seen, however, he is not merely concerned with the obvious fact that, if we behave in a consistently self-interested fashion, this will inevitably violate the liberty of others. He is also moved by the further consideration that, if we are blinded by the stratagems of corrupt leaders, or corrupted by collective self-deceit, this will have the effect of making us behave not merely in anti-social but in self-destructive ways. When he contends, therefore, that the indispensable means of preventing corruption is to invoke the coercive powers of the law, he is not merely endorsing the familiar observation that the law can be used to make us respect each other's freedom. He is also suggesting that the law can act to liberate us from our natural but self-destructive tendency to pursue our selfish interests. It can force us to promote the public interest in a genuinely *virtuoso* style, thereby enabling us to preserve our own liberty instead of undermining it. Machiavelli's further claim, in other words, is that the law can and must be used in addition to force us to be free.

Any consideration of this further possibility tends to be stigmatised by contemporary gothic theorists as an obvious – even a sinister – misunderstanding. Liberty, we are reminded, entails absence of constraint; so to speak of rendering people free by means of constraining them is simply to propagate a blatant confusion of terms.[80] Given the prevalence and prestige of these arguments, it is worth examining how Machiavelli nevertheless develops the case for saying that it is possible, and indeed essential, for the law to protect and enhance our liberty by means of coercing us.

The argument he develops is based on two assumptions I have already singled out. One is his generally pessimistic view of human nature, his view that it is wisest to regard our tendency to act corruptly as ineliminable. The other is his key contention that, since corruption is the antithesis of *virtù*, while *virtù* is indispensable for maintaining personal as well as public *libertà*, our corrupt behaviour must somehow be neutralised if a *vivere libero* (and hence our own *libertà*) are both to be preserved. The question is what the law can hope to achieve in the face of these difficulties. The answer, Machiavelli suggests, is that the law can be used to

---

[80] For a representative example of this argument, see Gribble 1969, pp. 158–60. Gribble's claims are discussed and endorsed in Allison 1981, pp. 390–1. For a similar commitment, see Parent 1974a, pp. 149–67. But for a classic corrective see MacCallum 1972 and cf. Taylor 1979.

coerce and direct us in just such a way that, even if we continue to act solely out of a corrupt desire to further our own individual or factional advantage, our motivations may be capable of being harnessed to serve the common good.

This process is not envisaged as one in which we are made to bring our desires in line with those of a higher self. On the contrary, Machiavelli assumes that we shall retain our selfish patterns of motivation and in consequence our self-destructive proclivities. All that happens is that the law operates to channel our behaviour in such a way that, although our reasons for action remain self-interested, our actions have consequences which, although not intended, are such as to promote the public interest. We are thereby enabled, by means of the coercive powers of the law, to attain the freedom we actually desire and to avoid the conditions of domination and servitude that our unconstrained behaviour would otherwise produce.[81]

There are two passages in Book I of the *Discorsi* in which Machiavelli relies on this precise structure of argument. The first occurs in the discussion of constitutional law in his opening chapters, a discussion that contrasts instructively with the handling of the same theme by current gothic theorists of liberty. It seems obvious to Machiavelli, no less than to contemporary theorists, that there must be one distinctive set of constitutional arrangements that offers those living under it the best prospect of maintaining their liberty. It is true that Machiavelli differs from current theorists in his views about how to uncover the nature of these arrangements. He believes that the surest method is to investigate the common elements of the most successful constitutional codes of antiquity. If the causes of their durability can be uncovered, it may in turn be possible to repeat their political success.[82] For a contemporary gothic theorist like John Rawls, by contrast, the aim is to stand at an Archimedean point outside history, with the result that Rawls prefers to reflect on his intuitions about justice at an imagined 'constitutional convention' in order to elucidate the legal foundations of a free society.[83]

Despite these divergent approaches, the fruits of Rawls's hypothetical convention and of Machiavelli's historical reflections turn out to be virtually the same – a fact so extraordinary as to cast doubt, perhaps, on

---

[81] Vatter 2000 p. 86 complains of my 'failure to distinguish between negative liberty and the desire not to be dominated'. But my point is that non-domination is a species of negative liberty. For a fuller elaboration see Skinner 1998.
[82] For this assumption see especially Machiavelli 1960, *Proemio*, pp. 123–5.
[83] Rawls 1971, pp. 196–9.

whether Rawls has really succeeded in freeing himself from the imaginative constraints imposed by the past. The conclusion at which they both arrive is that the optimum legal basis for a free polity consists of a republican constitution founded on a bicameral legislature,[84] a system to which Machiavelli adds the need for a strong consular or presidential element, while Rawls stresses in addition the need for an independent judiciary.[85]

If we turn, however, to their reasons for supposing that this structure will best serve to maximise our freedom, we encounter a deep disparity between the individualistic premises governing Rawls's theory and the more classical understanding of the relationship between law and liberty embodied in Machiavelli's account. For Rawls, the special value of the constitution he outlines is that it provides everyone, at least potentially, with equal access to power, equal means to prevent any encroachments upon their personal rights and an equal capacity in consequence to defend their liberties.[86] For Machiavelli, by contrast, the reason for preferring the same type of constitution lies in its unique potentiality for converting private vices into public benefits, thereby coercing us into respecting our own as well as other people's liberty.

This outcome is achieved, according to Machiavelli, essentially by exploiting the fact – which he again repeats – that 'in every type of civil association there are two divergent attitudes, that of the *grandi* and that of the ordinary people'.[87] By instituting a bicameral system, this rivalry can be exploited to the public advantage, as happened in republican Rome. The nobles held control of the Senate, while the establishment of the Tribunate 'not only gave to the ordinary people a share in the administration of the government, but constituted at the same time a guardian of Roman liberty'.[88] The two opposed groups, each representing opposed interests, maintained a continuous watch over each other, thereby ensuring that neither side was able to act simply to promote its own legislative programme. The outcome of this tensely balanced equilibrium was that 'all the laws that were enacted in favour of liberty arose from the disunion' between these two mutually hostile

---

[84] Machiavelli 1960, I. 2–4, pp. 129–38; Rawls 1971, pp. 222–4.
[85] Machiavelli 1960, I. 2, pp. 129–35; Rawls 1971, p. 224.
[86] This is the argument of section 36 of Rawls 1971.
[87] Machiavelli 1960, I. 4, p. 137: 'sono in ogni republica due umori diversi, quello del popolo e quello de' grandi'.
[88] Machiavelli 1960, I. 4, p. 138: 'oltre al dare la parte sua all'amministrazione popolare, furono constituiti per guardia della libertà romana'.

groups.⁸⁹ Even when both sides were motivated solely by a desire to advance their own ends, the constitution served to coerce them into acting in such a way that all purely sectarian proposals were blocked, and the interests of the whole community were in consequence upheld. By the force of law, the people were thereby liberated from the natural consequences of their own *corruzione* and channelled into acting in such a way that their individual as well as their civic liberties were preserved.

The other point at which Machiavelli considers how to force people to respect their own freedom is in his sequence of chapters on Roman religious practices. These chapters are placed immediately after the analysis of the Roman republican constitution in Book 1. The issue of religion arises in this context because of Machiavelli's belief – which he again shares with most contemporary theorists of liberty – that religious susceptibilities are peculiarly liable to pose a threat to well-ordered societies. A special series of *leggi e ordini* will therefore be needed to prevent this danger from materialising.

Once again, however, there is an instructive contrast to be drawn between Machiavelli's discussion of this issue and that of a modern gothic theorist such as John Rawls. Rawls assumes that the principal way in which the adherents of a particular sect are liable to jeopardise our freedom is by undermining what he calls 'the common interest in public order and security'.⁹⁰ He starts out from the observation that deeply religious people are prone to insist that 'others ought to recognise the same beliefs and first principles' as they do, and 'are grievously in error' if they fail to do so. This tends to breed intolerance, which in turn carries with it a danger of 'interference with the essentials of public order' and a consequential threat to the liberties of anyone who fails to endorse the outlook of the intolerant group.⁹¹

Machiavelli, by contrast, has a broader sense of the power of religion – and especially of Christianity – to threaten our liberty. To be deeply religious is to be motivated by the hope of going to heaven and the corresponding fear of incurring God's wrath and failing to be saved.⁹² But this means that true Christians care nothing for worldly glory or the welfare of their community in this present life. They care only for heavenly glory and their own welfare in the life to come. They have

---

⁸⁹ Machiavelli 1960, I. 4, p. 137: 'tutte le leggi che si fanno in favore della libertà, nascano dalla disunione loro'.
⁹⁰ Rawls 1971, p. 212.   ⁹¹ Rawls 1971, pp. 208, 213–18.
⁹² Machiavelli 1960, I. 11, pp. 160–3; I. 14, pp. 169–71; II. 2, pp. 282–3.

consequently taught us to despise the pagan ideals of 'greatness of spirit and bodily strength'.[93] Instead 'they glorify humble and contemplative men rather than men of action, and have set up humility, abjectness and contempt for worldly things as the greatest good'.[94]

Machiavelli's daring suggestion is thus that Christianity, as habitually practised, has served to encourage *ozio*, and has thereby acted as a corrupting influence on civic life. There is no reason, he insists, why the monkish leaders of the Christian faith should have been allowed so much licence 'to interpret our religion *secondo l'ozio* rather than *secondo la virtù*'.[95] But the fact is that the ideal of the Christian life we have inherited 'has rendered the world feeble and handed it over as a prey to the wicked'.[96] They in turn 'can control the world with full security, since the generality of men, hoping to go to Paradise, think more about enduring their injuries than avenging them'.[97]

The threat to liberty posed by any religion which, like Christianity, is based on our hopes and fears about the world to come is thus the threat of *corruzione*, not of intolerance. To preserve our liberty, we need above all to possess *virtù*; but to possess *virtù* is to be willing to place the salvation of our community above all personal considerations, whereas Christianity instructs us to treat our personal salvation as more important than anything else. 'Reflecting, then, on how it came about that peoples in ancient times were greater lovers of liberty than at the present time', Machiavelli concludes that Christianity must carry a considerable burden of the responsibility.[98] 'Having shown us' – he is careful to add – 'the truth and the true way of life', our religion has at the same time 'taught us to give little esteem to worldly honour', whereas in antiquity 'such honour was immensely esteemed and considered the greatest good'.[99]

---

[93] See Machiavelli 1960, II. 2, p. 282 on the admiration of the ancients for 'grandezza dello animo [e] fortezza del corpo'.

[94] Machiavelli 1960, II. 2, p. 282: 'ha glorificato più gli uomini umili e contemplativi che gli attivi [e] ha disposto il sommo bene nella umiltà, abiezione, e nel dispregio delle cose umane'.

[95] Machiavelli 1960, II. 2, p. 283: 'che hanno interpretato la nostra religione secondo l'ozio e non secondo la virtù'.

[96] Machiavelli 1960, II. 2, p. 282: 'Questo modo di vivere adunque pare che abbi renduto il mondo debole, e datolo in preda agli uomini scelerati.'

[97] Machiavelli 1960, II. 2, pp. 282–3: 'i quali sicuramente lo possono maneggiare, veggendo come l'università degli uomini per andare in Paradiso pensa più a sopportare le sue battiture che a vendicarle'.

[98] Machiavelli 1960, II. 2, p. 282: 'Pensando dunque donde possa nascere che in quegli tempi antichi i popoli fossero più amatori della libertà che in questi.'

[99] Machiavelli 1960, II. 2, p. 282: 'avendoci la nostra religione mostro la verità e la vera via, ci fa stimare meno l'onore del mono: onde i Gentili stimandolo assai, ed avendo posto in quello il sommo bene'.

As a result of these divergent views about the relationship between religion and civic freedom, Machiavelli presents an analysis completely at variance with that of most contemporary theorists of liberty when he goes on to consider what *leggi e ordini* are needed to prevent our religious susceptibilities from undermining our liberties. To a modern gothic theorist such as Rawls, the basic problem is that of adjudicating between the values of liberty of conscience and public tranquillity. Liberty of conscience must never be limited unless 'there is reasonable expectation that not doing so will damage the public order which the government should maintain'.[100] But as soon as it becomes clear that a given religion poses 'considerable risks to our own legitimate interests', then the law can and ought to intervene to 'force the intolerant to respect the liberty of others'.[101] For Machiavelli, by contrast, the laws required to regulate religion in the name of liberty will be such as are capable of harnessing the self-interested motivations of the religious in such a way as to enable the fear of God to be turned to public account. The basic question for Machiavelli, in short, is how to interpret religion *secondo la virtù*; how to prevent it from corrupting our public life and thereby threatening our liberty.

The fundamental requirement, according to Machiavelli, is to enact a series of *ordini* designed to encourage religious belief, or at least to compel the observance of religious practices.[102] As he explains in Book I chapter 11, unless the generality of the people are genuinely religious in their outlook there will obviously be no hope of manipulating their beliefs in such a way as to serve the common good. It follows that, 'just as the observation of divine worship is a cause of the *grandezza* of republics, so contempt for it is a cause of their ruin'.[103] The moral is emphatically drawn at the start of chapter 12:

> Those princes and those republics that wish to maintain themselves uncorrupted must above all else ensure that they maintain the ceremonies of their religion uncorrupted and at all times held in veneration. For there can be no surer sign of the ruin of a country than to see divine worship held in contempt.[104]

Although Machiavelli sometimes speaks with a seemingly ironic inflection about religious belief, whatever cynicism he may have felt is always

---

[100] Rawls 1971, p. 213.   [101] Rawls 1971, pp. 212, 219.
[102] Machiavelli 1960, I. 14–15, pp. 169–73.
[103] Machiavelli 1960, I. 11, p. 162: 'E come la osservanza del culto divino è cagione della grandezza delle republiche, così il dispregio di quello è cagione della rovina di esse.'
[104] Machiavelli 1960, I. 12, p 163: 'Quelli principi o quelle republiche le quali si vogliono mantenere incorrotte, hanno sopra ogni altra cosa a mantenere incorrotte le ceremonie della loro religione, e tenerle sempre nella loro venerazione; perché nessuno maggiore indizio si puote avere della rovina d'una provincia, che vendere dispregiato il culto divino.'

tempered by the thought that there can be no exploitation of piety unless there is piety to exploit.

As we have seen, however, piety according to Machiavelli is not only insufficient in itself; it is actually capable of undermining civic liberty. The further question is how to channel our fear of God and hope of salvation in such a way as to promote the common good instead of subverting it. Machiavelli gives his answer at the start of Book I chapter 11, the beginning of his sequence of chapters on Roman religion. It is essential that, whatever *ordini* a community enacts about religion, they must include a requirement that the absolute sanctity of oaths must be respected and recognised. It was due above all to the fact that the Romans 'had a much greater fear of breaking an oath than of breaking the laws' that their leaders were able to make use of religion 'to facilitate whatever undertaking the Senate or the *grandi* wanted to carry out'.[105]

An oath is a promise in which the name of God is invoked as a guarantee that the promise will be kept. We can readily see the political significance of such oaths if we consider the case, as Machiavelli does, of a body of citizens acting, or planning to act, in a corrupt and self-interested fashion in relation to some important public enterprise. It will be essential for their leaders to find some means of coercing them into upholding the public interest and hence their own liberty. Machiavelli's suggestion is that, as long as the prevailing religion emphasises the sanctity of oaths, it will always be open to the leaders of such a people to force them to overcome their natural selfishness by imposing an oath binding them to behave in the manner of genuinely *virtuosi* citizens. This will not of course have the effect of changing their basic attitudes. But it will certainly have the effect of making them more frightened of evading their public duties than of performing them, since their greatest desire, if they are truly religious, will be to keep their promise and avoid the wrath of God. By means of the *ordini* governing their religion, they will thus be coerced into acting, against their natural disposition, in such a way as to promote the freedom of their community and in consequence their own freedom at the same time. By means of coercion, in short, they will be assured of liberty.

Machiavelli cites numerous cases in which political leaders have successfully played on the religious susceptibilities of ordinary citizens in

---

[105] Machiavelli 1960, I. 11, p. 160: 'il che facilitò qualunque impresa che il Senato o quelli grandi uomini romani disegnassero fare [perché] quelli cittadini temevano più assai rompere il giuramento che le leggi'.

such a way as to force them to be free.[106] Of all his examples, however, perhaps the most striking – as we saw in chapter 5 – is that of Scipio Africanus and his conduct at the time of the second Punic war. After Hannibal defeated the Romans at Cannae, many citizens decided to give up and withdraw to Sicily. Hearing of this, Scipio met them with a naked sword in his hand and forced them to swear an oath not to abandon their native land. 'The result was that, although the love of their country and its laws had not been sufficient to keep them in Italy, they were kept there by the oath they were forced to take.'[107] Being forced, in other words, to become *virtuosi*, they stood their ground, eventually defeated Hannibal and thereby secured, by means of their enforced *virtù*, the liberty they had been ready to give up.

VI

Machiavelli's account of how to maintain civic (and hence individual) freedom reverses the relationship between liberty and the law expressed by most contemporary theorists of liberty. Among contemporary writers, the coercive apparatus of the law is generally pictured as an obvious affront to individual freedom. The power of the law to constrain us is only held to be justified if, in diminishing the extent of our natural liberty, it serves at the same time to assure more effectively our capacity to exercise the freedom that remains to us.[108] The proper relationship between the law and liberty is thus held to be expressed by saying that – as Isaiah Berlin puts it – the law should create a framework within which 'as many individuals as possible can realise as many of their ends as possible, without assessment of the value of those ends, save in so far as they may frustrate the purposes of others'.[109]

For a neo-Roman theorist like Machiavelli, by contrast, the law is in part justified because it serves to ensure a degree of personal freedom which, in its absence, would altogether collapse. If the coercive apparatus of the law were to be withdrawn, there would not be a greater degree

---

[106] See Machiavelli 1960, I. 11, p. 160 (on Lucius Manlius); I. 13, pp. 168–9 (on Titus Quintus); I. 15, pp. 169–73 (on the Samnites).

[107] Machiavelli 1960, I. 11, p. 161: 'E cosí quelli cittadini, i quali lo amore della patria le leggi di quella non ritenevano in Italia, vi furono ritenuti da un giuramento che furono forzati a pigliare.'

[108] As Gray 1980, p. 523 emphasises, this account of how coercion is to be justified constitutes a central feature of classical liberalism. Rawls 1971, p. 302 expresses it in the form of the axiom – which he calls the 'First Priority Rule' – that 'liberty can be restricted only for the sake of liberty'.

[109] Berlin 1969, p. 153n. Cf. also Berlin 1969, p. 161 for J. S. Mill's and Benjamin Constant's formulations of the point. The same commitment underlies Rawls 1971, pp. 235–43.

of personal liberty with a diminished capacity to enjoy it. Due to our self-destructive natures, there would rather be a diminution of personal liberty, a rapid slide towards a condition of complete servitude. The proper relationship between liberty and the law is not to be expressed, therefore, by treating the law as a neutral framework within which we pursue our own purposes. The law needs to be viewed in addition as a liberating agency. If our legislators have been wise, the law will constrain us in just such a way that we are released from the bondage that our natural selfishness would otherwise impose on us, and are granted our freedom by means of being coerced.

7

The idea of negative liberty: Machiavellian and modern perspectives

I

My aim is to explore a possible means of enlarging our present understanding of the concepts we employ in social and political argument. A prevailing orthodoxy bids us proceed by consulting our intuitions about what can and cannot be coherently said and done with the terms we generally use to express the concepts involved. But this approach might with profit be supplemented, I shall argue, if we were to confront these intuitions with a more systematic examination of the unfamiliar theories within which even our most familiar concepts have sometimes been put to work at different historical periods.

One way of proceeding with this line of thought would be to offer a general defence of this view about the 'relevance' of the history of philosophy for the understanding of contemporary philosophical debates. But I shall instead attempt to follow a more direct, if more modest, route by focusing on one particular concept which is at once central to current disputes in social and political theory and is at the same time overdue, it seems to me, for this type of historical treatment.

The concept I have in mind is that of political liberty, the extent of the freedom or liberty of action available to individuals within the confines imposed on them by their membership of civil associations.[1] The first point to be observed is that, among Anglophone philosophers of the present generation, the discussion of this topic has given rise to one conclusion which commands a remarkably wide measure of assent.

This chapter is a revised version of an essay that originally appeared under the title 'The Idea of Negative Liberty: Philosophical and Historical Perspectives' in *Philosophy in History*, ed. Richard Rorty, J. B. Schneewind and Quentin Skinner (Cambridge, 1984), pp. 193–221.

[1] Discussing this concept, some philosophers (for example Oppenheim 1981) prefer to speak of social freedom, while others (for example Rawls 1971) always speak of liberty. As far as I can see nothing hangs on this difference of terminology. Throughout the following argument I have accordingly felt free (or at liberty) to treat these two terms as synonyms and to use them interchangeably.

This is that – to cite the formula originally owed to Jeremy Bentham and more recently made famous by Isaiah Berlin – the concept of liberty is essentially a 'negative' one. Its presence is said to be marked by the absence of something; specifically, by the absence of some impediment that inhibits the agent concerned from being able to act in pursuit of his or her chosen ends. As Gerald MacCallum expresses the point, in a form of words that has become standard in the recent literature, 'whenever the freedom of some agent or agents is in question, it is always freedom from some constraint or restriction on, interference with, or barrier to doing, not doing, becoming or not becoming something'.[2]

It would be no exaggeration to say that this assumption – that the only coherent idea of liberty is the negative one of being unimpeded – has underpinned the entire development of modern contractarian political thought. We already find Thomas Hobbes expressing it at the outset of his chapter 'Of the Liberty of Subjects' in *Leviathan*, in which he presents an extremely influential statement of the claim that 'Liberty, or Freedome, signifieth (properly) the absence of Opposition' and signifies nothing more.[3] The same assumption, often couched specifically in terms of MacCallum's triadic analysis, continues to run throughout the current literature. Benn and Weinstein, for example, implicitly adopt MacCallum's framework in their important essay on freedom as the non-restriction of options, as does Felix Oppenheim in his discussion of social freedom as the capacity to pursue alternatives.[4] The same analysis is likewise invoked – with direct reference to MacCallum's classic article – in John Rawls's *Theory of Justice*, in Joel Feinberg's *Social Philosophy* and in many other accounts.[5]

It is true that, in spite of this basic and long-standing agreement, there have always been disputes among proponents of the 'negative' thesis about the nature of the circumstances in which it is proper to say that the freedom of some particular agent has or has not been restricted or infringed. For there have always been divergent beliefs as to what counts as opposition, and thus as the sort of constraint that limits the freedom as opposed to merely limiting the ability of agents to act. Far more important, however, for the purposes of my present argument is the widespread endorsement of the conclusion that – as Charles Taylor has put it in his attack on the consensus – the idea of liberty should be construed as a pure 'opportunity concept', as nothing but the absence of constraint,

---

[2] MacCallum 1972, p. 176. [3] Hobbes 1996, p. 145.
[4] Benn and Weinstein 1971, p. 101; Oppenheim 1981, p. 65.
[5] Rawls 1971, p. 202; Feinberg 1973, pp. 11, 16.

and hence as unconnected with the pursuit of any determinate ends or purposes.[6]

It is typical of negative theorists – Hobbes is again a classic example – to spell out the implications of this central commitment in polemical terms. The aim of doing so has generally been to repudiate two contentions about social freedom – both occasionally defended in the history of modern political philosophy – on the grounds of their incompatibility with the basic idea that the enjoyment of social freedom is simply a matter of being unobstructed. One of these has been the suggestion that individual liberty can be assured only within a particular form of self-governing community. Put most starkly, the claim is that (as Rousseau expresses it in *Du Contrat Social*) the maintenance of personal freedom depends on the performance of public services. The other and connected suggestion often targeted by negative theorists is that the qualities needed on the part of each individual citizen to ensure the effective performance of these duties must be the civic virtues. To put it starkly once more (as Spinoza does in *Tractatus Politicus*), the claim is that freedom presupposes virtue; that only the virtuous are truly or fully capable of assuring their own liberty.

By way of responding to these paradoxes, some contemporary theorists of negative liberty have simply followed Hobbes's lead. They have argued that, since the liberty of subjects must involve, in Hobbes's phrase, 'Immunitie from the service of the Commonwealth', any suggestion that freedom might involve the performance of such services, and the cultivation of the virtues necessary to perform them, must be totally confused.[7] Isaiah Berlin remarks, for example, that to speak of rendering myself free by virtuously performing my social duties, thereby equating duty with interest, is simply 'to throw a metaphysical blanket over either self-deceit or deliberate hypocrisy'.[8]

The more usual and more moderate riposte, however, has been to suggest that, whatever may be the merits of the two heterodox claims I have singled out, they are certainly not consistent with a negative analysis of the concept of freedom. They must point to a different conception – perhaps even a different concept – of political liberty. This appears to be Berlin's own view in an earlier section of his essay about the two allegedly different concepts of liberty. He concedes that we might entertain a secularised version of the belief that God's service is perfect freedom 'without thereby rendering the word "freedom" wholly meaningless'.

[6] Taylor 1979, p. 177.   [7] Hobbes 1996, p. 149.   [8] Berlin 1969, p. 171.

But he adds that the meaning we should then be assigning to the term cannot possibly be the one required by a theory of negative liberty.[9]

Despite these strictures, the more fairminded defenders of negative liberty have sometimes conceded the possibility of constructing a coherent – even if unfamiliar – theory of social freedom in which the liberty of individuals might be connected with ideals of virtue and public service.[10] As Berlin has emphasised, all that need be added if we wish to make sense of such claims is the ultimately Aristotelian suggestion that we are moral beings with certain true ends and rational purposes. If this is so, then it might certainly make sense to suggest that we can only hope in the fullest sense to enjoy our liberty if we live in such a community and act in such a way that those ends and purposes are realised as completely as possible.[11]

Some contemporary writers have added that we ought in fact to insert this further premise. We ought to recognise that (in Charles Taylor's words) freedom is not merely an 'opportunity' but an 'exercise' concept. We are free only 'in the exercise of certain capacities', so that we 'are not free, or less free, when these capacities are in some way unfulfilled or blocked'.[12] Having made this move, such theorists characteristically go on to suggest that this commits us to considering the reinstatement of both the claims about social freedom so firmly repudiated by Hobbes and his modern disciples. First of all, as Taylor observes, if human nature does indeed have an essence, it is certainly not implausible to suppose that its full realisation may only be possible 'within a certain form of society'. We may need, that is, to serve and uphold such a society if our true natures, and hence our own individual liberty, are to reach their fullest development.[13] And secondly, as Benjamin Gibbs, for example, has put it in his book *Freedom and Liberation*, certain conclusions about the relations between freedom and virtue then become hard to resist. Once we acknowledge that our liberty depends upon 'attaining and enjoying those cardinal goods appropriate to our natures', the virtues may well appear indispensable to the performance of just those morally worthwhile actions that serve to mark us out as 'consummately free'.[14]

---

[9] Berlin 1969, pp. 160–2.
[10] But by no means all have been so broadminded. Strict followers of Hobbes (such as Steiner 1974–5, Day 1983 and Flew 1983) insist that the only coherent account we can hope to give of the concept of liberty is a negative one. And, insofar as MacCallum's analysis suggests a negative understanding of freedom as the absence of constraints upon an agent's options (which it does), this is also the implication of his account and of those which depend on it.
[11] Berlin 1969, pp. 145–54.   [12] Taylor 1979, p. 179.
[13] Taylor 1979, p. 193.   [14] Gibbs 1976, pp. 22, 129–31.

Much of the debate between those who think of social freedom as a negative 'opportunity' concept and those who think of it as a positive 'exercise' concept may thus be said to stem from a deeper dispute about human nature. The argument is *au fond* about whether we can hope to distinguish an objective notion of *eudaimonia* or human flourishing.[15] Those who dismiss this hope as illusory – such as Berlin and his many sympathisers – conclude that this makes it a dangerous error to connect individual liberty with the ideals of virtue and public service. Those who believe in real or identifiably human interests – Taylor, Gibbs and others – respond by insisting that this at least makes it arguable that only the virtuous and public-spirited citizen is in full possession of his or her liberty.

This in turn means, however, that there is one assumption shared by virtually all the contributors to the current debate. Even Charles Taylor and Isaiah Berlin are able to agree on it. It is that we must be able to give some content to the idea of objective human flourishing if we are to make sense of any theory purporting to connect the concept of individual liberty with virtuous acts of public service.

The thesis I propose to defend is that this shared and central assumption is unjustified. By way of defending it, I shall turn to what I take to be the lessons of history. I shall try to show that, in an earlier and now discarded strand of thinking about social freedom, the concept of negative liberty was combined with the ideals of virtue and public service in just the manner nowadays assumed to be impossible without incoherence.[16] I shall thereby try to supplement and correct our prevailing and misleadingly restricted sense of what can and cannot be said and done with the concept of negative liberty by examining the record of the very different things that have been said and done with it at earlier phases in the history of our own culture.

II

Before embarking on this task, one obvious query about this way of proceeding needs first to be answered. It might well be asked why I propose to examine the historical record at this juncture instead of attempting directly to develop a more inclusive philosophical analysis of negative

---

[15] For emphasising that some such conception lies at the heart of most 'positive' views of liberty I am much indebted to Baldwin 1984.

[16] But for a critique of this contention see Herzog 1986. See also the valuable discussions in Spitz 1995, pp. 125–269 and in Senellart 1995.

liberty. My answer is not that I suppose such purely conceptual exercises to be out of the question. On the contrary, they have I think been among the most probing and original contributions to the contemporary debate.[17] It is rather that, in consequence of certain widespread assumptions about the best methods of studying social and political concepts, it is apt to seem much less convincing to suggest that a concept *might* be coherently used in an unfamiliar way than to show that it *has in fact* been put to unfamiliar but coherent uses.

The nature of the assumptions I have in mind can readily be illustrated from the current literature on the concept of liberty. The basic postulate of the writers I have so far mentioned is that to explicate a concept such as that of social freedom is to give an account of the meanings of the terms habitually used to express it. To understand the meanings of such terms, it is further agreed, is a matter of understanding their correct usage, of grasping what can and cannot be said and done with them.[18]

So far so good; or rather, so far so Wittgensteinian, which I am prepared to suppose amounts in these matters to much the same thing. These procedures tend to be equated, however, with giving an account of how *we* generally employ the terms involved. What we are enjoined to study is 'what we normally would say' about liberty, and what we find 'we do not want to say' when we reflect about the uses of the term in an adequately self-conscious way.[19] We are adjured to stay 'as close to ordinary language as possible', the reason being that the highroad to understanding a concept such as that of liberty is to grasp 'what we normally mean' by the term 'liberty'.[20]

This is not to say that 'ordinary language' is allowed to have the last word. Most of the writers I have cited are at pains to distance themselves from so widely discredited a belief. Rather it is assumed that, once we begin to move towards a position of equilibrium between our intuitions about concepts and the demands of current usage, it may well prove necessary to adjust the one in the light of the other. We may need, that is, to revise what we are disposed to say about liberty in the light of what we

---

[17] I have in mind especially MacCallum 1972 and Baldwin 1984.
[18] For explicit presentations of these postulates, applied to the case of 'explicating' the concept of freedom, see for example Parent 1974a, pp. 149–51 and Oppenheim 1981, pp. 148–50, 179–82.
[19] Parent 1974b, pp. 432–3. Cf. also Benn and Weinstein 1971, p. 194 on the need to study 'what in general one can appropriately say' about the term 'freedom' in order to understand the concept, and their criticism of Parent's account (Parent 1974b, p. 435) on the grounds that it is 'so evidently contrary to standard usage' that 'one is bound to mistrust the characterisation of freedom which makes it even possible'.
[20] For this injunction see Oppenheim 1981, p. 179.

find ourselves saying about other and closely connected concepts such as rights, responsibility, coercion and so forth. The true goal of conceptual analysis – as Joel Feinberg, for example, formulates it – is thus to arrive, by way of reflecting on 'what we normally mean when we employ certain words', at a more finished delineation of 'what we had better mean if we are to communicate effectively, avoid paradox and achieve general coherence'.[21]

As the above quotations reveal, however, the question is still about what *we* are capable of saying and meaning without incoherence. Given this approach, it is easy to see how it comes about that any purely analytical attempt to connect the idea of negative liberty with the ideals of virtue and service is liable to appear unconvincing, and vulnerable to being dismissed out of hand. For it is obvious that *we* cannot hope to connect the idea of liberty with the obligation to perform virtuous acts of public service except at the unthinkable cost of giving up, or making nonsense of, our intuitions about individual rights. But this in turn means that, in the case of all the writers I have been considering, only one of two responses can be offered to someone who insists on trying to explicate the concept in such a counter-intuitive way. The kinder is to suggest that – as Isaiah Berlin for example tends to put it – they must really be talking about something else; they must 'have a different concept' of liberty.[22] But the more usual is to contend – as for example William Parent does – that they must simply be confused. To connect the idea of freedom with such principles as virtue or rational self-mastery, as Parent patiently reminds us, fails to convey or even connect with 'what we ordinarily mean' by the term liberty. From which he takes it to follow that any attempt to forge such links will only result in a confused misunderstanding of the concept involved.[23]

It is in the hope of preventing myself from being ruled out of order in this fashion that I propose to eschew conceptual analysis and turn instead to history. Before doing so, however, one further preliminary note of warning must be sounded. If there is to be any prospect of invoking the past in the manner I have sketched – as a means of questioning rather than underpinning our current beliefs – we shall have to reconsider, and indeed repudiate, the reasons usually given for studying the history of philosophy by many of its leading practitioners at the present time.

---

[21] See Feinberg 1973, p. 2. For similar commitments see Parent 1974a, p. 166; Raz 1970, pp. 303–4; and Oppenheim 1981, pp. 179–80, who cites both Feinberg and Raz with approval.

[22] Berlin 1969, esp. pp. 154–62. Cf. Ryan 1980, p. 497.

[23] Parent 1974a, pp. 152, 166; and 1974b, p. 434. Cf. also Gray 1980, p. 511, who insists that, by reflecting on 'intelligible locutions having to do with freedom', we can dismiss MacCallum's contention that the term always denotes a triadic relationship.

For a representative discussion of these reasons, consider the Introduction to J. L. Mackie's revealingly titled book, *Problems from Locke*. This opens by articulating the basic presupposition of much contemporary work in the history of philosophy. There is a certain determinate range of problems, we are told, that go to make up the discipline of philosophy. We can therefore expect to find a corresponding range of historical treatments of these problems, some of which may prove to be 'of continuing philosophical interest'.[24] It follows that, if we want a usable history, there are two guidelines to be observed. The first is that we should concentrate on just those historical texts, and just those sections of just those texts, in which it is immediately apparent that familiar concepts are being deployed to construct familiar arguments with which we can then take direct issue. Mackie gives clear expression to this rule in the methodological Introduction to his book. He remarks that he 'makes no attempt to expound or study Locke's philosophy as a whole, or even that part of it which is to be found in the *Essay*'. This is because he is exclusively concerned with 'a limited number of problems of continuing philosophical interest' that happen to be raised and examined at various moments in Locke's texts.[25]

The underlying assumption is thus that the reason for exhuming the great philosophers of the past is to help us arrive at better answers to our own questions. The second guideline we are exhorted to observe then follows from this commitment. We must be prepared to recast the thought of the philosophers we are investigating in our own idiom, seeking to produce a rational reconstruction of their beliefs rather than a picture of full historical authenticity when these two projects begin to collide. Mackie offers a particularly clear statement of this further rule, observing that the main purpose of his work 'is not to expound Locke's views or to study their relations with those of his contemporaries and near contemporaries, but to work towards solutions of the problems themselves'.[26]

The value of following these rules, we are finally assured, lies in their capacity to provide us with a ready and easy way of dividing up our intellectual heritage. Suppose we come upon a philosophical text, or even a section of an otherwise interesting text, in which the author begins to discuss a topic which (as Mackie puts it) 'is not a live issue for us'. The right response at this juncture is to reallocate the text for study under the separate heading of 'the history of ideas'.[27] This is held to be the name

---

[24] See Mackie 1976, p. 1 and for a similar commitment cf. O'Connor 1964, p. ix.
[25] Mackie, 1976, p. 1.   [26] Mackie 1976, p. 2.   [27] Mackie 1976, p. 4.

of a distinct discipline that concerns itself with issues 'of purely historical' as opposed to 'intrinsically philosophical' significance.[28] Sometimes it is rather strongly implied that it is hard to see how these issues (not being 'live') can have much significance at all. But it is usually allowed that they may well be of interest to those who happen to be interested in such things. It is just that such people will be historians of ideas; they will not be engaged in an enquiry of any relevance to philosophy.

I have no wish to question the obvious truth that there are large continuities in the history of modern philosophy, so that it may sometimes be possible to sharpen our wits by arguing directly with our elders and betters. I do wish to suggest, however, that there are at least two reasons for questioning the assumption that the history of philosophy should be written as though it is not really history.

It seems to me in the first place that to recover what a given philosopher may have said about some particular issue can never be sufficient to provide us with an historical understanding of their work. I have already sought to explain this commitment in volume 1 chapter 6 of the present work. Here I need only observe that to mount an argument is always, I take it, to argue with someone, to reason for or against a certain conclusion or course of action. This being so, the business of interpreting any text that contains such forms of reasoning will always require us (to speak over-schematically) to follow two connected lines of approach. The initial task is obviously to recapture the substance of the argument itself. If we wish, however, to arrive at an interpretation of the text, an understanding of why its contents are as they are and not otherwise, this still leaves us with the further task of recovering what the writer may have meant by advancing that particular argument. We need, that is, to be able to give an account of what they were *doing* in presenting their argument: what conclusion or course of action they were supporting or defending, attacking or repudiating, ridiculing with irony, scorning with polemical silence, and so on, and on through the entire gamut of speech acts embodied in the vastly complex act of intended communication that any work of discursive reasoning will comprise.

One of my doubts about the prevailing approach to the history of philosophy is that it systematically ignores this latter aspect of the interpretative task. I now turn to my other criticism, which I propose to treat at much greater length. It is that the notion of 'relevance' embodied in

---

[28] For a statement of the issue in these exact terms see Scruton 1981, pp. 10–11.

the orthodox approach is a needlessly constricting and philistine one. According to the view I have been outlining, the history of philosophy is only 'relevant' if we can use it as a mirror to reflect our own beliefs and assumptions back at us. If we can do this, the subject takes on 'intrinsic philosophical significance'; if we cannot, it remains 'of purely historical interest'. The only way to learn from the past, in short, is to appropriate it. I wish to suggest instead that it may be precisely those aspects of the past which appear at first glance to be without contemporary relevance that may prove upon closer acquaintance to be of the most immediate philosophical significance. For their relevance may lie in the fact that, instead of supplying us with our usual and carefully contrived pleasures of recognition, they enable us to stand back from our own beliefs and the concepts we use to express them, perhaps forcing us to reconsider, to recast or even (I shall next seek to suggest) to abandon some of our current beliefs in the light of these wider perspectives.

To open the pathway towards this broader notion of 'relevance', I am pleading for a history of philosophy which, instead of purveying rational reconstructions in the light of current prejudices, tries to avoid them as much as possible. Doubtless they cannot be avoided altogether. It is deservedly a commonplace of recent hermeneutic theories that, as Hans Georg Gadamer in particular has emphasised, we are likely to be constrained in our imaginative grasp of historical texts in ways that we cannot even be confident of bringing to consciousness. All I am proposing is that, instead of bowing to this limitation and erecting it into a principle, we should fight against it with all the weapons that historians have already fashioned in their efforts to reconstruct without anachronism the alien *mentalités* of earlier periods.

III

The above remarks are excessively programmatic and in danger of sounding shrill. I shall now attempt to give them some substance by relating them to the specific example I have raised, the example of what can and cannot be coherently said and done with our concept of negative liberty. As I have already intimated, my thesis is as follows. We need to look beyond the confines of the present disputes about positive *versus* negative liberty in order to investigate more fully the range of arguments about social freedom that arose in the course of modern European political philosophy. This quest, I hope to show, will bring us to a line of argument about negative liberty which has largely been lost to view in the course of the present debate, but which serves to cast some doubt on the terms of that debate itself.

The missing line of argument I should like to reinstate is the one embedded in the classical and especially the Roman republican theory of citizenship. Before becoming engulfed by more individualistic styles of political reasoning, the Roman vision of freedom and civic equality enjoyed a brief but brilliant revival within the republican regimes of early-modern Europe. Within the Italian city-republics, the most incisive and influential articulation of what I shall describe as the neo-Roman case[29] was provided by Niccolò Machiavelli in his *Discorsi* on Livy's history of Rome. After England was proclaimed 'a Commonwealth and free state' in 1649, a similar style of neo-Roman thinking came briefly to the fore, with James Harrington in his *Commonwealth of Oceana* offering the most systematic reworking of the Machiavellian line of argument. Meanwhile the success of the Dutch revolt against Imperial Spain helped to bring the same strand of thinking to still greater prominence in the Netherlands, with Spinoza in his *Tractatus Politicus* making by far the most significant contribution to the debate.

This is the tradition, I shall argue, that we need to retrieve if we wish to provide a corrective to the dogmatism about the topic of social freedom that has marked the writings of more recent theorists of natural and human rights. By way of attempting this act of retrieval, I have chosen to concentrate on Machiavelli's presentation of the neo-Roman case in his *Discorsi* on Livy. I have made this choice in part for reasons of space, but also because the *Discorsi* seems to me the text in which – as Spinoza long ago observed – we encounter the most acute and helpful reworking of the classical theory of citizenship.[30] I shall thus be concerned to develop an historical thesis about Machiavelli's intentions in the *Discorsi* as well as a more general argument about the value of trying to recover what I take to be his line of thought. My historical thesis is that, while there are many things that Machiavelli may be said to be doing in the *Discorsi*, perhaps his most central concern is to address – partly to question, but chiefly to reiterate and amplify – that view of *libertas* which had lain at the heart of Roman republican thought. My more general thesis I have already stated: that to recapture the structure of this theory as far as possible in its own terms may in turn

---

[29] For this suggested terminology, and for an account of the fortunes of the neo-Roman theory after the Renaissance, see Skinner 1998.
[30] Spinoza 1958, p. 313.

help us to enlarge our own understanding of the concept of negative liberty.[31]

Machiavelli begins to consider what it means to be in possession of our liberty in the opening two chapters of Book I of his *Discorsi*. But his main discussion is launched in his ensuing sequence of chapters, in which he examines what ends and purposes we commonly seek within civil associations, and in consequence what grounds we have for valuing our liberty. This is the stage at which he introduces the psychological generalisations I have already discussed in chapter 6. He observes, that is, that in all known polities there have been two distinguishable types of citizen with contrasting dispositions and correspondingly different reasons for prizing their liberty. On the one hand are the *grandi*, who typically desire to obtain power for themselves and to avoid ignominy at all costs. Their principal aim is accordingly to remain as free as possible from any interference (*sanza ostaculo*) in the pursuit of their ascendancy.[32] On the other hand are the ordinary citizens, the *plebe* or *popolo*, whose main objective is simply to live in security. Their principal aim is likewise to remain as free as possible from interference, but in their case in the name of following so far as possible an undisturbed way of life.[33]

This account of why everyone values their freedom is at the same time an account of what Machiavelli means by speaking of individual freedom within civil associations. The *grandi* and *popolo* alike aim to be free in the sense of being unobstructed in the pursuit of the particular goals they choose to set themselves. As Machiavelli puts it in the opening chapter of Book I, the crucial contrast is thus between 'free men' and 'those who depend on others'.[34] To possess one's liberty is to be free in the ordinary 'negative' sense of being unconstrained by other agents. It is therefore to be free – as Machiavelli adds in his next chapter with reference to collective agents – to act 'according to one's own will and judgement'.[35]

It is important to underline this point, if only because it contradicts two claims often advanced by commentators on the *Discorsi*. One is that Machiavelli introduces the key term *libertà* into his discussion 'without taking the trouble to define it', so that the sense of the word only emerges gradually in the course of the argument.[36] The other is that, as soon as

---

[31] For an analysis and critique of my ensuing argument see Senellart 1995.
[32] Machiavelli 1960, I. 16, pp. 173–6 and I. 46, pp. 235–6.
[33] Machiavelli 1960, I. 16, pp. 173–6.
[34] Machiavelli 1960, I. 1, p. 126: 'uomini liberi o che dependono da altri'.
[35] Machiavelli 1960, I. 1, p. 129: 'governate per loro arbitrio'.
[36] Renaudet 1956, p. 186. For similar judgements see Pocock 1975, p. 196; Cadoni 1962, p. 462n; Colish 1971, pp. 323–4.

Machiavelli begins to make his meaning clear, it transpires that the term *libertà* as he uses it 'does not bear the sense' we should nowadays attribute to it; on the contrary, 'it must be taken in a wholly different sense'.[37]

Neither of these contentions seems warranted. As we have just observed, Machiavelli begins by stating exactly what he means by speaking of liberty: he means absence of constraint, especially absence of any limitations or obstructions imposed by other agents on one's capacity to act independently in pursuit of one's chosen goals. But as we saw at the outset, there is nothing unfamiliar about assigning the term 'liberty' this particular sense. To speak of liberty as a matter of being unconstrained by other social agents, and in consequence able to pursue one's own ends, is to echo a formula employed by many contemporary theorists of negative liberty, with whose basic framework of analysis Machiavelli appears to have no quarrel at all.

Given that we all have various goals we are minded to pursue, it will obviously be in our interests to live in whatever form of community best assures us the freedom to pursue them. So we next need to know under what type of regime we can most reliably hope to maximise our liberty to attain our chosen ends. By way of answering this question, Machiavelli introduces – at the start of Book 2 – an unfamiliar but pivotal claim into his discussion of individual liberty. The only form of polity, he maintains, in which we can hope to retain our freedom to follow our own pursuits will be one of which it makes sense to say that the community itself is free. Only in such communities can ambitious citizens hope to acquire power and glory for themselves, 'rising by means of their *virtù* to positions of prominence'.[38] Only in such communities can ordinary members of the *popolo* hope to live in security, 'without having any anxiety that their property will be taken away from them'.[39] Only in a free community, a *vivere libero*, are such benefits capable of being freely enjoyed.[40]

It remains to ask what Machiavelli means by speaking not merely of individuals but of communities as living, or not living, a free way of life. The short answer is that he means the same in both cases. As he makes clear at the start of Book 1, a political body, like a natural body, is free if and only if it is able to act according to its own will and in pursuit of its chosen ends. To speak of a free city or a free state is thus to speak of a

---

[37] Guillemain 1977, p. 321; Cadoni 1962, p. 482. For similar judgements see Hexter 1979, pp. 293–4; Prezzolini 1968, p. 63.
[38] Machiavelli 1960, II. 2, p. 284: 'ch'ei possono mediante la virtù loro diventare principi'.
[39] Machiavelli 1960, II. 2, p. 284: 'non dubitando che il patrimonio gli sia tolto'.
[40] Machiavelli 1960, I. 16, p. 174.

community which is 'not subject to the control of anyone else', and is thus able, in virtue of being unconstrained, 'to govern itself from the outset according to its own will, whether as a republic or a principality'.[41]

What, then, is the type of regime best suited to upholding such a free way of life? Machiavelli thinks it possible, at least in theory, for a community to live in liberty under a monarchical form of government. He sees no reason in principle why a king should not organise the laws of his kingdom in such a way as to reflect the general will – and thereby promote the common good – of the community as a whole.[42] But in practice Machiavelli is deeply sceptical about the capacity of princes to promote our liberty, as he makes clear in a crucial summarising passage at the start of Book 2. 'It is not the pursuit of individual good, but of the common good, that makes cities great, and it is beyond doubt that it is only in republics that this ideal of the common good is properly served, because everything that promotes it is followed out.'[43] Machiavelli's resounding conclusion is thus that, if we wish to see the common good fostered, and our individual liberty in consequence upheld, we must make sure that we institute and maintain a system of self-government. We can never hope to live a free way of life unless we live under a republican regime.

This conclusion represents the heart and nerve not merely of the *Discorsi* but of all neo-Roman theories of freedom and citizenship. Among more recent proponents of negative liberty, however, this commitment has usually been dismissed as an obvious absurdity. Hobbes, for example, seeks to dispose of it by sheer assertion, declaring in *Leviathan* that 'Whether a Common-wealth be Monarchicall, or Popular, the Freedome is still the same.'[44] This contention has in turn been reiterated by many defenders of negative liberty in the course of the contemporary debate, most of whom have explicitly denied that there is any necessary connection between the maximising of individual liberty and the upholding of any particular form of government. Our next task must therefore be to enquire into the reasons Machiavelli offers for insisting that, on the contrary, the preservation of individual liberty requires the maintenance of one particular type of regime.

---

[41] Machiavelli 1960, I. 2, p. 129: 'si sono subito governate per loro arbitrio, o come republiche o come principato'.

[42] Machiavelli 1960, I. 11, p. 154; I. 36, pp. 193–4; III. 5, pp. 388–90. For an excellent discussion see Colish 1971, p. 345.

[43] Machiavelli 1960 II, 2, p. 280: 'non il bene particulare ma il bene comune è quello che fa grandi le città. E sanza dubbio questo bene comune non è osservato se non nelle republiche: perché tutto quello che fa a proposito si esequisce.'

[44] Hobbes 1996, p. 149.

IV

The key to Machiavelli's reasoning at this stage is to be found in his account of the place of *ambizione* in public life.[45] As we have already seen, he believes that the exercise of ambition is invariably fatal to the liberty of anyone against whom it is successfully directed. This is because it takes the form of a *libido dominandi*, a willingness to coerce others and use them as means to one's own ends. We next need to recognise that this disposition to act ambitiously arises, according to Machiavelli, in two distinct forms, neither of which we have any possibility of fending off unless we live as citizens of an elective and self-governing republic.

One of these forms we have already encountered. It arises – to cite Machiavelli's terminology – 'from within' a community, and reflects the desire of the *grandi* to achieve power at the expense of their fellow-citizens. This is an ineliminable threat, for the *grandi* we have always with us, and they will always pursue these selfish goals. These they characteristically seek to attain by gathering around themselves groups of partisans, aiming to use these 'private forces' to wrest control of the government out of the hands of the public and seize power for themselves.[46]

Machiavelli distinguishes three main ways in which ambitious *grandi* can manage to acquire such partisans. The first, which he considers in Book 1, is that they can use their high social standing to overawe their fellow-citizens and persuade them to adopt measures more conducive to the promotion of sectional interests than the good of the community as a whole.[47] The other two possibilities are raised in the course of Book 3. One is that the *grandi* can seek to have themselves re-elected to public offices for excessive periods, so becoming sources of increasing patronage as well as objects of increasing personal loyalty.[48] The other is that they can lay out their exceptional wealth to purchase the support and favour of the *popolo* at the expense of the public interest.[49] As Machiavelli summarises at the outset of his discussion, in every case the same chain-reaction is set up. 'From partisans arise factions in cities, and from factions their ruin'.[50] The moral is that 'such is the ambitiousness of the *grandi*

---

[45] For systematic analyses of Machiavelli's employment of this term see Price 1982 and Price 1988.
[46] Machiavelli 1960, III. 22, pp. 448–54 and III. 28, pp. 463–4.
[47] Machiavelli 1960, I. 33, pp. 206–9 and I. 46, pp. 235–6.
[48] Machiavelli 1960, III. 22, pp. 448–54 and III. 24, pp. 455–6.
[49] Machiavelli 1960, III. 28, pp. 463–4.
[50] Machiavelli 1960, I. 7, p. 148: 'da partigiani nascono le parti nella cittadi, da parti la rovina di quelle'.

that, unless a city devises various ways and means of beating it down, they will quickly bring it to ruin'.[51]

The other form of *ambizione* Machiavelli describes is said to threaten free communities 'from outside'. At this stage the pervasive image of the body politic carries the full weight of the argument, since the parallel between natural and corporate bodies is said to extend to their having the same dispositions and natures. Just as some individuals seek the quiet life while others go in quest of power and glory, so too with bodies politic. Some attempt 'to live quietly and enjoy their liberty within their own boundaries', but others seek to dominate their neighbours and coerce them into acting as client states.[52] As always, ancient Rome is cited as the best illustration of this general truth. Due to their ambitiousness, the Romans waged continuous war on the peoples surrounding them, attaining their 'supreme greatness' by conquering each neighbour in turn, overthrowing their liberty and subjecting them to the service of Rome.[53]

As in the case of individual *grandi*, so too with entire communities, this disposition to act ambitiously is altogether natural and ineliminable. Some communities always seek to dominate others, from which it follows that 'neighbouring princes and neighbouring republics harbour natural feelings of hatred for one another, the product of this ambition to dominate'.[54] Moreover, just as the clients of ambitious *grandi* find themselves coerced into serving their patron's ends, so too the citizens of any polity that becomes the client of another will automatically forfeit their personal liberty. They will find themselves forced into doing their conqueror's bidding as soon as their community is reduced to servitude.[55]

There are, in short, two distinct threats to personal as well as civic liberty arising from the omnipresence of ambitiousness. How can they be fought off? Consider first the danger of servitude arising 'from outside'. To meet this threat, the members of a free community must obviously follow the methods and cultivate the qualities needed for effective defence. These Machiavelli takes to be the same for political as for natural bodies. The right method is to establish military ordinances to ensure that all

---

[51] Machiavelli 1960, I. 37, p. 218: 'perché gli è tanta l'ambizione de' grandi, che se per varie vie ed in vari modi ella non è in una città sbattuta, tosto riduce quella città alla rovina sua'.
[52] See Machiavelli 1960, II. 19, pp. 334–5, where he warns that this course cannot be followed: 'è impossibile che ad una republica riesca lo stare quieta e godersi la sua libertà e gli pochi confini'.
[53] Machiavelli 1960, II. 2, p. 279 and II. 6, p. 294.
[54] Machiavelli 1960, III. 12, p. 426: 'e' naturali odii che hanno i principi vicini e le republiche vicine l'uno contro l'altro: il che procede da ambizione di dominare'.
[55] Machiavelli makes this point in each of the three books of the *Discorsi*. See, for example, Machiavelli 1960, I. 2, pp. 129–34; II. 19, pp. 333–8; III. 12, pp. 425–8.

citizens act as the defenders of their own liberty, thereby preventing them from adopting the lazy and effeminate alternative of hiring soldiers to fight on their behalf.[56] To rely on mercenaries, Machiavelli repeatedly warns, is a sure way to ruin your city and forfeit your liberty, simply because their only motive for fighting is the small amount of pay you give them. This means that they will never be so much your friends as to be willing to lay down their lives in your cause. By contrast, a citizen army will always be striving for its own glory in attack and its own freedom in defence, and will therefore be far more willing to fight to the death.[57]

Machiavelli is not of course saying that a city which defends its body with its own arms will thereby guarantee its citizens their liberty. Against overwhelming odds, as the Samnites discovered in their struggles against Rome, there is ultimately no hope of avoiding defeat and enslavement.[58] But he is certainly admonishing us that, unless we are willing personally to contribute to the defence of our community against external aggression, we shall 'become so weak as to lay ourselves open as a prey to anyone who chooses to attack'.[59] As a consequence of this effeminate feebleness, we can expect to find ourselves, sooner rather than later, reduced to a state of servitude.[60]

As for the personal qualities we need to cultivate in order to defend our liberty, Machiavelli singles out two above all. We first of all need to be wise. But the wisdom we require is by no means that of the consciously sage and sapient, the *savi*, whom Machiavelli (following Livy) usually treats with marked disdain and irony. To be *savio* is generally to lack precisely those qualities of wisdom which are essential in military (and indeed in civil) affairs.[61] The relevant qualities are those required for the forming of practical judgments, the careful and effective calculation of chances and outcomes. They are, in a word, the qualities of *prudenza*. Prudence tells you when to go to war, how to conduct a campaign, how to bear its changing fortunes.[62] It is one of the qualities by which the greatest commanders have always been distinguished. As usual, Machiavelli is thinking in particular of the military leaders of early Rome, leaders such as Tullius and Camillus, each of whom was *prudentissimo* in his generalship.[63]

[56] Machiavelli 1960, I. 21, pp. 186–7.
[57] Machiavelli 1960, I. 43, p. 231; II. 10, pp. 302–5; II. 30, pp. 368–71.
[58] Machiavelli 1960, II. 2, pp. 279–80 and II. 3, pp. 285–7.
[59] Machiavelli 1960, I. 6, p. 144: 'ei diventa si vile che tu sei preda di qualunque ti assalta'.
[60] Machiavelli 1960, II. 10, p. 304; II. 19, pp. 334–6; II. 30, p. 369.
[61] See, for example, Machiavelli 1960, II. 24, p. 349 and II. 27, p. 461.
[62] See, for example, Machiavelli 1960, II. 12, p. 302; II. 14, p. 314; II. 27, p. 362.
[63] Machiavelli 1960, I. 21, p. 186; III. 12, p. 428.

The other quality indispensable for effective defence is *animo*, courage, which Machiavelli sometimes couples with *ostinazione*, sheer determination and persistence. Courage is the other leading attribute of the greatest military commanders, as Machiavelli repeatedly stresses in explaining the military successes of early Rome. When Cincinnatus, for example, was called from his plough to mount the defence of his city, he at once assumed the Dictatorship, raised an army, marched forth and defeated the enemy in a dramatically short space of time. The quality that brought him this decisive victory was *la grandezza dello animo*, his high courage.[64] Courage is also the quality that must above all be instilled in every individual soldier if victory is to be grasped. Nothing is more likely to bring defeat than the kind of accident that has the effect of taking away the courage of an army and leaving it terrified.[65] As the conduct of the French in battle above all reminds us, 'natural fury' is never enough; what is needed is fury disciplined by persistence or, in a word, courage.[66]

Even if 'external' ambition is successfully fought off, there is still the more insidious danger that the same malign disposition will arise 'from within' your city, in the breasts of its leading citizens, and thereby reduce you to servitude. How is this to be forestalled? Machiavelli again argues that, in the first instance, this is a matter of establishing the right laws and ordinances, and again alludes to the metaphor of the body politic in describing what laws are required. They must be such as to prevent any single limb or member of the body from exercising an undue or coercive influence over its will. The laws governing the behaviour of the community must express its general will, not merely the will of its active and most ambitious part. But this in turn means that, as Cicero had stressed, there must be specific laws and institutions capable of serving as a *temperamento* – a curb, a means of tempering selfish ambition and factiousness.[67] For as Machiavelli repeatedly affirms – citing a metaphor much invoked by Virgil as well as Cicero – unless the *grandi* are 'bridled' and 'held in check' their natural intemperance will quickly lead to disorderly and tyrannical results.[68]

---

[64] Machiavelli 1960, III. 25, p. 458.   [65] Machiavelli 1960, III. 37, pp. 486–7.
[66] Machiavelli 1960, III. 36, pp. 484–5.
[67] On the Tribunate as *un grande temperamento* on the nobility under the Roman republic, see Machiavelli 1960, III. 11, p. 423. Machiavelli's source appears to be the discussion of the Tribunes as a *temperamentum* in Cicero 1928, III. X. 24, p. 486.
[68] See Machiavelli 1960, I. 16, p. 173, where he appears to allude to Virgil 1999–2000, I, line 54, p. 266. There we are told that Aeolus holds the winds in his power and curbs them with prison chains – 'imperio premit ac vinclis et carcere frenat'. Machiavelli speaks throughout Book I of the need for a *freno* to curb the nobility. See Machiavelli 1960, I. 3, p. 136; I. 6, p. 142; I. 18, p. 180; I. 37, p. 218; I. 49, p. 243; I. 55, p. 257.

Besides the right *leggi e ordini*, there are certain personal qualities that everyone in public life must cultivate if they are to act as vigilant guardians of their own liberty. Once more Machiavelli singles out two above all. One is again said to be wisdom, but again this is not the wisdom of the professional sage. Rather it is the worldly wisdom or prudence of the experienced statesman, the person with practical ability to judge the best courses of action and follow them out. This quality is not merely indispensable for effective political leadership. It is also a central thesis of Machiavelli's political theory that no community can hope to be 'well-ordered' unless it is 'brought to order' by such a *prudente ordinatore*, such a worldly wise organiser of its civic life.[69] Furthermore, it is no less crucial that every citizen who aspires to take a hand in government, to help in upholding the freedom of the community, should be prudent by nature. Suppose we ask, for example, how it came about that ancient Rome was able, over so long a period, 'to institute all the laws that maintained her in liberty'.[70] The answer is that the city was continually organised and reorganised 'by so many leaders who were *prudenti*' that this constituted the key to her success.[71]

The other quality that every citizen must cultivate is a willingness to avoid all forms of intemperate and disorderly conduct, thereby ensuring that civic affairs are debated and decided in an orderly and well-tempered style. Taking up the Roman ideal of *temperantia*, Machiavelli closely follows his classical sources – notably Livy and Cicero – in dividing his discussion at this juncture into two parts. One aspect of *temperantia*, as Cicero had explained in *De Officiis*, consists of those qualities that enable a citizen to advise and act in a truly statesmanlike way. The most important of these, he repeatedly declares, are *modestia* and *moderatio*.[72] Machiavelli completely agrees:

I see no other way for those who offer advice to republics than to consider everything in a moderate way, not to lay claim to any undertaking as their own idea, and to give their opinion without passion, and then modestly and without passion to defend it.[73]

Machiavelli is scarcely less emphatic than Cicero about the value of conducting public affairs in a dispassionate style.

[69] Machiavelli 1960, I. 2, pp. 129–30; I. 9, pp. 153–5.
[70] Machiavelli 1960, I. 49, p. 241: 'provedere a tutte quelle leggi che la mantengono libera'.
[71] Machiavelli 1960, I. 49, p. 244.
[72] Cicero 1913, I. XXVII. 93, p. 96; I. XXVII. 96, p. 98; I. XL. 143, p. 146; I. XLV. 159, p. 162.
[73] Machiavelli 1960, III. 35, p. 482: 'Non ci veggo altra via [sc. per quegli che consigliano una republica] che pigliare le cose moderatamente, e non ne prendere alcuna per sua impresa, e dire la opinione su sanza passione, e sanza passione con modestia difenderla.'

PLATES 1–8 AMBROGIO LORENZETTI, *BUON GOVERNO*, FRESCO CYCLE, SALA DEI NOVE, PALAZZO PUBBLICO, SIENA

Plate 1 *The city and countryside under tyranny* (western wall)

Plate 2 *The rule of tyranny* (western wall)

Plate 3 *The rule of virtuous government* (northern wall)

Plate 4 *Justice and Concord* (detail of Plate 3)

Plate 5 *The effects of virtuous government in the city* (eastern wall)

Plate 6 *The effects of virtuous government in the countryside* (eastern wall)

Plate 7 *The effects of tyranny in the city* (western wall)

Plate 8 *Siena as Supreme Judge of the Sienese* (detail of Plate 3)

Plate 9 Giotto, *The Last Judgement*, fresco (western wall, Cappella degli Scrovegni, Padua)

Plate 10 *Dancers in the city* (detail of Plate 5)

Plate 11 Giotto, *Justice*, fresco (southern wall, Cappella degli Scrovegni, Padua)

Plate 12 Andrea di Bonaiuto, *Allegory of the Church*, fresco (Cappellone degli Spagnoli, Santa Maria Novella, Florence)

The other requirement of *temperantia*, Cicero had added, is that everyone should behave 'with orderliness',[74] a sentiment echoed by Livy with his frequent insistence on the need to act *recte et ordine*, in a right and orderly way. Again Machiavelli completely agrees. To maintain a *vivere libero*, the citizens must avoid all *disordine* and conduct themselves *ordinariamente*, in an orderly way. If intemperate and disorderly methods (*modi straordinari*) are permitted, tyranny will result; but as long as orderly and temperate methods (*modi ordinari*) are followed, freedom can be successfully preserved over long periods of time.[75]

Machiavelli helpfully summarises his argument towards the end of Book I in the course of explaining why he believes that the cities of Tuscany could easily have introduced a *vivere civile* if only a prudent leader with a knowledge of ancient statecraft had arisen to command them. As grounds for this judgement he mentions the fact that the Tuscan communes have always displayed *animo*, courage, and *ordine*, temperance and orderliness. From which it follows that, if only the missing ingredient of *prudente* leadership had been added, they would have been able to maintain their liberty.[76]

V

Hobbes insists in *Leviathan* that the classical and neo-Roman theory of liberty I have been considering is in danger of leaving us confused:

> The Liberties, whereof there is so frequent, and honourable mention, in the Histories, and Philosophy of the Antient Greeks, and Romans, and in the writings, and discourse of those that from them, have received all their learning in the Politiques, is not the Libertie of Particular men; but the Libertie of the Common-wealth.[77]

We can now see, however, that Hobbes has either failed to grasp the point of the classical and neo-Roman argument I have sought to reconstruct or else is deliberately distorting it. For the point of the argument is of course that the liberty of the commonwealth and the liberty of particular men cannot be separately assessed in the way that Hobbes and his epigoni among contemporary theorists of negative liberty assume. The essence of the neo-Roman case is that, unless a commonwealth is maintained 'in a state of liberty' (in the ordinary sense of being free from constraint

---

[74] Cicero 1913, I. XL. 142, p. 144.
[75] Machiavelli 1960, I. 7, pp. 146–9. See also Machiavelli 1960, I. 22, p. 188; I. 24, p. 191; I. 49, pp. 242–4.
[76] Machiavelli 1960, I. 55, p. 257.   [77] Hobbes 1996, p. 149.

to act according to its own will) then the individual members of such a body politic will find themselves stripped of their personal liberty (again in the ordinary sense of losing their freedom to seek their own goals). The grounds for this conclusion are that, as soon as a body politic forfeits the capacity to act according to its general will, and becomes subject to the will of either its own *grandi* or some ambitious neighbouring community, its citizens will find themselves treated as means to their masters' ends, and will thereby lose their freedom to pursue their own purposes. The enslavement of a community thus brings with it the inevitable loss of individual liberty. Conversely, the liberty of particular men, *pace* Hobbes, can only be assured under a 'free commonwealth', an elective and self-governing form of republican regime.

To grasp this point is at the same time to see that there is no difficulty about defending both the claims about social freedom which, as we saw at the outset, contemporary philosophers have been apt to stigmatise as paradoxical, or at least as incompatible with a negative understanding of individual liberty.

The first was the suggestion that freedom is connected with service — that only those who place themselves wholeheartedly at the service of their community are capable of assuring their own liberty. We can now see that, from the perspective of classical and neo-Roman thought, this is not a paradox but a perfectly straightforward truth. For a writer like Machiavelli, the liberty of individual citizens depends in the first place on their capacity to fight off servitude arising 'from outside'. But this can only be done if they are willing to undertake the defence of their polity themselves. A readiness to perform one's military service, to volunteer for active service, to join what we still call the armed services, constitutes a necessary condition of maintaining one's own individual freedom from servitude. Unless we are prepared to act 'in such a way as to exalt and defend our fatherland', we shall find ourselves conquered and enslaved.[78]

The maintenance of personal liberty also depends according to Machiavelli on preventing the *grandi* from coercing the *popolo* into serving their ends. But the only way to prevent this from happening is to organise the polity in such a way that every citizen is equally able to play a part in determining the actions of the body politic as a whole. This in turn means that a readiness to serve in public office, to pursue a life of public service, to perform voluntary services, constitutes a further necessary condition of maintaining one's own liberty. Only if we are prepared

---

[78] Machiavelli 1960, II. 2, p. 283 on the need to promote 'la esaltazione e la difesa della patria'.

'to do good for the community', to 'help forward' and 'act on behalf of' the common good, can we hope in turn to avoid a state of tyranny and personal dependence.[79]

Cicero had laid it down in his *De Officiis* that individual and civic liberty can only be preserved if we are prepared to act 'as slaves to the public interest'.[80] There are several echoes in Livy's history of the same use of the vocabulary of slavery to describe the condition of political liberty.[81] Machiavelli is simply reiterating the same classical oxymoron: the price we have to pay for enjoying any degree of personal freedom with any degree of continuing security is voluntary public service.

I turn to the other contention that contemporary writers have generally held to be incompatible with a negative understanding of individual liberty. This is the connected suggestion that the attributes required of each individual citizen in order to perform these public services must be the virtues, and thus that only those who behave virtuously are capable of assuring their own freedom. If we revert to Machiavelli's account of the qualities we need to cultivate in order to serve our polity in war and peace, we can readily see that this too appears, from the perspective of classical and neo-Roman thought, to be a perfectly straightforward truth.

According to Machiavelli we stand in need of three qualities above all: courage to defend our liberty; temperance and orderliness to maintain free government; and prudence to direct our civic and military undertakings to the best effect. As we saw in chapter 5, however, this is to speak of three of the four 'cardinal' virtues invariably singled out by the Roman historians and moralists. They had all agreed that – to cite Cicero's formulation in *De Inventione* – the overarching concept of *virtus generalis* can be divided into four components, and that these are prudence, justice, courage and temperance.[82]

It is true that Machiavelli's analysis differs from Cicero's in one immensely important respect. He silently makes one alteration – small in appearance but overwhelming in significance – to the classical analysis of the virtues needed to serve the common good. He erases the quality of justice, the quality that Cicero in *De Officiis* had described as the crowning splendour of virtue.[83]

---

[79] Machiavelli 1960, I. 9, pp. 153–4 on the indispensability of citizens who 'giovare...al bene comune' and act 'per il bene comune'.
[80] Cicero 1913, I. X. 31, p. 32: 'communi utilitati serviatur'.
[81] For example, Livy 1924, V. X. 5, vol. 3, p. 34. For a fuller exploration of this point see Skinner 1998.
[82] Cicero 1949, II. LIII. 159, p. 326.   [83] Cicero 1913, I. VII. 20, p. 20.

This is not to say that Machiavelli fails to discuss the concept of justice in the *Discorsi*. On the contrary, he follows the Ciceronian analysis of the concept almost word for word. As we saw in chapter 5, Cicero had argued in his *De Officiis* that the essence of justice consists in the avoidance of *iniuria* or harm contrary to right. Such harm can arise in one of two ways: either as the product of fraud or of 'brutal' and 'inhumane' cruelty and violence. To observe the dictates of justice is thus to avoid both these vices, and this duty lies equally upon us at all times. For in war, no less than in peace, good faith must always be kept and cruelty eschewed. Finally, the observance of these duties is also said to be in our interests. If we behave unjustly, we shall not only cheat ourselves of honour and glory; we shall undermine our ability to promote the common good and thereby uphold our own liberty.[84]

Machiavelli fully agrees with this account of what constitutes the virtue of justice. But he flatly repudiates the crucial contention that the observance of this virtue is invariably conducive to serving the common good. As we saw in chapter 5, he regards this belief as an obvious and disastrous mistake, a dissenting judgement that takes us to the heart of his originality and his subversive quality as a theorist of statecraft. He responds in the first place by making a firm distinction between justice in war and peace, arguing that in warfare both forms of *iniuria* are frequently indispensable. Fraud is often crucial to victory, and to treat it as inglorious is absurd.[85] The same is no less true of cruelty, a quality that marked the very greatest of Rome's generals, such as Camillus and Manlius, and proved in each case to be vital to their success.[86] Moreover, the same lessons apply with almost equal force in civic affairs. Although fraud in this case is detestable, it is often essential to the achievement of great things.[87] And although cruelty may similarly stand as an accusation against anyone who practises it, there is no denying that it will often have to be practised, and will always have to be excused, if the life and liberty of free communities are to be successfully preserved.[88]

This represents an epoch-making break with the classical analysis of the cardinal virtues; its suddenness and completeness can hardly be overemphasised. But it is scarcely less important to emphasise that this

---

[84] For this analysis see above, chapter 5 section II, and cf. Cicero 1913, I. XI. 34 to I. XIV. 45, pp. 36–48.
[85] Machiavelli 1960, III. 40, pp. 493–4. [86] Machiavelli 1960, III. 22, pp. 448–54.
[87] Machiavelli 1960, II. 13, pp. 311–13.
[88] Machiavelli 1960, I. 9, pp. 153–5; I. 16, p. 175; II. 13, pp. 311–13; III. 30, pp. 466–9; III. 41, pp. 494–5.

represents Machiavelli's sole quarrel with his Roman authorities. The rest of his analysis of *virtù* and its connections with *libertà* is impeccably Ciceronian in character. He not only centres his entire account around the qualities of courage, temperance and prudence, but he regularly refers to these attributes as elements of virtue as well as preconditions of liberty. When generals or entire armies are described as exhibiting *animo*, they are also said to be displaying an element of *virtù*.[89] When communities and their members are said to be *bene ordinata*, they are again said to be in possession of an element of *virtù*.[90] When civic and military leaders are commended for *virtuoso* behaviour, this is often because they are said to have exhibited exceptional *prudenza*.[91] In all these cases, the qualities that assure liberty are cardinal virtues.

It is true that this is to offer an unorthodox reading of Machiavelli's views about the meaning and significance of *virtù*.[92] Federico Chabod summarises the more usual view when he declares that '*virtù*, in Machiavelli, is not a "moral" quality as it is for us; it refers instead to the possession of energy or capacity to decide and act'.[93] But I am not denying this; as far as it goes, this seems to me correct. The widest use to which Machiavelli consistently puts the term *virtù* is in speaking of the means by which we achieve particular results; the means, as we still say, by virtue of which they are achieved.[94] As a result, when he comes to speak of the results in which he is principally interested in the *Discorsi* – the preservation of liberty and the attainment of civic greatness – he consistently uses the term *virtù* to describe the human qualities needed for these successes to be achieved. Speaking of *virtù* in these connections, he is thus speaking of abilities, talents, capacities. Of generals and armies he frequently remarks that the quality which enables them to defeat their enemies, to win great victories, is their *virtù*.[95] When discussing the role of *virtù* in civic affairs, he likewise uses the term to describe the talents needed to found cities, to prevent faction, to avoid corruption, to maintain decisive leadership, to impose orderly government and to uphold the other arts of peace.[96]

---

[89] See, for example, Machiavelli 1960, I. 43, p. 231; II. 12, p. 310; III. 36, p. 484.
[90] See, for example, Machiavelli 1960, III. I, p. 380.
[91] See, for example, Machiavelli 1960, I. 1, pp. 125–9; I. 21, p. 186; III. 23, p. 454.
[92] For a recent and contrasting analysis see Mansfield 1996, pp. 6–52.
[93] Chabod 1964, p. 248.
[94] For representative examples see Machiavelli 1960, I. 15, p. 172; II. 6, p. 295; II. 24, p. 354; III. 1, p. 381.
[95] For representative examples see Machiavelli 1960, I. 19, p. 184; II. 2, p. 279; III. 22, p. 452.
[96] For representative examples see Machiavelli 1960, I. 1, p. 127; I. 9, p. 154; I. 17, pp. 178–9.

My objection to Chabod's type of analysis is merely that it does not go far enough.[97] We still need to ask about the specific nature of the talents or abilities that serve to bring about these great results in civic and military affairs. If we press this further question we find, as we have seen, that Machiavelli's answer comes in two parts. We first need a certain ruthlessness, a willingness to discount the demands of justice when this is necessary to uphold the common good. But the remaining qualities we need are courage, temperance and prudence. At the heart of Machiavelli's political theory there is thus a purely classical message, framed in the same play on words that the ancient theorists had all exploited. If we ask in virtue of what qualities, what talents or abilities, we can hope to assure our own liberty and contribute to the common good, the answer is: in virtue of the virtues.

VI

In the light of the above attempt to outline the structure of a classical and neo-Roman theory of freedom, I now wish to revert to the current disputes about the idea of negative liberty from which I started out. The historical materials I have presented, I shall conclude by suggesting, are relevant to these disputes in two related ways.

They show us, in the first place, that the terms of the contemporary debate have become confused. It is agreed on all hands that a theory of liberty connecting the idea of social freedom with the performance of virtuous acts of public service would have to begin by positing certain ends as rational for everyone to pursue, and then seek to establish that the attainment of those ends would leave us in the fullest or truest sense in possession of our liberty. This is of course a possible way of connecting the concepts of freedom, virtue and service. It is widely (though I think mistakenly)[98] held to be Spinoza's way of doing so in his *Tractatus Politicus*, and it certainly appears to be Rousseau's way of doing so in *Du Contrat Social*. It is by no means the only way of doing so, however, as present-day analytical philosophers are apt to suppose. In a theory such as Machiavelli's, the point of departure is not a vision of *eudaimonia* or real human interests, but simply an account of the 'humours' or dispositions

[97] The same seems to me to apply to Price 1973, although this is the best available discussion of the uses of the term *virtù* throughout Machiavelli's political works.
[98] Because such interpretations underestimate the extent to which Spinoza is restating classical republican ideas, especially as developed by Machiavelli in the *Discorsi*. But for an excellent corrective see Haitsma Mulier 1980.

that prompt us to choose and pursue our various ends. Machiavelli has no quarrel with the Hobbesian assumption that the capacity to pursue such ends without obstruction is what the term 'liberty properly signifieth'. He merely argues that the performance of public services, and the cultivation of the virtues needed for performing them, prove upon examination to be instrumentally necessary to the avoidance of coercion and servitude, and thus to be necessary conditions of assuring any degree of personal liberty in the ordinary Hobbesian sense of the term.

This brings me to the other way in which the classical and neo-Roman theory is relevant to contemporary arguments. As a consequence of overlooking the possibility that a theory of negative liberty might coherently have the structure I have sketched, a number of philosophers have proceeded to enunciate further claims about the concept which they take to be statements of general truths, but which are in fact true only of their own particular theories of negative liberty.

One of these has been the Hobbesian claim that any theory of negative liberty must in effect be a theory of individual rights. As we have seen, this has acquired the status of an axiom in many contemporary discussions of negative liberty. Liberty of action, we are assured, 'is a right'; there is a 'moral right to liberty'; we are bound to view our liberty both as a natural right and as the means to secure our other rights.[99] As will by now be evident, these are mere dogmas. A neo-Roman theory such as Machiavelli's helps us to see that there is no conceivable obligation to think of our liberty in this particular way. Machiavelli's is a theory of negative liberty, but he develops it without making any use whatever of the concept of individual rights. While he often speaks of that which is *onesto*, or morally right, I know of no passage in his entire political writings where he speaks of individual agents as the bearers of *diritti* or rights.[100] On the contrary, the essence of his theory could be expressed by saying that the attainment of social freedom cannot be a matter of securing personal rights, since it indispensably requires the performance of social duties.

Machiavelli's scholastic contemporaries and their contractarian descendants have tended to respond to these arguments in a similar way. The best means, they suggest, to secure our personal liberty must

---

[99] For these claims see respectively Day 1977, p. 270; Day 1983, p. 18; McCloskey 1965, pp. 404–5.
[100] Colish 1971, pp. 345–6 claims that 'Machiavelli often connects *libertà* with certain private rights' and 'clearly identifies freedom with the protection of private rights'. But I can find no textual warrant for these assertions. For a good corrective to such anachronistic claims see Sasso 1958, pp. 333–41.

nevertheless be to conceive of it as a right, as a species of moral property, and to defend it absolutely against all forms of external interference. But to this objection the classical and neo-Roman theorists of freedom have a strong retort. To adopt this attitude, they maintain, is not merely the epitome of corrupt citizenship, but is also (like all derelictions of social duty) in the highest degree an instance of imprudence. All prudent citizens recognise that, whatever degree of negative liberty they may enjoy, it can only be the outcome of – and if you like the reward of – a steady recognition and pursuit of the public good at the expense of all purely individual and private ends.

As we have seen, however, contemporary theorists of negative liberty have not lacked their own retort at this point. They have gone on to denounce the underlying suggestion that it may be in our interests to perform our duties as dangerous metaphysical nonsense. But it will now be evident that this too is a mistake. Machiavelli believes of course that as citizens we have a specific duty (*ufficio*) to perform, that of advising and serving our community to the best of our abilities. So there are many things, he repeatedly tells us, that we ought to do and many others that we ought to avoid. But the reason he gives us for cultivating the virtues and serving the common good is never that these are our duties. The reason is always that these represent, as it happens, the best and indeed the only means for us 'to do well' on our own behalf, and in particular the only means of securing any degree of personal liberty to pursue our chosen ends. There is thus a perfectly clear and unmetaphysical sense in which, although Machiavelli never speaks of interests, it would be fair to say that he believes our duty and our interests to be one and the same. He is celebrated, moreover, for the chilling emphasis which he places on the idea that all men are evil, and can never be expected to do anything good unless they can see that it will be for their own advantage. So his final word is not merely that the apparent paradox of duty as interest enunciates, once more, a straightforward truth. Like his Roman authorities, he also believes that it states the most fortunate of all moral truths. For unless the generality of evil men can be given selfish reasons for behaving virtuously, it is unlikely that any of them will perform any virtuous actions at all.

8

Thomas More's Utopia *and the virtue of true nobility*

I

Almost everything about Thomas More's *Utopia* is debatable, but at least the general subject-matter of the book is not in doubt. More announces his theme on the title-page, which reads: *De optimo reipublicae statu deque nova insula Utopia*.[1] His concern, that is, is not merely or even primarily with the new island of Utopia; it is with 'the best state of a commonwealth'.

To say that this is More's concern is at once to raise what has always been seen as the main interpretative puzzle about his book. Does he intend us to take the description of Utopia in Book 2 as an account of a commonwealth in its best state? Are we intended to share and ratify the almost unbounded enthusiasm that Raphael Hythloday, the traveller to Utopia, displays for that island and its way of life?

Until recently More's interpreters tended to answer in the affirmative. One theory has been that More aimed to picture the best state that reason can hope to establish in the absence of revelation.[2] A yet more influential suggestion has been that he not only sought to portray a perfectly virtuous commonwealth, but wished at the same time to convey that, in spite of their heathenism, the Utopians are more truly and genuinely Christian than the nominally Christian states of western Europe.[3] While disagreeing on the extent to which More holds up Utopia as an ideal, both schools of thought accept that Utopia must in some sense be regarded as an ideal commonwealth. Of late, however, the

---

This chapter is a revised and updated version of an essay that originally appeared under the title 'More's *Utopia* and the Language of Renaissance Humanism' in *The Languages of Political Theory in Early-Modern Europe*, ed. Anthony Pagden (Cambridge, 1986), pp. 123–57.

[1] More 1965, p. cxcv. On the apparently Senecan allusion in the title see Parrish 1997.

[2] This interpretation was originally propounded in Chambers 1935 and has since been adopted by numerous commentators. For a list see Skinner 1978a, p. 257n.

[3] This is Hexter's thesis, originally put forward in Hexter 1952, p. 57 and fully developed in Hexter 1965, pp. lxviii–lxxvi. See Skinner 1967 for a discussion and Skinner 1978a, pp. 255–62 for a broad endorsement.

best scholarship on *Utopia* has instead laid all its emphasis on the doubts and equivocations in More's text.[4] Some commentators have stressed the inherently ambiguous character of the dialogue form that More chooses to employ;[5] others have underlined the moments at which he seems to criticise his own analysis of the 'best state',[6] and even to treat it as a futile theory which is doomed to 'get nowhere'.[7] From several different perspectives, scholars have converged on the suggestion that (as Brendan Bradshaw has expressed it) More must be taken to be expressing 'serious reservations about the ideal system' which Hythloday describes.[8] More's final aim (in W. S. Allen's words) must have been to leave us 'with an ambivalent and puzzled view' about Utopian life as a whole.[9]

There can be no doubt that this new approach has added significantly to our understanding of More's text, especially by insisting on the implications of the fact that the figure of More in the dialogue disagrees with Hythloday at several important points.[10] Nevertheless, the new orthodoxy seems to me to embody an unacceptable view of More's basic purposes. I shall accordingly try in what follows to restate the case for saying that, for all the ironies and ambiguities in More's text, his principal aim was to challenge his readers at least to consider seriously whether Utopia may not represent the best state of a commonwealth.

II

More's handling of the theme of the *optimus status reipublicae* undoubtedly contains many unusual and puzzling elements. But it is important to note at the outset that there was nothing unusual about More's decision to consider that particular theme. More's text is sometimes approached as if he introduced a completely new topic into Renaissance political thought.[11] But in fact the question of what constitutes the best state of a commonwealth had been a standard subject of debate throughout the era of the Renaissance. We find the question posed by a number of scholastic political philosophers in the wake of Aristotle's discussion

---

[4] For a critical survey of the recent literature see Logan 1994, pp. 203–58. Guy 2000 provides a fine survey of the question-marks that hang over every aspect of More's life.
[5] See Bevington 1961, pp. 496–509; Surtz 1965a, pp. cxxxiv–cxlvii. On More's use of the dialogue form see also Logan 1983, esp. pp. 121–3 and references.
[6] Logan 1983, pp. 257–62 sees *Utopia* less as a discussion of More's views about the *optimus status* than as a critical analysis of the classical and Renaissance literature on the theme.
[7] Fenlon 1975, p. 124.   [8] Bradshaw 1981, p. 25.   [9] Allen 1976, p. 118.
[10] Sylvester 1968 emphasises this point. See also Logan 1983, pp. 4–6 and references.
[11] Davis 1981, pp. 43, 61; Bradshaw 1981, p. 18.

in the *Politics*.¹² We also find it raised by an even wider range of so-called 'humanist' writers – that is, by those whose primary intellectual allegiances were owed to the *studia humanitatis*, and hence to the moral and political philosophy of Rome rather than Greece.¹³

This in turn suggests a way of approaching the complexities of More's text. If Utopia is an instance of a familiar genre of Renaissance political theory, it may be best to begin not with More's text but rather with some attempt to indicate the assumptions and conventions characteristic of the genre as a whole. Beginning in this way, we may eventually be able to gain a better sense of More's own basic purposes. For we may be able to see how far he is accepting and reiterating common assumptions, or perhaps rephrasing and reworking them, or perhaps criticising and repudiating them altogether in order to attain a new perspective on a familiar theme. It is this approach which I shall now attempt to put to work.

Among political theorists of the Renaissance, whether scholastic or humanist in allegiance, there was little debate over what constitutes the *optimus status reipublicae*. A state will be in its best state, it was widely agreed, if and only if two claims can appropriately be made about it. One is that its laws are just and thereby serve to promote the common good of its citizens. The other is that its citizens are in consequence able to pursue their own happiness, 'living and living well' in the manner most befitting the nature and dignity of mankind.¹⁴

As soon as writers of this period turn, however, to ask how these conditions can be brought about, large differences of opinion begin to emerge. Among these, the most basic concerned the form of government that needs to be set up if a commonwealth is to have any chance of

---

[12] For a scholastic discussion of the fruits of different forms of government as *optimi* or *pessimi*, see for example Marsilius 1928, I. 1, pp. 2–3.

[13] Seneca uses the phrase in *De Beneficiis*, telling us that a city is in its *optimus status* under the rule of a just king. See Seneca 1928–35, vol. 2, II. XX. 2, p. 92. Cicero mentions in his *Tusculanae Disputationes*, that Plato enquired into the *optimum rei publicae statum*. See Cicero 1927, II. XI. 27, p. 174. He adds in *De Finibus* that Aristotle also discussed the *optimus rei publicae status*. See Cicero 1931, V. IV. 11, p. 402. Drawing on such sources, humanist political writers of the *quattrocento* frequently employed the same phrase as well as debating the same theme. Erasmus and his circle speak in the same terms. Erasmus in his *Institutio Christiani Principis* compares the *pessimus* with the *optimus status reipublicae*. See Erasmus 1974, pp. 162, 194. Thomas Starkey examines the question at length in his *Dialogue*. See Starkey 1948, especially the summary at p. 63.

[14] This was the standard scholastic viewpoint. See, for example, Marsilius 1928, I. 4 and 5, pp. 11–21 on the need for the law to promote the *commune conferens*, thereby allowing each citizen *vivere et bene vivere*. The same assumptions recur among the Erasmian humanists of More's day. See for example Starkey 1948, esp. pp. 61–5. This was also More's viewpoint in *Utopia*. See More 1965, esp. pp. 236, 238, 240.

attaining and remaining in its best state. One widely held belief was that the only sure method is to assign all the affairs of the *res publica* to a wise guardian, a *Pater patriae*. His duty is to take upon himself the burdens of the *vita activa*, leaving everyone else free to pursue their own higher purposes and so attain happiness. As we saw in chapter 5, this was the view of the earliest generation of self-styled humanists, including Petrarch himself in his last political testament,[15] and of such younger contemporaries as Pier Paolo Vergerio and Giovanni da Ravenna, both of whom lived and wrote – as did Petrarch in the closing years of his life – under the patronage of the Carrara lords of Padua in the final decades of the fourteenth century.[16]

It was the belief of all these writers that, as Giovanni expresses it, 'the government of a single individual is always to be preferred, even when the person in question is only a moderately good man'.[17] One of his grounds for this belief is that 'where one person is in complete control, everyone else is able to pursue his own affairs in an untroubled way, and remains entirely free from public business'.[18] One reason for supposing this to be a desirable state of affairs is that a life of *otium*, of freedom from public duty, is indispensable for the achievement of our highest ends and hence our greatest happiness.[19] But a further reason derives from the fact that the alternative, the life of *negotium* as lived by courtiers, public servants and advisers to princes, is inherently corrupt. 'No life is more miserable, more uncertain, more self-deceiving.'[20] Flattery takes the place of truth, while approval is constantly sought for the most disgraceful policies, including violations of peace and betrayals of trust.[21] The moral is said to be obvious: 'if you wish to remain pious, just, a respecter of truthfulness and innocence, remove yourself from the life of the court'.[22]

These commitments remained an enduring element in humanist political theory, and became increasingly popular after Marsilio Ficino's translations in the 1480s made Plato's political doctrines widely available for the first time. We find the ideal of the philosopher-king espoused even

---

[15] See Petrarch 1554b and cf. the discussion in chapter 5 section II above.
[16] For biographical and bibliographical details on Vergerio see Robey 1973, pp. 8–9, 20–1; on Giovanni see Kohl 1980, pp. 22–9.
[17] Ravenna 1980, p. 106: 'Unius... vel mediocriter boni eligibilius esse regimen arbitror.'
[18] Ravenna 1980, p. 132: 'Nam ubi unus dominatur, suo quisque negotio prorsus publici securus vacat.'
[19] Ravenna 1980, pp. 138–40.
[20] Ravenna 1980, p. 166: 'nulla alia miserior, incertior... magis suique prorsus ignara'.
[21] Ravenna 1980, pp. 84–8, 94–6.
[22] Ravenna 1980, p. 96: 'Exeat aula qui vult esse pius, etiam qui iustus, qui vericola, qui innocens.'

by a number of Florentine humanists in this period.[23] The connected suggestion that, under any less perfect system, the philosopher must remain aloof from politics recurs even more prominently among northern humanists in the opening decades of the sixteenth century.

Within More's own intellectual circle, for example, we find the claim that a princely regime is always to be preferred, together with the claim that a life of *otium* is best for everyone else, both being eloquently defended. Erasmus's *Institutio Christiani Principis*, published in the same year as More's *Utopia*, contends that the only means to attain the *optimus status reipublicae* is to ensure 'that there is a prince whom everyone obeys, that the prince obeys the laws and that the laws answer to our ideals of *honestas* and equity'.[24] More's younger contemporary, Thomas Starkey, writing his *Dialogue Between Pole and Lupset* in the early 1530s, likewise begins by presenting the related ideal of *otium* as the outlook to be expected from a fashionable humanist intellectual trained in Italy. Pole opens the discussion by announcing that he desires no part in public life. He wishes to imitate 'the old and antique philosophers, who forsook the meddling with matters of common weals, and applied themselves to the secret studies and searching of nature'.[25] He offers two main reasons for his preference, both very familiar by this stage in the development of humanist culture. One is that the life of *negotium* inhibits us from attaining our highest ends and thereby cheats us of our fullest happiness. This is because 'the perfection of man resteth in the mind and in the chief and purest part thereof', and in consequence requires a life dedicated to *otium* and the pursuit of truth.[26] The other reason 'which hath caused many great, wise and politic men to abhor from common weals'[27] is that the life of *negotium* forces the philosopher, whose concern is with the truth, into a world of compromise, hypocrisy and lies. It leaves the wise man 'nothing obtaining but only to be corrupt with like opinions as they be which meddle therewith' and is therefore to be shunned in the same way that a good man shuns the company of thieves.[28]

This strand of humanism was always opposed, however, by a school of thought which argued that it can never be safe or even just to entrust our happiness to others. The exponents of this position generally concluded,

---

[23] Scala 1940 opens (p. 259) with an invocation of Cosimo de' Medici as 'pater patriae noster sapientissimus civis'. For a discussion of Scala's Platonism see Brown 1979, pp. 310–16.
[24] Erasmus 1974, p. 194: '[felicissimus est status] cum principi paretur ab omnibus atque ipse princeps paret legibus, leges autem ad archetypum aequi et honesti respondent'.
[25] Starkey 1948, p. 23.   [26] Starkey 1948, p. 23.   [27] Starkey 1948, p. 36.
[28] Starkey 1948, p. 37.

by contrast, that the only possible means of bringing about the *optimus status reipublicae* must be to train an active citizenry and cleave to a fully participative system of republican government.[29]

As we saw in chapter 5, this so-called 'civic' humanism tends to be associated in particular with the city-republics of Renaissance Italy, and above all with fifteenth-century Florence.[30] But the movement was of much broader significance, and it even penetrated the princely courts of northern Europe in the early years of the sixteenth century. For example, while Starkey's *Dialogue* opens with Pole's Platonist defence of *otium*, the figure of Lupset quickly repudiates it. If a man allows himself to be 'drawn by the sweetness of his studies' away from 'the cure of the common weal', then 'he doth manifest wrong to his country and friends, and is plain unjust and full of iniquity, as he that regardeth not his office and duty, to the which above all he is most bounden by nature'.[31]

Nor was this civic scale of values simply a product of the Renaissance. The ideals in question, as well as the vocabulary used for expressing them, were taken more or less wholesale from the last great defenders of the Roman republic – from Livy, from Sallust and above all from Cicero, whose *De Officiis* furnished virtually the whole framework for civic humanist discussions of the active life.

The *De Officiis* had taught in the first place that the highest aim of a good citizen must be to embrace the four cardinal virtues, since these are the qualities needed for the effective performance of our duties.[32] To possess these qualities is to be *honestus*, Cicero's general and most honorific term for someone who succeeds in cultivating the virtues and performing the *officia* they prescribe.[33] For Cicero, however, it was also a crucial principle that 'all the praise of *virtus* derives from action'.[34] From this he inferred that our highest earthly duty must be to place our talents in the service of our community.[35] We must learn to recognise that 'every duty that tends to preserve society and uphold the unity of mankind must be given preference over any duty to forward knowledge and science'.[36] Acting on this insight, we must train ourselves to discharge with *industria* all the *officia* of war and peace.[37] We must labour for our *res publica* in

[29] On the need for useful citizens as a typical motif of Renaissance Utopias see Eliav-Feldon 1982, pp. 58–64.
[30] Baron 1966, pp. 443–62; Pocock 1975, pp. 83–330. [31] Starkey 1948, p. 22.
[32] Cicero 1913, I. IV. 14 to I. V. 17, pp. 14–18.   [33] Cicero 1913, I. XVIII. 61, pp. 62–4.
[34] Cicero 1913, I. VI. 19, p. 20: 'Virtutis enim laus omnis in actione consistit.'
[35] Cicero 1913, I. XLIII. 153, p. 156.
[36] Cicero 1913, I. XLIV. 158, p. 162: 'omne officium, quod ad coniunctionem hominum et ad societatem tuendam valet, anteponendum est illi officio, quod cognitione et scientia continetur'.
[37] Cicero 1913, I. XXXIV. 122, p. 124.

everything that conduces to *honestas* and a well-ordered life.³⁸ We must make it our principal task 'to respect, defend and preserve concord and unity within the whole community of mankind'.³⁹

But what of the Platonist objection that this will cheat us of happiness, since it will carry us away from the life of *otium*, the way of life best suited to the nature and dignity of man? Cicero directly addresses this central contention of Greek ethics in Book 1 of *De Officiis* and offers an answer that was destined to be endlessly cited by the civic humanists of the Renaissance.

He admits that 'the noblest and greatest philosophers' have always 'withdrawn themselves from public affairs'.⁴⁰ They have held that, if you are a sage, it is essential 'that you should be able to live as you wish' (*sic vivere, ut velis*).⁴¹ But he firmly repudiates this scale of priorities. Near the start of his discussion he roundly declares that 'it is contrary to one's duty to permit oneself to be drawn away by one's studies from taking an active part in public life'.⁴² He later reiterates the argument in far more positive terms. The life of *negotium* is not merely of more importance than that of *otium*, but it also calls for greater abilities.⁴³ As a result, it is not only 'more fruitful' as a way of life, but is also capable of bringing us greater fulfilment and happiness.⁴⁴ Daringly, Cicero concludes with a direct criticism of Plato:

So it appears that what Plato says about philosophers is not really adequate. Although they secure one kind of justice, in that they do no positive harm, in another way they fail; for their studies prevent them from living an active life, so causing them to abandon those whom they ought to defend.⁴⁵

If the life of *otium* is to be justified, in other words, it must be because it helps to improve the life of *negotium*.

What of the further objection that a life of *negotium* is degrading to those of philosophical talents, since they will be obliged, in an imperfect world, to abandon the cause of truth in the name of playing a role and accommodating to the times? Again Cicero has a direct

---

³⁸ Cicero 1913, I. XXXIV. 124, p. 126.
³⁹ Cicero 1913, I. XLI. 149, p. 152: 'communem totius generis hominum conciliationem et consociationem colere, tueri, servare debemus'.
⁴⁰ Cicero 1913, I. XX. 69, p. 70: 'a negotiis publicis se removerint... nobilissimi philosophi'.
⁴¹ Cicero 1913, I. XX. 70, p. 70.
⁴² Cicero 1913, I. VI. 19, p. 20: 'studio a rebus gerendis abduci contra officium est'.
⁴³ Cicero 1913, I. XXVI. 92, p. 94.
⁴⁴ Cicero 1913, I. XXII. 74–8, pp. 74–80; I. XLIII. 153 to I. XLV. 160, pp. 156–64.
⁴⁵ Cicero 1913, I. IX. 28, p. 28: 'Itaque videndum est, ne non satis id, quod apud Platonem est in philosophos dictum... Nam alterum [iustitiae genus] assequuntur, ut inferenda ne cui noceant iniuria, in alterum incidunt; discendi enim studio impediti, quos tueri debent, deserunt.'

answer, and again it was endlessly echoed by the civic humanists of the Renaissance.

The truly wise person, Cicero retorts, is someone who recognises that all the world's a stage. 'Actors select for themselves not the best plays, but those in which they are best able to accommodate their talents.'[46] The relevance of the image is that 'if a player looks to this consideration in the theatre, should not a wise man look to the same consideration in life?'[47] Surely we must recognise that 'necessity will sometimes thrust roles upon us which we do not in the least feel to be suitable'.[48] But we must recognise at the same time that our duty in such a situation is to do the best we can, 'serving with as little indecorousness as can be mustered' in the adverse circumstances.[49]

These debates about the type of regime best suited to bringing about the *optimus status reipublicae* provide us, I suggest, with a context for understanding some at least of the complexities of More's text. In particular, they help us to make sense of what he is doing in Book I, the dialogue between Hythloday and the figure of More himself. We can now hope to recognise some of what is at stake in their argument: what orthodoxy More is questioning, what response he is offering, what exact position he is occupying on the spectrum of political debate.

Like his younger contemporary Thomas Starkey, More begins by allowing a fashionably Platonist commitment to be fully aired. This is done through the altogether Platonist figure of Hythloday. When we first encounter him, we are told that he is no ordinary traveller. Rather he is a voyager in the manner of Plato, a man in quest of the truth about political life.[50] After this introduction, the next fact we learn about him is that he adopts an unequivocal stance on what we have seen to be one of the major debates in Renaissance moral philosophy, the debate as to whether the truth about political life is more readily to be gleaned from Greek or Roman sources. Hythloday 'is by no means ignorant of the Latin language', we are told, 'but he is exceptionally learned in Greek, which he has studied with far greater attention than Latin. This is because he has devoted himself completely to philosophy, and in Latin

---

[46] Cicero 1913, I. XXXI. 114, p. 116: 'Illi [scaenici] enim non optimas, sed sibi accommodatissimas fabulas eligunt.'
[47] Cicero 1913, I. XXXI. 114, p. 116: 'Ergo histrio hoc videbit in scaena, non videbit sapiens vir in vita?'
[48] Cicero 1913, I. XXXI. 114, p. 116: 'aliquando necessitas nos ad ea detruserit, quae nostri ingenii non erunt'.
[49] Cicero 1913, I. XXXI. 114, p. 116: 'ut ea ... quam minime indecore facere possimus'.
[50] More 1965, p. 48. Cf. Bradshaw 1981, pp. 21–2.

has found nothing of the least significance on that subject except for some bits of Seneca and Cicero.'[51]

Hythloday then begins to recount what he has learnt on his travels, at which point his interlocutors urge him to place his wisdom at the disposal of the public by entering the service of a king.[52] Hythloday responds in precisely the tones which, as we have seen, Cicero had particularly associated with the admirers of Platonic philosophy. According to Cicero, the view adopted by that greatest of all philosophers had been that, if you are a sage, you must seek your happiness by living as you please – *vivere, ut velis*. Hythloday completely agrees. 'I live as I please' (*vivo ut volo*), he replies, and in consequence live more happily (*felicior*) than a life of public service would ever permit.[53]

When the figure of More in the dialogue presses him, he later offers a further – and again a purely Platonist – reason for refusing to enter public life. Being a philosopher, he says, 'I wish to speak the truth'.[54] If I were to become a courtier, 'I should instead have to approve openly of the worst possible decisions and endorse the most disgraceful decrees'.[55] The invariable outcome of such a way of life, he insists, is that 'rather than being able to do any good, you find yourself among colleagues who are easily able to corrupt even the best of men before reforming themselves'.[56] Plato was right, he concludes; he showed us 'why the wise are right to take no part in public affairs'.[57]

Having allowed these standard arguments in favour of *otium* to be fully laid out, the figure of More in the dialogue then attacks them point by point. He does so, moreover, not merely from the general perspective of a Ciceronian civic humanist, but in precisely the vocabulary which, as we have seen, Cicero had originally put into currency in his defence of the active life.[58]

---

[51] More 1965, pp. 48–50: '& latinae linguae non indoctus, & graecae doctissimus (cuius ideo studiosior quam Romanae fuit, quoniam totum se addixerat philosophiae: qua in re nihil quod alicuius momenti sit, praeter Senecae quaedam, ac Ciceronis extare latine cognovit)'. Later we learn (More 1965, p. 180) that the Utopians agree with these judgements.

[52] More 1965, p. 54.   [53] More 1965, pp. 54, 56.

[54] More 1965, p. 100: 'vera loqui volo'.

[55] More 1965, p. 102: 'approbanda sunt aperte pessima consilia, & decretis pestilentissimis subscribendum est'.

[56] More 1965, p. 102: 'in quo prodesse quicquam possis, in eos delatus collegas, qui vel optimum virum facilius corruperint, quam ipsi corrigantur'.

[57] More 1965, p. 102: 'cur merito sapientes abstineant a capessenda Republica'.

[58] It is perhaps worth underlining the claim I am making, especially in view of the comments in Logan 1983, p. 84n. on Skinner 1967. I am claiming only that the argument presented by the figure of More is also to be found in Cicero's *De Officiis* – and also, of course, in the writings of Cicero's numberless imitators and disciples. I am claiming, in short, that by More's time the argument had become part of the common currency of humanist debate.

The figure of More first assures Hythloday that 'if only you could induce yourself not to shun the courts of princes, you would be able to do the greatest good for the commonwealth by means of your advice'.[59] To this he adds in sterner tones – echoing *De Officiis* almost word for word – that 'there is in fact no greater duty than this one incumbent upon you as a good man'.[60] The Platonist objection that such a life cheats us of happiness is met with the lie direct. A life of public service 'not only constitutes the means by which you can help people both as private individuals and as members of the community, but is also the means to secure your own greater happiness'.[61] The further Platonist fear that this will betray the cause of truth by forcing the philosopher to accommodate to the times is met with a strong rebuke, one that again echoes the sentiments and even the imagery of *De Officiis* almost word for word.[62] What this betrays, the figure of More retorts, is nothing more than a kind of scholasticism. But the wise are aware that 'there is another and more practical kind of philosophy, one that understands its place on the stage, accommodates itself to whatever play is already in hand, and seeks to discharge whatever roles are assigned to it as decorously as possible'.[63] The same considerations, he goes on, 'apply equally in the case of the commonwealth and in the matter of giving advice to princes. Even if you cannot pull out evil opinions by the roots, even if you cannot manage to reform well-entrenched vices according to your own beliefs, you must never on that account desert the cause of the commonwealth.'[64]

There are, I think, two morals to be drawn from this first part of the story. The first is that the labels 'humanist' and even 'Christian humanist' have been applied too loosely to More's text even in some of the best

---

[59] More 1965, p. 86: 'si animum inducas tuum, uti ne ab aulis principum abhorreas, in publicum posse te tuis consiliis plurimum boni conferre'.

[60] More 1965, p. 86: 'quare nihil magis incumbit tuo, hoc est boni viri, officio'.

[61] More 1965, p. 54: 'eam tamen ipsam esse viam, qua non aliis modo & privatim, & publice possis conducere, sed tuam quoque ipsius conditionem reddere feliciorem'. It cannot be right to translate the last word (as in More 1965, p. 55) as 'more prosperous'. Where More wishes to speak of living prosperously – as he does for example in More 1965, p. 102 – he uses the term *prospere*.

[62] As noted in Surtz 1965b, p. 372, Erasmus also echoes Cicero's image of the world as a stage. See Erasmus 1551, Adag. XCI, 'Servire scenae', which opens (p. 54) by quoting Cicero on the need to accommodate to the times ('M. Tullius servire scenae dixit, pro eo quod est servire tempori, & rebus praesentibus sese accommodare').

[63] More 1965, p. 98: 'est alia philosophia civilior, quae suam novit scenam, eique sese accommodans, in ea fabula quae in manibus est, suas partes concinne & cum decoro tutatur'.

[64] More 1965, p. 98: 'Sic est in Republica sic in consultationibus principum. Si radicitus evelli non possint opiniones pravae, nec receptis usu vitiis mederi queas, ex animi tui sententia, non ideo tamen deserenda Respublica est.'

recent scholarship.⁶⁵ More's stance in the opening Book of *Utopia* is undoubtedly that of a humanist, and includes some explicit criticisms of scholastic philosophy. But we cannot simply speak of Hythloday as 'the ideal type of Christian humanist';⁶⁶ nor can we say that, in defending the importance of counselling princes, More's position is 'in all respects the orthodox humanist one'.⁶⁷ The question whether philosophers ought to counsel princes was a subject of intense debate among Christian humanists, and no specific answer to the question can be called orthodox. If we are to speak more precisely, we must recognise that what More is doing in Book I is reviving one particular set of humanist beliefs – those of a 'civic' or Ciceronian humanism – and sharply opposing them to a more fashionable and broadly Platonist outlook that was threatening to undermine the element of political commitment in the humanism of More's own time. The figure of More in the dialogue is restating the case for a humanist ideal to which the courts of northern Europe were proving increasingly inhospitable: the ideal of civic self-government, based on an active and politically educated citizenship.

The other moral suggested by this first part of the story concerns the relationship between Book I of *Utopia* and More's own personal circumstances at the time of writing it. In 1515, the year in which *Utopia* was conceived, More was employed on an embassy to Flanders; in 1516, the year of its publication, he was first offered a pension by Henry VIII; in the course of 1518, after much apparent hesitation, he accepted a place on the privy council and embarked on his career at court.⁶⁸ The arguments about *otium* and *negotium* in Book I have often been seen as a dramatisation of 'the moral tension' induced by the 'temptation' to give up the ideals of humanism embodied in the figure of Hythloday in favour of just such a worldly life.⁶⁹

It is arguable, however, that this is to misunderstand the nature of More's humanist allegiances. So far from viewing the choice of a public career as a temptation, the figure of More in the dialogue clearly regards it, in good Ciceronian style, as the one means of fulfilling the highest *officium* of a true humanist philosopher. If we are to relate this first half of *Utopia* to More's own life, my suggestion is that More should not necessarily be seen as expressing doubts about the decision he was in the process of making. If we can identify him at this juncture with the opinions

---

⁶⁵ Bradshaw 1981, p. 23; Logan 1983, pp. 235, 254.   ⁶⁶ Hexter 1965, p. xcii.
⁶⁷ Logan 1983, p. 41.   ⁶⁸ Chambers 1935, pp. 111–14, 144–6, 162–3.
⁶⁹ Hexter 1965, pp. lxxxiv, xci. See also Greenblatt 1980, pp. 11–73, who takes More to be crafting a public role and at the same time trying to escape from the identity so crafted.

expressed by the figure of More in the dialogue, it is arguable that we should instead see him as offering a justification for that decision as the outcome of a true understanding of the proper relationship between philosophy and public life.[70]

III

I turn to a second debate among Renaissance political theorists about the *optimus status reipublicae*. This arose within the ranks of those who agreed that the best state can only be attained if we live as active citizens within a self-governing commonwealth. The further question they raised concerns the range of attributes we need to possess as citizens if we are to discharge our civic *officia* to the best effect. To phrase it in the form in which it was habitually discussed, the question is about the qualities that make a citizen best fitted to serve the common good, and in consequence most deserving of honour, esteem and praise. Or, to put it in the precise vocabulary that the Renaissance writers liked to use, the question is about the qualities that serve to identify a truly noble citizen, a citizen of *vera nobilitas* whose conduct is worthy of honour, esteem and praise.

The humanists inherited an unambiguous answer to these questions from scholastic and ultimately Aristotelian sources. It became one of their favourite literary strategies to dramatise their doubts about this intellectual inheritance by way of writing dialogues about the concept of *vera nobilitas*, dialogues in which they counterpoised their own ideal against the more commonly accepted point of view. This genre first attained widespread popularity among the civic humanists of *quattrocento* Florence. Buonaccorso de Montemagna's *Controversia de Nobilitate* of the 1420s is one of the earliest examples, while Poggio Bracciolini's *De Nobilitate* of c.1440 is perhaps the best known. Thereafter the topic became a standard one, with many leading humanists of the second half of the *quattrocento* contributing to the debate. As we saw in chapter 5, such well-known figures as Cristoforo Landino, Bartolomeo Sacchi and Antonio de Ferrariis all wrote dialogues on the meaning of true nobility.[71]

If we turn to the earliest exponents of the *studia humanitatis* in England, and thus to More's immediate intellectual background, we find the same topic widely taken up. John Tiptoft made an English translation of

---

[70] On this point see Mermel 1977; Bradshaw 1981, p. 24; Logan 1983, p. 16n. On the ambiguities of More's position see Guy 2000, pp. 42–61.
[71] Landino 1970; Sacchi 1540, II, pp. 41–64. For Antonio de Ferrariis, *De Nobilitate* (1495) see Savino 1941, pp. 119–23. For a slightly later humanist treatise along the same lines see Clichtove 1512.

Buonaccorso's *Controversia* as early as the 1460s,[72] and by the start of the new century the question of *vera nobilitas* had begun to be much discussed in Erasmian circles.[73] Erasmus himself raises the issue in his *Institutio Principis Christiani*, and within a few years we find it recurring in such works as Henry Medwall's *Fulgens and Lucrece*, John Heywood's *Gentleness and Nobility*, Sir Thomas Elyot's *Book of the Governor* and many other writings of a similar humanist character.

The problem addressed by all these writers (as Tiptoft's translation of Buonaccorso puts it) is how to identify those who should 'of right' hold the 'offices of estate and worship' in the commonwealth.[74] According to the commonly accepted view – which a number of humanists continued to endorse[75] – the answer is that those citizens who are noblest and worthiest to occupy such honourable positions will be those who are possessed of high lineage and ancient wealth. As Tiptoft more succinctly expresses it, the suggestion is that 'noblesse resteth in blood and riches'.[76]

Although lineage was held to be important, the defence of this position principally centred on the claim that wealth is one of the conditions of true nobility. One tenet on which everyone agreed was that, if wealth is indeed a criterion, it must be inherited wealth. If it is instead the product of one's own acquisitive talents, this robs one of any title to be regarded as a citizen of the highest worthiness. As the figure of Niccolò explains in Poggio's *De Nobilitate*, 'I certainly cannot see what kind of nobility can be acquired by trade, for trade is judged by the wise to be vile and base, and nothing that can be regarded as contemptible can be related to nobility in any way.'[77]

The positive argument purporting to connect nobility with wealth was essentially Aristotelian in character. To possess extensive riches, but without exercising the contemptible abilities required to amass them, is to be in a position to serve and benefit one's friends and community in a truly noble style of splendour and magnificence altogether denied to

---

[72] Mitchell 1938, pp. 213–41.
[73] On the debt of More's *Utopia* to Erasmian humanism, and in particular to Erasmus's *Adagia*, see Wootton 1998.
[74] Tiptoft 1938, pp. 220, 223.
[75] Kristeller stresses that these views particularly commended themselves to Venetian and Neapolitan humanists writing in defence of their own class. For example, the Venetian noble Lauro Quirini wrote three dialogues in the mid-*quattrocento* defending the nobility of family and wealth. See Kristeller 1985, pp. 73, 177, 321–39.
[76] Tiptoft 1938, p. 221.
[77] Bracciolini 1964–9a, p. 70: 'At vero ex mercatura non video quae nobilitas acquiratur... quod vile atque abiectum sapientes arbitrati sunt... quod aliquo modo vituperari potest, nunquam admiscebitur cum nobilitate.'

those who live in more modest circumstances. As Lorenzo de' Medici – the protagonist of the Aristotelian case – emphasises in Poggio's dialogue, a rich man is in a unique position, 'both in time of war and peace, whenever the spending of money is of the utmost importance, to acquire glory for himself by that means, thereby winning the nobility that arises from that source'.[78]

The underlying assumption is that wealth, far from being a hindrance to civic virtue, is one of the means to ensure its effective exercise. This had been Aristotle's contention in the *Politics*, and Aquinas had influentially restated and enlarged on the argument in his *Quaestio* entitled *De Honestate* in the *Summa Theologiae*. Beginning with the claim that 'honour is due to many other things besides virtue',[79] Aquinas declares in his *responsio* that this position is essentially correct. Some objects other than virtue are rightly honoured because, like God, they are of even greater significance than virtue itself. 'But others are rightly honoured, even though they are of lesser significance, on the grounds that they are helpful to the exercise of virtue, and these include nobility, power and wealth.'[80]

As will by now be evident, this scholastic view of true nobility rests not merely on strong beliefs about the importance of inheritance, but also on aristocratic assumptions about the proper uses of extensive wealth. As in Aristotle, an ethic of display and splendour, of liberality and magnificence, lies at the heart of the argument.[81] Aquinas in the *Summa* once again proved to be a highly influential intermediary in the transmission of these values. As he insists in his *Quaestio* entitled *De Magnificentia* 'the achievement of anything great – from which the term magnificent arises – appropriately relates to the idea of virtue, from which it follows that the term "magnificent" denotes a virtue'.[82]

The same assumptions frequently reappear in humanist dialogues about *vera nobilitas*, where they usually figure not merely as scholastic

---

[78] Bracciolini 1964–9a, p. 77: 'bello quoque et pace, in quibus pecuniarum sumptus maxime sunt necessarii, gloria acquiritur, a qua descendit nobilitas'.
[79] Aquinas 1962, II^a. II^{ae}, Qu. 145, art. 1, 2, p. 629: 'multis aliis debetur honor quam virtuti'.
[80] Aquinas, 1962, II^a. II^{ae}, Qu. 145, art. 1, ad 2, p. 629: 'Alia vero, quae sunt infra virtutem, honorantur, inquantum coadiuvant ad operationem virtutis: sicut nobilitas, potentia et divitiae.'
[81] See for example Bracciolini 1964–9a, pp. 77, 81, where the figure of Lorenzo, the protagonist of the Aristotelian point of view, insists on the indissoluble links between *nobilitas* and the capacity to display both *splendor* and *magnificentia*. It seems important to underline this point, if only because of the influential but misleading claim in Hexter 1952, pp. 36–7, that none of More's contemporaries 'would have maintained for a moment that what mattered in a commonwealth was splendor, magnificence and majesty'.
[82] Aquinas, 1962, II^a. II^{ae}, Qu. 134, art. 1, resp., p. 596: 'Et ideo operari aliquid magnum, ex quo sumitur nomen *magnificentiae*, proprie pertinet ad rationem virtutis. Unde magnificentia nominat virtutem.'

arguments but as widely accepted beliefs. In Buonaccorso's *Controversia*, for example, the first speaker ends by explaining that his reason for treating wealth as a criterion for true nobility is that 'the chief and highest part of noblesse must rest in liberality', and that 'he paineth himself vainly to exercise liberality to other folks which hath not whereof to use it to himself'.[83] 'If you deny this view', as Lorenzo adds in Poggio's dialogue, 'you will be rejecting what is agreed about this matter by everyone.'[84]

Among a number of humanist intellectuals, however, this view was in fact rejected. It was challenged with a claim that soon became a slogan of a particular strand of humanist political thought: the claim that *virtus vera nobilitas est*, that the possession of virtue constitutes the only possible grounds for regarding someone as a person of true nobility.

This is not to say that the humanists in general had any quarrel with the assumptions about private property and its hereditability underpinning the Aristotelian and scholastic case. On the contrary, they strongly endorse Aquinas's classic account in the *Summa* of the indispensability of private property in any well-ordered commonwealth. Drawing once more on Aristotle, Aquinas had argued in his *Quaestio* entitled *De Furto et Rapina* that private property is not merely legitimate but essential to the satisfactory conduct of political life. One reason he gives is that, if all things are instead held in common, everyone will avoid working and in consequence help to bring about a state of gratuitous poverty. But his main contention is that, in the absence of private property, endless confusion and quarrelling will be sure to arise, a state of disorder that can never be regulated and stabilised except by recognising that some goods must be held privately and not treated as part of the common stock.[85]

The humanists found little to say about the first of these claims, although Cicero in *De Officiis* had insisted that one of the prime duties of our rulers must be to ensure that there is an abundance of goods, a commitment he had announced in the course of his own defence of private property.[86] But they firmly underline Aquinas's second line of reasoning, making it a commonplace of humanist political theory that no satisfactory social order can ever be maintained unless the values of 'degree, priority and place' are unequivocally upheld.[87] As always, Cicero's arguments in *De Officiis* furnish them with their highest authority.

---

[83] Tiptoft 1938, p. 221.
[84] Bracciolini 1964–9a, p. 66: 'si negas ex his... communi omnium sensu repugnas'.
[85] Aquinas, 1962, II^a. II^{ae}, Qu. 66, art. 2, resp., p. 325.
[86] Cicero 1913, II. XXI. 74, pp. 248–50.
[87] On the need for 'degree' if 'order' is to be preserved see Skinner 1978a, pp. 238–41 and references there.

'What plague could ever be worse', Cicero had asked, than to favour an equal distribution of goods?[88] He had answered his own question with considerable vehemence in denouncing the idea of enforcing equal distributions of land:

> Those who seek in this way to become the friends of the people are undermining the foundations of the commonwealth. For in the first place they are destroying harmony, which cannot possibly be sustained where money is taken from one person and given to someone else. And in the second place they are subverting equity, which will altogether collapse if it ceases to be lawful for people to hold their own goods.[89]

For Cicero, perhaps the highest duty of the state is to guarantee to all its citizens the undisturbed enjoyment of their private property.

Despite their endorsement of these commonly accepted beliefs about the social basis of nobility, the humanists completely repudiate the related claim that the quality of nobility itself is in any way connected with lineage or inherited wealth. They permit themselves a tone of pure amazement at the idea that ancient lineage might be supposed relevant. As Niccolò puts it in Poggio's dialogue, 'what can conceivably be thought noble about a man who merely boasts numerous ancestors and a long account of his family history?'[90] Erasmus in his *Institutio* later allowed himself a similar note of surprise. He concedes that he has no wish 'to take away honour from those of high lineage, provided that they are formed in the image of their ancestors and excel in those qualities that originally made them members of the nobility'.[91] But he adds that this gives us no reason at all 'to allow the title of nobility' to those who merely happen to be members of a leisured class and live a life of *iners otium*, sluggish idleness.[92]

The main point the humanists make, however, is that it is even more ridiculous to suppose that the possession of inherited wealth can in any way entitle someone to be regarded as truly noble. Niccolò flatly declares in Poggio's dialogue that 'riches cannot in the least ennoble us',[93] while Erasmus in the *Institutio* offers an anatomy of true nobility that serves to underline the same judgement. 'There are three forms of nobility', he

---

[88] Cicero 1913, II. XXI. 73, p. 248: 'qua peste quae potest esse maior?'
[89] Cicero 1913, II. XXII. 78, pp. 252–4: 'Qui vero se populares volunt... labefactant fundamenta rei publicae, concordiam primum, quae esse non potest, cum aliis adimuntur, aliis condonantur pecuniae, deinde aequitatem, quae tollitur omnis, si habere suum cuique non licet.'
[90] Bracciolini 1964–9a, p. 70: '[qui enim fieri potest ut] vir... maioribus tantum ac stirpis origine fisus possit ullo esse pacto nobilis?'
[91] Erasmus 1974, p. 198: 'Non quod bene natis suum honorem detraham, si respondeant maiorum imaginibus et iis rebus praecellant, quae primum nobilitatem pepererunt.'
[92] Erasmus 1974, p. 198: 'nec iners ocium [sic] nobilitatis titulo donandum'.
[93] Bracciolini 1964–9a, p. 71: 'nobilitare ergo nos [opes] minime possunt'.

maintains, 'one of which arises from virtue and good deeds, while the next derives from an understanding of those studies which are *honestissimae* and the third from ancestral portraits and long lineage, or else from the possession of wealth. But this third and lowest degree is so low that it really amounts to nothing at all unless it has arisen out of virtue itself.'[94]

If lineage and inherited wealth are both irrelevant, what gives rise to the quality of true nobility? Erasmus's analysis already supplies the answer, and in putting it forward he was able to draw on a century of civic humanist argument. As Niccolò had already declared in triumph at the end of Poggio's dialogue, 'it is virtue alone upon which the palm of nobility deserves to be bestowed'.[95] He summarises his response to Lorenzo de' Medici's contrasting argument as follows:

> It is thus the judgement of the wise that nobility arises neither from a life of *otium* nor from contemplative solitude, nor even from the possession of great wealth. It arises exclusively from the study of virtue, a quality we are much better able to exercise when living in cities and amid the fellowship of mankind.[96]

These conclusions, Niccolò adds, have been demonstrated by Seneca and by 'our Cicero' beyond any shadow of doubt.[97]

As before, my suggestion is that this aspect of the debate about the *optimus status reipublicae* supplies us with a context that helps to make sense of some further complexities in More's *Utopia*. In particular, it helps us to explain the connections between the two Books into which *Utopia* is divided, and at the same time to reconsider what has always been the chief interpretative puzzle about the book. As we saw at the outset, the puzzle is to understand how far More intends us to admire the portrait of Utopian society sketched by Hythloday in Book 2. What emerges, I suggest, is that one of More's concerns in *Utopia* is to intervene in the precise debate we have so far been considering, the debate about the meaning of true nobility. To grasp the nature of his intervention, I shall argue, is at the same time to uncover at least one part of the serious message that underlies the seemingly detached and ironic surface of his text.

---

[94] Erasmus 1974, p. 146: 'tria sint nobilitatis genera: unum, quod ex virtute recteque factis nascitur; proximum, quod ex honestissimarum disciplinarum cognitione proficiscitur; tertium, quod natalium picturis et maiorum stemmatis aestimatur aut opibus... quod sic infimum est, ut nullum omnino sit, nisi et ipsum a virtute fuerit, profectum'.

[95] Bracciolini 1964-9a, p. 80: 'soli virtuti palma nobilitatis tribuenda est'.

[96] Bracciolini 1964-9a, p. 72: 'Non enim solitudine, aut ocio ignavo, vel opum magnitudine, sed virtutis studio comparandam sapientes censent, quam magis in urbibus & hominum coetu exercere possumus.'

[97] See Bracciolini 1964-9a, p. 80, citing 'noster Cicero' and quoting from the *Epistulae Morales* of Seneca ('vir sapientissimus').

The figure of Raphael Hythloday engages with the issue of *vera nobilitas* at two connected but distinguishable points. First of all, he provides us with a picture of what he describes as the true and the counterfeit images of nobility,[98] together with a description of the contrasting social consequences that naturally flow from espousing one or other of them.

The moment at which he draws this contrast most forcefully is in the closing pages of the book. After outlining the Utopian way of life, Hythloday ends by discussing with the figure of More the significance of the story he has told. The first claim that Hythloday makes at this juncture is that, in his judgement, the Utopians have in fact attained the *optimus status reipublicae*.[99] Their laws and institutions seriously aim at the common good, as a result of which they are able to live *felicissime*, as happily as possible.[100]

How have they managed it? Hythloday answers in essentially negative terms. They have managed by not organising their society according to 'the unjust ideas of justice' that prevail everywhere else.[101] These unjust ideas take the form of 'lavishing great gifts' upon nobles, rich merchants and other 'so-called gentlemen'[102] who either live a life of *otium* and 'do no work at all', or else occupy themselves with 'wholly superfluous forms of *negotium*' that contribute nothing of value to the commonwealth.[103] 'For this they are rewarded with a luxurious and a splendid life.'[104] By contrast, we find no thanks, no benefits, no feelings of kindness[105] accorded to those who work 'with unceasing labour' at tasks 'so essential to the commonwealth that it would not last a single year without them'.[106] 'The lives they lead are so full of misery that the condition of beasts of burden might seem altogether preferable.'[107]

We can perhaps rephrase what Hythloday appears to be claiming at this summarising moment in his argument. He is telling us that the Utopians owe their happiness to their avoidance of mistaken beliefs

---

[98] More 1965, p. 168 uses the term *fucatus*.
[99] See More 1965, p. 236 on the Utopian hope that the *optima forma* has been achieved.
[100] See More 1965, p. 238 on how the citizens of Utopia 'seriously concern themselves with public affairs' ('serio publicum negotium agunt') and p. 244 on how, as a result, they live 'felicissime'.
[101] See More 1965, p. 238 comparing Utopian with 'aliarum iustitiam gentium'.
[102] See More 1965, p. 240 on how 'tanta munera' are lavished on 'generosis ut vocant'.
[103] See More 1965, p. 238 on the *otium* and *supervacuum negotium* of the nobles and rich merchants.
[104] More 1965, p. 238: 'lautam et splendidam vitam... consequatur'.
[105] More 1965, p. 240 on the lack of *benignitas* or *beneficia* and the failure 'referre gratiam'.
[106] See More 1965, p. 238 on those whose work is 'tam necessario, ut sine eo ne unum quidem annum possit ulla durare Respublica'.
[107] More 1965, p. 238: 'vitam adeo miseram ducunt, ut longe potior videri possit conditio iumentorum'.

about the qualities that truly deserve to be regarded as noble and praiseworthy, as opposed to the qualities that merely happen to be displayed by the so-called gentry and nobility. Nor is this to put words into Hythloday's mouth. If we turn back to the account he gives in Book 2 of the Utopians' social attitudes, we find him phrasing his description in exactly these terms. The Utopians are distinguished by their belief that to connect nobility with *splendor*, with richness of apparel or other conspicuous displays of wealth,[108] 'such that someone will think himself nobler if the texture of his garments is finer', is nothing other than insane.[109] The Utopians 'not only think it extraordinary, they actually detest the insanity of those who pay almost divine honours to the rich, especially when those who do so owe the rich nothing, are under no obligation to them, but behave towards them in that fashion simply because they happen to be rich'.[110]

Rejecting this counterfeit view of nobility, the view that the Utopians espouse is exactly the one we have already encountered in Cicero and his humanist disciples, and is couched in exactly the same terms. The Utopians believe that what is alone noble and deserving of honour is a willingness to labour for the common good.[111] The qualities they think of as truly noble are accordingly the qualities of virtue that are indispensable for performing such civic tasks. As a result, the laws and customs of Utopia not only forbid *otium* and require *negotium* from everyone.[112] They also ensure that the elements of civic virtue are encouraged, praised and admired above all. The Utopians, we learn, are all trained in virtue.[113] They are encouraged to follow a virtuous way of life by the fact that virtue is so highly honoured in their society.[114] They are especially incited to virtue by the fact that statues of great figures who have performed outstanding services to the community are erected in their marketplaces.[115] Any magistrate who serves with particular virtue is rewarded with honour and praise.[116] The priests, who are chosen for their outstanding virtue,

---

[108] See More 1965, p. 154 on the amusement caused by the *splendor* of the foreign *nobiles* who visited Utopia.

[109] More 1965, p. 156: 'ipsum denique solem liceat intueri, aut quemquam tam insanum esse, ut nobilior ipse sibi ob tenuioris lanae filum videatur'.

[110] More 1965, p. 156: 'mirantur, ac detestantur insaniam qui divitibus illis, quibus neque debent quicquam, neque sunt obnoxii, nullo alio respectu, quam quod divites sunt, honores tantum non divinos impendunt'.

[111] More 1965, pp. 130, 134.

[112] See More 1965, esp. p. 126 on the absence of *otium* in Utopia and the enforcement by the magistrates of the obligation of *negotium* upon everyone.

[113] More 1965, p. 184.   [114] More 1965, p. 192.

[115] More 1965, p. 192.   [116] More 1965, p. 196.

are regarded for that reason as persons of true *maiestas*.¹¹⁷ The whole society is portrayed as one in which the quality of virtue has been made the ruling principle. It is a society in which the women, the magistrates and the heads of families are all described as possessing *honestas*, the highest term of praise among Ciceronian humanists for those who attain the full range of the virtues and deploy them upon the betterment of our common life.¹¹⁸

As a result of substituting this view of what is truly noble for the commonly accepted one, the Utopians have managed to avoid a number of baleful social consequences that stem, according to Hythloday, from endorsing the counterfeit belief. Hythloday lists them when first mentioning the existence of Utopia at the end of Book 1, and reiterates them when summarising his argument in the closely parallel passage at the end of Book 2. One is poverty, which is unknown in Utopia, a society in which 'it has dwindled away completely', leaving 'no poor men, no beggars',¹¹⁹ but 'abundance of everything for everyone'.¹²⁰ The other is social disorder, the inevitable concomitant of poverty. This too has 'perished completely' in Utopia,¹²¹ leaving 'a people so well-ordered that if you had seen them, you would say that there is no good order anywhere else'.¹²²

We can summarise the scale of values Hythloday is describing – as he does himself when first mentioning Utopia – by saying that Utopia is a society in which *virtuti precium sit*, in which 'virtue has its reward'.¹²³ For it is a society in which virtue is regarded, as it ought to be, as the one quality truly deserving of honour, esteem and praise.

I am suggesting, then, that Hythloday's description of Utopia in Book 2 can be read as an account of the social benefits that flow from espousing the true instead of the counterfeit view of nobility. By contrast, his oft-cited analysis of the injustices of English society in Book 1 forms a perfectly balanced account of the dire effects that stem from accepting the counterfeit view in its place.

That the English endorse the counterfeit view is emphatically asserted in the course of Book 2, especially at the stage when Hythloday compares 'what is now believed' about the ideal of nobility with the Utopian attitudes we have just examined. 'What is now believed is that nothing else

---

¹¹⁷ More 1965, pp. 228, 230.   ¹¹⁸ More 1965, pp. 126, 188, 196.
¹¹⁹ More 1965, pp. 238, 242.   ¹²⁰ More 1965, p. 102: 'rebus omnia abundent omnibus'.
¹²¹ More 1965, p. 242.
¹²² More 1965, p. 106: 'populum recte institutum nusquam alibi te vidisse quam illic'.
¹²³ More 1965, p. 102.

counts as nobility' than 'being descended from a long line of ancestors who have been rich over a long period of time, especially if they have been rich in landed estates'.[124] The result is that men of high lineage and inherited wealth 'believe themselves to be noble' in the sense of being entitled to honour and respect, entitled to be met with bared heads and bent knees.[125]

Hythloday not only characterises this belief as 'sweetly insane';[126] he also treats it as the cause of all the woes afflicting English society that are analysed in Book 1. Not only does he start by directing his accusations specifically against 'the great number of nobles' and their 'immense crowds of idle retainers';[127] he subsequently confines himself almost entirely to illustrating how these particular social groups have been the ruin of English society.

The most obvious consequence of their ascendancy is widespread poverty. Recognising that their title to respect depends on their capacity to live a life of *splendor* and *magnificentia*, the nobles are driven into 'evil greed' as the only means of satisfying their pride.[128] 'They are not content, living in *otium* and luxury, to do no good for their community; they actually do it positive harm.'[129] To ensure the highest profits from their lands, 'they leave no arable at all, but enclose everything for pasture, demolishing houses, destroying towns' and evicting tenants who are then left to starve.[130] Desperate and gratuitous hardship is the price that others pay for their noble and aristocratic way of life.

The other and consequential outcome is endemic social unrest. The armies of retainers kept by the aristocracy form a serious part of the problem, for they live in idleness, never learn any kind of trade, devote themselves to the arts of war and 'continually make trouble and disturb the peace'.[131] Still worse are the disorders caused by those evicted from their lands and livelihoods. 'For what remains for them, in the last resort,

---

[124] More 1965, p. 168: 'quod eiusmodi maioribus nasci contigerit, quorum longa series dives (neque enim nunc aliud est nobilitas) habita sit, praesertim in praediis'.
[125] See More 1965, p. 168 on the 'nudatus alterius vertex, aut curvati poplites' of those who wait upon the nobility.
[126] More 1965, p. 168: 'suaviter insaniunt'.
[127] More 1965, p. 62: 'Tantus est ergo nobilium numerus... [et] verum immensam quoque ociosorum stipatorum turbam'.
[128] See More 1965, p. 68 on their 'improba cupiditas'.
[129] More 1965, p. 66: 'nec habentes satis, quod ociose ac laute viventes, nihil in publicum prosint, nisi etiam obsint'.
[130] More 1965, p. 66: 'arvo nihil relinquunt, omnia claudunt pascuis, demoliuntur domos diruunt oppida'.
[131] More 1965, p. 64 on 'turbam alere, quod infestat pacem'.

but to steal and then be hanged – justly, no doubt – or else to wander and beg?'[132]

Hythloday completes this aspect of his argument when he points, at the end of Book 2, to the principles that must inevitably govern any society founded on this view of nobility. As we have seen, to base a society on the true view, as the Utopians do, is to make virtue its ruling principle. By contrast, to base a society on the counterfeit view is to ensure that its citizens cultivate the worst of the vices. Of these the deadliest is pride, 'that serpent from hell which coils itself round the hearts of mortal men'.[133] To connect nobility with wealth is to place 'this chief and progenitor of all plagues' at the centre of our social life.[134] For pride 'measures prosperity not by her own advantages, but by the disadvantages suffered by others',[135] and therefore loves to live 'in circumstances where her happiness can shine more brightly by comparison with their miseries'.[136] Moreover, once the life of magnificence demanded by pride becomes our highest aspiration, the other ruling passion of our society can only be avarice. For everyone will be forced to act 'with insatiable cupidity' to ensure that the demands of pride are adequately satisfied.[137]

So far, Hythloday has simply reiterated and defended a conventional humanist equation between virtue and true nobility. As I began by observing, however, his contrast between the rival views of nobility only represents one of two ways in which he engages with the debate about *vera nobilitas*. When we turn to the further claim he wishes to advance, we find ourselves moving beyond the confines of humanist orthodoxy, confronting an argument at once more radical and explicitly Platonist in character.

Hythloday signals this further commitment in the form of two images introduced at the end of Book 1. He remarks that hitherto he has been talking about the diseases of bodies politic. He now wishes to consider 'how to return them to a healthy state'.[138] But there is no hope of such a cure, he adds, unless we can first identify the seeds of evil in social life and pluck them out by the roots.[139]

---

[132] More 1965, p. 66: 'quid restat aliud denique, quam uti furentur, & pendeant iuste scilicet aut vagentur atque mendicent'.
[133] More 1965, p. 242: 'haec averni serpens mortalium pererrans pectora'.
[134] More 1965, p. 242: 'omnium princeps parensque pestium superbia'.
[135] More 1965, p. 242: 'haec non suis commodis prosperitatem, sed ex alienis metitur incommodis'.
[136] More 1965, p. 242: 'quorum miseriis praefulgeat ipsius comparata felicitas'.
[137] More 1965, p. 240: 'cum inexplebili cupiditate'.
[138] More 1965, p. 104: 'ut sanentur vero atque in bonum redeant habitum'.
[139] For this image see More 1965, pp. 86, 242.

What then is the evil that needs to be rooted out? After surveying the Utopian system, Hythloday answers his own question in a single word. At the root of social injustice lies a mistaken belief about what should count as *privatus*, the realm of private as opposed to public interests. Describing Utopia as a community in which the *optimus status reipublicae* has in fact been realised, Hythloday at once adds that it is a society of which it can also be said that *nihil privati est*, that there is nothing of the private about it at all.[140] There is in fact a deep suspicion of privacy in Utopia. The Utopians never eat in private, but always in public halls.[141] They seem to prefer public to private worship.[142] They live in private houses, but these are kept public by virtue of a design that 'gives admission to anyone who wishes to enter'.[143] They even insist that, before marriage, the private parts of the body must be made public to the partner involved.[144]

What they have recognised above all, however, is that no community can ever hope to attain its best state unless the institution of private property and the money economy sustaining it are both abolished.[145] We can now see the force of Hythloday's metaphor: money, he is saying, is the root of all evil, and must be eradicated if there is to be any prospect of serving public as opposed to private interests. As Hythloday observes at the end of Book 1, this is what Plato recognised. 'As that wisest of all men easily foresaw, the one and only road to public welfare is by way of an equality of goods.'[146] Hythloday emphatically agrees, and goes on to spell out the implications of the argument. 'I am fully persuaded that no just and equal distribution of goods will ever be possible, nor will happiness ever be found in mortal affairs, until the institution of private property is totally overthrown.'[147] To state his belief at its simplest and most resonant, what he is saying is that we have no hope of establishing a genuine commonwealth unless we base it on a system of common wealth.

As Book 2 goes on to show, this is the insight that the Utopians have put into practice. As a result, Hythloday affirms at the close of his account, they not only live *felicissime*, as happily as possible; it also seems likely that their happiness will last *aeternum duratura*.[148] The right way to translate

---

[140] More 1965, pp. 102, 104, 238.   [141] More 1965, pp. 128, 138.
[142] More 1965, pp. 222–4, 232, 236.
[143] More 1965, p. 120: 'quemvis intromittunt, ita nihil usquam privati est'.
[144] More 1965, p. 188.   [145] More 1965, p. 102.
[146] More 1965, p. 104: 'Siquidem facile praevidit homo prudentissimus, unam atque unicam illam esse viam ad salutem publicam, si rerum indicatur aequalitas.'
[147] More 1965, p. 104: 'Adeo mihi certe persuadeo, res aequabili ac iusta aliqua ratione distribui, aut feliciter agi cum rebus mortalium, nisi sublata prorsus proprietate, non posse.'
[148] More 1965, p. 244. For an account of life in Utopia, sensitive to the nuances of More's vocabulary, see Baker-Smith 1991, pp. 151–200.

that last phrase is surely by observing that Hythloday ends in just the way that such stories are supposed to end, by assuring us that everyone lived happily ever after.

IV

Hythloday's conclusion is a sufficiently resounding one, but it still leaves us with the problem of assessing where the author of *Utopia* stands in relation to it. Are we to take it that Thomas More endorses the claim that the Utopians have succeeded in establishing a perfectly virtuous society? Are we even to suppose, as some commentators have lately argued, that the description of Utopia is intended as the portrait of a perfectly Christian commonwealth? Or must we conclude, as the best recent scholarship has claimed, that More's irony and indirection reflect his own deep feelings of ambiguity about the Utopian way of life?

If we are to reconsider these questions, we need to start by reminding ourselves of the precise topic More addresses in his book. As I began by observing, it is surely uncontentious to say that his basic concern is with the best state of a commonwealth. But to say that this is his theme is at the same time to insist that he is not primarily concerned with a number of other distinct though closely related questions that also preoccupied Erasmian humanists at the time. He does not begin – as Erasmus does in the *Enchiridion* – by telling us that his topic will be 'the right way of life, such that, if you are instructed in it, you can attain that state of mind which is worthy of a true Christian'.[149] Nor does he announce – as, for example, Thomas Starkey does in his *Dialogue* – that his aim will be to examine the relationship between the best state of a commonwealth and the attainment of that way of life 'wherein lieth the perfection of man'.[150] More's concern, as his title page informs us, is purely and simply with the best state of a commonwealth in itself.

Once we recognise the precise focus of More's enquiry, and the need to distinguish it from other topics of debate within the Christian humanist movement, we can hope to re-examine some of the interpretations of

---

[149] Erasmus 1525, p. 14: 'quandam vivendi rationem [praescriberem] qua instructus, possis ad mentem Christo dignam pervenire'. This was perhaps the central question of Erasmian humanism in More's time, but it is not the question addressed in *Utopia*. Cf. McConica 1965, esp. pp. 13–43, and Bradshaw 1981.

[150] Starkey 1948, pp. 23, 26. The discussion of this relationship, as distinct from the discussion of the perfect life, was a long-established *topos* of humanist political thought. For an early example see Ravenna 1980, pp. 164–6: 'Sed presens intentio non de his qui, defecatis usquequaque desideriis, e ceno temporali in superna rapiuntur...sed de his qui in vita civili versantur.' ('But my present concern is not with those who, released from all their passions, are transported from this temporal slime heavenwards, but only with those who are engaged in civil life.')

More's text suggested by recent scholarship. In particular, we can hope to reconsider J. H. Hexter's thesis that, for all the heathenism of Utopia, it was More's intention to portray the Utopians as living a perfectly virtuous and hence a truly Christian way of life.

This interpretation cannot survive an examination of what Hythloday tells us about the place of religion in Utopian life. The chief point he makes is that, insofar as the Utopians have any shared religion, their religious beliefs are at the same time dictates of rationality. They all think it obvious that the world is governed by divine providence.[151] Likewise, they all agree 'that the soul is immortal; that it is destined by God's mercy for a life of happiness; and that there will be punishments after this present life for our crimes as well as rewards for our virtues and good deeds'.[152] But they think that 'although these principles belong to religion, reason also leads us to the judgement that they are worthy to be believed and accepted'.[153] This makes the Utopians willing to enforce these particular principles, for they feel that to deny them 'would be to sink below the dignity of human nature'.[154] But it also leads them to acknowledge that, apart from these obvious exceptions, nothing about religion is certain and everything ought therefore to be tolerated.[155]

The first comment Hythloday offers on this outlook is that even the Utopians admit that it may not be altogether satisfactory. They recognise that moral arguments depend in part on religious premises.[156] They also concede that, 'if religious sanctions were to be withdrawn, no one would be so foolish as not to pursue their own pleasure by fair means or foul'.[157] Although they think that the religious principles they introduce into their own discussions about human happiness are such that 'no truer viewpoint can be attained by the processes of human reasoning alone',[158] they concede that their conclusions have been arrived at 'in the absence of a heaven-sent religion'.[159] They acknowledge, moreover, that such a

---

[151] More 1965, p. 220.
[152] More 1965, pp. 160–2: 'Animam esse immortalem, ac dei beneficentia ad felicitatem natam, virtutibus ac bene factis nostris praemia post hanc vitam, flagitiis destinata supplicia.'
[153] More 1965, p. 162: 'Haec tametsi religionis sint, ratione tamen censent ad ea credenda, & concedenda perduci.' For a discussion see Logan 1983, pp. 163–4.
[154] More 1965, p. 220: 'ab humanae naturae dignitate degeneret'.   [155] More 1965, p. 220.
[156] More 1965, p. 160. We are told that the Utopians 'never discuss the idea of happiness without taking their principles from religion as well as philosophy'. ('Neque enim de felicitate disceptant unquam, quin principia quaedam ex religione deprompta, tum philosophia.') As noted in Skinner 1967, p. 159, the translation in More 1965 is at fault in this passage.
[157] More 1965, p. 162: 'quibus e medio sublatis, sine ulla cunctatione pronunciant neminem esse tam stupidum, qui non sentiat petendam sibi per fas ac nefas voluptatem'. As noted in Skinner 1967, pp. 159–60, the translation in More 1965 is again at fault in this passage.
[158] More 1965, p. 178: 'nullam investigari credunt humana ratione veriorem'.
[159] More 1965, p. 178: 'caelitus immissa religio'.

religion might well be able 'to inspire mankind with something more holy' than the beliefs they currently accept.[160]

Hythloday goes on to make it clear that in his view the religious and, in consequence, the moral attitudes of the Utopians are certainly flawed. He thereby introduces into his analysis a distinction familiar to classical humanists: a distinction between the optimal conduct of public affairs on the one hand and the optimal conduct of one's own individual life on the other. The former he believes the Utopians have already attained; on the latter point, however, he feels that they still need to be further instructed.

Hythloday is explicit in the first place about the incompleteness of religious understanding in Utopia. Before his arrival, the Utopians knew nothing of the Incarnation, being wholly ignorant of 'the name and the doctrine and the nature and the miracles of Christ'.[161] Even after his voyages, they still lacked access to the Sacraments or the Scriptures, thus remaining cut off from the Church's mediating powers and from any understanding of the divine positive law and the soteriological scheme outlined in the Bible.[162]

Hythloday is equally emphatic about the resulting limitations of the Utopian moral code. These derive from the one feature of Utopian life he directly criticises, namely their view of human happiness. Basing themselves on reason alone, and knowing nothing of God's purposes as disclosed in the Bible, 'they show themselves more inclined than is right'[163] to conclude that individual happiness must simply consist 'in leading as carefree and joyful a life as possible while helping others to do the same'.[164] One implication of their outlook is that in certain circumstances they are ready to permit and even encourage both suicide and euthanasia. 'If someone has a disease which is not only incurable but a source of continual agony and distress',[165] then 'the priests and magistrates

---

[160] More 1965, p. 178: 'sanctius aliquid inspiret homini'.
[161] More 1965, p. 216: 'CHRISTI nomen, doctrinam, mores, miracula'.
[162] More 1965, pp. 180–2 lists the books that Hythloday subsequently took with him to Utopia. He never brought the Bible, which might seem strange until one reflects that its omission is essential if More is to make his point about the limitations of a moral creed founded purely on reason. See also More 1965, p. 218, reporting that Hythloday's party at no point included a priest, with the result that the Utopians still lack the Sacraments.
[163] More 1965, p. 160: 'At hac in re propensiores aequo videntur.' This is the sole point at which Hythloday criticises any feature of the Utopian way of life. The translation in More 1965 suggests a further criticism at p. 145, but only because 'aliquanto procliviores' is translated as 'somewhat too much inclined' instead of 'somewhat more inclined' as the context requires.
[164] More 1965, p. 162: 'nos ut vitam quam licet minime anxiam, ac maxime laetam ducamus ipsi, caeterisque omnibus ad idem obtinendu adiutores'.
[165] More 1965, p. 186: 'si non immedicabilis modo morbus sit verumetiam perpetuo vexet atque discrutiet'.

exhort the person concerned' either to commit suicide and 'free themselves from their bitter life' or else 'voluntarily to allow others to free them from it'.[166] Such decisions are regarded not merely as wise but as 'pious and holy', and those who take them are honoured for doing so.[167]

Given their view of human happiness, this attitude strikes the Utopians as perfectly reasonable. But it is a case in which their reliance on reason alone, without the benefit of Christian revelation, leads them seriously astray.[168] Although they have no means of knowing it, the actions they regard as pious and honourable are at once mortal sins and a negation of an important aspect of Christian soteriology. The Utopians lack any understanding of the intrinsic value of suffering, a value which – under the symbol of the Cross – is central to the soteriological scheme presented in the New Testament. At the same time they fail to recognise, as Hythloday remarks in his tirade against the English practice of hanging thieves, that 'God has not only forbidden us to kill', but 'has withdrawn from us the right to bring about our own death as well as the death of others'.[169] Although reason might incline us to allow certain exceptions – as the Utopians do in their ignorance – the divine positive law made known by God in the Mosaic Code, and renewed by Christ in the New Testament, is completely unambiguous. 'Thou shalt not kill.'

It cannot, then, have been More's intention, in emphasising the heathenism of Utopia, to point ironically to the fact that the heathen Utopians, 'far more than the nominal Christians of Europe, have succeeded in establishing a truly Christian commonwealth'.[170] The irony of the situation seems rather to be registered by the figure of More in the dialogue when he initially tells us at the start of Book 1 about his conversations with Hythloday. He reports that Hythloday 'told me of many mistaken customs to be found among the newly-discovered peoples'.[171] But he adds at once that Hythloday 'also informed me of not a few customs that could well serve as examples to our own cities, nations, peoples and kingdoms, thereby enabling us to correct our own mistakes'.[172] Possessing as we do the benefits of revelation as well as reason, we ought

---

[166] More 1965, p. 186: 'sacerdotes et magistratus hortantur hominem'.
[167] More 1965, p. 186: such an act is held to be 'prudenter facturum' and 'pie sancteque facturum' and is thus regarded as 'honorificum'.
[168] See Duhamel 1955, pp. 99–126 and Logan 1983, pp. 218–20.
[169] More 1965, p. 72: 'Deus vetuit occidi quenquam ... deus non alienae modo, verum etiam suae cuique mortis ius ademerit.'
[170] As I argued in Skinner 1978a, p. 233.
[171] More 1965, p. 54: 'multa apud novos illos populos adnotavit perperam consulta'.
[172] More 1965, p. 54: 'haud pauca recensuit, unde possint exempla sumi corrigendis harum urbium, nationum, gentium, ac regnorum erroribus idonea'.

to be able to surpass such heathen communities in all respects. The irony – and the scandal – lies in the fact that we have so much to learn from them.[173]

The Utopians have not attained the ideal of a perfectly Christian life. But it does not follow that they have not attained the best state of a commonwealth. Reason and revelation are both indispensable for the first, but reason alone suffices for the second, and reason is a universal possession of mankind, one common to heathens and Christians alike. It is certainly possible, therefore, that More intends us to accept that the Utopians have in fact achieved a correct view of what constitutes true nobility, have avoided the baleful consequences of espousing the counterfeit view, and have arrived as a result at the *optimus status reipublicae*.

As we have seen, it is certainly Hythloday's belief that this is the case. But the question, as before, is whether Thomas More, the author of *Utopia*, intends us to endorse that belief. The answer appears to be contained in a single, highly charged passage at the end of the book, a passage in which the figure of More in the dialogue comments directly on the lessons that Hythloday has drawn from his own narrative. 'When Raphael finished his story, many things occurred to me that seemed absurdly established in the customs and laws of the people he had described.'[174] Among these many absurdities, the figure of More singles out one above all:

> The one that struck me most was the feature that constitutes the foundation of their entire social structure: their common life and mode of subsistence, based on having no money transactions at all. If this were to be established, it would overthrow all the nobility, magnificence, splendour and majesty that represent, according to the commonly accepted opinion, the true decorations and ornaments of any commonwealth.[175]

This is a highly ambiguous as well as a highly charged passage, but it certainly contains one objection to Hythloday's analysis to be expected

---

[173] Here I revert to an interpretation that used to be widely accepted. See the references in Logan 1983, p. 141 n. For an excellent restatement see Bradshaw 1981, pp. 6–14. The point was often made by other humanists. Erasmus on several occasions (for example, in the Preface to his edition of Cicero's *De Officiis*) notes the almost scandalous extent to which certain pagan authors are able to instruct us. See too the complaint in Vives 1973, p. 27: 'Senecam, hominem gentilem, Christianos edocentem quae illum conveniebat potius a Christianis discere.' ('Seneca, a pagan, teaching Christians things it would be more appropriate for him to learn from them.')

[174] More 1965, p. 244: 'Haec ubi Raphaël recensuit, quanquam haud pauca mihi succurrebant, quae in eius populi moribus, legibusque perquam absurde videbantur instituta.'

[175] More 1965, p. 244: 'in eo quoque ipso maxime, quod maximum totius institutionis fundamentum est vita scilicet, victuque communi, sine ullo pecuniae commercio, qua una re funditus evertitur omnis nobilitas, magnificentia, splendor, maiestas, vera ut publica est opinio decora atque ornamenta Reipublicae'.

from a good Ciceronian humanist – the *persona* that, as we have seen, the figure of More sustains throughout the dialogue.[176] The objection implicitly raised by the figure of More is in fact no different from the one we have already seen him making at the end of Book I. Philosophy, he had told Hythloday, must seek to be useful in civic life. But in order to be useful it must accommodate to the times. It must work with commonly accepted opinions and try to make them 'as little bad as possible'.[177] But as we have seen, the most commonly accepted opinion in More's time about nobility, magnificence, splendour and majesty was that they are all interconnected. It is precisely Hythloday's contention, however, that the ideal of nobility will have to be separated from these other values if the *optimus status reipublicae* is ever to be attained. The figure of More is thus raising an objection which is in part a purely practical one: what is absurd about Hythloday's advocacy is the fact that it takes no account whatever of what is generally believed.[178]

It seems clear, however, that Thomas More, the author of *Utopia*, is offering a deeper comment on Hythloday's story, and the question of what further comment he wishes to make has become a subject of intense debate. Some recent commentators have straightforwardly identified him with the views expressed by the figure of More in the dialogue. They have accordingly concluded that he is criticising the Utopian system for failing to recognise the importance of nobility, magnificence, splendour and majesty in social life.[179] But this thesis has I think nothing to recommend it. In the first place it is not what the figure of More says in the crucial passage. He merely says that the Utopian system would overthrow 'the commonly accepted opinion' of these values – the opinion that they are all indissolubly linked with each other. As I have laboured to demonstrate, however, it was one of the characteristic ambitions of humanist political theory to dissolve those very links in the name of upholding the rival opinion that true nobility derives from virtue alone. To suppose that the author of *Utopia* was aligning himself at this crucial moment with the orthodoxy that his fellow humanists were overwhelmingly concerned to attack is not merely to go beyond anything said in the text.

---

[176] Bradshaw 1981, pp. 25 and 27 claims that the role in which More casts himself in the dialogue is that of 'the practical man of affairs'. But this seems to me to misunderstand More's views about the role of the humanist intellectual in public life. It is as a committed 'civic' humanist, not a mere man of business, that More presents himself.

[177] More 1965, p. 100: 'ut sit quam minime malum'.

[178] Here I am influenced by Bradshaw 1981, pp. 25–6.

[179] Bradshaw 1981, p. 25 claims that the passage must be taken at face value as an expression of 'More's serious reservations about the ideal system which Hythloday has just outlined'. Cf. Allen 1976, pp. 116–18 for a similar argument.

It is also to render incoherent the fundamentally humanist allegiances displayed throughout the book.[180]

The clue to More's meaning lies instead, I suggest, in examining the implications of his argument from the point of view of his fellow humanists.[181] His argument (to repeat) is that if the Utopian system were to be instituted – forbidding the use of money and abolishing private property – the effect would be to overthrow the values conventionally attached to the concepts of nobility, magnificence, splendour and majesty. As I have been emphasising, however, it was precisely the ambition of More's fellow humanists to overthrow just those conventional values. The implication seems inescapable: More is pointing out that, although the Utopian system may look absurd at first sight, it provides a means of overturning those very values which, according to the humanists themselves, were standing in the way of their own equation between virtue and true nobility, and in consequence standing in the way of enabling the best state of the commonwealth to be realised.

It appears, then, that what More is doing is putting a challenge to his fellow humanists, and in particular raising a doubt about the coherence of their political thought. On the one hand they liked to claim that they wanted above all to prevent inherited wealth from being treated as a criterion of true nobility. But on the other hand they continued to insist on the indispensability of private property, of hereditability and in general of 'degree, priority and place' as preconditions of any well-ordered society. The question we are left with at the end of *Utopia* is whether we can really have it both ways. If we are serious about the claim that virtue constitutes the only true nobility, it may be incoherent simply to endorse the usual justifications for private property. It may instead be necessary to consider the Utopian case for abolishing it in the name of ensuring that virtue alone is honoured, and that the best state of the commonwealth is thereby attained.

There is one obvious objection, however, to supposing that this is the fundamental message that the author of *Utopia* intends to leave with us at the end of his book. This is the fact that the figure of More appears throughout the dialogue in the guise of a good Ciceronian humanist. As I have shown, that school of thought consistently and vehemently opposed

---

[180] For this reason, I cannot accept the claim in Surtz 1965b, p. 454 that, in using the term 'nobilitas' pejoratively, More 'is emphasising the gulf between the high ideal and the accepted standard'. As I have tried to show, what he is doing is opposing a humanist standard to the accepted one.

[181] Here I argue against my own previous interpretation of the passage. See Skinner 1978a, pp. 256–9, an account endorsed in Logan 1983, p. 242.

the Platonist claim that the attainment of the *optimus status reipublicae* might require the abolition of private property. Moreover, when Hythloday first speaks of the Platonist commitment at the end of Book 1, the figure of More responds in precisely the terms I have shown to be characteristic of humanist (and scholastic) theories about the indispensability of private property in any well-ordered commonwealth. 'It is quite impossible to live a satisfactory way of life', the figure of More retorts, 'where everything is held in common.'[182] One reason is that gratuitous poverty will result. 'For how can there ever be an adequate supply of goods where individuals are no longer spurred onwards by the motive of personal gain, and become sluggish through trusting to the industry of others?'[183] A further reason is that 'endless quarrelling and sedition' will be sure to arise, especially because 'the authority of magistrates and any reverence for their office will have been completely undermined'.[184]

But the element which has not been sufficiently noticed in the structure of More's *Utopia* is that Hythloday's entire contribution can – and I think should – be read as an ironic inversion of precisely these two central assumptions of scholastic as well as humanist political thought. What Hythloday shows in Book 1 is that, even if you uphold the rights of private property, you do not necessarily avoid the twin dangers of poverty and disorder. For in England, where the rights of property-holders are defended with extreme violence, the country nevertheless suffers from exactly those two social diseases. By contrast, what Hythloday shows in Book 2 is that, even if you abolish private property, you do not necessarily contract these social diseases at all.[185] For in Utopia, where everything is held in common, the community is nevertheless described as one in which – as Hythloday revealingly expresses it in his summary – there is no disorder, and where there is abundance of everything for everyone.

There is, moreover, a carefully contrived asymmetry between the figure of More's response to these claims at the end of Book 1 and his later response to exactly the same claims at the end of Book 2. At

---

[182] More 1965, p. 106: 'ibi nunquam commode vivi posse, ubi omnia sint communia'.
[183] More 1965, p. 106: 'Nam quo pacto suppetat copia rerum, unoquoque ab labore subducente se? utpote quem neque sui quaestus urget ratio, & alienae industriae fiducia reddit segnem.' As I have sought to show, these were the principal objections that scholastic and humanist political theorists alike registered about Platonic communism. It seems to me anachronistic to dismiss them – as Logan 1983, p. 127 does – as 'ineffectual' and 'feeble'.
[184] More 1965, p. 106: 'necesse est perpetua caede ac seditione ... Sublata praesertim autoritate ac reverentia magistratuum'.
[185] But Hexter 1952, p. 42, makes a point similar in relation to Book 2. See also Bradshaw 1981, pp. 17 and 25 for valuable comments and the summary of Hexter's discussion in Logan 1983, p. 128 and note.

the end of Book 1 he confidently replies by putting the standard case in favour of private property. By the end of Book 2, however, his confidence has completely evaporated in the face of Hythloday's arguments. He makes no attempt to restate his earlier case,[186] but instead brings the discussion to a close by making fully explicit the two judgements we have seen to be implicit in his earlier comments on Hythloday's narrative.[187] On the one hand he reiterates his purely practical doubts. 'I cannot have any hope', he says, of seeing many features of the Utopian commonwealth adopted.[188] But on the other hand he leaves us to wonder whether this may not be entirely to our loss. For the book ends with the figure of More saying that 'I readily confess that there are very many features of the Utopians' commonwealth which, although I cannot have any hope of seeing, I should nevertheless like to see, realised in our own communities'.[189]

Like his fellow-humanists, Thomas More acknowledges the impracticability of seeking to abolish the institution of private property. Unlike them, however, he implies that such realism is purchased at a very high price. To concede the practical point, he shows us, is to close off one of the means – perhaps, Hythloday suggests, 'the one and only means' – of bringing about the *optimus status reipublicae*.[190] As a result, *Utopia* concludes on a wistful and elegiac note. Doubtless we have no hope of ever living in the manner of the Utopians; but the thought we are left with is that, for all that, theirs may nevertheless be the best state of a commonwealth.

---

[186] A point excellently made in Bradshaw 1981, p. 25.
[187] There seems to me no textual warrant for the claim in Bradshaw 1981, p. 26 that the dialogue is 'simply broken off' at the end.
[188] More 1965, p. 246.
[189] More 1965, p. 246: 'ita facile confiteor permulta esse in Utopiensium republica, quae in nostris civitatibus optarim verius quam sperarim'.
[190] See More 1965, p. 104 on the 'una atque unica via' to attain this goal.

9

Humanism, scholasticism and popular sovereignty

I

The sixteenth century has rightly been seen as a pivotal moment in the evolution of modern theories of constitutionalism and the right of resistance. There was admittedly nothing new in the idea that a body of people can justifiably resist or even remove a ruler judged to be behaving tyrannically. But the exercise of this power had usually been treated as a temporary response to some specific crisis of legitimacy. What was lacking was the idea that the people constitute the ultimate authority from which all legitimate governments must derive. Although, as we saw in chapter 2, this conception became well entrenched in the city-republics of the *Regnum Italicum* in the course of the thirteenth century, the apologists of monarchy in northern Europe generally continued to regard the institution of kingship as divinely ordained. It was not until the sixteenth century that there rose to prominence a more radical vision of monarchical government, a vision in which kings and other rulers were viewed as agents or mandatories of the people, who were in turn held to possess a continuing right not merely to limit but to control their rule. Only in this period, in consequence, do we begin to encounter the idea that the power to resist and remove tyrannical kings must be regarded as a moral right possessed at all times by the body of the people – and perhaps even its individual members – in virtue of their standing as the ultimate holders of sovereignty.

These developments have often been associated with the rise of revolutionary Calvinism in the latter part of the sixteenth century. Julian Franklin has argued that it was 'in the political crises touched off by the spread of the Reformation' that these ideas first appeared in their fully

The original (but very different) version of this chapter appeared under the title 'The Origins of the Calvinist Theory of Revolution' in *After the Reformation*, ed. Barbara Malament (London, 1980), pp. 309–30.

developed form.¹ They initially emerged, he adds, most clearly and fully in France, and above all in the works of such leading Huguenot revolutionaries as Theodore Beza, François Hotman and the anonymous author of the *Vindiciae, Contra Tyrannos* of 1579. Michael Walzer in his classic study, *The Revolution of the Saints*, likewise emphasises the causal role played by a new and specifically Calvinist theory of revolution. Walzer begins by speaking of 'the appearance of revolutionary organisation and radical ideology' as one of the 'startling innovations of sixteenth-century political history'. He goes on to argue that 'it was the Calvinists who first switched the emphasis of political thought' from the figure of the prince to that of the revolutionary, and in consequence 'formed the basis for the new politics of revolution'.² My aim in what follows will be to reconsider these claims about the special contribution of Calvinism to the development of modern views of popular sovereignty.

II

There are I think two aspects of Franklin's and Walzer's interpretation that no one would wish to challenge. There is no doubt in the first place that most of the leading protagonists of political resistance in mid-sixteenth-century Europe were Calvinists, or at least took some trouble to present themselves as defenders of Calvinism. This is hardly surprising, given that most of the political struggles to which the Reformation gave rise were struggles against the domination of the Catholic church. This applies to the attempted *coups d'état* in Scotland and England in the 1550s as well as to the upheavals in Holland and France in the 1570s. The leaders of all these movements were professed Calvinists, and their principal ideologists were Calvinist preachers and publicists. The roll-call of the theorists involved is impressive: John Knox and George Buchanan in Scotland, John Ponet and Christopher Goodman in England, Theodore Beza and Philippe du Plessis Mornay in France,³ Philip Marnix and Jacob van Wesembeeke in the Netherlands.⁴

The other contention not in doubt is that, in connection with these movements, a number of Calvinist writers defended the claim that there must be a moral right on the part of entire communities – and even their individual members – to assert their sovereignty by overthrowing tyrannical governments. It is true that this most radical version of the

---

¹ Franklin 1969, pp. 11–15. ² Walzer 1965, pp. 1, 2.
³ For these writers see Skinner 1978b, esp. pp. 323–38.
⁴ For these writers see Gelderen 1992, esp. pp. 115–26.

Calvinist theory of revolution was less frequently affirmed in the course of the sixteenth century than is sometimes implied. Consider, for example, the most celebrated Calvinist revolutionary of the age, John Knox. If we turn to his most violent call to arms, his *Appellation* of 1558, we encounter scarcely any trace of these arguments. Knox describes the establishment of political society as a work of God himself, and accordingly treats the lawfulness of forcible resistance not as a moral right but as an aspect of the people's religious duty to uphold the law of God.[5] Consider, similarly, the Huguenot treatises published in the wake of the St Bartholomew's Day massacre in 1572. Although the Huguenot revolutionaries usually accept that forcible resistance to tyranny is a moral right, they take great care to deny that any such right remains lodged with the body of the people. When, for example, the author of the *Vindiciae* describes the nature of the contracts that inaugurate civil associations, he emphasises that the signatories must be the chosen ruler on the one hand and 'the officers of the kingdom' on the other, without any direct intervention from the people as a whole.[6] This in turn means that, when he defends the right of forcible resistance, he insists that it is possessed only by the officers to whom the people have transferred their authority. It is only to these officers that a ruler makes a promise to rule justly; it is only they who may in consequence be said to have a right to defend the commonwealth from oppression if this promise is not kept.[7]

There can be no doubt, however, that in a number of Calvinist treatises of the later sixteenth century we do encounter the claim that a moral right of forcible resistance remains lodged with the body of the people, and even with its individual members as well. The earliest treatise[8] in which this position is taken up is the Latin dialogue by George Buchanan entitled *De Iure Regni apud Scotos*, which was written in Scotland during the 1560s, in the immediate aftermath of the first successful Calvinist revolution.[9] Buchanan begins by stressing that political societies are in no sense directly ordained by God. All civil associations are instituted by their own members for the improvement of their welfare and the greater security of their rights. The proof lies in the fact that the original condition of mankind was not a political one. Alluding to the *De Inventione*,

---

[5] Knox 1994, pp. 83–4, 95–8. See, on this theme, Burns 1996, pp. 122–52.
[6] *Vindiciae* 1994, pp. 129–37.   [7] *Vindiciae* 1994, pp. 155–8, 169–72.
[8] Caprariis 1959, p. 113 and Kingdon 1967, pp. 153–5 both refer to a still earlier tract, *The Civil and Military Defence of the Innocents and of the Church of Christ*, published in Lyon in 1562, which evidently allowed for resistance by the whole body of the people. But the tract has not survived.
[9] Trevor-Roper 1966 argues that Buchanan sketched the *De Iure* late in 1567, although it remained unpublished until 1579. But for further discussion see McFarlane 1981, pp. 392–6.

the figure of Buchanan rhetorically asks his docile interlocutor, Thomas Maitland: 'Do you not think that once upon a time people lived in huts and even in caves, and wandered about like so many aliens, having neither laws nor even any fixed dwelling-places?'[10] As soon as Maitland agrees, Buchanan sweeps on to infer that all legitimate political societies must therefore have arisen out of human desires and decisions, and specifically out of a recognition that some common benefit would be secured that could not be gained from a solitary way of life.[11]

There is a conspicuous absence in this account of the assumption that the people or their leaders must have sworn a covenant with God at the formation of their commonwealth in order to ensure the rule of righteousness.[12] Buchanan concedes that peoples must originally have been induced to congregate not merely by considerations of utility but also by natural feelings of sociability implanted by God.[13] But he adds that 'considerations of Utility also have great force in helping to establish and maintain human societies'.[14] The body of the people will consent to the election of a ruler and the inauguration of a law-making authority as soon as they recognise the convenience of having someone to deliberate and concern themselves with the affairs of the community as a whole.[15]

Buchanan's humanist vision of the origins of political society is matched by a radically populist analysis of the proper relationship between government and the governed. The people are pictured as consenting to the establishment of a commonwealth essentially in order to secure (but not to alter) their existing system of rights. It follows that rulers must in turn be governed by laws,[16] and must have the status not of overlords but merely of officials or 'elected guardians of society'.[17] There is no question of creating a sovereign who is *legibus solutus*, since 'the people, who grant to the king his power to make laws, prescribe to him the form of his power' in advance.[18] Nor is there any question of alienating or 'transmitting' any rights in the act of instituting a king. Since

---

[10] Buchanan 1579, p. 8: 'putas ne tempus quoddam fuisse, cum homines in tuguriis atque etiam antris habitarent: ac sine legibus, sine certis sedibus palantes vagarentur?' As befits a leading humanist, Buchanan holds to a Ciceronian rather than an Aristotelian view of the origins of political society. His account very closely follows Cicero 1949, I. I. 1 to II. II. 3, pp. 2–8.
[11] Buchanan 1579, p. 9.
[12] See for example the discussion of this covenant in *Vindiciae* 1994, pp. 21–34.
[13] Buchanan 1579, pp. 9–11.
[14] Buchanan 1579, p. 9: 'Magnam profecto videtur quibusdam Utilitas habere vim ad societatem publicam humani generis & constituendam & continendam.'
[15] Buchanan 1579, pp. 15–16. [16] Buchanan 1579, pp. 19–20.
[17] See Buchanan 1579, p. 25 on the *rex* as *custos societatis*.
[18] Buchanan 1579, p. 32: 'populo, qui ei imperium in se dedit... eius imperii modum ei praescribat'.

the people are only electing a 'minister' or representative, it is clear that 'just as they originally had the power to create their kings, so they must also have the power to regulate their behaviour' after appointing them.[19]

When Buchanan turns to the limits of political obligation, he proceeds to endorse an almost anarchistic view of the right of forcible resistance. He has argued that the people only delegate and never alienate their original sovereignty. Those who nowadays rule as kings 'accepted from our ancestors not a wide but a limited power, restrained within definite bounds, while the people retained a perpetual right which has never been taken away from them by any public decree'.[20] The figure of Buchanan in the dialogue is therefore convinced that, as he declares, 'all nations that have ever elected kings and obeyed them must have held this belief in common, that whatever the people may grant to anyone in the way of legal right can always be taken away again if there are just causes for doing so'.[21] Citing instances from Scottish history, he concludes that, if ever the members of a nation find that they have elected not a king but a tyrant, and thus a mere wielder of unjust force, they can always 'shake off his violent power as soon as they gain sufficient confidence in their own strength'.[22] As Buchanan had earlier implied, however, our rulers have a duty to protect not merely the welfare of the community but the rights of individual members at the same time. His other and still more radical conclusion is thus that the right to repel unjust force with force must be lodged 'not merely with the whole body of the people, but even with each individual citizen as well'.[23]

Although George Buchanan was both a Calvinist and a revolutionary, we still need to pause before concluding that his *De Iure Regni* illustrates Michael Walzer's thesis about 'the origins of radical politics'. According to Walzer, it was due to their Calvinist allegiances that writers like Buchanan felt moved to adopt their radical stance. But we still need to ask whether the theory of politics they espoused had its origins within the Calvinist movement itself, or whether they merely adopted and developed it from earlier sources and authorities. Granted that the *writers*

---

[19] Buchanan 1579, p. 62: 'fuerit potestas populi in regibus creandis, & in ordinem redigendis'.
[20] Buchanan 1579, p. 66: 'non immensam, sed intra certos terminos constrictam, & finitam potestatem reges nostros a maioribus accepisse ... & perpetui iuris a populo usurpatio, nullo unquam decreto publico reprehensa'.
[21] Buchanan 1579, p. 80: 'Omnes nationes, quae regibus a se electis parent, hoc communiter sentiunt, quicquid iuris alicui populus dederit, idem eum iustis de causis posse reposcere.'
[22] Buchanan 1579, p. 62: 'populus quoque ubi primum suis viribus coeperit confidere violentum illud imperium poterit excutere'.
[23] Buchanan 1579, p. 97: 'ius est non modo universo populo, sed singulis etiam'. Cf. also Buchanan 1579, pp. 61, 79, 81, and see Burns 1951, pp. 65–7.

who mounted and theorised about the revolutions of sixteenth-century Europe were in general self-proclaimed Calvinists, was it also the case that the *arguments* they invoked were specifically Calvinist in provenance and character?

One of Walzer's main contentions is that this further question must also be answered in the affirmative. Walzer treats the theories of political resistance espoused by the Catholic polemicists of the same period as little more than a reiteration of medieval beliefs. Francisco Suárez is taken as the paradigm of the Catholic outlook, and his view of forcible resistance is said to be that it amounts to nothing more than 'a temporarily necessary form of legal violence' which is brought to an end as soon as order is restored.[24] This backward-looking attitude is sharply contrasted with the 'new politics' of Calvinism, a politics centring on the revolutionary attempt to 'set legality and order aside' in order to accommodate the theory and practice of 'permanent warfare'.[25] The implication of the contrast is said to be that 'the origins of radical politics' must be sought in a specifically Calvinist set of beliefs and experiences. It was Calvinism that 'taught previously passive men the styles and methods of political activity'.[26]

As it stands, however, this argument embodies a *non sequitur*. Walzer may be right to claim that the revolutionary theories of the Calvinists were in no way adopted from their Catholic adversaries. But it does not follow that the theories they articulated must have been the products of a distinctively Calvinist set of beliefs and experiences. There remains the possibility that their outlook may have represented one instance of a more general response by the leaders of the Protestant Reformation to the threat of persecution by the defenders of the Catholic church. What remains to be investigated is the possibility that the theories espoused by the Calvinists may have originated with the Lutherans, from whom the Calvinists may have adopted their arguments.[27]

It is easy to explain why this possibility has so often been overlooked. It has widely been assumed that, as Walzer himself argues, Luther was 'a political conservative', whose followers 'turned away from politics' and left the kingdom of earth, as Luther himself wrote, 'to anyone who wants to take it'.[28] But in fact neither Luther nor the other leading

---

[24] Walzer 1965, p. 111 and note.   [25] Walzer 1965, pp. 111–12.
[26] Walzer 1965, p. 18. For a similar view see Baron 1939, pp. 40–2.
[27] For a further but complementary doubt, emphasising the debt of Calvinism to humanist traditions of thought, see Todd 1987.
[28] Walzer 1965, pp. 23, 26. For a classic statement of the view that Luther was wholly committed to a doctrine of passive political obedience see Figgis 1960, pp. 73–93.

protagonists of the Lutheran Reformation were consistent in adopting such an unworldly stance. When faced in 1530 and again after 1546 with the threat of an imperial campaign designed to crush their church, they decisively abandoned their earlier posture of political passivity.[29] They not only responded by vindicating the lawfulness of forcible resistance, but argued in terms of one of the leading principles later adopted by the Calvinist revolutionaries. Since all rulers, they maintained, are assigned their authority on condition that they institute the rule of justice, any ruler who betrays this trust 'ceases in that to be a Magistrate', as John Locke was later to put it, and may thus be lawfully opposed as a tyrannical wielder of unjust force.[30]

This argument is stated by Luther himself in his *Warnung an seine lieben Deutschen* of 1531. The specific warning that Luther issues is that the emperor may be about to start a war, which indeed seemed probable at the time. Luther declares that, if this happens, it will no longer be possible to accept the emperor as a lawful magistrate. He will no longer be imposing lawful authority but will merely be exercising the power of the fist. Once this characterisation is established, the conclusion in favour of forcible resistance readily follows. Luther announces that, if war breaks out, he will not reprove those who decide to fight the imperialist murderers and bloodthirsty papists. He will accept their action as an instance of self-defence, since it will not amount to rebellion against a lawful magistrate but merely a case of repelling unjust force with force.[31]

This conclusion has sometimes been dismissed as an uncharacteristic outburst in a moment of crisis, an outburst that failed to exercise any lasting influence.[32] But if we turn to the later theoretical writings of Philipp Melanchthon, Luther's chief lieutenant in the Wittenberg Reformation, we find the same line of argument even more plainly set out. Consider, for example, Melanchthon's *Prolegomena* to Cicero's *De Officiis*, a work he originally published in 1530 and reissued in a revised and radicalised form in 1542.[33] One of the new sections he added specifically deals with the office of rulers and magistrates. The discussion opens by pointing to the fact that 'animals have a natural instinct to repel violence, due to the fact that God has implanted in their nature an

---

[29] This point is emphasised in Skinner 1978b, pp. 191–224 and in Kingdon 1991, pp. 200–6.
[30] Locke 1988, II, 202, p. 400.
[31] See Luther 1910 and for a discussion see Brecht 1990, pp. 411–21.
[32] See the accounts of Luther's *volte face* in 1530–31 in Baron 1937, p. 422 and Mesnard 1969, p. 228.
[33] See Melanchthon 1850 and for publishing details see Bindseil 1850.

appetite for conserving themselves, while in mankind we also find the same inclination to repulse unjust violence'.[34] This 'natural knowledge' is said to be 'the testimony which God has given to us for discriminating between justice and injustice'.[35] Melanchthon proceeds to argue the standard humanist case that the reason for instituting civil associations is to guarantee the rule of justice, and thus that the office of rulers and magistrates automatically excludes any right to inflict 'manifest injuries' on their subjects.[36] This allows him to restate the crucial conclusion at which Luther had already arrived:

> It is lawful to repel unjust force by means of a kind of force that has been ordained, that is to say, through the office of the magistrate when he is able to call on help, or else by one's own hand if the magistrate cannot act, in the manner of someone who kills thieves.[37]

As Melanchthon explicitly affirms, the lawful power to resist unjust force is not merely lodged with ordained magistrates. It is a power possessed *in extremis* by every individual subject, this being in accordance with the truth of the maxim that 'nature permits us to repel force with force'.[38]

The same arguments were subsequently restated by a number of Lutheran publicists in the face of Emperor Charles V's campaign against the Schmalkaldic League after 1546. The most important treatise to revive these claims was the *Confessio et Apologia* issued by the pastors of Magdeburg. This was probably written by Luther's close associate Nicholas von Amsdorf, and was published in German and Latin in April 1550.[39] The second section of the *Confessio* takes as its point of departure the justification of forcible resistance already offered by Luther in his *Warnung* nearly twenty years before.[40] Amsdorf first emphasises that all the powers that be are ordained to fulfil a particular office. He then argues that, since magistrates are ordained by God to be an honour to good works and a terror to the bad, it follows that if they begin to honour the bad and persecute the good they cannot

---

[34] Melanchthon 1850, p. 573: 'Bestiae naturale inclinatione repellunt violentiam, quia cuilibet naturae insita est a Deo appetito conservandi sese: in homine autem [est inclinatio] ad depulsionem iniustae violentiae.'
[35] Melanchthon 1850, p. 573: 'testimonia de Deo, ostendentia discrimen inter iusta et iniusta'.
[36] See Melanchthon 1850, p. 574 on 'iniuria manifesta'.
[37] Melanchthon 1850, p. 573: 'vim iniustam repellere licet vi ordinata, scilicet officio magistratus, cum eius auxilio uti potest, aut manu propria, si desit magistratus, ut si quis incidat in latrones'.
[38] Melanchthon 1850, p. 573: 'Verum est igitur dictum, vim vi repellere natura concedit'.
[39] [Amsdorf] 1550. My ascription is based on the fact that Amsdorf's name stands first in the list of pastors who signed the tract at the end.
[40] [Amsdorf] 1550, Sig. A. 2^r.

be accounted genuine magistrates.[41] This again is taken to license the conclusion that anyone who resists such actions will not be resisting lawful authority, but merely a wielder of unjust force who may be lawfully repulsed.[42]

III

It might seem that Michael Walzer's thesis about the origins of radical politics could still be rescued if it were now restated in more general terms. Although there may be little that was distinctively Calvinist about the revolutionary arguments of the mid-sixteenth century, it might still be argued that these arguments were the product of a distinctively *Protestant* psychology and experience. But even this, I think, would be to claim too much. Walzer's basic distinction between the backward-looking philosophy of the Catholic schoolmen during this period and the 'modern' outlook associated with the Reformation cannot be sustained. If we turn to the schoolmen of the early sixteenth century, we find them enunciating the same theory of resistance as was later espoused by such humanist converts to Calvinism as George Buchanan and still later enshrined in such classic restatements of the Calvinist theory as John Locke's *Two Treatises of Government*. The schoolmen of the generation immediately preceding the Reformation have received little attention,[43] but it is the main argument of this chapter that they need to be brought centre-stage if we are to gain a better understanding of the evolution of radical politics in early-modern Europe.

The radical arguments deployed by the schoolmen largely stem from two prominent strands of later medieval thought. One was the discussion among civil lawyers of the conditions under which the infliction of violence need not constitute legal injury. The *Digest* of Roman law contains a classic statement of the claim – later taken up by Lutheran as well as Calvinist theorists – that it is always legitimate to repel unjust force with force: *vim vi repellere licere*. The maxim itself appears in Book 43 under the title *De Vi et de Vi Armata*, where Ulpian is quoted as follows:

---

[41] [Amsdorf] 1550, Sig. F. 3ʳ.
[42] On Amsdorf's tract and its significance see Skinner 1978b, pp. 206–11.
[43] This was true when this chapter was originally written, but there is now a large and distinguished literature on Almain and Mair. On Almain see Carlyle and Carlyle 1936, pp. 241–7; Burns 1983, Burns 1994; Brett 1997, pp. 116–22. On Mair see Burns 1954 and Burns 1981. See also Oakley 1962 and Oakley 1965, two valuable articles in which Almain and Mair are treated together, and Oakley 1984, a collection of these and related articles. For another valuable treatment of Almain and Mair see Tierney 1997, pp. 236–54.

Cassius writes that it is lawful to repel force with force, and that this is permitted by the law of nature. From which it appears, he says, that armed force may lawfully be repelled with armed force.[44]

The implications of the dictum are spelled out in the analysis of the *Lex Aquilia* in Book 9, where the main example considered is that of robbery with violence. If I kill a thief who is attacking me, there will be no question of my being liable for murder, because natural reason permits everyone to protect themselves from danger. Even if it is only my property rather than my life which is in jeopardy, it may still be lawful for me to kill a thief who comes in the night, provided that I give fair warning.[45]

It is true that none of the jurists intended this justification of private violence to be applicable in the public sphere. But this was not enough to deter a number of writers from adapting and extending their arguments in such a way as to generate a theory of political resistance. Nearly two centuries before Luther and Melanchthon made their appeal to the maxim *vim vi repellere licere*, we already find William of Ockham arguing in the same fashion in his *Octo Quaestiones de Potestate Papae*. Discussing the jural relationship between the pope and the emperor in his second *Quaestio*, Ockham considers the parallel question of the relationship between a kingdom and its king. He concedes that 'the king is superior to his whole kingdom in the ordinary course of events'.[46] But he instantly qualifies this doctrine with the claim that 'in certain circumstances he is inferior to the kingdom'.[47] This is said to be proved by the fact that 'in cases of dire necessity it is lawful for the subjects of a kingdom to depose their king and keep him in custody'.[48] And this in turn is said to be justified by the fact that 'we have it from the law of nature that anyone may lawfully repel force with force'.[49]

The other and even stronger foundation for the arguments of the early sixteenth-century schoolmen was provided by the theorists of the Conciliar movement. At the time of the Great Schism at the end of the fourteenth century, Jean Gerson and his followers had adapted the Roman Law theory of corporations in such a way as to defend a thesis

---

[44] *Digest* 1985, XLIII. XVI. I. 27, vol. 4, p. 584: 'Vim vi repellere licere Cassius scribit idque ius natura comparatur: apparet autem, inquit, ex eo arma armis repellere licere.'
[45] *Digest* 1985, IX. II. 4, vol. 1, p. 278.
[46] Ockham 1940, p. 86: 'Rex enim superior est regulariter toto regno suo.'
[47] Ockham 1940, p. 86: 'tamen in casu est inferior regno'.
[48] Ockham 1940, p. 86: 'regnum in casu necessitatis potest regem suum deponere et in custodia detinere'.
[49] Ockham 1940, p. 86: 'ex iure naturali habet quod cuilibet vim vi repellere licet'.

of popular sovereignty in the church.⁵⁰ They had argued that, as Gerson puts it in his treatise *De Potestate Ecclesiastica* of 1417, the highest power to govern the church must at all times be lodged with the general council as the representative assembly of the faithful, with the pope's *plenitudo potestatis* being assigned to him merely as a matter of convenience.⁵¹ The first inference Gerson draws is that 'if the general council represents the universal church, it is integrally necessary that its power should include the authority of the pope'.⁵² This being so, the pope cannot be considered as the *caput* or head of the members of the church, 'for each of these, as the Apostle says, is also given a duty to perform'.⁵³ Rather the council must be in all ways *maior* or greater than the pope, 'including in coercive power',⁵⁴ and its authority must extend even to deposing and removing the pope from office.⁵⁵ Gerson chooses not to spell out the implications of his theory for other types of *societates perfectae*, such as political communities. But he leaves us with an analysis of ecclesiastical power which, if transferred to the civil sphere, would yield the conclusion that the highest authority to make laws must remain lodged with the people or their representatives at all times.

Early in the sixteenth century these legal and conciliarist ideas were duly applied to the civil sphere by a group of avowed followers of Ockham and Gerson at the University of Paris.⁵⁶ The occasion for this development was the quarrel that the French king, Louis XII, picked with Pope Julius II after the collapse of the League of Cambrai in 1510.⁵⁷ Alarmed by Louis' victory over the Venetians in the previous year, Julius decided to repudiate the alliance he had formed with the French in 1508. Louis responded by appealing over the pope's head to a general council of the church, summoning the council to meet at Pisa in May 1511.⁵⁸ (This in turn alarmed the Florentines, and Machiavelli was one of the emissaries sent to plead for the council to be held elsewhere.)⁵⁹ Besides demanding that a general council should go into session, Louis called on the University of Paris to confirm his claim that the church as a body possesses

---

⁵⁰ On the Schism see Flick 1930, vol. 1, pp. 262, 271, 312. On Gerson and his followers see Morrall 1960. For earlier conciliarist ideas see Tierney 1955.
⁵¹ Gerson 1965, pp. 217, 222, 232–3.
⁵² Gerson 1965, p. 222: 'si generale concilium repraesentet universalem Ecclesiam sufficienter et integre necesse est ut includat auctoritatem papalem'.
⁵³ Gerson 1965, p. 239: 'non ita ut caput, ... quibus singulis, ut ait Apostolus, proprium datum est officium'.
⁵⁴ Gerson 1965, p. 240: 'maior in coercitiva potestate'.   ⁵⁵ Gerson 1965, p. 223.
⁵⁶ For a classic study of the Sorbonne in this period see Renaudet 1953.
⁵⁷ La Brosse 1965, pp. 58–9.   ⁵⁸ Jedin 1957–61, vol. 1, pp. 32–4.
⁵⁹ Renaudet 1922, pp. 469–76.

greater authority than the pope.⁶⁰ The professors at the Sorbonne duly responded with a number of systematic works of political theory, defending the idea of popular sovereignty as a claim not merely about the government of the church but about the location of authority in civil associations as well.⁶¹

The first and most radical exponent of this position was Jacques Almain (c.1480–1515), known to his contemporaries as 'Splendor Academiae'. Almain was commissioned by the university to furnish its official reply to the king, which was published as *Libellus de Autoritate Ecclesiae* in 1512.⁶² It seems that Almain may have won this commission as the result of a more wide-ranging disputation he had already conducted on the subject of natural, civil and ecclesiastical power. This latter work was first published in 1518 as *Questio in Vesperiis Habita*⁶³ and was later reprinted under the more descriptive title of *Quaestio Resumptiva... de Dominio Naturali, Civili, & Ecclesiastico*.⁶⁴ Of still greater importance in these debates was the figure of John Mair (c.1467–1550). Mair was Almain's teacher, and probably collaborated with him in the writing of his *Libellus*. Later he published similar views about the concept of popular sovereignty,⁶⁵ initially outlining them in his commentary on the fourth book of Peter Lombard's *Sentences* in 1516⁶⁶ and subsequently restating them in a more accessible style in his *Historia Majoris Britanniae* in 1521.⁶⁷

John Mair has largely been neglected by historians of political theory,⁶⁸ but he is arguably of pivotal significance in the evolution of early-modern theories of popular sovereignty. He not only adopted and developed the

---

⁶⁰ For the dependence of the ensuing discussions of popular sovereignty by the Sorbonnists (especially Almain and Mair) on the works of Gerson and his associates, see Oakley 1964, pp. 203–4, 213–15; La Brosse 1965, Part II; Brett 1997, pp. 76–87, 116–22.
⁶¹ For the immediate context of these works see Burns and Izbicki 1997.
⁶² My citations are taken from Almain 1706a, the version of the tract issued (under the title *Tractatus* rather than *Libellus*) in 1606 and again in 1706 as an appendix to the works of Jean Gerson. For a translation see Almain 1997a.
⁶³ Almain 1518, 4th pagination, fos. lxii–lxvii.
⁶⁴ This was the title under which the work appeared when it too was republished as an appendix to the works of Jean Gerson. See Almain 1706b. For a translation see Almain 1997b.
⁶⁵ For these and other biographical details see Mackay 1892, pp. xxxiii–xxxviii. For Mair's date of birth see Burns 1954, p. 83.
⁶⁶ Mair originally published his commentary in 1509, but first added his radical political arguments to the edition of 1516, republishing this version in 1519 and again in 1521. My translations are taken from the 1519 edition.
⁶⁷ See Mair 1521 and cf. Mair 1892, the version from which I quote. The title embodies a pun on *Major*, the Latinised version of Mair's name. On Mair as an historian see Burns 1996, pp. 59–75.
⁶⁸ This was true when this chapter was originally written, but we now have Burns 1981, Oakley 1984 and Tierney 1997, all important discussions of Mair's political works.

arguments already adumbrated by his acknowledged masters, William of Ockham and Jean Gerson, but also served as a channel through which their ideas passed into the age of the Reformation and beyond. When Mair began teaching theology at the Collège de Montaigu in the early years of the sixteenth century, one of his pupils there was Jean Calvin himself.[69] Even more suggestively, when he returned to his native Scotland in 1518, one of the students whom he taught as professor of philosophy and divinity at the University of Glasgow was John Knox.[70] Most suggestively of all, when he transferred to the University of St Andrews in 1522, one of the young scholars who followed him there 'to sit at his feet' was George Buchanan.[71]

For Almain as well as Mair, the point of departure in the analysis of civil associations is with the idea of the original freedom of the people. Mair offers the fullest account of the natural condition of mankind in the later editions of his commentary on the fourth book of Lombard's *Sentences*. He agrees with Gerson that Adam enjoyed a paternal but not a political form of dominion, since there was no need for coercive authority in a sinless world.[72] He accordingly reiterates – as Gerson had done – the patristic view that the need for secular communities must originally have arisen in consequence of the Fall. Wandering and congregating in different parts of the world, men found it expedient for their own protection 'to constitute a single head for themselves and to live under kingly forms of government'.[73] Later, however, they discovered to their cost that kingship tends to degenerate into tyranny, and at that stage Mair imagines a further development. 'Very many kings, it seems to me, must then have been introduced by the consent of the people, and were able justly to maintain their government only by popular consent.'[74]

The chief corollary drawn by Almain and Mair is that no rulers placed in power by a free people can ever possess absolute sovereignty, since they must originally have been installed on agreed terms to serve as delegates or 'ministers' of the community that appointed them. The doctrine is most clearly summarised by Almain at the start of his *Quaestio Resumptiva*. He agrees that the capacity to establish 'civil dominion' must originally have been granted to mankind after the Fall, and he

---

[69] Ganoczy 1966, pp. 39–41. [70] Ridley 1968, pp. 15–16.
[71] Burns 1954, pp. 85, 92–3; McFarlane 1981, pp. 27–8. [72] Mair 1519, fo. cii^v.
[73] Mair 1519, fo. ciii^r: 'possent inter se constituere unum caput, & in regia politia vivere'.
[74] Mair 1519, fo. ciii^r: 'Aliqui autem reges & plurimi, ut opinor, introducti sunt consensu populi: & ... non poterant iuste tenere regimen sine populi consensu.'

proceeds to note five corollaries. The second states that the *ius gladii* or 'right of the sword' must remain lodged with the *communitas* or body of the people at all times, since 'no perfect Community can abdicate this power, just as no individual person can abdicate the power they possess to conserve themselves in being'.[75] His third corollary adds that the jurisdictional standing of the ruler of any such community must therefore 'be merely that of an official' appointed by the people.[76] Almain concedes in his fifth corollary that 'because it is not possible for the whole Community regularly to congregate, it has been thought appropriate that they should delegate this power to a certain person, or group of persons, who are able to meet together easily'.[77] But he insists in his fourth corollary that such persons can never have a higher standing than delegates of the people, since 'the power that the Community has over the Prince whom it has instituted is one that it is impossible for it to renounce'.[78]

There are two implications that Almain – more explicit and radical than Mair – is particularly anxious to underline. The first, evidently directed against the more conservative outlook of the Thomists, is that we cannot speak of any new rights of sovereignty being established at the inauguration of commonwealths. The Thomists had originally put forward – and Suárez was later to repeat – a strongly contrasting argument. No individual, they had observed, possesses the right to kill, but it is unquestionable that any lawful ruler possesses, in the *ius gladii*, just such a right. They inferred that, although it is true that the people must originally have instituted the legal powers under which they live, the act of doing so must have involved them in creating an authority greater than themselves. Almain retorts that this doctrine is incoherent, on the grounds that 'no one can give what they do not already possess'.[79] This leads him to argue that, since there is undoubtedly a right of judicial execution in any commonwealth, a similar right must already have existed before the commonwealth was brought into existence.[80] 'Because it is the Community that gives authority to the Prince to kill, it follows that

---

[75] Almain 1706b, col. 964: 'Nulla Communitas perfecta hanc potestatem a se abdicare potest, sicut nec singularis homo potestatem quam habet ad se conservandum in esse.'
[76] Almain 1706b, col. 964: 'dominium Jurisdictionis Principum est solum ministeriale'.
[77] Almain 1706b, col. 965: 'quia Communitas regulariter facile congregari non potest ... congruum fuit, ut eam delegaret alicui, aut aliquibus, qui facile congregari possunt'.
[78] Almain 1706b, col. 963: 'Non potest renunciare Communitas potestati quam habet super suum Principem ab ea constitutum.'
[79] Almain 1706b, col. 964: '*Nemo dat quod non habet*.' Cf. also Almain 1706a, col. 978.
[80] Almain 1706b, cols. 963–4.

this authority must originally have been possessed by the Community itself, and not in the way of a grant from anyone else, unless we think of it as a grant from God.'[81]

Drawing on the theory of natural rights already outlined by Ockham and Gerson,[82] Almain puts forward a remarkably individualistic argument in proof of this conclusion.[83] He presents his case most fully at the start of his *Libellus de Autoritate Ecclesiae*. First he declares that every individual person in the pre-political state of nature 'must have been endowed with a natural right or power to do anything necessary to sustain and conserve themselves, and to repel all harmful things'.[84] This latter right must have extended, he specifically adds, to include 'the power of killing anyone who makes an unjust attack on us'.[85] Almain then argues that exactly the same right or power must, by analogy, be possessed by the body of the people, 'since any individual person can be compared with the entire Community as a part to a whole'.[86] The community must therefore have a natural and inalienable right to repel unjust force with force, 'even to the extent of cutting off by death anyone who may perturb the community' or threaten its capacity to preserve itself.[87]

The other implication Almain underlines is that, since any legitimate ruler must be a mere delegate of the people, the act performed by the whole community in setting up a commonwealth can never be one that involves them in the alienation of their rights. The fullest statement of this claim is again to be found in the opening chapter of the *Libellus de Autoritate Ecclesiae*. Here too Almain appears to be opposing the more conservative outlook of the Thomists. They had argued – and Suárez was later to reiterate – that when a body of people (in Suárez's words)

---

[81] Almain 1706b, col. 964: 'cum Communitas det Principi auctoritatem occidendi, sequitur quod est prius in Communitate, & non ex datione cuiuscumque alterius, nisi dicatur Dei'.
[82] Brett 1997, p. 119.
[83] The argument is laid out in Almain 1706a col. 977 and again in Almain 1706b, cols. 961–2.
[84] Almain 1706a, col. 977: 'hominem condidit cum naturali Iure, seu potestate, ea quae suae sustentationi ac conservatione necessaria sunt sumendi, necnon & ea quae nociva sunt repellendi'.
[85] Almain 1706a, col. 977: 'potestas eum, qui iniuste aggreditur, interimendi'.
[86] Almain 1706a, col. 977: 'Cum ergo quaelibet persona singularis comparetur ad totam Communitatem, sicut pars ad totum.' Almain's argument is thus that the reason why the community must possess this power is that, by analogy with its individual members, any community must possess whatever rights are necessary for preserving itself. This is not to say (as I originally suggested in Skinner 1980) that the community acquires this power from the fact that its individual members possess it. Burns 1983 supplies this correction. But the inference seems a natural one, and a number of sixteenth-century schoolmen (for example, Domingo de Soto) duly went on to draw it.
[87] Almain 1706a, col. 977: 'eos quorum vita est in perturbationem Communitatis, etiam per mortem praescindere'.

'makes a transfer of power to a prince' this will involve them 'not in a delegation but rather in a kind of alienation or absolute gift' of their rights, and thus in the creation of a sovereign above the law, not a mere delegate of the sovereign people.[88] Almain retorts that 'the Power that any perfect Community possesses is one that it can never abdicate, any more than an individual person can voluntarily relinquish their Power to preserve themselves'.[89] This enables him to insist once more that 'the Power which a King has at his disposal is simply the Power of the Community', and thus that 'the Power of Princes can never be greater than that of the holder of an office'.[90]

It is important to distinguish Almain's and Mair's arguments from those of the humanist writers we examined in chapters 2 and 5. Mair specifically notes in his commentary on Lombard's *Sentences* that the people of ancient Rome elected their consuls, and that the people of modern Venice continue to elect their Doges as leaders drawn from the ranks of the citizen-body itself.[91] But he makes it clear that he is not himself arguing in favour of the neo-Roman thesis that free peoples must ensure that their rulers take their turn at being ruled. He is content to assume that he is talking, as he says, about *regia politia*, about monarchical forms of government. The thesis on which he insists is simply that, whatever type of monarchy we institute, we must ensure that the powers allotted to our kings are consistent with the fact that the body of the people remains the ultimate bearer of sovereignty at all times.

The upshot of Mair's argument, and even more clearly of Almain's, is thus that our rulers must be 'ministers', elected on condition that they protect and uphold the rights of the sovereign people. They accordingly go on to argue that, should our rulers fail to discharge these duties, they can lawfully be resisted and removed. Almain states the inference with his usual briskness at the start of his *Libellus de autoritate ecclesiae*. 'A Prince who rules not for the benefit but for the destruction of the Polity can be deposed.'[92] Mair endorses the conclusion in his commentary on the fourth book of Lombard's *Sentences*. Here he treats

---

[88] Suárez 1975, III. IV. 11, p. 49: 'Quodcirca translatio huius potestatis a republica in principem non est delegatio, sed quasi alienatio seu perfecta largitio.'
[89] Almain 1706a, col. 978: 'Nulla Communitas perfecta hanc Potestatem a se abdicare potest, sicut nec singularis homo quam habet Potestatem ad se conservandum.'
[90] Almain 1706a, col. 979: 'Potestas qua Rex utitur, est Potestas Communitatis [ergo] *Dominium Principum esse ministeriale*.' Cf. also Almain 1706b, col. 964.
[91] Mair 1519, fo. ciii^r.
[92] Almain 1706a, col. 978: 'eum [sc.Principem] (si non in aedificationem, sed in destructionem Politiae regat) deponere potest'.

the right of political resistance, using a favourite and homely simile, as a straightforward corollary of his doctrine of popular sovereignty. Since any ruler is in effect an administrative official, 'who cannot have the same free power over his kingdom as I have over my books', it follows that 'the whole people must be above the king and can in some cases depose him'.[93]

Two features of this doctrine need to be underlined. One is that the argument is conducted in wholly secular terms. Since Almain and Mair both view the creation of civil associations essentially as a device for protecting the rights and welfare of the people, they defend the lawfulness of resistance entirely as a moral right, wholly bypassing the language of religious duties. The other notable feature of their argument is its radically populist character. The authority to exercise the right of forcible resistance is said to be lodged not merely with the people's representatives but with the body of the people themselves. It is true that Mair is extremely hesitant and in consequence inconsistent at this vital point. When discussing the right of deposition in his *History*, he concludes by warning us that, unless there has been 'a solemn consideration of the matter by the three Estates', even a tyrannical king 'is not to be deposed'.[94] At an earlier stage in his argument, however, he had suggested that, even though 'the chief men and the nobility who act for the common people' should normally be responsible for checking an evil ruler, his power is ultimately 'dependent upon the whole people'. This leads him to accept the more radical conclusion that 'the whole people must be above the king and in some cases can depose him', and that 'a people may deprive their king and his posterity of all authority, when the king's worthlessness calls for such a course, just as at first it had the power to appoint him king'.[95]

If we turn finally to the younger and less cautious Almain, we find the same doctrine put forward with much greater confidence. He announces his commitment – again with characteristic briskness – at the start of the *Quaestio Resumptiva*. He has already established, he claims, that it must be the body of the people who institute their rulers to protect their interests. So it must be the same body that retains the perpetual power to resist and remove tyrannical rulers if they fail to discharge the duties they were elected to perform. 'Given that the Community cannot renounce the power it possesses over any Prince whom it has constituted, it follows

---

[93] Mair 1519, fos. cii^v–ciii^r.   [94] Mair 1521, p. 219. Cf. Oakley 1962, p. 18.
[95] Mair 1521, pp. 213, 214, 215; cf. also Mair 1519, fo. ciii^r.

that it must be the Community that has the power to depose him (if he rules not for its benefit but for its destruction), this being a natural power of the Community itself.'[96]

IV

The study of radical politics in early-modern Europe has for some time been dominated by the concept of the 'Calvinist theory of revolution'. But I have now suggested that in some respects the label is a misleading one. It is true that the political upheavals of sixteenth-century Europe were largely engineered by professed Calvinists, but the theories in terms of which they explained and justified their actions were not, at least in their main outlines, specifically Calvinist at all. When the humanist George Buchanan stated for the first time on behalf of the reformed churches a fully secularised and populist theory of resistance, he was largely restating a series of arguments already mounted by the scholastic theologians at the Sorbonne over a half a century before.[97] John Mair and his associates bequeathed to the era of the Reformation the leading elements of the early-modern theory of revolution in its most radical form. It only remained for Buchanan – Mair's own pupil – to take over the concepts and arguments he had learnt from his scholastic teachers and press them into service on behalf of the Calvinist cause.

Once this background is brought into focus, it may even seem that recent studies have been asking the wrong question about the so-called Calvinist theory of revolution. They have generally asked what could have prompted the Calvinists to develop their distinctive analysis and justification of revolutionary activity. Perhaps they ought instead to have asked what prompted the Calvinists to appeal so extensively to the theories already developed by their Catholic adversaries. The significance of the question lies in the fact that it hints at a different view of the relationship between the ideology of the radical Calvinists and their revolutionary practice. Because Michael Walzer, for example, thinks of their ideology as distinctively Calvinist, he sees it as the key to their self-definition and as the fundamental motive for their behaviour.[98] Once

---

[96] Almain 1706b, col. 964: 'Non potest renunciare Communitas potestati quam habet super suum Principem ab ea constitutum, qua scilicet potestate eum (si non in aedificationem, sed ad destructionem regat) deponere potest, cum talis potestas sit naturalis.'
[97] McFarlane 1981, pp. 403-4.
[98] See, for example, Walzer 1965, p. 2, speaking of the Calvinists as 'moved by new and revolutionary ideologies'.

we see, however, how little of their ideology was distinctively Calvinist, we are bound to ask whether they may have been engaged not merely in a process of self-definition, but also in a more outward-looking ideological exercise designed to appeal to the uncommitted, to reassure those who might be thinking of joining the cause, and above all to neutralise their ideological enemies by showing how far the Calvinist revolutionary programme could be legitimated by reference to accepted beliefs.

It would require a great deal of further research to test such an hypothesis. But if we recall for a moment the situation in which the Calvinists found themselves, we can at least end by making two points about the plausibility of such an argument. Characteristically the Calvinists were in a small minority, trying to promote illegal and subversive behaviour, and confronting a hostile majority dedicated to claiming that their actions were wholly at odds with good and godly government. Given this predicament, it would not be surprising if the Calvinists were in fact motivated, at least in part, by a felt need to try to broaden the basis of their support, and to defuse so far as possible the condemnation of Catholic Europe.

The other point worth making is that, if these were indeed among their motives, it would have been rational for the Calvinists to act in precisely the way in which they acted. When they presented themselves as exponents of a political theory already articulated by a number of Catholic schoolmen, they were arguably adopting the best available means of legitimising their cause. Perhaps this was their own perception; and perhaps it is in this perception that we should be looking, at least in part, for the secret of their success.

10

Moral ambiguity and the Renaissance art of eloquence

I

If we consider the leading works of English philosophy written in the age of the scientific revolution, we can hardly fail to be struck by the anxiety they frequently register about what John Locke, in his *Essay Concerning Human Understanding*, calls the 'doubtfulness and uncertainty', the 'great uncertainty and obscurity' afflicting the application of moral terms.[1] This sense of increasing ambiguity and confusion about the description and appraisal of human actions was, for example, widespread within the early Royal Society. It underlies John Wilkins's plan of 1668 for the construction of what he called a philosophical language,[2] and it surfaces in the *History* of the society published by Thomas Sprat in the previous year, in which he complains that the use of ambiguous and over-elaborate language has 'already overwhelm'd most other *Arts* and *Professions*'.[3]

A similar disquiet pervades Locke's analysis in Book 3 of the *Essay* of what he calls 'the imperfections and abuses' of words:

Men's Names, of very compound *Ideas*, such as for the most part are moral Words, have seldom, in two different Men, the same precise signification; since one Man's complex *Idea* seldom agrees with anothers, and often differs from his own, from that which he had yesterday, or will have tomorrow.[4]

This chapter is a much revised and extended version of an article that originally appeared under the same title in *Essays in Criticism* 44 (1994), pp. 267–92.

[1] Locke 1979, III. IX. 4 and 6, p. 477.
[2] Slaughter 1982 rightly sees the rise of universal language projects as a response to perceived linguistic inadequacies. But in discussing John Wilkins she concentrates on his aspiration to produce fixed definitions and taxonomies in the sciences. It needs to be stressed that he harboured similar ambitions for moral and religious discourse. For a discussion of his wish to unmask the 'wild errors' in religion that 'shelter themselves under the disguise of affected phrases' see Shapiro 1969, esp. p. 219. For his attempt to provide a fixed typology of the virtues and vices see Wilkins 1668, pp. 206–13. For further discussions of Wilkins's project see Knowlson 1975, pp. 91–107 and Stillman 1995, pp. 228–62.
[3] Sprat 1959, p. 111.   [4] Locke 1979, III. IX. 6, p. 478.

As a result of these confusions, Locke goes on, there is 'scarce any Name, of any very complex *Idea*, (to say nothing of others,) which, in common Use, has not a great latitude, and which keeping within the bounds of Propriety, may not be made the sign of far different *Ideas*'.[5]

Some time before Locke issued these warnings in 1690, we already find Thomas Hobbes considering the same problem in terms that Locke appears at various moments to follow almost word for word. As early as 1640 Hobbes had observed in *The Elements of Law* 'how unconstantly names have bene settled, and how subject they are to equivocation', and how these ambiguities act as a barrier to the construction of a genuine civil science.[6] By the time he came to publish his *Leviathan* in 1651 he was ready to carry the argument much further. He not only reasserts the fact that everyone continually disagrees about the application of evaluative terms, so much so that 'the same man, in divers times, differs from himselfe; and one time praiseth, that is, calleth Good, what at another time he dispraiseth, and calleth Evil'.[7] He now goes so far as to add that this explains why the natural condition of mankind must necessarily be one of mutual hostility, since such differences are the principal causes of 'Disputes, Controversies, and at last War'.[8]

These considerations bring me to the question I want to address. Why was there so much anxiety in this period about what was seen as the increasing inability to agree about the proper application of evaluative terms? The question has lately been much debated by intellectual historians, and one particular answer has won increasing acceptance. The anxiety, we are told, was a response to the growing interest in, and even acceptance of, the doctrines of Pyrrhonian scepticism, an interest that quickened towards the end of the sixteenth century with the rediscovery of the texts of Sextus Empiricus and their exploitation by such writers as Montaigne and Pierre Charron.[9]

---

[5] Locke 1979, III. IX. 8, p. 479.
[6] Hobbes 1969b, p. 23. While Hobbes 1969b is the standard edition, it contains so many transcription errors that I have preferred to quote from BL Harl. MS 4235, arguably the best surviving manuscript, although my page references are to the 1969 edition.
[7] Hobbes 1996, pp. 110–11.   [8] Hobbes 1996, p. 111.
[9] There are interesting discussions in Brunschvicg 1944, pp. 113–54; Battista 1966, pp. 135, 145, 172–5; and Curley 1978, who valuably relates this background to Descartes' philosophy. But the argument has chiefly been developed by Richard Popkin. See Popkin 1979, and for a full list of his contributions see Popkin 1988. The argument has been applied specifically to Hobbes by a number of more recent commentators. See Missner 1983; Sarasohn 1985; Kahn 1985, pp. 154, 181; Tuck 1989, pp. 64, 93, 102; Hampsher-Monk 1992, pp. 4–6; Hanson 1993, pp. 644–5; Flathman 1993, pp. 2–3, 43–7, 51–2. But for an excellent corrective see Sorell 1993.

This has certainly proved a fruitful hypothesis, but it has I think led to an overemphasis on this particular strand of thought. Such writers as Hobbes, Wilkins and Locke were not merely or even primarily responding to a set of epistemological arguments. Rather they were reacting against the entire rhetorical culture of humanism within which the vogue for scepticism had developed. Nor were they mainly concerned with the technical arguments put forward by the sceptics, whether of a Pyrrhonian or an Academic stamp. Rather they were seeking to overcome a more generally sceptical outlook encouraged by the emphasis placed by the humanists on the *Ars rhetorica*, with its characteristic insistence that there will always be two sides to any question, and thus that in moral reasoning it will always be possible to construct a plausible argument *in utramque partem*, on either side of the case. One of the most obvious ways in which Hobbes in particular remains enmeshed in Renaissance rhetorical culture is that he always aspires to control interpretation, to limit the play of ambiguity and to arrive at authorised versions of potentially subversive texts.

My hypothesis is thus that the anxieties expressed by seventeenth-century philosophers about moral ambiguity stem less from the rise of Pyrrhonism than from the Renaissance revival of the classical art of eloquence.[10] Indeed I am tempted to insist that this is not so much a hypothesis as a fact. When Hobbes asks himself in *De Cive* about 'the true character of those who stir up the populace and incite them to follow new ways', he replies that what invariably distinguishes such trouble-makers is 'a powerful form of eloquence separated from a true knowledge of things'.[11] When Locke in Book 3 of the *Essay* enquires into the sources of ambiguities and misdescriptions, he too lays most of the blame on 'Rhetorick, that powerful instrument of Error and Deceit'.[12] He ends by proclaiming that 'all the Art of Rhetorick, besides Order and Clearness, all the artificial and figurative application of Words Eloquence hath invented, are for nothing else but to insinuate wrong *Ideas*, move the Passions, and thereby mislead the Judgment'.[13] Summing up the general view, Sprat similarly declares in his *History* that eloquence is 'fatal to Peace and good Manners', so fatal that it 'ought to be banish'd out of all civil Societies'.[14]

---

[10] For an attempt to pursue this argument in the case of Hobbes see Skinner 1996.
[11] See Hobbes 1983a, XII. XII, p. 193 on '*eloquentia potens, separata a rerum scientia*' as '*verus character sit eorum qui populum ad res novas sollicitant & concitant*'.
[12] Locke 1979, III. X. 34, p. 508.   [13] Locke 1979, III. X. 34, p. 508.   [14] Sprat 1959, p. 111.

II

To understand this fear and dislike of the *Ars rhetorica*, we need to begin by reverting to its governing assumption: that in any discussion about moral or civil affairs it will always be possible to mount a plausible argument on either side of the case. From this it follows that, if I am to convince you that I am in the right, I shall need to find some means of shifting or moving you round to my side. This is one of the themes most prominently discussed in Cicero's *De Oratore*, his fullest and most important dialogue on the art of eloquence. The various characters in the discussion repeatedly speak of the need for advocates in a court of law to drive or impel the judge, to sway or move him, to press or coerce him into adopting their point of view.[15] (It hardly needs stressing that both judge and advocate are invariably assumed to be male.) The figure of Antonius even adds that, should an orator find himself confronting a judge 'who is actively hostile to his cause and friendly to his adversary', he must 'try to swing him round as if by some kind of machinery' until he is forced to see things from a different perspective.[16]

But how can we hope – as we still put it – to induce people to stand where we stand on some particular issue? According to the classical rhetoricians, we can never hope to speak persuasively if we are lacking in wisdom and the associated capacity for effective reasoning. Without these intellectual talents, Cicero insists, our discourse will be no better than garrulous and inane.[17] But we can never hope to rely on the force of reason alone to carry us to victory in the war of words, simply because it will always be possible to adduce good reasons *in utramque partem*. The inescapable conclusion, according to the rhetoricians, is that if we are to speak 'winningly' we shall have to master the art of persuasion, learning how to empower our reason with the moving force of eloquence.

By far the most influential summary of this fundamental belief is furnished by Cicero himself in the opening pages of his *De Inventione*, a discussion to which the rhetorical theorists of the English Renaissance endlessly return. Cicero concedes that 'eloquence in the absence of wisdom is never of the least advantage to civil communities'.[18] But he insists that, since wisdom in itself 'is silent and powerless to speak', wisdom in the absence

---

[15] Cicero 1942a, II. XLII. 178, vol. 1, p. 324; III. VI. 23, vol. 2, p. 18; III. XIV. 55, vol. 2, p. 44.
[16] Cicero 1942a, II. XVII. 72, vol. 1, p. 252: when the judge is 'amicus adversario et inimicus tibi', then 'tanquam machinatione aliqua ... est contorquendus'.
[17] Cicero 1942a, I. V. 17, vol. 1, pp. 12–14 and I. VI. 20, vol. 1, p. 16.
[18] Cicero 1949, I. I. 1, p. 2: 'civitatibus, eloquentiam vero sine sapientia ... prodesse numquam'.

of eloquence is of even less use.[19] What is needed 'if a commonwealth is to receive the greatest possible benefits' is *ratio atque oratio*, powerful reasoning allied to powerful speech.[20] 'A large and crucial part' of any civil science must therefore be occupied by the art of eloquence, and especially 'by that form of artistic eloquence which is generally known as rhetoric, the function of which is evidently that of speaking in a manner calculated to persuade'.[21]

The idea of eloquence as a moving force, a force capable of impelling a doubting or hostile audience to come round to our side, was taken up with much enthusiasm by the vernacular rhetoricians of the English Renaissance.[22] Thomas Wilson refers in his pioneering *Arte of Rhetorique* of 1554 to the orator's ability to 'stir' his hearers, to press or push them towards the adoption of some particular standpoint.[23] George Puttenham in his *Arte of English Poesie* of 1589 likewise speaks of the orator's power to 'lead on' an audience,[24] while Henry Peacham in his *Garden of Eloquence* of 1593 similarly extols the power of figurative language to 'prevaile much in drawing the mindes' of an audience, thereby helping the orator to 'move them to be of his side, to hold with him, to be led by him'.[25] This sense of eloquence as a physical force became encapsulated in a set of metaphors that have remained with us ever since as a way of dramatising the *vis verborum* or power of persuasive utterance. We still refer to the capacity of eloquent speakers to seize the attention of an audience; we also speak of the power of eloquent speech to sway us, to transport us, to carry us away.

It remains to ask by what means the force of eloquence can shift or move us to do what reason commands. According to the classical theorists of rhetoric, it chiefly does so by adding *pathos* to *logos*, by appealing to the passions or affections in such a way as to excite them against our opponents and in favour of our own cause. The figure of Antonius in Cicero's *De Oratore* puts the crucial point with disarming frankness. After capturing the attention of our auditor, we must try 'to shift or impel him

---

[19] See Cicero 1949, I. II. 3, p. 6 on *sapientia* as 'tacita' and 'inops dicendi'.
[20] See Cicero 1949, I. II. 3, p. 6 and I. IV. 5, p. 12 on the need for *ratio atque oratio* to ensure that 'ad rem publicam plurima commoda veniunt'.
[21] Cicero 1949, I. V. 6, pp. 12–14: 'magna et ampla pars est artificiosa eloquentia quam rhetoricam vocant ... officium autem eius videtur esse dicere apposite ad persuasionem'.
[22] For further details about the vernacular rhetoricians discussed here see Crane 1965 and Skinner 1996, pp. 51–65.
[23] Wilson 1554, Preface, Sig. A 2^v; cf also fos. 34^v, 63^r, 73^r.
[24] Puttenham 1970, pp. 147, 151, 189. For the attribution of the *Arte* to Puttenham see Willcock and Walker 1970, pp. xvi–xliv.
[25] Peacham 1593, p. 121.

so that he becomes ruled not by deliberation and judgement but rather by sheer impetus and perturbation of mind'.[26] Quintilian later expresses the same commitment when discussing the role of the emotions in Book 6 of his *Institutio Oratoria*. It is through arousing the passions, he maintains, 'that the force of oratory is able to display itself to the greatest effect'.[27] 'This is the power', he proclaims, 'that dominates tribunals, this is the style of eloquence that rules over all.'[28]

A deliberate ambiguity in the use of the word *move* may thus be said to lie at the heart of the classical conception of persuasive speech. The essential task of the orator is to shift or move an audience to come round to his point of view. But the surest means of accomplishing this task will be to speak in such a way that the audience is not merely convinced but 'greatly moved'. As Cicero summarises when speaking in his own person in the *De Partitione Oratoria*, 'that speech which has the greatest effect in shifting or moving our hearers will be the one that moves their minds'.[29]

Drawing on these classical authorities, the Tudor rhetoricians continually come back to the same basic point. Richard Sherry lays it down in his *Treatise of Schemes and Tropes* of 1550 that an orator must always be 'appoynted and readye thorowlye to move and turne mens myndes'.[30] Thomas Wilson agrees in his *Arte of Rhetorique* that an orator 'muste perswade, and move the affeccions of his hearers' if he is to ensure 'that thei shalbe forced to yelde unto his saiying'.[31] Henry Peacham similarly stresses in *The Garden of Eloquence* that one of the orator's principal aims must be to 'move to the love of the thing', to 'force and move the mind forward, to a willing consent'.[32]

We still need to know how we can hope in practice to write or speak in such a moving style. Not without some misgivings, the rhetoricians answer that there is only one possible way. We must find some means of 'amplifying' the facts, of stretching or exaggerating them to make them appear more favourable to our cause than they are in strict truth.[33] The figure of Antonius puts the point with his accustomed frankness in Book 1 of *De Oratore*:

---

[26] Cicero 1942a, II. XLII. 178, vol. 1, p. 324: 'ipse sic moveatur, ut impetu quodam animi et perturbatione, magis quam iudicio aut consilio regatur'.
[27] Quintilian 1920–2, VI. II. 3, vol. 2, p. 416: 'quo nihil adferre maius vis orandi potest'.
[28] Quintilian 1920–2, VI. II. 4, vol. 2, p. 418: 'hoc est quod dominetur in iudiciis, haec eloquentia regnat'.
[29] Cicero 1942b, VI. 22, p. 328: 'maximeque movet ea quae motum aliquem animi miscet oratio'.
[30] Sherry 1961, p. 22.   [31] Wilson 1554, fo. 2ᵛ.   [32] Peacham 1593, pp. 63, 65, 77.
[33] For the admission that exaggeration – even 'beyond all reason' – is indispensable, see Wilson 1554, fos. 63ᵛ, 65ʳ, 78ᵛ.

By his choice of words the orator must succeed in making all those things which in ordinary life are felt to be bad, troublesome and thus to be avoided seem very much graver and more irksome than they are, while managing at the same time by his manner of speaking to amplify and embellish all those things which are generally felt to be most desirable and worthwhile.[34]

Quintilian makes the point even more forthrightly in the course of conceding that, as critics of the *Ars rhetorica* complain, 'this is an art which relies on moving the emotions by saying that which is false'.[35] He admits that such extreme methods can only be justified 'if there is no other possibility of ensuring that the judge is led to arrive at a fair verdict'.[36] But he freely acknowledges that, 'since those who sit in judgement are often ignorant, it will often be necessary to speak in such a way as to deceive them if they are not to make mistakes'.[37]

This use of the term 'amplification' to cover the entire process of arousing the emotions by way of stretching the truth recurs even more prominently among the Tudor rhetoricians. Richard Sherry assigns the topic a section of its own, placing it before (and implicitly contrasting it with) the notion of rhetorical proof. His main contention is that amplification comprises 'a greate parte of eloquence', since an orator will always and inevitably be concerned with 'increasing and diminynshing' the facts in the name of winning over an audience.[38] Thomas Wilson likewise argues that the best means of achieving an 'apte movyng of affections' is by means of 'Amplificacion', the term he employs for the technique of 'augmentyng and vehemently enlargyng' our arguments so as to 'set the Judge or hearers in a heate, or els to mitigate and asswage displeasure conceived'.[39] Henry Peacham later develops a similar understanding of the term, arguing that all such 'increasing and diminishing' is the work of amplification, the means 'whereby the hearers might the sooner be moved to like of that which was spoken'.[40]

There were generally held to be two principal methods of amplification, both of which are treated by the rhetoricians as parts of *ornatus* and hence as aspects of *elocutio*, the third of the five elements in the classical

---

[34] Cicero 1942a, I. LI. 221, vol. 1, p. 156: 'Orator autem omnia haec, quae putantur in communi vitae consuetudine, mala, ac molesta, et fugienda, multo maiora et acerbiora verbis facit; itemque ea, quae vulgo expetenda atque optabilia videntur, dicendo amplificat atque ornat.'
[35] Quintilian 1920–2, II. XVII. 26, vol. 1, p. 336: 'et falsum dicat et adfectus moveat'.
[36] Quintilian 1920–2, II. XVII. 27, vol. 1, p. 336: 'si aliter ad aequitatem perduci iudex non poterit'.
[37] Quintilian 1920–2, II. XVII. 28, vol. 1, p. 336: 'Imperiti enim iudicant et qui frequenter in hoc ipsum fallendi sint, ne errent.'
[38] Sherry 1961, p. 70.   [39] Wilson 1554, fos. 63^r and 71^v.   [40] Peacham 1593, pp. 119, 121.

theory of eloquence.[41] The more important is said to be the use of the figures and tropes to lend additional colour to our utterances, thereby making them more persuasive or 'colourable'.[42] The other and contrasting method is that of challenging and replacing descriptions instead of enhancing them. The orator's aim in the latter case is to redescribe a given action or situation in such a way as to augment or extenuate its moral significance, thereby hoping to alter the attitude of his audience and enlist them in his cause. It is this contrasting technique, involving what Hobbes was to describe as the 'rhetorication' of moral discourse,[43] on which I now wish to concentrate.

As we have already seen in volume 1 chapter 10, the fullest and most influential account of this technique had been furnished by Quintilian, who first discusses it in Book 4 of his *Institutio Oratoria* in the course of considering how best to present a narrative of facts. Suppose we find ourselves facing an opponent who has managed to recount the facts of a case 'in such a way as to rouse up the judges and leave them full of anger against us'.[44] How should we respond? We must restate the same facts, Quintilian suggests, but not in the same way. 'We must assign different causes, a different state of mind and a different motive for what was done.'[45] Above all, 'we must try to elevate the action as much as possible by the words we use: for example, prodigality must be more leniently redescribed as liberality, avarice as carefulness, negligence as simplicity of mind'.[46] We must attempt, in short, to replace the descriptions offered by our adversaries with a set of terms that picture the action no less plausibly, but serve at the same time to place it in a contrasting moral light.

Quintilian's analysis was taken up by all the Tudor rhetoricians I have singled out. Richard Sherry refers us directly to Quintilian in the course

---

[41] See *Ad C. Herennium* 1954, I. II. 3, p. 6 for perhaps the most influential summary of the view that rhetoric is a five-fold *Ars*, with *elocutio* (incorporating *ornatus*, i.e., the figures and tropes) as its third element. For a discussion of the place of *elocutio* in classical and Renaissance rhetoric see Vickers 1981.

[42] On *ornatus* as colouring, and on the relations between adding colouring and improving the colourability of arguments, see for example Wilson 1554, fo. 86^r, fos. 89^v to 810^r [*recte* 90^r] and fo. 111^v. For a fuller discussion of this aspect of the theory of persuasive speech see Skinner 1996, pp. 181–211.

[43] Hobbes 1983b, p. 26. The phrase is of course due to Hobbes's translator, who has now been identified in Malcolm 2000 as the poet Charles Cotton.

[44] Quintilian 1920–2, IV. II. 75, vol. 2, p. 90: 'incendit [iudices] et plenos irae reliquit'.

[45] Quintilian 1920–2, IV. II. 76–7, vol. 1, p. 90: 'eadem [exponemus] sed non eodem modo; alias causas, aliam mentem, aliam rationem dabo'.

[46] Quintilian 1920–2, IV. II. 77, vol. 2, pp. 90–2: 'Verbis elevare quaedam licebit; luxuria liberalitatis, avaritia parsimoniae, negligentia simplicitatis nomine lenietur.' For an account of how this analysis was taken up by later Roman rhetorical theorists see below, volume 3, ch. 4, section I.

of examining, under the heading of 'Diminution', the process by which 'greate matters are made lyghte of by wordes, as when he was wel beaten by a knave, that knave wyll saye he dyd but a lytle stryke hym'.[47] Later he adds a number of other examples to illustrate the technique:

The first way of increasyng or diminishing is by chaungynge the worde of the thynge, when in encreasyng we use a more cruell worde, and a softer in diminyshynge, as when we call an evyll man a thiefe, and saye he hathe kylled us, when he hathe beaten us. And it is more vehemente if by correccion we compare greater wordes wyth those that we put before, as: Thou haste broughte not a thyefe, but an extortioner, not an adulterer but a ravysher, etc.[48]

Although he makes no mention of the fact, Sherry is taking his illustrations almost word for word from the opening of Quintilian's section on amplification.

Thomas Wilson follows Quintilian's analysis scarcely less closely in his *Arte of Rhetorique*. He begins by observing that 'the firste kinde of Amplification is when by chaunging a woorde, in augmentynge we use a greater, but in diminishynge we use a lesse'.[49] Among examples of how to use the device in extenuation, he suggests calling 'him that is a cruell or mercilesse man somewhat soore in judgement', or 'a naturall foole a playne symple man', or 'a notable flatterer a fayre spoken man, a glutton a good felowe at hys table, a spende all a liberall gentilman, a snudge or pynche penye a good husbande, a thriftye man'.[50]

After these pioneering discussions in the 1550s, we find the same arguments and examples widely taken up.[51] Henry Peacham includes a list of 'extenuating' redescriptions in the first edition of his *Garden of Eloquence* in 1577 by way of illustrating how we can best hope to 'excuse our own vices, or other mens whom we doe defend'.[52] George Puttenham speaks in very similar terms in his *Arte of English Poesie* of 1589 about 'wordes and sentences of extenuation or diminution' that we can hope to use 'to excuse a fault, & to make an offence seeme less then it is'.[53] His examples include saying 'of a great robbery, that it was but a pilfry matter: of an arrant ruffian that he is a tall fellow of his hands: of a prodigall foole, that he is a kind hearted man: of a notorious unthrift, a lustie youth, and such like phrases of extenuation'.[54]

While all these writers view this technique as having immense rhetorical significance, they have differing views about how it should be named

---

[47] Sherry 1961, p. 61. [48] Sherry 1961, pp. 70–1. [49] Wilson 1554, fo. 66^v; cf. also fo. 69^r.
[50] Wilson 1554, fos. 66^v, 67^r. Cf. Ascham 1970, pp. 206–7. [51] See Cox 1989.
[52] Peacham 1971, sig. N, iiii^v. [53] Puttenham 1970, p. 220. [54] Puttenham 1970, p. 220.

and classified. Aristotle's original suggestion in Book 3 of *The 'Art' of Rhetoric* had been that, when we augment or diminish an action by redescribing it, we should think of ourselves as employing a species of metaphor.[55] He was thus inclined to treat the device as one of the tropes of speech. But this was not a proposal that found much favour with the Roman theorists of eloquence. As we have seen, Quintilian's initial suggestion was that the technique should perhaps be categorised neither as a figure nor as a trope but rather as a distinct form of *amplificatio*.[56] But he later changed his mind, concluding that it ought probably to be grouped among the *schemata* or figures of speech. He adds that those who argue for this classification generally agree that the name of the *figura* we employ 'when we call someone wise rather than astute, or courageous rather than overconfident, or careful instead of avaricious'[57] is Παραδιαστολή, a term he translates as *distinctio* and defines as 'the means by which similar things are distinguished from each other'.[58]

Quintilian's terminology was widely adopted by the Tudor rhetoricians, although they generally preferred to transliterate his Greek than to offer translations of their own, and hence invented the term *paradiastole*. Henry Peacham agrees that, whenever 'by a mannerly interpretation we doe excuse our own vices, or other mens whom we doe defend, by calling them virtues', we are using the figure of paradiastole.[59] George Puttenham similarly explains that, 'if such moderation of words tend to flattery, or soothing, or excusing, it is by the figure *Paradiastole*', the name of the device we apply when we seek to lessen or abate the force of words.[60]

It is on the figure of paradiastole that, in the rest of this chapter, I now wish to concentrate. One reason for focusing on it is that so far it has attracted little attention even from historians of rhetoric.[61] But my main reason is that it occupies, I have come to see, a place of major importance in the development of early-modern moral and political thought. I would go so far as to say that most of the anxieties expressed by the philosophers I began by citing about the dangerous implications

---

[55] Aristotle 1926, III. II. 10, pp. 355-7.
[56] Quintilian 1920-2, VI. II. 23, vol. 2, p. 430; cf. VIII. IV. 9-14, vol. 3, pp. 266-70.
[57] Quintilian 1920-2, IX. III. 65, vol. 3, p. 482: 'Cum te pro astuto sapientem appelles, pro confidente fortem, pro illiberali diligentem.'
[58] See Quintilian 1920-2, IX. III. 65, vol. 3, p. 482 on *distinctio*, 'qua similia...discernuntur'. For a history of the term see below, volume 3, ch. 4, section II.
[59] Peacham 1971, sig. N, iiii^v. [60] Puttenham 1970, p. 184.
[61] For valuable comments, however, see Cox 1989, esp. pp. 53-5 and Whigham 1984, pp. 40-2 and 204-5, and for more recent discussions see Condren 1994, pp. 78-84 and Skinner 1996, pp. 138-80.

of the *Ars rhetorica* were directed against this particular device. Rhetorical redescription was seen by devotees of scientific discourse such as Wilkins no less than by proponents of civil science such as Hobbes as one of the persuasive techniques they most of all needed to neutralise or overcome.

III

There are several obvious questions to ask about the technique of paradiastole, and I shall proceed by considering how the rhetoricians and philosophers set about answering them. It seems worth asking in the first place how we can hope to employ such a method of redescription at all. It might seem, that is, that a virtue such as courage and its opposed vice, cowardice, are the names of actions that are categorically distinct. How can we hope rhetorically to redescribe the one as the other without its becoming obvious that we have ceased to talk about the action concerned?

The answer given by the rhetoricians reflects the continuing influence of Aristotle on the moral as well as the rhetorical thought of the Renaissance. The clue is said to lie in recognising that many of the virtues, and many of the terms we consequently employ to describe and appraise human actions, constitute a mean between two extremes of vice. The crucial implication is that many virtues and vices must therefore stand in a relationship of proximity with each other. As Hobbes was to put it in his Latin translation of Aristotle's *Rhetoric*, they may be said to 'confine' upon one another: like neighbouring countries, they may be described as sharing certain confines or boundaries.[62]

The Roman rhetoricians place much emphasis on this implication, generally stating it in the form of the claim that good qualities often appear as *vicinae* or neighbours of the vices. Cicero expresses the point in just these terms when discussing the key concept of *honestas* in Book 2 of his *De Inventione*. The dispositions to be avoided if we wish to act well 'are not only the opposite of the virtues, as courage is of cowardice and justice of injustice, but also those which appear close to virtues, and to border on them'.[63] For example, 'diffidence is the opposite of confidence

[62] Hobbes MSS (Chatsworth) MS D 1, p. 24: 'Confinia virtutibus vitia.' This manuscript is a Latin paraphrase of Aristotle's text that Hobbes evidently made for teaching purposes in the early 1630s. For further details about this manuscript see below, volume 3, ch. 1 note 27 and ch. 2 note 79.

[63] Cicero 1949, II. LIV. 165, p. 332: 'non ea modo quae his [sc. virtutibus] contraria sunt, ut fortitudini ignavia et iustitiae iniustitia, verum etiam illa quae propinqua videntur et finitima esse'.

and is accordingly a vice, but audacity is not its opposite but is similar and close to it, but is nevertheless a vice. So too with the other virtues, each of which will be found to have a vice bordering on it.'[64] Quintilian outlines a similar argument in his *Institutio Oratoria*, illustrating it specifically from the art of oratory. When considering the merits of untrained orators in Book 2 he repeats that 'there is a certain neighbourly quality between a number of the virtues and vices'.[65] He goes on to quote (although without acknowledgement) three of Aristotle's examples from *The 'Art' of Rhetoric*: 'slander can pass for frankness, recklessness for courage, extravagance for copiousness'.[66]

With these contentions about virtue and vice as *vicinae*, the rhetoricians arrive at their explanation of why we can always hope to use the technique of paradiastole to excite the feelings of an audience. Because of these neighbourly relations, a clever orator can always challenge the proffered description of an action with some show of plausibility. For he can always extenuate an evil action by imposing on it the name of an adjoining virtue. Alternatively, he can always denigrate a good action by redescribing it with the name of a neighbouring vice. The upshot, as Cicero puts it in *De Partitione Oratoria*, is that 'we need to take great care lest we find ourselves deceived by those vices which appear to imitate virtue'.[67] We can easily fall victim to the fact that 'cunning imitates prudence, insensibility imitates temperance, pride in attaining honours and superciliousness in looking down on them both imitate magnanimity, extravagance imitates liberality and audacity imitates courage'.[68]

The poets and moralists of Tudor England offer a very similar analysis of what makes rhetorical redescription possible. They reveal a special fondness for images of disguise, stressing how the nearness of good and evil makes it all too easy for the vices to mask themselves by hiding under a mantle of goodness. Perhaps the earliest English writer to comment on the technique of paradiastole in this way was Sir Thomas Wyatt in

---

[64] Cicero 1949, II. LIV. 165, p. 332: 'fidentiae contrarium est diffidentia et ea re vitium est; audacia non contrarium, sed appositum est ac propinquum et tamen vitium est. Sic uni cuique virtuti finitimum vitium reperietur.'
[65] Quintilian 1920–2, II. XII. 4, vol. 1, p. 284: 'Est praeterea quaedam virtutum vitiorumque vicinia.'
[66] Aristotle 1926, I. IX. 28–9, pp. 96–8. Cf. Quintilian 1920–2, II. XII. 4, vol. 1, p. 284: 'maledictus pro libero, temerarius pro forti, effusus pro copioso accipitur'.
[67] Cicero 1942b, XXIII. 81, p. 370: 'Cernenda autem sunt diligenter, ne fallunt ea nos vitia, quae virtutum videntur imitari.'
[68] Cicero 1942b, XXIII. 81, p. 370: 'Nam et prudentiam malitia et temperantiam immanitas in voluptatibus aspernandis et magnitudinem animi superbia in nimis extollendis et despicientia in contemnendis honoribus et liberalitatem effusio et fortitudinem audacia imitatur.'

the version he made in 1536 of Luigi Alammani's satire on court life.[69] Wyatt is anxious to disclaim the courtly arts himself, but he explains at the same time that courtiers must understand how to conceal their vices under a mantle of virtues:

> My wit is naught. I cannot learn the way.
> And much the less of things that greater be,
>   That asken help of colours of device
>   To join the mean with each extremity:
> With the nearest virtue to cloak away the vice.[70]

These reflections were echoed by many moralists of the next generation. Thomas Nashe is one writer who makes extensive play with similar metaphors of masking and concealment. He maintains, for example, in his *Anatomie of Absurditie* that, if Englishmen would only become 'halfe so much Italianated as they are', the vices would no longer find it so easy to 'maske under the visard of virtue'.[71] Thomas Lodge is another conservative moralist who speaks in similar terms. He explains, for example, in the Preface to his translations of Seneca that the reason why we stand in so much need of Seneca's teachings is that nowadays we perceive virtue 'but in a shadow, which serves for a vaile to cover many vices'.[72]

A second question it seems natural to ask about the technique of paradiastole relates to the point or purpose of using it. Why would anyone want deliberately to introduce such ambiguities into moral and political argument? The Tudor rhetoricians invariably respond by pointing to the value of the device as a method of extenuation, a means of augmenting what can be said in favour of an action or diminishing what can be said against it. When Thomas Wilson discusses 'the first kinde of Amplification' – that of 'augmentynge' or 'diminishynge' the force of an utterance 'by chaunging a woorde' – he assumes that the aim of speaking in this way will always be to exonerate or excuse.[73] George Puttenham similarly alludes to the idea of smoothing out blemishes or faults when he proposes to rename the figure of paradiastole 'the *Curry-favell*'.[74] To 'curry' means to groom or comb out, while Fauvel was the name of the horse in Gervais de Bus's fourteenth-century poem *Le Roman de Fauvel*

---

[69] For Alammani, and for a reprinting of the poem used by Wyatt, see Mason 1986, pp. 260–3. On the 'self-fashioning' involved in Wyatt's rejection of courtly cynicism see Greenblatt 1980, esp. pp. 127–56.
[70] Wyatt 1978, p. 187. Cf. Whigham 1984, p. 204, and for a commentary Mason 1986, pp. 283–9.
[71] Nashe 1958, vol. 1, p. 10.   [72] Lodge 1614, Sig. XX, 1^r.
[73] Wilson 1554, fos. 66^v to 67^r.   [74] Puttenham 1970, p. 184.

whose initials spell the vices of Flatérie, Avarice, Vilanie, Variété, Envie and Lascheté.[75]

To employ the curry-favell, according to Puttenham, is thus to exculpate or at least to extenuate the vices. No doubt owing to the influence of such discussions, the poets and moralists of the period likewise concentrate on the power of rhetorical redescriptions to mitigate and excuse. Sir Thomas Wyatt even refers specifically to the flattering of Fauvel when listing the courtly wiles of those who 'join the mean with each extremity':

> As drunkenness good fellowship to call;
> The friendly foe with his double face
> Say he is gentle and courteous therewithal;
> And say that Favel hath a goodly grace
>   In eloquence; and cruelty to name
>   Zeal of justice and change in time and place.[76]

Wyatt's bitter reflections on courtly hypocrisy are strongly echoed in the next generation by Sir Philip Sidney in the old *Arcadia*. When Prince Basilius loses his way out hunting, he encounters the foolish Dametas, whose rude and violent speech he mistakes for shrewdness. The prince is greatly delighted, and introduces Dametas to his Court 'with apparent show of his good opinion'. Sidney sardonically describes the outcome: 'The flattering courtier[s] had no sooner taken the prince's mind but that there were... shadows of virtues found for Dametas. His silence grew wit, his bluntness integrity, his beastly ignorance virtuous simplicity.'[77] As in Wyatt, one of the marks of a successful courtier is said to be a mastery of paradiastole, the talent for excusing vices by redescribing them as virtues.[78]

It is obviously one-sided, however, to suppose that paradiastole can actually be *defined* – as Henry Peacham claims – as an 'instrument of excuse'.[79] As Aristotle had originally observed in his *Rhetoric*, there is no reason why the same device should not be used to perform the opposite task of amplifying what can be said against a given course of action by depreciating its apparently virtuous qualities. To cite Aristotle's own example, it may be possible to denigrate the behaviour of a habitually cautious man by claiming that he is really a person of cold and designing temperament.[80] The anonymous translation of Aristotle's *Rhetoric* issued

---

[75] Harman, Milner and Mellers 1962, p. 121.
[76] Wyatt 1978, pp. 187–8.   [77] Sidney 1973, p. 31.
[78] For the symbolic significance of the episode see Worden 1996, pp. 146, 151–2, 217–19.
[79] Peacham 1593, p. 169.   [80] Aristotle 1926, I. IX. 28, p. 96.

as *A Briefe of the Art of Rhetorique* in c.1637 succinctly summarises the general point: the same technique can equally well be used to 'make the best of a thing' or else to 'make the worst of it'.[81]

Although the Tudor rhetoricians ignore this latter and more disquieting possibility, a number of the poets and moralists place their main emphasis on it. Sir Philip Sidney in *Astrophil and Stella* mournfully asks to be told whether, even in the celestial regions, the highest virtues are re-described, as they are on earth, in such a way as to leave them upbraided and mocked:

> Is constant *Love* deem'd there but want of wit?
> Are Beauties there as proud as here they be?
> Do they above love to be lov'd, and yet
>   Those Lovers scorne whom that *Love* doth possesse?
> Do they call Vertue there ungratefulnesse?[82]

We encounter some strikingly similar sentiments in John Lyly's hyperbolically Ciceronian *Euphues* of 1579. Lyly frequently refers to the technique of paradiastole, and invariably points to its use as a means of persuading an audience to view the conventional virtues in a doubtful or ambiguous light. When he speaks in his own person at the outset of his story about 'those of sharpe capacity', one of his criticisms is that, if anyone seeks to 'argue with them boldly, then he is impudent: if coldly, an innocent'.[83] When the figure of Euphues later addresses his 'cooling' oration to his friend Philautus and all fond lovers, one of the complaints he makes against women is that they are too ready to redescribe the finest manly qualities in such a way as to depreciate them. If a man 'be cleanlye, then term they him proude; ... if bolde, blunt; if shamefast, a cowarde'.[84]

A generation before Lyly was writing, we already find Wyatt speaking in similar terms in his satire on court life. Although he begins by criticising those who attempt 'with the nearest virtue to cloak away the vice', he immediately goes on to describe the contrasting rhetorical possibility:

> And, as to purpose likewise it shall fall,
> To press the virtue that it may not rise.[85]

---

[81] [Hobbes(?)] 1986, p. 109. For this translation see above, note 62.
[82] Sidney 1962, sonnet 31, p. 180.   [83] Lyly 1868, p. 46.
[84] Lyly 1868, p. 115.   [85] Wyatt 1978, p. 187.

Having mentioned both stratagems, he concludes by exemplifying each of them:

> And he that suffereth offence without blame
> Call him pitiful, and him true and plain
> That raileth reckless to every man's shame:
> Say he is rude that cannot lie and feign,
> The lecher a lover, and tyranny
> To be the right of a prince's reign.[86]

Wyatt's shocking examples illustrate the doubly alarming power of paradiastole not merely to excuse the vices but, more directly, to mock the virtues.

Once we recognise that this is the point or purpose of using paradiastole, a further question arises about its role in moral and political argument. What should we think of the technique? Is it to be admired and encouraged, or is it best avoided and shunned? If we turn with these questions in mind to the writers I have been considering, we encounter two sharply conflicting responses. Among the rhetoricians, we find an understandable disposition to point with pride to the technique as one of the most effective means of blurring distinctions between actions and thereby persuading people to view them in unfamiliar ways. George Puttenham, for example, commends the use of paradiastole as one of the most helpful means 'to make the best of a bad thing, or turne a signification to the more plausible sence'.[87] At this juncture, however, the rhetoricians found themselves in a small minority. Among the educated classes of early-modern England, the fact that an awareness of paradiastole was deliberately inculcated as part of the rhetorical training provided in schools and Universities came to be viewed as a matter of grave concern. As politics and public debate increasingly polarised in the early years of the seventeenth century, a number of commentators began to speak of the technique and its uses not merely with anxiety but with growing frustration and resentment.

One of the sources of this polarisation was the disaffection felt by those of puritan temperament towards the government of the English church and the values of English society more generally. We accordingly find those sympathetic to the puritan cause expressing a growing distaste for prevailing ideals of civilised conduct, complaining in particular about the pride, the licentiousness and the extravagance of the nobility and the court. As a number of these commentators observed, moreover, the

[86] Wyatt 1978, p. 188. [87] Puttenham 1970, pp. 184-5.

technique of rhetorical redescription was used with disgraceful frequency to excuse and even to glorify these typical vices of the age. Joseph Hall, a Caroline bishop who was nevertheless a puritan sympathiser, makes the point with great vehemence in a sermon of 1624 entitled *The Great Imposter*:

> The naturall man knowes well how filthy all his brood is, and therefore will not let them come forth, but disguised with the colours and dresses of good; so as now every one of natures birds is a Swan; Pride is handsomnesse, desperate fury, valour; lavishnesse is noble munificence, drunkennesse civility, flattery complement, murderous revenge, justice; the Curtizan is *bona femina*, the Sorcerer a wise man, the oppressor a good husband; *Absolom* will goe pay his vowes; *Herod* will worship the Babe.[88]

What Hall objects to is the use of paradiastole to mislead the pious by deceitfully redescribing a number of prevailing vices as neighbouring virtues.

Still more agonising to those of puritan sensibility was the feeling that they were living in an impious age in which the godly were increasingly viewed with contempt. Again Joseph Hall is a witness to these feelings, and again he refers specifically to the use of rhetorical redescription as a means of mocking and dismissing true piety:

> Would the Israelites be devout? they are idle; Doth *David* daunce for joy before the Arke? He is a foole in a Morris: Doth Saint *Paul* discourse of his heavenly Vision? too much learning hath made him mad. Doe the Disciples miraculously speake all the tongues of Babel? They are full of new wine: Doe they preach Christs Kingdome? they are seditious; The resurrection? they are bablers. Is a man conscionable? he is an Hypocrite: is he conformable? he is unconscionable: Is he plaine dealing? he is rudely uncivill: Is he wisely insinuative? he is a flatterer: In short, such is the wicked craft of the heart, that it would let us see nothing in it[s] owne forme; but faine would shew us evill faire, that we might be inamoured of it, and vertue ugly, that we might abhorre it.[89]

Hall expresses his disgust not merely at the use of rhetorical redescription to excuse vice, but also to perform the still more impious task of scorning and ridiculing virtue. As he summarises, 'such is the envy of nature, that where shee sees a better face than her owne, she is ready to scratch it, or cast dirt in it; and therefore knowing that all vertue hath a native beauty in it, she labours to deforme it'.[90]

Of all the divisions in English society at this time, the most destructive in the longer term arose from the mounting opposition in Parliament

---

[88] Hall 1624, p. 33. [89] Hall 1624, pp. 34–5. [90] Hall 1624, pp. 33–4.

to the policies of the crown, and especially to its allegedly excessive use of the royal prerogative. Seeing their own campaign as an attempt to secure freedom and justice, the crown's opponents were outraged at the opprobrious terms in which their behaviour was continually redescribed by the government. When, for example, Charles I sought to prevent debate about the Petition of Right in 1628, Christopher Wandesford responded by proposing a direct appeal to the king, complaining at the same time that the justice of their cause was being unfairly dismissed:

Let us make our remonstrance for our right. We are his counsellors. We are fallen into a dangerous time; some call evil men good, and good men evil, and bitter sweet. Justice is now called popularity and faction[91] ... popularity and puritanism is objected to the best subjects.[92]

A graduate of Cambridge, where he would have received a training in the *Ars rhetorica*, Wandesford specifically directs his complaint against the use of paradiastole to undermine the standing of those criticising the government.

John Milton levels the same charge in his invective against Charles I's misgovernment in his *Eikonoklastes* of 1649. He makes the point in thunderous terms in his chapter on the king's hatred of those who dared to question his prerogative:

That trust which the Parlament faithfully discharg'd in the asserting of our Liberties, he calls *another artifice to withdraw the people from him, to their designes*. What piece of Justice could they have demanded for the people, which the jealousie of a King might not have miscall'd, a designe to disparage his Government, and to ingratiat themselves?[93]

Once again the objection is to the use of paradiastole to make the virtuous conduct of Parliament appear self-seeking and corrupt.

Among the supporters of the crown, however, precisely the same accusation was flung at the leaders of the opposition in Parliament. They were denounced for employing the same technique, cloaking and disguising their wicked and self-interested motives under the names of neighbouring virtues. We already encounter the charge in a letter from Sir Henry Wotton to Sir Edmund Bacon giving a satirical account of the Parliament of 1614. Wotton relates that John Hoskins was one of four members of

---

[91] *Commons Debates 1628*, vol. 4, p. 115.
[92] This further phrase comes from the report in the Stowe MSS. See *Commons Debates 1628*, vol. 4, p. 119.
[93] Milton 1962, p. 501.

the Commons 'committed close prisoners to the Tower' at the end of the session, the offence in his case being 'licentiousness baptized freedom'. Wotton goes on: 'For I have noted in our House, that a false or faint patriot did cover himself with the shadow of equal moderation, and on the other side, irreverent discourse was called honest liberty; so as upon the whole matter "no excesses want precious names".'[94] Ben Jonson makes a comparable but more intemperate charge when he speaks in his *Discoveries* about those who dare 'to censure their sovereign's actions'. The outcome, he complains, is that 'all the councils are made good or bad by the events', so that 'it falleth out, that the same facts receive from them the names; now, of diligence; now, of vanity; now, of majesty; now, of fury: where they ought wholly to hang on his mouth'.[95]

Such accusations only intensified after the outbreak of the civil war in 1642. When John Bramhall published his *Serpent Salve* in 1643, a response to Henry Parker's *Observations* in support of Parliament, he claimed to see exactly the same rhetorical technique at work in Parker's hypocritical protestations of patriotism and loyalty. 'We are now God knowes in this way of Cure' for the country's ills, Bramhall retorts, a way in which 'Ambition, Covetousnesse, Envy, Newfanglednesse, Schisme shal gain an opportunity to act their mischievous intentions, under the cloake of Justice and zeal to the Common-wealth'.[96] Benjamin Whichcote makes the same accusation – with an even clearer reference to the rhetorical device in play – in his sermon denouncing those 'who hold the Truth in Unrighteousness'.[97] One way of committing this sin, he declares, is by 'doing *that* under one notion, which a Man's own Judgement will not let him do, under another', thereby placing our actions 'under a disguise'. For example, it is a grave case of the sin 'when any Man is *Conceited*, or of a *Turbulent Spirit in Religion*, for him to please himself with a notion of *Zeal for Truth*'.[98]

Among those who felt so much anxiety about paradiastole, one further question naturally suggested itself. If its cultivation carries with it such grave dangers to the stability of commonwealths, what can be done to limit or neutralise its effects? I turn to this question in volume 3 of the present work – in particular chapter 4 section VI – where I consider the answer offered by such divines as Benjamin Whichcote, Robert South and others who preached specifically against the perils of paradiastolic

---

[94] Wotton 1907, vol. 2, p. 37. As Wotton himself notes, his closing phrase quotes Pliny, *Natural History* XXXVII. 12.
[95] Jonson 1988, p. 404.   [96] Bramhall 1643, p. 55.
[97] The text of the sermon is Romans 1.8.   [98] Whichcote 1698, p. 80.

speech. Here I simply offer, by way of introduction to my later analysis, a summary of their general line of argument.

Although such critics often professed to fear that the prevalence of paradiastolic speech might lead us into a world of complete moral arbitrariness, they generally agreed that the danger can fairly readily be staved off. We first need to recall that words serve as the names of things and states of affairs, and that moral words serve as the names of moral states of affairs.[99] We then need to ensure, in any dispute about the application of such evaluative terms, that there is agreement both about the facts of the case and about the definitions of the terms involved. If we can succeed in bringing together such definitions and facts, we can hope to see which terms can properly be applied and which redescriptions can in consequence be ruled out. As Robert South summarises, provided that we are willing 'to consider and weigh circumstances, to scatter and look through the mists of error, and so separate appearances from realities', we can always hope to arrive at 'a full discovery of the true goodness and evil of things'.[100]

I need to end by stressing, however, that this optimistically 'realist' line of reasoning was confronted within early-modern philosophy by one deeply sceptical and challenging voice. The voice was that of Thomas Hobbes,[101] who insists in *Leviathan* that all such attempts at a realist solution must be misconceived, simply because words are not the names of things but merely the names of our conceptions of things.[102] When it comes to moral words, moreover, we have to reckon with the fact that our conceptions are in turn affected by our emotional states and attitudes. 'For though the nature of that we conceive, be the same; yet the diversity of our reception of it, in respect of different constitutions of body, and prejudices of opinion, gives every thing a tincture of our different passions.'[103] Hobbes traces the implications in a passage of exceptional importance from the perspective of my present argument:

And therefore in reasoning, a man must take heed of words; which besides the signification of what we imagine of their nature, have a signification also of the nature, disposition, and interest of the speaker; such as are the names of Vertues, and Vices; For one man calleth *Wisdome*, what another calleth *feare*; and

---

[99] For an account of how the doctrine that words stand for things animated Wilkins's project for a philosophical language see Slaughter 1982, pp. 161–3.
[100] South 1823a, pp. 130–1.
[101] Hobbes's engagement with the problems raised by paradiastolic speech is taken up at greater length in volume 3, ch. 4, section V.
[102] For a contrast with Locke's position on this issue see Ashworth 1981, pp. 299–326.
[103] See Hobbes 1996, p. 31 and cf. James 1997, pp. 131–6.

one *cruelty*, what another *justice*; one *prodigality*, what another *magnanimity*; and one *gravity*, what another *stupidity*, &c. And therefore such names can never be true grounds of any ratiocination.[104]

Here Hobbes not only recurs to the problem of paradiastole and repeats a number of examples already made familiar by the ancient and Renaissance theorists of eloquence. He also goes to the extreme of declaring that the power of the technique to generate ambiguity is such that any genuine argument about vice and virtue is thereby ruled out.

A scepticism so deep admits of only two possible solutions, each of which might be thought a *reductio ad absurdum*. One would be to abandon any attempt to map our existing language onto the world. This is the solution implicit in John Wilkins's *Essay*, as Jonathan Swift was later to observe in his satire on the philosophical projectors encountered by Gulliver in his voyage to Laputa. Like the philosophers we have been considering, the members of the Grand Academy of Lagado acknowledge that words rarely succeed in referring unambiguously to things. But whereas Wilkins proposed the construction of a new language, the academicians propose that, 'since words are only names for things, it would be more convenient for all men to carry about them such things as were necessary to express the particular business they are to discourse on'. Theirs is in short 'a scheme for entirely abolishing all words whatsoever'.[105]

The other solution, scarcely less draconian, is the one put forward by Hobbes in *Leviathan*. Since our moral appraisals and the terms we use to express them are invariably affected by our emotions, those who call for the acceptance of their own appraisals are merely calling for 'every of their passions, as it comes to bear sway in them, to be taken for right Reason'.[106] The inevitable outcome is that 'their controversie must either come to blowes, or be undecided, for want of a right Reason constituted by Nature'.[107] But this in turn suggests that, if we are to avoid such hostilities, the only alternative is that 'the parties must by their own accord, set up for right Reason, the Reason of some Arbitrator, or Judge, to whose sentence they will both stand'.[108]

If we ask who can serve as such an arbitrator, Hobbes's response is that the only possible candidate is the absolute sovereign to whom we submit in the act of instituting a commonwealth. He draws the inference

---

[104] Hobbes 1996, p. 31.
[105] Swift 1967, p. 230, possibly picking up the unfortunate remark in Wilkins 1668, Sig. a, 2^r to the effect that 'things are better than words'.
[106] Hobbes 1996, p. 33.   [107] Hobbes 1996, p. 33.   [108] Hobbes 1996, pp. 32-3.

most clearly in a crucial summarising passage from the final chapter of *The Elements of Law*:

> But this is certayne, seeing right reason is not existent, the reason of some man, or men, must supply the place thereof; and that man, or men, is he or they, that have the Soveraigne power, as hath bene already proved; and Consequently the civill Lawes are to all subjects the measures of their Actions, whereby to determine, whether they be right or wronge, profittable or unprofittable, vertuous or vitious; and by them the use, and definition of all names not agreed upon, and tending to Controversie, shall be established.[109]

Putting Hobbes's conclusion the other way round, we can point at the same time to a remarkable and little-noticed feature of his theory of sovereignty. One reason, Hobbes is telling us, why it is indispensable to institute an absolute sovereign, whose judgements in all matters pertaining to the being and well-being of the Commonwealth we must agree in advance to endorse, is that nothing short of this will enable us to overcome the ambiguities attendant on the use of paradiastolic speech.

Faced with the challenge of linguistic ambiguity, Wilkins proposed the creation of a new language, the academicians of Laputa proposed the abolition of language altogether, while Hobbes proposed the regulation of meanings and definitions by fiat. What these hyperbolical solutions have in common is the belief that the problem of moral ambiguity is too intractable to be solved within the framework of our existing linguistic resources. It is hard to imagine a greater tribute to the power assigned by the culture of the Renaissance to the art of eloquence.

[109] Hobbes 1969b, pp. 188-9.

11

John Milton and the politics of slavery

I

King Charles I was executed on 30 January 1649, and on 17 March the Rump Parliament took the still more revolutionary step of abolishing the office of kingship, arguing that 'for the most part, use hath been made of the regal power to oppress and impoverish and enslave the subject'.[1] Two days later, by a further Act of Parliament, the House of Lords was declared 'useless and dangerous' and was likewise 'wholly abolished'.[2] After pausing anxiously for two months, Parliament went on to draw the obvious inference and duly proclaimed that 'the people of England, and of all the dominions and territories thereunto belonging' now constituted 'a Commonwealth and Free State' governed solely by the people's elected representatives.[3] With this sequence of decisions, a republic was founded for the first and (so far) the only time in British history.

These unprecedented events stood in urgent need of legitimation, and several different strands of political thinking were immediately pressed into service. Some defenders of the commonwealth, including the Rump itself, sought to occupy the highest possible constitutional ground. They argued that Charles I had broken his contract with his people, and that the people's representatives had simply removed a tyrant and re-established lawful authority under their own command.[4] Others argued, more concessively, that all governments are manifestations of the will of God, and thus that the new regime, no less than its predecessor, ought to be regarded as providentially ordained. (I shall return to examine this line of thought in detail in volume 3 chapter 10.) Still others suggested in yet more pragmatic vein that no government can hope to survive an

---

This chapter is a revised and extended version of an article that originally appeared under the same title in *Prose Studies* 23 (2000), pp. 1–22.

[1] *Constitutional Documents 1625–1660*, pp. 384–7.   [2] *Constitutional Documents 1625–1660*, p. 387.
[3] *Constitutional Documents 1625–1660*, p. 388.   [4] *Constitutional Documents 1625–1660*, pp. 377–80.

examination of its original right to rule, and thus that the capacity of the new regime to protect its subjects should be accepted as a sufficient title to be obeyed. (I shall return to this further argument in volume 3 chapters 6 and 9.)

Alongside these contentions, a number of apologists for the commonwealth instead attempted to defend it in classical and, more specifically, in Roman law terms. According to this version of events, the British people had been living in a state of servitude under the rule of Charles I. The abolition of the monarchy was therefore interpreted as an act of self-liberation on the part of an enslaved people who had thereby succeeded in regaining their birthright of freedom. Historians have found much less to say about these arguments, but there are at least two reasons for paying close attention to them. One is that, as I shall attempt to show in chapter 12, they formed a crucial but neglected element in the attack on the royal prerogative under the early Stuarts, and in consequence helped to legitimise the decision by Parliament to take up arms in 1642. My other reason brings me to the theme of the present chapter. John Milton, incomparably the greatest writer to speak out in defence of the regicide, drew extensively on these classical ideas in the tracts he published on behalf of the commonwealth between 1649 and 1651.[5] My first aim in what follows will accordingly be to sketch the origins and development of this neo-Roman vision of the British polity. My eventual aim will be to illustrate the continuities between this analysis and Milton's arguments in defence of the regicide. My underlying aspiration is to offer a new account of the sources and character of Milton's theory of free citizens and free states.

II

When anxieties were first voiced about 'fundamental' liberties in the early Stuart Parliaments, the language in which these complaints were generally couched was that of the common law.[6] Faced with a government inclined to construe their liberties as privileges, the common lawyers in the House of Commons retorted that – in the words of Sir Edward Coke – the people possess their freedom as a matter not of grace but of legal right.[7] The common law case was perhaps best summarised by

---

[5] On the general theme of Milton's classical republicanism see Dzelzainis 1995.
[6] The classic work is Pocock 1987, but for important revisions see Burgess 1992 and Sommerville 1999, pp. 81–104.
[7] *Commons Debates 1628*, vol. 3, p. 95.

John Glanville in a speech he was asked to make on behalf of the House at the time of the presentation of the Petition of Right in 1628. There are certain 'lawful and just liberties', Glanville maintains, which give us the status of 'free subjects of this realm'.[8] They are fundamental in the sense that they are 'absolutely the rights' of free subjects, and are at once declared and confirmed in Magna Carta, from which we can trace 'an inherent right and interest in liberty and freedom in the subjects of this realm as their birthright and inheritance'.[9]

One of the complaints voiced in the Parliament of 1628, and strongly echoed in 1640, was that these rights were being 'miserably violated', especially by the exercise of the royal prerogative to imprison subjects without trial and impose taxes without consent.[10] A deeper grievance was that the very existence of these prerogatives posed a threat to fundamental liberties, leaving them in a state of perpetual danger and insecurity.[11] When the Commons debated its Petition in 1628, Sir Edward Coke argued that the remedy lay in rejecting the crown's understanding of the prerogative as a set of 'regal' as opposed to 'legal' rights. 'Magna Carta and all other statutes', Coke replied, 'are absolute without any saving of sovereign power', so that outside the *lex terrae* there can be no prerogative powers at all.[12] When the Long Parliament met in November 1640, the common lawyers and their allies duly pushed through a series of Acts designed to convert this theory into constitutional practice: they abolished the prerogative courts and outlawed the use of prerogative powers to collect taxes without parliamentary consent.

It has recently been argued that, in so far as Parliament had a legal case in favour of taking up arms against Charles I in 1642, it was this conception of the common law and its supremacy on which they relied.[13] But this interpretation overlooks the presence in the Parliamentary debates of what I have characterised as a classical vision, and more specifically a neo-Roman vision, of fundamental liberties. If the crown, according to this rival analysis, possesses any discretionary powers capable of undermining fundamental liberties, what we have to say is not that these liberties are thereby left in a state of jeopardy. What we have to say is that we do not possess any such liberties, since the very existence of such prerogative powers reduces us to a level below that of free subjects.

As I have already intimated, this argument was taken not from the common law but from the law of Rome. John Milton himself draws

---

[8] *Commons Debates 1628*, vol. 3, p. 562.   [9] *Commons Debates 1628*, vol. 3, pp. 564-5.
[10] *Commons Debates 1628*, vol. 3, p. 565.
[11] *Commons Debates 1628*, vol. 3, pp. 496, 528-9, 532-3, 562.
[12] *Commons Debates 1628*, vol. 3, p. 494.   [13] Cromartie 1999, pp. 78-9, 86, 112, 118.

attention to this fact in one of the entries in his Commonplace Book dating from the early 1640s. He notes that, if we wish to see 'what lawyers declare concerning liberty', we must turn to the discussions of freedom and servitude in the *Codex* of Justinian.[14] There we learn that 'the fundamental division within the law of persons', as the *Digest* puts it, 'is that all men and women are either free or are slaves'.[15] After this comes a formal definition of the concept of slavery. 'Slavery is an institution of the *ius gentium* by which someone is, contrary to nature, subject to the dominion of someone else.'[16] This in turn is held to yield a definition of individual liberty. If everyone in civil associations is either bond or free, then a *civis* or free subject must be someone who is not under the dominion of anyone else, but is *sui iuris*, capable of acting in their own right.[17] It likewise follows that what it means for someone to lack personal liberty must be for that person not to be *sui iuris*, but instead to be under the power or subject to the will of someone else.

While this understanding of civil liberty received its definitive articulation in Justinian's *Codex*, we already encounter it at a much earlier date among the philosophers and especially the historians of ancient Rome. Sallust and Livy both discuss the transition from the servitude imposed on the Roman people by their early kings to the state of liberty they came to enjoy under their 'free commonwealth',[18] while Tacitus later examined the causes of their return to servitude under the principate.[19] A further and closely connected issue raised by these writers relates to the social consequences of losing the status of *cives* or free subjects. We can never hope, they maintain, to find any notable exploits – any deeds of glory or greatness – performed by peoples living in conditions of servitude. Livy[20] and Tacitus[21] both issue this warning, but it is Sallust who places the weightiest emphasis on it. His main reason for believing that individual freedom is a necessary condition of civic greatness appears at the outset of his *Bellum Catilinae*, where he explains that powerful kings invariably feel envious and hostile towards any subjects who exhibit notable civic virtues. To cite John Heywood's translation of 1608, 'absolute

---

[14] Milton 1953, pp. 410, 470.
[15] *Digest* 1985, I. V. 3. 35, vol. 1, p. 15: 'Summa itaque de iure personarum divisio haec est, quod omnes homines aut liberi sunt aut servi.'
[16] *Digest* 1985, I. V. 4. 35, vol. 1, p. 15: 'Servitus est constitutio iuris gentium, qua quis dominio alieno contra naturam subicitur.'
[17] *Digest* 1985, I. VI. 1. 36, vol. 1, p. 17: 'Some persons are in their own power, some are subject to the power of others, such as slaves, who are in the power of their masters.' ['quaedam personae sui iuris sunt, quaedam alieno iuri subiectae sunt ... in potestate sunt servi dominorum ...']
[18] Sallust 1931a, VI–VII, pp. 10–14; Livy 1919, II. I–III, pp. 218–28.
[19] Tacitus 1925, I. I–III, pp. 2–8.   [20] Livy 1919, II. I, pp. 218–20.
[21] Tacitus 1925, I. II, p. 6.

Princes are alwaies more jealous of the good, then of the badde, because another mans Vertue (as they take it) is a diminution of their respectivenesse, and therefore dangerous'.[22] The implications of Sallust's diagnosis are later spelled out by Tacitus at the start of his *Historiae*. Under absolute monarchies the exercise of civic virtue becomes (in the words of Henry Savile's translation of 1591) 'the readie broade way to most assured destruction'.[23] Those who live at the mercy of such rulers learn to curb the very qualities that need to be given the freest rein if civic greatness is to be achieved. The alternative, Tacitus grimly adds, is to learn from experience that under tyranny the possession of outstanding qualities is 'a capitall crime'.[24] With virtue effectively proscribed, we are condemned to living in a servile society in which flatterers and time-servers flourish unopposed.

These arguments were much invoked in the years immediately following the execution of Charles I. Before then, however, critics of the royal prerogative preferred to focus on a different reason given by Sallust for believing that individual liberty is a precondition of political glory and greatness. Sallust had offered this further reflection in his *Bellum Iugurthinum*, putting it into the mouth of Gaius Memmius in a speech upbraiding the plebs for allowing themselves to be dominated by the Roman nobility. The outcome of living for many years without security for life or liberty, Memmius tells them, is that they have become so anxious and dispirited that all civic virtue has been lost. If 'care of liberty had possessed your courages', as Heywood's translation puts it, 'the Common-wealth should not, as now lie disgraced'. But the whole populace has fallen into 'slavish patience', becoming 'so corrupted with the same sloth and cowardice' that they have learned to 'tollerate so vile a servitude'.[25]

As soon as critics of the early Stuart monarchy began to feel anxious about fundamental liberties, they increasingly turned to these accounts of slavery and the servile behaviour to which it allegedly gives rise. The contention that the mere existence of prerogative rights converts free subjects into slaves was loudly voiced in the Parliamentary debates about Impositions in 1610. As opponents of the government stressed, the use of the prerogative to impose customs and other charges presupposes that the right to hold property remains subject to the will of the king. But to live subject to the will of another person, as the *Digest* had

---

[22] Sallust 1608, first pagination, p. 17 [*recte* p. 7]. [23] Tacitus 1591, p. 2.
[24] Tacitus 1591, p. 2. [25] Sallust 1608, second pagination. pp. 29–30.

explained, is what it means to live in servitude. Sir Thomas Hedley duly drew the inference in the great speech he delivered immediately after Sir Francis Bacon had spoken in favour of the prerogative.[26] If, Hedley warns, you 'take away the liberty of the subject in his profit or property', then 'you make a promiscuous confusion of a freeman and a bound slave'.[27] Towards the end of the session an attempt was made to introduce a Bill for the protection of fundamental liberties, the aim being to 'leave a monument behind us that may shew to posterity we do unwillingly endure servitude'.[28]

The same objections resurfaced in 1628 in the course of the protests against the levying of the Forced Loan two years earlier. We are told, Sir Dudley Digges remarked at the outset of the Commons debate, that 'he is no great monarch' who cannot take 'whatsoever he will'. But any king who 'is not tied to the laws' and thereby rules by mere caprice is nothing better than 'a king of slaves'.[29] Sir Robert Phelips went on to denounce the employment of the lord lieutenants to collect the Loan. 'What a miserable grievance is that of lieutenancies, when by an arbitrary warrant I shall have my goods taken away from me as if I were a poor slave.'[30] Referring to Livy's cautionary tale of the Decemvirs, Phelips added that 'there's now a decemvir in every county, and amongst that decemvir there's some Appius Claudius that seek their own revenges'. Sir John Eliot – also invoking Livy's history – reverted to the same issue later in the debate, stressing once more that the very fact of being 'liable to the command of a higher power' is what takes away our liberty.[31]

Still more fundamental than the freedom to hold and dispose of property, everyone agreed, was the value of personal liberty. This commitment gave rise to a further criticism of the government in the Parliament of 1628 for undermining the status of free subjects. The principal grievance was held to be the crown's use of prerogative powers to imprison without declaring a cause. As Richard Creshald objected, if such a power is permitted we 'become bondage', and this condition 'I am sure is contrary to and against the law of nature'.[32] Speaking in support, Sir John Eliot agreed that without this 'common right of the subject' we are nothing

[26] For a perceptive analysis of Hedley's speech see Peltonen 1995, pp. 220–8.
[27] *Proceedings in Parliament 1610*, vol. 2, p. 192.
[28] *Proceedings in Parliament 1610*, vol. 2, p. 329.   [29] *Commons Debates 1628*, vol. 2, p. 66.
[30] Here I have made a conjectural emendation, for the manuscript reads not 'slave' but 'snake'. See British Library, Stowe MS 366 fo. 10ᵛ (and cf. *Commons Debates 1628*, vol. 2, p. 69). But the comparison with 'a poor snake' makes no sense, and given that the rest of the speech is about slavery I assume that the copyist of the notes taken at the debate must have misread 'slave'.
[31] *Commons Debates 1628*, vol. 2, p. 72.   [32] *Commons Debates 1628*, vol. 2, p. 149.

better than bondmen.³³ Later in the session, Sir Roger North put it to the Commons that their principal duty was to halt these encroachments and thereby 'save ourselves and them that sent us from being slaves'.³⁴

The anxieties voiced by the Roman historians about the social consequences of living in servitude likewise surfaced at numerous moments in these debates. We already find Sir Thomas Hedley speaking in 1610 of the need for 'spirit and courage' to be sustained if civic greatness is to be achieved, and warning against the dire effects of failing to uphold the freedom that enables such virtues to flourish. 'If the liberty of the subject be in this point impeached, that their lands and goods be any way in the king's absolute power to be taken from them', this will leave them 'little better than the king's bondmen', as a result of which 'they will use little care or industry to get that which they cannot keep and so will grow both poor and base-minded like to the peasants in other countries'.³⁵ The same moral was later drawn with even more patriotic assurance by Sir Dudley Digges in the Parliament of 1628:

> That king that is not tied to the laws is a king of slaves. I have been in employments abroad. For the propriety of goods and of liberty, see the mischief of the contrary in other nations. In Muscovy one English mariner with a sword will beat five Muscovites that are likely to eat him. In the states where there are no excises, as in trades, they are most free and noble. If these be brought, the king will lose more than he gains.³⁶

The self-congratulating tendency to speak of the free world (by contrast with that of the Muscovites) has a long pedigree.

III

With the recall of Parliament in 1640, similar protests about the undermining of fundamental liberties broke out anew. As soon as the Short Parliament assembled in April, Sir Francis Seymour returned to the attack with an angry speech denouncing evil counsellors for treasonously telling the king that 'his prerogative is above all Lawes' and thus that 'his Subjects are but slaves'.³⁷ By the time Parliament decided on armed resistance in the summer of 1642, the claim that the people were living in servitude had become a staple of debate. When Charles I issued his Commission of Array on 1 July, summoning his subjects to the defence of the realm, the Commons retorted that this command imposed a

---

³³ *Commons Debates 1628*, vol. 2, p. 6.   ³⁴ *Commons Debates 1628*, vol. 2, p. 269.
³⁵ *Proceedings in Parliament 1610*, vol. 2, pp. 194–5.   ³⁶ *Commons Debates 1628*, vol. 2, p. 66.
³⁷ *Proceedings of the Short Parliament of 1640*, p. 142.

'heavier Yoke of Bondage upon the People, than that of Ship-money'.[38] Rather than merely taking away the right to dispose of their property, it presumed 'a Power in the King without limitation, not only to impose Arms, but to command the Persons of the subjects at pleasure'.[39] Such a power, the Commons added, implies a subjugation of the people 'to far greater Bondage' than ever before.[40]

During these months the war of words similarly intensified outside Parliament, with Henry Parker coming forward as the most lucid and resourceful opponent of the royalist cause. Parker is habitually (and rightly) described as the leading pamphleteer in favour of Parliament at this climacteric time.[41] But it is important to recognise that what he principally defended was not the claim that the prerogative should be brought within the ambit of the common law, but the more unsettling suggestion that the very existence of the prerogative leaves everyone enslaved.[42] The latter charge is vehemently pressed in his earliest tract, *The Case of Shipmony Briefly Discoursed*, which he published to coincide with the convening of the Long Parliament in November 1640. Charles I's use of prerogative powers to collect ship money is roundly denounced as 'incompatible with popular liberty'.[43] The King's policy is such that 'to his sole indisputable judgement it is left to lay charges as often and as great as he pleases'. But the effect of this policy will be to turn us into 'the most despicable slaves in the whole world' (pp. 98, 108).

As Parker insists at several points in *The Case of Shipmony*, it is not the oppressive exercise but the mere existence of such prerogatives that reduces us to servitude. His is a conditional anxiety about what *could* be done by any government that enjoys 'a controlling power over all Law' and consequently 'knowes no bounds but its owne will' (p. 109). If the king's prerogative extends thus far, we are left entirely at his mercy; all our liberties are enjoyed 'at the king's meere discretion'. But as Parker rhetorically asks, if this is our predicament, 'wherein doe we differ in condition from the most abject of all bondslaves?' (p. 109).

Parker also takes up the suggestion originally explored by Sallust and Tacitus about the social consequences of living in servitude. His most important tract, his *Observations* of July 1642, begins by proclaiming it 'a great and fond error in some Princes to strive more to be great over

---
[38] Rushworth 1691, vol. 1, p. 661.   [39] Rushworth 1691, vol. 1, p. 665.
[40] Rushworth 1691, vol. 1, p. 665.
[41] For this judgement see Sirluck 1959, pp. 19–25. See also Mendle 1995, pp. 32–50, 70–89.
[42] For a contrasting attempt to relate Parker's arguments to the common law tradition see Cromartie 1999, pp. 81, 114.
[43] [Parker] 1999, p. 96. References to this tract are hereafter given in the body of the text.

their people, then in their people'.⁴⁴ The reason why this is such a grave mistake is that no mighty exploits can ever be expected from subjects condemned to living in an impoverished or demoralised state. It is only 'by infranchising their Subjects' that kings can hope 'to magnifie themselves'. The 'most great and glorious' king will always be the one who 'hath the most and strongest subjects, and not he which tramples upon the most contemptible vassals'. To appreciate the folly of preferring to lord it over an enslaved nation, we need look no further than France. 'Were the Peasants there more free, they would be more rich and magnanimous, and were they so, their King were more puissant' and less 'adulterate' in his greatness (p. 168).

As we have seen, such fears had already been expressed in the parliamentary debates of 1610 and especially of 1628. During the early months of 1642, however, a new and more far-reaching argument began to emerge. Critics of the government began to turn their attention specifically to the prerogative of the 'negative voice', the right of the king to give or withhold his assent to any proposed act of legislation. As we shall see in chapter 12, the occasion for this development was the king's refusal to accept the Militia Ordinance sent for his approval in February 1642. Stunned at first by this exercise of the royal veto, the king's opponents eventually gave their response in a Remonstrance of 19 May 1642. The negative voice permits the king to 'make his own understanding or reason the rule of his government' and thereby enables him to ignore 'the wisdom of both houses of parliament'.⁴⁵ But this leaves the representative body of the nation dependent in its highest decisions upon the king's mere will and caprice, thereby reducing the whole body of the people at a single stroke to a condition of servitude.

As we shall see in chapter 12, these arguments were increasingly made to carry the weight of Parliament's attack on the crown in the summer of 1642. The implications were finally spelled out in the Declaration of 2 August in favour of taking up arms. The king is now alleged to be wholly under the control of the so-called malignant party, whose ambition is to 'alter the government of this kingdom, and reduce it to the condition of some other countries, which are not governed by parliaments, and so not by laws; but by the will of the prince, or rather of those who are about him'.⁴⁶ The policy of the malignants is to 'take all parliaments away; or, which is worse, make them the instruments of slavery, to confirm it by

⁴⁴ [Parker] 1933, p. 168. References to this tract are hereafter given in the body of the text.
⁴⁵ *Parliamentary History of England*, vol. 2, p. 1267.
⁴⁶ *Parliamentary History of England*, vol. 2, p. 1439.

law, and leave the disease incurable'.[47] Their basic aim is thus to make themselves 'masters of our religion and liberties' and thereby 'make us slaves'.[48]

To speak of Britain as an enslaved nation, however, was scarcely sufficient in itself to yield a justification for armed resistance. Too many people believed that the conduct of our rulers, be they good or evil, must be accepted without question as a part of God's design. Some royalists even went so far as to maintain that slavery itself is ordained by God. When William Ball published his reply to Parker's *Observations* in September 1642 under the title *A Caveat for Subjects*, he explicitly insisted that, when God established 'power and dominion', he not only intended 'that some should bee masters and others servants', but that 'some should become slaves to tyrants'. God sometimes calls us 'to servility', and when he does so the condition must be uncomplainingly endured.[49]

A stronger argument was clearly required if such extreme beliefs about the inviolability of our rulers were to be countered. Those edging towards armed resistance found their answer in the claim that, far from being ordained powers, all rulers are entrusted by their subjects – sometimes in the form of an explicit contract – to govern them in such a way as to promote their safety and benefit. Any king who fails to uphold the *salus populi* may thus be said to have betrayed his trust and thereby forfeited any title to allegiance. This doctrine had been widely debated ever since the 'monarchomach' writers of the French religious wars had developed it a generation earlier,[50] and we find it increasingly invoked by Parliament in the spring of 1642. When the two Houses resolved on 20 May 'that the king, seduced by wicked counsel, intends to make war against the parliament' they explicitly declared that the king's recent actions constituted 'a breach of the trust reposed in him by his people' and that this in turn justified a resort to defensive arms.[51]

Once more, however, the clearest statement of the argument can be found in Henry Parker's *Observations* of July 1642. Parker begins with the crucial contention that, 'in this contestation between Regall and Parliamentary power', we need to recognise that political authority 'is originally inherent in the people' (p. 167). If it is now held by anyone else, this can only be because of a 'paction' or 'contract' by which

---

[47] *Parliamentary History of England*, vol. 2, p. 1437.
[48] *Parliamentary History of England*, vol. 2, p. 1439. [49] Ball 1642, p. 12.
[50] For the evolution of this theory see Skinner 1978b, pp. 302–48; for its introduction into early Stuart England see Salmon 1959, pp. 58–79.
[51] *Parliamentary History of England*, vol. 2, p. 1241.

the people 'by common consent' assigned it to them (pp. 167, 170). The only possible motive a sovereign people could have for entering into such an agreement would be that of improving the safety and security of their 'lives, lands and liberties' (pp. 168–9, 178). It follows that all lawful contracts of government must be 'conditionate and fiduciary' (p. 170). 'Kings receive all royalty from the people' in the form of 'a speciall trust of safety and libertie' expressly limited by the requirement that they preserve the *salus populi* (p. 171). If instead they endanger the safety of the people or undermine their liberties, the people are 'ipso facto absolved of all allegiance' and become 'bound by higher dutie, to seeke their own preservation by resistance and defence' (p. 170).

It is in the light of this argument that Parker proclaims the right – even the duty – of Parliament to take up arms against the king. This is not to say, however, that he thereby abandons his earlier reliance on Roman law doctrines about freedom and slavery. If we turn to consider how he defends his pivotal assumption that any lawful contract of government must be 'fiduciary' in character, we find the distinctions drawn at the start of the *Digest* lying at the heart of his case.

As we have seen, the *Digest* had laid it down that to live in subjection to the discretion of a lord or master is what it means to live in servitude. Parker not only reiterates the argument but draws on the terminology of Roman law to express it. If any nation, he declares, agrees to submit 'to the meer discretion' of a king, it will effectively 'resigne its owne interest to the will of one Lord, as that that Lord may destroy it without injury' (pp. 174, 180). But to enter into such an unlimited contract will be to 'indure that thraldome which uses to accompany unbounded & unconditionate royalty'. Any nation, in other words, which covenants 'to give away its owne proprietie in it selfe absolutely' will be consenting to 'subject it selfe to a condition of servility' (p. 186).

The *Digest* had gone on to stigmatise the institution of slavery as contrary to the law of nature. Here again Parker picks up the argument, claiming that it would be 'unnaturall' for any nation 'to give away its owne proprietie in it selfe absolutely' and thereby 'contribute its owne inherent puissance, meerely to abet Tiranny, and support slavery' (pp. 182, 186). The idea of an unconditional contract of government must therefore be 'contrarie to the supreme of all Lawes', the law of nature (p. 186). So deeply, indeed, does Parker believe that such agreements are 'rebellious to nature' that he even concludes, rather optimistically, that it would not only be unjust but impossible 'for any nation so to inslave it selfe' (p. 174).

Parker next uses these considerations as a lens through which to inspect the government of Charles I. The king, he concludes, has in fact enslaved the nation and thereby violated his trust. One obvious sign of the people's servitude is the king's possession of a negative voice, a prerogative which 'at one blow confounds all Parliaments, and subjects us to as unbounded a regiment of the Kings meere will as any Nation under Heaven ever suffered under' (p. 175). We cannot imagine a free people ever consenting to such an unbounded contract of government. To hand over so much authority would be 'contrary to the originall, end, and trust of all power and Lawe', for it would create 'as vast and arbitrary a prerogative as the Grand Seignior has' and thereby condemn us to servitude (p. 183). It is therefore unquestionable that in these circumstances we are justified 'in taking up armes for our own safety' in accordance with the highest of all laws, 'the principles of Nature' (pp. 183, 210).

IV

As we saw at the outset, the revolution set in train in the summer of 1642 reached its climax in the opening months of 1649, when the monarchy was abolished and the 'Commonwealth and Free state' was proclaimed. Although, as we have seen, the Rump Parliament did not lack for support in its attempts to legitimise these events, it was anxious to supply its own justification for what it had done, and called on John Milton among others to write officially in its defence. Milton initially responded on his own initiative in *The Tenure of Kings and Magistrates*, which he began while Charles I was still on trial, publishing it within a fortnight of the king's death. For this effort he was rewarded by the Council of State with the post of Secretary for Foreign Tongues, and in that capacity he was subsequently commissioned to produce two further treatises in defence of the new regime: *Eikonoklastes*, which appeared in October 1649, and *Pro Populo Anglicano Defensio*, his ambitious address to the learned of Europe, which was first published in February 1651.[52]

The *narratio* of Milton's *Tenure* contains the clearest statement of his theory of free government, a theory subsequently reiterated in more informal terms at various moments in *Eikonoklastes* and the *Defensio*.[53] As a number of scholars have rightly emphasised, what Milton offers is essentially a restatement of the 'monarchomach' view of lawful government as it had been elaborated by critics of the Stuart monarchy at the start

[52] For the narrative of Milton's pamphleteering at this juncture see Hughes 1962.
[53] See Milton 1962, pp. 485–7, 524–5 and cf. Milton 1932, pp. 270–2, 358–62, 378–82.

of the civil wars.⁵⁴ This is not to say that Milton inertly recapitulates these earlier lines of thought. He is at once more individualistic in his premises than a writer like Henry Parker and at the same time more broadly concerned with popular sovereignty than merely with the right of resistance.⁵⁵ Nevertheless, the outlines of Milton's argument are familiar enough. He opens with the ringing affirmation that no one 'can be so stupid as to deny that all men naturally were born free'.⁵⁶ He infers that, if we are now subject to legitimate government, this can only be because we consented to our own subjection by a 'bond or Covnant' (p. 9). The only motive a free people could have for making such an agreement would be the expectation that 'the public safety' and 'the common good' would be the better served (p. 10). This in turn means that the bond in question must be a conditional one: we owe allegiance if and only if we (or our elected representatives)⁵⁷ agree that our rulers are indeed performing their side of the bargain. There cannot be a political covenant specifying that we hand over power absolutely to a ruler who is thereby rendered unaccountable.⁵⁸ It follows that, if we or our representatives judge that our ruler is not acting for our benefit, we are automatically 'disengag'd' from our allegiance and can choose to 'retaine him or depose him' as we will (p. 13).

As with Henry Parker and other protagonists of Parliament in 1642, Milton's account of free government is in turn based on a classical analysis of what it means to live 'in a free state'. But this aspect of Milton's argument has, I think, been less satisfactorily handled in the recent literature. There has been almost no discussion of what precisely he may have understood by the concepts of freedom and unfreedom,⁵⁹ and there has even been a tendency to deny that his theory of free government owes anything to classical models at all.⁶⁰ My aim in what follows will be to try to remedy these deficiencies, at least in a preliminary way. Specifically, I shall argue that the concept of freedom lying at the heart of Milton's

---

⁵⁴ See, for example, Sirluck 1964, pp. 211–12, 219, 223; Sanderson 1989, pp. 131–5; Dzelzainis 1991, pp. xii–xix.

⁵⁵ These points are excellently brought out in Dzelzainis 1999, pp. 80–1.

⁵⁶ Milton 1991, p. 8. References to this treatise are hereafter given in the body of the text.

⁵⁷ As Sirluck 1964, pp. 213–14 notes, Milton faced the embarrassing fact that a majority of the House of Commons had opposed the execution of the king. He is left having to distinguish between mere majorities and the majority of the uncorrupted. See, for example, Milton 1932, p. 356.

⁵⁸ Milton 1991, pp. 11, 12, 15.

⁵⁹ Dzelzainis 1995 and Dzelzainis 1999 constitute important exceptions to this stricture.

⁶⁰ See Corns 1995, pp. 26–7 and cf. the comment on Kevin Sharpe's work in Norbrook 1999, p. 209n.

defence of the commonwealth is identical with the classical understanding of the concept we have already encountered in earlier critics of the Stuart monarchy.

The simplest way to trace these intellectual allegiances will be to begin by asking what reasons Milton gives for insisting that the bond or covenant underlying a free commonwealth must always be of a limited or conditional character. His answer in *The Tenure* turns out to be wholly dependent on Roman ideas about freedom and slavery. As in the case of Parker, we can distinguish three steps by which the concept of an unconditional trust or covenant is dismissed. Milton first observes that, were we to hand over power absolutely, 'our lives and estates' would be left at the 'meer grace and mercy' of our ruler, and hence 'in the tenure and occupation of another inheriting Lord' (pp. 11–12, 32). But this, he next argues, would be to condemn ourselves to living 'under tyranny and servitude' in the manner of 'slaves and vassals born', without 'that power, which is the root and sourse of all liberty' (p. 32). His third point is that the act of consenting to such servitude would be contrary to the law of nature, and would thus be a moral impossibility. Given that 'all men naturally were born free', such a covenant would involve 'a violation of their natural birthright' and would thus be 'a kinde of treason against the dignitie of mankind' (pp. 8, 10–11).

Milton also reformulates with exceptional clarity the classical assumption that freedom is to be contrasted not with actual but with possible constraint. This too is a point worth underlining, if only because his commentators have paid little attention to the unfamiliar way in which he handles the concept of liberty. Suppose you find yourself living at the 'meer grace and mercy' of a king, so that you are liable to the loss of your fundamental liberties with impunity at any time. If this is your predicament, Milton argues, you have already forfeited your status as a free subject. This is because any government, even if it is 'not illegal, or intolerable', leaves its citizens 'no better than slaves and vassals born', if it 'hangs over them as a lordly scourge' (p. 32).

We find the same assumptions even more clearly at work in the memorable passage from chapter 11 of *Eikonoklastes*, in which Milton steps back from his anti-Stuart tirade and offers us a definition of a free commonwealth:

Every Common-wealth is in general defin'd, a societie sufficient of it self, in all things conducible to well being and commodious life. Any of which requisit things if it cannot have without the gift and favour of a single person, or without leave of his privat reason, or his conscience, it cannot be thought sufficient of it self, and by consequence no Common-wealth, nor free; but a multitude of Vassalls in the possession and domaine of one absolute Lord.[61]

Here again it is the mere fact of owing our well-being and commodious life to the discretion of a ruler which is taken to cancel our liberty.

Attempting a yet further clarification of the same argument, Milton later appeals in his *Defensio* to one of his most cherished classical authorities. 'Listen', he commands, 'to the words of Cicero in his fourth *Philippic*: "What cause of waging war can be more just than that of repudiating slavery? For the most wretched thing about this condition is that, even if the master happens not to be oppressive, he can be so if he should choose." '[62] Once again, it is the mere fact of our dependence that proclaims and seals our servitude.

Having outlined the nature of a free commonwealth in *The Tenure*, Milton proceeds in *Eikonoklastes* to apply these general considerations to the reign of Charles I. The outcome is a virulent denunciation of the king and his evil counsellors for reducing the people to slavery. Charles I's aspiration was 'to set up an arbitrary Government of his own', so that 'all Britain was to be ty'd and chain'd to the conscience, judgement, and reason of one Man'.[63] His aim, in other words, was to 'tred down all other men into the condition of Slaves'.[64] He was 'diligent and careful' to bring it about that 'we should be slaves',[65] thereby forcing us into a 'fatal struggling for Libertie and life'.[66]

As with the earlier writers I considered, the main evidence for this conclusion is said to be Charles's refusal to give up the prerogative of the negative voice.[67] The very existence of this power leaves 'our highest consultations and purpos'd laws' subject to being 'terminated by the Kings will'.[68] But this makes 'the will of one man our Law', after which 'no suttletie of dispute can redeem the Parliament, and Nation from being Slaves'.[69] To live under such a government is to live in a 'servil condition' in which we are obliged 'to submit like bond slaves'.[70] Since any decisions made by the people's representatives can always be overturned, Parliament is left with 'no more freedom than if it sate in his Noose, which when he pleases to draw together with one twitch of his

---

[61] Milton 1962, p. 458.
[62] Milton 1932, p. 96: 'Audi igitur verba Ciceronis in 4 Philip. *Quae causa iustior est belli gerendi, quam servitutis depulsio? In qua etiamsi non sit molestus dominus, tamen est miserrimum posse si velit.*'
[63] Milton 1962, p. 359.
[64] Milton 1962, p. 412. The claim is repeated in the *Defensio*, in which Milton repeatedly speaks of the *servitus* of the people under Charles I. See Milton 1932, pp. 4, 64, 510, 542, *et passim*.
[65] Milton 1962, p. 455. [66] Milton 1962, p. 569. [67] Milton 1962, pp. 408–18.
[68] Milton 1962, p. 462. [69] Milton 1962, p. 462. [70] Milton 1962, pp. 577, 580.

Negative, shall throttle a whole Nation, to the wish of *Caligula* in one neck'.[71]

Milton accordingly has no hesitation in defending the regicide and the establishment of the commonwealth. The people were undoubtedly justified in throwing off the slavery imposed on them by their tyrannical king in violation of the laws of nature and the inherently limited character of legitimate government. The inference is perhaps drawn most explicitly in chapter 5 of the *Defensio*, at the moment when Milton responds to Salmasius's jibe that the execution of Charles I dishonoured the nation. The true situation, Milton retorts, was that 'with the country almost ruined by debauchery – by which means its slavery was to have been made more bearable – and with its laws overthrown and its religion sold off, the English people liberated themselves from servitude'.[72]

There is one further way in which Milton shows himself a faithful follower of the classical arguments that Henry Parker and other supporters of the Parliamentary cause had earlier invoked. This is in his account of the social consequences of living in servitude. He strongly endorses the belief that no deeds of glory can ever be expected from the enslaved subjects of tyrannical governments. We need the highest courage and civic spirit to perform such deeds, and these qualities can never be found except among those living in a free state. These claims are already present in the *Areopagitica* of 1644, in which Milton speaks of liberty as 'the nurse of all great wits', and solemnly apostrophises its benign influence:

This is that which hath rarify'd and enlighten'd our spirits like the influence of heaven; this is that which hath enfranchis'd, enlarg'd and lifted up our apprehensions degrees above themselves.

He goes on to declare that, liberated as we have been by Parliament from the tyranny of the malignant party, 'our hearts are now more capacious, our thoughts more erected to the search and expectation of greatest and exactest things'.[73]

The same connections are subsequently traced in both the *Tenure* and the *Defensio*. In the *Tenure* Milton speaks of 'the voice of our Supreme Magistracy, calling us to liberty' as the means enabling us to perform 'the flourishing deeds of a reformed Common-wealth'.[74] And in one of the grandest passages of exhortation in the *Defensio* he repeats that 'if you want wealth, freedom, peace and power', you must make sure that you

---

[71] Milton 1962, p. 579.
[72] Milton 1932, pp. 282–4: 'Immo luxu pene perditam, quo tolerantior servitutis esset, extinctis deinde legibus, et mancipata religione, [Angli] servientem liberarunt.'
[73] Milton 1959, p. 559.   [74] Milton 1991, p. 32.

live in liberty, for 'to hope for these goods under kingly domination is to hope in vain'.[75] Those who think otherwise 'are merely confessing that they have been born body and soul to a life of servitude'.[76]

V

My thesis has been that, in his vision of a free commonwealth, Milton combines a classical – and more specifically a Roman law – conception of freedom and slavery with a 'monarchomach' understanding of lawful government. This enabled him to restate, in defence of the regicide, a series of arguments already made familiar by Parker and other parliamentary theorists at the outbreak of the civil war. To leave the story there, however, would be to overlook one important way in which Milton was able at the same time to supplement and transform these earlier presentations of the case. Writing after the abolition of the monarchy, he was in a position to draw more freely on the anti-monarchical prejudices of his Roman authorities, and was able in consequence to add significantly to previous discussions about the relations between individual liberty and the true greatness of kingdoms and states.

We can best approach this further theme by asking why it is, according to Milton, that we cannot hope to find any glorious deeds performed by those living under tyranny. As we have seen, earlier critics of the Stuart monarchy had generally picked up Sallust's suggestion that such subjects will feel too discouraged, too demoralised, to cultivate the necessary civic virtues. Milton at first endorses this simple explanation when, in *Areopagitica*, he issues his thundering denunciation of the Long Parliament's Order of 1643 requiring all books to be officially licensed. The effect, he protests, will be 'to dishearten utterly and discontent' those who seek 'that lasting fame and perpetuity of praise' which accrues to 'those whose publisht labours advance the good of mankind'.[77] Such inventive spirits will simply give up in the face of potential persecution, as has already happened 'in other Countries, where this kind of inquisition tyrannizes'.[78] By way of illustrating his argument, Milton recalls the visit he paid to Italy some ten years before:

I have sat among their lerned men, for that honor I had, and bin counted happy to be born in such a place of *Philosophic* freedom, as they suppos'd England was,

---

[75] Milton 1932, p. 542: 'si opes, si libertatem, si pacem, si imperium vultis, ... haec omnia ... sub regio dominatu neequicquam sperare'.
[76] Milton 1932, p. 542: 'corpore atque animo ad servitutem natos fatentur esse'.
[77] Milton 1959, p. 531.   [78] Milton 1959, p. 537.

while themselvs did nothing but bemoan the servil condition into which lerning amongst them was brought; that this was it which had dampt the glory of Italian wits; that nothing had bin there writt'n now these many years but flattery and fustian.[79]

Once again, Milton stresses that liberty is jeopardised not merely by actual but by possible constraint. If we fear that some harm might befall us if we were to voice our less conventional thoughts, that in itself will be sufficient to inhibit us from voicing them.

As we have seen, however, Sallust's principal claim about the effects of living under monarchy had been far more explicitly republican in tone. He had suggested – as had Tacitus – that kings as well as tyrants can be relied upon to be actively envious of their most talented subjects. As a result, such subjects will find it far too dangerous to reveal or cultivate the qualities required for performing deeds of greatness or renown. Before the outbreak of the civil war we encounter no hint of this further suggestion, even in so radical a critic of the monarchy as Henry Parker. After the regicide, however, the argument suddenly became thinkable, with Milton coming forward as one of the earliest writers to apply it in defence of the commonwealth.

Milton instantly refers us at the start of *The Tenure of Kings and Magistrates* to Sallust's statement of the case.[80] The opening paragraph of the *Tenure* echoes the key passage from *Bellum Catilinae* so closely as to amount almost to a translation of it:

Tyrants are not oft offended, nor stand much in doubt of bad men, as being all naturally servile; but in whom vertue and true worth most is eminent, them they feare in earnest, as by right thir Maisters, against them lies all thir hatred and suspicion.[81]

If we turn to *Eikonoklastes*, we find the same passage from Sallust quoted on the title-page, and a further paraphrase in the chapter describing Charles I's alleged hatred of those who dared to question his misgovernment:

That trust which the Parliament faithfully discharg'd in the asserting of our Liberties, he calls *another artifice to withdraw the people from him, to their designes*. What piece of Justice could they have demanded for the people, which the jealousie of a King might not have miscall'd, a designe to disparage his Goverment, and to

---

[79] Milton 1959, pp. 537–8.
[80] On Sallust's influence on Milton at this period see Armitage 1995, esp. pp. 209–14. On Sallust's general presence in the political writings of the 1650s see Armitage 2000, pp. 132–9.
[81] Milton 1991, p. 3.

ingratiat themselves?[82] To be more just, religious, wise, or magnanimous then the common sort, stirrs up in a Tyrant both feare and envy; and streight he cries out popularitie, which in his account is little less then Treason.[83]

Milton is now prepared to go at least as far as his classical authorities in suggesting that kings may be no different from tyrants in their envy of the qualities that contribute to civic greatness.

Sallust and Tacitus had gone on to suggest that, because the civic virtues will effectively be proscribed under tyrannies, those living under such regimes will eventually be reduced to torpor and servility. Here too Milton not only invokes their arguments but turns them against the rule of kings as well as tyrants. Tacitus had opened his *Annals* with an especially melancholy statement of the case, and Milton duly quotes it against Salmasius in chapter 5 of his *Defensio*:

After the victory of Actium, the condition of the commonwealth was turned upside down. Nothing in the way of ancient or upright manners anywhere remained. With civic equality laid aside, everyone instead began to follow the commands of the prince.[84]

For Milton no less than Tacitus, the moral is that the imposition of slavery invariably breeds servility and slavishness.

We find this insight further developed when Milton turns in *Eikonoklastes* to consider the behaviour of his fellow-citizens under the yoke of Charles I. He is shocked by the extent to which, habituated to a life of servitude, they showed themselves ready to 'choose rather to be the Slaves and Vassals of his will, then to stand against him, as men by nature free'.[85] He is even more shocked by the slavish attitudes they revealed at the moment of their liberation, a weakness he denounces in one of his fiercest bursts of invective:

But now, with a besotted and degenerate baseness of spirit, except some few, who yet retain in them the old English fortitude and love of Freedom, and have testifi'd it by thir matchless deeds, the rest, imbastardiz'd from the ancient nobleness of thir Ancestors, are ready to fall flatt and give adoration to the Image and Memory of this Man, who hath offer'd at more cunning fetches to undermine our Liberties, and putt Tyranny into an Art, then any British King before him.[86]

---

[82] For the figure of speech (paradiastole) against which Milton is here complaining, see above, chapter 10 section III.
[83] Milton 1962, p. 501.
[84] Milton 1932, p. 318, quoting Tacitus *Annals* I. IV: '*Post Actiacam victoriam, verso civitatis statu, "nihil usquam prisci aut integri moris; omnes exuta aequalitate iussa principis aspectare"*.'
[85] Milton 1962, p. 543. [86] Milton 1962, p. 344.

Milton's deepest anxiety is that, rendered abject and ignoble by the tyranny of the Stuarts, the people may no longer be able to summon the qualities needed to take advantage of their new-found liberty.

Fearing and despising the multitude,[87] Milton remained haunted by the thought that, even after their triumph over Charles's tyranny, they might still fall back into accepting the rule of kings. He exhorts them at the end of *Eikonoklastes* to see that this would be a shamefully servile as well as a self-destructive act. They would 'shew themselves to be by nature slaves, and arrant beasts; not fitt for that liberty which they cri'd out and bellow'd for'.[88] Little more than a year later, however, he makes it clear in the *Defensio* that this is precisely the outcome he fears:

> Any form of slavery is shameful to a freeborn man; but for you, after recovering your freedom with God as your champion and through your own prowess, and after so many brave exploits, and after making such a memorable example of such a powerful King, to wish to return again to slavery, contrary to your destiny, will not only be the height of shamefulness, but will also be both impious and wicked.[89]

While inveighing against the return of kingship, Milton already seems almost to be predicting it.

Milton's deepest fears were of course fully realised. His final blueprint for a republican government in *The Ready and Easy Way to Establish a Free Commonwealth* appeared in April 1660 while preparations were already under way to welcome the returning Charles II. Throughout *The Ready and Easy Way*, his last political tract, Milton expresses a burning rage against 'the inconsiderate multitude' who now seem 'madd upon' returning to kingship[90] and 'thir once abjur'd and detested thraldom'.[91] He professes himself incredulous as well as horrified. Accepting the rule of a king, he is now prepared unequivocally to assert, is strictly equivalent to deciding to enslave oneself. The people are agreeing to become 'the slaves of a single person', to 'change thir noble words and actions, heretofore so becoming the majesty of a free people, into the base necessitie of court flatteries and prostrations'.[92] Still echoing his classical authorities, he points once more to the self-defeating consequences:

---

[87] On Milton's 'aristocratic' bias see Fixler 1964, pp. 163–71 and Sanderson 1989, pp. 138–41.
[88] Milton 1962, pp. 581, 601.
[89] Milton 1932, p. 542: 'Et servitus quidem omni homini ingenuo turpis est; vobis autem post libertatem Deo vindice, vestroque marte recuperatam, post tot fortia facinora, et exemplum in Regem potentissimum tam memorabile editum, velle rursus ad servitutem, etiam praeter fatum, redire, non modo turpissimum, sed et impium erit et sceleratum.'
[90] Milton 1980, p. 446.   [91] Milton 1980, p. 422.   [92] Milton 1980, pp. 428, 448.

After ten or twelve years prosperous warr and contestation with tyrannie, basely and besottedly to run their necks again into the yoke which they have broken, and prostrate all the fruits of thir victorie for naught at the feet of the vanquished, besides our loss of glorie, and such an example as kings or tyrants never yet had the like to boast of, will be an ignomine if it befall us, that never yet befell any nation possessd of thir libertie; worthie indeed themselves, whatsoever they be, to be for ever slaves.[93]

Once again Milton echoes Sallust's warning that, in the absence of freedom, there will be no hope of attaining civic glory and greatness.

The Roman historians had entertained one further and yet more tragic thought about the effects of living in servitude. Provided that our loss of liberty is accompanied by a life of ease, they had argued, we may fall into such a state of corruption that we may cease even to wish for the more strenuous life of freedom and greatness. Sallust reports that Catiline taunted the people of Rome by declaring that they would fail to follow him only if 'your spirits bee so basely dejected, that you had rather live in subjection, then command with Honour'.[94] Following Sallust's lead as so often, Tacitus enlarges on the danger when discussing the conquest of Gaul and England in his *Agricola*. As Savile's translation puts it, 'the French also were once, as we reade, redoubted in warre, till such time as giving themselves over to peace and idlenesse cowardice crept in, and shipwracke was made both of manhood and liberty togither'.[95] As for the English, Tacitus adds that under the thumb of the Romans 'by little and little they proceeded to those provocations of vices' which 'the ignorant termed civilitie' but which were in truth nothing more than 'a point of their bondage'.[96] Still more shameful, Tacitus declares at the start of his *Annals*, is the fact that the Roman nobility behaved in no less craven a fashion after Augustus ended the civil wars and took all power into his hands. This revolution was effected, in the words of Grenewey's translation, 'without contradiction of any: the stowtest by war or proscriptions alreadie spent. And the rest of the nobilitie, by how much the more serviceable, by so much the more bettered in wealth, and advanced in honors.'[97]

In his political tracts Milton has nothing explicit to say about this worst betrayal of the birthright of freedom. But after the restoration of Charles II in 1660, and especially after the re-entrenchment of a base and servile Court, he became deeply preoccupied by the theme. He speaks of it with anguish in *Samson Agonistes*, which first appeared in 1671, especially

[93] Milton 1980, p. 428.   [94] Sallust 1608, first pagination, p. 20.
[95] Tacitus 1591, p. 243.   [96] Tacitus 1591, p. 250.   [97] Tacitus 1598, p. 1.

at the moment when the enslaved Samson meditates on Judah's failure to take part in a fight for deliverance:

> Had Judah that day joined, or one whole tribe,
> They had by this possessed the towers of Gath,
> And lorded over them whom now they serve;
> But what more oft in nations grown corrupt,
> And by their vices brought to servitude,
> Than to love bondage more than liberty,
> Bondage with ease than strenuous liberty... [98]

Despite the Biblical setting, it is hard not to feel that Milton is here offering his last and bitterest reflection on the failure of the good old cause.

---

[98] Milton 1998, lines 265–71, p. 472.

12

Classical liberty, Renaissance translation and the English civil war

I

Shortly after the publication of Hobbes's *Leviathan* in the spring of 1651, Benjamin Worsley received a letter from his friend William Rand expressing strong agreement with one important element in Hobbes's argument. 'I am of opinion & have long bin with Mr Hobbs,' Rand wrote, 'that the reading of such bookes as Livy's History has bin a great rub in the way of the advancement of the Interest of his Leviathanlike Monarchs.'[1] Hobbes's judgement to this effect had been delivered in chapter 21 of *Leviathan*, in which he had presented it in the form of a cautionary tale about the origins of the English civil war:

> It is an easy thing, for men to be deceived, by the specious name of Libertie; ... And when the same errour is confirmed by the authority of men in reputation for their writings in this subject, it is no wonder if it produce sedition, and change of Government. In these westerne parts of the world, we are made to receive our opinions concerning the Institution, and Rights of Common-wealths, from *Aristotle, Cicero*, and other men, Greeks and Romanes, ... And by reading of these Greek, and Latine Authors, men from their childhood have gotten a habit (under a false shew of Liberty,) of favouring tumults, and of licentious controlling the actions of their Soveraigns; and again of controlling those controllers, with the effusion of so much blood; as I think I may truly say, there was never any thing so deerly bought, as these Western parts have bought the learning of the Greek and Latine tongues.[2]

No modern historian has to my knowledge placed anything like this degree of emphasis on the role of the classics, and especially the Latin classics, in helping to legitimise (and hence to bring about) the outbreak of the English civil war in 1642. Like William Rand, however, I have come to see that there is a great deal to be said for Hobbes's

---

[1] Rand to Worsley, 11 August 1651, Hartlib Papers (Sheffield) 62/21/2A. On Rand see Webster 1975, p. 301.
[2] Hobbes 1996, pp. 149–50.

explanation, and my principal aim in what follows will be to examine and assess it.

II

It is not hard to see why Hobbes's explanation has come to be so completely discounted. Recent historians have insisted on treating the debates about the liberties of subjects prior to the civil war as if they were couched entirely in the language of common law.[3] As I began to argue in chapter 11, however, this interpretation overlooks the presence in these debates of a strongly contrasting thesis about fundamental liberties.[4] If the crown, according to this rival analysis, possesses any discretionary powers capable of undermining such liberties, what we have to say is not that they are thereby left in a state of jeopardy as Sir Edward Coke and his associates maintained. What we have to say is that we do not possess any such liberties, since the very existence of such prerogatives reduces us below the level of free subjects.

It is true that some common lawyers included one element of this argument in their criticisms of the prerogative. According to common law theories of land tenure, one way in which a subject may lack the status of a free man is if his property is held not in fee simple but at the discretion of a lord. To be a free man requires, in other words, that you be a 'freeman', not a mere villein 'appendant' to a manor or place. The distinction can already be found in Henry de Bracton's *De Legibus et Consuetudinibus Angliae*,[5] and it is significant that, after its initial printing in 1569, Bracton's treatise was next republished in 1640.[6] During the early decades of the seventeenth century, however, the most widely cited discussion of villeinage was that of Sir Thomas Littleton in his fifteenth-century treatise, *Un lyver de exposicion de parcell de les tenures*.[7] Littleton's analysis, which seems to have attained a broad readership after it was translated into English in 1600, is founded on a sharp contrast between 'a free man' and a 'villein to another'.[8] A villein is not a slave, since it is

---

[3] See, for example, Burgess 1992 and Cromartie 1999.
[4] For a survey of debates in Parliament under the early Stuarts see Smith 1999, pp. 101–21.
[5] See Bracton 1640, I. VI. 4, fos. 4^v–5^r for the distinctions between *servus*, *villanus* and *liber homo*. Bracton's discussion is treated as authoritative by John Cowell in his pioneering law dictionary of 1607. See Cowell 1607, Sig. YYY, 4^r.
[6] See Bracton 1640.
[7] This is the heading in Cambridge University Library MS Mm. v. 2, fo. 2^r, the earliest extant manuscript of Littleton's treatise.
[8] [Littleton] 1600, II, 10, fo. 37^v.

only his property, not his person, which is *sub potestate domini*.⁹ But a villein is less than a free subject, since his property is held 'at the will of his lord', so that if the lord 'commeth within the house of the villeine where such goods be, & there openly among the neighbours claime the same goods to be his', then 'this is said a good seisin in the law'.¹⁰ The same distinction was repeated by Sir Thomas Smith in his *De Republica Anglorum* of 1583, although Smith adds the important rider that, while the law continues to recognise the category of 'appendantes of the manor or place', the fact is that 'so fewe there be, that it is not almost worth the speaking'.¹¹

These distinctions were picked up in the early Stuart Parliaments by a number of common lawyers as part of their assault on the alleged prerogative right to impose taxes without consent.¹² This prerogative first came under heavy fire in the Parliaments of 1610 and 1614, mainly in consequence of the crown's prosecution of the London merchant John Bate in 1606.¹³ When the Levant Company, which had been trading with Venice in currants, was forced to surrender its monopolistic charter, the crown recouped its losses by imposing a custom on the import of these foodstuffs. John Bate refused to pay and was sued in the Court of Exchequer. Giving judgement in favour of the crown, the Exchequer Barons ruled that the king had an 'absolute' power to levy such impositions in the name of the common good.¹⁴ They thereby touched off an explosion in the Parliament of 1610 – which continued to reverberate in 1614 – over whether the royal prerogative lawfully extended to 'imposing' on profits or property.¹⁵

It was in relation to this question that a number of common lawyers appealed to the distinction between villeins and free subjects.¹⁶ To defend prerogative taxes, they argued, is to presuppose that our money and goods can rightfully be taken from us at the will of the king. But this is to imply that our relationship to the king is that of a villein to his lord, and

---

⁹ This phrase, echoing the *Digest*, already occurs in Bracton 1640, I. VI. 4, fo. 4ᵛ.
¹⁰ [Littleton] 1600, II, 10, fo. 38ʳ.
¹¹ Smith 1982, p. 136. Smith's discussion is cited in Cowell 1607, Sig. YYY, 3ᵛ.
¹² See Holmes 1992, pp. 129–37 on the crown's efforts to exploit this prerogative during this period. For a survey of James I's relations with his Parliaments see Smith 1973.
¹³ See Smith 1999, pp. 53–4 for details about Bate's case and cf. Peck 1993, pp. 91–4 for the general issue.
¹⁴ See the judgement of Chief Baron Fleming in *Constitutional Documents of the Reign of James I*, pp. 340–5. Burgess 1996, pp. 80–6 claims that such 'absolute' power was still subject to legal constraint, but Sommerville 1999, pp. 140–2, 150–1, 247–8 convincingly reaffirms that 'absolute' power was by definition *solutus*, free of law.
¹⁵ For the debates on this issue in 1610 and 1614 see Smith 1999, pp. 106–8.
¹⁶ For analogous arguments about the status of foreigners (neither slaves nor citizens) see Kim 2000, pp. 1–15.

is thus to undermine our status as free subjects. Sir Thomas Hedley put the case in his great speech to the Commons of June 1610:[17]

But now in point of profit or property of lands and goods, there is a great difference between the king's free subjects and his bondmen; for the king may by commission at his pleasure seize the lands or goods of his *villani*, but so can he not of his free subjects. And therefore, 22 *Assisarum*, such commissions are adjudged void and against the law, for the lands or goods of a freeman cannot be taken from him without his consent.[18]

The lawyers and their associates continued to hammer away at the point in the Parliament of 1614. Sir Edwin Sandys declared that 'this liberty of imposing' must be agreed 'to trench to the foundation of all our interests', because it 'makes us bondmen, gives use but no propriety'.[19] Referring explicitly to the law of tenures, William Jones reinforced the argument. 'Tenants in ancient demesne' are 'but the King's villeins', and the effect of impositions is to reduce free subjects to the same servile state.[20] Later in the session the moral was yet more succinctly drawn by Sir Dudley Digges: 'Impositions imply villeinage.'[21]

During the 1620s, still urgently in need of funds, the government resolved to impose a Forced Loan, authorising the lord lieutenants to employ their own agents to collect the tax.[22] This policy not only prompted a renewed attack on non-parliamentary levies in the Parliament of 1628, but caused the policy to be singled out in the Petition of Right as one of the principal misuses of the royal prerogative. 'Your subjects' as the Petition complained, 'have inherited this freedom, that they should not be compelled to contribute to any tax, tallage, aid, or other like charge, not set by common consent in Parliament.' But in spite of this right, 'divers other charges have been laid and levied upon your people in several counties by Lord Lieutenants' in violation of 'the laws and free customs of this realm'.[23]

Leading this further battle against the crown, Sir Edward Coke reverted to the claim that to defend such prerogatives is to presuppose that the relationship between the king and his subjects is that of villeins to

---

[17] On the common law features of this speech see Pocock 1987, pp. 270–7; on its more classical elements see Peltonen 1995, pp. 220–8.
[18] *Proceedings in Parliament 1610*, vol. 2, p. 192.
[19] *Proceedings in Parliament 1614*, p. 147, quoted in Sommerville 1999, p. 144.
[20] *Proceedings in Parliament 1614*, p. 311.
[21] *Proceedings in Parliament 1610*, vol. 2, p. 419. On Digges, Sandys and their antagonism in the 1614 Parliament see Moir 1958, pp. 19, 59–60, 159–60; Raab 1998, pp. 176–92.
[22] For details see Cust 1987. One of these agents was Thomas Hobbes. See Skinner 1996, pp. 224, 229.
[23] *Constitutional Documents 1625–1660*, p. 67.

their lord. By 1628 Coke had published the first volume of his *Institutes of the Lawes of England*, in which he had reprinted Littleton's treatise on tenures together with a translation and a commentary.[24] Speaking in the Parliament of 1628, Coke leant heavily on Littleton's authority. 'While it is true of "villeins *in nativo habendo*" ', he explained, that 'their lord may tax them high or low', such taxation 'is against the franchise of the land for freemen'. To possess such a franchise is to possess liberty in respect of the disposal of land, and no freeman may legally be 'put out of his liberty or franchise'. It follows that 'no benevolence nor aid shall be but by assent of the realm', for to impose such a tax is to reduce free subjects to villeinage.[25]

III

During the same period, we begin to encounter a much more far-reaching criticism of the royal prerogative on the grounds of its incompatibility with individual liberty. This further attack was grounded not on common law conceptions of villeinage but on classical and especially Roman law distinctions between free citizens and slaves.[26] As I began by noting, one reason for emphasising this further argument is that the constitutional debates of this period have too readily been treated as if they were couched entirely in the language of common law.[27] A further reason is that, insofar as Roman law arguments have been detected in these early Stuart debates, they have usually been associated with the defence of the allegedly absolute powers of the crown.[28] As we shall see, however, the most radical arguments in favour of the liberty of subjects were largely taken from the legal and political writers of ancient Rome.[29]

---

[24] See Coke 1628, *sub* 'Villenage', ch. 11, sects. 172–212, fos. 116^r–141^v.

[25] *Commons Debates 1628*, vol. 2, p. 64.

[26] For the idea that liberty should be contrasted not with coercion but with enslavement see Pettit 1999, esp. pp. 17–41, 51–73, an analysis to which I am greatly indebted. See also the valuable discussion in Ivison 1997, pp. 24–52.

[27] A point made against G. R. Elton, Conrad Russell and their admirers in Sommerville 1996a and Sommerville 1996b. The assumption nevertheless persists, and underlies much of the argument of Burgess 1996 and Cromartie 1999.

[28] It used to be generally agreed that Roman law mainly served as a prop to absolutism. See for example Mosse 1950 and Simon 1968, p. 267, claiming that the study of the *Corpus Juris* 'put the civil lawyers in the royalist camp'. More recently, thanks largely to Levack 1973, it has been recognised that the situation was more complicated. See, for example, Burgess 1992, pp. 121–30 and Burgess 1996, pp. 63–90. But even Levack 1973, p. 88 and Burgess 1996, pp. 75, 78 still appear to assume a basic consonance between Roman law and royalist thought.

[29] For valuable surveys of Roman *libertas* and its revival in early-modern English political theory see Sellers 1994, pp. 69–98; Sellers 1998, pp. 7–11, 17–22; and the important analysis in Peltonen 1995.

To this extent, Hobbes's account in *Leviathan* of the ideological resources on which the parliamentarians drew in 1642 is much closer to the mark than has generally been recognised.

As we saw in chapter 11, we find the Roman law distinction between free citizens and slaves laid out most systematically under the rubric *De statu hominis* at the start of Justinian's *Digest*. There we learn that slavery can be defined as 'an institution of the *ius gentium* by which someone is, contrary to nature, subjected to the dominion of someone else'.[30] This in turn is said to yield a definition of individual liberty. If everyone in a civil association is either bond or free, then a *civis* or free subject must be someone who is not under the dominion of anyone else, but is *sui iuris*, capable of acting in their own right.[31] It likewise follows that what it means for someone to lack the status of a free subject must be for that person not to be *sui iuris* but instead to be *sub potestate*, under the power or subject to the will of someone else.[32]

While this understanding of civil liberty received its definitive articulation in the *Digest*, we already encounter it at a much earlier date among the historians and philosophers of ancient Rome, and especially in the writings of Cicero, Sallust, Livy and Tacitus.[33] Anyone in early seventeenth-century England who had received a university education would have been required to study these texts in their original Latin,[34] but it is worth recalling that it was in this period that all these writers were made available in English for the first time. Nicholas Grimalde's translation of Cicero's *De Officiis* was issued as early as 1556,[35] but it only became a best-seller when it appeared in a dual-language version in 1558, after which it went through at least five editions before the end of the century.[36] Meanwhile Henry Savile's translation of Tacitus's *Historiae* and *Agricola* had been published in 1591, with Richard Grenewey's versions of the *Annals* and *Germania* following in 1598.[37] Two years later Philemon Holland issued his enormous folio containing

---

[30] *Digest* 1985, I. V. 4. 35, vol. 1, p. 15: 'Servitus est constitutio iuris gentium, qua quis dominio alieno contra naturam subicitur.'
[31] *Digest* 1985, I. VI. 1. 36, vol. 1, p. 17: 'Some persons are in their own power, some are subject to the power of others, such as slaves, who are in the power of their masters.' ['quaedam personae sui iuris sunt, quaedam alieno iuri subiectae sunt... in potestate sunt servi dominorum...']
[32] Wirszubski 1950, pp. 1–3.   [33] Wirszubski 1950, pp. 9–15.   [34] Feingold 1997, pp. 246–56.
[35] See Cicero 1556. See also Cicero 1534, a much freer translation of *De Officiis* issued by Robert Whytinton and reprinted in 1540.
[36] See Cicero 1558 and cf. Conley 1927, p. 19n, who notes that the dual-language version was reprinted in 1568, 1575, 1583, 1596 and perhaps 1600.
[37] See Tacitus 1591 and Tacitus 1598 and cf. Peltonen 1995, pp. 124–35 on these translations and their influence.

the whole of the extant books of Livy's *History*,[38] while in 1608 Thomas Heywood published his translations of Sallust's *Bellum Catilinae* and *Bellum Iugurthinum*.[39] The themes of Livy's *History* became even better known when Edmund Bolton published his translation of Florus's *Roman Histories* in 1618 (with further editions in 1621 and 1636), thereby putting into circulation an epitome heavily reliant on Livy's text.[40]

Among these writers it is Cicero who is most interested in formal definitions of *libertas* and *servitus*, freedom and servitude. The fear of enslavement figures as a running theme of his speeches denouncing Marcus Antonius as a public enemy of Rome's traditional *civitas libera* or free state.[41] These so-called *Philippics* became one of the most popular of Cicero's works in the early-modern period, with a dozen or more editions appearing by the middle of the sixteenth century.[42] Cicero repeatedly exhorts the Roman people to reassert the *libertas* they forfeited when they fell under the domination of Julius Caesar, and violently denounces Antonius for aspiring to reduce his fellow citizens to a renewed condition of slavery. Not only does Cicero organise his argument around the contrast between freedom and servitude, but he emphasises that the loss of liberty suffered by slaves is not merely or even basically a matter of being oppressed or coerced. He makes the point most explicitly in a passage from the eighth philippic that became a key text for defenders of the English commonwealth after the abolition of the monarchy in 1649:[43]

Do you call servitude peace? Our ancestors took up arms not only to be free, but also to win power. You think that our arms should now be thrown away in order that we should become slaves. But what cause of waging war can be more just than that of repudiating slavery? For the most miserable feature of this condition is that, even if the master happens not to be oppressive, he can be so should he wish.[44]

---

[38] See Livy 1600; on Holland's translation see Matthiessen 1931, pp. 182–216 and Peltonen 1995, pp. 135–6.
[39] Sallust 1608. But as Conley 1927, pp. 37, 136 notes, Sallust's *Bellum Iugurthinum* had already been translated by Alexander Barclay in c.1520.
[40] Florus 1618.
[41] Cicero 1926, III. VI. 14, p. 202 formally brands Antonius a public enemy of the commonwealth.
[42] Information from British Library catalogue.
[43] See, for example, Milton 1932, p. 96: 'Audi igitur verba Ciceronis in 4 [*recte* 8] Philip. *Quae causa justior est belli gerendi, quam servitutis depulsio? In qua etiamsi non sit molestus dominus, tamen est miserrimum posse si velit*.'
[44] Cicero 1926, VIII. IV. 12, p. 374: 'servitutem pacem vocas? Maiores quidem nostri, non modo ut liberi essent, sed etiam ut imperarent, arma capiebant; tu arma abicienda censes, ut serviamus. Quae causa justior est belli gerendi, quam servitutis depulsio? in qua etiamsi non sit molestus dominus, tamen est miserrimum posse, si velit.'

As Cicero's closing remark makes clear, to possess *de facto* freedom of action is not necessarily to enjoy personal or political liberty. If your freedom is held at the discretion of anyone else, such that you continue to be subject to their will, then you remain a slave. To enjoy your liberty, in other words, it is not sufficient to be free from coercion or the threat of it; it is also necessary to be free from the possibility of being threatened or coerced.

Cicero was at least as much interested in his *Philippics* in the contrasting ideal of the *civitas libera* or free state, but for the best-known statement of his views about the meaning of civil or public liberty we must turn to his *De Officiis*. We learn in Book 2 that, as Grimalde's translation puts it, 'libertie be all to shaken' when 'the lawes bee sounke by some mans might' and citizens are made to depend on the will of a ruler instead of on the rule of law.[45] By contrast, as Cicero had already laid down in Book 1, free men can be defined as those who are not dependent on anyone else, but are able 'to use their owne libertie: whose propertie is, to lyve as ye list'.[46] Summarising in Book 3, Cicero left his early-modern readers to ponder an almost treasonably anti-monarchical inference. Anyone desiring to be a king 'alloweth the overthrow of law, and libertie', so that 'it is not honest to raign as king in that citie, which both hath been & ought to be free'.[47]

Cicero's analysis is very obviously indebted to Aristotle's discussion of freedom and tyranny in *Politics*, and it is a further striking fact that Aristotle's text likewise became available in English for the first time at the end of the sixteenth century. Louis le Roy's French translation was turned into English in 1598, and in this version we are told that kingship degenerates into an enslaving form of tyranny whenever a king 'dooth absolutely commaund and raigne over such as are equall, and all that are better; respecting his owne, and not the subjects profit, and therefore is not voluntarie: for no person that is free dooth willingly endure such a state'.[48] Later we are given an account of the 'tokens' of political liberty – an account that Cicero follows almost word for word. According to Aristotle, 'obeying and governing by turns, is one token of libertie', so that we may say that 'the end and foundation of the popular state, is Libertie'. To which he adds that 'another token of libertie is, to live as men list', since 'the propertie of bondage is, not to live according to a man's own discretion'.[49]

---

[45] Cicero 1558, fo. 81ʳ. Grimalde is here translating II. VII. 24.
[46] Cicero 1558, fo. 31ʳ. Grimalde is here translating I. XX. 70.
[47] Cicero 1558, fo. 149ʳ. Grimalde is here translating III. XXI. 83.
[48] Aristotle 1598, IV. X, p. 208.   [49] Aristotle 1598, VI. II, pp. 339–40.

Besides drawing on Aristotle, Cicero refers at several points in *De Officiis* to the Law of the Twelve Tables, which he takes to be the earliest legal code established in the *civitas libera* after the expulsion of the kings from Rome.[50] Cicero alludes to the Twelve Tables again in his *De Legibus*, in Book 3 of which he outlines an ideal constitution for a free state and proceeds to enunciate two golden rules. 'When giving laws to free peoples', he reminds us once again, we must first ensure that they are never dominated by the wills of their magistrates.[51] We must ensure that they are entirely ruled by laws, so that 'just as the magistrates govern the people, so the laws govern the magistrates'.[52] The other golden rule is said to be the one explicitly stated in the Twelve Tables, according to which the highest duty of magistrates is encapsulated in the maxim *salus populi suprema lex esto*, 'the safety of the people must be treated as the supreme law'.[53]

The Roman historians were less interested than Cicero in formal definitions of freedom and servitude, but they thought about these concepts in very similar terms. Sallust at the start of his *Bellum Catilinae* describes how the rule of the early kings degenerated into *dominatio* and thereby enslaved the Roman people.[54] But the people managed – in the words of Heywood's translation – to turn this slavery under 'the Government of one' into a 'forme of limited pollicy', thereby establishing 'this form of Liberty in Government'.[55] Tacitus in his *Annals* provides a contrasting description of how the Roman people were forced back into slavery under the early principate, and likewise equates their loss of liberty with the re-imposition of arbitrary will as the basis of government.[56] As Grenewey's translation puts it, after the ascendancy of Augustus 'there was no signe of the olde laudable customes to be seene: but contrarie, equalitie taken away, every man endevored to obey the prince', so that 'the Consuls, the Senators, and Gentlemen ranne headlong into servitude'.[57] Tacitus admits that some later emperors liked to invoke the traditional *praecepta* of the free state, as when Vitellius adjured Meherdates before the Senate 'that he should not thinke himselfe a Lord and maister to commaund over his subjects as slaves; but a guide, and they citizens'.[58] But as Tacitus's tone continually makes clear, he regards such rhetorical flights

---

[50] Cicero 1913, I. XII. 37, p. 40 and III. XXXI. 111, p. 390.
[51] Cicero 1928, III. II. 4, p. 460: 'nos autem, quoniam leges damus liberis populis...'
[52] Cicero 1928, III. I. 2, p. 460: 'ut enim magistratibus leges, ita populo praesunt magistratus'.
[53] Cicero 1928, III. III. 8, p. 466.   [54] Sallust 1931a, VI–VII, pp. 10–14.
[55] Sallust 1608, p. 17 [*recte* p. 7].   [56] Tacitus 1925, I. I–III, pp. 2–8.
[57] Tacitus 1598, pp. 2–3.   [58] Tacitus 1598, p. 158.

as little better than a mockery of the liberty that the Roman people had lost.

In the opening Books of his *History* Livy offers a fuller account of both these processes. Book 2 begins with a much-cited account of the transition from the *dominatio* of the early kings to the liberty enjoyed by the Roman people under their 'free state'. Livy equates this transformation with the establishment of the rule of law and the consequent ending of any dependence on the discretion of the king.[59] Having expelled the Tarquins, the Romans established 'a free state now from this time forward'. 'Which freedom of theirs', as Holland's translation goes on, was due to the fact that 'the authoritie and rule of laws' was now 'more powerfull and mightie than that of men'.[60] Bolton's translation of Florus offers a more ingenuous account of the same pivotal episode:

It was agreed, that whereas the authority had before beene single, and perpetuall; it should bee now but from yeere to yeere, and bipartite, least either by singularitie, or continuance it should be corrupted: and for Kings they styled them Consuls, that they might remember *the dutie of their place was* to consult, and provide for their Countrey. Such joy was conceived for this new freedom, that they could hardly beleeve the change.[61]

Livy's analysis of this crucial transition concludes with an ironic account of how the slavery of the people and the licentious freedom of the king's courtiers were alike brought to an end. The courtiers 'made mone and complained one to another' that the king had been someone 'at whose hands one might obtain somewhat, as need required, were the cause right or were it wrong'. But 'as for laws, they are things deafe and inexorable: more holsome and commodious to the poore than to the rich and mightie'. The complaint of those 'seeking to enjoy the same licentious life' under the republic was thus that 'the libertie of others turned to their servitude'.[62]

Livy draws on this understanding of freedom and slavery in many later passages, but he illustrates the danger of falling back into servitude most fully in his account of the Decemvirate. The Tribunes initially called for the establishment of this magistracy on the grounds that the rule of the consuls was 'too absolute, and in a free state intolerable', since they were able to 'rule of themselves, and use their owne will and licentious lust in steede of law'.[63] But within a year of receiving special authority to reform the laws, the Decemvirs instead yielded to the malign influence

---

[59] Livy 1919, II. I, pp. 218–20 and II. III, pp. 226–8. [60] Livy 1600, p. 44.
[61] Florus 1618, pp. 33–4. [62] Livy 1600, p. 45. [63] Livy 1600, p. 87.

of their leader Appius Claudius and seized power for themselves. As a result, the people who in their reforming zeal had been 'gaping greedily after libertie' found themselves 'fallen and plunged into servitude and thraldome'.[64] This reversion to slavery, Livy repeats, occurred when they lost the protection of the laws and found themselves subjected once more to arbitrary power. 'The meaner persons went to the wals, and with them they dealt according to their lust and pleasure right cruelly. The person wholy they regarded, and never respected the cause, as with whom favour and friendship prevailed as much as equity and right should have done.'[65]

By contrast, Livy always defines the liberty of cities as well as citizens in terms of not living in subjection to the power or discretion of anyone else. When, for example, he describes the surrender of the Collatines to the people of Rome, he stresses that they were able to take this decision because they were 'in their owne power', and hence 'at libertie to doe what they will'.[66] The same view emerges yet more clearly from the much later passage in which he discusses the efforts of the Greek cities to restore their good relations with Rome. To be able to enter into such negotiations, one of their spokesmen is made to say, presupposes the possession of 'true libertie', the name of that condition in which a people 'is able to stand alone and maintain it selfe, and dependeth not upon the will and pleasure of others'.[67]

IV

By the time the English Parliament met in 1610, these observations by the Roman historians about 'free states' and the attendant dangers of enslavement had all been turned into works of English political thought. Carrying with them the unparalleled prestige accorded to the wisdom of antiquity, these works provided at the same time an explicitly anti-monarchical perspective from which the English could begin if they chose to reflect anew on their own political experiences.[68] As Hobbes rightly perceived, such reflections were almost certain in the end to have a destabilising impact on the Stuart monarchy. Those who felt threatened by the crown's understanding of its prerogatives now had available to them a way of thinking about their grievances in the light of which

---

[64] Livy 1600, p. 112. For a very similar account see Florus 1618, ch. 24, pp. 101–2.
[65] Livy 1600, p. 111.   [66] Livy 1600, p. 28.   [67] Livy 1600, p. 907.
[68] On the resulting capacity to imagine republics see Sanders 1998, pp. 11–33 and Norbrook 1999, pp. 34–62.

the crown's policies could easily be represented as nothing less than an aspiration to reduce a free people to servitude.[69]

Among those who began to view their predicament through the lens supplied by these classical arguments, it is possible to distinguish two main groups. It is remarkable in the first place to find how many common lawyers showed a readiness to argue at least partly in these neo-Roman terms. Historians have generally treated the common and Roman lawyers as opposed to each other, but many of the former drew freely on Roman sources when discussing the liberty of subjects. This is not to say that we encounter this syncretism among such leading common lawyers as John Selden or Sir Edward Coke. But when Selden argued in the Parliament of 1628 in favour of relying exclusively on common law, Sir Henry Marten appears to have spoken for many when he responded that 'the common law is the daughter, the civil law is the mother' and that there is no need 'to see such a strangeness between them'.[70]

The other group of critics who made prominent use of classical arguments were those whom Hobbes was later to stigmatise in *Behemoth* as the 'Democratical Gentlemen'.[71] Hobbes's characterisation is in one way misleading, for it gives the impression that the gentlemen in question were self-conscious exponents of a radical ideology designed to limit the powers of the crown. To read their speeches and pamphlets, however, is to be struck not by their radicalism but by their defensive and even reactionary outlook, by their bewilderment as well as outrage as they confronted what they took to be the crown's assault on their standing in the community, and above all by their determination to exploit any arguments tending to uphold their traditional privileges. Hobbes was undoubtedly right, however, to see that their characteristic reliance on classical arguments about liberty and servitude eventually pushed them into adopting a standpoint so radical as to be virtually republican in its constitutional allegiances.[72] Hobbes bitterly summarises the position into which they stumbled as a result of seeking to defend their interests by recklessly drawing on 'the books written by famous men of the

---

[69] The anxiety remained throughout the constitutional upheavals of the century. See Tully 1980, pp. 111–14, 135–46 on the fact that John Locke's reply to Sir Robert Filmer in his *Two Treatises* reiterates the claim that Filmer's views about property and political power have the effect of reducing free citizens to slaves.

[70] *Commons Debates 1628*, vol. 2, p. 568. As Levack 1973, pp. 117–21 stresses, although Marten was a civilian he came to agree with much of the common law case against the prerogative.

[71] St John's College Oxford, MS 13, p. 24; cf. Hobbes 1969a, p. 26.

[72] This perspective on the significance of the early Stuart Parliaments is beginning, rightly in my view, to be revived. See, for example, the excellent discussion in Rabb 1998, pp. 60–3 and references there.

ancient Grecian and Roman commonwealths'.[73] They found themselves committed to arguing that the very existence of discretionary powers was straightforwardly incompatible with individual liberty, and thus that 'all that lived under Monarchy were slaves'.[74]

The first prerogatives to be targeted in these neo-classical terms were those which subjected the goods of freemen to the discretion of the king. The earliest moment at which we find the authority of the ancient writers widely invoked is accordingly in the debates about Impositions in the Parliament of 1610. Defending the need for such a debate, Thomas Wentworth declared that, unless we are permitted to question this prerogative, then we might as well be sold for slaves.[75] Later he went on to object that, if we allow the prerogative 'of imposing, even upon our lands and goods', the effect will be to leave us 'at the mercy' of the king.[76] Sir Thomas Hedley agreed that such a prerogative places the property of free subjects 'in the absolute power and command of another'.[77] As their classical authorities had explained, however, to live at the mercy or under the absolute power of another is what it means to live in servitude. Hedley duly reminded the Commons that Cicero ('though an heathen yet a wise man') and Tacitus had both drawn exactly this distinction between freedom and servitude. Nor was Hedley willing to concede the usual common law claim that, even if our property is held at the discretion of the king, we are not strictly speaking lowered to the condition of slavery, since our personal liberty remains untouched. To have the power to take away our property, Hedley retorts, is to have the power to take away our means of sustenance, and is thus to have control over those things which 'are rightly called a man's living, for that without these, the natural life cannot be maintained'. The effect, therefore, of placing our lands and goods under the control of another 'is not so much to lose all a man's wealth as the power of holding it', and this is 'nothing else but bondage'.[78] Hedley already gestures at a definition that was later to become of absolutely central importance: that to speak of 'property' is not merely to speak of our estates but of our very being or 'substance', and is thus to speak of our lives and liberty as well.[79]

---

[73] St John's College Oxford, MS 13, p. 3; cf. Hobbes 1969a, p. 3.   [74] Hobbes 1996, p. 150.
[75] *Proceedings in Parliament 1610*, vol. 2, p. 83; cf. Sommerville 1999, p. 97.
[76] *Proceedings in Parliament 1610*, vol. 2, p. 108.   [77] *Proceedings in Parliament 1610*, vol. 2, p. 196.
[78] *Proceedings in Parliament 1610*, vol. 2, p. 194.
[79] Sir Edward Coke later picked up the point in the Parliament of 1628. See *Commons Debates 1628*, vol. 2, p. 64. For a parallel concern with the connections between the status of freeholder and the possession of civil liberty see Kupperman 1989, pp. 30–2.

During the next session of Parliament in 1614, Christopher Neville found himself imprisoned in the Tower for delivering what appears to have been a bravura indictment of Impositions in the same neo-classical style.[80] Neville's was one of several interventions stigmatised by the king as 'better becoming a Senate of Venice' than a civil body whose members bear 'the natural capacity of subjects'.[81] Neville's speech is known only by report, but it seems to have been a full-scale rhetorical oration in which (as Sir Henry Wotton somewhat drily observed) he 'gathered together divers Latin sentences against kings' and 'interlarded them with certain Ciceronian exclamations'.[82] According to a further report by Sir John Holles, Neville explictly drew at the same time on the analysis of liberty and slavery to be found in the *Digest* of Roman law. According to Holles, Neville not only 'shewed the miseries of the times and lamented them' but also 'shewed by the civil lawyers' definition the difference between free and bond men, in which state impositions had cast us'.[83]

The same arguments resurfaced in the protests against the Forced Loan in 1628.[84] Sir Francis Seymour declared that the right to demand such loans is incompatible with the security of property, and thus with the independence of subjects, for if the king 'is pleased to take what he thinks fit', then 'we do not know what we enjoy'.[85] Later in the session, a number of democratical gentlemen felt driven to express a more general anxiety about the impact of such prerogatives on the freedom of subjects. Sir John Scudamore ruminated on 'how often have I heard it that we could not fall to a resolution to supply his Majesty till we knew whether we were slaves or bondmen; that our vital liberties did in a manner want life'.[86] Speaking soon afterwards in the debate about the Petition of Right, Sir John Strangeways reaffirmed that such prerogatives undoubtedly serve to enslave, roundly concluding that 'the great work of this day, you know, is to free the subject'.[87] Speaking in a similar spirit, Sir John Eliot drew the attention of the Commons to Livy's account of how liberties come to be infringed, adding that Livy's explanation 'now reflects upon us'.[88] After the session of 1629, at the close of which Eliot was imprisoned in the Tower, he occupied himself by writing *The Monarchie of Man*, in

---

[80] Moir 1958, pp. 146–7.   [81] This reaction is reported in Wotton 1907, vol. 2, pp. 36–7.
[82] Wotton 1907, vol. 2, p. 38.   [83] Holles 1923, p. 138.
[84] For a full analysis of the 1628 debates see Russell 1979, pp. 323–89.
[85] *Commons Debates 1628*, vol. 2, p. 66. On Digges see Underdown 1996, p. 27; on Seymour's opposition see Smith 1994, pp. 45–7 and cf. pp. 60–3 for his subsequent adoption of a 'constitutionally royalist' position.
[86] *Commons Debates 1628*, vol. 3, p. 193.   [87] *Commons Debates 1628*, vol. 3, p. 214.
[88] *Commons Debates 1628*, vol. 2, p. 72.

which he continued to reflect on the same classical themes. Turning again to Livy, but above all to Tacitus – and quoting him in Grenewey's translation[89] – Eliot devoted the first half of his work to a learnedly neo-classical comparison between tyranny and true monarchy. As well as referring to the Roman historians, he made much use of Aristotle and Cicero, citing the latter as his chief authority for the view that, under monarchy as opposed to tyranny, 'nothing should be taken either of the goods or person of a subject without a judgement of the Senate (who are the makers of the Lawes), or of them who are constituted Judges'.[90]

During the same disputatious session of 1628, a further prerogative was similarly targeted on the grounds that it reduces free subjects to slavery. The power in question, explicitly denounced in the Petition of Right, was that of imprisoning suspects 'without any cause showed' if the king judged their imprisonment to be necessary for public security.[91] This issue had risen to renewed prominence in 1627 after a number of those arrested for refusing to pay the Forced Loan had been left in prison without trial.[92] As Edward Littleton argued at the Committee of Both Houses on 3 April 1628, the effect was to make what he described as 'personall libertye' dependent on the will of the king, so permitting the 'invasion' of the most fundamental freedom 'established & confirmed by the whole State'.[93] Such dependence, many of the democratical gentlemen went on to insist, is the clearest possible sign of thralldom and servitude. As Henry Sherfield summarised, 'if the King may imprison a freeman without a cause', then 'he is in worse case than a villein', for a villein at least enjoys personal liberty, whereas 'to be imprisoned without cause, that is a thraldom'.[94]

V

After the brief and stormy session of 1629,[95] Charles I summoned no further Parliaments until the need for revenue forced his hand in 1640. As soon as the Short Parliament assembled in April of that year, a renewed campaign was mounted on the royal prerogative, in the course

---

[89] For the reference to Grenewey see Eliot 1879, vol. 2, p. 47 and for other quotations from Tacitus see Eliot 1879, vol. 2, pp. 12, 15, 32, 37–8, 46, 57, 60, 62, 66.
[90] Eliot 1879, vol. 2, p. 49. Cf. Sommerville 1999, p. 147.
[91] *Constitutional Documents 1625–1660*, p. 67.   [92] Sommerville 1999, pp. 134, 153–8.
[93] Cambridge University Library MS Ii. 5. 32, fos. 218^{r-v}, 221^{v}.
[94] *Commons Debates 1628*, vol. 2, pp. 189, 208. See also *Commons Debates 1628*, vol. 2, p. 357 for the repetition of the point by Sir Edward Coke.
[95] See Smith 1999, pp. 118–19.

of which the classical arguments we have been considering were again brought to the fore. At first the king responded by ordering an immediate dissolution, but he quickly found that his worsening financial difficulties left him no such easy avenue of escape. A new Parliament was convened in November 1640, and in less than two years the renewed quarrelling led to civil war.

We need to distinguish two separate phases in this renewed attack on the prerogative mounted by the democratical gentlemen and their allies.[96] They began by reverting to what they took to be the crown's continuing disregard for the fundamental liberties of individual subjects, above all their personal freedom and property rights. When Sir John Holland spoke at the start of the Long Parliament about 'the great and manifold grievances of this kingdom', he principally emphasised the need for the Commons to preserve 'our *Rights*, our ancient *Rights*, the *Rights* of our Inheritances. Our *Liberties*, our *Priviledges*, our *Proprieties*'.[97] A few days later, Sir Edward Dering in his opening speech likewise reminded the Commons that every subject 'hath long prayed for this houre in hope to be relieved; and to know hereafter whether any thing hee hath (besides his poore part and portion of the common Ayre he breatheth) may be truly called his owne'.[98]

As things turned out, the question of personal liberty did not prove to be a major stumbling-block until the eve of the civil war. But the issue of property rights, and especially the question of how far the holding of property may be subject to the will of the king, became a focus of debate from the moment when Parliament first reassembled in the spring of 1640. The main reason for this renewed concern was that, in the course of the 1630s, the crown had extended its policy of raising non-parliamentary revenues, in particular by turning the Ship Money levy into what the government's critics regarded as a general tax. When in 1636 John Hampden declined to pay, the government reluctantly decided to turn his refusal into a test case.[99] Hampden was sued in the King's Bench in 1637, and in the following year a majority of the royal

---

[96] When quoting from official Declarations issued by the King and Parliament I basically rely on Husbands *et al.* 1643. However, I cross-reference to *Parliamentary History of England*, vol. 2, a less satisfactory but more readily available text.

[97] Holland 1640, p. 5. Thomason notes on the title-page of his copy (Thomason Tracts, British Library) that the speech was delivered on 7 November 1640.

[98] Dering 1640, p. 2. Thomason notes on the title-page of his copy that Dering delivered the speech 'before ye 23 November' 1640.

[99] The government would have preferred the case not to come to court, but the manoeuvrings of Lord Saye and Sele forced their hand.

justices returned the inflammatory verdict that in times of danger the king possessed the prerogative right to impose additional charges at will, and that the king himself must be 'sole judge both of the danger, and when and how the same is to be prevented and avoided'.[100]

When George Peard, a common lawyer, rose in the Short Parliament to speak against this judgement, he reverted to the argument earlier advanced by Sir Thomas Hedley to the effect that the imposing of non-parliamentary levies takes away 'not onely our goods but persons likewise', so reducing us from free subjects to slaves.[101] As we saw in chapter 11, however, the most powerful repudiation of the policy from the same neo-classical standpoint appeared in *The Case of Shipmony Briefly Discoursed*, a pamphlet anonymously issued by Henry Parker to coincide with the opening of the Long Parliament in November 1640.[102] Continuing to press the case, the Long Parliament itself went on to produce a general statement to the effect that we forfeit our freedom whenever our properties are made dependent on the will of the king. The occasion for this resolution was the dispute that arose in the opening months of 1642 over the decision by Parliament to take into its own hands the royal arsenal at Hull. When the governor, Sir John Hotham, closed the city gates against the king, Charles I reacted by accusing him of treason, arguing that as sovereign he possessed 'the same title to His Town of Hull, which any of His Subjects have to their Houses or Lands'.[103] The response of the two Houses – in their Remonstrance of 26 May 1642 – was to proclaim this view of the prerogative blankly inconsistent with the liberty of subjects. Picking up the claim that any threat to the property of freemen is at the same time a threat to their living and substance, Parliament went on to speak – in the litany later made famous by John Locke – of the inherent conflict between such prerogatives and our 'lives, Liberties and Estates'.[104] Kings are prone to believe 'that their Kingdoms are their own, and that they may do with them what they will'.[105] But this principle 'is the Root of all the Subjects misery, and of the invading of their just Rights and Liberties'. It undermines 'the very Foundation of the liberty, property and interest of every Subject in particular, and of

---

[100] *Constitutional Documents 1625–1660*, p. 109. Cf. Kenyon 1966, pp. 87–8. On Sir Robert Berkeley's judgement see Sommerville 1999, pp. 151–2.
[101] *Proceedings of the Short Parliament of 1640*, p. 172.
[102] Mendle 1995, pp. 32–50 gives an account of the precise political context in which Parker's tract appeared.
[103] Husbands *et al.* 1643, p. 266. Cf. *Parliamentary History of England*, vol. 2, col. 1300.
[104] Husbands *et al.* 1643, p. 264. Cf. *Parliamentary History of England*, vol. 2, col. 1298.
[105] Husbands *et al.* 1643, p. 266. Cf. *Parliamentary History of England*, vol. 2, col. 1301.

all the Subjects in generall'. To say that a king can dispose of these rights at will is to say that they are held by mere grace, which in turn is to say that we are not free subjects at all.[106]

The need to secure life, liberty and estates against such encroachments continued to be asserted throughout the period up to the start of the fighting in the autumn of 1642. During the opening months of that year, however, the democratical gentlemen and their allies suddenly shifted the focus of their attack. As we began to see in chapter 11, they turned to challenge in the name of popular liberty a power of the crown hitherto regarded as sacrosanct by all parties. The prerogative they began to question was that of the 'Negative Voice', the right of the king to give or withhold his assent to any proposed acts of legislation put to him by the two Houses of Parliament.

The democratical gentlemen plunged into this further phase of their campaign over the question of who should control the militia. After the outbreak of the Irish rebellion in October 1641, and after the king's abortive but violent attempt to arrest five members of Parliament in January 1642, the two Houses claimed to be anxious about their own security. Following their decision in January to take over the arsenal at Hull, they proceeded at the beginning of February to draw up a Militia Ordinance which they sent to the king for his assent. Protesting about 'the bloody counsels of Papists and other ill-affected persons', they proposed that 'for the safety therefore of His Majesty's person, the Parliament and kingdom at this time of imminent danger', the control of the militia should be vested exclusively in persons approved by the two Houses of Parliament. They went on to list their local nominees, granting them extensive powers to muster, train and arm the people 'for the suppression of all rebellions, insurrections and invasions that may happen'.[107]

As every good royalist knew, the control of the militia was one of the indisputable 'marks' of sovereignty listed by Jean Bodin in his *Six livres de la république*. Although Charles had hitherto accepted a number of bills limiting his prerogative, this further demand at first elicited from him and his advisers a stunned silence.[108] While the king temporised, however, Parliament made an astonishing move that wholly changed the

[106] Husbands *et al.* 1643, p. 266. Cf. *Parliamentary History of England*, vol. 2, col. 1300.
[107] *Constitutional Documents 1625–1660*, pp. 245–6 prints the Ordinance of 5 March, but notes that the same provisions already appear in the version sent for the royal assent on 16 February. Husbands *et al.* 1643, pp. 73–5 prints the list (12 February) of those whom Parliament proposed to entrust with the organisation of the militia.
[108] See Husbands *et al.* 1643, p. 80 for the king's initial response, in which he asks for more time 'to consider of a particular Answer for a matter of so great weight'.

terms of the debate. Voting the king's delay a direct denial,[109] the two Houses passed the Militia Ordinance on their own authority on 5 March 1642,[110] and ten days later pronounced it legally binding on the people notwithstanding its failure to secure the royal assent.[111]

'I am so much amazed', exclaimed the king (an unfortunate echo of Shakespeare's *Richard II*) 'that I know not what to Answer.'[112] As recently as December 1641 John Pym had explicitly conceded that the prerogative of the Negative Voice was a pillar of the constitution and beyond dispute, assuring the king that it rests 'only in his power, to pass or refuse the votes of Parliament'.[113] Less than three months later, we find the two Houses voting in effect to set this prerogative aside. The outcome was an instant crisis of legitimacy. How could Parliament possibly defend its decision to trample on such a fundamental and hitherto unquestioned flower of the crown?

The answer is that the principles in the light of which the two Houses justified their action were entirely drawn from the legal and moral philosophy of ancient Rome. The resulting campaign mounted by the democratical gentlemen and their allies may in turn be said to have moved forward in two distinct steps. They began by taking their stand squarely on the fundamental maxim that Cicero had cited from the Law of the Twelve Tables: that, in legislating for a free state, s*alus populi suprema lex esto*, the safety of the people must be treated as the supreme law. They maintained that the nation was at present in a state of dire emergency, and that the safety of the people would be further imperilled if the control of the militia were to be assigned to anyone other than the two Houses themselves. From this they inferred that they had a positive duty, in the name of *salus populi*, to take over the militia even in the absence of the king's assent.

But what exactly was the dire emergency that justified this revolutionary step? The democratical gentlemen evidently feared that, if the king controlled the militia, he might use it to crush their continuing dissent. But they could scarcely voice this anxiety without appearing to accuse the king of plotting against his own people, and they remained anxious

---

[109] *Parliamentary History of England*, vol. 2, col. 1108.
[110] *Constitutional Documents 1625–1660*, pp. 245–7.
[111] Husbands *et al.* 1643, p. 112. Cf. *Parliamentary History of England*, vol. 2, col. 1129.
[112] Husbands *et al.* 1643, p. 94. Cf. *Parliamentary History of England*, vol. 2, col. 1110. The alleged parallels with Richard II were explicitly pointed out in *The Life and Death of King Richard the Second, Who Was deposed of His Crown, by reason of His not regarding the Councell of the Sage and Wise of His Kingdome, but followed the advice of wicked and lewd Councell*, a parliamentary tract of July 1642.
[113] *Parliamentary History of England*, vol. 2, col. 1003.

at this juncture not merely to uphold the principle that the king can do no wrong,[114] but also to insist that they were still doing the king's (true) business.[115] As a result, they found themselves driven into arguing that, although the king was undoubtedly innocent of any designs against his subjects, he had nevertheless surrounded himself with a group of evil counsellors bent on subverting the Protestant religion and the privileges of Parliament. This, they insisted, was the dire emergency that made it essential for them to take control of the militia, thereby ensuring that *salus populi* was preserved and the kingdom protected from so terrible a threat.

The House of Commons first began to speak in these terms in the wake of Charles's attempt to arrest the five Members in January 1642. Denouncing this unparalleled assault on their privileges, they declared that anyone attempting to perpetrate any further violence would be branded 'a publike enemy of the Common-wealth'.[116] They clearly intended to recall the exact words used by Cicero in his third philippic to denounce Marcus Antonius's violence against the Senate and people of Rome. But they took a step too far in attempting to apply the vocabulary of Roman republicanism so directly to the English polity. Charles I was able to respond in his loftiest tones that, in describing his advisers as 'Enemies to the Common-wealth', the Commons had used 'an English phrase We scarcely understand'.[117]

Forced to reconsider their terminology, the two Houses began to speak instead of a malignant party whose leaders had seduced the innocent but misguided king. In their Petition of 1 March they assured the king that he stood in need of immediate protection against 'the most malignant enemies of Gods true Religion, and of the peace and safety of Your Selfe, and your Kingdom'.[118] Answering his subsequent refusal to pass the Militia Ordinance as a bill, they struck a yet more alarmist note. 'The heads of the Malignant party', they now maintained, believe that 'by new practices, both of force and subtilty' they can make a prey of 'the Religion and Liberty of this Kingdome'.[119] The people of England are facing a 'desperate and mischievous Plot of the malignant party',[120]

---

[114] For the continuing importance of this principle see Husbands *et al.* 1643, p. 199 and cf. *Parliamentary History of England*, vol. 2, col. 1253.
[115] As Kishlansky 1977 has shown, the Parliamentarians only gradually abandoned the claim that they were continuing to work in the best interests of a misguided king.
[116] Husbands *et al.* 1643, p. 39. Cf. *Parliamentary History of England*, vol. 2, col. 1043.
[117] Husbands *et al.* 1643, p. 177. Cf. *Parliamentary History of England*, vol. 2, col. 1246.
[118] Husbands *et al.* 1643, p. 93. Cf. *Parliamentary History of England*, vol. 2, col. 1109.
[119] Husbands *et al.* 1643, p. 195. Cf. *Parliamentary History of England*, vol. 2, col. 1250.
[120] Husbands *et al.* 1643, p. 214. Cf. *Parliamentary History of England*, vol. 2, col. 1268.

in consequence of which the kingdom is in 'eminent danger, both from enemies abroad, and a Popish and discontented partie at home'.[121]

It was hard for the two Houses to avoid a hint of paranoia as they strove to establish the gravity of the menace, and it proved correspondingly easy for Charles and his advisers to satirise their rhetoric. No doubt it is true, the king observed in his Answer to the Declaration of 19 May, that 'the rumour and discourse of Plots and Conspiracies may have bin necessary to the Designes of particular men'.[122] But the fact remains that, 'after eight Moneths amusing the Kingdom with the expectation of a discovery of a Malignant Party', the two Houses have still been unable to name a single member of it.[123] Charles's Answer to the Remonstrance of 26 May adopts a yet more sarcastic tone, ridiculing the view 'that Calamitie proceeds from evill Counsellors, whom no body can name; from Plots and Conspiracies, which no man can discover; and from Fears and Jealousies, which no man understands'.[124] 'The *Malignant Party*', the king goes on to suggest, appears to be nothing more than the name given by the refractory Commons to 'all the Members of both Houses, who agree not with them in their Opinion' about the prerogative.[125]

Among those who felt convinced, however, that a party of malignants was definitely at work, the constitutional solution proposed by the democratical gentlemen evidently carried much weight. As a result, we find the two Houses putting forward their solution with growing confidence in their numerous declarations about the militia in the spring of 1642. They invariably begin by alluding to *salus populi* as the most fundamental of all the fundamental laws of the land. The vote calling for the Militia Ordinance to be obeyed as a law speaks of 'the safeguard both of his Majestie, and his People' as paramount,[126] while the Petition of a week later repeats that none of their plans can 'bee perfected before the Kingdome be put into safetie, by setling the *Militia*'.[127] Summarising their grievances in the Declaration of 19 May, they repeat once more that the fundamental purpose of government is 'the safeguard both of his Majesty, and his people', the maintenance of 'the good and safetie of the whole'.[128]

---

[121] Husbands *et al.* 1643, p. 207. Cf. *Parliamentary History of England*, vol. 2, col. 1261. This passage from the Declaration of 19 May quotes the Vote of the two Houses of 15 March, on which see Husbands *et al.* 1643, p. 112 and *Parliamentary History of England*, vol. 2, col. 1129.
[122] Husbands *et al.* 1643, p. 241. Cf. *Parliamentary History of England*, vol. 2, col. 1282.
[123] Husbands *et al.* 1643, p. 247. Cf. *Parliamentary History of England*, vol. 2, col 1288.
[124] Husbands *et al.* 1643, p. 292. Cf. *Parliamentary History of England*, vol. 2, col. 1339.
[125] Husbands *et al.* 1643, p. 283. Cf. *Parliamentary History of England*, vol. 2, col. 1330.
[126] Husbands *et al.* 1643, p. 112. Cf. *Parliamentary History of England*, vol. 2, col. 1129.
[127] Husbands *et al.* 1643, p. 123. Cf. *Parliamentary History of England*, vol. 2, col. 1138.
[128] Husbands *et al.* 1643, p. 207. Cf. *Parliamentary History of England*, vol. 2, cols. 1261–2.

The upholding of *salus populi*, they concede, normally requires the two Houses to act in concert with the king. We still find this understanding of the mixed constitution unhesitatingly put forward even in the markedly hostile Declaration of 19 May:

> The Kingdome must not be without a meanes to preserve it selfe, which that it may be done without confusion, this Nation hath intrusted certaine hands with a Power to provide in an orderly and regular way, for the good and safetie of the whole, which power, by the Constitution of this Kingdome, is in his Majestie and in his Parliament together.[129]

The two Houses accept, in short, that England is a mixed monarchy, and that in normal circumstances the highest legislative authority can be exercised only when King and Parliament act together as the three Estates of the realm and hence as the joint bearers of sovereignty.[130]

The two Houses next insist, however, that the crisis in which the nation currently finds itself is such that this fundamental principle of the mixed constitution can no longer be upheld. Although the nation is facing a dire emergency, the king is incapable of recognising the gravity of the situation, so completely has he been hoodwinked by the malignant party.[131] Given this predicament, with one of the three Estates effectively disabled from pursuing the public good, it becomes the positive duty of the other two Estates to act together in the name of *salus populi*, even if this involves defying the sadly misguided king.

With this contention, the two Houses arrive at their revolutionary conclusion that, at least in conditions of emergency, the highest legislative authority lies not with the King-in-Parliament but with Parliament alone.[132] The principle is already implicit in the Militia Ordinance, and soon afterwards we find it explicitly stated by a number of the democratical gentlemen. Sir Simonds D'Ewes heard Henry Marten 'take the

---

[129] Husbands *et al.* 1643, p. 207. Cf. *Parliamentary History of England*, vol. 2, col. 1262. During the early seventeenth century there was some dispute (or perhaps merely confusion) about the character of the mixed constitution. Some argued that the Three Estates comprised the Lords spiritual, the Lords temporal and the Commons, with the king acting as their head. See Mendle 1985, pp. 108–10, 112–13 and cf. Sommerville 1999, pp. 165–6. After the exclusion of the Bishops from the House of Lords in February 1642, however, those who wished to defend the theory of the mixed constitution naturally took the three estates to be King, Lords and Commons. See Mendle 1985, esp. pp. 166–8, 176–7.

[130] For other statements of the theory at this juncture see Mendle 1985, p. 177.

[131] This claim is first strongly stated in the Petition about the Militia presented to the king on 1 March 1642. See Husbands *et al.* 1643, pp. 92–4 and cf. *Parliamentary History of England*, vol. 2, col. 1109.

[132] On this dramatic revision of the theory of the mixed constitution see Mendle 1985, esp. pp. 176–83. As Mendle 1993 rightly adds, this move in the spring of 1642 undoubtedly involved the two Houses in claiming that sovereignty lay with them alone.

boldnes' to affirm, as early as 8 February 1642, 'that the Kings consent should bee included in the Votes of the Lords howse'.[133] D'Ewes also records that Nathaniel Fiennes, in a similar speech of 1 April, declared 'that the King had no negative voice in passing those Acts of Parliament which both howses had agreed unto but was to assent to them'.[134] The Militia Ordinance had presupposed that no such assent is necessary, whereas Fiennes evidently believed that the king was obliged to assent to anything voted by Parliament, but constitutionally the outcome was the same: the king was denied any standing as a separate Estate endowed with the right to accept or reject any proposed legislation put to him.[135]

This doctrine reached a wider public with the appearance on 21 April[136] of a brief but remarkable pamphlet entitled *A Question Answered*.[137] Once again the basic principle invoked – in strikingly classical terms – is that of *salus populi*, 'the good and preservation of the Republique'.[138] The king can never possess any lawful power to act other than in the name of this basic principle. 'For it cannot be supposed that the *Parliament* would ever by Law intrust the King with the *Militia* against themselves, or the Commonwealth, that intrusts them to provide for their weale, not for their woe.' Drawing a parallel that was later much invoked, the author next tells us that the position of a king is similar to that of an army commander-in-chief. He is assigned the highest powers of command, but only on condition that they are rightly and equitably used:

Nor need this equity be expressed in the Law, being so naturally implyed and supposed in all Laws that are not merely Imperiall. . . . And therfore when the Militia of an Army is committed to the Generall, it is not with any expresse condition, that he shall not turn the mouths of his Cannons against his own Souldiers, for that is so naturally and necessarily implyed, that it is needlesse to be expressed.

We can readily see the force of the analogy, we are told, if we think about the implication of allowing the king to turn aside any proposals

---

[133] BL Harl. MS 162, fo. 375ᵛ. Cf. Mendle 1985, pp. 177–8.
[134] BL Harl. MS 163, fo. 452ᵛ [repaginated 58ᵛ]. The passage has been crossed out but is still legible.
[135] A distinction valuably stressed in Mendle 1985, pp. 178–9.
[136] Various dates have been suggested. I follow the one entered by Thomason in his own copy of the tract.
[137] Mendle 1985, Appendix 2, pp. 187–8 argues in favour of Henry Parker's authorship, but Mendle 1995, p. 194 more cautiously lists it under the tracts 'perhaps by Parker'. It is true that one of the arguments in the tract recurs in Parker's *Observations*, but it is striking that Thomason's copy contains no attribution, especially as he would have been well-placed to know if Parker had written it.
[138] *A Question Answered* is a single-sheet broadside, catalogued in the Thomason Tracts, British Library, as 669. f. 6 (7).

put to him by both Houses of Parliament for assuring the safety of the people. The effect would be to convert 'the legall and mixt *Monarchy*' into 'the greatest *Tiranny*', for 'if Laws invest the King in an absolute power, and the letter be not controled by the equity', our kings would have 'a Tiranny confer'd upon them legally, and so the very end of Laws, which is to give bounds and limits to the exorbitant wills of Princes, is by the Lawes themselves disapointed'.

The clear implication of *A Question Answered* is that, if the king attempts to act contrary to the good and safety of the people, the other two Estates in 'the legall and mixt *Monarchy*' have a duty to prevent him by acting alone. There is no such thing, in other words, as a royal veto over measures enacted by the two Houses in the name of the common good. These implications remain inexplicit, however, and it was left to the two Houses themselves to spell them out in their Declaration of 19 May, which they proceeded to do with the utmost confidence. 'The Prince being but one person', they now explain, he 'is more subject to accidents of nature and chance, whereby the Common-Wealth may be deprived of the fruit of that trust which was in part reposed in him'.[139] When 'cases of such necessity' arise, 'the Wisdome of this State hath intrusted the Houses of Parliament with a power to supply what shall bee wanting on the part of the Prince'.[140] The need for this power is obvious in the case of natural disability, but 'the like reason doth and must hold for the exercise of the same power in such cases, where the Royall trust cannot be, or is not discharged, and that the Kingdome runs an evident and imminent danger therby'.[141] But this is to speak, they go on, of the very predicament in which, as a result of the machinations of the malignant party, the nation now finds itself. Given that the nation now faces this danger, the two Houses can and must act according to their own judgement, and 'there needs not the authority of any person or Court to affirme; nor is it in the power of any person or Court to revoke, that judgement'.[142] If one of the three Estates cannot or will not act for the common good, the sovereign power to preserve the commonwealth automatically devolves upon the other two, which acquire the power *in extremis* to act alone.[143] As the Declaration of 26 May confirms, where 'the publike Weal, and good of the Kingdom' is concerned, the

---

[139] Husbands *et al.* 1643, pp. 207–8. Cf. *Parliamentary History of England*, vol. 2, col. 1262.
[140] Husbands *et al.* 1643, p. 208. Cf. *Parliamentary History of England*, vol. 2, col. 1262.
[141] Husbands *et al.* 1643, p. 208. Cf. *Parliamentary History of England*, vol. 2, col. 1262.
[142] Husbands *et al.* 1643, p. 208. Cf. *Parliamentary History of England*, vol. 2, col. 1262.
[143] For the growing belief in this period that the preservation of the state ought to be assigned paramount importance see Baldwin 1998.

two Estates of Parliament 'are the most proper Judges', since they 'are sent from the whole Kingdom for that very purpose'. Nor, we are now assured, has the crown ever questioned their possession of this ultimate sovereign power, 'otherwise then is expressed in that usuall Answer, *Le Roy l'avisera*, which signifies rather a suspension then a refusall of the Royall Assent'.[144]

VI

By the end of May 1642, the democratical gentlemen and their allies had fully articulated their revolutionary vision of the mixed constitution. Even the core prerogative of the Negative Voice, they were now prepared to argue, can be set aside by Parliament if the safety of the people might otherwise be jeopardised. We next need to note that, in the course of the months that followed, the two Houses proceeded to open up a different and yet more radical line of attack on the government. Moving beyond their simple invocations of *salus populi*, they began to delve more deeply into their classical heritage, and in particular to appeal yet again to Roman ideas about freedom and servitude.

This further development was prompted by the fact that the government in the meantime succeeded in mounting a damaging counter-attack on their initial line of argument. As Charles I and his advisers soon perceived, the control of the militia was constitutionally a side issue. The key constitutional question was raised by Parliament's underlying rejection of the prerogative of the Negative Voice. Responding to this revolutionary move, the king's advisers began by conceding the basic premises of the Parliamentary case.[145] They agreed that *salus populi* is *suprema lex*, and thus that the need to uphold 'Peace and safety', the need to be 'vigilant enough for the Publike safetye', must be recognised as the fundamental duty of government.[146] They were even prepared to accept that the king may be said to have a sacred obligation to act 'for the good and safety' of his subjects, and spoke emphatically of 'the Power wherewith he is trusted' and of 'the great trust that, by God and

[144] Husbands *et al.* 1643, p. 269.
[145] As Mendle 1985, pp. 5–6 notes, the chief writer on the king's behalf in the spring of 1642 was Edward Hyde.
[146] See Husbands *et al.* 1643, p. 158 (and cf. *Parliamentary History of England*, vol. 2, col. 1201) for the king's message of 28 April refusing to pass the Militia Ordinance as a bill. See also Husbands *et al.* 1643, p. 175 (and cf. *Parliamentary History of England*, vol. 2, col. 1245) for the king's answer to Parliament's Declaration of 5 May about the militia.

Mans Law is committed to the King, for the Defence and Safety of His People'.[147]

Having made these concessions, however, Charles and his advisers went vigorously on the offensive. They did not fail in the first place to invoke the idea of the king's divine right to rule. While acknowledging that the king is entrusted with power to procure *salus populi*, they rejected any suggestion that this trust is imposed on him by his own subjects, thereby blocking any possible implication that the foundations of lawful government may be contractual in character. The king's trust, they replied, is imposed on him directly by God, which makes him answerable to God alone for the manner in which he discharges it. As Charles himself pronounced, his is a trust 'which God and the Law hath granted to Us and Our Posterity for ever'.[148]

To these considerations the king and his advisers added a strictly constitutional retort. No one, they maintained, can be obliged to obey a mere bill or ordinance, even if it has been passed by both Houses, if it fails to secure the royal assent. To argue otherwise is to forget that, according to the fundamental laws and customs of the realm, the power to make laws is at all times vested jointly in King-in-Parliament. This was the blank wall that John Pym encountered as soon as he proposed in the debate of 15 March that the Militia Ordinance should be binding on all subjects. 'Divers spake against it', Sir Simonds D'Ewes records, 'and said nothing but a law could binde the Subiect to which was requisite as well the Kings roiall assent as the assent of both howses.'[149] We find the same understanding of the constitution implicit in several of the king's replies to Parliament of May 1642,[150] but for the classic exposition of the argument we must turn to the *Answer to the XIX Propositions* composed for the king by Viscount Falkland and Sir John Culpeper and issued on 18 June.[151] The *Answer* unequivocally asserts that 'in this kingdom the Laws are jointly made by a King, by a House of Peers, and by a House

---

[147] See Husbands *et al.* 1643, p. 181 (and cf. *Parliamentary History of England*, vol. 2, col. 1223) for the king's reply to Parliament's Answer of 9 May about Hull. See also Husbands *et al.* 1643, pp. 287, 290 (and cf. *Parliamentary History of England*, vol. 2, cols. 1334, 1337) for the king's answer to Parliament's Remonstrance of 26 May.

[148] Husbands *et al.* 1643, p. 287. Cf. *Parliamentary History of England*, vol. 2, col. 1334.

[149] BL Harl. MS 163, fo. 427ʳ [repaginated 33ʳ].

[150] See Husbands *et al.* 1643, pp. 163–4 (and cf. *Parliamentary History of England*, vol. 2, col. 1213) for the king's answer to Parliament's Declaration of 4 May about Hull. See also Husbands *et al.* 1643, pp. 175–6 (and cf. *Parliamentary History of England*, vol. 2, col. 1245) for the king's answer to Parliament's Declaration of 5 May about the militia. For the adoption of the same vocabulary by royalist pamphleteers after April 1642 see Mendle 1985, pp. 180–2.

[151] Mendle 1985, p. 6.

of Commons chosen by the People, all having free Votes and particular Priviledges'.[152] Furthermore, the essence of the king's standing as one of the three Estates derives from the fact that he possesses a Negative Voice. It is an indispensable aspect of 'the King's Regalitie' that, when presented by Parliament with a proposed Act of legislation, he has the right 'to grant or deny such of their Petitions as pleaseth himself'.[153] Speaking in his own person, Charles adds that any attempt to bypass or even question his veto would amount to denying 'the freedom of Our Answer', when 'We have as much right to reject what We think unreasonable, as you have to propose what you think convenient or necessary'. By the terms of the mixed constitution 'the Manage of Our Vote is trusted by the Law, to our Own Judgement and Conscience', and 'most unreasonable it were that two Estates, proposing something to the Third' should be able to bind the third to act according to their will.[154]

Charles I's *Answer* has sometimes been viewed as a concessive and conciliatory document.[155] If we place it, however, in the context of Parliament's attack on the royal veto, it appears as an aggressive reaffirmation of the crown's place in the mixed constitution, and as the culmination of a powerful series of responses to the democratical gentlemen and their allies.[156] The crown's replies were admirably written, witty and ironic in tone, highly effective at mocking the hypocrisies of the two Houses as they fulminated against their unnamed enemies. Still more important, the *Answer* contained an unimpeachable account of how the process of legislation was normally carried out, and one in which the prerogative of the Negative Voice was shown to play a pivotal role that no one had previously called in doubt.

It was at this moment that the democratical gentlemen sought to regain the ideological initiative by delving yet more deeply into their classical heritage, and in particular by extending their earlier discussions of freedom and servitude. The main credit for engineering this crucial move appears to be due to Henry Parker, whose *Observations upon some of his Majesties late Answers and Expresses* first appeared anonymously on

---

[152] Charles I 1999, p. 168.
[153] Charles I 1999, p. 155. Fukuda 1997, pp. 24–5 sees in this passage the earliest 'Polybian' definition of the English constitution. But the language of the *Answer* closely echoes the Parliamentary declarations to which it was a response.
[154] Charles I 1999, p. 164. [155] Weston 1965, pp. 5, 26, 29.
[156] Weston 1965, pp. 29–30 overlooks Parliament's earlier claims about the right of the two Houses to act alone, and consequently treats that argument as a radical response to Charles I's *Answer*. But the *Answer* was a counterblast to the radical argument, which as we have seen had already been advanced by Parliament.

2 July 1642.[157] The *Observations* is Parker's most important tract, and, as we shall see, its neo-classical analysis of freedom and free commonwealths exercised an immediate and pervasive influence on other writers in favour of the parliamentary cause.

Parker's is an unusually complex text, however, and it would be misleading to imply that his account of freedom and slavery carries the main burden of his case. Rather he seems to have taken his principal task to be that of lending full support to the radical interpretation of the mixed constitution already put forward by the two Houses of Parliament. He accordingly begins by reaffirming that *salus populi* is 'the Paramount Law that shall give Law to all humane Lawes', enunciating the principle in exactly the terms that Cicero had employed in his *De Legibus*.[158] Parker next concedes that in normal circumstances 'the legislative power of this Kingdome is partly in the King, and partly in the Kingdome', and that 'when it concerns not the saving of the people from some great danger or inconvenience, neither the King can make a generall binding Law or Ordinance without the Parliament, or the Parliament without the King' (p. 182). He then insists, however, that 'where this ordinary course cannot be taken for the preventing of publike mischiefes, any extraordinary course that is for that purpose the most effectuall, may justly be taken and executed' in accordance with the paramount duty to ensure that *salus populi* is preserved. If the king should happen to be deaf to some grave crisis in the state, there must be a right in the two Houses of Parliament to act, even 'without his concurrence', to uphold *salus populi* by way of making 'any temporary orders for putting the Kingdome into a posture of defence'.[159]

Besides restating this earlier line of thought, however, Parker goes on to develop a further and explicitly neo-classical attack on the prerogative of the Negative Voice. If this prerogative, he declares, is indeed pivotal to the operation of the mixed constitution, then we cannot speak of the English as a free nation at all. The effect of the Negative Voice is to take away the liberty not merely of individual subjects but of the people as a whole. It converts the English from a free people into a nation of slaves.

This further argument runs as a groundswell through Parker's text, but it may be helpful to distinguish two elements in it. One hinges on the nature of the relationship between the king and Parliament presupposed

---

[157] Mendle 1995, pp. 70–89 gives an account of the precise context in which Parker's text appeared.
[158] [Parker] 1933, p. 169. Cf. Cicero 1928, III. I. 1–3, pp. 458–60.
[159] [Parker] 1933, p. 182. As Mendle 1995, p. 48 puts it, the argument amounts to a defence of 'full-blown bicameral parliamentary absolutism'.

by the claim that the crown possesses a Negative Voice. With this prerogative, Parker objects, the king 'assumes to himselfe a share in the legislative power' so great as to open up 'a gap to as vast and arbitrary a prerogative as the Grand Seignior has' in Constantinople (pp. 182–3). For he assumes a power to 'take away the being of Parliament meerely by dissent', thereby making it 'more servile then other inferior Courts' (p. 187). To allow the Negative Voice, in short, is to render Parliament dependent on the king and thereby reduce it to servitude.

The other element in Parker's argument flows from his assumption that 'the Lords and Commons represent the whole Kingdome' and 'are to be accounted by the vertue of representation as the whole body of the State' (pp. 175, 211). If we allow that the king has a Negative Voice, then 'without the Kings concurrence and consent', the two Houses are reduced to 'livelesse conventions without all vertue and power'. But this is to take away the political virtue and power of the people as a whole. Tracing the implications of this disenfranchisement, Parker closely follows two different formulae used by his classical authorities to describe the onset of national servitude. As we have seen, Livy had equated this condition with the substitution by our rulers of 'their owne will and licentious lust in steede of law'.[160] Parker repeats that the Negative Voice subjects the entire nation 'to as unbounded a regiment of the Kings meere will, as any Nation under Heaven ever suffered under'. For 'what remains, but that all our lawes, rights, & liberties, be either no where at all determinable, or else onely in the Kings breast?' (pp. 175–6). The other formula to which Parker refers is Aristotle's claim that (as the English translation of the *Politics* had put it) we fall into a condition of slavery whenever we become subject to the discretion of others, since 'the propertie of bondage is, not to live according to a man's own discretion'.[161] Parker agrees that, if we permit the king 'to be the sole, supream competent Judge in this case, we resigne all into his hands, we give lifes, liberties, Laws, Parliaments, all to be held at meer discretion' and thereby leave ourselves in bondage (pp. 209–10).

Charles I had complained in his *Answer to the XIX Propositions* that without the Negative Voice he would be reduced from the status of 'a King of *England*' to a mere 'Duke of *Venice*'.[162] Parker daringly picks up the objection as a means of clinching his argument about national servitude. 'Let us look upon the Venetians, and other such free Nations', he responds, and ask ourselves why it is that they are 'so extreamly jealous

---

[160] Livy 1600, p. 87.   [161] Aristotle 1598, VI. II, pp. 339–40.   [162] Charles I 1999, p. 167.

over their Princes'. It is because they fear 'the sting of Monarchy', which stems (as Livy had said) from the power of monarchs to 'dote upon their owne wills, and despise publike Councels and Laws' (p. 192). The jealousy of the Venetians arises, in other words, from their recognition that under a genuine monarchy they would be reduced to slavery. It is 'meerely for fear of this bondage' that they prefer their elected dukes to the rule of hereditary kings (p. 192).

Perhaps foreseeing the conflict to come, Parker adds in minatory tones that no self-respecting people can be expected to endure such servitude. He reiterates that, if a nation is made 'to resigne its owne interest to the will of one Lord, as that that Lord may destroy it without injury', this is to say that the nation in question has been made 'to inslave it selfe' (p. 174). Once more we hear strong echoes of the English translation of Aristotle's *Politics*, which had warned that 'no person that is free dooth willingly endure such a state'.[163] Parker similarly warns that 'few Nations will indure that thraldome which uses to accompany unbounded & unconditionate royalty' (p. 180). The reason, he adds, is that it is 'contrarie to the supreme of all Lawes' for 'any Nation to give away its owne proprietie in it selfe absolutely' and thereby 'subject it selfe to a condition of servilitie below men' (p. 186). If kings impose this servitude, Parker implies, they must not be surprised if their subjects throw off this unnatural yoke.

While Parker's intervention was of crucial importance, his neo-classical line of argument was not without precedent. The parliamentary Remonstrance of 26 May 1642 had already contained a warning that, if Parliament becomes wholly dependent on the will of the king and his evil counsellors, the English will be no better than a nation of slaves:

> We shall likewise address our Answer to the Kingdom, not by way of appeal (as we are charged) but to prevent them from being their own executioners; and from being perswaded, under false colours of defending the law, and their own Liberties to destroy both with their own hands, by taking their lives, Liberties, and Estates out of their hands, whom they have chosen and entrusted therewith; and resigning them up unto some evill Counsellors about his Majesty, who can lay no other foundation of their own greatnesse, but upon the ruine of this, and, in it, of all Parliaments, and in them of the true Religion, and the freedome of this Nation.[164]

The Remonstrance ends by calling on the people to reflect on the treasonous designs of the malignant party and ask themselves 'whether if they could master this Parliament by force, they would not hold up the

---

[163] Aristotle 1598, IV. X, p. 208.
[164] Husbands et al. 1643, pp. 263–4. Cf. *Parliamentary History of England*, vol. 2, cols. 1298–9.

same power to deprive Us of all Parliaments; which are the ground and Pillar of the Subjects Liberty, and that which onely maketh *England* a free Monarchy'.[165]

A similar line of argument can be found in the speech delivered by Denzil Holles to the House of Lords on 15 June at the impeachment of the peers who had joined the king at York:

> I come hither unto your Lordships in the behalfe of the *Parliament*; or rather in the behalfe of the whole *Kingdome*, labouring with much distraction, many feares, great apprehensions of evill and mischiefe intended against it, and now hatching and preparing by that Malignant party, which thirsts after the destruction of *Religion, Laws*, and *Liberty*; all which are foulded up, cherished, and preserved in the carefull bosome of the Parliament.[166]

The members of the malignant party, Holles goes on, are fully aware that 'if they can take away Parliaments' then 'all will be at their mercy', for 'not only the Peace, and Happinesse and well-being, but the very *Being* of this Kingdome, can have no other bottom to stand upon, but the Parliament'.[167] The two Houses provide us with 'the only meanes to continue us to be a Nation of freemen, and not slaves, to be owners of any thing; that we may call our wives, our children, our estates, nay our bodies our own'.[168]

After the publication of Parker's *Observations*, these neo-classical hints about public freedom and its forfeiture were far more confidently taken up. The Declaration issued by the two Houses on 14 July[169] maintains that the stark choice now facing 'the free-born English Nation' is either to adhere to the cause of Parliament or else 'to the King seduced by Jesuiticall Counsell and Cavaliers, who have designed all to slavery and confusion'.[170] The Declaration of 4 August presents the dilemma in still more lurid terms.[171] We are being invited to 'yield our selves to the cruel mercy of those who have possessed the King against us',[172] although it is obvious that their aspiration is 'to cut up the freedom of Parliament by the root, and either take all Parliaments away, or which is worse, make them the instruments of slavery'.[173] The final Declaration issued by Parliament before the king raised his standard of war on 22 August recurs to the same theme. The leaders of the malignant party 'have now

---

[165] Husbands *et al*. 1643, p. 279. Cf. *Parliamentary History of England*, vol. 2, col. 1313.
[166] Holles 1642, p. 1.   [167] Holles 1642, p. 2.   [168] Holles 1642, p. 4.
[169] For the date see Rushworth 1692, p. 756.
[170] Husbands *et al*. 1643, p. 464. Cf. *Parliamentary History of England*, vol. 2, col. 1413.
[171] For the date see Rushworth 1692, p. 761.
[172] Husbands *et al*. 1643, p. 492. Cf. *Parliamentary History of England*, vol. 2, col. 1434.
[173] Husbands *et al*. 1643, p. 494. Cf. *Parliamentary History of England*, vol. 2, col. 1437.

advised and prevailed with his Majesty by this Proclamation, to invite his Subjects to destroy his Parliament and good people by a Civill War; and, by that meanes to bring ruine, confusion, and perpetuall slavery upon the surviving part of a then wretched Kingdome'.[174]

It would be an overstatement, however, to suggest that these references to slavery and national servitude necessarily reflect any direct acquaintance with classical theories of liberty. These Declarations perhaps imply, but they certainly do not state, the distinctive Roman law assumption that the mere fact of living in dependence on the goodwill of others is sufficient to take away our liberty. We find a very different picture, however, if we turn to the numerous pamphlets and treatises published in defence of Parliament in the weeks immediately following the appearance of Parker's *Observations* at the start of July. A considerable number of these writers reveal a clear understanding of the classical theory of freedom and slavery, and in several instances they put forward this theory as the essence of their increasingly anti-royalist stance.

One of the most forthright statements of the neo-classical case can be found in the anonymous tract of 1 August 1642 entitled *Reasons why this kingdome ought to adhere to the Parliament.*[175] Despite the calumnies put about by the malignant party, the two Houses are said to remain the people's 'onely Sanctuary of their Religion, Lawes, Liberties, and properties' (p. 6). Referring directly to Parker's 'most excellent' *Observations* (p. 2), the author goes on to assail the prerogative of the Negative Voice as uniquely destructive of the nation's liberties. If any decision made by Parliament can be frustrated by the exercise of the royal veto, this gives the king 'an unlimited declarative power of Law above all Courts, in his own breast'. But this means that 'the last Appeale must be to his discretion and understanding, and consequently, the Legislative power His alone' (p. 11). If we now comply with this view of the constitution, the effect will not only be to 'forsake this Parliament, and leave it to the mercy of the Malignants'; it will also be to leave our 'Religion, Lawes, Liberties, and properties open to the spoyle and oppression of an Arbitrary Government' (p. 12). It is just this openness to being spoiled and oppressed, however, that serves in itself to take away our liberty. If Parliament allows the king a Negative Voice, 'this whole Kingdome shall consist only of a King, a Parliament, and Slaves' (p. 14).

Less than two weeks later, the two Houses ordered the printing of a very similar argument put forward in *A Remonstrance in defence of the*

---

[174] Husbands *et al.* 1643, p. 509. Cf. *Parliamentary History of England*, vol. 2, col. 1443.
[175] Thomason adds the date of publication on the title-page of his copy.

Lords and Commons in Parliament.[176] The anonymous author calls on the whole nation to adhere to the two Houses, 'who are the eyes, eares and understanding of the Common wealth' (pp. 5–6). If instead we allow the malignants to obtain the power they seek, this will bring 'the ruine of the Parliament, the destruction of the Kingdome, and the Lawes and liberties of the Subject' (p. 3). By defending the Negative Voice, the malignants hope to 'change the forme of Government of this Kingdome, and make it subject to the Arbitrary power of the king'. But to make a kingdom subject to arbitrary power is to reduce it to servitude. The malignants are in effect planning to 'become masters of our Religion and liberties to make us slaves' (p. 5).

A further plea to recognise that the very existence of the Negative Voice enslaves the nation can be found in the tract published on 17 August 1642 under the title *Considerations for the Commons in This Age of Distractions*.[177] The Negative Voice gives rise to a consequence that 'must needs sound harsh in the eares of a free people'. This harsh consequence is that 'the King withdrawne by evill Councell may at pleasure take away the very essence of Parliaments meerely by his owne dissent, thereby stripping them of all power in matters of judicature that they may not determine any thing for the good and safety of the Kingdome'. If this prerogative is allowed, 'it must needs follow, that its both vaine and needlesse to trouble the whole Kingdome to make choice of its representative body', for whatever decisions it may reach can always be set aside by the mere dissenting will of the king. The reason why this cannot fail to sound harsh in the ears of a free people is that any king who may 'at pleasure' set aside the laws in this fashion is a king of slaves. If Parliament now accommodates with the king, 'let the World judge what were likely to be the portion of the Communalty of this Kingdom'. No doubt the two Houses will 'live like Princes, but we like slaves'.[178]

Of all the neo-classical defences of Parliament, however, by far the fullest and most sophisticated was the anonymous treatise published on 15 October 1642 under the title *The Vindication of the Parliament And their Proceedings*.[179] The two enemies now facing each other are said to be the malignant party and the two Houses of Parliament. Quoting the Declaration of 2 August, the author first explains that the goal of the

---

[176] Thomason adds on the title-page of his copy that this tract appeared on 11 August 1642.
[177] Thomason adds the date of publication on the title-page of his copy.
[178] All quotations from *Considerations* 1642, Sig. A, 3ᵛ.
[179] Thomason adds the date of publication on the title-page of his copy. Because of the muddled pagination of *Vindication*, I have given references by signature mark rather than by page.

malignant party is 'to cut up the freedome of *Parliament* by the root, and either to take all *Parliaments* away, or (which is worse) make them the instruments of slavery'.[180] An easy means of attaining this goal lies ready to hand in the alleged prerogative of the Negative Voice. With this prerogative 'the sole power of managing the affaires of the *Kingdome*' belongs 'onely unto the *King*, and nothing at all to *either*, or *both Houses*'.[181] But to grant the king this 'arbitrary power, to rule us, according to the dictates of his own conscience' is to run the risk of turning ourselves into 'most miserable and wretched slaves'.[182]

As the author is at pains to underline, the mere fact that the king possesses this Negative Voice is sufficient in itself to reduce us to slavery. Speaking in Aesopian vein, he reminds us that, as we can readily learn from the birds and their predators, it is all too easy to live in servitude without suffering actual oppression or constraint:

For as the Crane had better to keepe his head out of the Wolves mouth, then to put it into his mouth, and then stand at his mercy, whither he will bite off his neck or not, so it is better for every wise man, rather to keepe and preserve those immunities, freedomes, prerogatives, and priviledges, which God, and nature hath given unto him, for the preservation, prosperity and peace of his posterity, person and estate, then to disenfranchize himselfe and relinquish and resigne all in to the hands of another, and to give him power either to impoverish or enrich, either to kill him or keepe him alive.[183]

An absolute ruler may choose to enrich you rather than kill you, but you are none the less a slave for that. What takes away your liberty is your awareness that you are living at the mercy of someone else.

Although the author of the *Vindication* assures us that he is writing in the hope of averting 'these *Civill Wars* threatning',[184] he concludes by maintaining that the prospect of enslavement is undoubtedly sufficient to justify a resort to arms. The King has surrounded himself with papists and evil counsellors who 'perswade him that it is lawfull for him to doe what he list'. As a result, the choice now facing the people is between '*Popery, or Protestantisme*' and between '*slavery or liberty*'.[185] But it would be 'unnaturall, that any Nation should be bound to contribute its own inherent puissance meerely to abet tyranny, and support slavery'.[186] From which it follows that a defensive war would now be justified. We must

---

[180] *Vindication* 1642, Sig. B, 4ʳ.   [181] *Vindication* 1642, Sig. C, 2ᵛ.
[182] *Vindication* 1642, Sig. D, 3ʳ.   [183] *Vindication* 1642, Sig. D, 3ᵛ.
[184] *Vindication* 1642, Sig. A, 2ᵛ.   [185] *Vindication* 1642, Sig. D, 4ᵛ.
[186] *Vindication* 1642, Sig. E, 1ʳ. Here the author quotes [Parker] 1933, pp. 169–70, although without acknowledgement.

stand ready to take up arms, and not to lay them down until 'we are assured of a firme peace, and to be ruled as becommeth a free people, who are not borne slaves'.[187]

VII

By the time the *Vindication* had reached print, the two Houses of Parliament had already taken the resolve to raise an army and resist the king by force. The plots of the malignant party and other evil counsellors left them no alternative, they proclaimed, but to 'Declare and Ordaine, that it is, and shall be lawfull for all His Majesties loving Subjects, by force of Armes to resist the said severall parties, and their Accomplices'.[188] Those engaging in such acts of resistance will not only be defending 'the Religion of Almighty God' against the aspiration of the malignant party to replace it with popery. They will also be foiling their evil designs by defending 'the Liberties and Peace of the Kingdom' against the imposition of arbitrary government.[189]

Historians have generally claimed that the arguments used to justify this final decision to resist were essentially contractual in character.[190] The king had broken the terms of his covenant with his people, who had never given up their natural right to set down whatever form of government they originally consented to set up. There is no doubt that such arguments were brought forward at this juncture. As we saw in chapter 11, Henry Parker in his *Observations* made particularly emphatic use of them.[191] But it is striking that Parliament itself and many of its supporters preferred to justify their decision to go to war in neo-classical rather than in contractarian terms. The final Declarations issued by Parliament in August 1642 make no mention of the natural rights of the sovereign people. They instead speak of the need to liberate the people from being mastered and enslaved by the 'Malignant Party of Papists, those who call themselves Cavaliers, and other ill-affected persons' who have deliberately driven the country into civil war:

The intention being still the same, not to rest satisfied with having *Hull*, or taking away the ordinance of the *Militia*; But to destroy the Parliament, and be masters of our religion and liberties, to make us slaves, and alter the Government of this

---

[187] *Vindication* 1642, Sig. E, 1ʳ.
[188] See Husbands *et al.* 1643, p. 499, in which the declaration is dated to 8 August 1642.
[189] Husbands *et al.* 1643, p. 499.
[190] See for example Salmon 1959, pp. 80–8; Sanderson 1989, esp. pp. 18–21.
[191] [Parker] 1933, pp. 167–71.

Kingdom, and reduce it to the condition of some other countries, which are not governed by Parliaments, and so by Laws, but by the will of the Prince, or rather of those who are about him.[192]

It is in the name of staving off such perpetual slavery, they declare, that they have now decided to raise an army under the Earl of Essex, 'with whom, in this Quarrell we will live and dye'.[193] From the parliamentary perspective, the civil war began as a war of national liberation from servitude.

[192] Husbands *et al.* 1643, p. 497. Cf. *Parliamentary History of England*, vol. 2, col. 1439.
[193] Husbands *et al.* 1643, p. 498. Cf. *Parliamentary History of England*, vol. 2, col. 1440.

13

Augustan party politics and Renaissance constitutional thought

I

In the discussion of his political career, as in his career itself, Lord Bolingbroke has been less fortunate than his lifelong rival, Sir Robert Walpole. Walpole's rise to power and the conduct of his administration have been classically analysed in the two volumes of Sir John Plumb's biography,[1] but the conduct of Bolingbroke's opposition has been less satisfactorily discussed. This can no longer be explained by citing Edmund Burke's sneering dismissal: 'Who now reads Bolingbroke?' A growing number of scholars do, and a lengthening list of studies have in consequence been devoted in recent years to establishing the facts about Bolingbroke's career and to analysing his political works.[2] What seems unsatisfactory about these studies is not that they have failed to agree about the facts or in general to present them fairly and well. It is rather that the facts seem to have been fitted into inappropriate schemes of explanation.[3] Accordingly, my aim in what follows will not primarily be to provide new information about Bolingbroke and his party of opposition to Walpole's government. It will rather be to argue that the existing facts fit a theory about the behaviour of Bolingbroke and his party which does not seem to have been entertained by any of Bolingbroke's interpreters, but which seems to me to offer the best explanation of his political career.

The thesis I wish to advance can be stated in a general as well as a more specific form. My specific claim is that the prevailing explanations of Bolingbroke's opposition appear to misunderstand the nature of the

---

This chapter is an abbreviated and extensively revised version of an essay that originally appeared under the title 'The Principles and Practice of Opposition: The Case of Bolingbroke versus Walpole' in *Historical Perspectives*, ed. Neil McKendrick (London, 1974), pp. 93–128.

[1] Plumb 1956, 1960. See also Plumb 1967, pp. 159–89.
[2] The list has become much longer since this chapter was originally written. For the best guide to the more recent literature see Armitage 1997, pp. xxx–xxxviii.
[3] For an important exception, however, to which I am greatly indebted, see Pocock 1971, pp. 104–47.

connections between his professed principles and his political behaviour. My broader claim is that these misunderstandings arise from a more general incapacity – shared by much recent political history – to give a coherent account of the relations between political thought and action. Correspondingly, my specific aim will be to provide a new account of the role that needs to be assigned to Bolingbroke's professed principles in explaining his opposition to Walpole's government. My broader aim will be to provide a framework capable of being applied more generally in discussions about the interplay between principle and practice in public life.

II

The relevant facts about the opposition to Walpole's ministry can be found in any of the recent studies of Bolingbroke's career, and will be set out here as briefly as possible. The campaign took two main forms. The first began in earnest in December 1726 with the founding of *The Craftsman*, the periodical set up by Bolingbroke and William Pulteney to expose the crafts by which Walpole governed.[4] The other line of attack was mounted in Parliament itself and began to gather momentum during the opening session of the new reign in 1728.[5] Bolingbroke himself was obliged to pour his energies into the journalistic campaign, for in spite of the pardon he had received in 1723 for his Jacobite adventures he was still debarred from taking his seat in the House of Lords.[6] He was able, however, to gather around him a brilliant coterie of sympathisers at his retreat at Dawley[7] as well as a considerable following in the House of Commons itself. The core of his parliamentary support was formed by William Pulteney, William Bromley, Samuel Sandys and Lord Morpeth,[8] who were sometimes joined for crucial divisions by such prominent high Tories as William Shippen and Sir William Wyndham.[9] Both lines of attack were unremittingly kept up until the life

---

[4] Kramnick 1968, pp. 17–24; Dickinson 1970, pp. 185, 188–9. For the government side of the journalistic war see Hanson 1936, pp. 106–18 and Burtt 1992, pp. 110–27. For the best and most up-to-date analysis of the literary attack on Walpole's government see Gerrard 1994, pp. 3–45.

[5] Plumb 1960, pp. 157–72, 176–85. The first session was opened on 23 January 1728. See *Parliamentary History of England*, vol. 8, p. 607.

[6] Hart 1965, pp. 45–59; Jackman 1965, pp. 34–42; Dickinson 1970, pp. 154–83. For Walpole's attitude towards Bolingbroke's pardon see Plumb 1960, pp. 124–7.

[7] Hart 1965, pp. 61–3; Dickinson 1970, pp. 212–19.

[8] But cf. Gerrard 1994, p. 111, who stresses that Bolingbroke's opposition was part of a more complex campaign.

[9] While the Tories were thus prepared to take up some 'whig' issues, there were distinctively Tory grounds for opposition to the ministry as well. On the content of Toryism in this period see Colley 1982, pp. 85–117.

of the Parliament ran out in 1734. Bolingbroke's leadership of this most concerted effort to unseat the whig oligarchy came to an end only after the general election of that year, in which Walpole was duly returned to power with a still comfortable majority.[10] The opposition ground on in the new Parliament,[11] but Bolingbroke suddenly lost heart and retired to France to enjoy the consolations of philosophy in his second exile.[12]

Bolingbroke and his party made use of every available expedient to embarrass the ministry. As Plumb puts it, writing of the particularly troublesome session of 1730, Walpole found himself confronted and denounced on a bewildering variety of issues: 'gaols, the renewal of the East India Company charter, the Africa Company, the complaints of London shopkeepers, the peculiarly difficult by-election petition from Liverpool'.[13] Underlying this whirling cut-and-thrust, however, there were several 'perennial' topics to which the opposition continually returned. As Plumb observes, these were the issues 'dear to independents', the issues that could absolutely be relied upon to excite their deepest prejudices. The demand that they should be debated became 'almost a part of the formal ritual of the Parliamentary session'.[14]

The members of the opposition took especially grave exception to two particular policies. One was that, even after the conclusion of Britain's involvement in any major European wars, the government was still maintaining a sizeable land force, and was even prepared to pay for Hessian mercenaries.[15] This policy was targeted in virtually every session of Parliament. An attempt was made in the opening session to prevent the addition of eight thousand men to the existing land forces.[16] During the second session Pulteney and Shippen opposed the vote to maintain the army at its existing strength,[17] while in the next session Shippen returned to the same point.[18] The fifth session saw Lord Morpeth's successful demand for an additional debate on the issue,[19] while in the sixth he launched yet another assault, prompting Walpole himself to reply and both Shippen and Wyndham to counter-attack.[20]

---

[10] Plumb 1960, pp. 314–24.
[11] So did *The Craftsman*, but with diminished success. It eventually changed sides.
[12] He took up residence at Chanteloup, where he died in 1751. See Dickinson 1970, pp. 247–96.
[13] Plumb 1960, p. 216.   [14] Plumb 1960, pp. 216, 303, 305.   [15] Plumb 1960, pp. 207–8.
[16] See *Parliamentary History of England*, vol. 8, pp. 642–3 and for the debate about the Hessian troops see pp. 643–4.
[17] *Parliamentary History of England*, vol. 8, pp. 677–80.
[18] *Parliamentary History of England*, vol. 8, pp. 771–3.
[19] *Parliamentary History of England*, vol. 8, pp. 882–911. Lord Morpeth raised the issue on 26 January (p. 882). Lord Hervey promptly opposed the motion (pp. 882–3) and a full-scale debate ensued.
[20] *Parliamentary History of England*, vol. 8, pp. 1184–90.

The seventh and last session saw Wyndham return to the same argument, once again supported by Pulteney and other sympathisers with the opposition's cause.[21]

The other policies opposed with no less consistency related to the ministry's control of the House itself. The climax came in the final session, in the course of which William Bromley (evidently prompted by Bolingbroke himself) put forward a motion to repeal the Septennial Act. The Act had first been passed by the whigs in 1717, and the opposition rightly saw it as the lynchpin of Walpole's managerial success.[22] Meanwhile the other policy that came under repeated fire was that of granting pensions and offices of profit to members of Parliament willing to offer the government their unwavering support. During the third session Samuel Sandys brought in a bill 'for disabling persons from being chosen Members of, or sitting and voting in, the House of Commons, who have any Pension ... or any offices, held in trust for them, from the crown'.[23] This motion actually passed the Commons, and Walpole had to rely on the Bishops to throw it out of the Lords. During the fourth session Sandys returned to the attack. He failed in his efforts to publish a list of members who were holding pensions, but he again succeeded in getting a Pensions Bill past the Commons, and again Walpole had to use the Lords to throw it out.[24] During the fifth and sixth sessions Sandys introduced yet further bills, eventually forcing Walpole to reply on behalf of the government.[25] Finally, in the closing session Sandys altered his tactics and instead sought leave 'to bring in a Bill for securing the freedom of Parliament, by limiting the number of officers in that House'. This too found support from Wyndham and the Tories, and although it was voted down it proved to be the first in a series of place bills that the indefatigable Sandys continued to introduce.[26]

Bolingbroke's biographers have been inclined to describe him as willing to take up 'any and every expedient and issue, real or imagined' with

---

[21] *Parliamentary History of England*, vol. 9, pp. 262–83.
[22] *Parliamentary History of England*, vol. 9, pp. 394–479. On the role played by Bolingbroke see Kramnick 1968, pp. 29–30 and Dickinson 1970, p. 243.
[23] *Parliamentary History of England*, vol. 8, p. 789.
[24] For the attempt to publish the list see *Parliamentary History of England*, vol. 8, p. 857; for the bill see p. 841. For Walpole's use of the Lords in connection with this and the earlier bill see Foord 1964, pp. 183–4.
[25] *Parliamentary History of England*, vol. 8, pp. 882, 992, 1177–84.
[26] *Parliamentary History of England*, vol. 9, p. 366. See also Foord 1964, p. 184, noting that this was followed by other place bills, all brought in by Sandys, in the sessions of 1735, 1736, 1740 and 1741.

which to denounce the government.[27] As the above account suggests, however, this assessment is not entirely accurate. Bolingbroke and his sympathisers also followed a pattern of opposition, a pattern so consistent that within a few years it had become entirely predictable. One of Lord Chesterfield's pieces of advice to his son, when he was about to enter Parliament, was to rehearse a speech either about the size of the land forces or about the award of pensions and places by the government. The reason why these were regarded as the best subjects for prepared eloquence was that these were the issues on which it was certain that a debate could be forced.[28]

Besides concentrating on this pattern of opposition, Bolingbroke and his supporters consistently professed the same principle for the sake of which, they declared, they were pursuing their campaign. They claimed to be activated wholly by what they described as the spirit of patriotism.[29] This term did not suffer at the time from any of the equivocal and potentially ironic overtones with which it has since become invested. It was a strongly favourable evaluation to apply to anyone's behaviour, and one with a clear meaning. By the concept of patriotism Bolingbroke and his followers understood the ideal of acting in such a way as to defend the established constitution and the political liberties of those living under it. When, for example, Bolingbroke's admirers wished to celebrate his own patriotism after his death, they chose an epitaph stressing his 'zeal to maintain the liberty and to restore the ancient prosperity of Great Britain'.[30] Bolingbroke's whig opponents did not, of course, accept for a moment that any of his professions of patriotism were sincere, but they agreed about what it meant to be a patriot. They agreed, that is, that if it could sincerely be said of someone that they had 'a mighty concern for the public good',[31] and specifically that they cared about 'the spirit of liberty'[32] and worked for 'the support and defence of our liberties',[33] then it would undoubtedly be right to dignify their behaviour with 'the honourable name of patriotism'.[34]

---

[27] Dickinson 1970, pp. 113, 193–4.   [28] Chesterfield 1901, Letter of 26 March 1754, vol. 2, p. 341.
[29] There are several excellent discussions of the language of patriotism in this period. See in particular Colley 1989; Cunningham 1989; Gerrard 1994, esp. pp. 3–6; and for an historiographical survey Clark 2000.
[30] Jackman 1965, p. 3; Hart 1965, p. 82. For a near contemporary analysis along similar lines see Berkeley 1953, pp. 253–5. Writing in 1750, Berkeley begins (p. 253) with the warning that 'Being loud and vehement either against a court, or for a court, is no proof of patriotism.' The prevailing definition of patriotism in terms of the defence of constitutional liberty is well brought out in Dobrée 1949 and Kemp 1966, pp. 37–46.
[31] [Gibson] 1731, p. 4. On Gibson's support for Walpole see Colley 1982, pp. 104, 193–4.
[32] [Yonge] 1731, pp. vii, 38.   [33] [Hervey] 1734, p. 7.   [34] [Arnall] 1735, pp. 9, 16.

III

If those are the relevant facts, the questions I want to raise can now be introduced. What was the nature of the connection between the ideals for the sake of which Bolingbroke and his party claimed to be acting and the specific courses of action they pursued? What role was played by their professed principles in governing their actions? Or, to put the question the other way round, what weight should be placed on their professions of principle in seeking to explain their behaviour?

Due in large measure to the influence of Sir Lewis Namier, one answer to these questions until recently enjoyed the status of an orthodoxy. The basic premise of the Namierite case is that Bolingbroke's tactics and those of his party were solely motivated 'by an insatiable ambition for power'.[35] From this it is said to follow that, since their professions of principle were mere rationalisations of this 'ambition born of hate',[36] we should assign them no weight at all in attempting to explain their behaviour.[37]

Namier himself treated it as virtually an axiom about political life that those who engage in it are driven solely by a desire to acquire and exercise power. He accordingly insisted that professed principles – or 'party names and cant', as he characteristically preferred to put it – offer no guide to the 'underlying realities' of politics.[38] Such principles are invoked merely to ensure that the 'unconscious promptings' and 'inscrutable components' of personal ambition and the quest for domination[39] are 'invested *ex post facto* with the appearance of logic and rationality'.[40] As Namier summarises in his essay *Human Nature in Politics*, 'what matters most is the underlying emotions, the music, to which ideas are a mere libretto, often of very inferior quality'.[41]

Namier 'empties Hanoverian Whiggery of principle',[42] and this approach has in turn had a profound impact on the study of eighteenth-century politics. The same assumptions are clearly embodied, for example, in John Brooke's analysis of political parties in the period. The aim of the politicians, we are told, 'was simply to get into office'. They dignified this 'struggle for power' as 'a conflict between opposing political ideas', but their professed principles were merely 'a respectable façade'

---

[35] Robertson 1947, p. 3.   [36] Laski 1920, p. 90.
[37] Walcott 1964, p. 90 remarks that to do so would be 'off the track'.
[38] Namier 1957, p. vii. Walcott 1964, p. 90 also speaks of 'cant' and criticises those who take Bolingbroke's writings 'at their face value'.
[39] Namier 1955, p. 3.   [40] Namier 1930, p. 147.
[41] Namier 1955, p. 4.   [42] Taylor 1952, p. 17.

behind which they ruthlessly pursued their interests.[43] The same assumptions govern Archibald Foord's discussion of Bolingbroke's opposition to Walpole. He too insists that Bolingbroke's professed principles were mere rationalisations 'manufactured as debating points'; and he too infers that, since they merely 'sprang from calculations of advantage', they are 'in the final analysis irrelevant' to the explanation of Bolingbroke's behaviour.[44]

There is something obviously unsatisfactory about these Namierite accounts. If not actually mistaken, they seem incomplete, for they seem incapable of explaining the specific characteristics of Bolingbroke's campaign. The Namierites are able to tell us why Bolingbroke and his party chose to conduct some form of opposition to Walpole's government. But they are unable to explain why Bolingbroke conducted his campaign according to a specific pattern, concentrating so doggedly on the issues of the land forces and the control of the House of Commons. The Namierites recognise, of course, that the policies pursued by Bolingbroke in the name of patriotism had a specific content, but they refuse to take their content seriously. Namier himself dismissed the issues singled out by the opposition as mere 'flapdoodle',[45] while Brooke's analysis likewise invokes the question-begging idea that there are 'fashions' in opposition.[46] Foord's explanation falls back on the equally question-begging suggestion that 'all political programmes need an altruistic keynote',[47] while Lucy Sutherland speaks in a puzzled but dismissive tone of the fact that Bolingbroke's programme expressed 'an archaic, academic Whiggism'.[48]

Suppose we concede, however, that Bolingbroke's professions of patriotic principle amounted to nothing more than fashionable (or perhaps archaic) flapdoodle. There is still a decision on the part of Bolingbroke and his party to be explained, a decision to propagate one particular brand of flapdoodle rather than another, and to do so with such single-mindedness. We need to be able, in other words, to explain a further belief that Bolingbroke and his party evidently held, besides their belief that denouncing Walpole's ministry constituted a rational means of gaining power for themselves: the belief that it was rational, granted this desire, to carry out their campaign in one particular way.

Once this lacuna is identified, we are left with two possible ways of accounting for it, and thus of trying to replace the Namierite approach with a better explanatory scheme. Either the form of the Namierite argument

---

[43] Brooke 1961, pp. 21–2, 245. Cf also Brooke 1956, p. 218 and Brooke 1963–4.
[44] Foord 1964, pp. 78–9, 114n, 136, 150.   [45] Namier 1930, p. 95.
[46] Brooke 1956, p. 25.   [47] Foord 1964, p. 150.   [48] Sutherland 1956, p. 58.

would bring about a loss of freedom.⁶¹ Dickinson similarly speaks of Bolingbroke's 'genuine concern' about 'the increasing numbers of placemen in Parliament' and maintains that his worries about the corruption of the constitution provided 'a constant motivating force in his political career'.⁶²

These anti-Namierite lines of interpretation account for Bolingbroke's behaviour in exactly the same way as he always accounted for it himself. This is perhaps enough in itself to make one suspicious, and the gain in explanatory power provided by this approach is certainly more than outweighed by the loss of plausibility involved in having to rest the entire interpretation of Bolingbroke's career on the presumption of his unwavering sincerity. I shall not attempt, however, to disprove these claims on behalf of Bolingbroke and his party as men of principle. They would be hard to rebut, just as they would be hard to substantiate (and have not of course been substantiated, but merely asserted, by the scholars I have cited). What I wish to suggest is rather that there is a shared and mistaken assumption underlying the Namierite and the anti-Namierite lines of argument.

The key assumption shared by the Namierites and their critics can be summarised as follows. If and only if we can show that a given principle serves as a motive for an action can we hope to establish the need to refer to the principle to explain the action. The Namierites assume that such principles seldom if ever function as motives, and thus seldom need to be cited. The revisionist view is that such principles function as motives more often than not, and thus usually need to be cited. What I next wish to question, however, is this shared assumption itself. I wish, in other words, to question not the accuracy but the validity of the Namierite argument.

IV

We need to begin by taking note of a crucial fact about the constitutional conventions of eighteenth-century Britain. To engage in the sort of 'formed opposition' conducted by Bolingbroke and his party between 1728 and 1734 was to engage in an activity which (as Namier himself put it) was regarded at the time as 'immoral' and 'tainted with disloyalty'.⁶³ Bolingbroke's whig opponents left him in no doubt as

---

⁶¹ Mansfield 1965, p. 11; cf. also pp. 46, 66. ⁶² Dickinson 1970, pp. 184, 188.
⁶³ Namier 1930, p. 58. See also Robbins 1958, pp. 505–29; Walcott 1964, p. 87; Mansfield 1965, pp. 11–12, 112–16; Kramnick 1968, pp. 155–62.

to the unconstitutional nature of his campaign. Their accusations – conveniently summarised in the title of William Arnall's pamphlet *Opposition No Proof of Patriotism* – took two main forms. First and most dramatically, they accused Bolingbroke in a more or less explicit way of fomenting sedition and treason. As an anonymous pamphleteer put it, the leaders of the opposition are engaged in 'such notorious acts as call their loyalty in question', since they are offering 'treasonable insolencies towards the throne'.[64] The most unguarded accusations were mounted by Walpole's friend Sir William Yonge in his pamphlet *Sedition and Defamation Displayed*. The opposition, Yonge claims, are 'attempting to raise sedition or rebellion'. They are 'infamous retailers' of 'sedition and treason', who 'publish seditious and traitorous libels against the Government and his Majesty himself'. They may appear to be acting under a veil of patriotism, but once this disguise is torn off we see that 'sedition and treason stalk abroad'.[65]

The other and more telling line of attack took the form of pointing out that the very idea of a 'formed' or 'general' opposition was in itself of doubtful legality. William Arnall raised the objection in the form of a rhetorical question. 'Can there be a more unjust thing than opposing measures necessary to the support and being of a State?' Later in the pamphlet he supplied his own answer. 'Where the laws rule, where liberty flourishes', as is the case in England, then '*General Opposition* ought to be out of countenance and cease'.[66] Bolingbroke's 'general opposition' is 'repugnant to patriotism', and 'all calm and disinterested men' must condemn it.[67]

Faced with such accusations, it was clearly essential for Bolingbroke and his party to supply a rival account of their own behaviour. They needed to supply their whig opponents with a reason for believing that, in spite of any *prima facie* appearance of unconstitutionality, their campaign of opposition was justifiable in the circumstances. So they needed to be able to show that their conduct could be redescribed in such a way as to defeat or at least to override the strongly unfavourable interpretations being placed upon it.

It will by now be evident why Bolingbroke and his party needed to exhibit a plausible relationship between some political principle and their actual behaviour, even if they were not in fact motivated by any principles at all. They needed to be able to refer to some accepted principle both as a means of redescribing their opposition and their motives for engaging in

---

[64] *Coalition of Patriots Delineated* 1735, p. 4.   [65] [Yonge] 1731, pp. 1–2, 20, 33.
[66] [Arnall] 1735, p. 11.   [67] [Arnall] 1735, pp. 7, 11. See also *Persuasive to Impartiality* 1731, p. 26.

it, and at the same time as a means of legitimising it. It will also be clear why it was rational for them to redescribe their behaviour specifically by professing the principle of patriotism. If they could plausibly claim to be defending the political liberties of their fellow-countrymen, they could hope to use this redescription to defeat, or at least to override, the unfavourable evaluations placed on their conduct by their adversaries. They could certainly hope to defeat the wilder accusations of treason. For a course of action that can properly be described as patriotic cannot also be described as treasonous. They could also hope to override the one major criticism they could not hope to defeat, namely that they were engaged in a 'formed' or 'general' opposition. For no whig would dare to suggest that the maintenance of a constitutional convention ought to be ranked higher as a political value than the preservation of the political liberties of Englishmen.

This brings me to what I take to be Bolingbroke's great *coup* as a politician. He not only recognised the inescapable need to claim (however disingenuously) that he was motivated by some accepted political principle. He also recognised that a special plausibility would attach to claiming that the specific principle motivating his behaviour was that of patriotism. What he recognised was that, if he were to concentrate on denouncing the size of the land forces and the control of the House of Commons, this would give him the best chance of making the whig ministry's conduct look unpatriotic in the light of their own most cherished beliefs about political liberty.

The essence of Bolingbroke's *coup* was thus to perceive that, according to whig beliefs about the nature of the agencies by which the liberties of citizens are most readily undermined, the whig ministry could plausibly be claimed to be pursuing a number of policies inimical to such liberties. Bolingbroke's strategy then consisted of focusing on just those policies, magnifying them with a good deal of cynical emphasis, and insisting that his 'formed' opposition was in the circumstances the act of a true patriot, since it was the act of someone anxious to prevent the liberties of Englishmen from being subverted and overthrown.

The precise mechanics of this *coup* can readily be illustrated if we turn to the great tradition of whig political theory, and thus to the nature of the beliefs that Bolingbroke's adversaries had inherited about the preservation and subversion of liberty.[68] The origins of their beliefs lay deep in the constitutional theories of the Renaissance. As we

---

[68] On the 'whig canon' see Robbins 1959, Pocock 1975. For the seventeenth-century background see Fink 1962. For the canon and early-modern moral theory see Schneewind 1993. For a recent survey see Geuna 1998, pp. 116–32.

saw in chapters 2 and 5, these theories had in turn been adapted from classical and especially Roman sources, and as we further saw in chapter 11 they were later revived and developed in England, especially in the years following the execution of Charles I in 1649.[69] Among the defenders of the English 'free state' at that crucial juncture, perhaps the most influential was James Harrington in his *Commonwealth of Oceana*, first published in 1656.[70] Harrington's views on political liberty, which owed a great deal to Machiavelli's *Discorsi*, were thereafter propagated by a group of 'neo-Harringtonians' associated with the Earl of Shaftesbury at the time of the Exclusion Crisis,[71] a group including Henry Neville and William Petyt among political writers and Lord Somers among the whig grandees.[72]

The most formative period, however, for the propagation of these neo-classical ideas about public liberty came in the closing years of the seventeenth century.[73] The beginnings of this development can perhaps be traced to the reprinting in 1694 of Henry Neville's translation of Machiavelli's political works, originally issued some twenty years before.[74] The same year saw the publication of James Tyrrell's *Bibliotheca Politica*[75] and Robert Molesworth's *Account of Denmark*, with its Machiavellian analysis of Denmark's loss of liberty in the *coup d'état* of 1660.[76] But the most important years for the establishment of the whig canon were between 1697 and 1700. The year 1697 saw the publication of Andrew Fletcher's first political tract,[77] as well as the start of John Trenchard's collaboration with Walter Moyle, at that time sitting as an independent whig in the House of Commons.[78] The following year saw the appearance of further tracts by Andrew Fletcher[79] and John Trenchard,[80] as well as the posthumous publication of the *Discourses Concerning Government* by the whigs' own martyr, Algernon Sidney,[81] and

---

[69] On these writers see Skinner 1998, pp. 11–16.   [70] Pocock 1977, p. xi.
[71] For this group, and its modifications of Harrington's doctrine, see the exceptionally valuable article in Pocock 1971, pp. 104–47. For Machiavelli's apparent influence on Harrington see Raab 1964, pp. 185–217.
[72] Neville 1969; [Petyt] 1680; Somers 1681.
[73] But see Goldie 1980 and Pocock 1985, pp. 215–30 for important discussions of the period between 1688 and 1694.
[74] See [Neville] 1694 and cf. [Neville] 1675.
[75] [Tyrrell] 1692–4, an attack on patriarchalism and an account of the whig view of the constitution issued in the form of thirteen dialogues between 1692 and 1694. See Pocock 1987, pp. 187–93.
[76] [Molesworth] 1694.   [77] [Fletcher] 1697.
[78] [Trenchard and Moyle] 1697. Cf. Kramnick 1968, pp. 244 and 254–6.
[79] See [Fletcher] 1997 and cf. Robertson 1997, pp. xxxii–xxxiii.   [80] [Trenchard] 1698.
[81] See Sidney 1990 and cf. West 1990, p. xvii. On the composition of the *Discourses* see Scott 1991, esp. pp. 201–14.

of Edmund Ludlow's republican *Memoirs* of the civil war period.[82] The climax was reached in 1700 with the appearance of the first collected edition of James Harrington's political works.[83] The editor was John Toland, who also contributed in his own right to the establishment of the whig canon with his *Danger of Mercenary Parliaments* in 1695 and his *Art of Governing by Parties* in 1701.[84]

The attitudes voiced by these writers were in turn reiterated and developed in a number of works that were published in the years surrounding the crisis of the South Sea Bubble. Neville's translation of Machiavelli and Ludlow's *Memoirs* were both reissued in 1720. The following year saw the appearance of Molesworth's essay on the principles of an independent whig,[85] as well as the beginning of the collaboration between John Trenchard and Thomas Gordon out of which arose *Cato's Letters* in 1724.[86] Two years later there appeared a collected edition of Walter Moyle's works,[87] and two years after that an edition of Tacitus by Thomas Gordon in which the purportedly whig implications of Tacitus's *Histories* were underlined in a series of introductory Discourses.[88]

It remains the case, however, that the most important moment for the crystallising of 'true whig' ideology was around the year 1700, and I shall mainly concentrate on the writings of that period. When the theorists I have cited turn to the topic of political liberty, they generally put forward three connected arguments. They maintain in the first place that freedom is secured when the constitution of a nation is balanced between its executive and legislative parts, and is threatened whenever that balance is encroached upon or lost. There is a clear source for this belief in Machiavelli's *Discorsi*, with their constant stress on the need for the overweening powers of the nobility to be balanced by the populace, and on the importance of sustaining a constitution capable of holding the self-interest of both parties in check.[89] This analysis was broadly

---

[82] Ludlow 1894. For the most relevant sections see vol. 1, pp. 114–15, 151–67, 203–5, 245–6.
[83] Harrington 1700.   [84] [Toland] 1695 and [Toland] 1701.
[85] [Molesworth] 1721, pp. i–xxxvi.
[86] Between January 1720 and June 1721 they issued a weekly, *The Independent Whig*, and between November 1720 and July 1723 they published a series of letters, first in the *London Journal*, later in the *British Journal*, which appeared in book form (with additions by Gordon) as *Cato's Letters* in 1724. See Trenchard and Gordon 1995.
[87] His previously unpublished works were issued in Moyle 1726; his previously published works in Moyle 1727.
[88] Gordon 1728. Discourse 3 (pp. 34–42) is on Julius Caesar's tyranny, while Discourse 5 (pp. 52–68) is on the difference between 'Governments free and arbitrary'. The Discourses are commended in Bolingbroke 1844a, p. 315.
[89] [Neville] 1694, I. 4–6, pp. 273–7.

adopted by James Harrington in the 'Preliminaries' to his *Oceana*, both sections of which open with a contrast between the balanced constitutions of antiquity and the instability of modern 'gothic' governments.[90] Machiavelli, we are told at the outset, is 'the only politician' who has properly recognised the value of mixed constitutions amid the gothic barbarism of modern Europe.[91]

From *Oceana* these assumptions passed into the whig canon as a whole. Algernon Sidney insists in his *Discourses* that 'mixed and popular governments' are always to be preferred if we wish to maintain peace, to avoid civil disorder and to promote the public good.[92] Robert Molesworth's chapter on the Danish form of government is based on the claim that the balance between elective kingship and frequent meetings of the estates alone enabled Denmark to uphold her liberties.[93] John Toland's denunciation of mercenary parliaments likewise includes a warning to his fellow-countrymen that they will 'fruitlessly bewail' the loss of their liberties if they fail to maintain 'a poise and balance' in the constitution and prevent 'encroaching power'.[94] Dedicating his edition of Harrington's works to the Lord Mayor and Aldermen of London, Toland begins with a further declaration to the effect that 'liberty is the true spring' of their 'prodigious trade', and that this freedom is in turn owed to the balanced workings of the constitution.[95]

A second claim advanced by the whig writers is that, if we wish to understand how liberty is gained and lost, we must attend above all to the lessons of history. We need in particular to examine the histories of the numerous European states that have passed from popular freedom into the slavery of absolutism. This commitment again has a clear source in Machiavelli's *Discorsi*, which begins by deploring 'our ignorance or inadvertency in History' and by expressing the hope that (as Neville translates it) 'they which shall peruse these my Discourses, may extract such Advantage and Document as is necessary for their proficiency and improvement'.[96] One of Machiavelli's principal aspirations is to show how the polities of antiquity waxed under conditions of self-government and waned under princely rule.[97] Here too his approach was adopted and developed by James Harrington in *Oceana*, the latter part of which is largely given over to outlining a fictional history of England in which

---

[90] Harrington 1977, pp. 161–9, 188–98.   [91] Harrington 1977, p. 161
[92] Sidney 1990, pp. 195–202, 217–51, 270–9.   [93] [Molesworth] 1694, esp. pp. 44–5.
[94] [Toland] 1695, pp. 1–2. Cf. [Toland] 1701, the opening chapter of which contains a tribute to the liberties of the subject guaranteed by the mixed constitution.
[95] Harrington 1700, Dedication, pp. ii–iii.   [96] [Neville] 1694, Introduction, p. 268.
[97] [Neville] 1694, II. 2, pp. 335–7.

the relations between the shifting balance of property and the balance of political power provide the major theme.[98]

This stress on the lessons of history likewise passed into the whig canon as a whole. Of the three major sections into which Algernon Sidney divided his *Discourses*, the second includes a series of chapters on the rise of Rome under her republican constitution and her decline under her empire,[99] while the third is largely given over to a whig history of the English constitution in which the acceptance of Magna Carta, the rise of Parliament and the rule of law are all assigned a pivotal place.[100] James Tyrrell's *Bibliotheca Politica* is similarly organised in the form of a whig history of the ancient constitution, while John Toland's *Art of Governing by Parties* reveals how the black art of arousing factions 'was set on foot among us' under the Stuart monarchy and inevitably led to disastrous results.[101] The assumption underlying all these discussions is spelled out by Robert Molesworth in the Preface to his *Account of Denmark*, in which he recommends a combination of travel and historical study on the grounds that this will 'teach a gentleman who makes right use of it by what steps slavery has within these last two hundred years crept upon Europe'.[102]

The third main argument advanced by all these writers concerns the nature of the agencies which, as history shows, have been employed with the greatest frequency to alter the balance of free constitutions and extinguish the liberties of those living under them. There are generally taken to be two such agencies, the more blatant of which is said to be the employment by kings and courts of standing mercenary armies. Machiavelli again provides an obvious source for this anxiety, with his constant denunciations of auxiliary and mercenary troops and his corresponding insistence that free nations must always defend themselves by means of their own citizen militias.[103] The theme is again taken up by James Harrington, two of whose formulae in his *Aphorisms Political* of 1659 summarise the significance of the Machiavellian argument. The first contends that 'Where the spirit of the people is impatient of a government by arms and desirous of a government by laws, there the spirit of the people is not unfit to be trusted with their liberty.'[104] The contrasting aphorism asserts that 'Where there is a standing army, and not a formed government, there the army of necessity will have dictatorian power.'[105]

[98] Harrington 1977, pp. 210–340. [99] Sidney 1990, pp. 144–9, 157–66.
[100] Sidney 1990, pp. 456–501, 524–78.
[101] See [Toland] 1701, p. 8 and cf. p. 119 for a list of historical examples.
[102] [Molesworth] 1694, Preface, Sig. B, 3r.
[103] [Neville] 1694, I. 2, pp. 270–2; I. 43, p. 312; II. 10, pp. 344–6; II. 20, pp. 359–60; II. 30, pp. 372–3.
[104] Harrington 1977, Aphorism 7, p. 762. [105] Harrington 1977, Aphorism 98, p. 775.

This emphasis on the danger of standing armies, and on the need to permit citizens to bear arms in the name of liberty, likewise became entrenched not merely in the whig canon but also, with ironic consequences, in that most Harringtonian of official documents, the American Constitution.[106] Algernon Sidney in his *Discourses* offers a Tacitean analysis of how the republican constitution of ancient Rome was corrupted by the power of the soldiery,[107] and later explains the plight of modern France and Denmark in similar terms. It was 'the strength of a mercenary soldiery' that allowed the king of Denmark to overthrow 'all the laws of his country', while the power of the standing army in France has become such that the people cannot even 'defend their own rights' against their kings.[108] Molesworth repeats the claim about Denmark, arguing that the reason why the Danes lost their political liberties, and cannot be expected to regain them, is that their king now maintains against them 'a standing army composed for the most part of foreigners'.[109] Ludlow and Tyrrell draw the same moral from much closer to home. Ludlow's *Memoirs* includes an account of the behaviour of the army during the Interregnum that scared every good whig for generations,[110] while Tyrrell's savagely hostile account of the reign of James II includes the charge that one of the king's 'Arbitrary proceedings' was to raise a standing army with the aim of encouraging his soldiers 'to Fight against the Religion and Liberties of their own Country'.[111]

Several whig writers, including Andrew Fletcher, Walter Moyle and John Trenchard, concentrate virtually all their attention on the threat of standing armies to political liberty.[112] Andrew Fletcher's *Discourse* reflects on 'the alteration of Government which happened in most countries of Europe about the year fifteen-hundred' and 'was fatal to their liberty'. There was originally 'a balance that kept those Governments steady' and 'an effectual provision against the encroachments of the crown'. But liberty gave way to tyranny as soon as this balance was disrupted, and the chief agency of this disruption was that princes 'were allowed to raise armies of volunteers and mercenaries', so that 'the power of the sword was transferred from the subject to the

---

[106] For this pedigree of ideas see Robbins 1959 and Bailyn 1967.   [107] Sidney 1990, pp. 454–6.
[108] Sidney 1990, pp. 187, 198.   [109] [Molesworth] 1721, p. 268.
[110] They are cited, for example, in [Trenchard] 1698, p. 1 with the exhortation to read them 'if any man doubt whether a standing army is slavery'.
[111] [Tyrrell] 1692–4, p. 687; cf. also p. 666.
[112] On their arguments, and those of their opponents, and on the background to the debate, see Miller 1946, Western 1965, Schwoerer 1974.

King'.[113] John Trenchard and Walter Moyle take up the same issue in *An Argument, Shewing, that a Standing Army is inconsistent with a Free Government* in 1697. Speaking of Europe's relapse into absolutism, they conclude that 'if we enquire how these unhappy nations have lost that precious jewel, liberty', the answer is that they all 'permitted a standing army to be kept among them', so that the balance between rulers and people was tilted and liberty overthrown.[114] Walter Moyle reiterates the conclusion in his *Second Part*, claiming that 'in all ages and parts of the world, a standing army has been the never-failing instrument of enslaving a nation'.[115] John Trenchard later draws the same moral from the history of England, claiming that standing armies 'have brought us from one tyranny to another'.[116] The groundswell of the argument, as Trenchard and Moyle summarise it, is thus that 'to know whether a people are free or slaves, it is necessary only to ask whether there is an army kept amongst them'.[117]

I turn to the other and more insidious way in which the liberties of free nations are said to be most readily lost. This invariably happens, we are told, if their citizens are prevented from involving themselves in a free and independent spirit in the activity of government. Machiavelli had laid it down in Book I of the *Discorsi* that to be vigorously involved in public life, even at the cost of provoking 'tumults', is to be a citizen of *virtù*, while to lose or forfeit this involvement is to be politically corrupt.[118] James Harrington takes over both these technical terms, as well as Machiavelli's underlying belief that political liberty can only be assured when such corruption is held in check. Harrington's 'model' of a Commonwealth in *Oceana* is accordingly filled with detailed suggestions as to the devices needed to ensure that the people remain actively involved in politics – devices of annual election, rotation of office and the whole paraphernalia of constitutional checks and balances.

This emphasis on active citizenship likewise became a leading element in the whig vision of political life. Algernon Sidney speaks in two closely connected sections about liberty as the cause of civic virtue, and civic virtue as the means to offset corruption. Where such virtue and a willingness to serve the common good are lost, no commonwealth can hope to maintain its freedom and greatness for any length of time.[119]

[113] [Fletcher] 1697, pp. 5–6, 9, 114–15.   [114] [Trenchard and Moyle] 1697, p. 4.
[115] [Moyle] 1697, p. 10.   [116] [Trenchard] 1698, pp. iv–v.
[117] [Trenchard and Moyle] 1697, p. 11.
[118] [Neville] 1694, I. 3–6, pp. 272–7 on virtue; I. 16–18, pp. 288–92 on corruption.
[119] Sidney 1990, pp. 134–44 and 144–9.

Robert Molesworth likewise explains how Denmark lapsed into absolutism by referring to 'the enslaving of the spirits of the people' and the consequent ease with which their king was able to trick them into signing away their political rights.[120] John Toland's similar anxiety about 'mercenary Parliaments' is that they encourage 'supineness and base neglect', the outcome of which is that the people, having lost any independence or political involvement, 'give away with their own breath and free consent all their rights to their estates and lives'.[121] A people imbued with civic virtue will always be able to 'check and curb' any such 'ambitious and overgrown statesmen', and will thus be able to uphold their rights. But a people who have allowed themselves to become 'unconcerned spectators' of the nation's political life will readily submit to the 'debauching of their honest principles' at the hands of those who aim to subvert their liberties.[122]

Suppose we now turn to Bolingbroke's own political works, and in particular to his *Remarks on the History of England* and his *Dissertation upon Parties*, both of which he wrote during the most active period of his opposition to Walpole's government. We not only find him referring specifically to a number of the writers we have been considering, including Machiavelli, James Harrington and Algernon Sidney;[123] we also find him deploying exactly the same arguments about the value of political liberty. First of all, we find in the *Remarks* a fulsome endorsement of the whig belief in the importance of balanced constitutions. Bolingbroke summarises the doctrine in a much-cited epigram to the effect that 'in a constitution like ours, the safety of the whole depends on the balance of the parts; and the balance of the parts on their mutual independency on each other'.[124] To this he adds in *A Dissertation upon Parties* that, so long as this 'balance of power' is maintained, we shall be able to 'secure to ourselves, and to our latest posterity, the possession of that liberty which we have long enjoyed'. But if we allow this balance to be disrupted, we shall rapidly bring about the collapse of our liberties.[125] This is the lesson that Bolingbroke continually seeks to derive from his outline of English history. The unique grandeur of Elizabeth's reign was based on her exact understanding of the link between political liberty and the balance of the constitution. The undermining of popular liberty in the Wars of the Roses

---

[120] [Molesworth] 1694, Preface, Sig. B, 3a. See also the Conclusion, in which Molesworth stresses (p. 267) that the king of Denmark has 'taken care' to make 'all the people poor in Spirit, as well as in purse'.
[121] [Toland] 1695, p. 8.   [122] [Toland] 1695, pp. 4–5.
[123] Bolingbroke 1997a, pp. 46–7, 69, 98, 111, 171.
[124] Bolingbroke 1844a, p. 331.   [125] Bolingbroke 1997a, p. 118.

and later under the Stuarts was brought about by an alteration of the balance, first in the direction of feudal power and later in the direction of absolutism.[126]

Bolingbroke likewise endorses the whig belief that any study of the way in which these liberties are gained or lost needs to be historical in approach. His main political works are accordingly couched in the form of histories. The *Remarks* examines the vicissitudes of the mixed constitution over several centuries, while *A Dissertation upon Parties* includes a sequence of chapters tracing the loss of liberty in ancient Rome, modern Spain and modern France.[127] Bolingbroke may also have coined the epigram summarising the value of this approach when he observed, at the start of his *Letters on the Study and Use of History*, that 'history is philosophy teaching by examples'.[128]

The most important belief from the whig canon that Bolingbroke endorses relates to the nature of the agencies by which our liberties can most readily be undermined. The same weapon was used, he maintains, to deliver the *coup de grâce* to popular freedom in ancient Rome and modern Spain: the use of 'the force of an army' against the people.[129] In Rome 'the principal men' brought about the collapse of the republic when they 'employed the commands they had of armies' as well as their positions in the state to further their own factional ends.[130] In Spain the standing army played an even more direct role in the subversion of liberty. Despite an ordinance of the Cortes 'against increasing the standing forces of the kingdom', the kings continually found 'pretences for keeping armies on foot'. The fatal outcome was finally reached when Ferdinand, who had raised 'a regular, disciplined army' ostensibly to defend Navarre against the French, turned it upon his own people, 'marched into Castile, defeated the commons, and extinguished liberty'.[131] The general moral, as Bolingbroke announces towards the end of his *Remarks*, is that 'standing armies have been generally the instruments of overturning free governments'.[132]

Bolingbroke also endorses the whig belief that the other most efficacious means of subverting political liberty consists of corrupting the people, thereby preventing them from playing an independent and

---

[126] Bolingbroke 1844a, pp. 335–41, 413–21, 428. Cf. Bolingbroke 1997a, pp. 152–61.
[127] Bolingbroke 1997a, 122–51.
[128] Bolingbroke 1844b, p. 177. On Bolingbroke's use of history see Jackman 1965, pp. 44–69 and Kramnick 1967, pp. 33–56.
[129] Bolingbroke 1997a, p. 143. [130] Bolingbroke 1844a, p. 304.
[131] Bolingbroke 1997a, p. 138.
[132] Bolingbroke 1844a, p. 427. See also Bolingbroke 1844a, pp. 341, 371.

public-spirited role in their nation's affairs.¹³³ He follows Machiavelli in attributing the collapse of the Roman republican constitution to its 'want of a third estate', and thus to the incapacity of the people to check and balance the power of the executive.¹³⁴ He makes the same point in discussing the drift of the French constitution towards absolutism. 'The great, original defect of having but two estates to share the supreme power' with 'the constant desire of encroaching' and the lack of popular surveillance is the mortal weakness 'common to the Roman, and to the French constitution'.¹³⁵

It is in discussing the case of modern Spain, however, that Bolingbroke puts forward the most unequivocally Machiavellian analysis of the constitutional devices that modern rulers have used to enslave their subjects. The Castilians originally possessed in the Cortes 'an assembly, that may be more truly compared to a British Parliament than the assembly of the states of France', an assembly that guaranteed the citizens their liberties so long as they remained active and independent in running it.¹³⁶ But their freedom was struck down with 'an incurable, fatal wound' when 'prostitute wretches were found' who were prepared to maintain 'that the necessary independency of the prince could not be supported, without allowing a corrupt dependency of the Cortes on him'. This soon entrenched 'the custom of bribing the representatives of the Commons, by gifts and promises, and so securing a majority to the court'.¹³⁷ Once 'corrupt majorities were thus secured', the people were unable to check the encroaching power of the court and its dependent ministers with their 'titles, places, pensions and grants'.¹³⁸ The result was that the king gained 'such an influence over the Cortes, as overturned at last the whole constitution' and enslaved the formerly free Castilian people.¹³⁹ The moral is that 'though it be proper in all limited monarchies to watch and guard against all concessions, or usurpations, that may destroy the balance of power, on which the preservation of liberty depends; yet it is certain that concessions to the crown from the other constituent parts of the legislature are almost alone to be feared'.¹⁴⁰

---

¹³³ For Bolingbroke on the theme of civic virtue see Burtt 1992, pp. 87–109. The need to offer uncorrupt service to the public, and the incapacity of the government to offer it, likewise provides Bolingbroke with his central theme in his letter *On the Spirit of Patriotism*, which he composed in 1736 shortly after his retirement to France. See Bolingbroke 1997b, esp. pp. 205–7.
¹³⁴ Bolingbroke 1997a, p. 130.   ¹³⁵ Bolingbroke 1997a, p. 143.
¹³⁶ Bolingbroke 1997a, p. 132.   ¹³⁷ Bolingbroke 1997a, p. 133.
¹³⁸ Bolingbroke 1997a, pp. 133, 137.   ¹³⁹ Bolingbroke 1997a, p. 137.
¹⁴⁰ Bolingbroke 1997a, p. 135.

V

With this survey of the beliefs about political liberty held by the writers in the whig canon, we are now in a position, I believe, to trace the nature of the connections between the principle for the sake of which Bolingbroke and his party claimed to be acting (that of patriotism) and the lines of opposition they consistently pursued (that of denouncing the size of the land forces and the control of the Commons).

We can hope in the first place to explain why Bolingbroke and his party adopted and consistently carried out this particular programme. According to the writers in the whig canon, the two policies most liable to undermine political liberty are the maintenance by the crown of a standing mercenary army, and the interference by the executive with the people's capacity to engage freely and independently in the nation's political life. This in turn helps to explain first of all why the opposition chose to focus on the issue of the land forces. They perceived that this would make it plausible to imply that what the government was doing in maintaining a large professional force in time of peace was seeking to create a standing army dependent on the crown. We can also explain why they concentrated the rest of their fire on the award of pensions and places. They perceived that this would similarly make it plausible to imply that what the government was doing in offering such rewards was interfering with the balance of the constitution by corrupting the legislature. Bolingbroke was too cautious, of course, to claim that these were the ministry's intended goals. But he was able to convey the strong impression that this must be the case by stressing that the ministry was engaged in a set of policies known to be particularly liable to bring about exactly these results.[141]

We can also explain why Bolingbroke endorsed so many whig beliefs in his own political works. A number of interpreters have commented on the apparent paradox that it was Bolingbroke, the arch-enemy of the whigs, who provided the most stylish summary of a number of key whig beliefs. The explanation usually offered is that Bolingbroke must have been a 'pseudo-whig' himself,[142] or else that he must after all have been a genuine 'neo-Harringtonian' who shared the whig vision of political life.[143] A better explanation, I suggest, is that Bolingbroke

---

[141] On altering the balance of the constitution see Bolingbroke 1844a, pp. 306, 333-4, 417. On corruption see Bolingbroke 1997a, pp. 93-7, 137-9, 177-86.

[142] Robbins 1959, p. 284; Jackman 1965, p. 142.

[143] Pocock 1971, p. 134 speaks of Bolingbroke as 'the most spectacular of the neo-Harringtonians', a view adopted in Kramnick 1968, pp. 177, 180 and Dickinson 1970, pp. 184-5.

was seeking to remind his whig enemies of the views held by the accredited theorists of their own party about the concept of political liberty, thereby seeking to establish that their behaviour as a government was gravely out of line with the political principles in which they professed to believe.

Finally, we can also explain why it was the principle of patriotism for the sake of which Bolingbroke and his party consistently claimed to act. As I have suggested, the essence of Bolingbroke's *coup* lay in matching this principle to his party's practice in such a way as to convey the impression that the whig government was pursuing at least two policies known to every good whig to be liable to endanger English liberties. This enabled him to leave the impression that, in opposing these policies, he was concerned above all to ensure that English liberties were preserved. But to be concerned with the preservation of English liberties was agreed on all hands to be the clearest sign of patriotic zeal. Bolingbroke and his party were thus able to claim that they were genuinely motivated by the spirit of patriotism, thereby justifying their apparently unconstitutional policy of conducting a 'formed opposition' to the king's ministry.[144]

I have argued that, unless we put ourselves in a position to explain why Bolingbroke and his party evidently felt it rational to act as they did, we cannot hope to explain their behaviour. I have further argued that the reason why they evidently felt it rational to behave as they did is that it *was* rational in the circumstances. I have not tried, however, to vindicate the honesty or sincerity of their conduct. I see no convincing evidence for saying that Bolingbroke and his party genuinely believed that English liberties were in jeopardy, nor that they felt any deep nostalgia for the passing of an older and less commercialised way of life. My argument goes even further in this direction than that of the Namierites. For I have implied that Bolingbroke's political writings may chiefly have been designed to remind the whigs of their own political principles rather than to set out any principles in which he himself necessarily believed. But in another way my account is completely opposed to that of the Namierites. For I have insisted that it does not follow from the fact that Bolingbroke's professions of principle may have been *ex post facto* rationalisations that these principles can be by-passed when we come to explain his behaviour.

The general belief I have thus been concerned to isolate and criticise is that it is only if an agent's professed principles can be shown to have served as motives that we need to refer to those principles in order to explain

---

[144] For Bolingbroke's insistence that a formed opposition, in the political situation he describes, would be the act of a true patriot, see Bolingbroke 1844a, pp. 357, 428–9, 447, 450–3.

the agent's behaviour. As I have sought to show, an agent's principles will also make a difference to their actions whenever there is a need to provide an explicit justification for them. This will make it necessary for such an agent to limit and direct their behaviour in just such a way as to render their actions *compatible* with the claim that they were motivated by some accepted principle. This in turn means that such an agent's professed principles invariably need to be treated as causal conditions of their actions, even if the agent professed those principles in a wholly disingenuous way.

14

From the state of princes to the person of the state

I

The English translation of Thomas Hobbes's *De Cive*, first published in 1651, begins by promising to undertake 'a more curious search into the rights of States, and duties of Subjects'.[1] The Introduction to *Leviathan*, first published in the same year, similarly announces that the aim of the work will be to anatomise 'that great LEVIATHAN, called a COMMON-WEALTH, or STATE'.[2] Since that time, the idea that the confrontation between individuals and states furnishes the central topic of political theory has come to be almost universally accepted. This makes it easy to overlook the fact that, when Hobbes spoke in these terms, he was self-consciously setting a new agenda for the discipline he claimed to have invented, the discipline of political science.[3] His suggestion that the duties of subjects are owed to an agency called the state, rather than to the person of a ruler, was still a relatively new and highly contentious one. So was his implied assumption that our duties are owed exclusively to the state, rather than to a multiplicity of jurisdictional authorities, local as well as national, ecclesiastical as well as civil in character. So, above all, was his use of the term *state* to denote this highest source of authority in matters of civil government.

Hobbes's declaration can thus be viewed as marking the end of one phase in the history of political theory and the beginning of another and more familiar one. It announces the end of an era in which the concept of public power had been analysed in more personal and charismatic terms. It points to a simpler and more abstract vision of sovereignty as

---

This chapter is an extensively revised and much expanded version of an essay that originally appeared under the title 'The State' in *Political Innovation and Conceptual Change*, ed. Terence Ball, James Farr and Russell L. Hanson (Cambridge, 1989), pp. 90–131.

[1] Hobbes 1983b, Preface, p. 32. On the translation see Warrender 1983, pp. 1–4. On the author of the translation (the poet Charles Cotton) see Malcolm 2000.
[2] Hobbes 1996, Introduction, p. 9.   [3] Hobbes 1839, p. ix.

the property of an impersonal agency, a vision that has remained with us ever since and has come to be embodied in the use of such terms as *état, stato, Staat* and state. My aim in what follows will be to sketch the historical circumstances out of which these linguistic and conceptual transformations arose.[4]

II

As early as the fourteenth century, the Latin term *status* – together with such vernacular equivalents as *estat, stato* and *state* – can already be found in general use in a variety of political contexts. During this formative period, these terms were predominantly employed to refer to the state or standing of rulers themselves.[5] One important source of this usage was the rubric *De statu hominum* from the opening of the *Digest* of Roman law. There the authority of Hermogenianus is adduced for the claim that, 'since all law is established for the sake of human beings, we first need to consider the status of such persons, before we consider anything else'.[6] Following the revival of Roman law studies in twelfth-century Italy, the word *status* came in consequence to designate the legal standing of all sorts and conditions of men, with rulers being described as enjoying a distinctive 'estate royal', *estat du roi* or *status regis*.[7]

When the question of a ruler's status was raised, the reason for doing so was generally to emphasise that it ought to be viewed as a state of majesty, a high estate, a condition of stateliness. Within the well-established monarchies of France and England, we encounter this formula in chronicles and official documents throughout the latter half of the fourteenth century. Jean Froissart recalls in Book I of his *Chroniques* that, when the young king of England held court to entertain visiting dignitaries in 1327, 'the queen was to be seen there in an *estat* of great noblece'.[8] The same usage recurs poignantly in the speech made by William Thirnyng to Richard II in 1399, in which he reminds his former sovereign 'in what presence you renounced and ceased of the state of King, and of lordship and of all the dignity and worship that [be]longed thereto'.[9]

---

[4] But for a critique of this approach see Nederman 1985.
[5] Hexter 1973, p. 155.
[6] *Digest* (1985), I. V. 2, vol. 1, p. 15: 'Cum igitur hominum causa omne ius constitutum sit, primo de personarum statu ac post de ceteris... dicemus.'
[7] Post 1964, pp. 333–67, 368–414.
[8] Froissart 1972, p. 116: 'La [*sc.* la reine] peut on veoir de l'estat grand noblece.'
[9] *Rotuli Parliamentorum 1278–1503*, vol. 3, p. 424, col. 1.

Underlying the suggestion that a distinctive quality of stateliness 'belongs' to kings was the prevailing belief that sovereignty is intimately connected with display, that the presence of majesty serves as an ordering force. This was to prove the most enduring of the many features of charismatic leadership eventually subverted by the emergence of the modern concept of an impersonal state.[10] As late as the end of the seventeenth century, it is still common to find political writers using the word *state* to point to a connection between the stateliness of rulers and the efficacy of their rule. As one might expect, exponents of divine-right monarchy such as Bossuet continue to speak of the *état* of *majesté* in just such terms.[11] But the same assumptions survived even among the enemies of kingship. When John Milton, for example, describes in his *History of Britain* the immortal moment when King Canute ordered the ocean to 'come no further upon my land', Milton observes that the king sought to give force to his extraordinary command by speaking 'with all the state that royalty could put into his countenance'.[12]

By the end of the fourteenth century, the term *status* was also in regular use to refer to the state or condition of a realm or commonwealth.[13] This conception of the *status reipublicae* was likewise classical in origin, and can be found in the histories of Livy and Sallust[14] as well as in Cicero's orations and political works.[15] It can also be found in the Codex of Roman law, most notably in the opening rubric of the *Digest*, where the analysis begins with Ulpian's contention that law is concerned with two arenas, the public and the private, and that 'public law is that which pertains to the *status rei Romanae*'.[16]

With the revival of Roman law studies, this further piece of legal terminology likewise passed into general currency. It became usual in the fourteenth century, both in France and in England, to discuss 'the state of the realm' or *estat du roilme*.[17] Speaking of the year 1389, for example, Froissart remarks that the king decided 'to reform the country *en bon état*, so that everyone would be contented'.[18] The idea of linking the

---

[10] For a comparison between systems of state power in which the ordering force of display is proclaimed, and those in which (as in the modern West) it is obscured, see Geertz 1980, pp. 121–3, whose formulation I have adopted.
[11] Bossuet 1967, pp. 69, 72.   [12] Milton 1971, p. 365.
[13] See Ercole 1926, pp. 67–8; Rubinstein 1971, pp. 314–15; Hexter 1973, p. 155.
[14] See, for example, Livy 1949, XXX. II. 8, p. 372; Sallust 1931a, XL. 2, p. 68.
[15] See, for example, Cicero 1913, II. I. 3, p. 170.
[16] *Digest* 1985, I. I. 2, vol. 1, p. 1: 'publicum ius est quod ad statum rei Romanae spectat'.
[17] Post 1964, pp. 310–22.
[18] Froissart 1824–6, vol. 12, p. 93: 'Le roi... réforma le pays en bon état, tant que tous s'en contentèrent.'

good state of a king and his kingdom soon became a commonplace. By the middle of the fifteenth century, petitioners to the English parliament regularly ended their pleas by promising the king that they would 'tenderly pray God for the good estate and prosperity of your most noble person of this your noble realm'.[19]

If we turn from northern Europe to the Italian city-republics, we encounter the same terminology at an even earlier date. As we saw in chapter 2, the earliest advice-books for *podestà* and other city magistrates were produced in the opening decades of the thirteenth century. These manuals already make it clear that their principal concern is with the *status civitatis*, the state or condition of the city as an independent political entity. The *Oculus Pastoralis* repeatedly employs the phrase,[20] as does Giovanni da Viterbo in his treatise *De Regimine Civitatum* of c.1250.[21] By the start of the fourteenth century we begin to encounter the same concept in the vernacular, with writers of *Dictamina* such as Filippo Ceffi offering extensive instructions to magistrates on how to maintain the *stato* of the city given into their charge.[22]

Discussing the state or standing of such communities, the advice generally tendered by these writers is that magistrates have a duty to maintain their cities in a good, happy and prosperous state.[23] The ideal of upholding the *bonus* (or even the *optimus*) *status reipublicae* was again Roman in origin; the phrase occurs with some frequency in Cicero and Seneca.[24] The author of the *Oculus Pastoralis* similarly speaks of the need to preserve one's city in a happy, advantageous, honourable and prosperous *status*.[25] Giovanni da Viterbo likewise insists on the desirability of maintaining the *bonus status* of one's community,[26] while Filippo Ceffi writes with equal confidence in the vernacular of the obligation to sustain one's city in 'a good *stato* and complete peace'.[27]

---

[19] Shadwell 1912, vol. 1, p. 64 (Petition from the abbey of Syon). See also Shadwell 1912, vol. 1, pp. 66, 82 *et passim*.
[20] *Oculus* 1966, pp. 26, 27, 28 *et passim*.
[21] Viterbo 1901, pp. 230, 231, 232 *et passim*. For the date see Sorbelli 1944.
[22] Ceffi 1942, 27, 47, 48 *et passim*.
[23] Ercole 1926, pp. 67–8; Post 1964, pp. 18–24, 310–32, 377–81; Rubinstein 1971, pp. 314–16; Mansfield 1996, pp. 284–6.
[24] For references to the *optimus status reipublicae* see Cicero 1927, II. XI. 27, p. 174 and Cicero 1931, V. IV. 11, p. 402. For the *optimus civitatis status* see Seneca 1929–35, II. XX. 2, vol. 3, p. 92.
[25] *Oculus* 1966, p. 26: 'ad . . . comodum ac felicem statum civitatis huius', and p. 28: 'ad honorabilem et prosperum statum huius comunitatis'.
[26] See Viterbo 1901, p. 230 on the 'bonus status totius communis huius civitatis'.
[27] Ceffi 1942, p. 47: 'in tutta pace e buono stato'.

These writers also provide the earliest restatements of the classical view of what it means for a city or *respublica* to attain its best state.²⁸ Our magistrates must follow the dictates of justice in all their public acts, so that the common good is promoted, the cause of peace upheld and the happiness of the people assured. This line of reasoning is later taken up by Aquinas and his Italian disciples at the end of the thirteenth century. Aquinas presents the argument at several points in his *Summa* as well as in his commentary on Aristotle's *Politics*. 'A judge has care of the good of the community, based on justice, which is why he desires death for the criminal, because this has the character of good in relation to the common *status*.'²⁹ The same line of reasoning had already been put forward a generation earlier by the writers of advice-books for city magistrates. Giovanni da Viterbo speaks in very similar vein of the *optimus status* in his treatise *De Regimine Civitatum*, while Brunetto Latini reiterates Giovanni's argument in his chapter *Dou gouvernement des cités* at the end of his encyclopaedic *Li Livres dou trésor* in 1266.³⁰

This vision of the *optimus status reipublicae* later became central to *quattrocento* humanist accounts of the well-ordered political life. When Giovanni Campano (1427–77)³¹ analyses the dangers of faction in his tract *De Regendo Magistratu*, he declares that 'there is nothing I count more unfavourable to the *status* and safety of a *respublica*'.³² If the right *status* of a community is to be preserved, all factional advantage must be subordinated to the pursuit of the common good.³³ Filippo Beroaldo (1453–1505) endorses the same conclusion in a treatise to which he actually gave the title *De Optimo Statu*. The best *status*, he agrees, can be attained if and only if our magistrates 'set aside the pursuit of their own advantages and ensure that they act in everything in such a way as to promote the public benefit'.³⁴

---

[28] Note that they begin to discuss this issue nearly a century earlier than such chroniclers as Giovanni Villani, one of the earliest sources usually cited in this context. See Ercole 1926, pp. 67–8; Rubinstein 1971, pp. 314–16; Hexter 1973, p. 155 and cf. Villani 1802–3, vol. 3, p. 159; vol. 4, p. 3 *et passim*.
[29] Aquinas 1952, Iª. II^ae, Qu. 19, art. 10, Resp., p. 104: 'nam iudex habet curam boni communis, quod est iustitia, et ideo vult occisionem latronis, quae habet rationem boni secundum relationem ad statum communem'.
[30] Viterbo 1901, pp. 220–2. Cf. Latini 1948, pp. 402–5, paraphrasing Giovanni's account.
[31] In providing dates for the more obscure humanists I have relied on Cosenza 1962.
[32] Campano 1502, fo. xxxxvii^r: 'nihil existimem a statu et salute reipublicae alienius'.
[33] Campano 1502, fo. xxxxvii^r–v.
[34] Beroaldo 1508, fo. xv^v: 'oblitis suorum ipsius commodorum ad utilitatem publicam quicquid agit debet referre'.

The Erasmian humanists imported the same values and vocabulary into northern Europe in the early decades of the sixteenth century. Erasmus himself contrasts the *optimus* with the *pessimus reipublicae status* in his *Institutio Principis Christiani* of 1516,[35] arguing that 'the happiest *status* is reached when everyone obeys the prince, when the prince obeys the laws and when the laws answer to our ideals of honesty and equity'.[36] His younger contemporary Thomas Starkey offers a similar account in his *Dialogue* of what constitutes 'the most prosperous and perfect state that in any country, city or town, by policy and wisdom may be established and set'.[37] And in Thomas More's *Utopia* the figure of Raphael Hythloday likewise insists that, because the Utopians live in a society in which the laws embody the principles of justice and allow everyone to live 'as happily as possible',[38] we are justified in saying that the Utopians have attained the *optimus status reipublicae*, the best state of a commonwealth.[39]

III

I now turn to examine how these early uses of *status* and its vernacular equivalents mutated in such a way as to give these terms their modern range of reference.[40] Historians who have addressed this question have generally concentrated on the evolution of legal theories about the *status* of rulers in the fourteenth and fifteenth centuries.[41] It was rare, however, even for civil lawyers to use the Latin word *status* without qualification, and it was virtually unknown for political writers to employ such a barbarism at all.[42] Even when we encounter the term *status* in political contexts, it is almost always evident that what is at issue is the state or standing of a king or kingdom, not in the least the idea of the state as the institution

---

[35] Erasmus 1974, p. 162.
[36] Erasmus 1974, p. 194: 'felicissimus est status, cum principi paretur ab omnibus atque ipse princeps paret legibus, leges autem ad archetypum aequi et honesti respondent'.
[37] Starkey 1948, p. 63.
[38] More 1965, p. 244 states that their *Reipublicae fundamenta* have been established *felicissime*.
[39] More 1965, p. cxcv.
[40] On the term 'state' and the modern concept of the state see also Dyson 1980, pp. 18–19, 25–8, 206–14.
[41] See Kantorowicz 1957, pp. 207–32, 268–72; Post 1964, pp. 247–53, 302–9; Strayer 1970, pp. 57–9; Wahl 1977, p. 80. But for a valuable corrective see Ullmann 1968–9, pp. 43–4. For a survey of discussions about medieval origins see Fell 1991.
[42] François Hotman loftily dismisses such usages as late as the 1570s. See Hotman 1972, p. 332, observing that the powers of the Public Council extend 'to all those matters which the common people in vulgar parlance nowadays call Affairs of State' – 'de iis rebus omnibus, quae vulgus etiam nunc Negotia Statuum populari verbo appellat'.

in whose name legitimate government is exercised. If we wish to trace the origins of this transformation, it seems to me that we need to begin by focusing not on legal writings but rather on the advice-books for magistrates on which I have already commented, and above all on the mirror-for-princes literature to which they eventually gave rise.[43] It was within this latter tradition of practical political reasoning that the terms *status* and *stato* first began to be used in new and significantly extended ways.[44]

As we saw in chapter 5, the writers of handbooks for princes were generally preoccupied with two related questions of statecraft. Their loftiest aim was to explain how rulers can hope to attain the goals of honour and glory for themselves while at the same time managing to promote the happiness and welfare of their subjects.[45] But their main concern was with a more basic and urgent question of politics: how to advise the *signori* of Italy, often in highly unsettled circumstances, on how to hold on to their *status principis* or *stato del principe*, their state or standing as effective rulers of their existing territories.

As a result, the use of the term *stato* to denote the political standing of rulers, together with the discussion of how such rulers should behave if they wish *mantenere lo stato*, began to resound through the chronicles and advice-books of *trecento* Italy. When Giovanni Villani speaks in his *Istorie Fiorentine* of the civic dissensions that scarred the city during the 1290s, he observes that they were largely directed against the people in their *stato e signoria*.[46] When Ranieri Sardo in his *Cronaca Pisana* describes the accession of Gherardo d'Appiano in 1399, he remarks that the new *capitano* continued to enjoy the same *stato e governo* as his father had enjoyed before him.[47] By the time we reach Machiavelli's *Il Principe* of 1513, the question of what rulers should do to maintain their political standing had become the chief topic of debate. Machiavelli's advice is almost entirely directed at new princes who wish *mantenere lo stato*, to uphold their positions in whatever territories they may have managed to inherit or acquire.[48]

If such rulers are to prevent their state or standing from being altered to their disadvantage, they must clearly be able to fulfil a number of

---

[43] But for a critique of this proposal and a discussion of medieval uses of *status* and *état* see Harding 1994.
[44] Dowdall 1923, p. 102; Skinner 1978b, pp. 352–8; Ornaghi 1995, pp. 349–58. But for a critique of this thesis see Coleman 1997.
[45] For an early statement of these twin ideals see Petrarch 1554b, pp. 420–1, 428. For a classic restatement see Machiavelli 1960, p. 102.
[46] Villani 1802–3, vol. 4, pp. 24, 190–4.   [47] Sardo 1845, pp. 240–1.
[48] For these phrases see Machiavelli 1960, pp. 16, 19, 22, 25–6, 27, 28, 35 *et passim*.

preconditions of effective government. If we turn to examine how these preconditions were formulated and discussed, we shall find that the terms *status* and *stato* were employed in an increasingly extended manner to refer to these various aspects of political power.[49]

One precondition of maintaining one's standing as a ruler is obviously that one should be able to preserve the character of one's existing regime. We accordingly find the terms *status* and *stato* being used from an early period to refer not merely to the state or condition of princes, but also to the presence of particular forms of government. This usage in turn appears to have arisen out of the habit of employing the term *status* to classify the types of rule described by Aristotle. Aquinas has sometimes been credited with popularising this development, since there are versions of his *Expositio* of Aristotle's *Politics* in which oligarchies are described as *status paucorum* and the rule of the people as the *status popularis*.[50] Such usages later became widespread in *quattrocento* humanist political thought. Filippo Beroaldo begins his *De Optimo Statu* with a typology of legitimate regimes, speaking of the *status popularis*, the *status paucorum* and even the *status unius* when referring to monarchies.[51] Francesco Patrizi of Siena (1412–94) opens his *De Regno* with a similar typology, one in which monarchy, aristocracy and democracy are all characterised as different types of *status*.[52] Writing in the vernacular at the same period, Vespasiano da Bisticci (1421–98) contrasts the rule of *signori* with the *stato populare*,[53] while Francesco Guicciardini invokes the same distinction a generation later in his *Discorsi* on the government of Florence.[54] Machiavelli likewise uses *stato* in just this fashion in a number of passages in *Il Principe*,[55] most notably in the opening sentence of the book, in which he informs us that 'all the *stati*, all the dominions that have had or now have power over men, either have been or are republics or principalities'.[56]

By this time the term *stato* was also in widespread use as a way of referring to prevailing regimes. When Giovanni Villani notes that in

---

[49] Rubinstein 1971 has already analysed some of these usages. While I have avoided duplicating his examples I am much indebted to his account.
[50] See Aquinas 1966, III. V, 385, p. 136 on the contrast between living 'in statu populari' and 'in statu paucorum'; VI. IV, 973, p. 319 on the 'status popularis'; VI. VI, 1008, p. 328 on the 'status paucorum'. Rubinstein 1971, p. 322 credits Aquinas with popularising these usages, but they were largely the product of humanist revisions of his text in the 1490s. See Cranz 1978 pp. 169–73 and cf. Mansfield 1996, p. 346 and further references there.
[51] Beroaldo 1508, fos. xi^r and xii^v.   [52] Patrizi 1594a, pp. 16–17, 19, 21.
[53] Vespasiano 1970–6, vol. 1, p. 406.   [54] Guicciardini 1932, p. 274.
[55] See Machiavelli 1960, pp. 28–9 on the *stato di pochi*.
[56] Machiavelli 1960, p. 15: 'Tutti li stati, tutti e' dominii che hanno avuto et hanno imperio sopra li uomini, sono stati e sono o republiche o principati.'

1308 'it was the members of the *parte Nera* who held control' in Florence, he speaks of the government they established as *lo stato de' Neri*.⁵⁷ When Ranieri Sardo writes about the fall of the Nove in Siena in 1355, he describes the change of regime as the loss of *lo stato de' Nove*.⁵⁸ When Vespasiano relates how the enemies of Cosimo de' Medici managed to set up a new government in 1434, he characterises the *coup* as a change of *lo stato*.⁵⁹ By the time we come to such theorists as Machiavelli's friend Francesco Vettori, writing in the early years of the sixteenth century, we find these usages firmly entrenched. Vettori employs the term *stato* not only to refer to different forms of government, but also to describe the prevailing regime in Florence that he wished to see defended.⁶⁰

A second precondition of maintaining one's state as a ruler is obviously that one should suffer no loss or alteration of the territories given into one's charge. As a result of this further preoccupation, we find the terms *status* and *stato* pressed into service as a way of referring to the areas over which a ruler or chief magistrate needs to exercise control. When the author of the *Oculus Pastoralis* admonishes magistrates to care for the welfare of their cities, he speaks of their duty to maintain *suos status*.⁶¹ When the authors of the *Gratulatio* addressed the people of Padua in 1310 to express the hope that the province will continue to live in peace, they declare that they are praying for the tranquillity of the whole *status*.⁶² And when Ambrogio Lorenzetti explains in the verses accompanying his frescoes in the Sala de' Nove in Siena that all *signori* must cultivate the virtues, he gives as his reason that this is how they must act *per governar suo stato*.⁶³

These usages proliferate in the chronicles and handbooks of the high Renaissance. When Ranieri Sardo wants to describe how the Pisans made peace in their territories in 1290, he says that the truce extended throughout the *stato*.⁶⁴ When Francesco Guicciardini remarks in his *Ricordi* that the French revolutionised warfare in Italy after 1494, producing a situation in which the loss of a single campaign brought with it the forfeiture of all one's lands, he describes such defeats as leading to the loss of *lo stato*.⁶⁵ So too with Machiavelli, who frequently uses the term *lo stato* in *Il Principe* to denote the lands or territories of princes. He writes at length in chapter 3 about the methods a wise prince must adopt if he

---

⁵⁷ Villani 1802–3, vol. 4, pp. 25, 190–1. Cf. Villani 1802–3, vol. 8, p. 186.
⁵⁸ Sardo 1845, p. 125.   ⁵⁹ Vespasiano 1970–6, vol. 2, pp. 171, 173.
⁶⁰ Vettori 1842, pp. 433, 436. Rubinstein 1971, p. 318 notes that these were already standard usages in late *quattrocento* Florence.
⁶¹ *Oculus* 1966, p. 24.   ⁶² *Gratulatio* 1741, p. 131.
⁶³ Starn and Partridge 1992, Appendix I, p. 264.   ⁶⁴ Sardo 1845, p. 91.
⁶⁵ Guicciardini 1933, p. 298.

wishes to acquire new *stati*; and he asks in chapter 24 why so many of the princes of Italy have lost their *stati* in the course of his own lifetime.[66]

Due in large measure to these Italian influences, the same usages can be found in northern Europe by the early decades of the sixteenth century. Guillaume Budé in his *L'Institution du prince* equates the range of *les pays* commanded by Augustus after his victory over Antonius with the extent of *son estat*.[67] Thomas Starkey in his *Dialogue* speaks of the need to establish a Council in England to 'represent the whole state'.[68] And when Lawrence Humfrey wishes to warn us in *The Nobles* that a ruler's bad behaviour can easily corrupt his entire kingdom, what he says is that his vices can spread 'into the whole state'.[69]

As these writers emphasise, however, by far the most important precondition of maintaining one's state as a ruler must be to keep one's hold over the existing institutions of government within one's *regnum* or *civitas*. This gave rise to the most important linguistic innovation that can be traced to the chronicles and political treatises of Renaissance Italy. The crucial development took the form of an extension of the term *stato* to refer not merely to prevailing regimes but also, and more specifically, to the institutions of government and the means of coercive control that serve to preserve order within political communities.

Vespasiano speaks on several occasions in his *Vite* of *lo stato* as just such an apparatus of political authority. In his life of Alessandro Sforza he describes how Alessandro conducted himself in the government of *lo stato*,[70] and in his life of Cosimo de' Medici he praises Cosimo for recognising how difficult it is to hold power over *uno stato* when opposed by influential citizens.[71] Guicciardini in his *Ricordi* similarly asks why the Medici lost control of *lo stato* in 1527, and later observes that they found it much harder than Cosimo had done to maintain their hold over *lo stato di Firenze*.[72] Castiglione likewise makes it clear in his *Libro del Cortegiano* that he thinks of *lo stato* as a power structure that a prince needs to control and dominate. He speaks in Book 2 of the need for courtiers 'to be prudent and wise when taking part in discussions about *stati*',[73] and he explicitly

---

[66] Machiavelli 1960, pp. 18, 22, 24, 97.
[67] Budé 1966, p. 140. Delaruelle 1907, p. 201 notes that, although Budé's *Institutio* was not published until 1547, it was completed by the start of 1519.
[68] Starkey 1948, p. 167.   [69] Humfrey 1563, Sig. Q, 8ᵛ.
[70] Vespasiano 1970–6, vol. 1, p. 426.
[71] Vespasiano 1970–6, vol. 1, pp. 177, 192. On the latter passage see Rubinstein 1971, p. 318.
[72] Guicciardini 1933, pp. 287, 293. Guicciardini – but not Machiavelli – also speaks explicitly of *ragione di stato*. See Maffei 1964, pp. 712–20. For the subsequent history of the concept in *cinquecento* Italy see Meinecke 1957, pp. 65–145 and Borrelli 1993.
[73] Castiglione 1981, II. XXII, p. 151: '... nei discorsi de' stati prudente e savio'. Hoby's translation of 1561 renders this as 'discourses uppon states'. See Castiglione 1994, p. 125.

distinguishes at the outset of Book 4 between ruling families and the states over which they rule.[74]

Of all these writers of advice-books, it is Machiavelli in *Il Principe* who shows the most consistent willingness to distinguish the institutions of *lo stato* from those who have charge of them. He thinks of *stati* as having their own foundations, and speaks in particular of each *stato* as having its own particular laws, customs and ordinances.[75] He is willing in consequence to speak of *lo stato* as an independent agent, and describes it as capable, among other things, of choosing courses of action and calling in times of crisis on the loyalty of its citizens.[76] As he makes clear at several points, what he takes himself to be discussing in *Il Principe* is not merely how princes ought to behave. He also sees himself as writing more abstractly about statecraft (*dello stato*) and about *cose di stato* or affairs of state.[77]

It has often been argued that, with these observations of Machiavelli's, we already encounter an understanding of the state not merely as an apparatus of power but as an agent whose existence remains independent of those who exercise its authority at any given time.[78] There is not much evidence, however, to support this vision – originally Burckhardt's vision – of the Italian Renaissance as the crucible in which the modern idea of the state was formed.[79] Machiavelli and his contemporaries undoubtedly engineered an important innovation when they used the term *stato* to refer to the institutions of government, and thus to a distinct apparatus of power. But even Machiavelli usually takes pains to emphasise that the power in question remains that of the prince, and thus that in speaking of *lo stato* he is speaking of *il suo stato*, of the prince's own state or condition of rulership.[80] For all the importance of the writers I have been considering, none of them ever conceives of the state as the name of an agent distinguishable at once from rulers and ruled.[81]

---

[74] See Castiglione 1981, IV. II, p. 365, distinguishing 'la felicità della casa e dello stato'. Hoby renders this as 'the happines of the house and of the State'. See Castiglione 1994, p. 292.

[75] Machiavelli 1960, pp. 53, 76, 84.   [76] Machiavelli 1960, pp. 48, 92.

[77] Machiavelli 1960, pp. 21, 25.

[78] Cassirer 1946, pp. 133–7; Chiappelli 1952, p. 68; Chabod 1962, pp. 146–55; D'Entrèves 1967, pp. 30–2; Mansfield 1996, pp. 288–94.

[79] Burckhardt 1990, p. 23 speaks of the emergence in *trecento* Italy of 'the purely modern fiction of the omnipotence of the state', and adds (p. 73) that Machiavelli's Florence was 'the most important workshop' in which 'the modern European spirit' was formed. See also Chittolini 1979.

[80] Machiavelli 1960, pp. 16, 47, 87, 95.

[81] Even in France this arguably remains true until the 1570s. See Lloyd 1983, pp. 146–53. In Spain the old assumptions survive at least until the middle of the seventeenth century, *pace* Maravall 1961. See Elliott 1984, pp. 42–5, 121–2. Shennan 1974, pp. 113–14 notes that in Germany a patrimonial concept of government survived even longer.

IV

To trace the process by which the state eventually came to be viewed as an independent agent and as the seat of sovereignty, we need to turn away from the practical political literature on which I have so far concentrated. We need to turn first to consider two overlapping strands of constitutionalist theory that likewise rose to prominence in the course of the fifteenth and sixteenth centuries. One of these (which I shall examine in section V) was the contractarian theory associated with the so-called 'monarchomach' or king-killing writers of the later sixteenth century. The other was the tradition of Italian republicanism, a tradition that remained in contestation with the theory of princely government throughout the era of the Renaissance in Italy and beyond.

Turning first to the republican tradition, we need to recall that, as we saw in chapter 2, there were two distinct idioms in which the basic ideal of self-government was articulated. One was the juristic idiom of the legal commentators, many of whom made it their business to adapt the Roman law theory of *imperium* to the conditions of the Italian city-republics. The other was the more moralistic style of writing adopted by the admirers of Sallust, Cicero and the other defenders of the *vera respublica* in ancient Rome. As we have already seen, this was the idiom initially employed by the writers of treatises for city magistrates, and it was subsequently carried to new peaks of eloquence with the flowering of classical republicanism in the high Renaissance.

If there is any basic assumption shared by these two strands of republican thought, it is that all power corrupts and that absolute power corrupts absolutely. Any individual or group, once granted sovereignty over a community, will tend to promote their own interests at the expense of the common good. The only way to ensure that the laws promote the good of the community at large will therefore be to leave the citizens in charge of their own affairs. If their government is instead controlled by an authority external to their community, that authority will be sure to subordinate the good of the community to its own purposes. The same outcome will be no less likely under the rule of hereditary *signori* or princes. Since they will generally seek their own ends rather than the common good, the community will again forfeit its liberty to act in pursuit of whatever goals it may wish to set itself.

This basic insight was followed up in two distinct ways. It was used in the first place to justify assertions of civic autonomy, and hence to defend the *libertas* of the Italian cities against external interference. This demand was initially directed against the Empire and its claims to feudal suzerainty over the *Regnum Italicum*. As we saw in chapter 2, the argument was mounted in detail by such jurists as Azo, and later by Bartolus, Baldus and their followers in the fourteenth century. Seeking to vindicate what Bartolus called 'the *de facto* refusal of the cities of Tuscany to recognise any superior in temporal affairs',[82] they evolved a legal theory according to which the ultimate bearer of sovereignty in any independent city must be the *universitas* or corporation of the people as a whole.[83]

This call for *libertas* was at the same time directed against potential rivals as sources of coercive jurisdiction within the cities themselves. One target was the power of local feudatories, who continued to be viewed, as late as Machiavelli's *Discorsi*, as the most dangerous of all the enemies of free states.[84] But the same hostility was no less vehemently displayed towards the jurisdictional pretensions of the church. The most radical response, embodied for example in Marsilius's *Defensor Pacis* of 1324, took the form of insisting that all coercive power must be secular by definition, and thus that the church can have no civil jurisdiction at all.[85] But even in the earliest treatises on city government, such as Giovanni da Viterbo's *De Regimine Civitatum* of c.1250, we already encounter a refusal to allow the church any say in civic affairs. The reason, as Giovanni expresses it, is that the ends of temporal and ecclesiastical authority are wholly distinct. If the church lays claim to any jurisdiction in political matters, it will simply be 'putting its sickle into another man's harvest'.[86]

The other way in which the basic insight of the republican tradition was developed was in the form of a positive claim about the type of regime we need to institute if we are to retain our *libertas*. The essence of the republican case is that the only form of government under which a city can hope to remain 'in a free state' will be a *respublica* in the strictest sense. The community must retain ultimate sovereignty, assigning its rulers and magistrates a status no higher than that of elected functionaries. These officials must in turn recognise that they are mere agents or *ministri* of justice, charged with the duty of ensuring that the laws established by the community for the promotion of its own good are equitably enforced.

[82] Bartolus 1562, XLVII. XXII, p. 779 on the 'civitates Tusciae, quae non recognoscunt de facto in temporalibus superiorem'. For Baldus on *de facto* sovereignty see Canning 1987, pp. 93–131.
[83] Michaud-Quantin 1970; Wahl 1977; Canning 1983, pp. 8–17; Canning 1987, pp. 185–97. For analogous reinterpretations of the Decretals see Mochi Onory 1951. For a valuable survey see Tierney 1982.
[84] Machiavelli 1960, I. 55, pp. 254–8. [85] Marsilius 1928, II. 4, pp. 128–43.
[86] Viterbo 1901, p. 266: 'in alterius messem falcem suam mittere'.

This contrast between the freedom of republican regimes and the servitude implied by any form of monarchical government has often been viewed as the distinctive contribution of *quattrocento* Florentine thought.[87] As we saw in chapter 2, however, the underlying assumption that 'a free state' can only be achieved under a republic was already present in a number of much earlier writings on behalf of the Italian communes. It is certainly true, however, that the argument was worked out with the fullest assurance by the protagonists of the Venetian and Florentine republics in the era of the high Renaissance. Among Venetian writers, Gasparo Contarini furnished the best-known statement of the case in his *De Republica Venetorum* of 1543. Owing to the city's elective system of government, he declares, in which 'a mixture of the *status* of the nobility and of the people' is maintained, 'there is nothing less to be feared in the city of Venice than that the head of the republic will interfere with the *libertas* or activities of any of the citizens'.[88] Among Florentine theorists, Machiavelli in his *Discorsi* provided the most influential restatement of the same argument. 'It is easy to understand', as he confides at the start of Book 2, 'whence the love of living under a free constitution springs up in peoples, for experience shows that no cities have ever increased in dominion or in riches except when they have been established in liberty.'[89] The reason, he goes on, 'is easy to understand, for it is not the pursuit of individual advantage but of the common good that makes cities great, and there is no doubt that it is only under republican regimes that this ideal of the common good is followed out'.[90]

From the point of view of my present argument, two aspects of this republican tradition are of special significance. First of all, it is among these writers that we first encounter the claim that there is a distinct form of 'civil' or 'political' authority which is autonomous, which exists to regulate the public affairs of an independent community, and which brooks no rivals as a source of coercive power within its own territories. We encounter, in other words, the familiar understanding of the state as the monopolist of legitimate force. This view of civil government was

---

[87] This is, for example, the main thesis of Baron 1966. For a reaffirmation see Witt 1996.
[88] Contarini 1626, pp. 22, 56: 'temperandam ... ex optimatum & populari statu ... nihil minus urbi Venetae timendum sit, quam principem reipublicae libertati ullum unquam negocium facessere posse'. On Contarini see Pocock 1975, pp. 320–8.
[89] Machiavelli 1960, II. 2, p. 280: 'E facil cosa è conoscere donde nasca ne' popoli questa affezione del vivere libero: perché si vede per esperienza le cittadi non avere mai ampliato né di dominio né di ricchezza se non mentre sono state in libertà.'
[90] Machiavelli 1960, II. 2, p. 280: 'La ragione è facile a intendere: perché non il bene particulare ma il bene comune è quello che fa grandi le città. E sanza dubbio questo bene comune non è osservato se non nelle republiche.'

taken up in France and England at an early stage in their constitutional development. It underlies their hostility to the jurisdictional powers of the church, culminating in France in the Concordat of 1516 and in England in the Marsiglian assumptions governing the Henrician Reformation, especially the Act in restraint of Appeals in 1533. The same view underpins the repudiation by France and England of the Holy Roman Empire and its claims to exercise jurisdiction within their territories.[91] This connected attack on the ideal of universal empire had already been central to the work of such Italian jurists as Andreas de Isernia and Oldradus da Ponte in the early fourteenth century. It was their defence of the Neapolitan kingdom in its struggle for independence from the Empire that originally gave rise to the dictum, subsequently invoked in every affirmation of national sovereignty, that *Rex in regno suo est Imperator regni sui*; that all kings within their own kingdoms may be said to exercise full imperial authority. [92]

The other way in which the republican tradition contributed to crystallising an understanding of the state as an independent agency was of even greater significance. According to the writers I have been considering, no community can hope to remain in a free state unless it succeeds in imposing strict conditions on its rulers and magistrates. They must always be elected; they must always be subject to the laws and institutions of the community that elects them; and they must act to promote the common good – and hence the peace and happiness – of the citizens as a whole. As a result, the republican theorists no longer equate the idea of governmental authority with the powers of particular rulers or magistrates. Rather they think of the powers of civil government as embodied in a structure of laws and institutions which our rulers and magistrates are entrusted to administer in the name of the common good. They cease in consequence to speak of rulers 'maintaining their state' in the sense of preserving their personal ascendancy over the apparatus of government. Rather they speak of the *status* or *stato* as the name of that apparatus of government which our rulers have a duty to maintain and preserve.

There are already some hints of this momentous transition in the earliest treatises designed for city magistrates. Brunetto Latini insists in his *Trésor* of 1266 that cities must always be ruled by elected officials if the *bien commun* is to be fostered. He further insists that these *sires* must follow the laws and customs of the city in all their public acts.[93] Such a

---

[91] On the struggle against church and Empire as formative in the construction of modern European states see the survey in Creveld 1999, pp. 62–87.
[92] On the Neapolitan jurists see Calasso 1957, Costa 1969, Canning 1983.
[93] Latini 1948, pp. 392, 402, 408, 412, 415.

system is indispensable not only to maintaining such officials in a good *estat*, but also to maintaining 'the *estat* of the city itself'.⁹⁴ A similar hint can be found in Giovanni da Vignano's *Flore de Parlare* of the 1270s. One of Giovanni's model letters, designed for the use of ambassadors seeking military help, describes the government of such communities as their *stato*, and appeals for support 'in order that our good *stato* can remain in wealth, honour, greatness and peace'.⁹⁵ The same hint recurs soon afterwards in Matteo de' Libri's *Arringhe*, in which he sets out a similar speech for ambassadors to deliver, advising them to appeal for help 'in order that our good *stato* may be able to remain in peace'.⁹⁶

It is only with the final flowering of Renaissance republicanism, however, that we find the terms *status* and *stato* used with full confidence to refer to an independent apparatus of government. Even at this stage, moreover, the development was largely confined to the vernacular literature. Consider, by contrast, a work such as Alamanno Rinuccini's Latin dialogue of 1479, *De Libertate*. This includes a classic restatement of the claim that individual as well as civic liberty is possible only under the laws and institutions of a republic. But Rinuccini never stoops to using the barbarous term *status* to describe the laws and institutions involved.⁹⁷ The same is true of such Venetian writers as Gasparo Contarini in his *De Republica Venetorum*. Although Contarini has a clear conception of the apparatus of government as a set of institutions independent of those who have control of them, he always speaks in a similar way of such institutions as those of the *respublica*, never those of the *status* or state.⁹⁸

If we turn, however, to the less pure latinity of such writers as Francesco Patrizi in his *De Institutione Reipublicae*, we come upon a significant change. Patrizi lays it down that the basic obligation of magistrates is to act 'in such a way as to promote the common good', and argues that this above all requires them to uphold 'the established laws' of the community.⁹⁹ He then summarises by saying that this is how magistrates must act if they are to prevent the *status* from being overturned.¹⁰⁰ The vernacular

---

⁹⁴ See Latini 1948, p. 403 on 'l'estat de vous et de cette ville' and p. 411 on remaining 'en bon estat'.
⁹⁵ Vignano 1974, p. 247: 'che 'l nostro bom stato porà remanere in largheça, honore, grandeça e reponso'.
⁹⁶ Libri 1974, p. 12: 'ke 'l nostro bon stato potrà remanire in reposo'.
⁹⁷ Rinuccini 1957.
⁹⁸ See Contarini 1626, pp. 28 and 46, two passages where, in Lewkenor 1599, *respublica* is rendered as 'state'. On Lewkenor's translation see Fink 1962, pp. 41–2.
⁹⁹ See Patrizi 1594b, p. 281 on the duty to uphold 'veteres leges' and to act 'pro communi utilitate'.
¹⁰⁰ See Patrizi 1594b, pp. 279 and 292 on how to act 'ne civitatis status evertatur'.

writers of the next generation strongly consolidate this terminological shift. Francesco Guicciardini's *Discorso* on how the Medici should act to improve their grip on Florence provides a suggestive example. He advises them to gather around them a group of advisers loyal to the *stato* and willing to act on its behalf. The reasoning behind this strategy, he says, is that 'every *stato*, every sovereign power, needs dependents' who are willing 'to serve the *stato* and benefit it in everything'.[101] If the Medici base their regime on such a group, they will be able to establish 'the most powerful bulwark and basis for the defence of the *stato*' that anyone could aspire to set up.[102]

Machiavelli uses the term *stato* with still greater assurance in his *Discorsi* to denote the same kind of agency and authority. It is true that he largely continues to employ the term in traditional ways to refer to the state or condition of a city and its way of life.[103] Even when he mentions *stati* in the context of describing systems of government, his usages are still largely traditional: he is generally speaking either about a species of regime,[104] or about the general area or territory over which a prince or a republic holds sway.[105] But there are several moments, especially in the analysis of constitutions at the start of Book 1, when he appears to go further. The first is when he writes in chapter 2 about the founding of Sparta. He emphasises that the laws promulgated by Lycurgus remained distinct from, and served to control, the kings and magistrates entrusted with enforcing them, and he characterises Lycurgus's achievement in creating such a system by saying that 'he established *uno stato* which then endured for more than eight hundred years'.[106] The next instance occurs in chapter 6, where Machiavelli asks whether the institutions of government in republican Rome could have been set up in such a way as to avoid the *tumulti* that disrupted the city's political life. He puts the question in the form of asking 'whether it might have been possible to establish *uno stato* in Rome' without such an apparent weakness.[107] The last and most revealing instance occurs in chapter 18, in which he considers the difficulty of maintaining *uno stato libero* within a corrupt city. Not only does he mark an explicit distinction between the authority

---

[101] Guicciardini 1932, pp. 271–2: 'ogni stato ed ogni potenzia eminente ha bisogno delle dependenzie... che tutti servirebono a beneficio dello stato'.
[102] Guicciardini 1932, p. 273: 'uno barbacane e fondamento potentissimo a difesa dello stato'.
[103] Machiavelli 1960, I. 3, p. 135; I. 6, pp. 142–3; I. 25, p. 192; I. 26, p. 194 *et passim*.
[104] Machiavelli 1960, I. 2, pp. 130–2; I. 18, p. 182; II. 25, p. 357.
[105] Machiavelli 1960, II. 24, pp. 351–3.
[106] Machiavelli 1960, I. 2, p. 133: 'Licurgo... fece uno stato che durò più che ottocento anni.'
[107] Machiavelli 1960, I. 6, p. 141: 'se in Roma si poteva ordinare uno stato...'.

of the magistrates under the Roman republic and the authority of the laws 'by means of which, together with the magistrates, the citizens were kept under control'.[108] He also declares that the latter set of institutions and practices can best be described as 'the order of the government or, rather, of *lo stato*'.[109]

It has often been noted that, with the reception of Renaissance republicanism in northern Europe, we begin to encounter similar assumptions among Dutch and English protagonists of 'free states' in the middle of the seventeenth century.[110] It has less often been recognised that the same assumptions, couched in the same vocabulary, can already be detected more than a century earlier among the first writers to introduce some elements of classical republicanism into English political thought. Thomas Starkey, for example,[111] distinguishes at several points in his *Dialogue* between the state itself and 'they which have authority and rule of the state'.[112] The 'office and duty' of rulers, Starkey goes on, is to 'maintain the state established in the country' over which they hold sway, 'ever looking to the profit of the whole body' rather than their own good.[113] The only method, he concludes, of 'setting forward the very and true commonweal' is for everyone to recognise, rulers and ruled alike, that they are 'under the same governance and state'.[114] The same assumptions recur in John Ponet's *Shorte Treatise of Politike Power* of 1556. He too speaks of rulers as the holders of a particular office, and describes the duty attaching to their office as that of upholding the state. He is thus led to contrast the behaviour of 'an evil persone comyng to the governement of any state' with a good ruler who will recognise that he has been 'to suche office called for his vertue, to see the hole state well governed, and the people defended from injuries'.[115]

Perhaps most significantly, we encounter the same phraseology in Tudor translations of the leading Italian treatises on republican government. When Lewes Lewkenor issued his English version of Gasparo

---

[108] Machiavelli 1960, I. 18, p. 180: 'le leggi dipoi che con i magistrati frenavano i cittadini'.
[109] Machiavelli 1960, I. 18, p. 180: 'l'ordine del governo o vero dello stato'.
[110] Fink 1962, pp. 10–20, 56–68; Raab 1964, pp. 185–217; Pocock 1975, pp. 333–422; Haitsma Mulier 1980, pp. 26–76.
[111] I see no justification for the claim in Mayer 1985, p. 25 that Starkey merely 'dressed up' his *Dialogue* in humanist form. Cf. Skinner 1978a, pp. 213–42 for an attempt to place Starkey's ideas in a humanist context.
[112] Starkey 1948, p. 61.   [113] Starkey 1948, p. 64.
[114] Starkey 1948, p. 71. For a (sceptical) discussion of the significance of these passages see Mayer 1989, pp. 124–8.
[115] [Ponet] 1556, Sig. G, 1ᵛ. For the ascription to Ponet and other biographical details see Garrett 1938 and Hudson 1942, pp. 36–90.

Contarini's *De Republica Venetorum* in 1599, he found himself in need of an English term to render Contarini's basic contention that the authority of the Venetian government inheres at all times in the citizen-body of the *respublica*, with the Doge and Council merely serving as their elected representatives. Following standard humanist practice, Lewkenor generally expresses this concept by using the term 'commonwealth'. But in speaking of the relationship between the commonwealth and its own citizens, he sometimes prefers to speak of the state. When he mentions the possibility of enfranchising additional citizens, he explains that this can only happen when someone can be shown to have been especially 'dutifull towardes the state'. And when he discusses the Venetian ideal of citizenship, he feels able to allude in even broader terms to 'the citizens, by whom the state of the Cittie is maintained'.[116]

Despite the obvious importance of these theorists, it would still be misleading to conclude that their use of the term *status* and its vernacular equivalents expressed a modern understanding of the state as an authority distinct from rulers and ruled. The republican writers embrace only one half of this doubly abstract notion of public power. On the one hand, they constitute the earliest group of political writers who speak with full self-consciousness of a categorical distinction between states and governments, and at the same time express this distinction as a claim about the independent structures of *stati*, *états* and states. But on the other hand, they make no comparable distinction between the powers of states and the powers of the communities over which they rule. On the contrary, the whole thrust of republican theory is towards an ultimate equation between the two. This undoubtedly yields a recognisable concept of the state, one that many Marxists and exponents of direct democracy continue to espouse. But it involves a repudiation of the most distinctive element in the mainstream theory of the modern state: the claim that it is the state itself, rather than the community over which it holds sway, that constitutes the seat of sovereignty.

The explicit rejection of this further contention is an important feature of many treatises in praise of 'free states'. Consider again one of the earliest English works of this character, John Ponet's *Shorte Treatise of Politike Power*. As we have seen, Ponet makes a firm distinction between the office and person of the ruler, and even uses the term 'state' to describe the form of civil authority that our rulers have a duty to uphold. But he makes no analogous distinction between the power of the state

---

[116] Lewkenor 1599, pp. 18, 33.

and that of the people. Not only does he maintain that 'Kinges, Princes and governours have their autoritie of the people',[117] but he insists that the highest political power resides at all times in 'the body or state of the Realme or common wealthe'.[118]

We find the same commitment upheld even by the most sophisticated defenders of 'free states' in the seventeenth century. A good example is furnished by John Milton's *Ready and Easy Way to Establish a Free Commonwealth* of 1660. If we are to maintain 'our freedom and flourishing condition', Milton argues, and establish a government 'for preservation of the common peace and libertie', it is essential that the people's sovereignty must never be 'transferrd'. It must be 'delegated only, and as it were deposited' with a governing Council of State.[119] The ruling institutions of the state are thus conceived as nothing more than a means of expressing the powers of the people in an administratively more convenient guise. As Milton had earlier emphasised in *The Tenure of Kings and Magistrates* in 1649, whatever authority our rulers may possess is merely 'committed to them in trust from the People, to the Common good of them all, in whom the power yet remains fundamentally' at all times.[120]

V

I turn to the second and overlapping tradition of constitutionalism that needs to be investigated. As I have already noted, the writers we next need to consider are the so-called monarchomachs or king-killers, a term of abuse first employed by William Barclay in his *De Regno* of 1600.[121] The monarchomachs rose to sudden prominence in the latter part of the sixteenth century in the course of the religious wars in France and the Low Countries,[122] although the intellectual roots of their constitutionalism lay deep in the legal and scholastic theory of corporations, as we saw in chapter 9. Few of the monarchomachs were republicans in the strict sense of believing that self-rule is a necessary condition of public and private liberty. They were generally content to assume that the right to exercise sovereignty will be vested in a monarchical form of government, although they almost always spoke of the need to ensure that such monarchs are elected. Writing in a more religious idiom, they

---

[117] [Ponet] 1556, Sig. G, 5^v–6^r.   [118] [Ponet] 1556, Sig. G, 5^r.
[119] Milton 1980, pp. 432–3, 456.   [120] Milton 1991, p. 10.   [121] See Barclay 1600.
[122] For the Dutch theorists see Gelderen 1992, pp. 110–65; for the French see Skinner 1978b, pp. 302–48.

were chiefly concerned to vindicate the rights of peoples, especially under conditions of sectarian oppression, to resist and remove even lawfully constituted rulers if they could be shown to be governing tyrannically. From the point of view of my present argument, however, the significance of these writers derives from the fact that some of them eventually felt driven to defend their co-religionists by way of espousing a theory of popular sovereignty.[123]

The French Calvinists increasingly edged towards this position in the 1570s, especially after the Catholic government under Catherine de' Medici allegedly ordered the massacre of St Bartholomew's Day in 1572, in which over two thousand Calvinists were murdered in Paris and perhaps as many as ten thousand more in the provinces.[124] The great summarising document of the ensuing protest movement was the *Vindiciae, Contra Tyrannos*, almost certainly written by Hubert Languet and Philippe du Plessis Mornay.[125] The text was drafted in 1574 immediately after the publication of several other leading Huguenot treatises, including the anonymous *Reveille-matin des François* and François Hotman's *Francogallia*.[126] It was subsequently revised and extended to take account of changing political circumstances and eventually appeared in 1579.[127]

Within a few years, the continuing effort in the Low Countries to throw off the rule of Spain gave rise to a number of comparable treatises. Perhaps the most important was Johannes Althusius's *Politica Methodice Digesta*, in which the authority of the *Vindiciae* is invoked at numerous points.[128] Althusius's massive treatise was first published in 1603 when he was teaching law at the Academy of Herborn, founded by Count John of Nassau, and was subsequently reissued in a more extended version in 1610 and again in 1614.[129] Meanwhile a similar form of constitutionalism had been espoused by Catholic writers in England as well as France. After Henry of Navarre, an avowed Huguenot, became heir to the French throne in 1584, a number of monarchomach treatises began to appear

---

[123] My analysis of this movement in Skinner 1978b, pp. 239–75, 302–48 has been criticised in Kossmann 1981 and Eire 1986 for allegedly exaggerating the extent to which it was based on a theory of popular sovereignty. But it can hardly be denied that the movement *included* such theories, and it is with these that I am solely concerned in my present argument.

[124] Skinner 1978b, p. 242.

[125] On the authorship of the *Vindiciae* see Garnett 1994, pp. lv–lxxvi. For a fuller analysis of its argument see Skinner 1978b, pp. 315–18, 329–43 and Garnett 1994, pp. xix–liv.

[126] Garnett 1994, pp. lxviii–lxix, lxxv.

[127] On these revisions see Garnett 1994, pp. lxviii, lxxv.

[128] Althusius 1932, pp. 146, 157, 184, 261, 382, 388, 391 *et passim*.

[129] Carney 1965, pp. xiv–xvi. On Althusius as a theorist of popular sovereignty see Tierney 1982, pp. 71–9.

in defence of the Catholic cause, the most violent being Jean Boucher's *De Iusta Henricii Tertii Abdicatione* of 1589, in which large sections were lifted directly out of the *Vindiciae*.[130] After the defeat of the Spanish Armada in 1588 a similar movement of Catholic protest began to gather momentum in England, with the Jesuit Robert Persons issuing the most inflammatory of the resulting monarchomach tracts in the form of his *Conference about the Next Succession to the Crowne of Ingland* in 1594.[131]

The founding principle of politics according to all these writers is that everyone is by nature free of subjection to government. It is not only manifest, the *Vindiciae* proclaims, that 'a people can exist of itself, and is prior in time to a king' but that 'men are free by nature, impatient of servitude, and are born more to command than to obey'.[132] If we find such peoples living as subjects of government, this can only be because they must at some stage have decided to accept this form of subjection and must have freely consented to its terms. The exemplary instance is that of the people of ancient Israel, who covenanted with God and with their kings to establish a righteous commonwealth. From this we can infer, the *Vindiciae* declares, 'that the people constitutes kings, confers kingdoms, and approves the election by its vote'.[133]

These writers further insist that, because every individual member of the populace originally lived in freedom, we cannot imagine them entering into a contract with their rulers by which they relinquish their original powers of self-government. To hand over their rights unconditionally, in effect selling themselves into slavery, would not only be a manifest irrationality but inconsistent with the laws of nature. From the fact of the original freedom of the people the monarchomachs accordingly infer that the contract of government must always have the effect of imposing terms and conditions on the exercise of public power. As the *Vindiciae* puts it, the anointment of David serves in particular to remind our rulers that, although they are confirmed in their office by God, it is 'by the people and for the people that they rule'. Not only are they 'constituted by the people' but their authority is 'conferred by the people', who retain the right to resist and remove them if they govern tyrannically.[134]

We next need to highlight a crucial presupposition of this view of the political covenant. If a multitude of individuals or families in a pre-political condition possesses the ability to covenant with a chosen ruler,

---

[130] Garnett 1994, p. xx.
[131] The tract appeared under the pseudonym 'R. Doleman'. On Robert Persons and his authorship of the *Conference* see Holmes 1982, pp. 130–4, 147–65, 214–20.
[132] *Vindiciae* 1994, pp. 71, 92.   [133] *Vindiciae* 1994, p. 68.   [134] *Vindiciae* 1994, pp. 69, 70, 71, 74.

this can only be because they have the capacity to exercise a single will and make decisions with a single voice. The usual way of expressing this assumption was to say that such a *populus* can be regarded as 'one', as a union or unified form of society. Sometimes the argument was couched more specifically in the form of the claim – adapted from the Roman law theory of corporations – that such a *populus* can be described as an *universitas*.[135] This is the term invariably employed in the *Vindiciae*, and later in Althusius's *Politica*, to express the idea that, as the *Vindiciae* repeatedly asserts, any body of people must be capable of acting 'all together as a whole' in setting the terms of its subjection to government.[136]

If a *populus* can be considered as one, and hence as capable of speaking with a single voice, we can equally well describe it according to these writers as bearing the character of a single person. Bartolus, Baldus and their followers had already arrived at this conclusion two centuries earlier. They had begun by arguing that a *populus* can be viewed as a corporation, and hence as a distinct legal entity. This had led them to suggest that, if a body of people can in this way be distinguished from the individuals who compose it, the body must amount legally speaking to *una persona*. It must possess a capacity to act through the agency of its members, who must in turn possess an ability to express not merely their own wills but the will of the *persona* of the *populus* as a whole.[137]

This use of the term *persona* derives from a number of classical usages that Thomas Hobbes was later to examine with exceptional acuity in *Leviathan*. Hobbes presents his analysis in chapter 16, *Of Persons, Authors, and things Personated*, a discussion without parallel in any of the earlier recensions of his civil science. That Hobbes considered this chapter to be of special significance is signalled by the pivotal place he assigns to it in his general argument. He makes it the closing chapter of Part 1, using it at once to round off his account of the world of natural persons and to pave the way for his exploration of the artificial world of politics in Part 2.

Hobbes begins by pointing out that the word *persona* started life as a piece of theatrical terminology, signifying 'the *disguise*, or *outward*

---

[135] On the evolving uses of the term *universitas* see Michaud-Quantin 1970, pp. 11–44; on the *universitas* and the *stato* or state, see Canning 1983; Black 1992; Najemy 1994b.
[136] See *Vindiciae* 1579, p. 13 for its first use of the term *populus universus* and cf. *Vindiciae* 1994, p. 22. See also *Vindiciae* 1579, pp. 51, 65 on the *populus* as an *universitas* and cf. *Vindiciae* 1994, pp. 50, 59.
[137] Garnett in his edition of the *Vindiciae* valuably singles out the passages in the *Digest* that were made to bear this interpretation by Bartolus, Baldus and their monarchomach followers. See *Vindiciae* 1994, p. 38 n.17; p. 47 n. 73; p. 59 n. 148; p. 90 n. 153. For the views of the post-glossators see Michaud-Quantin 1970; Canning 1980; Canning 1987, pp. 185–97.

appearance of a man, counterfeited on the Stage; and sometimes more particularly that part of it, which disguiseth the face'.[138] From being used to denote a mask, the term came to be applied more generally to refer to the *dramatis personae* in a play, in which usage 'a *Person*, is the same that an *Actor* is, both on the Stage and in common Conversation'.[139] Finally, by an obvious metaphorical extension, the term came to be used to describe the different offices and duties discharged by individual citizens in public life, a usage in which Hobbes is particularly interested:

To *Personate*, is to *Act*, or *Represent* himselfe, or an other; and he that acteth another, is said to beare his Person, or act in his name; (in which sense *Cicero* useth it where he saies, *Unus sustineo tres Personas; Mei, Adversarii, & Iudicis*, I beare three Persons; my own, my Adversaries, and the Judges).[140]

As Hobbes was well aware, Cicero had been especially fond of using *persona* in this final sense. One illuminating example occurs in Book 3 of *De Officiis*, in which he considers the predicament of a judge who finds himself trying a case in which one of his friends is involved. He must be careful, Cicero warns, not to do anything contrary to the interests of the *respublica*, remembering that 'when he takes upon himself the *persona* of a judge, he lays aside the *persona* of a friend'.[141]

It was due to a further metaphorical extension of these usages that the term *persona* eventually acquired its juristic meaning, and it is this meaning that we encounter in the writings of the monarchomachs. The *Vindiciae* draws explicitly on Bartolus's account of legal *personae* in the course of describing the exemplary covenant between God and the chosen people of Israel. The people were able to make such a pledge because 'an *universitas* of men sustains the role of, and acts in the manner of, a single person'.[142] Althusius likewise describes the *populus* in the Preface to his *Politica* as a single body or unified group, and hence as having one character.[143] He later cites a number of authorities who claim that, when

---

[138] Hobbes 1996, ch. 16, p. 112. [139] Hobbes 1996, ch. 16, p. 112.
[140] Hobbes 1996, ch. 16, p. 112, quoting (slightly inaccurately) Cicero 1942a, II. XXIV. 102, vol. 1, p. 274. Hobbes had already made the distinction between acting *ex propria persona* and *in persona non sua* in his *Critique* of Thomas White. For the date of this manuscript (1642–3) see Jacquot and Jones 1973, pp. 43–5; for the relevant passage see BN Fonds Latin MS 6566A, fo. 6ᵛ and cf. Hobbes 1973, p. 107.
[141] Cicero 1913, III. X. 43, p. 310: 'ponit enim personam amici, cum induit iudicis'. Cf. Cicero 1913, I. XXX. 107, p. 108 and I. XXXII. 115, pp. 116–18.
[142] *Vindiciae* 1579, p. 37: 'universitas enim hominum unius personae vicem sustinet'. Cf. *Vindiciae* 1994, p. 38. (But I have supplied my own translation, highlighting the theatrical metaphor.)
[143] See Althusius 1932, p. 5 on the *populus universus* and its proprietorship of *maiestas*. Cf. Gierke 1957, pp. 250, 255, 256–7.

such a group lives together under settled laws, this type of *universitas* can be described both as a *civitas* and as a *persona*.[144] His chapter on the powers of magistrates adds that we may say 'of such administrators and rectors, who have been appointed by the body of the people, that they serve as representatives who act the part of the *persona* constituted by the people as a whole'.[145]

The same vocabulary recurs even more prominently among Althusius's immediate successors, notably in Johann Werdenhagen's *Politica Generalis* of 1632, a work published in Amsterdam while Werdenhagen was teaching at the University of Leiden.[146] Werdenhagen devotes Book 2 chapter 6 to furnishing an exceptionally full anatomy of the various 'modes' in which the term *persona* can be used.[147] After discussing the vexed question of the *tres personae* of the Holy Trinity, he notes that, in the sixth mode of its use, the term *persona* 'can be applied not merely to an individual human being but also to the whole body of the people'.[148] This leads him to isolate, as its seventh mode, a distinctive legal usage according to which 'an *universitas* can be considered in law just as if it is a single *persona*'.[149]

This image of the populace as a *persona*, and hence as capable of consenting to the terms of its own government, was used by the monarchomachs to introduce a general account of the powers required to sustain kingdoms and commonwealths. They treat the founding covenant – the *foedus* or *pactum* – as the source of a structure of public institutions that evolve and solidify over time.[150] This structure is said to include a *dominium publicum* or public domain, which needs to be sufficiently large to defray the costs of government and above all of defence. As the *Vindiciae* explains, alluding to Tacitus, 'peace cannot be sustained without war, nor war without soldiers, nor soldiers without pay, nor pay without tribute', so that a public domain had to be instituted 'in order to support the burdens of peace'.[151] A further element in the same structure is said to be the judicial system of courts and their functionaries, a system

---

[144] Althusius 1932, ch. 5, p. 39.
[145] Althusius 1932, ch. 18, p. 140: 'administratores & rectores, universalis consociationis, seu totum & universum populum, a quo constituti sunt, repraesentant... eiusque personam gerunt'.
[146] Voigt 1965, pp. 7, 10.
[147] Werdenhagen 1632, II. 6, p. 123: 'De distinctione Populi & Societate ac Personis istius in genera.'
[148] Werdenhagen 1632, II. VI. 23, p. 131: 'Non tantum uni homini, sed etiam toti populi applicatur.'
[149] Werdenhagen 1632, II. VI. 23, p. 132: 'In Iure tota Universitas tanquam Una persona consideretur.' Cf. Gierke 1957, pp. 245, 252.
[150] The *Vindiciae* generally speaks of the *foedus*, but sometimes of the *pactum* and sometimes even of the *contractus*. See, for example, *Vindiciae* 1579, pp. 159, 168 and cf. *Vindiciae* 1994, pp. 129, 138.
[151] *Vindiciae* 1994, p. 115. Cf. *Vindiciae* 1994, pp. 89–90, 113 and Tacitus 1931, LXXIV, p. 146.

indispensably required, as the *Vindiciae* adds, if justice is to be impartially administered and if the laws are to 'speak with one and the same voice to all'.[152]

Reflecting on these institutions, the monarchomachs invariably insist, no less than the classical republicans had done, on a strong distinction between the office and the person of any ruler or functionary entrusted with administering them. No ruler can count as the proprietor or even the usufructuary of the public patrimony. As the *Vindiciae* puts it, 'a true king is a curator of public affairs', so that 'he can no more alienate or squander the royal domain than the kingdom itself'.[153] Nor can a ruler be regarded as standing above the laws, since the basic duty of his office is to enforce whatever laws the people may have agreed to be necessary for the assurance of their own welfare and benefit. As the *Vindiciae* explains, any king is merely 'a minister and executor of the law', who 'receives from the people the laws which he is to protect and observe'.[154]

When writing in Latin, these theorists normally describe this permanent structure of institutions as the structure of the *regnum*, the kingdom or commonwealth.[155] When writing in the vernacular, however, they sometimes echo the language of the classical republicans and speak of the structure in question as that of the state. Robert Persons uses the term in his chapter outlining the French and English laws of succession in his *Conference* of 1594. His chapter heading states that, when we survey the history of these laws, we are surveying the practice 'of the States of France and England'.[156] To which he adds that, when we examine particular cases, we are speaking of decisions made by 'the whole state'.[157] The same usage recurs among the supporters of Parliament at the outbreak of the English civil war. When Henry Parker, for example, addressed his *Observations* to Charles I in 1642,[158] he justified the Long Parliament's arrogation of sovereignty on the grounds that 'the State hath an Interest Paramount in cases of publique extremity',[159] and that in England the Parliament is given ultimate charge of 'matters of Law and State'.[160]

Some scholars have inferred that it is within this tradition of thought that we first encounter a clear understanding of the state as an apparatus of government distinct from both rulers and ruled.[161] Some have gone

---

[152] *Vindiciae* 1994, pp. 96, 97–9.   [153] *Vindiciae* 1994, p. 119.
[154] *Vindiciae* 1994, pp. 74, 96, 99, 104.   [155] *Vindiciae* 1579, p. 83; cf. *Vindiciae* 1994, p. 76.
[156] [Persons] 1594, p. 164. It is possible, however, that by 'states' in this instance Persons means the Estates or Parliament.
[157] [Persons] 1594, p. 168.
[158] On Parker as author of the *Observations* see Mendle 1995, pp. 82–5, 192.
[159] [Parker] 1933, p. 199.   [160] [Parker] 1933, p. 202.   [161] For example Lloyd 1983, p. 155.

even further, arguing that such an understanding can already be found in the Bartolist theory of corporations from which the monarchomachs drew so much of their intellectual strength.[162] There is certainly something to be said in favour of these arguments. It is true that, like the classical republicans, the monarchomachs separate the office and the person of the prince in such a way as to distinguish those who possess authority over the institutions of a community from those institutions themselves. It is also true that, even more clearly than the republicans, the monarchomachs and their legal authorities think of sovereignty as the property of a legal person, thereby distinguishing it from the powers of any natural persons who may be assigned the right to exercise it at any given time.

Although they separate sovereignty from sovereigns, however, the monarchomachs make no comparable distinction between the powers of sovereignty and the powers of the people. Like the classical republicans, they embrace only one half of the doubly abstract notion of state authority. While they stress that sovereignty is the property of a legal person, the person whom they treat as the bearer of sovereignty is always the *persona* constituted by the corporate body of the people, never the impersonal body of the *civitas* or *respublica* itself. We find this commitment underlined with particular clarity in the *Vindiciae*. There we are repeatedly told that, although our rulers are undoubtedly *maior singulis*, greater in power than any individual members of the populace, they remain *minor universis*, lesser in power than the populace as a whole.[163] The body of the people remains at all times the possessor of 'supreme lordship', and thus remains 'the lord of the commonwealth'.[164] Neither in the *Vindiciae* nor even in later monarchomach treatises such as Althusius's *Politica* do we find any distinction drawn between the powers of the people as an *universitas* and the powers of the *civitas* itself. The aim is always to insist, no less firmly than the defenders of 'free states', on an ultimate equation between the two.

VI

If we wish to witness the moment at which the powers of the state were finally described as such, and were distinguished not merely from the powers of rulers but from those of the community, we need to direct our

---

[162] Calasso 1957, pp. 83–123; Wahl 1977; Canning 1983, pp. 23–7; Najemy 1994b.
[163] *Vindiciae* 1579, pp. 89, 193; cf. *Vindiciae* 1994, pp. 78, 156.
[164] *Vindiciae* 1994, pp. 75, 77, 165.

attention away from the constitutional theorists on whom I have so far concentrated. We need to turn instead to a strongly contrasting group of legal and political philosophers who made it their business to address themselves critically to the thesis of popular sovereignty, whether in its republican guise as a claim about 'free states' or in its legal and neo-scholastic form as a claim about the inalienable rights of communities. We need to turn, that is, to those theorists whose aspirations included a desire to legitimise the more absolutist forms of government that began to prevail in western Europe in the early part of the seventeenth century.[165] It was as a by-product of their arguments, and in particular of their efforts to insist that the powers of government must be something other than the powers of the governed under another guise, that the concept of the state as a distinct person and as the seat of sovereignty was finally articulated with full self-consciousness.[166]

Some of these theorists saw themselves chiefly as enemies of the republican vision of free states. This is true to some degree of Thomas Hobbes, who sharply retracts in *Leviathan* the admiration he had expressed in his earlier *Elements of Law* for classical theories of freedom and citizenship. In *The Elements* he had allowed that Aristotle 'saith well' that 'noe man can partake of Liberty, but onely in a Popular Common wealth'.[167] But in *Leviathan* he mounts a furious attack on Aristotle, and even more on Cicero and his followers, for equating monarchy with tyranny. As we saw in chapter 12, he came to believe that the willingness of schools and universities to inculcate this calumny had been the cause of ruinous conflicts throughout the commonwealths of western Europe.

To most of these writers, however, it was the monarchomachs who seemed to pose the gravest and most immediate threat. This is what we learn from Jean Bodin in his *Six livres de la république*, first published in 1576 and translated into English as early as 1606.[168] Bodin tells us that he felt

---

[165] For a similar perspective see Black 1992. For a critique see Najemy 1994b. Note that, in what follows, I see no need (by contrast with the implications of Burgess 1996) to avoid the term 'absolutist' when discussing these writers, provided that it is not taken to mean anything like 'unbridled'. They frequently employed the term themselves when referring to their theory of sovereignty. See for example Bodin 1962, p. 84; Blackwood 1588, p. 89; Hobbes 1996, ch. 21, p. 143; ch. 29, pp. 222–3; ch. 42, p. 379.

[166] On this juristic understanding of the state as a distinct moral person see Dyson 1980, pp. 14–15, 218–20 and Runciman 1997.

[167] Hobbes 1969b, p. 170. As I noted in chapter 10, although Hobbes 1969b remains the standard edition, it contains an unacceptable number of transcription mistakes. I have therefore preferred to quote from BL Harl. MS 4235, arguably the best surviving manuscript, although my page references are to the 1969 edition.

[168] This translation (by Richard Knolles) is the version from which I quote.

moved to write 'when I perceived on every side that subjects were arming themselves against their princes' and that 'books were being brought out openly' which taught that 'princes sent by providence to the human race must be thrust out of their kingdoms under a pretense of tyranny, and that kings must be chosen not by their lineage, but by the will of the people'.[169] One of his chief aspirations, he explains, is to refute the widespread but treacherous opinion 'that the power of the people is greater than the prince', this being 'a thing which oft times causeth the true subjects to revolt from the obedience which they owe unto their soveraigne prince, & ministreth matter of great troubles in Commonweals'.[170]

A yet more direct attack on the monarchomachs was mounted soon afterwards by the so-called Pont-à-Mousson writers on sovereignty, among whom the leaders were Adam Blackwood and William Barclay, two Scotsmen teaching civil law in France.[171] Blackwood first trained at Toulouse, after which he taught at Paris,[172] while Barclay taught first at Bourges and later at Pont-à-Mousson.[173] There he became a colleague of Pierre Gregoire, the author of another important anti-monarchomach treatise on sovereignty, the *De Republica* of 1596.[174] Barclay and Blackwood were greatly exercised by the deposition of Mary Queen of Scots, an act confirmed by the Scottish Parliament in 1567. As we saw in chapter 9, George Buchanan had defended these proceedings in one of the most radical of all the monarchomach tracts, his *De Iure Regni apud Scotos* of 1579.[175] Adam Blackwood replied in a treatise entitled *Adversus Georgii Buchanani... pro regibus Apologia*, which first appeared at Paris in 1581 and was reissued in a revised and extended form in 1588.[176] William Barclay also replied to Buchanan (much less respectfully) in his *De Regno* of 1600, an immense tome in which the term 'monarchomach' was originally coined, and which subsequently caused its author to be singled out by John Locke in his *Two Treatises* as 'the great Champion of Absolute Monarchy'.[177] As Barclay's full title resoundingly proclaims, his championing was directed not merely against George Buchanan, but against the

---

[169] Bodin 1962, pp. A71–2.
[170] Bodin 1962, p. 95; cf. p. 224. On Bodin's *Six livres* as an ideological reaction to the menace of Huguenot constitutionalism see Franklin 1973; Salmon 1973; and Skinner 1978b, pp. 284–301.
[171] On this school of thought see Collot 1965 and Salmon 1991, esp. pp. 233–6.
[172] Church 1941, pp. 245–6.   [173] Gierke 1957, pp. 401–2.
[174] On Gregoire see Church 1941, pp. 245–6, 247–9; on Gregoire and Barclay see Collot 1965.
[175] See Burns 1996, pp. 185–209 for Buchanan's defence and p. 191n. for references to earlier discussions of his work.
[176] Church 1941, p. 245 and note.   [177] Locke 1988, II. 239, p. 424.

author of the *Vindiciae*, against Boucher's *De Iusta Abdicatione* and against 'all the other monarchomachs'.[178]

A similar defence of monarchy began to gather strength in England in the early years of the seventeenth century. Sir John Hayward published his *Answer* to Robert Persons's *Conference* in 1603,[179] and similar treatises by other civil lawyers punctuated the ensuing decades, one of the most important being Calybute Downing's *Discourse* of 1633 on civil and ecclesiastical power.[180] With the outbreak of civil war in 1642 it became a matter of still greater urgency to answer the monarchomach case, and a number of tracts in defence of monarchical power duly began to appear. One of the most searching was Dudley Digges's *The Unlawfulnesse of Subjects taking up Armes*, which was published anonymously in 1643. Digges stigmatises as 'evidently false' the claim that rulers are *universis minor*,[181] a doctrine he associates above all with Buchanan, Hotman, the author of the *Vindiciae* and their English counterparts such as Henry Parker and other supporters of the parliamentary cause.[182] But by far the most important writer to come forward at this critical juncture as a theorist of royalism was Thomas Hobbes, first in *The Elements of Law* in 1640 and then in *De Cive* in 1642. Hobbes is no less anxious than Bodin to warn his fellow-citizens that – as he later puts it in *Leviathan* in words closely echoing the *Six livres* – although the condition of political subjection may appear miserable, the greatest misery that can possibly befall us as subjects 'is scarce sensible, in respect of the miseries, and horrible calamities, that accompany a Civill Warre'.[183]

Although these writers are fervent believers in monarchy, none of them takes the shortest way with the monarchomachs by arguing that our rulers are simply the direct gifts of God.[184] They all agree that the people must originally have been free of government. They accept in consequence that every form of legitimate government must arise out of some kind of contract or covenant. As a result, they all insist that legitimate rulers must be regarded as public persons with a duty to act in

---

[178] See Barclay 1600. [179] On Hayward as a civil lawyer see Levack 1973, pp. 237–8.
[180] On Downing as a civil lawyer see Levack 1973, p. 225. For his 'absolutist' views see Sommerville 1999, pp. 40, 67. Downing's treatise was reissued in 1634, and it is from that edition that I quote.
[181] [Digges] 1643, p. 33.
[182] [Digges] 1643, p. 58 names these and other monarchomachs and at pp. 62–4 replies specifically to Henry Parker.
[183] Hobbes 1996, ch. 18, p. 128.
[184] Here I correct the misleading account of Barclay and Blackwood given in Skinner 1978b, p. 301.

such a way as to procure the safety and benefit of those over whom they rule. What none of them can tolerate, however, is the further suggestion that the covenant underpinning the authority of our governors has the effect of imposing terms and conditions on the exercise of government. For the anti-monarchomach writers, the crucial polemical task is to show that this alleged inference can somehow be denied.

How, then, do they deny it? The writers I am considering may be said to explore two contrasting possibilities. Some respond by challenging the monarchomach contention that no free people would ever agree to a covenant obliging them to relinquish their original powers and rights. This, for example, is the principal line of attack pursued by William Barclay in his *De Regno* of 1600. Barclay agrees that it is appropriate to think of the people as originally free of government.[185] He further agrees that we can think of them as an *universitas* capable of choosing their rulers and covenanting to establish the terms of their rule.[186] But he sees no reason to infer that the resulting covenant need necessarily embody any limitations on the exercise of public authority. As he points out, we are unambiguously told in the *Digest* that, in the exemplary instance of the Roman people, the terms of the *Lex regia* were such that the populace agreed to the conferment, and hence the total relinquishment, of all their original *imperium* and *ius*. The inference Barclay draws is that the bearer of ultimate sovereignty in any kingdom or commonwealth must therefore be the *publica persona* of the *princeps* himself.[187]

By contrast with this orthodox retort, a number of absolutists made a different and crucial move, a move that eventually led them to embrace the idea of the sovereignty of the state. Rather than questioning the nature of the covenant negotiated by the *persona* of the people, they questioned the underlying image of the populace as a single *persona* capable of negotiating the terms of a covenant. Rather, we find them arguing, it is only as a result of submitting to government that an aggregate of individuals ever becomes converted into a unified body of people. Jean Bodin in his *Six livres* lays out exactly this argument in the course of making his fundamental distinction between the government of families and of *républiques*. It is only the acceptance of 'soveraintie of power', he maintains, 'which uniteth in one body all the members and families'

---

[185] Barclay 1600, III. II, pp. 110–11.
[186] Barclay 1600, III. IV, p. 124 on the act being 'de ipso populo universo'.
[187] Barclay 1600, III. II, pp. 112–13; III. III, pp. 115–16; III. IV, pp. 123–31. Blackwood also has recourse to this argument. See Blackwood 1588, ch. 8 (*recte* 9), pp. 80–5 and ch. 9 (*recte* 10), pp. 89–98.

of a *civitas* or *république*.¹⁸⁸ It is an error to suppose that the people owe their unity to the fact of living together as members of a single society or as denizens of a single place. 'For it is neither the wals, neither the persons, that maketh the city, but the union of the people under the same soveraigntie of government.'¹⁸⁹ In the absence of such a union 'the same is no more a commonweale, neither can by any means long endure'.¹⁹⁰

Bodin later underlines his argument in the course of analysing the concept of citizenship. We can only speak of citizens and recognise that they have 'made a Commonweale' when we find a group of people 'governed by the puissant soveraigntie of one or many rulers'.¹⁹¹ This is because, he insists once more, 'the enclosure of wals make not a citie, (as many have written) no more than the wals of a house make a familie'. What alone creates 'one very citie' out of a multitude of individuals is the acceptance of their common subjection 'unto the command of their soveraigne lords, and unto their edicts and ordinances'.¹⁹²

Thomas Hobbes refers admiringly to Bodin in discussing the concept of sovereignty in *The Elements of Law*,¹⁹³ and goes on to elaborate a strikingly similar analysis of the act of covenanting in *Leviathan*. As he argues in chapter 17, there is only one way in which a multitude can attain unity, and hence act in the manner of a single person. This is by agreeing, each with each, 'to conferre all their power and strength upon one Man, or upon one Assembly of Men, that may reduce all their Wills, by plurality of voices, unto one Will'.¹⁹⁴ It is only by this means that they can hope to transform themselves from a multitude with many conflicting wills into '*One Person*', thereby attaining 'a reall Unitie of them all, in one and the same Person, made by covenant of every man with every man'.¹⁹⁵ The error of the monarchomachs, in short, is to suppose that the covenant tells us the terms of our subjection; it merely tells us the name of the man or assembly to whom we have agreed to subject ourselves.

Hobbes further corroborates his argument in the closing chapters of Part 2 of *Leviathan*. If the essential rights of sovereignty are taken away, 'the Commonwealth is thereby dissolved, and every man returned into the condition, and calamity of a warre with every other man'.¹⁹⁶ Without a sovereign, the people are so far from being an *universitas* that they amount to nothing at all. 'A Common-wealth, without Soveraign Power, is but a word, without substance, and cannot stand.'¹⁹⁷ This is

---

¹⁸⁸ Bodin 1962, p. 9.   ¹⁸⁹ Bodin 1962, p. 10.   ¹⁹⁰ Bodin 1962, p. 10.
¹⁹¹ Bodin 1962, p. 49.   ¹⁹² Bodin 1962, pp. 49–50, 51.   ¹⁹³ Hobbes 1969b, pp. 172–3.
¹⁹⁴ Hobbes 1996, ch. 17, p. 120.   ¹⁹⁵ Hobbes 1996, ch. 17, p. 120.
¹⁹⁶ Hobbes 1996, ch. 30, p. 231.   ¹⁹⁷ Hobbes 1996, ch. 31, p. 245.

because, as Hobbes has already explained in chapter 16, 'it is the *Unity* of the Representer, not the *Unity* of the Represented, that maketh the Person *One*', and '*Unity* cannot otherwise be understood in Multitude'.[198]

Some time before Hobbes gave final shape to these thoughts in *Leviathan*, Dudley Digges had already developed a similar line of attack on the monarchomachs in his *Unlawfulnesse of Subjects taking up Armes*. He too begins by maintaining that the only way in which a multitude can 'reduce themselves into a civill unitie', and thereby act in the manner of a single person, is 'by placing over them one head, and making his will the will of them all'.[199] He goes on to explain that 'this submission of all to the will of one; or this union of them agreed upon, is to be understood in a politique sense'.[200] It is only by creating a political union under a sovereign that a people ceases to be a mere multitude. 'The sinews of government, by which they were compacted into one' is what converts them from a warring collection of individuals into a well-ordered people.[201] 'For government is an effect not of a peoples divided naturall powers, but as they are united and made one by civill constitution.'[202]

The thesis advanced by all these writers is thus that the act of submitting to a sovereign is what converts us from a multitude into a union, and thus into one person. What, then, is the name of this person? Jean Bodin's answer is that, whenever we engender a 'union of the people' by way of accepting a sovereign, the name of the person we create is the *état* or state. Bodin gestures at this final crystallising of the concept at several points in his *Six livres*, as does Adam Blackwood in his *Apologia* and Pierre Gregoire in his *De Republica*.[203] Blackwood still prefers to speak of the *respublica* rather than the *status*, responding to George Buchanan's contention that any *populus* remains *maior* than its king by arguing that 'the king alone takes upon himself the *persona* of the *respublica* as a whole'.[204] But in Bodin we already find the word *estat* used on several occasions

---

[198] Hobbes 1996, ch. 16, p. 114.   [199] [Digges] 1643, p. 4.   [200] [Digges] 1643, p. 4.
[201] [Digges] 1643, p. 7.   [202] [Digges] 1643, p. 7.
[203] Lloyd 1983, pp. 156–62. Fell 1983, pp. 92–107, 175–205 lays all his emphasis on Bodin's contemporary Corasius, although without investigating the extent to which he uses the term *status* to express his concept of 'the legislative state'. By the next generation the use of the vernacular term *état* (or *estat*) to express such a concept had become well established in France. See Church 1972, pp. 13–80; Keohane 1980, pp. 54–82, 119–82. Dowdall 1923, p. 118 singled out the contribution of Charles Loyseau's *Traité des seigneuries* (1608), which has subsequently been much discussed. See Church 1972, pp. 33–4; Basdevant-Guademet 1977; Lloyd 1981; Lloyd 1983, pp. 162–8; Lloyd 1994, pp. xi–xxv.
[204] Blackwood 1588, ch. 32, p. 281: '[rex] solus reipublicae personam agit'. He later adds (ch. 33, p. 296) that, within a *respublica*, 'the people undoubtedly resembles a body while the king resembles its soul' – 'Populus certe corpori similis est, rex animo.'

as a synonym for *république*, while Pierre Gregoire uses the Latin word *status* in a similar way. Gregoire is quite explicit that, when a people takes on a unified character under the sovereignty of a ruler, the name of the resulting union is '*una Respublica seu status*'.[205] Still more significantly, Bodin feels able to speak in his *Six livres* of *l'estat en soi*, 'the state in itself', and to describe it both as a form of authority independent of particular types of government and as the seat of 'indivisible and incommunicable sovereignty'.[206] It is notable, moreover, that when Richard Knolles came to translate these passages in 1606, he not only used the word *state* in all these instances, but also in a number of passages in which Bodin had continued to speak in more traditional style about the *cité* or *république*.[207]

Calybute Downing in his *Discourse* of 1633, as well as Sir John Hayward in his earlier *Answer* to Robert Persons, both appear to gesture towards the same conclusion, although the direction of their thinking is admittedly far from clear. Downing argues that 'distinct and settled societies' can only hope to flourish in peace 'where a State is so framed that they are all united in one head'.[208] Hayward likewise maintains that the creation of an effective structure of government and obedience requires 'union of the authoritie which doth command'.[209] This union, he goes on, is founded on communal amity, 'which is the onely bande of this collective body', and arises 'when many doe knit in one power and will'.[210] Later he suggests that the union created by this amity can best be described as that of the state. Sovereigns are assigned their authority to 'execute this high power of state'[211] and are presented to the people by 'the lawes of the State'.[212]

By contrast with these stumbling observations, Dudley Digges speaks without hesitation of the state as the name of the institution we create by the act of submitting to government. He first does so in the course of defending the claim that the state 'hath full power to restraine the license of resisting, for the preservation of order and publique tranquillity':

---

[205] Bodin 1576, pp. 219, 438. Cf. Gregoire 1596, 1. 2, p. 12: '*De origine & progressu societatis, coniunctionis & coitionis populi in unam Rempublicam, seu statum communem.*'

[206] Bodin 1576, pp. 282–3: 'Et combien que le gouvernement d'une Republique soit plus ou moins populaire, ou Aristocratique, ou Royale, si est-que l'estat en soi ne reçoit compairison de plus ni de moins: car toujours la souveraineté indivisible et incommunicable est à un seul.' Cf. Bodin 1576, pp. 281 and 414 for the phrase 'en matière d'estat'. Hobbes 1996, ch. 18, p. 127 similarly speaks of the 'incommunicable, and inseparable' powers of sovereigns.

[207] Bodin 1962, pp. 184, 250, 451; cf. also Bodin 1962, pp. 10, 38, 409, 700 for additional uses of 'state'.

[208] [Downing] 1634, p. 46. [209] [Hayward] 1603, Sig. B, 3ᵛ.

[210] [Hayward] 1603, Sig. B, 4ʳ. [211] [Hayward] 1603, Sig. L, 1ᵛ.

[212] [Hayward] 1603, Sig. T, 3ᵛ.

That it should lay such an obligation upon all Subjects, there is evident reason, because what the supreame power, that is the State (in order to those things wherein supremacy consists) does, is truly the act of all, and none can have just cause of quarrell for dislike of what they themselves doe; and moreover necessity inforces it. Because without this the essence and being of a State were destroyed.[213]

Digges subsequently confirms his analysis with impressive concision when discussing the supremacy of those who hold sovereignty: 'that which makes a State one, is the union of supreame power'.[214]

Digges may possibly have been writing with some knowledge of Hobbes's *Elements of Law*, in which Hobbes had claimed it as one of his major discoveries that the person we engender when we submit to government is the person of the city or commonwealth:

The errour concerning mixt government hath proceeded from want of understanding of what is meant by this word body Politique, and how it signifieth not the Concord, but the union of many men. And though in the Chapters of subordinate Corporations, a Corporation be declared to be one Person in lawe, yet the same hath not been taken note of in the body of a Commonwealth, or City, nor have any of those innumerable writers of Politics observed any such union.[215]

It is true that Hobbes still speaks in this passage of the commonwealth rather than the state, and that he continues to speak in these terms at many points in *Leviathan*. He refers in his chapter *Of Civill Lawes* to the '*Persona Civitatis*, the Person of the Common-wealth' and subsequently explains that the reason why a civil association is generally 'called a *Common-wealth*' is 'because it consisteth of men united in one person'.[216] It is a striking fact about the composition of *Leviathan*, however, that as Hobbes's argument unfolds he increasingly speaks of the possessor of sovereignty not as the person of the commonwealth but as the person of the state. When he discusses 'the Laws and Authority of the Civill State' in Part 3, he informs us that sovereignty is 'Power in the State' and that this form of power is expressed in 'the Civill Laws of the State'.[217] To which he adds in his critique of vain philosophy in Part 4 that those who 'enjoy the benefit of the Laws' are being 'protected by the Power of the Civill State'.[218]

---

[213] [Digges] 1643, p. 32.   [214] [Digges] 1643, p. 65. Cf. also [Digges] 1643, pp. 40, 59.
[215] Hobbes 1969b, pp. 173–4.
[216] Hobbes 1996, ch. 26, p. 183; ch. 33, p. 268. On 'the Person of the Common-wealth' see also Hobbes 1996, ch. 15, p. 104; ch. 17, pp. 120–1; ch. 31, p. 252.
[217] Hobbes 1996, ch. 42, pp. 345, 361, 379.   [218] Hobbes 1996, ch. 46, p. 469; ch. 47, p. 476.

Hobbes confirms this understanding of state sovereignty when he turns in Part 3 of *Leviathan* to consider the alleged power of churches over those who exercise sovereign power. He consistently distinguishes between 'the Pastorall Function' and 'power in the Civill State', arguing that every true sovereign must be recognised as 'the Governour both of the State and of the Religion' established in that state.[219] As a result, he continually insists that all priests and pastors receive their authority 'from the Civill State'. They are 'subject to the State' and possess no power 'distinct from that of the Civill State'.[220]

Hobbes is not the first philosopher to speak of the person of the state as the true holder of sovereignty, but he is arguably the first to recognise the full extent of the conceptual difficulties raised by this new and epoch-making commitment. I shall return to these difficulties in analysing his theory of artificial personality in chapter 5 of volume 3, but it is necessary to say a preliminary word about them here. For it is due to Hobbes's clear recognition of these problems, and to the nature of his response to them, that he is perhaps entitled to be regarded as the first philosopher to enunciate a fully systematic and self-conscious theory of the sovereign state.

Hobbes's initial problem is to explain how it is possible for the person of the state to be the true bearer of sovereignty if, as he concedes, the state 'hath no will', and 'can do nothing' of its own accord.[221] Hobbes gives his answer in chapter 16 of *Leviathan* by way of introducing what he describes as his theory of attributed action.[222] The state is able to exercise sovereign power because it is represented by a sovereign whose actions can validly be attributed to the state. The sovereign is an actor who plays the role of the state and thereby acts in its name. The actions performed by the sovereign in his or her public capacity can therefore be attributed to the state, and are in fact (by attribution) the actions of the state. This, then, is how it comes about that, although the state is 'but a word', it is nevertheless the name of the person possessed of sovereign power.[223] Hobbes summarises in chapter 26, his chapter on the concept of civil law. On the one hand, the state or commonwealth 'is no Person, nor has capacity to doe any thing, but by the Representative'. But on the other hand, since the state or commonwealth 'praescribes, and commandeth

---

[219] Hobbes 1996, ch. 39, p. 322; ch. 47, p. 480.
[220] Hobbes 1996, ch. 42, p. 374; ch. 46, p. 474; ch. 47, p. 482. On 'the Civill State' see also Hobbes 1996, ch. 39, p. 321; ch. 47, pp. 475, 481.
[221] Hobbes 1996, Introduction, p. 9; ch. 24, p. 171; ch. 31, p. 253.
[222] Hobbes 1996, ch. 16, p. 111. [223] Hobbes 1996, ch. 26, p. 184; ch. 31, p. 245.

the observation of those rules, which we call Law', the true legislator is the state or commonwealth itself.[224]

Hobbes's other problem is how to distinguish the representation from the misrepresentation of the state's authority. What enables a sovereign to claim, when he or she performs an act of sovereign power, that such an act can properly and validly be attributed to the person of the state? Hobbes answers in chapter 16 of *Leviathan* by way of introducing his fundamental concept of authorisation and, more specifically, of *being the Author* of an action performed by someone else.[225] When the members of a multitude covenant, each with each, to hand over their conjoined powers to a sovereign, they perform two actions at the same time. They bring into existence the person of the state by way of agreeing who shall be sovereign, and at the same time they authorise their sovereign to act in the name of the state. As a result, they remain the authors of all the actions of the sovereign, and hence (by attribution) of the actions of the state. The validity of the sovereign's actions accordingly stems from the fact that they are at the same time the actions of each and every member of the multitude.[226] It makes no sense for the members of the multitude to criticise the actions of their sovereign, for in doing so they are simply criticising themselves. 'He that complaineth of injury from his Soveraigne, complaineth of that whereof he himselfe is Author; and therefore ought not to accuse any man but himselfe.'[227]

With these contentions, Hobbes is finally able to offer us his formal definition of a commonwealth or state. A state is '*One Person, of whose Acts a great Multitude, by mutuall Covenants one with another, have made themselves every one the Author, to the end he may use the strength and means of them all, as he shall think expedient, for their Peace and Common Defence*'.[228] More clearly than any previous writer on public power, Hobbes enunciates the doctrine that the legal person lying at the heart of politics is neither the *persona* of the people nor the official person of the sovereign, but rather the artificial person of the state.[229]

---

[224] Hobbes 1996, ch. 26, p. 184.
[225] Hobbes 1996, ch. 16, p. 112: 'Of Persons Artificiall, some have their words and actions *Owned* by those whom they represent. And then the Person is the *Actor*; and he that owneth his words and actions, is the AUTHOR: in which case the Actor acteth by Authority.'
[226] Hobbes 1996, ch. 16, p. 114: 'because the Multitude naturally is not *One*, but *Many*; they cannot be understood for one; but many Authors, of every thing their Representative saith, or doth in their name'.
[227] Hobbes 1996, ch. 18, p. 124.   [228] Hobbes 1996, ch. 17, p. 121.
[229] Gierke 1957, p. 139 claims that the thesis 'that the State-personality, in itself, was the real "Subject" of sovereignty' was 'first propounded by Hobbes, and never forgotten afterwards'.

VII

I have argued that the idea of supreme political authority as the authority of the state was originally the outcome of one particular theory of civil association, a theory at once absolutist and secular-minded in its ideological allegiances. This theory was in turn the product of the earliest major counter-revolutionary movement in modern European history, the movement of reaction against the ideologies of popular sovereignty initially developed in the Dutch and French religious wars and subsequently restated in the course of the English constitutional upheavals of the mid-seventeenth century.[230] It is not surprising, therefore, to find that both the ideology of state power and the new terminology employed to express it served to provoke a series of doubts and criticisms that have never been altogether stilled.

Some of the initial hostility stemmed from conservative theorists anxious to uphold the venerable ideal of *un roi, une foi, une loi*. They repudiated any suggestion that the aims of public authority should be purely civil in character, and sought to reinstate a closer relationship between allegiance in church and state. Some wished in addition to make it clear that sovereigns are of far higher standing than mere representatives, and to insist that the powers of the state must be understood to inhere in them and not in the person of the state.[231]

Much of the initial hostility, however, came from radical theorists who wished to reassert the ideal of popular sovereignty in place of the sovereignty of the state. The contractarian writers of the next generation, including John Locke and such admirers as Benjamin Hoadly, sought to avoid the terminology of state power altogether, preferring to speak of 'civil government' or 'supreme civil power'.[232] Echoing similar suspicions, the so-called commonwealthmen maintained their loyalty to the classical ideal of the self-governing republic throughout much of the eighteenth century, and likewise eschewed the vocabulary of state power in favour of continuing to speak of civil associations and commonwealths.[233]

---

[230] For a commentary on this view about the acquisition of the concept of the state see Geuss 2001, pp. 48–52.

[231] See Rowen 1961.

[232] Locke 1988, p. 135 speaks on his title-page of taking 'Civil-Government' as his theme; Hoadly 1773 speaks of 'civil authority' (p. 189), 'civil government' (p. 191) and 'supreme civil power' (p. 203). On Locke as a theorist not of the state but of 'political society' see Dunn 1969, pp. 120–47.

[233] Robbins 1959, pp. 125, 283; Kramnick 1968, pp. 236–60; Pocock 1975, pp. 423–505.

It is true that, at the end of the eighteenth century, a renewed counter-revolutionary effort was made to neutralise these various populist doubts. Hegel and his followers argued that the English contractarian theory of popular sovereignty merely reflected a failure to distinguish the powers of civil society from those of the state, and a consequent failure to recognise that the independent authority of the state is indispensable if the purposes of civil society are to be fulfilled. But this hardly provided an adequate reassurance. On the one hand, the anxiety of liberal theorists about the relationship between the powers of states and the alleged sovereignty of citizens gave rise to confusions which have never been resolved. And on the other hand, a deeper criticism arose out of these Hegelian roots, according to which the state's vaunted independence from its own agents as well as from the members of civil society amounts to nothing more than a pious fraud. Sceptics in the tradition of Michels and Pareto, no less than socialists in the tradition of Marx and Engels, have never ceased to insist that modern states are in truth nothing more than the executive arms of their own ruling class.

Given the importance of these rival ideologies, it is remarkable how quickly the Hobbesian conception of the state nevertheless succeeded in establishing itself at the heart of political discourse throughout western Europe. This is not to say that the concept was always well understood even by those who made prominent use of it. Rather it gave rise to a serious confusion which has continued to bedevil the analysis of public power ever since. The chief architects of the confusion were those self-consciously commonsensical writers who felt it obvious that the powers of the state must be reducible to the powers of some identifiable person or apparatus of government. Within the Anglophone tradition, the classic statement of this commitment can be found in John Austin's *Province of Jurisprudence Determined* of 1832. When Austin turns to the state, he begins with his usual confidence by informing us of 'the meaning which I annex to the term':

> '*The* state' is usually synonymous with '*the* sovereign'. It denotes the individual person, or the body of individual persons, which bears the supreme powers in an independent political society.[234]

Although Austin pronounces himself a deep admirer of Hobbes,[235] his definition of the state has the effect of obliterating the very distinction on which Hobbes's theory is based.

[234] Austin 1995, p. 190 note.   [235] Austin 1995, p. 229 and note.

By contrast with the positivism of so much English legal theory,[236] the Hobbesian view of the person of the state as the seat of sovereignty won immediate acceptance among a broad range of writers on natural jurisprudence in continental Europe. Perhaps the most important conduit for the transmission of this doctrine was Samuel Pufendorf's treatise of 1672, *De Iure Naturae et gentium*, which appeared in an English version by Basil Kennet together with Jean Barbeyrac's explanatory notes in 1717.[237] Pufendorf explicitly draws our attention to the fact that (as Kennet's version puts it) 'Mr *Hobbes* hath given us a very ingenious Draught of a Civil State, conceived as an *Artificial Man*'.[238] Although Pufendorf is critical of Hobbes at many points, he goes on to offer an analysis of state power which is at once Hobbesian in character and at the same time succeeds in resolving any lingering ambiguities in Hobbes's own account.

Pufendorf begins by offering a much fuller account than Hobbes had done of the two different worlds we simultaneously inhabit. One is the world of nature, while the other is the artificial world we construct for ourselves when we agree to follow a common life and regulate it by the rule of law. A number of Renaissance philosophers of language had already maintained that one of the distinctive powers of the human mind is that of calling into existence a moral world by the act of recognising and distinguishing moral entities. Pufendorf offers an unusually extensive exploration of this world of artifice, which he takes to be created by the imposition of moral names backed by an understanding of the properties they denote, all of which are 'fram'd with Analogy to Substance'.[239] Some of the moral persons inhabiting this world are described as 'simple'. Their existence is merely a reflection of the fact that all natural persons will find themselves playing a variety of roles, 'at home a Householder, a Senator in Parliament, an Advocate in the Halls of Justice, and a Counsellor at Court'.[240] But other moral persons are described as compound entities. They are brought into existence 'when several Individual Men are so united together, that what they *will* or *act* by virtue of that Union, is esteem'd a single Will, and a single Act, and no more'.[241]

---

[236] The same assumptions continue to underlie recent historical discussions of the state. Harding 1994, p. 58 complains that, in speaking of the state as a person distinct from both rulers and ruled, I introduce 'a mysterious new entity which deserves the attention of Ockham's razor'. But the concept of the state as we have inherited it *is* a mysterious entity, and I want to try to penetrate the mystery rather than dismiss it.
[237] See Pufendorf 1717. It is from this version that I quote.
[238] Pufendorf 1717, VII. II. XIII, p. 475.   [239] Pufendorf 1717, I. I. XII, p. 7.
[240] Pufendorf 1717, I. I. XIV, p. 9.   [241] Pufendorf 1717, I. I. XIII, p. 8.

When Pufendorf turns in Book 7 to apply this general theory of *entia moralia* to civil societies, he particularly singles out that 'Union of Wills and of Forces' which gives rise to 'a Common wealth, or Civil State, the strongest of all *Moral Persons*, or *Societies*'.[242] With this characterisation, he at once reiterates and places in a broader framework the Hobbesian analysis of the person of the state. He thereby arrives at what he takes to be 'the most proper Definition of a Civil State', according to which 'it is a compound Moral Person, whose Will, united and tied together by those Covenants which before pass'd among the Multitude, is deem'd the Will of all; to the End, that it may use and apply the Strength and Riches of private Persons towards maintaining the common Peace and Security'.[243]

As Pufendorf subsequently confirms, it follows that we cannot speak of the holders of sovereign power, even when acting in their public capacities, as the true bearers of sovereignty. Rather the 'subject' of sovereign power must be the person of the state, in whose name and on whose behalf the sovereign's actions are performed:

> The State in exerting and exercising its Will, makes use either of a single Person, or of a Council, according as the Supreme Command hath been conferr'd, either on the former or on the latter. Where the Sovereignty is lodg'd in one Man, there the State is supposed to chuse and desire whatever that one man (who is presumed to be Master of perfect Reason,) shall judge convenient; in every Business or Affair, which regard the End of Civil Government, but not in others.[244]

Although every act of the state must be performed by the sovereign, the will in the light of which the sovereign conducts himself remains 'that one Will, which we attribute to the State'.[245] The role of the sovereign, as in Hobbes, is that of 'representing the Will of the State'.[246]

By the middle of the eighteenth century, this vision of the state had become widely accepted in continental Europe. Perhaps the clearest reflection of this acceptance can be found in the attempt made by Louis de Jaucourt to summarise conventional wisdom in the article he contributed to the *Encyclopédie* in 1756 under the title *L'Etat*. There we read that '*The state* can be defined as a civil society by means of which a multitude of men are united together through their dependence upon a sovereign.'[247] After this definition there follows a recognisably Hobbesian account of the distinction between a state and a mere aggregate of individuals:

---

[242] Pufendorf 1717, VII. II. V, p. 468.   [243] Pufendorf 1717, VII. II. XIII, p. 475.
[244] Pufendorf 1717, VII. II. XIV, p. 476.   [245] Pufendorf 1717, VII. IV. II, p. 491.
[246] Pufendorf 1717, VII. II. XIV, p. 476.
[247] Jaucourt 1756, p. 19: 'on peut définir l'*état*, une société civile, par laquelle une multitude d'hommes sont unis ensemble sous le dépendance d'un souverain'.

This union of many persons in a single body, a union produced by putting together the wills and powers of every individual, is what distinguishes the *state* from a multitude. A multitude is nothing more than an assemblage of various persons, among whom each has a particular will. But the *state* is a society animated by a single soul which directs all its movements in a constant manner and in such a way as to procure the benefit of all.[248]

Like Pufendorf, Jaucourt concedes that, if the state is to be animated in this way, it stands in need of a sovereign to act on its behalf. The capacity of the state to remain in being depends on 'the establishment of a superior power' by means of which 'this union of individual wills is held in place'.[249] Nevertheless, the powers assigned to such sovereigns remain the powers of the state, which can thus 'be considered as a distinct moral person, of which the sovereign is the head and all individuals are the members'.[250] The state is accordingly seen, once again, as the true bearer of sovereignty, the possessor of 'certain rights which are distinct from those of each individual citizen, and which no individual or group of citizens can arrogate to themselves'.[251]

By this time, the idea of the state as the seat of sovereignty was beginning to be accepted even by English writers on jurisprudence. Perhaps the most distinguished example is furnished by Sir William Blackstone's *Commentaries on the Laws of England*, the first volume of which appeared in 1765. Blackstone's opening discussion of 'the very end and institution of civil states' strongly echoes Hobbes. 'A state', Blackstone declares, 'is a collective body, composed of a multitude of individuals, united for their safety and convenience, and intending to act together as one man.'[252] Blackstone goes on to pinpoint the difficulty to which this analysis gives rise. If the state is to act as one man, 'it ought to act by one uniform will', but because political communities 'are made up of many natural persons, each of whom has his particular will and inclinations, these several wills cannot by any *natural* union be joined together'.[253] The only solution, Blackstone repeats, is for the members of the multitude to convert

---

[248] Jaucourt 1756, p. 19: 'Cette union de plusieurs personnes en un seul corps, produite par le concours des volontés & des forces de chaque particulier, distingue l'*état*, d'une multitude: car une multitude n'est qu'un assemblage de plusieurs personnes, dont chacune a sa volonté particulière; au lieu que l'*état* est une société animée par une seule âme qui en dirige tous les mouvemens d'une maniere constante, relativement à l'utilité commune.'

[249] See Jaucourt 1756, p. 19 on 'l'établissement d'un pouvoir supérieur' by which 'l'union des volontés [est] soûtenue'.

[250] Jaucourt 1756, p. 19: 'On peut considérer l'*état* comme une personne morale, dont le souverain est la tête, & les particuliers les membres.'

[251] Jaucourt 1756, p. 19: 'certains droits distincts de ceux de chaque citoyen, & que chaque citoyen, ni plusieurs, ne sauroient s'arroger'.

[252] Blackstone 1857, p. 38.   [253] Blackstone 1857, p. 38.

themselves into a single person by way of replacing their individual wills by the will of a sovereign representative. They must seek 'by the consent of all persons to submit their own private wills to the will of one man, or of one or more assemblies of men, to whom the supreme authority is intrusted'.[254] By acting in this way, they can hope to make good their lack of natural union by instituting the purely political union of the state, a union in which the sovereign is the representative while the union itself remains the seat of sovereignty.

VIII

The immediate outcome of the conceptual revolution I have traced was to set up a series of reverberations in the wider political vocabularies of the western European states. Once the term *state* came to be accepted as the master noun of political discourse, a number of other concepts and assumptions bearing on the analysis of sovereignty had to be reorganised or in some cases given up. To round off this analysis, we need to examine the process of displacement and redefinition that accompanied the entrenchment of the concept of the state as an artificial person and as the bearer of sovereignty.

One concept that underwent a consequential process of redefinition was that of political allegiance. A subject or *subditus* had traditionally sworn allegiance to his sovereign as a liege lord. But with the acceptance of the idea that sovereignty is lodged not with rulers but with the state, this was replaced by the familiar view that citizens owe their loyalty to the state itself. This is not to say that those who originally advanced this argument had any desire to give up speaking of citizens as *subditi* or subjects. On the contrary, the earliest theorists of the state retained a strong preference for this traditional terminology, using it as a means of countering both the monarchomach inclination to speak of the sovereignty of the *universitas* and the classical republican contention that we ought to speak only of *civitates* and *cives*, of cities and their citizens. Hobbes, for example, declares with his usual cunning in his first published treatise on civil science that he is writing specifically 'about the citizen': *De Cive*. Yet it is one of his most important polemical claims that, as the English translation expresses it, 'each *Citizen*, as also every *subordinate civill Person*' ought properly to regard himself as 'the SUBJECT of him who hath the *chiefe command*'.[255]

---

[254] Blackstone 1857, p. 38.   [255] Hobbes 1983b, V. XI, p. 90.

Hobbes is in complete agreement with his radical opponents, however, when he goes on to argue that citizens ('that is to say, Subjects')[256] ought not to think of their allegiance as due to the natural persons who exercise sovereign power. The monarchomachs had already insisted that, as Hotman had put it, the holders of offices under a monarchy must be viewed as councillors of the kingdom, not of the king, and as servants of the crown, not of the person wearing it.[257] Hobbes elaborates the same argument when he declares with much emphasis in *De Cive* that the absolute obedience owed by each and every subject is due not to the person of their ruler, but rather to the *civitas* itself as 'a civill Person' and thus as the seat of supreme power.[258]

A further and closely connected concept that underwent a comparable process of transformation was that of treason. As long as the concept of allegiance remained connected with the doing of homage, the crime of treason remained that of behaving treacherously towards a sovereign lord. By the end of the sixteenth century, however, this was coming to seem less and less adequate. Even in the case of England, still bound by the Statute of 1352 in which treason had been defined to include the crime of compassing or imagining the king's death, the judges began to place increasingly wide constructions upon the meaning of the original Act. The aim in almost every case was to establish a view of treason essentially as an offence committed against the king in the discharge of his office.[259]

Meanwhile the political writers, untrammelled by the need to wrestle with precedents, arrived by a more direct route at the familiar view of treason as a crime not against the king but against the state. As so often, it is Hobbes who states the new understanding most unequivocally. He declares at the end of his analysis of dominion in the English version of *De Cive* that those who are guilty of treason are those who refuse to perform the duties 'without which the State cannot stand'.[260] Subsequently he takes this assumption for granted in *Leviathan*, observing in chapter 28 that anyone who commits treason 'suffers as an enemy of the Commonwealth',[261] and adding in his Review and Conclusion that a spy can be defined as someone who acts as an 'Enemy of the State'.[262]

The acceptance of state sovereignty also had the effect of devaluing the more charismatic elements of political leadership which, as I

---

[256] Hobbes 1983b, XII. VIII, p. 151.   [257] Hotman 1972, pp. 254, 298, 402.
[258] Hobbes 1983b, V. VII–XII, pp. 88–90.
[259] On this process see Holdsworth 1922–72, vol. 8, pp. 307–33.
[260] Hobbes 1983b, XIV. XX, p. 181.   [261] Hobbes 1996, ch. 28, p. 216.
[262] Hobbes 1996, Conclusion, p. 485.

indicated at the outset, had earlier been of central importance to the theory and practice of government throughout western Europe. Among the assumptions that suffered displacement, the most important was the claim that sovereignty is conceptually connected with display, that majesty serves in itself as an ordering force. Even Machiavelli still assumes that a ruler can expect to derive protection from *la maestà dello stato*, from a connection between his condition of stateliness and his capacity to maintain his state.[263] It proved impossible, however, for such beliefs about the charisma attaching to public authority to survive the transfer of that authority to the impersonal agency – Rousseau's 'purely moral person'[264] – of the modern state. By the start of the eighteenth century, we already find conservative writers lamenting that, as Lord Bolingbroke observes in an evident allusion to *Leviathan*, 'the state is become, under ancient and known forms, a new and undefinable monster', with the result that a monarchy like England finds itself left with 'a king without monarchical splendor' as head of state.[265]

It was of course possible to transfer the attributes of majesty to the state's representatives, permitting them to conduct state openings of parliament, to be granted state funerals, to lie in state and so forth. Once it became accepted, however, that even heads of state are simply holders of offices, the ascription of so much pomp and circumstance to mere functionaries came to seem not merely inappropriate but even absurd, a case not of genuine pomp but of mere pomposity. This insight was first elaborated by the defenders of 'free states' in their anxiety to insist that, in John Milton's phrase, rulers should never be 'elevated above thir brethren' but should 'walk the streets as other men'.[266] Thomas More's *Utopia*, for example, contains an early and devastating portrayal of public magnificence as nothing more than a form of infantile vanity.[267] John Ponet's *Shorte Treatise* of *Politike Power* includes a more minatory reminder of the punishments visited by God upon the Israelites for demanding 'a galaunt and pompous king'.[268] And Milton in *The Ready and Easy Way* speaks with withering contempt of those rulers who aspire 'to set a pompous face upon the superficial actings of State'.[269]

---

[263] See Machiavelli 1960, p. 74, and cf. pp. 76, 93. The same applies even more strongly to Machiavelli's contemporaries among 'mirror-for-princes' writers. See, for example, Pontano 1952, pp. 1054–6; Sacchi 1608, p. 68.
[264] See Rousseau 1966, p. 54 on 'la personne morale qui constitue l'État'.
[265] Bolingbroke 1844b, p. 333.   [266] Milton 1980, p. 425.
[267] See More 1965, pp. 152–6 on the reception of the Anemolian ambassadors.
[268] [Ponet] 1556, Sig. F, 4ʳ.   [269] Milton 1980, p. 426.

The state of princes to the person of the state

One outcome of distinguishing the authority of the state from that of its agents was thus to sever a time-honoured connection between the presence of majesty and the exercise of majestic powers.[270] Displays of stateliness eventually came to be seen as mere 'shows' or 'trappings' of power, not as features intrinsic to the workings of power itself.[271] When, for example, Gasparo Contarini concedes that the Doge of Venice is permitted to uphold the dignity of his office with a certain magnificence, he emphasises that this is just a matter of appearances, using a phrase that Lewes Lewkenor was to translate by saying that the Doge is allowed a 'royall appearing shew'.[272] Speaking with much greater hostility, Milton agrees that a monarch 'sits only like a great cypher', his 'vanitie and ostentation' having nothing to contribute to the ordering force of public authority.[273]

For the most self-conscious rejection of the older images of power, as well as the most unblinking vision of the state as a purely impersonal authority, we cannot do better than to end by turning once again to Thomas Hobbes. Discussing these concepts in chapter 10 of *Leviathan*, Hobbes deploys the idea of an effective power to command in such a way as to absorb every other element traditionally associated with the notions of public honour and dignity. To hold dignities, he declares, is simply to hold 'offices of Command'; to be held honourable is nothing more than 'an argument and signe of Power'.[274] Here, as throughout, it is Hobbes who first speaks systematically and unapologetically in the abstract and unmodulated tones of the modern theorist of the sovereign state.

---

[270] Foucault 1977 popularised an alleged contrast between the modern repudiation of power as spectacle and its centrality in the Renaissance. See also Greenblatt 1981. But as Pye 1984 observes, this arguably underestimates the extent to which, even in the Renaissance, the theatrical conception was already in contestation with a more abstract understanding of state authority.
[271] On the distinctiveness of this conception of public power see Geertz 1980, pp. 121–3.
[272] See Lewkenor 1599, p. 42, translating 'specie regia' from Contarini 1626, p. 56.
[273] Milton 1980, pp. 426, 429.   [274] Hobbes 1996, ch. 10, pp. 63–4, 65.

Bibliographies

MANUSCRIPT SOURCES

BIBLIOTHEQUE NATIONALE, PARIS

Fonds Latin MS 6566A: *Hobs* [Marked on spine; no title-page]

BRITISH LIBRARY

Add. MS 22041, fos. 324r–325v: Martinus, *Formula Vit[a]e Honest[a]e*
Harl. MS 162: *This first Tome or volume of the Journall of the howse of Commons... collected... by Sr Simonds D'Ewes* [7 November 1640 to 24 February 1641]
Harl. MS 163: *The second Tome or volume of the Journall of the howse of Commons... collected... by Sr Simonds D'Ewes* [6 April 1641 to 6 October 1642]
Harl. MS 4235: Thomas Hobbes, *The Elements of Law, Naturall and Politique*
Stowe MS 366, fos. 10^r–11^r [Speech of Sir Robert Phelips to House of Commons, 22 March 1628]

CAMBRIDGE UNIVERSITY LIBRARY

MS Mm. v. 2, fos. 2–77: [Sir Thomas Littleton], *Un lyver de exposicion de parcell de les tenures*
MS Ii. 5. 32, fos. 218^r–221^v: *Mr Littletons Argument concerning the personall libertye of the Subject* [A speech delivered 'in the painted chamber at a committee of both Houses 3. Apr 4. Car 1628'.]

CHATSWORTH, DERBYSHIRE

Hobbes MS D. 1: *Latin Exercises* [Bound MS volume: *Ex Aristot: Rhet.*, pp. 1–143]

ST JOHN'S COLLEGE, OXFORD

MS 13: *Behemoth or the Long Parliament. By Thomas Hobbes of Malmsbury* [Fair copy in hand of James Wheldon, additions and excisions in hand of Hobbes]

UNIVERSITY OF SHEFFIELD

Hartlib Papers 62/21/1A–2B: Rand to Worsley, 11 August 1651

PRINTED PRIMARY SOURCES

Ad C. Herennium de Ratione Dicendi (1954). Ed. and trans. Harry Caplan, London.
Alamanni, Lodovico (1955). *Discorso* [1516] in *Das florentinische Staatsbewusstsein im Übergang von der Republik zum Prinzipat*, ed. Rudolf von Albertini, Bern, pp. 362–71.
Alberti, Leon Battista (1971). *I Libri della Famiglia* [c.1430], ed. Ruggiero Romano and Alberto Tenenti, Turin.
Alciato, Andrea (1621). *Emblemata, cum commentariis*, Padua.
Almain, Jacques (1518). *Questio in Vesperiis Habita* in *Opuscula*, ed. Vincent Doesmier, Paris, sect. 4, fos. lxii–lxvii.
  (1706a). *Tractatus de Autoritate Ecclesiae* in Jean Gerson, *Opera Omnia*, ed. Louis Ellies du Pin, 5 vols., Antwerp, vol. 2, cols. 976–1012.
  (1706b). *Quaestio Resumptiva... de Dominio Naturali, Civili & Ecclesiastico* in Jean Gerson, *Opera Omnia*, ed. Louis Ellies du Pin, 5 vols., Antwerp, vol. 2, cols. 961–76.
  (1997a). *A Book concerning the Authority of the Church* in *Conciliarism and Papalism*, ed. J. H. Burns and Thomas M. Izbicki, Cambridge, pp. 134–200.
  (1997b). *Questions at Vespers*, trans. Arthur S. McGrade in *Cambridge Translations of Renaissance Philosophical Texts*, ed. Jill Kraye, 2 vols., Cambridge, vol. 2, pp. 14–35.
Althusius, Johannes (1932). *Politica Methodice Digesta*, ed. Carl J. Friedrich, Cambridge, Mass.
[Amsdorf, Nicholas von] (1550). *Confessio et Apologia Pastorum et Reliquorum Ministrorum Ecclesiae Magdeburgensis*, Magdeburg.
Aquinas, St Thomas (1952). *Summa Theologiae, Pars Prima et Prima Secundae*, ed. Piero Caramello, Turin.
  (1962). *Summa Theologiae, Pars II^a II^{ae}*, ed. Piero Caramello, Turin.
  (1966). *In Octo Libros Politicorum Aristotelis Expositio*, ed. R. M. Spiazzi, Turin.
  (1973). *De Regimine Principum ad Regem Cypri* in *Opuscula Philosophica*, ed. R. M. Spiazzi, Turin, pp. 257–358.
Aristotle (1598). *Aristotles Politiques, or Discourses of Government*, trans. I. D., London.
  (1872). *Politicorum Libri Octo*, trans. William of Moerbeke, ed. Franz Susemihl, Leipzig.
  (1926). *The 'Art' of Rhetoric*, ed. and trans. John Henry Freese, London.
  (1972). *Ethica Nicomachea*, trans. Robert Grosseteste, ed. R. A. Gauthier, Leiden.
  (1996). *The Politics* and *The Constitution of Athens*, ed. Stephen Everson, Cambridge.
[Arnall, William] (1735). *Opposition No Proof of Patriotism*, London.
Arnobius (1953). *Adversus Nationes*, ed. Concetto Marchesi, 2nd edn, Milan.

Ascham, Roger (1970). *The Scholemaster* in *English Works*, ed. William A. Wright, Cambridge, pp. 171-302.
Augustine, St (1957-72). *De Civitate Dei Contra Paganos*, ed. and trans. George E. McCracken *et al.*, 7 vols., London.
Austin, John (1995). *The Province of Jurisprudence Determined* [1832], ed. Wilfred E. Rumble, Cambridge.
Azo, Portius (1888). *Quaestiones*, ed. Ernst Landsberg, Freiburg.
  (1966a). *Summa super codicem*, ed. Mario E. Viora, Turin.
  (1966b). *Lectura super codicem*, ed. Mario E. Viora, Turin.
Ball, William (1642). *A Caveat for Subjects, Moderating the Observator*, London.
Barbarossa, Frederic (1979-85). *Frederici I Diplomata* in *Diplomata Regum et Imperatorum Germaniae*, ed. Heinrich Appelt, 3 vols., Hanover.
Barclay, William (1600). *De Regno et regali potestate adversus Buchananum Brutum Boucherium et reliquos monarchomachos, Libri Sex*, Paris.
Bartolus of Sassoferrato (1562). *Digestum Novum Commentaria*, Basel.
  (1588). *In II Partem Digesti Novi Commentaria* in *Opera Omnia*, 12 vols., Basel.
Beacon, Richard (1594). *Solon his Follie, or a Politique Discourse, Touching the Reformation of Common-weales Conquered, Declined or Corrupted*, Oxford.
Berkeley, George (1953). *Maxims Concerning Patriotism* in *The Works of George Berkeley Bishop of Cloyne*, vol. 6, ed. T. E. Jessop, London, pp. 253-5.
Beroaldo, Filippo (1508). *Libellus de Optimo Statu* in *Opuscula*, Venice, fos. x-xxxiiii.
Blackstone, Sir William (1857). *Commentaries on the Laws of England*. Vol. 1. *Of the Rights of Persons* [1765], ed. Robert Malcolm Kerr, London.
Blackwood, Adam (1588). *Adversus Georgii Buchanani... pro regibus Apologia*, 2nd edn, Paris.
Boccalini, Traiano (1948). *Ragguagli di Parnaso* [1613], ed. Luigi Firpo, 3 vols., Bari.
Bodin, Jean (1576). *Les Six Livres de la république*, Paris.
  (1962). *The Six Books of a Commonweale*, trans. Richard Knolles, ed. Kenneth D. McRae, Cambridge, Mass.
Bolingbroke, Henry St John, Viscount (1844a). *Remarks on the History of England* in *The Works of Lord Bolingbroke*, 4 vols., London, vol. 1, pp. 292-455.
  (1844b). *Letters on the Study and Use of History* in *The Works of Lord Bolingbroke*, 4 vols., London, vol. 2, pp. 173-334.
  (1997a). *A Dissertation upon Parties* in *Bolingbroke: Political Writings*, ed. David Armitage, Cambridge, pp. 1-191.
  (1997b). *On the Spirit of Patriotism* in *Bolingbroke: Political Writings*, ed. David Armitage, Cambridge, pp. 193-216.
Bologna, Hugh of (1863). *Rationes Dictandi* [c.1120] in *Briefsteller und Formelbücher des Elften bis Vierzehnten Jahrhunderts*, ed. Ludwig Rockinger, 2 vols., Munich, vol. 1, pp. 53-94.
Bossuet, J.-B. (1967). *Politique tirée des propres paroles de l'Ecriture Sainte*, ed. Jacques Le Brun, Geneva.
Bracciolini, Poggio (1964-9a). *De Nobilitate* [c.1440] in *Opera Omnia*, ed. Riccardo Fubini, 4 vols., Turin, vol. 1, pp. 64-83.

(1964–9b). *Historiae Florentini Populi* in *Opera Omnia*, ed. Riccardo Fubini, 4 vols., Turin, vol. 2, pp. 85–495.

(1964–9c). *In Laudem Rei Publicae Venetorum* [1459] in *Opera Omnia*, ed. Riccardo Fubini, 4 vols., Turin, vol. 2, pp. 925–37.

(1997). *In Praise of the Venetian Republic*, trans. Martin Davies in *Cambridge Translations of Renaissance Philosophical Texts*, ed. Jill Kraye, 2 vols., Cambridge, vol. 2, pp. 135–45.

Bracton, Henry de (1640). *De Legibus et Consuetudinibus Angliae, Libri Quinque* [1259], London.

Braga, Martin of (1950). *Formula Honestae Vitae* in *Martini Episcopi Bracarensis Opera Omnia*, ed. Claude W. Barlow, New Haven, Conn., pp. 236–50.

Bramhall, John (1643). *The Serpent Salve, or, A Remedie For the Biting of an Aspe*, n.p.

Brescia, Albertano da (1507). *De Amore et Dilectione* [1238] in *Albertani moralissimi Opus*, Cuneus, fos. 25–61.

(1873). *Trattati Morali*, trans. Andrea da Grosseto, ed. Francesco Selmi, Bologna.

Breves Officialium Comunis Senensis [1250], ed. Luciano Banchi (1866) in *Archivio Storico Italiano* 3, pp. 7–104.

Bruni, Leonardo (1952). *Ad Petrum Paulum Histrum Dialogus* in *Prosatori latini del Quattrocento*, ed. Eugenio Garin, Milan, pp. 44–99.

(1968). *Laudatio Florentinae Urbis* [1403–4] in Hans Baron, *From Petrarch to Leonardo Bruni*, Chicago, Ill., pp. 217–63.

Buchanan, George (1579). *De Iure Regni apud Scotos, Dialogus*, Edinburgh.

Budé, Guillaume (1966). *De l'institution du prince* [1547], Farnborough.

Campano, Giovanni (1502). *De Regendo Magistratu* in *Opera Omnia*, Venice, fos. xxxxiii–xxxxviii.

Capua, Thomas of (1929). *Ars Dictandi* [c.1230], ed. Eming Heller, Heidelberg.

Carafa, Diomede (1971). *Dello Optimo Cortesano* [c.1470], ed. Gioacchino Paparelli, Salerno.

Cassian, Johannes (1886). *Conlationes I–X*, ed. Michael Petschenig, Vienna.

(1965). *De Institutis Coenobiorum*, ed. and trans. Jean-Claude Guy, Paris.

Castiglione, Baldassare (1981). *Il Libro del Cortegiano* [1528], ed. Nicola Longo, Milan.

(1994). *The Book of the Courtier* [1561], trans. Thomas Hoby, ed. Virginia Cox, London.

Cavalcanti, Giovanni (1973). *Trattato Politico-Morale*, ed. M. T. Grendler, Geneva.

Ceffi, Filippo (1942). *Dicerie* [c.1330], ed. Giuliana Giannardi in *Studi di Filologia Italiana* 6, pp. 27–63.

Charles I (1999). *XIX. Propositions Made By both Houses of Parliament, to the Kings most Excellent Majestie: With his Majesties Answer thereunto* [1642] in *The Struggle for Sovereignty: Seventeenth-Century English Political Tracts*, ed. Joyce Lee Malcolm, 2 vols., Indianapolis, Ind., vol. 1, pp. 145–78.

Chesterfield, The Earl of (1901). *The Letters of the Earl of Chesterfield to his Son*, ed. Charles Strachey and Annette Calthrop, 2 vols., London.

Cicero (1534). *The Thre Bookes of Tullyes Offices both in latyne tonge & in englysshe lately translated by Roberte Whytinton*, London.
  (1556). *Thre Bokes of Duties, to Marcus his sonne, turned oute of latine into english, by Nicolas Grimalde*, London.
  (1558). *Thre Bookes of Duties, to Marcus his sonne, turned out of latine into english, by Nicolas Grimalde. Wherunto the latine is adjoyned*, London.
  (1913). *De Officiis*, ed. and trans. Walter Miller, London.
  (1926). *Philippics*, ed. and trans. Walter C. A. Ker, London.
  (1927). *Tusculanae Disputationes*, ed. and trans. J. E. King, London.
  (1928). *De Legibus*, ed. and trans. Clinton Walker Keyes, London.
  (1931). *De Finibus Bonorum et Malorum*, ed. and trans. H. Rackham, London.
  (1942a). *De Oratore*, ed. and trans. E. W. Sutton and H. Rackham, 2 vols., London.
  (1942b). *De Partitione Oratoria*, ed. and trans. H. Rackham, London, pp. 310–420.
  (1949). *De Inventione*, trans. H. M. Hubbell, London.
  (1976). *In Catilinam I–IV*, ed. and trans. C. Macdonald, London.
Clichtove, Josse (1512). *De Vera Nobilitate*, Paris.
Coalition of Patriots Delineated, A (1735). London.
Coke, Sir Edward (1628). *The First Part of the Institutes of the Lawes of England. Or, a Commentarie upon Littleton*, London.
Commons Debates 1628, volume 2: *17 March–19 April 1628*, ed. Robert C. Johnson and Maija Jansson Cole (1977), New Haven, Conn.
Commons Debates 1628, volume 3: *21 April–27 May 1628*, ed. Robert C. Johnson, Mary Frear Keeler, Maija Jansson Cole and William B. Bidwell (1977), New Haven, Conn.
Commons Debates 1628, volume 4: *28 May–26 June 1628*, ed. Mary Frear Keeler, Maija Jansson Cole and William B. Bidwell (1978), New Haven, Conn.
Compagni, Dino (1939). *La Cronica*, ed. Isidoro del Lungo, Florence.
Conches, Guillaume de (1929). *Moralium Dogma Philosophorum*, ed. John Holmberg, Uppsala.
  (1965). *Glosae super Platonem*, ed. Edouard Jeauneau, Paris.
Considerations for the Commons in This Age of Distractions (1642). London.
Constitutional Documents of the Puritan Revolution 1625–1660, ed. Samuel Rawson Gardiner (1906), 3rd edn, Oxford.
Constitutional Documents of the Reign of James I, A.D. 1603–1625 with an historical commentary, ed. J. R. Tanner (1930), Cambridge.
Contarino, Gasparo (1626). *De Republica Venetorum Libri quinque*, Amsterdam.
  (1968). *Opera* [Paris, 1571], reprinted Farnborough.
Cowell, John (1607). *The Interpreter: Or Booke Containing the Signification of Words*, Cambridge.
Dante Alighieri (1965). *Monarchia*, ed. P. G. Ricci, Milan.
  (1966). *Inferno* in *La Commedia*, ed. Giorgio Petrocchi, Milan.
  (1967a). *Purgatorio* in *La Commedia*, ed. Giorgio Petrocchi, Milan.

(1967b). *Paradiso* in *La Commedia*, ed. Giorgio Petrocchi, Milan.

(1995). *Convivio*, ed. Franca Brambilla Ageno, 3 vols., Florence.

Decembrio, Pier Candido (1731). *Philippi Mariae... Vita* [c.1435] in *Rerum Italicarum Scriptores*, ed. Lodovico Muratori, Milan, vol. 20, pp. 986–1020.

(1958). *De Laudibus Mediolanensis Urbis Panegyricus* [c.1435] in *Rerum Italicarum Scriptores*, ed. Lodovico Muratori, new edn ed. Giosue Carducci and Vittorino Fiorini, Bologna, vol. 20, pt. 1, pp. 1013–25.

De Laude Civitatis Laudae [c.1250]. Ed. Georg Waitz (1872) in *Monumenta Germaniae Historica*, vol. 22, Hanover, pp. 372–3.

Dering, Sir Edward (1640). *The First Speech Made by Sir Edward Deering in the House of Commons*, London.

Digest of Justinian, The, ed. Theodor Mommsen and Paul Krueger, trans. Alan Watson (1985), 4 vols., Philadelphia, Penn.

[Digges, Dudley] (1643). *The Unlawfulnesse of Subjects taking up Armes against their Soveraigne, in what case soever*, n.p.

[Downing, Calybute] (1634). *A Discourse of the State Ecclesiasticall of this Kingdome, in relation to the Civill*, 2nd edn, Oxford.

Eliot, Sir John (1879). *The Monarchie of Man*, ed. Alexander B. Grosart, 2 vols., London.

Erasmus, Desiderius (1525). *Enchiridion Militis Christiani*, Strasbourg.

(1551). *Adagia*, Basel.

(1974). *Institutio Christiani Principis* [1516], ed. Otto Herding in *Opera Omnia*, pt. 4, vol. 1, Amsterdam, pp. 95–219.

(1997). *The Education of a Christian Prince*, ed. Lisa Jardine, Cambridge.

Faba, Guido (1889). *Parlamenti ed Epistole* [1243–3], ed. Augusto Gaudenzi in *I Suoni, le Forme e le Parole dell' Odierno Dialetto della Città di Bologna*, Turin, pp. 127–60.

(1892). *Dictamina Rhetorica* [1226–8], ed. Augusto Gaudenzi in *Il Propugnatore* 5, pt. 1, pp. 86–129; pt. 2, pp. 58–109.

(1893). *Epistole* [1239–41], ed. Augusto Gaudenzi in *Il Propugnatore* 6, pt. 1, pp. 359–90; pt. 2, pp. 373–89.

(1956). *Summa de Viciis et Virtutibus*, ed. Virgilio Pini in *Quadrivium* 1, pp. 97–152.

Ferreti, Ferreto de' (1920). *Le Opere*, ed. Carlo Cipolla, 3 vols., Rome.

[Fletcher, Andrew] (1697). *A Discourse Concerning Militias and Standing Armies*, London.

(1997). *A Discourse of Government with Relation to Militias* in *Political Works*, ed. John Robertson, Cambridge, pp. 1–31.

Florus, Lucius Iulius (1618). *The Roman Histories*, trans. E. M. B[olton], London.

Froissart, Jean (1824–6). *Chroniques*, ed. J. A. C. Buchon, 14 vols., Paris.

(1972). *Chroniques: debut du premier livre*, ed. G. T. Diller, Geneva.

Gerson, Jean (1965). *De Potestate Ecclesiastica* [1417] in *Oeuvres Complètes*, vol. 6: *L'oeuvre ecclésiologique*, ed. Palémon Glorieux, Paris, pp. 210–50.

Giamboni, Bono (1968). *Il Libro de' Vizi e delle Virtudi*, ed. Cesare Segre, Turin.

[Gibson, Edmund] (1731). *The Lord Bishop of London's Caveat against Aspersing Princes and their Administration*, London.
Gordon, Thomas (1728). *The Works of Tacitus. Volume 1: Containing the Annals. To which are prefixed, Political Discourses upon that Author*, London.
Gratulatio Patavini potestatis atque reipublicae Patavinae (1741). In *Antiquitates Italicae*, ed. Lodovico Muratori, vol. 4, Milan, pp. 131–2.
Gregoire, Pierre (1596). *De Republica, libri sex et viginti*, Pont à Musson.
Grosseto, Andrea da (1873). *Trattati Morali di Albertano da Brescia*, trans. Andrea da Grosseto, ed. Francesco Selmi, Bologna.
Guicciardini, Francesco (1932). *Discorsi del Reggimento di Firenze* in *Dialogo e Discorsi del Reggimento di Firenze* [c.1520], ed. Roberto Palmarocchi, Bari, pp. 173–281.
  (1933). *Ricordi* in *Scritti Politici e Ricordi*, ed. Roberto Palmarocchi, Bari, pp. 239–336.
  (1945). *Ricordi Politici e Civili*, ed. Adolfo Faggi, Turin.
  (1965). *Selected Writings*, ed. Cecil and Margaret Grayson, London.
Haechtanus, Laurentius (1579). *Microcosmos: Parvus Mundus*, Amsterdam.
Hall, Joseph (1624). *The Great Imposter, Laid Open in a Sermon at Grayes Inne*, London.
Harrington, James (1700). *The Oceana ... and his Other Works*, ed. John Toland, London.
  (1977). *The Political Works of James Harrington*, ed. J. G. A. Pocock, Cambridge.
[Hayward, John] (1603). *An Answer to the First Part of a Certaine Conference, Concerning Succession*, London.
Helinandus of Froidmont (1855). *De Bono Regimine Principis* [c.1200] in *Patrologiae Cursus Completus*, ed. J.-P. Migne, vol. 212, Paris, pp. 735–46.
[Hervey, Lord] (1734). *The Conduct of the Opposition and the Tendency of Modern Patriotism*, London.
Hoadly, Benjamin (1773). *The Original and Institution of Civil Government Discussed* in *The Works*, ed. John Hoadly, 3 vols., London, vol. 2, pp. 182–286.
Hobbes, Thomas (1839). *Elements of Philosophy. The First Section, Concerning Body* in *The English Works of Thomas Hobbes*, ed. Sir William Molesworth, London.
  (1969a). *Behemoth or The Long Parliament*, ed. Ferdinand Tönnies, 2nd edn, introd. M. M. Goldsmith, London.
  (1969b). *The Elements of Law Natural and Politic* [1640], ed. Ferdinand Tönnies, 2nd edn, introd. M. M. Goldsmith, London.
  (1973). *Critique du 'De Mundo' de Thomas White*, ed. Jean Jacquot and Harold Whitmore Jones, Paris.
  (1983a). *De Cive* [1642]: *The Latin Version*, ed. Howard Warrender, Clarendon Edition, vol. 2, Oxford.
  (1983b). *De Cive* [1642]: *The English Version*, ed. Howard Warrender, Clarendon Edition, vol. 3, Oxford.
  (1996). *Leviathan, Or The Matter, Forme, & Power of a Common-Wealth Ecclesiasticall and Civill* [1651], ed. Richard Tuck, Cambridge.

[Hobbes, Thomas (?)] (1986). *A Briefe of the Art of Rhetorique* in *The Rhetorics of Thomas Hobbes and Bernard Lamy*, ed. J. T. Harwood, Carbondale and Edwardsville, Ill.
Holland, Sir John (1640). *His Speech in Parliament Declaring the great and manifold Grievances of this Kingdom*, London.
Holles, Denzell (1642). *The Speech Delivered at the Lords Barr, Wednesday the 15th of June*, London.
Holles, Sir John (1923). *A Summary of what was done in the Parliament begun the 5 of April, 1614* in *Historical Manuscripts Commission Report on the Manuscripts of His Grace the Duke of Portland*, London, vol. 9, pp. 132–9.
Hotman, François (1972). *Francogallia*, trans J. H. M. Salmon, ed. Ralph E. Giesey, Cambridge.
Humfrey, Lawrence (1563). *The Nobles or of Nobilitye*, London.
Husbands, Edward, Warren, T. and Best, R. (eds.) (1643). *An Exact Collection of all Remonstrances, Declarations, Votes, Orders, Ordinances, Proclamations, Petitions, Messages, Answers, and other Remarkable Passages betweene the Kings most Excellent Majesty, and his High Court of Parliament beginning at his Majesties return from Scotland, being in December 1641, and continued untill March the 21, 1643*, London.
Il Costituto del Comune di Siena dell'anno 1262, ed. Lodovico Zdekauer (1897), Milan.
Jaucourt, Louis de (1756). *Etat* in *Encyclopédie, ou Dictionnaire raisonné, des Sciences, des Arts et des Métiers*, ed. Denis Diderot and Jean d'Alembert, Paris, vol. 6, p. 19.
Jonson, Ben (1988). *Timber: or Discoveries* in *The Complete Poems*, ed. George Parfitt, London, Appendix 1, pp. 373–458.
Kenyon, J. P. (ed.) (1966). *The Stuart Constitution: Documents and Commentary*, Cambridge.
King, Margaret L. and Rabil, Albert (eds.) (1983). *Her Immaculate Hand: Selected Works By and About The Women Humanists of Quattrocento Italy*, New York.
Knox, John (1994). *The Appellation* in *John Knox: On Rebellion*, ed. Roger A. Mason, Cambridge, pp. 72–114.
Landino, Cristoforo (1952). *Disputationes Camaldulenses* [c.1470] in *Prosatori Latini del Quattrocento*, ed. Eugenio Garin, Milan, pp. 716–91.
  (1970). *De Vera Nobilitate* [c.1480], ed. M. T. Liaci, Florence.
Latini, Brunetto (1948). *Li Livres dou trésor* [1266], ed. Francis J. Carmody, Berkeley, Calif.
Lewkenor, Lewes (1599). *The Commonwealth and Government of Venice. Written by the Cardinall Gasper Contareno, and translated out of Italian into English, by Lewes Lewkenor Esquire*, London.
Liber de Laudibus Civitatis Ticinensis [c.1320]. In *Rerum Italicarum Scriptores*, ed. Lodovico Muratori, new edn ed. Giosue Carducci and Vittorino Fiorini (1903), Città di Castello, vol. 11, pt. 1, pp. 1–52.
Libri, Matteo de' (1974). *Arringhe* [c.1275], ed. Eleonora Vincenti, Milan, pp. 3–227.
Lisini, Alessandro (ed.) (1903). *Il Costituto del Comune di Siena Volgarizzato nel 1309–1310*, 2 vols., Siena.

[Littleton, Sir Thomas] (1600). *Littleton's Tenures in English. Lately perused and amended*, London.
Livy (1600). *The Romane Historie*, trans. Philemon Holland, London.
    (1919). *Books I and II*, ed. and trans. B. O. Foster, London.
    (1924). *Books V, VI and VII*, ed. and trans. B. O. Foster, London.
    (1949). *Books XXVIII–XXX*, ed. and trans. Frank Gardner Moore, London.
Locke, John (1979). *An Essay Concerning Human Understanding* [1690], ed. Peter H. Nidditch, Oxford.
    (1988). *Two Treatises of Government* [1690], ed. Peter Laslett, Cambridge.
Lodge, Sir Thomas (1614). *To the Courteous Reader* in *The Workes both Morrall and Natural*, London.
Lodi, Orfino da (1869). *De Regimine et Sapientia Potestatis* [c.1240], ed. Antonio Ceruti in *Miscellanea di Storia Italiana* 7, pp. 33–94.
Ludlow, Edmund (1894). *Memoirs*, ed. C. H. Firth, 2 vols., Oxford.
Luther, Martin (1910). *Warnung an seine lieben Deutschen* in *Werke*, Weimar, vol. 30, pt. 3, pp. 276–320.
Lyly, John (1868). *Euphues* [1579], ed. Edward Arber, London.
Machiavelli, Niccolò (1960). *Il Principe e Discorsi Sopra la Prima Deca di Tito Livio*, ed. Sergio Bertelli, Milan.
    (1961). *Lettere*, ed. Franco Gaeta, Milan.
    (1962). *Istorie Fiorentine*, ed. Franco Gaeta, Milan.
Macrobius (1893). *Commentarii in Somnium Scipionis*, ed. Franz Eyssenhardt, Leipzig.
Maio, Giuniano (1956). *De Maiestate* [1492], ed. Franco Gaeta, Bologna.
    (1997). *On Majesty*: ch. 19. *On Magnificence* in *Cambridge Translations of Renaissance Philosophical Texts*, ed. Jill Kraye, 2 vols., Cambridge, vol. 2, pp. 110–13.
Mair, John (1519). *In Quartum Sententiarum Quaestiones Utilissimae*, Paris.
    (1521). *Historia Majoris Britanniae tam Angliae quam Scotia*, Paris.
    (1892). *A History of Greater Britain, as well England as Scotland*, ed. and trans. Archibald Constable, Edinburgh.
Mamertinus, Claudius (1964). *Gratiarum Actio* in *XII Panegyrici Latini*, ed. R. A. B. Mynors, Oxford, pp. 121–44.
Marsilius of Padua (1928). *Defensor Pacis* [1324], ed. C. W. Previté-Orton, Cambridge.
Melanchthon, Philipp (1850). *In Officia Ciceronis Prolegomena* in *Corpus Reformatorum*, vol. 16, ed. H. E. Bindseil, Halle, pp. 533–614.
Milton, John (1932). *Johannis Miltoni Angli Pro Populo Anglicano Defensio* [1651] in *The Works of John Milton*, ed. Frank Allen Patterson *et al.*, vol. 7, New York.
    (1953). *Commonplace Book* in *Complete Prose Works*, vol. 1, *1624–1642*, ed. Don M. Wolfe, New Haven, Conn., pp. 362–513.
    (1959). *Areopagitica* [1644] in *Complete Prose Works*, vol. 2, *1643–1648*, ed. Ernest Sirluck, New Haven, Conn., pp. 486–570.
    (1962). *Eikonoklastes* [1649] in *Complete Prose Works*, vol. 3, *1648–1649*, ed. Merritt Y. Hughes, New Haven, Conn., pp. 337–601.

(1971). *History of Britain* in *Complete Prose Works*, vol. 5, *1648–1671*, part 1, ed. French Fogle, New Haven, Conn.

(1980). *The Ready and Easy Way to Establish a Free Commonwealth* [1660] in *Complete Prose Works*, vol. 7, *1659–1660*, ed. Robert W. Ayers, New Haven, Conn., pp. 405–63.

(1991). *The Tenure of Kings and Magistrates* [1649] in *John Milton: Political Writings*, ed. Martin Dzelzainis, Cambridge, pp. 1–48.

(1998). *Samson Agonistes* in *The Complete Poems*, ed. John Leonard, London, pp. 463–511.

[Molesworth, Robert] (1694). *An Account of Denmark, As it was in the Year 1692*, London.

Molesworth, Robert (1721). *Franco Gallia . . . translated . . . by the Author of the Account of Denmark, The second edition, with additions and a New Preface by the Translator*, London.

Montagnone, Geremia da (1505). *Compendium Moralium Notabilium* [c.1300], Venice.

More, Thomas (1965). *Utopia* [1516] in *The Complete Works of St. Thomas More*, vol. 4, ed. Edward Surtz and J. H. Hexter, New Haven, Conn.

Morosini, Domenico (1969). *De Bene Instituta Re Publica* [c.1500], ed. Claudio Finzi, Milan.

[Moyle, Walter] (1697). *The Second Part of an Argument, Shewing, that a Standing Army is inconsistent with a Free Government*, London.

Moyle, Walter (1726) *The Works of Walter Moyle Esq.*, ed. Thomas Sargent, 2 vols., London.

(1727). *The Whole Works of W. Moyle Esq.*, ed. Anthony Hammond, London.

Mussato, Albertino (1727). *De Gestis Italicorum Post Mortem Henrici VII Caesaris Historia* in *Rerum Italicarum Scriptores*, ed. Lodovico Muratori, vol. 10, Milan, cols. 569–768.

(1900). *Ecerinis*, ed. Luigi Padrin, Bologna.

Nashe, Thomas (1958). *The Anatomie of Absurditie* [1589] in *The Works of Thomas Nashe*, ed. Ronald B. McKerrow, 5 vols., Oxford, vol. 1, pp. 3–49.

[Neville, Henry] (trans.) (1675). *The Works of the Famous Nicolas Machiavel*, London.

(1694). *The Discourses of Nicolas Machiavel, upon the First Decade of Titus Livius* in *The Works of the Famous Nicolas Machiavel*, London, pp. 267–430.

Neville, Henry (1969). *Plato Redivivus: or, a Dialogue Concerning Government* in *Two English Republican Tracts*, ed. Caroline Robbins, Cambridge, pp. 65–200.

Ockham, William of (1940). *Octo Quaestiones de Potestate Papae* in *Opera Politica*, vol. 1, ed. J. G. Sikes, Manchester, pp. 1–221.

Oculus Pastoralis [c.1220], ed. Dora Franceschi (1966) in *Memorie dell'Accademia delle Scienze di Torino* 11, pp. 19–70.

Ovid (1977–84). *Metamorphoses*, ed. and trans. Frank J. Miller, revised G. P. Goold, 2 vols., London.

Palmieri, Matteo (1997). *Civil Life: Book 2*, trans. David Marsh in *Cambridge Translations of Renaissance Philosophical Texts*, ed. Jill Kraye, 2 vols., Cambridge, vol. 2, pp. 150–72.

[Parker, Henry] (1933). *Observations upon some of his Majesties late Answers and Expresses* [1642] in *Tracts on Liberty in the Puritan Revolution 1638–1647*, ed. William Haller, New York, vol. 2, pp. 167–213.

(1999). *The Case of Shipmony briefly discoursed* [1640] in *The Struggle for Sovereignty: Seventeenth-Century English Political Tracts*, ed. Joyce Lee Malcolm, 2 vols., Indianapolis, Ind., vol. 1, pp. 93–125.

Parliamentary History of England, from the Earliest Period to the Year 1803 ... vol. 2: *AD 1625–1642*, ed. William Cobbett and T. C. Hansard (1807), London.

Parliamentary History of England, from the Earliest Period to the Year 1803 ... vol. 8: *AD 1722–1733*, ed. William Cobbett and T. C. Hansard (1811), London.

Parliamentary History of England, from the Earliest Period to the Year 1803 ... vol. 9: *AD 1733–1737*, ed. William Cobbett and T. C. Hansard (1811), London.

Paruta, Paolo (1852). *Opere Politiche*, ed. Cirillo Monzani, 2 vols., Florence.

Patrizi, Francesco (1594a). *De Regno et Regis Institutione*, Strasbourg.

(1594b). *De Institutione Reipublicae* [c.1460], Strasbourg.

Peacham, Henry (1593). *The Garden of Eloquence*, 2nd edn, London.

(1971). *The Garden of Eloquence* [1577], ed. R. C. Alston, Menston.

Perrault, Guillaume (1618). *Summae Virtutum ac Vitiorum*, ed. Rodolph Clutius, Mainz.

[Persons, Robert] (1594). *A Conference about the Next Succession to the Crowne of Ingland*, n.p.

Persuasive to Impartiality and Candour in Judging of the Present Administration, A (1731). London.

Petrarch (1554a). *De Vita Solitaria* in *Opera Quae Extant Omnia*, Basel, pp. 256–331.

(1554b). *De Republica Optime Administranda Liber* [1373] in *Opera Quae Extant Omnia*, Basel, pp. 419–35.

(1975). *Opere Latine*, ed. Antonietta Bufano, 2 vols., Turin.

[Petyt, William] (1680). *The Ancient Right of the Commons of England Asserted*, London.

Pico della Mirandola, Giovanni (1942). *De Hominis Dignitate, Heptaplus, De Ente et Uno, e Scritti Vari*, ed. Eugenio Garin, Florence.

Plato (1929). *Timaeus*, ed. and trans. R. G. Bury, London.

[Ponet, John] (1556). *A Shorte Treatise of Politike Power*, Strasbourg.

Pontano, Giovanni (1952). *De Principe* [1468] in *Prosatori Latini del Quattrocento*, ed. Eugenio Garin, Milan, pp. 1023–63.

(1997). *On the Prince*, trans. Nicholas Webb in *Cambridge Translations of Renaissance Philosophical Texts*, ed. Jill Kraye, 2 vols., Cambridge, vol. 2, pp. 69–87.

Proceedings in Parliament 1610, ed. Elizabeth Read Foster (1966), 2 vols., New Haven, Conn.

Proceedings in Parliament 1614 (House of Commons), ed. Maija Jansson (1988) in *Memoirs of the American Philosophical Society*, vol. 172, Philadelphia, Penn.

Proceedings of the Short Parliament of 1640, ed. Esther S. Cope with Willson H. Coates (1977), The Royal Historical Society, Camden 4th series, vol. 19, London.
Prudentius (1949–53). *Psychomachia* in *Prudentius*, ed. and trans. H. J. Thomson, 2 vols., London, vol. 1, pp. 274–342.
Pseudo-Apuleius (1981). *De Monarchia*, ed. Benjamin G. Kohl and Nancy G. Siraisi in *Mediaevalia* 7, pp. 1–39.
Ptolemy of Lucca (1973). *De Regimine Principum ad Regem Cypri* in St Thomas Aquinas, *Opuscula Philosophica*, ed. R. M. Spiazzi, Turin, pp. 257–358.
Pufendorf, Samuel (1717). *Of the Law of Nature and Nations*, trans. Basil Kennet, 3rd edn, London.
Puttenham, George (1970). *The Arte of English Poesie* [1589], ed. Gladys Willcock and Alice Walker, Cambridge.
Question Answered, A (1642). London.
Quintilian (1920–2). *Institutio Oratoria*, ed. and trans. H. E. Butler, 4 vols., London.
Ravenna, Giovanni di Conversino da (1980). *Dragmalogia de Eligibili Vite Genere* [c.1400], ed. and trans. Helen L. Eaker, introd. Benjamin G. Kohl, Lewisburg, Ky.
Remigio de' Girolami (1959). *De Bono Pacis*, ed. Charles T. Davis in *Studi Danteschi* 36, pp. 123–36.
Rimini, Henry of (1472). *Tractatus de Quatuor Virtutibus Cardinalibus*, Strasbourg.
Rinuccini, Alamanno (1957). *Dialogus de Libertate* [1479], ed. Francesco Adorno in *Atti e Memorie dell' Accademia Toscana di Scienze e Lettere La Colombaria* 22, pp. 265–303.
Riva, Bonvesin de la (1974). *De Magnalibus Mediolani* [1288], trans. Giuseppe Pontiggia, ed. Maria Corti, Milan.
Rome, Giles of (1607). *De Regimine Principum Libri III* [c.1285], ed. H. Samaritani, Rome.
Rotuli Parliamentorum; ut et petitiones, et placita in Parliamento 1278–1503, ed. John Topham et al. (eds.) (1783), vol. 3, London.
Rousseau, Jean-Jacques (1966). *Du contrat social*, ed. Pierre Burgelin. Paris.
Rushworth, John (1691). *Historical Collections. The Third Part; in Two Volumes. Containing the Principal Matters which happened from the Meeting of the Parliament, November the 3d. 1640: to the End of the Year 1644*, London.
Sacchi, Bartolomeo [Platina] (1540). *De Vera Nobilitate* [c.1475] in *De Vitis et Gestis Summorum Pontificum*, Cologne, pt. 2, pp. 41–64.
  (1608). *De Principe Viro* [1471], Frankfurt.
  (1997). *On the Prince* [selections], trans. Nicholas Webb in *Cambridge Translations of Renaissance Philosophical Texts*, ed. Jill Kraye, 2 vols., Cambridge, vol. 2, pp. 89–108.
Salisbury, John of (1909). *Policraticus*, ed. C. C. J. Webb, 2 vols., Oxford.
Sallust (1608). *The Two most worthy and Notable Histories which remaine unmaimed to Posterity: (viz:) The Conspiracie of Cateline, undertaken against the government of the Senate of Rome, and The Warre which Iugurth for many years maintained against the same State*, trans. Thomas Heywood, London.
  (1931a). *Bellum Catilinae* in *Sallust*, ed. and trans. J. C. Rolfe, London, pp. 2–128.

(1931b). *Bellum Iugurthinum* in *Sallust*, ed. and trans. J. C. Rolfe, London, pp. 132–380.
Sardo, Ranieri (1845). *Cronaca Pisana* in *Archivio Storico Italiano* 6, pt. 2, pp. 73–244.
Scala, Bartolomeo (1940). *De Legibus et Iudiciis Dialogus* [1483], ed. Lambertus Borghi in *La Bibliofilia* 42, pp. 256–82.
 (1997). *Dialogue on Laws and Legal Judgements*, ed. David Marsh in *Cambridge Translations of Renaissance Philosophical Texts*, ed. Jill Kraye, 2 vols., Cambridge, vol. 2, pp. 174–99.
Seneca (1917–25). *Epistulae Morales*, ed. and trans. R. M. Gummere, 3 vols., London.
 (1928–35). *Moral Essays*, ed. and trans. John W. Basore, 3 vols., London.
Shadwell, L. L. (ed.) (1912). *Enactments in Parliament Specially Concerning the Universities of Oxford and Cambridge*, 4 vols., Oxford.
Sherry, Richard (1961). *A Treatise of Schemes and Tropes*, ed. H. W. Hildebrandt, Gainesville, Fa.
Sidney, Algernon, (1990). *Discourses Concerning Government*, ed. Thomas G. West, Indianapolis, Ind.
Sidney, Sir Philip (1962). *Astrophil and Stella* in *The Poems of Sir Philip Sidney*, ed. William A. Ringler, Jr., Oxford, pp. 163–237.
 (1973). *The Countess of Pembroke's Arcadia*, ed. Jean Robertson, Oxford.
Signa, Boncompagno da (1892). *Rhetorica Novissima* [1235], ed. Augusto Gaudenzi in *Bibliotheca Iuridica Medii Aevi*, 3 vols., ed. Augusto Gaudenzi, Bologna, vol. 2, pp. 247–97.
Smith, Sir Thomas (1982). *De Republica Anglorum* [1583], ed. Mary Dewar, Cambridge.
Somers, Lord (1681). *The Security of Englishmen's Lives*, London.
South, Robert (1823a). *The Fatal Imposture and Force of Words: set forth in a sermon preached on Isaiah V. 20* in *Sermons Preached upon Several Occasions*, 7 vols., Oxford, vol. 4, pp. 108–38.
 (1823b). *The Second Discourse on Isaiah V.20* in *Sermons Preached upon Several Occasions*, 7 vols., Oxford, vol. 4, pp. 203–88.
Spinoza, Benedict de (1958). *Tractatus Politicus* in *The Political Works*, ed. A. G. Wernham, Oxford, pp. 256–445.
Sprat, Thomas (1959). *History of the Royal Society*, ed. J. I. Cope and H. W. Jones, London.
Starkey, Thomas (1948). *A Dialogue Between Reginald Pole and Thomas Lupset* [c.1530], ed. K. M. Burton, London.
Suárez, Francisco (1975). *De Civili Potestate (III. 1–16)* in *De Legibus* [1612], ed. Luciano Pereña, Madrid.
Swift, Jonathan (1967). *Gulliver's Travels*, ed. P. Dixon and J. Chalker, Harmondsworth.
Tacitus (1591). *The Ende of Nero and Beginning of Galba. Fower Bookes of the Histories Of Cornelius Tacitus. The Life of Agricola*, trans. Henry Savile, Oxford.
 (1598). *The Annales of Cornelius Tacitus. The Description of Germanie*, trans. Richard Grenewey, London.

(1925). *The Histories, Books I–III*, ed. and trans. Clifford H. Moore, London.
(1931). *The Histories, Books IV–V*, ed. and trans. Clifford H. Moore, London.
Tiptoft, John (1938). *The Declamacion of Noblesse* in *John Tiptoft (1427–1470)*, ed. R. J. Mitchell, London, Appendix 1, pp. 213–41.
[Toland, John] (1695). *The Danger of Mercenary Parliaments*, n.p.
(1701). *The Art of Governing by Parties*, London.
Trebizond, George of (1970). *Praefatio in libros Platonis 'De Legibus'* [c.1450] in *Studi in Onore di Antonio Corsano*, ed. Francesco Adorno, Manduria, pp. 13–17.
[Trenchard, John] (1698). *A Short History of Standing Armies in England*, London.
[Trenchard, John and Moyle, Walter] (1697). *An Argument, Shewing, that a Standing Army is inconsistent with a Free Government*, London.
Trenchard, John and Gordon, Thomas (1995). *Cato's Letters*, ed. Ronald Hamowy, 2 vols., Indianapolis, Ind.
[Tyrrell, James] (1692–4). *Bibliotheca Politica*, London.
Valla, Lorenzo (1543). *Elegantiarum Latinae Linguae, libri sex* in *Opera*, Basel, pp. 1–235.
Valle, Guglielmo della (1782–6). *Lettere Senesi*, 3 vols., Rome.
Varro (1938). *De Lingua Latina*, ed. and trans. Roland G. Kent, 2 vols., London.
Vergerio, Pier Paolo (1934). *Epistolario*, ed. Leonardo Smith, Rome.
(1975). *De Republica Veneta* [c.1400], ed. David Robey and John Law in *Rinascimento* 15, pp. 38–49.
(1997). *The Venetian Republic* [selections] trans. Ronald G. Witt in *Cambridge Translations of Renaissance Philosophical Texts*, ed. Jill Kraye, 2 vols., Cambridge, vol. 2, pp. 118–27.
Vespasiano da Bisticci (1970–6). *Le Vite*, ed. Aulo Greco, 2 vols., Florence.
Vettori, Francesco (1842). *Parero* in *Archivio Storico Italiano* 1, pp. 433–6.
Vettori, Paolo (1955). *Ricordi al Cardinale de' Medici Sopra le Cose di Firenze* [1512] in *Das florentinische Staatsbewusstsein im Übergang von der Republik zum Prinzipat*, ed. Rudolf von Albertini, Bern, pp. 345–7.
(1997). *Memorandum to Cardinal de' Medici about the Affairs of Florence*, trans. Russell Price in *Cambridge Translations of Renaissance Philosophical Texts*, ed. Jill Kraye, 2 vols., Cambridge, vol. 2, pp. 239–44.
Vignano, Giovanni da (1974). *Flore de Parlare* [c.1290] in Matteo dei Libri, *Arringhe*, ed. Elenora Vincenti, Milan, pp. 229–325.
Villani, Giovanni (1802–3). *Istorie Fiorentine*, 8 vols., Milan.
Vindication of the Parliament And their Proceedings, The (1642). London.
Vindiciae, Contra Tyrannos (1579). Edinburgh [*recte* Basel].
Vindiciae, Contra Tyrannos (1994). Ed. and trans. George Garnett, Cambridge.
Virgil (1999–2000). *Aeneid*, ed. and trans. H. Rushton Fairclough, revised G. P. Goold, 2 vols., London.
Viterbo, Giovanni da (1901). *Liber de Regimine Civitatum* [c.1250], ed. Caietano Salvemini in *Bibliotheca Iuridica Medii Aevi*, 3 vols., ed. Augusto Gaudenzi, Bologna, vol. 3, pp. 215–80.
Vives, Ludovico (1973). *De Subventione Pauperum*, ed. Armando Saitta, Florence.
Wales, Gerald of (1891). *De Principis Instructione Liber* [c.1217], ed. G. F. Warner, London.

Werdenhagen, Johann (1632). *Introductio Universalis in omnes Respublicas sive Politica Generalis*, Amsterdam.
Whichcote, Benjamin (1698). *Sermon 3* in *Select Sermons of Dr Whichcot*, ed. Anthony, Third Earl of Shaftesbury, London, pp. 79–117.
Wilkins, John (1668). *An Essay Towards a Real Character And a Philosophical Language*, London.
Wilson, Sir Thomas (1554). *The Arte of Rhetorique, for the use of all suche as are studious of Eloquence, sette forth in English*, n.p.
Wotton, Sir Henry (1907). Letter to Sir Edmund Bacon in *The Life and Letters of Sir Henry Wotton*, ed. Logan Pearsall Smith, 2 vols., Oxford, vol. 2, pp. 36–8.
Wyatt, Sir Thomas (1978). *The Complete Poems*, ed. R. A. Rebholz, Harmondsworth.
Xenophon (1545). *Contentio Virtutis et Vitii pro Hercule* in *Catonis Dysticha*, Tübingen, Sig. L, 2v–5r.
[Yonge, Sir William] (1731). *Sedition and Defamation Displayed*, London.

SECONDARY SOURCES

Albertini, Rudolf von (1955). *Das florentinische Staatsbewusstsein im Übergang von der Republik zum Prinzipat*, Bern.
Alessio, Gian Carlo (1979). 'Brunetto Latini e Cicero (e i dettatori)', *Italia Medioevale e Umanistica* 22, pp. 123–69.
Alexander, Jonathan J. G. (1996). 'Dancing in the Streets', *Journal of the Walters Art Gallery* 54, pp. 147–62.
Allen, W. S. (1976). 'The Tone of More's Farewell to Utopia: A Reply to J. H. Hexter', *Moreana* 13, pp. 108–18.
Allison, Lincoln (1981). 'Liberty: A Correct and Authoritarian Account', *Political Studies* 29, pp. 376–91.
Armitage, David (1995). 'John Milton: Poet Against Empire' in *Milton and Republicanism*, ed. David Armitage, Armand Himy and Quentin Skinner, Cambridge, pp. 206–25.
  (1997). Introduction to *Bolingbroke: Political Writings*, ed. David Armitage, Cambridge, pp. vii–xliv.
  (2000). *The Ideological Origins of the British Empire*, Cambridge.
Artifoni, Enrico (1986). 'I Podestà Professionali e la Fondazione Retorica della Politica Comunale', *Quaderni Storici* 63, pp. 687–719.
  (1994a). 'Sull' Eloquenza Politica del Duecento Italiano' in *Federico II e le Città Italiane*, Palermo, pp. 144–60.
  (1994b). 'Retorica e Organizzazione del Linguaggio Politico nel Duecento Italiano' in *Le Forme della Propaganda Politica nel Due e nel Trecento*, ed. Paolo Cammarosano, Rome, pp. 157–82.
  (1997). 'Sapientia Salomonis: une forme de présentation du savoir rhétorique chez les *dictatores* italiens' in *La parole du prédicateur*, ed. Rosa Maria Dessì and Michel Lauwers, Nice, pp. 291–310.

Ashworth, E. J. (1981).'"Do Words Signify Ideas or Things?" The Scholastic Sources of Locke's Theory of Language', *Journal of the History of Philosophy* 19, pp. 299–326.
Ayers, Michael (1991). *Locke*, vol. 1: *Epistemology*, London.
Bailyn, Bernard (1967). *The Ideological Origins of the American Revolution*, Cambridge, Mass.
  (1968). *The Origins of American Politics*, New York.
Baker-Smith, Dominic (1991). *More's Utopia*, London.
Baldwin, Geoffrey (1998). The Self and the State, 1580–1651, PhD thesis, University of Cambridge.
Baldwin, Thomas (1984). 'MacCallum and the Two Concepts of Freedom', *Ratio* 26, pp. 125–42.
Baron, Hans (1937). 'Religion and Politics in the German Imperial Cities during the Reformation', *English Historical Review* 52, pp. 405–27, 614–33.
  (1939). 'Calvinist Republicanism and its Historical Roots', *Church History* 8, pp. 30–42.
  (1961). 'Machiavelli: The Republican Citizen and Author of *The Prince*', *English Historical Review* 76, pp. 217–53.
  (1966). *The Crisis of the Early Italian Renaissance*, 2nd edn, Princeton, N.J.
  (1968). *From Petrarch to Leonardo Bruni*, Chicago, Ill.
Basdevant-Gaudemet, Brigitte (1977). *Aux origines de l'état moderne: Charles Loyseau, 1564–1627, théoricien de la puissance publique*, Paris.
Battista, Anna Maria (1966). *Alle Origini del Pensiero Politico Libertino*, Milan.
Baxandall, Michael (1985). 'Art, Society and the Bouguer Principle', *Representations* 12, pp. 32–43.
Bellosi, Luciano (1974). *Buffalmacco e il Trionfo della Morte*, Turin.
Belting, Hans (1985). 'The New Role of Narrative in Public Painting of the Trecento: *Historia* and Allegory', *Studies in the History of Art* 16, pp. 151–68.
Benn, Stanley I. and Weinstein, W. L. (1971). 'Being Free to Act, and Being a Free Man', *Mind* 80, pp. 194–211.
Bentley, J. H. (1987). *Politics and Culture in Renaissance Naples*, Princeton, N.J.
Berges, Wilhelm (1938). *Die Fürstenspiegel des hohen und späten Mittelalters*, Leipzig.
Berlin, Isaiah (1969). *Four Essays on Liberty*, Oxford.
Berns, Thomas (2000). *Violence de la loi à la Renaissance: L'Originaire du politique chez Machiavel et Montaigne*, Paris.
Bertoni, Giulio (1947). *Il Duecento*, 3rd edn, Milan.
Bevington, D. M. (1961). 'The Dialogue in *Utopia*: Two Sides to the Question', *Studies in Philology* 58, pp. 496–509.
Billanovich, G. (1981). *La Tradizione del Testo di Livio e le Origini dell' Umanesimo*, Padua.
Bindseil, H. E. (1850). Introduction to Philipp Melanchthon, *In Officia Ciceronis Prolegomena* in *Corpus Reformatorum*, vol. 16, ed. H. E. Bindseil, Halle, pp. 529–34.
Black, Anthony (1984). *Guilds and Civil Society in European Political Thought from the Twelfth Century to the Present*, London.
  (1992). *Political Thought in Europe, 1250–1450*, Cambridge.

Bloomfield, Morton (1952). *The Seven Deadly Sins*, Ann Arbor, Mich.
Blythe, James M. (1992). *Ideal Government and the Mixed Constitution in the Middle Ages*, Princeton, N.J.
  (2000). ' "Civic Humanism" and Medieval Political Thought' in *Renaissance Civic Humanism*, ed. James Hankins, Cambridge, pp. 30–74.
Borrelli, Gianfranco (1993). *Ragion di Stato e Leviatano*, Bologna.
Borsook, Eve (1980). *The Mural Painters of Tuscany. From Cimabue to Andrea del Sarto*, 2nd edn, Oxford.
Bouwsma, William J. (1968). *Venice and the Defense of Republican Liberty*, Berkeley, Calif.
Bowsky, William M. (1981). *A Medieval Italian Commune: Siena under the Nine, 1287–1355*, London.
Bradshaw, Brendan (1981). 'More on *Utopia*', *Historical Journal* 24, pp. 1–27.
Brandi, Cesare (1955). 'Chiarimenti sul "Buon Governo" di Ambrogio Lorenzetti', *Bollettino d'Arte* 40, pp. 119–23.
Brecht, Martin (1990). *Martin Luther: Shaping and Defining the Reformation 1521–32*, trans. James L. Schaaf, Minneapolis, Minn.
Brett, Annabel S. (1997). *Liberty, Right and Nature: Individual Rights in Later Scholastic Thought*, Cambridge.
Bridgeman, Jane (1991). 'Ambrogio Lorenzetti's Dancing "Maidens": A Case of Mistaken Identity', *Apollo* 133, pp. 245–51.
Brooke, John (1956). *The Chatham Administration, 1766–1768*, London.
  (1961). 'Party in the Eighteenth Century', in *Silver Renaissance: Essays in Eighteenth-Century English History*, ed. Alex Natan, London, pp. 20–37.
  (1963–4). 'Namier and Namierism', *History and Theory* 3, pp. 331–47.
Brown, Alison (1979). *Bartolomeo Scala 1430–1479, Chancellor of Florence*, Princeton, N.J.
  (1994) Introduction to Francesco Guicciardini, *Dialogue on the Government of Florence*, Cambridge, pp. vii–xxviii.
  (2000). 'De-Masking Renaissance Republicanism' in *Renaissance Civic Humanism*, ed. James Hankins, Cambridge, pp. 179–99.
Brunschvicg, Léon (1944). *Descartes et Pascal, lecteurs de Montaigne*, Paris.
Burckhardt, Jacob (1990). *The Civilisation of the Renaissance in Italy*, trans. S. G. C. Middlemore, ed. Peter Burke and Peter Murray, London.
Burgess, Glenn (1992). *The Politics of the Ancient Constitution: An Introduction to English Political Thought, 1603–1642*, London.
  (1996). *Absolute Monarchy and the Stuart Constitution*, London.
Burke, Peter (1974). *Tradition and Innovation in Renaissance Italy: A Sociological Approach*, London.
Burns, J. H. (1951). 'The Political Ideas of George Buchanan', *Scottish Historical Review* 30, pp. 60–8.
  (1954). 'New Light on John Major', *Innes Review* 5, pp. 83–100.
  (1962). 'Bolingbroke and the Concept of Constitutional Government', *Political Studies* 10, pp. 264–76.
  (1981). '*Politia Regalis et Optima*: The Political Ideas of John Mair', *History of Political Thought* 2, pp. 31–61.

(1983). '*Jus Gladii* and *Jurisdictio*: Jacques Almain and John Locke', *Historical Journal* 26, pp. 369–74.
(1994). 'Jacques Almain on *Dominium*: A Neglected Text' in *Politics, Ideology and Law in Early Modern Europe: Essays in Honor of J. H. M. Salmon*, Rochester, N.Y., pp. 149–58.
(1996). *The True Law of Kingship: Concepts of Monarchy in Early-Modern Scotland*, Oxford.
Burns, J. H. and Izbicki, Thomas M. (1997). Introduction to *Conciliarism and Papalism*, ed. J. H. Burns and Thomas M. Izbicki, Cambridge, pp. vii–xxiii.
Burtt, Shelley (1992). *Virtue Transformed: Political Argument in England, 1688–1740*, Cambridge.
Butterfield, Herbert (1957). *George III and the Historians*, London.
Butters, H. C. (1985). *Governors and Government in Early Sixteenth-Century Florence, 1502–1519*, Oxford.
Cadoni, Giorgio (1962). 'Libertà, Repubblica e Governo Misto in Machiavelli', *Rivista Internazionale di Filosofia del Diritto* 39, pp. 462–84.
Calasso, Francesco (1957). *I Glossatori e la Teoria della Sovranità: Studi di Diritto Comune Pubblico*, 3rd edn, Milan.
Canning, J. P. (1980). 'The Corporation in the Political Thought of the Italian Jurists of the Thirteenth and Fourteenth Century', *History of Political Thought* 1, pp. 9–32.
(1983). 'Ideas of the State in Thirteenth- and Fourteenth-Century Commentators on the Roman Law', *Transactions of the Royal Historical Society* 33, pp. 1–27.
(1987). *The Political Thought of Baldus de Ubaldis*, Cambridge.
Caprariis, Vittorio de (1959). *Propaganda e Pensiero Politico in Francia Durante le Guerre di Religione, 1559–1572*, Naples.
Carli, Enzo (1950). *Le Tavolette di Biccherna*, Florence.
(1983). *Sienese Painting*, New York.
Carlyle, R. W. and Carlyle, A. J. (1936). *A History of Medieval Political Theory in the West*, vol. 6: *Political Theory from 1300 to 1600*, London.
Carmody, Francis J. (1948). Introduction to Brunetto Latini, *Li Livres dou trésor*, Berkeley, Calif., pp. xiii–lxii.
Carney, Frederick S. (1965). Translator's Introduction to *The Politics of Johannes Althusius*, London, pp. xiii–xxxvii.
Cassirer, Ernst (1946). *The Myth of the State*, New Haven, Conn.
Castellani, Arrigo (1955). 'Le Formule Volgari di Guido Faba', *Studi di Filologia Italiana* 13, pp. 5–78.
Catto, Jeremy (1976). 'Ideas and Experience in the Political Thought of Aquinas', *Past and Present* 71, pp. 3–21.
Cavalcaselle, G.-B. and Crowe, J.-A. (1885). *Storia della Pittura in Italia*, 3 vols., Florence.
Celli, Roberto (1980). 'Pour l'histoire des origines du pouvoir populaire: l'expérience des villes-états italiennes XIe–XIIe siècles', *Publications de l'Institut d'Etudes Médiévales: Université Catholique de Louvain* 3, pp. 1–63.

Chabod, Federico (1962). *L'Idea di nazione*, 2nd edn, Bari.
  (1964). *Scritti su Machiavelli*, Turin.
Chambers, R. W. (1935). *Thomas More*, London.
Chiappelli, Fredi (1952). *Studi sul Linguaggio del Machiavelli*, Florence.
Chittolini, Giorgio (1979). *La Crisi Degli Ordinamenti Comunali Origini dello Stato del Rinascimento*, Bologna.
Church, William Farr (1941). *Constitutional Thought in Sixteenth-Century France*, Cambridge, Mass.
  (1972). *Richelieu and Reason of State*, Princeton, N.J.
Clark, J. C. D. (2000). 'Protestantism, Nationalism, and National Identity, 1660–1832', *The Historical Journal* 43, pp. 249–76.
Coleman, Janet (1997). 'The Theory and Practice of Monarchies and Republics in Relation to Personal and Collective Liberty' in *The Propagation of Power in the Medieval West*, ed. Martin Gosman, Arjo Vanderjagt and Jan Veenstra, Gröningen, pp. 207–30.
  (1998). 'Some Relations Between the Study of Aristotle's *Rhetoric*, *Ethics* and *Politics* in Late Thirteenth- and Early Fourteenth-Century University Arts Courses and the Justification of Contemporary Civic Activities (Italy and France)' in *Political Thought and the Realities of Power in the Middle Ages*, ed. Joseph Canning and Otto Gerhard Oexle, Göttingen, pp. 127–57.
  (2000). *A History of Political Thought: From the Middle Ages to the Renaissance*, Oxford.
Colish, Marcia L. (1971). 'The Idea of Liberty in Machiavelli', *Journal of the History of Ideas* 32, pp. 323–50.
  (1978). 'Cicero's *De Officiis* and Machiavelli's *Prince*', *Sixteenth Century Journal* 9, pp. 81–94.
  (1999). 'Republicanism, Religion, and Machiavelli's Savonarolan Moment', *Journal of the History of Ideas* 60, pp. 597–616.
Colley, Linda (1982). *In Defiance of Oligarchy: The Tory Party 1714–60*, Cambridge.
  (1989). 'Radical Patriotism in Eighteenth-Century England' in *Patriotism: The Making and Unmaking of British National Identity*, ed. Raphael Samuel, 3 vols., London, vol. 1, pp. 169–87.
Collot, Claude (1965). *L'Ecole doctrinale de droit publique de Pont-à-Mousson – Pierre Gregoire et Guillaume Barclay*, Paris.
Condren, Conal (1994). *The Language of Politics in Seventeenth-Century England*, London.
Conley, C. H. (1927). *The First English Translations of the Classics*, New Haven, Conn.
Corns, Thomas N. (1995). 'Milton and the Characteristics of a Free Commonwealth' in *Milton and Republicanism*, ed. David Armitage, Armand Himy and Quentin Skinner, Cambridge, pp. 25–42.
Cosenza, Mario Emilio (1962). *Biographical and Bibliographical Dictionary of the Italian Humanists*. Vol. 5: *Synopsis and Bibliography*, Boston, Mass.
Costa, P. (1969). *Iurisdictio. Semantica del potere politico nella pubblicistica medievale 1100–1433*, Milan.

Cox, Virginia (1989). 'Rhetoric and Politics in Tasso's *Nifo*', *Studi Secenteschi* 30, pp. 3–98.
  (1994). Introduction to Baldassare Castiglione, *The Book of the Courtier*, trans. Thomas Hoby, ed. Virginia Cox, London, pp. xvii–xxxi.
  (1999). 'Ciceronian Rhetoric in Italy, 1260–1350', *Rhetorica* 17, pp. 239–88.
Cozzi, Gaetano (1970). 'Domenico Morosini e il *De Bene Instituta Re Publica*', *Studi Veneziani* 12, pp. 405–58.
Crane, W. G. (1965). 'English Rhetorics of the 16th Century' in *The Province of Rhetoric*, ed. Joseph Schwartz and John A. Rycenga, New York, pp. 212–26.
Cranz, F. Edward (1978). 'The Publishing History of the Aristotle Commentaries of Thomas Aquinas', *Traditio* 34, pp. 157–92.
Creveld, Martin van (1999). *The Rise and Decline of the State*, Cambridge.
Cromartie, Alan (1999). 'The Constitutionalist Revolution: The Transformation of Political Culture in Early Stuart England', *Past and Present* 163, pp. 76–120.
Cunningham, Hugh (1989). 'The Language of Patriotism' in *Patriotism: The Making and Unmaking of British National Identity*, ed. Raphael Samuel, 3 vols., London, vol. 1, pp. 57–89.
Curley, Edwin (1978). *Descartes Against the Skeptics*, Oxford.
Cust, Richard (1987). *The Forced Loan and English Politics 1626–1628*, Oxford.
Davis, Charles T. (1984). *Dante's Italy and Other Essays*, Philadelphia, Penn.
Davis, J. C. (1981). *Utopia and the Ideal Society*, Cambridge.
Day, J. P. (1977). 'Threats, Offers, Law, Opinion and Liberty', *American Philosophical Quarterly* 14, pp. 257–72.
  (1983). 'Individual Liberty' in *Of Liberty*, ed. A. Phillips Griffiths, Cambridge, pp. 17–29.
D'Entrèves, A. P. (1967). *The Notion of the State*, Oxford.
De Rosa, Daniela (1980). *Coluccio Salutati: Il Cancelliere e il Pensatore Politico*, Florence.
Delaruelle, Louis (1907). *Guillaume Budé: Les origines, les débuts, les idées maîtresses*, Paris.
DeWald, E. T. (1961). *Italian Painting 1200–1600*, New York.
Dickinson, H. T. (1970). *Bolingbroke*, London.
Diesner, H.-J. (1985). 'Die Virtu der Principe bei Machiavelli', *Zeitschrift für historische Forschung* 12, pp. 385–428.
Dobrée, Bonamy (1949). 'The Theme of Patriotism in the Poetry of the Early Eighteenth Century', *Proceedings of the British Academy* 35, pp. 49–65.
Donato, Maria Monica (1995). 'La "Bellissima Inventiva": Immagini e idee nella Sala della Pace' in *Ambrogio Lorenzetti: Il Buon Governo*, ed. Enrico Castelnuovo, Milan, pp. 23–41.
  (2001). 'Ancora sulle "Fonti" nel *Buon Governo* di Ambrogio Lorenzetti: dubbi, precisazioni, anticipazioni' in *Politica e Cultura nelle Repubbliche Italiane dal Medioevo all'età Moderna*, ed. Simonetta Adorni Braccesi and Mario Ascheri, Rome, pp. 43–79.

Dondaine, Antoine (1948). 'Guillaume Peyraut: vie et oeuvres', *Archivum Fratrum Praedicatorum*, 18, pp. 162–236.
Dowdall, H. C. (1923). 'The Word "State"', *The Law Quarterly Review* 39, pp. 98–123.
Duhamel, P. A. (1955). 'Medievalism of More's *Utopia*', *Studies in Philology* 52, pp. 99–126.
Dunn, John (1969). *The Political Thought of John Locke: An Historical Account of the Argument of the 'Two Treatises of Government'*, Cambridge.
Dyson, Kenneth (1980). *The State Tradition in Western Europe: A Study of an Idea and Institution*, London.
Dzelzainis, Martin (1991). Introduction to John Milton, *Political Writings*, ed. Martin Dzelzainis, Cambridge, pp. ix–xxv.
  (1995). 'Milton's Classical Republicanism' in *Milton and Republicanism*, ed. David Armitage, Armand Himy and Quentin Skinner, Cambridge, pp. 3–24
  (1999). 'Milton's Politics' in *The Cambridge Companion to Milton*, 2nd edn, ed. Dennis Danielson, Cambridge, pp. 70–83.
Eire, Carlos M. N. (1986). *War against the Idols: The Reformation of Worship from Erasmus to Calvin*, Cambridge.
Eliav-Feldon, Miriam (1982). *Realistic Utopias: The Ideal Imaginary Societies of the Renaissance 1516–1630*, Oxford.
Elliott, J. H. (1984). *Richelieu and Olivares*, Cambridge.
Emerton, Ephraim (1925). *Humanism and Tyranny*, Cambridge, Mass.
Eorsi, Anna (1978). 'Donne Danzanti sull' Affresco: Efficacia del buon governo in città di Ambrogio Lorenzetti' in *Acta Historiae Artium Academiae Scientiarum Hungaricae* 24, pp. 85–9.
Ercole, Francesco (1926). *La Politica di Machiavelli*, Rome.
  (1929). *Dal Commune al Principato: saggi sulla storia del diritto pubblico del rinascimento italiano*, Florence.
  (1932). *Da Bartolo all'Althusio*, Florence.
Fasoli, Gina (1958). 'Nascita di un Mito' in *Studi Storici in Onore di Gioacchino Volpe* 1, Florence, pp. 45–79.
Feinberg, Joel (1973). *Social Philosophy*, Englewood Cliffs, N. J.
Feingold, Mordechai (1997). 'The Humanities' in *The History of the University of Oxford*. Vol. 4: *Seventeenth-Century Oxford*, ed. Nicholas Tyacke, Oxford, pp. 211–357.
Feldges-Henning, Uta (1972). 'The Pictorial Programme of the *Sala della Pace*: A New Interpretation', *Journal of the Warburg and Courtauld Institutes* 35, pp. 145–62.
Fell, A. London (1983). *Origins of Legislative Sovereignty and the Legislative State*, vol. 1, Cambridge, Mass.
  (1991). *Origins of Legislative Sovereignty and the Legislative State*. Vol. 4: *Medieval or Renaissance Origins? Historiographical Debates and Deconstructions*, Westport, Conn.

Fenlon, Dermot (1975). 'England and Europe: *Utopia* and its Aftermath', *Transactions of the Royal Historical Society* 25, pp. 115–35.
Fieldhouse, H. N. (1938–9). 'Bolingbroke and the Idea of Non-Party Government', *History* 23, pp. 41–56.
Figgis, J. N. (1960). *Political Thought from Gerson to Grotius, 1414–1625*, New York.
Fink, Zera S. (1962). *The Classical Republicans*, 2nd edn, Evanston, Ill.
Fixler, Michael (1964). *Milton and the Kingdoms of God*, London.
Flanagan, Thomas (1972). 'The Concept of *Fortuna* in Machiavelli' in *The Political Calculus*, ed. Anthony Parel, Toronto, pp. 127–56.
Flathman, Richard E. (1993). *Thomas Hobbes: Skepticism, Individuality, and Chastened Politics*, London.
Flew, Anthony (1983).' "Freedom is Slavery": A Slogan for our New Philosopher Kings' in *Of Liberty*, ed. A. Phillips Griffiths, Cambridge, pp. 45–59.
Flick, A. C. (1930). *The Decline of the Medieval Church*, 2 vols., London.
Folena, Gianfranco (1959).' "Parlamenti" Podestarili di Giovanni da Viterbo', *Lingua Nostra* 20, pp. 97–105.
Foord, Archibald S. (1964). *His Majesty's Opposition, 1714–1830*, Oxford.
Foucault, Michel (1977). *Discipline and Punish: The Birth of the Prison*, trans. Alan Sheridan, London.
Franceschi, Dora (1966). Introduction to *Oculus Pastoralis* in *Memorie dell'accademia delle Scienze di Torino* 11, pp. 19–70.
Franklin, J. H. (1969). *Constitutionalism and Resistance in the Sixteenth Century*, New York.
  (1973). *Jean Bodin and the Rise of Absolutist Theory*, Cambridge.
Frati, Carlo (1913).' "Flore de Parlare" o "Somma d'arengare" attribuita a Ser Giovanni Fiorentino da Vignano', *Giornale Storico della Letteratura Italiana* 61, pp. 1–31, 228–65.
Frojmovič, Eva (1996). 'Giotto's Allegories of Justice and the Commune in the Palazzo della Ragione in Padua: A Reconstruction', *Journal of the Warburg and Courtauld Institutes* 59, pp. 24–47.
Frugoni, Chiara (1983). *Una Lontana Città: Sentimenti e Immagini nel Medioevo*, Turin.
  (1991). *Pietro and Ambrogio Lorenzetti*, trans. Lisa Pelletti, Florence.
Fukuda, Arihiro (1997). *Sovereignty and the Sword: Harrington, Hobbes and Mixed Government in the English Civil Wars*, Oxford.
Ganoczy, Alexandre (1966). *Le Jeune Calvin: Genèse et évolution de sa vocation reformatrice*, Wiesbaden.
Gardner, Julian (1979). 'Andrea di Bonaiuto and the Chapterhouse Frescoes in Santa Maria Novella', *Art History* 2, pp. 107–38.
Garin, Eugenio (1954). *Medioevo e Rinascimento*, Bari.
Garnett, George (1994). Editor's Introduction to *Vindiciae, Contra Tyrannos*, ed. and trans. George Garnett, Cambridge, pp. xix–lxxvi.
Garrett, C. H. (1938). *The Marian Exiles*, Cambridge.
Gaudenzi, Augusto (1895). 'Sulla Cronologia delle Opere Dei Dettatori Bolognesi', *Bullettino dell' Istituto Storico Italiano* 14, pp. 55–174.

Gauthier, R.-A. (1951). *Magnanimité*, Paris.
Geertz, Clifford (1980). *Negara: The Theater State in Nineteenth-Century Bali*, Princeton, N.J.
Gelderen, Martin van (1992). *The Political Thought of the Dutch Revolt, 1555–1590*, Cambridge.
Gerrard, Christine (1994). *The Patriot Opposition to Walpole: Politics, Poetry, and National Myth, 1725–1742*, Oxford.
Geuna, Marco (1998). 'La Tradizione Repubblicana e i Suoi Interpreti: Famiglie Teoriche e Discontinuità Concettuali', *Filosofia Politica* 12, pp. 101–32.
Geuss, Raymond (1981). *The Idea of a Critical Theory: Habermas and the Frankfurt School*, Cambridge.
  (2001). *History and Illusion in Politics*, Cambridge.
Giannardi, Giuliana (1942). 'Le "Dicerie" di Filippo Ceffi', *Studi di Filologia Italiana* 6, pp. 5–63.
Gibbs, Benjamin (1976). *Freedom and Liberation*, Brighton.
Gibbs, Robert (1999). 'In Search of Ambrogio Lorenzetti's *Allegory of Justice*: Changes to the Frescoes in the Palazzo Pubblico', *Apollo* 149, no. 447, pp. 11–16.
Gierke, Otto von (1957). *Natural Law and the Theory of Society 1500 to 1800*, trans. Ernest Barker, Boston, Mass.
Gilbert, Felix (1965). *Machiavelli and Guicciardini: Politics and History in Sixteenth-Century Italy*, Princeton, N.J.
  (1967). 'The Date of the Composition of Contarini's and Giannotti's Books on Venice', *Studies in the Renaissance* 14, pp. 172–84.
  (1977). *History: Choice and Commitment*, Cambridge, Mass.
Gilmore, Myron P. (1941). *Argument from Roman Law in Political Thought, 1200–1600*, Cambridge, Mass.
Godman, Peter (1998). *From Poliziano to Machiavelli: Florentine Humanism in the High Renaissance*, Princeton, N.J.
Goldie, Mark (1980). 'The Roots of True Whiggism 1688–94', *History of Political Thought* 1, pp. 195–236.
Grabmann, Martin (1916). *Forschungen über die Lateinischen Aristoteles Übersetzungen des XIII Jahrhunderts*, Münster.
  (1946). 'Guglielmo di Moerbeke O. P., il traduttore delle opere di Aristotele', *Miscellanea Historiae Pontificae* 11, pp. 111–13.
Grafton, Anthony (1991). 'Humanism and Political Theory' in *The Cambridge History of Political Thought 1450–1700*, ed. J. H. Burns and Mark Goldie, Cambridge, pp. 9–29.
Grafton, Anthony and Jardine, Lisa (1986). *From Humanism to the Humanities: Education and the Liberal Arts in Fifteenth- and Sixteenth-Century Europe*, London.
Gray, Hanna H. (1963). 'Renaissance Humanism: The Pursuit of Eloquence', *Journal of the History of Ideas* 24, pp. 497–514.
Gray, John (1980). 'On Negative and Positive Liberty', *Political Studies*, 28, pp. 507–26.
Greenblatt, Stephen (1980). *Renaissance Self-Fashioning: From More to Shakespeare*, Chicago, Ill.

(1981). 'Invisible Bullets: Renaissance Authority and its Subversion', *Glyph* 8, pp. 40-61.
Greenstein, Jack M. (1988). 'The Vision of Peace: Meaning and Representation in Ambrogio Lorenzetti's *Sala della Pace* Cityscapes', *Art History* 11, pp. 492-510.
Grendler, P. F. (1969). *Critics of the Italian World, 1530-1560*, Madison, Wis.
Gribble, J. (1969). *Introduction to the Philosophy of Education*, Boston, Mass.
Guarini, Elena Fasano (1990). 'Machiavelli and the Crisis of the Italian Republics' in *Machiavelli and Republicanism*, ed. Gisela Bock, Quentin Skinner and Maurizio Viroli, Cambridge, pp. 17-40.
Guillemain, Bernard (1977). *Machiavel: L'Anthropologie politique*, Geneva.
Guy, John (2000). *Thomas More*, London.
Haitsma Mulier, Eco (1980). *The Myth of Venice and Dutch Republican Thought in the Seventeenth Century*, trans. G. T. Moran, Assen.
Hampsher-Monk, Iain (1992). *A History of Modern Political Thought: Major Political Thinkers from Hobbes to Marx*, Oxford.
Hankins, James (1996). 'Humanism and the Origins of Modern Political Thought' in *The Cambridge Companion to Renaissance Humanism*, ed. Jill Kraye, Cambridge, pp. 118-41.
(2000). 'Rhetoric, History, and Ideology: The Civic Panegyrics of Leonardo Bruni' in *Renaissance Civic Humanism*, ed. James Hankins, Cambridge, pp. 143-78.
Hansen, Mogens Herman (2000). 'The Concepts of City-State and City-State Culture' in *A Comparative Study of Thirty City-State Cultures*, ed. Mogens Herman Hansen, Copenhagen, pp. 11-34.
Hanson, D. W. (1993). 'Science, Prudence, and Folly in Hobbes's Political Theory', *Political Theory* 21, pp. 643-64.
Hanson, Laurence W. (1936). *Government and the Press, 1695-1763*, London.
Harding, Alan (1980). 'Political Liberty in the Middle Ages', *Speculum* 55, pp. 423-43.
(1994). 'The Origins of the Concept of the State', *History of Political Thought* 15, pp. 57-72.
Harman, Alec, Milner, Anthony and Mellers, Wilfrid (1962). *Man and his Music: The Story of Musical Experience in the West*, London.
Harrison, Charles (1995). 'The Arena Chapel: Patronage and Authorship' in *Siena, Florence and Padua: Art, Society and Religion, 1280-1400*, ed. Diana Norman, 2 vols., London, vol. 2, pp. 83-103.
Hart, Jeffrey (1965). *Viscount Bolingbroke, Tory Humanist*, London.
Hertter, Fritz (1910). *Die Podestàliteratur italiens im 12. und 13. Jahrhundert*, Leipzig.
Herzog, Don (1986). 'Some Questions for Republicans', *Political Theory* 14, pp. 473-93.
Hexter, J. H. (1952). *More's 'Utopia': The Biography of an Idea*, New York.
(1965). Introduction to *The Complete Works of St. Thomas More*, vol. 4, ed. Edward Surtz and J. H. Hexter, New Haven, Conn, pp. xv-cxxiv.
(1973). *The Vision of Politics on the Eve of the Reformation: More, Machiavelli, and Seyssel*, New York.

(1979). *On Historians*, London.
Holdsworth, W. S. (1922–72). *A History of English Law*, 17 vols., London.
Hollis, Martin (1979). 'Rational Man and Social Science' in *Rational Action: Studies in Philosophy and Social Science*, ed. Ross Harrison, Cambridge, pp. 1–15.
Holloway, Julia Bolton (1993). *Twice-Told Tales: Brunetto Latini and Dante Alighieri*, New York.
Holmes, Clive (1992). 'Parliament, Liberty, Taxation, and Property' in *Parliament and Liberty from the Reign of Elizabeth to the English Civil War*, ed. J. H. Hexter, Stanford, Calif., pp. 122–54.
Holmes, Geoffrey (1967). *British Politics in the Age of Anne*, London.
Holmes, George (1973). 'The Emergence of an Urban Ideology at Florence', *Transactions of the Royal Historical Society* 23, pp. 111–34.
Holmes, Peter (1982). *Resistance and Compromise: The Political Thought of the Elizabethan Catholics*, Cambridge.
Hudson, Winthrop S. (1942). *John Ponet (1516?–1556): Advocate of Limited Monarchy*, Chicago, Ill.
Hughes, Merritt Y. (1962). Introduction to *Complete Prose Works* [of John Milton], vol. 3, *1648–1649* ed. Merritt Y. Hughes, New Haven, Conn., pp. 190–258.
Hull, Suzanne W. (1982). *Chaste Silent and Obedient: English Books for Women 1475–1640*, San Marino, Calif.
Hyde, J. K. (1965). 'Medieval Descriptions of Cities', *Bulletin of the John Rylands Library* 48, pp. 308–40.
(1966). *Padua in the Age of Dante*, Manchester.
(1972). 'Contemporary Views on Faction and Civil Strife in Thirteenth- and Fourteenth-Century Italy' in *Violence and Civil Disorder in Italian Cities 1200–1500*, ed. Lauro Martines, Berkeley, Calif., pp. 273–307.
Ivison, Duncan (1997). *The Self at Liberty: Political Argument and the Arts of Government*, Ithaca, N.Y.
Jackman, S. W. (1965). *Man of Mercury*, London.
Jacquot, Jean and Jones, Harold Whitmore (1973). Introduction to Thomas Hobbes, *Critique du 'De Mundo' de Thomas White*, Paris, pp. 9–102.
James, Susan (1997). *Passion and Action: The Emotions in Seventeenth-Century Philosophy*, Oxford.
Jedin, Hubert (1957–61). *A History of the Council of Trent*, trans. Ernest Graf, 2 vols., London.
Jones, Philip (1997). *The Italian City-State: From Commune to Signoria*, Oxford.
Kahn, Victoria (1985). *Rhetoric, Prudence and Skepticism in the Renaissance*, Ithaca, N.Y.
Kantorowicz, Ernst H. (1957). *The King's Two Bodies: A Study in Medieval Political Theology*, Princeton, N.J.
Katzenellenbogen, Adolf (1939). *Allegories of the Virtues and Vices in Medieval Art*, trans. A. Crick, London.
Kelly, Joan (1999). 'Did Women Have a Renaissance?' in *Feminism and Renaissance Studies*, ed. Lorna Hutson, Oxford, pp. 21–47.

Kemp, Betty (1966). 'Patriotism, Pledges and the People' in *A Century of Conflict 1850–1950: Essays for A. J. P. Taylor*, ed. Martin Gilbert, London, pp. 35–46.
Kempers, Bram (1989). 'Gesetz und Kunst: Ambrogio Lorenzettis Fresken im Palazzo Pubblico in Siena' in *Malerei und Stadtkultur in der Dantezeit*, ed. Hans Belting and Dieter Blume, Munich, pp. 71–84.
  (1992). *Painting, Power and Patronage: The Rise of the Professional Artist in Renaissance Italy*, trans. Beverley Jackson, London.
Keohane, Nannerl O. (1980). *Philosophy and the State in France: the Renaissance to the Enlightenment*, Princeton, N.J.
Kim, Keechang (2000). *Aliens in Medieval Law: The Origins of Modern Citizenship*, Cambridge.
King, Margaret L. (1980). 'Book-Lined Cells: Women and Humanism in the Early Italian Renaissance' in *Beyond their Sex: Learned Women of the European Past*, ed. Patricia Labalme, New York, pp. 66–90.
Kingdon, R. M. (1967). *Geneva and the Consolidation of the French Protestant Movement, 1564–1572*, Geneva.
  (1991). 'Calvinism and Resistance Theory, 1550–1580' in *The Cambridge History of Political Thought 1450–1700*, ed. J. H. Burns and Mark Goldie, Cambridge, pp. 193–218.
Kishlansky, Mark (1977). 'The Emergence of Adversary Politics in the Long Parliament', *Journal of Modern History* 49, pp. 617–40.
Knowlson, James (1975). *Universal Language Schemes in England and France 1600–1800*, Toronto.
Kohl, Benjamin G. (1980). Introduction to Giovanni di Conversino da Ravenna, *Dragmalogia de Eligibili Vite Genere*, ed. and trans. Helen L. Eaker, Lewisburg, Kentucky, pp. 13–46.
Kossmann, E. H. (1981). 'Popular Sovereignty at the Beginning of the Dutch Ancien Régime', *The Low Countries History Year Book* 14, pp. 1–28.
Kramnick, Isaac (1967). 'Augustan Politics and English Historiography: The Debate on the English Past, 1730–35', *History and Theory* 6, pp. 33–56.
  (1968). *Bolingbroke and his Circle: The Politics of Nostalgia in the Age of Walpole*, Cambridge, Mass.
Kristeller, Paul Oskar (1951). 'Matteo de' Libri, Bolognese Notary of the Thirteenth Century, and his *Artes Dictaminis*', *Miscellanea Giovanni Galbiati*, vol. 2, Milan, pp. 283–320.
  (1961). *Renaissance Thought: The Classic, Scholastic and Humanist Strains*, New York.
  (1962). 'Studies on Renaissance Humanism during the Last Twenty Years', *Studies in the Renaissance* 9, pp. 7–30.
  (1965). *Renaissance Thought II: Papers on Humanism and the Arts*, New York.
  (1979). 'Humanism and Scholasticism in the Italian Renaissance' in *Renaissance Thought and its Sources*, ed. Michael Mooney, New York, pp. 85–105.

(1980). 'Learned Women of Early Modern Italy: Humanists and University Scholars' in *Beyond their Sex: Learned Women of the European Past*, ed. Patricia Labalme, New York, pp. 91-116.

(1985). *Studies in Renaissance Thought and Letters II*, Rome.

(1988). 'Humanism' in *The Cambridge History of Renaissance Philosophy*, gen. ed. Charles Schmitt, Cambridge, pp. 113-37.

Kupperman, Karen Ordahl (1989). 'Definitions of Liberty on the Eve of Civil War: Lord Saye and Sele, Lord Brooke, and the American Puritan Colonies', *The Historical Journal* 32, pp. 17-33.

La Brosse, Olivier de (1965). *Le Pape et le concile*, Paris.

Larner, John (1971). *Culture and Society in Italy, 1290-1420*, London.

Laski, Harold J. (1920). *Political Thought in England: Locke to Bentham*, London.

Leuchovius, Deborah (1982). 'Notes on Ambrogio Lorenzetti's *Allegory of Good Government*', *The Rutgers Art Review* 3, pp. 29-35.

Levack, Brian P. (1973). *The Civil Lawyers in England 1603-1641: A Political Study*, Oxford.

Liaci, M. T. (1970). Introduction to Cristoforo Landino, *De Vera Nobilitate*, ed. M. T. Liaci, Florence.

Lloyd, Howell A. (1981). 'The Political Thought of Charles Loyseau (1564-1610)', *European Studies Review* 11, pp. 53-82.

(1983). *The State, France and the Sixteenth Century*, London.

(1994). Introduction to Charles Loyseau, *A Treatise of Orders and Plain Dignities*, ed. Howell A. Lloyd, Cambridge, pp. xi-xxv.

Logan, George M. (1983). *The Meaning of More's 'Utopia'*, Princeton, N.J.

(1994). 'Interpreting *Utopia*: Ten Recent Studies and the Modern Critical Traditions', *Moreana* 31, pp. 203-58.

Lottin, Odon (1942-60). *Psychologie et morale aux XIIe et XIIIe siècles*, 6 vols., Louvain.

MacCallum, Gerald (1972). 'Negative and Positive Freedom', in *Philosophy, Politics and Society*, 4th series, ed. Peter Laslett, W. G. Runciman and Quentin Skinner, Oxford, pp. 174-93.

Mackay, A. J. G. (1892). Life of the Author in John Mair, *A History of Greater Britain*, ed. and trans. Archibald Constable, Edinburgh, pp. xxix-cxv.

Mackie, J. L. (1976). *Problems from Locke*, Oxford.

Maffei, R. de (1964). 'Il Problema della "Ragion di Stato" nei suoi primi affioramenti', *Rivista Internazionale di Filosofia del Diritto* 41, pp. 712-32.

Malcolm, Noel (1997). Introduction to *The Origins of English Nonsense*, London, pp. 3-124.

(2000). 'Charles Cotton, Translator of Hobbes's *De Cive*', *Huntington Library Quarterly* 61, pp. 259-87.

Mansfield, Harvey (1965). *Statesmanship and Party Government: A Study of Burke and Bolingbroke*, Chicago, Ill.

(1996). 'Machiavelli's *Stato* and the Impersonal Modern State' in *Machiavelli's Virtue*, Chicago, Ill., pp. 281-94.

Maravall, José Antonio (1961). 'The Origins of the Modern State', *Journal of World History* 6, pp. 789-808.

Marchesi, Concetto (1904). *L'Etica Nicomachea nella Tradizione Latina Medievale*, Messina.
Mason, H. A. (1986). *Sir Thomas Wyatt: A Literary Portrait*, Bristol.
Matthiessen, F. O. (1931). *Translation, An Elizabethan Art*, London.
Mayer, Thomas F. (1985). 'Faction and Ideology: Thomas Starkey's *Dialogue*', *Historical Journal* 28, pp. 1–25.
 (1989). *Thomas Starkey and the Commonweal: Humanist Politics and Religion in the Reign of Henry VIII*, Cambridge.
McCloskey, H. J. (1965). 'A Critique of the Ideals of Liberty', *Mind* 74, pp. 483–508.
McConica, J. K. (1965). *English Humanists and Reformation Politics*, Oxford.
McFarlane, I. D. (1981). *Buchanan*, London.
Meinecke, Friedrich (1957). *Machiavellism*, trans. Douglas Scott, London.
Mendle, Michael (1985). *Dangerous Positions: Mixed Government, the Estates of the Realm, and the Making of the Answer to the XIX Propositions*, Alabama.
 (1993). 'Parliamentary Sovereignty: A Very English Absolutism' in *Political Discourse in Early Modern Britain*, ed. Nicholas Phillipson and Quentin Skinner, Cambridge, pp. 97–119.
 (1995). *Henry Parker and the English Civil War: The Political Thought of the Public's "Privado"*, Cambridge.
Mermel, Jerry (1977). 'Preparations for a Politic Life: Sir Thomas More's Entry into the King's Service', *Journal of Medieval and Renaissance Studies* 7, pp. 53–66.
Mesnard, Pierre (1969). *L'Essor de la philosophie politique au XVIe siècle*, 3rd edn, Paris.
Michaud-Quantin, Pierre (1970). *Universitas: Expressions du mouvement communautaire dans le moyen-âge latin*, Paris.
Michel, Suzanne (1932). *La Notion thomiste du bien commun*, Paris.
Miller, E. A. (1946). 'Some Arguments used by the English Pamphleteers, 1697–1700, Concerning a Standing Army', *Journal of Modern History* 18, pp. 306–13.
Milner, Stephen J. (2000). 'Citing the *Ringhiera*: The Politics of Place and Public Address in *Trecento* Florence', *Italian Studies* 55, pp. 53–82.
Minio-Paluello, Lorenzo (1956). 'Remigio Girolami's *De Bono Communi*', *Italian Studies* 11, pp. 56–71.
Missner, Marshall (1983). 'Skepticism and Hobbes's Political Philosophy', *Journal of the History of Ideas* 44, pp. 407–27.
Mitchell, R. J. (1938). *John Tiptoft (1427–1470)*, London.
Mochi Onory, Sergio (1951). *Fonti canonistiche dell' idea moderna dello Stato*, Milan.
Moir, Thomas L. (1958). *The Addled Parliament of 1614*, Oxford.
Monaci, Ernesto (1905). 'Sulle formole volgari dell' *Ars notaria* di Raniero di Perugia', *Rendiconti della Reale Accademia dei Lincei* 14, pp. 268–81.
Monfasani, John (1976). *George of Trebizond: A Biography and a Study of his Rhetoric and Logic*, Leiden.
 (1990). 'Lorenzo Valla and Rudolph Agricola', *Journal of the History of Philosophy* 28, pp. 181–200.

Morrall, J. B. (1960). *Gerson and the Great Schism*, Manchester.
Mosse, George L. (1950). *The Struggle for Sovereignty in England*, East Lancing, Mich.
Murphy, J. J. (1974). *Rhetoric in the Middle Ages*, Berkeley, Calif.
Nagel, Thomas (1970). *The Possibility of Altruism*, Oxford.
Najemy, John (1993). *Between Friends: Discourses of Power and Desire in the Machiavelli–Vettori Letters of 1513–1515*, Princeton, N.J.
  (1994a). 'Brunetto Latini's "Politica"', *Dante Studies* 112, pp. 33–51.
  (1994b). 'Stato, Comune e "Universitas"', *Annali dell'Istituto Storico Italo-germanico in Trento* 20, pp. 245–63.
Namier, L. B. (1930). *England in the Age of the American Revolution*, London.
  (1955). *Personalities and Powers*, London.
  (1957). *The Structure of Politics at the Accession of George III*, 2nd edn, London.
Nederman, Cary J. (1985). 'Quentin Skinner's State: Historical Method and Traditions of Discourse', *Canadian Journal of Political Science* 18, pp. 339–52.
  (1990). Introduction to John of Salisbury, *Policraticus*, ed. and trans. Cary J. Nederman, Cambridge, pp. xv–xxvi.
  (1991). 'Aristotelianism and the Origins of "Political Science" in the Twelfth Century', *Journal of the History of Ideas* 52, pp. 179–94.
  (1992). 'The Union of Wisdom and Eloquence Before the Renaissance: The Ciceronian Orator in Medieval Thought', *Journal of Medieval History* 18, pp. 75–95.
  (1995). 'Nature, Sin and the Origins of Society: The Ciceronian Tradition in Medieval Political Thought', *Journal of the History of Ideas* 49, pp. 3–26.
Newell, W. R. (1987). 'How Original is Machiavelli? A Consideration of Skinner's Interpretation of Virtue and Fortune', *Political Theory* 15, pp. 612–34.
Norbrook, David (1999). *Writing the English Republic: Poetry, Rhetoric and Politics 1627–1660*, Cambridge.
Norman, Diana (1995). '"Love justice, you who judge the earth": The Paintings of the Sala dei Nove in the Palazzo Pubblico, Siena' in *Siena, Florence and Padua: Art, Society and Religion, 1280–1400*, ed. Diana Norman, 2 vols., London, vol. 2, pp. 145–67.
Nozick, Robert (1974). *Anarchy, State and Utopia*, New York.
O'Connor, Daniel J. (1964). Preface to *A Critical History of Western Philosophy*, London, p. ix.
Oakley, Francis (1962). 'On the Road from Constance to 1688: the Political Thought of John Major and George Buchanan', *Journal of British Studies* 1, pp. 1–31.
  (1964). *The Political Thought of Pierre d'Ailly: The Voluntarist Tradition*, New Haven, Conn.
  (1965). 'Almain and Major: Conciliar Theory on the Eve of the Reformation', *American Historical Review* 70, pp. 673–90.
  (1984). *Natural Law, Conciliarism and Consent in the Later Middle Ages*, London.
Oertel, Robert (1968). *Early Italian Painting to 1400*, trans. Lily Cooper, London.

Oppel, John W. (1974). 'Peace vs. Liberty in the Quattrocento: Poggio, Guarino, and the Scipio-Caesar Controversy', *Journal of Medieval and Renaissance Studies* 4, pp. 221–65.
Oppenheim, Felix (1981). *Political Concepts: A Reconstruction*, Oxford.
Ornaghi, Lorenzo (1995). 'Per Una Teoria Politica dello Stato. Prime Notazioni e Chiarimenti', *Quaderni di Scienza Politica* 2, pp. 335–69.
Pächt, Otto (1950). 'Early Italian Nature Studies and the Early Calendar Landscape', *Journal of the Warburg and Courtauld Institutes* 13, pp. 13–47.
Pampaloni, Guido (1961). 'Fermenti di Riforme Democratiche nella Firenze Medicea del Quattrocento', *Archivio Storico Italiano* 119, pp. 11–62.
  (1962). 'Nuovi Tentativi di Riforme alla Costituzione Fiorentina Visti Attraverso le Consulte', *Archivio Storico Italiano* 120, pp. 521–81.
Panofsky, Erwin (1970). *Meaning in the Visual Arts*, Harmondsworth.
Parent, William A. (1974a). 'Some Recent Work on the Concept of Liberty', *American Philosophical Quarterly* 11, pp. 149–67.
  (1974b). 'Freedom as the Non-Restriction of Options', *Mind* 83, pp. 432–4.
Parrish, John M. (1997). 'A New Source for More's *Utopia*', *Historical Journal* 40, pp. 493–8.
Pearsall, Derek and Salter, Elizabeth (1973). *Landscapes and Seasons of the Medieval World*, London.
Peck, Linda Levy (1993). 'Kingship, Counsel and Law in Early Stuart Britain' in *The Varieties of British Political Thought, 1500–1800*, ed. J. G. A. Pocock, Gordon J. Schochet and Lois G. Schwoerer, Cambridge, pp. 80–115.
Peltonen, Markku (1995). *Classical Humanism and Republicanism in English Political Thought 1570–1640*, Cambridge.
Pettit, Philip (1999). *Republicanism: A Theory of Freedom and Government*, 2nd edn, Oxford.
Pfeiffenberger, Selma (1966). The Iconology of Giotto's Virtues and Vices at Padua, PhD thesis, Bryn Mawr College.
Pini, Virgilio (1956). 'La *Summa de Vitiis et Virtutibus* di Guido Faba', *Quadrivium* 1, pp. 41–152.
Plumb, J. H. (1956). *Sir Robert Walpole*, vol. 1: *The Making of a Statesman*, London.
  (1960). *Sir Robert Walpole*, vol 2: *The King's Minister*, London.
  (1967). *The Growth of Political Stability in England, 1675–1725*, London.
Pocock, J. G. A. (1971). *Politics, Language, and Time: Essays on Political Thought and History*, New York.
  (1975). *The Machiavellian Moment: Florentine Political Thought and the Atlantic Republican Tradition*, Princeton, N.J.
  (1977). Editorial Introduction to *The Political Works of James Harrington*, ed. J. G. A. Pocock, Cambridge, pp. xi–xviii.
  (1985). *Virtue, Commerce, and History: Essays on Political Thought and History, Chiefly in the Eighteenth Century*, Cambridge.
  (1987). *The Ancient Constitution and the Feudal Law: A Reissue with a Retrospect*, Cambridge.

Popkin, Richard H. (1979). *The History of Scepticism from Erasmus to Spinoza*, rev. edn, Berkeley, Calif.
　(1988). *The Sceptical Mode in Modern Philosophy*, ed. R. A. Watson and J. E. Force, Dordrecht.
Poppi, Antonino (1988). 'Fate, Fortune, Providence and Human Freedom' in *The Cambridge History of Renaissance Philosophy*, gen. ed. Charles Schmitt, Cambridge, pp. 641–67.
Post, Gaines (1964). *Studies in Medieval Legal Thought: Public Law and the State, 1100–1322*, Princeton, N.J.
Prezzolini, Giuseppe (1968). *Machiavelli*, London.
Price, Russell (1973). 'The Senses of *Virtù* in Machiavelli', *European Studies Review* 3, pp. 315–45.
　(1977). 'The Theme of *Gloria* in Machiavelli', *Renaissance Quarterly* 30, pp. 588–631.
　(1982). '*Ambizione* in Machiavelli's Thought', *History of Political Thought* 3, pp. 383–445.
　(1988). 'Self-Love, "Egoism" and *Ambizione* in Machiavelli's Thought', *History of Political Thought* 9, pp. 237–61.
Pye, Christopher (1984). 'The Sovereign, the Theater, and the Kingdome of Darknesse: Hobbes and the Spectacle of Power', *Representations* 8, pp. 84–106.
Raab, Felix (1964). *The English Face of Machiavelli: A Changing Interpretation 1500–1700*, London.
Rabb, Theodore K. (1998). *Jacobean Gentleman: Sir Edwin Sandys, 1561–1629*, Princeton, N.J.
Rawls, John (1971). *A Theory of Justice*, Cambridge, Mass.
Raz, Joseph (1970). 'On Lawful Governments', *Ethics* 8, pp. 296–305.
Renaudet, Augustin (1922). *Le Concile gallican de Pise-Milan: Documents Florentines (1510–1512)*, Paris.
　(1953). *Préréforme et humanisme à Paris pendant les premières guerres d'Italie (1494–1517)*, 2nd edn, Paris.
　(1956). *Machiavel*, 6th edn, Paris.
Ricciardi, Roberto (1968). 'Angelo Poliziano, Giuniano Maio, Antonio Calcillo', *Rinascimento* 8, pp. 277–309.
Ridley, Jasper (1968). *John Knox*, Oxford.
Robbins, Caroline (1958).' "Discordant Parties": A Study of the Acceptance of Party by Englishmen', *Political Science Quarterly* 73, pp. 505–29.
　(1959). *The Eighteenth-Century Commonwealthman*, Cambridge, Mass.
Robertson, G. C. (1947). *Bolingbroke*, The Historical Association, London.
Robertson, John (1997). Introduction to *Andrew Fletcher: Political Works*, ed. John Robertson, Cambridge, pp. ix–xlix.
Robey, David (1973). 'P. P. Vergerio the Elder: Republicanism and Civic Values in the Work of an Early Humanist', *Past and Present* 48, pp. 3–37.
Robey, David and Law, John (1975). 'The Venetian Myth and the *De Republica Veneta* of Pier Paolo Vergerio', *Rinascimento* 15, pp. 3–59.

Robinson, Duncan (1986). 'Fourteenth-Century Siena: The Iconography of a Medieval Commune' in *Civitas: Religious Interpretations of the City*, ed. Peter S. Hawkins, Atlanta, Ga., pp. 85–96.
Rowen, Herbert H. (1961)."'L'état, c'est à moi." Louis XIV and the State', *French Historical Studies* 2, pp. 83–98.
Rowley, George (1958). *Ambrogio Lorenzetti*, 2 vols., Princeton, N.J.
Rubinstein, Nicolai (1952). 'Florence and the Despots: Some Aspects of Florentine Diplomacy in the Fourteenth Century', *Transactions of the Royal Historical Society*, 5th series, 2, pp. 21–45.
  (1957). 'Some Ideas on Municipal Progress and Decline in the Italy of the Communes' in *Fritz Saxl, 1890–1948: A Volume of Memorial Essays*, ed. D. J. Gordon, London, pp. 165–83.
  (1958). 'Political Ideas in Sienese Art: The Frescoes by Ambrogio Lorenzetti and Taddeo di Bartolo in the Palazzo Pubblico', *Journal of the Warburg and Courtauld Institutes* 21, pp. 179–207.
  (1965). 'Marsilius of Padua and Italian Political Thought of his Time' in *Europe in the Late Middle Ages*, ed. J. R. Hale, J. R. L. Highfield and Beryl Smalley, London, pp. 44–75.
  (1971). 'Notes on the Word *stato* in Florence before Machiavelli' in *Florilegium Historiale: Essays Presented to W. K. Ferguson*, ed. J. G. Rowe and W. H. Stockdale, Toronto, pp. 313–26.
  (1982). 'Political Theories in the Renaissance' in *The Renaissance: Essays in Interpretation*, ed. André Chastel, London, pp. 153–200.
  (1985). 'The *De Optimo Cive* and the *De Principe* by Bartolomeo Platina' in *Tradizione Classica e Letteratura Umanistica: Per Alessandro Perosa*, 1, Rome, pp. 375–89.
  (1997). 'Le Allegorie di Ambrogio Lorenzetti nella Sala della Pace e il pensiero politico del suo tempo', *Rivista Storica Italiana* 109, pp. 781–802.
Runciman, David (1997). *Pluralism and the Personality of the State*, Cambridge.
Russell, Conrad (1979). *Parliaments and English Politics 1621–1629*, Oxford.
Ryan, Cheyney C. (1980). 'The Normative Concept of Coercion', *Mind* 89, pp. 481–98.
Ryan, Magnus (2000). 'Bartolus of Sassoferrato and Free Cities', *Transactions of the Royal Historical Society*, 6th series, 10, pp. 65–89.
Salmon, J. H. M. (1959). *The French Religious Wars in English Political Thought*, Oxford.
  (1973). 'Bodin and the Monarchomachs' in *Jean Bodin: Verhandlungen der internationalen Bodin Tagung in München*, ed. Horst Denzer, Munich, pp. 359–78.
  (1991). 'Catholic Resistance Theory, Ultramontanism, and the Royalist Response, 1580–1620' in *The Cambridge History of Political Thought 1450–1700*, ed. J. H. Burns and Mark Goldie, Cambridge, pp. 219–53.
Sanders, Julie (1998). *Ben Jonson's Theatrical Republics*, London.
Sanderson, John (1989). *'But the People's Creatures': The Philosophical Basis of the English Civil War*, Manchester.

Sapegno, Maria Serena (1984). 'Il Trattato Politico e Utopico' in *Letteratura Italiana*, vol. 3, 2: *Le forme del testo: la prosa*, ed. Alberto A. Rosa, Turin, pp. 949–1010.
Sarasohn, L. T. (1985). 'Motion and Morality: Pierre Gassendi, Thomas Hobbes and the Mechanical World-View', *Journal of the History of Ideas* 46, pp. 363–79.
Sasso, Gennaro (1958). *Niccolò Machiavelli: Storia del suo Pensiero Politico*, Naples.
Savino, E. (1941). *Un Curioso Poligrafo del Quattrocento*, Bari.
Schneewind, J. B. (1993). 'Classical Republicanism and the History of Ethics', *Utilitas* 5, pp. 185–207.
Schwoerer, Lois G. (1974). *No Standing Armies!: The Antiarmy Ideology in Seventeenth Century England*, Baltimore, Md.
Scott, Jonathan (1991). *Algernon Sidney and the Restoration Crisis, 1677–1683*, Cambridge.
Scruton, Roger (1981). *From Descartes to Wittgenstein: A Short History of Modern Philosophy*, London.
Seigel, Jerrold E. (1966).' "Civic Humanism" or Ciceronian Rhetoric? The Culture of Petrarch and Bruni', *Past and Present* 34, pp. 3–48.
 (1968). *Rhetoric and Philosophy in Renaissance Humanism*, Princeton, N.J.
Sellers, M. N. S. (1994). *American Republicanism: Roman Ideology in the United States Constitution*, New York.
 (1998). *The Sacred Fire of Liberty: Republicanism, Liberalism and the Law*, New York.
Senellart, Michel (1995). 'Républicanisme, *Eudaimonia* et liberté individuelle: le modèle machiavélien selon Quentin Skinner' in *Aristotelica et Lulliana*, ed. Fernando Domínguez, Ruedi Imbach, Theodor Pindl and Peter Walter, *Instrumenta Patristica* 26, The Hague, pp. 259–87.
Shapiro, Barbara J. (1969). *John Wilkins 1614–1672: An Intellectual Biography*, Berkeley, Calif.
Shaw, Prue (1996). Introduction to Dante, *Monarchy*, ed. Prue Shaw, Cambridge, pp. ix–xxxiv.
Shennan, J. H. (1974). *The Origins of the Modern European State, 1450–1725*, London.
Silvano, Giovanni (1985). '*Vivere Civile*' e '*Governo Misto*' *a Firenze nel Primo Cinquecento*, Bologna.
Simon, Jocelyn (1968). 'Dr Cowell', *Cambridge Law Journal* 26, pp. 260–72.
Siraisi, Nancy G. (1973). *Arts and Sciences at Padua*, Toronto.
Sirluck, Ernest (1959). Introduction to *Complete Prose Works* [of John Milton], vol. 2, *1643–1648*, ed. Ernest Sirluck, New Haven, Conn., pp. 1–216.
 (1964). 'Milton's Political Thought: The First Cycle', *Modern Philology* 61, pp. 209–24.
Skinner, Quentin (1967). 'More's *Utopia*', *Past and Present* 38, pp. 153–68.
 (1978a). *The Foundations of Modern Political Thought*, vol. 1: *The Renaissance*, Cambridge.
 (1978b). *The Foundations of Modern Political Thought*, vol. 2: *The Age of Reformation*, Cambridge.

(1980). 'The Origins of the Calvinist Theory of Revolution' in *After the Reformation: Essays in Honor of J. H. Hexter*, ed. Barbara C. Malament, Philadelphia, Penn., pp. 309–30.

(1981). *Machiavelli*, Oxford.

(1996). *Reason and Rhetoric in the Philosophy of Hobbes*, Cambridge.

(1998). *Liberty before Liberalism*, Cambridge.

Slaughter, M. M. (1982). *Universal Languages and Scientific Taxonomy in the Seventeenth Century*, Cambridge.

Smalley, Beryl (1971). 'Sallust in the Middle Ages' in *Classical Influences on European Culture AD 500–1500*, ed. R. R. Bolgar, Cambridge, pp. 165–75.

Smart, Alastair (1978). *The Dawn of Italian Painting, 1250–1400*, Oxford.

Smith, Alan G. R. (1973). 'Constitutional Ideas and Parliamentary Developments in England 1603–1625' in *The Reign of James VI and I*, ed. Alan G. R. Smith, London, pp. 160–76.

Smith, David L. (1994). *Constitutional Royalism and the Search for Settlement, c.1640–1649*, Cambridge.

(1999). *The Stuart Parliaments 1603–1689*, London.

Smith, Logan Pearsall (1907). *The Life and Letters of Sir Henry Wotton*, 2 vols., Oxford.

Sommerville, Johann (1996a). 'English and European Political Ideas in the Early Seventeenth Century: Revisionism and the Case of Absolutism', *Journal of British Studies* 35, pp. 168–94.

(1996b). 'The Ancient Constitution Reassessed: The Common Law, the Court and the Languages of Politics in Early Modern England' in *The Stuart Court and Europe: Essays in Politics and Political Culture*, ed. R. Malcolm Smuts, Cambridge, pp. 39–64.

(1999). *Royalists and Patriots: Politics and Ideology in England 1603–1640*, London.

Sommerville, Margaret (1995). *Sex and Subjection: Attitudes to Women in Early-Modern Society*, London.

Sorbelli, Albano (1944). 'I teorici del reggimento comunale', *Bullettino dell'Istituto Storico Italiano per il Medio Evo* 59, pp. 31–136.

Sorell, Tom (1993). 'Hobbes Without Doubt', *History of Philosophy Quarterly* 10, pp. 121–35.

Southard, Edna C. (1978). The Frescoes in Siena's Palazzo Pubblico, 1289–1539, PhD thesis, University of Indiana.

Spitz, Jean-Fabien (1995). *La Liberté politique: Essai de généalogie conceptuelle*, Paris.

Starn, Randolph and Partridge, Loren (1992). *Arts of Power: Three Halls of State in Italy, 1300–1600*, Berkeley, Calif.

Steiner, Hillel (1974–5). 'Individual Liberty', *Proceedings of the Aristotelian Society* 75, pp. 33–50.

Stillman, Robert E. (1995). *The New Philosophy and Universal Languages in Seventeenth-Century England: Bacon, Hobbes, and Wilkins*, Lewisburg, Ky.

Strayer, J. R. (1970). *On the Medieval Origins of the Modern State*, Princeton, N.J.

Surtz, Edward (1965a). Introduction to *The Complete Works of St. Thomas More*, vol. 4, ed. Edward Surtz and J. H. Hexter, New Haven, Conn., pp. cxxv–cxciv.
  (1965b). Commentary in *The Complete Works of St. Thomas More*, vol. 4, ed. Edward Surtz and J. H. Hexter, New Haven, Conn., pp. 257–570.
Sutherland, Lucy (1956). 'The City of London in Eighteenth-Century Politics', in *Essays Presented to Sir Lewis Namier*, ed. Richard Pares and A. J. P. Taylor, London, pp. 49–74.
Sylvester, R. S. (1968). 'Si Hythlodaeo Credimus: Vision and Revision in Thomas More's *Utopia*', *Soundings* 51, pp. 272–89.
Talamo, Roberta (1997). 'Quentin Skinner interprete di Machiavelli', *CroceVia* 3, pp. 80–101.
Tarr, Roger P. (1990). 'A Note on the Light in Ambrogio Lorenzetti's *Peaceful City* Fresco', *Art History* 13, pp. 388–95.
Taylor, A. J. P. (1952). *Rumours of War*, London.
Taylor, Charles (1979). 'What's Wrong with Negative Liberty' in *The Idea of Freedom*, ed. Alan Ryan, Oxford, pp. 175–93.
Thomas, Keith (1959). 'The Double Standard', *Journal of the History of Ideas* 20, pp. 195–216.
Tierney, Brian (1955). *Foundations of the Conciliar Theory*, Cambridge.
  (1982). *Religion, Law and the Growth of Constitutional Thought, 1150–1650*, Cambridge.
  (1997). *The Idea of Natural Rights: Studies on Natural Rights, Natural Law and Church Law 1150–1625*, Atlanta, Ga.
Todd, Margo (1987). *Christian Humanism and the Puritan Social Order*, Cambridge.
Trevor-Roper, H. R. (1966). 'George Buchanan and the Ancient Scottish Constitution', *English Historical Review* (Supp. 3), London.
Trinkaus, Charles (1970). *In Our Image and Likeness: Humanity and Divinity in Italian Humanist Thought*, 2 vols., London.
Tuck, Richard (1989). *Hobbes*, Oxford.
Tully, James (1980). *A Discourse on Property: John Locke and his Adversaries*, Cambridge.
  (1993). *An Approach to Political Philosophy: Locke in Contexts*, Cambridge.
Tuve, Rosemond (1963). 'Notes on the Virtues and Vices', *Journal of the Warburg and Courtauld Institutes* 26, pp. 264–303.
  (1966). *Allegorical Imagery*, Princeton, N.J.
Ullman, B. L. (1973). *Studies in the Italian Renaissance*, 2nd edn, Rome.
Ullmann, Walter (1968–9). 'Juristic Obstacles to the Emergence of the Concept of the State in the Middle Ages', *Annali di Storia del Diritto* 12–13, pp. 43–64.
  (1975). *Medieval Political Thought*, Harmondsworth.
  (1977). *Medieval Foundations of Renaissance Humanism*, London.
Underdown, David (1996). *A Freeborn People: Politics and the Nation in Seventeenth-Century England*, Oxford.
Valeri, Nino (1942). *La Libertà e la Pace: Orientamenti Politici del Rinascimento Italiano*, Turin.

Varese, Claudio (1961). *Storia e Politica nella Prosa del Quattrocento*, Turin.
Vatter, Miguel E. (2000). *Between Form and Event: Machiavelli's Theory of Political Freedom*, Dordrecht.
Ventura, Iolanda (1997). 'L'Iconografia Letteraria di Brunetto Latini', *Studi Medievali* 38, pp. 499–528.
Vickers, Brian (1981). 'Rhetorical and Anti-Rhetorical Tropes: On Writing the History of *Elocutio*', *Comparative Criticism* 3, pp. 105–32.
Viroli, Maurizio (1992). *From Politics to Reason of State: The Acquisition and Transformation of the Language of Politics 1250–1600*, Cambridge.
Voigt, Alfred (1965). *Über die Politica generalis des J. A. v. Werdenhagen*, Amsterdam.
Wahl, J. A. (1977). 'Baldus de Ubaldis and the Foundations of the Nation-State', *Manuscripta* 21, pp. 80–96.
Walcott, Robert (1964).' "Sir Lewis Namier Considered" Considered', *The Journal of British Studies* 3, pp. 85–108.
Waley, Daniel (1988). *The Italian City-Republics*, 3rd edn, London.
   (1991). 'Ambrogio Lorenzetti's Dancing "Maidens" ', *Apollo* 134, pp. 141–2.
Walzer, Michael (1965). *The Revolution of the Saints: A Study in the Origins of Radical Politics*, Cambridge, Mass.
Warrender, Howard (1983). Editor's Introduction to Thomas Hobbes, *De Cive: The English Version*, ed. Howard Warrender, Oxford, pp. 1–18.
Webster, Charles (1975). *The Great Instauration: Science, Medicine and Reform 1626–1660*, London.
Wenzel, Siegfried (1967). *The Sin of Sloth: Acedia in Medieval Thought and Literature*, Chapel Hill, N.C.
West, Thomas G. (1990). Foreword to Algernon Sidney, *Discourses Concerning Government*, ed. Thomas G. West, Indianapolis, Ind., pp. xv–xxxvi.
Western, J. R. (1965). *The English Militia in the Eighteenth Century*, London.
Weston, Corinne Comstock (1965). *English Constitutional Theory and the House of Lords 1556–1832*, London.
Whigham, Frank (1984). *Ambition and Privilege: The Social Tropes of Elizabethan Courtesy Theory*, Berkeley, Calif.
White, John (1966). *Art and Architecture in Italy 1250 to 1400*, Harmondsworth.
   (1967). *The Birth and Rebirth of Pictorial Space*, 2nd edn, London.
White, Jonathan (2000). *Italy: The Enduring Culture*, London.
White, Lynn Jr. (1969). 'The Iconography of *Temperantia* and the Virtuousness of Technology' in *Action and Conviction in Early Modern Europe*, ed. T. K. Rabb and J. E. Seigel, Princeton, N.J., pp. 197–219.
Wieruszowski, Helene (1971). *Politics and Culture in Medieval Spain and Italy*, Rome.
Wilkins, E. H. (1959). *Petrarch's Later Years*, Cambridge, Mass.
Willcock, Gladys and Walker, Alice (1970). Introduction to George Puttenham, *The Arte of English Poesie*, Cambridge, pp. ix–cii.
Williams, John R. (1957). 'The Quest for the Author of the *Moralium Dogma Philosophorum*, 1931–56', *Speculum* 32, pp. 736–47.
Wirszubski, Ch. (1950). *Libertas as a Political Idea at Rome during the Late Republic and Early Principate*, Cambridge.

Witt, Ronald G. (1970). 'Cino Rinuccini's *Risponsiva alla invettiva di Messer Antonio Lusco*', *Renaissance Quarterly* 23, pp. 133-49.
 (1971). 'The Rebirth of the Concept of Republican Liberty in Italy' in *Renaissance Studies in Honor of Hans Baron*, ed. Anthony Molho and John A. Tedeschi, Florence, pp. 173-99.
 (1982). 'Medieval *Ars dictaminis* and the Beginnings of Humanism: A New Construction of the Problem', *Renaissance Quarterly* 35, pp. 1-35.
 (1996). 'The *Crisis* after Forty Years', *American Historical Review* 101, pp. 110-18.
Wootton, David (1998). 'Friendship Portrayed: A New Account of *Utopia*', *History Workshop Journal* 45, pp. 29-47.
Worden, Blair (1996). *The Sound of Virtue: Philip Sidney's Arcadia and Elizabethan Politics*, London.
Yates, Frances (1969). *The Art of Memory*, London.
Zaccaria, Vittorio (1956). 'Sulle Opere di Pier Candido Decembrio', *Rinascimento* 7, pp. 13-74.
Zdekauer, Lodovico (1913). 'Iustitia: Immagine e Idea', *Bullettino Senese di Storia Patria* 20, pp. 384-425.

Index

Acciaiuoli, Donato, 134
Agathocles of Sicily, 143, 147
Alamanni, Lodovico, 143
Alamanni, Luigi, 276
Alberti, Leon Battista, 126, 134
Alciato, Andrea, 94n.
Alemannus, Hermannus, 42
Allen, W. S., 214
Almain, Jacques, 8, 256, 257–62
Althusius, Johannes, 388, 389, 391–2, 394
Ambrose, St, 61
Amsdorf, Nicholas von, 252–3
Amsterdam, 392
Answer to the Nineteen Propositions, 333–4, 336
Appius Claudius, 166, 168, 291, 318
Aquinas, St Thomas, 39, 40, 54, 61n., 65, 68–9, 108, 123
  De Regno, 30, 31, 32–4, 122
  Expositio [of Aristotle's *Politics*], 372, 375
  see also *Summa Theologiae*
Arezzo, 2, 4, 10, 81, 119
argumentum in utramque partem, 266, 267
Aristotle, 63, 134, 227, 322, 375, 395
  Art of Rhetoric, 273–5, 277–8
  Nicomachean Ethics, 42, 52, 66, 72–5, 91, 140
  Politics, 12, 30, 32–3, 36, 57, 91, 133, 214–15, 226, 315, 336, 337
Armada, Spanish, 389
armies
  citizen, 129, 144, 154, 201–2, 206, 359–61
  mercenary and standing, 346–7, 359–61, 363
Armitage, David, 303n., 344n.
Arnall, William, 354
Artifoni, Enrico, 10n., 18n.
Athens, 149
Augustine, St, 12, 48
Augustus, Roman emperor, 377
Austin, John, 406

Averroes, 52, 66
Azo, Portius, 38, 380
  Lectura, 15–16
  Quaestiones, 14
  Summa, 13–14, 16–17

Bacon, Edmund, 281
Bacon, Francis, 291
Baldus de Ubaldis, 380, 390
Baldwin, Tom., 190n., 191n.
Ball, William, 295
Barbeyrac, Jean, 407
Barclay, William, 387, 396, 397, 398
Baron, Hans, 12, 13n., 91, 92, 118n., 149n., 381n.
Bartolus of Sassoferrato, 17, 133, 380, 390, 391, 394
Bassanius, Johannes, 14
Bate, John, 310
Bellum Catilinae (Sallust)
  glory and greatness, 20, 26, 27, 110, 130, 150, 306
  justice, 26, 110
  liberty, 27, 130, 150, 163, 289–90, 306, 316
  monarchy and self-government, 27, 130, 289–90, 303, 304
Belting, Hans, 94n., 95n., 97n.
Benn, Stanley I., 187
Bentham, Jeremy, 187
Berkeley, George, 348n.
Berlin, Isaiah, 184, 187, 188–9, 190, 192
Beroaldo, Filippo, 372, 375
Beza, Theodore, 246
Bible (and Apocrypha)
  Book of Wisdom, 51, 72, 73
  Corinthians, 61, 108
  Galatians, 109n.
  Isaiah, 95n.
  John, 108n.
  Luke, 95n.
  Matthew, 111

Bible (and Apocrypha) (*cont.*)
  Philippians, 108n.
  Proverbs, 107
  Psalms, 111n.
  Revelations, 101n.
  Romans, 83n., 109n., 111n.
  Timothy, 83n.
Blackstone, William, 409
Blackwood, Adam, 396, 398n., 400
Boccalini, Traiano, 159
Bodin, Jean, 325, 395–6, 397, 398–9, 400–1
Bolingbroke, Henry St John, Viscount, 8, 344, 345–8, 349–55, 362–4, 412
Bologna, 4, 10
  University of, 11, 13, 17
Bologna, Hugh of, 18
Bolton, Edmund, 314, 317
Bonaiuto, Andrea di, 105
Bossuet, Jacques-Bénigne, 370
Botero, Giovanni, 158
Boucher, Jean, 389
Bourges, 396
Bracciolini, Poggio, 4, 140, 148
  De Nobilitate, 132, 133–4, 224, 225, 226, 227, 228–9
  Historiae, 23
  In Laudem . . . Venetorum, 138–9
Bracton, Henry de, 309
Bradshaw, Brendan, 214, 240n., 241n., 244n.
Braga, Martin of, 43, 51, 61n., 62, 63–4, 65–6, 83
Bramhall, John, 282
Brandi, Cesare, 89
Brescia, Albertano da, 94n., 101, 107, 108
Brett, Annabel, 253n., 256n.
Bridgeman, Jane, 103n., 104, 105, 106n.
Bromley, William, M. P., 345, 347
Brooke, John, 349, 350
Brucioli, Antonio, 148
Bruni, Leonardo, 4, 140, 149, 152, 155–6
  Dialogus, 2
  Laudatio, 20, 128–32, 134–5, 138
  Oratio, 134
Buchanan, George, 246, 253, 257, 262, 397
  De Iure Regni, 247–9, 396, 400
Budé, Guillaume, 377
Burckhardt, Jacob, 13, 378
Burgess, Glenn, 287n.
Burke, Edmund, 344, 351
Burke, Peter, 6n.
Burns, J. H., 253n., 256n., 259n., 351n.
Bus, Gervaise de, 276
Butterfield, Herbert, 351

Caesar, Julius, 27, 152, 160, 166, 167, 175, 314
Calvin, Jean, 257

Calvinism, and theory of revolution, 245, 246–7, 249–50, 253, 262–3
Campano, Giovanni, 372
Canute, king of England, 370
Capua, Thomas of, 18
Carafa, Diomede, 135, 136
Carrara, Francesco da, 120, 122, 123
Cary, Lucius, Viscount Falkland, 333
Cassian, Johannes, 107, 109, 112
Castiglione, Baldassare, 136, 377
Catholic Church, criticism of, 37, 380, 382
Ceffi, Filippo, 19, 22, 29–30, 42, 45, 119n., 371
Cerata, Laura, 126
Charles I, king of Great Britain and Ireland, 292, 293, 297, 304, 324
  execution of, 8, 286, 290, 301, 356
  on Militia Ordinance, 325, 326–7, 328
  Milton on, 303–5
  and Negative Voice, 294, 325, 332–4
  and Petition of Right, 281, 322
Charles II, king of Great Britain and Ireland, 305, 306
Charles IV, Holy Roman Emperor, 89
Charles V, Holy Roman Emperor, 252
Charron, Pierre, 265
Chesterfield, Philip Stanhope, Earl of, 348
Cicero, 2, 6–7, 18, 55, 56, 70, 71, 111, 131, 134, 147, 203, 221, 229, 231, 300, 320, 322, 326, 370, 371, 379, 395
  De Finibus, 48, 215n.
  De Inventione, 42, 51, 56, 62, 64, 86, 207, 247–8, 267–8, 274–5
  De Legibus, 316, 335
  De Oratore, 267, 268–9, 269–70
  De Partitione Oratoria, 269, 275
  De Republica, 48, 51, 54–5
  Philippics, 314–15, 327
  Somnium Scipionis, 63
  Tusculanae Disputationes, 63, 123, 215n.
  see also *De Officiis*
citizenship, 6–7, 9, 399, 410–11
  virtues and 131–3, 134, 140, 154–7, 224–5, 227–9, 231–2, 234, 242, 361–2
city-republics, Italian
  decline of, 5, 22–3, 118–19, 157–9
  humanists and, 126–34, 148–57, 196
  jurists and, 13–17
  pre-humanists and, 17–30, 41–56, 57–67, 109–11
  rise of, 4–5, 10–11, 39
  scholastics and, 30–8, 57
  see also Florence; Padua; Siena; Venice
civil war in England, outbreak of (1642), 288, 292–3, 294, 296, 297, 308–9, 323, 342–3
Coke, Edward, 287, 288, 309, 311–12, 319
Coleman, Janet, 10n., 374n.

Colish, Marcia, 197n., 199n., 211n.
Colley, Linda, 345n., 348n.
common good
   Machiavelli on, 151, 155, 163–4, 168–9, 174, 178, 208, 381
   pre-humanists on, 25–6, 47–8, 56, 61, 72, 99, 372, 379–80, 382
   representations of, 40–1, 76–7, 80, 81–2
   scholastics on, 34, 372
Compagni, Dino, 119
Conches, Guillaume de, 43n.
concord, civic, 22, 23–5, 31–2, 45–6, 48–50, 56
   representations of, 70–1, 95
   see also discord, civic; peace
consent, and origins of political associations, 15, 79, 257–8, 298, 389–90
Considerations for the Commons, 340
Constantinople, 336
Contarini, Gasparo, 128, 158, 381, 383, 385–6, 413
corruption, 7, 152, 212, 352, 361–2, 363–4, 365, 379
   Machiavelli on, 151, 164–70, 172–7, 180–4, 361
courage, *see* fortitude
courtiers, 135–6, 221–2, 277
Cox, Virginia, 273n.
Craftsman, The, 345
Creshald, Richard, MP, 291
Culpepper, John, 333
Curley, Edwin, 265n.

D'Ewes, Simonds, MP, 329–30, 333
dancing
   as expression of *gaudium*, 111–14, 115–17
   representations of, 97, 103–4, 105, 106
Dante Alighieri
   Convivio, 114, 133
   De Monarchia, 119–20
   Inferno, 88
   Purgatorio, 101n., 118–19
Davis, Charles T., 13n.
De Officiis (Cicero) 42, 43, 313
   common good, 46–7, 68, 155
   concord, 24–5, 48–9
   equity, 49
   justice, 26, 124–5, 207–8
   magistrates, 60–1, 316
   monarchy, 315
   otium and *negotium*, 219–20, 222
   private property, 227–8
   res publica, 27, 28, 218–19, 391
   self-government, 28, 29, 315–16
   virtues, 62–3, 64, 83, 86, 144–5, 204–5, 218–19

Decembrio, Pier Candido, 135
Decembrio, Uberto, 135
Denmark, loss of liberty in, 358–9, 360–1, 362
dependence, *see* slavery
Dering, Edward, MP, 323
Dickinson, H. T., 352, 353
dictatores, 3, 4–5, 18–19, 41, 92
   see also pre-humanists
Digest of Roman Law, 13
   equity, 49
   justice, 52
   law, 369, 370
   Lex regia, 15, 398
   liberty and slavery, 289, 290–1, 296, 310n., 313, 321
   self-defence, 253–4
   see also Justinian, Codex of
Digges, Dudley, the elder, 291, 292, 311
Digges, Dudley, the younger, 397, 400, 401–2
discord, civic, 22, 23–5, 45–6, 119
   representations of, 69–70, 95–6
Discorsi (Machiavelli) 6, 8, 126, 142
   ambition, 164–8, 173, 175, 200–1
   common good, 151, 155, 163–4, 168–9, 174, 178, 208, 381
   corruption, 151, 164–70, 172–7, 180–4, 361
   fortune, 159, 169, 171–2
   free states, 150–2, 153–4, 161–3, 176, 198–9
   glory and greatness, 149–50, 151–3, 170, 174, 180–2
   history, 358–9
   justice, 154–5, 207–8
   law, 173–6, 177–85
   liberty, 7, 150–1, 160–1, 170, 173–6, 177–84, 196–205, 206–10, 211–12, 356, 357–8, 361, 380
   lo stato, 384–5
   mixed constitutions, 153–4, 156–7, 178–80, 203, 357–8
   necessity, 145, 147, 154–5, 173–4
   religion, 157, 172–3, 180–4
   Rome, 150–5, 165, 167–8, 172, 174–5, 179, 202–3, 208
   self-government, 151, 162–3, 198–9, 381
   slavery, 162–3, 200–3
   Venice, 152–3
   virtù 154–6, 163–4, 170, 171, 177–8, 201–5, 207–10, 361
   see also Livy
Donato, Maria Monica, 69n., 93n.
Doni, Francesco, 159
Downing, Calybute, 397, 401
Dzelzainis, Martin, 298n.

Eliot, John, 291–2, 321–2
eloquence
　Hobbes on, 266
　as moving force, 267–9
　see also rhetoric
Elyot, Thomas, 225
Engels, Friedrich, 406
equity, 48, 49–51, 56, 70–1
Erasmus, Desiderius, 170, 222n., 240n.
　Enchiridion, 236
　Institutio, 215n., 217, 225, 228–9, 373

Faba, Guido, 18, 19, 41, 42, 45–6, 60, 72n., 94n., 109
　Epistole, 21
　Summa, 63, 64, 108
Falkland, *see* Cary
Feinberg, Joel, 187, 192
Ferdinand of Aragon, 143
Ferrariis, Antonio de, 135, 140, 224
Ferreti, Ferreto de', 120
Ficino, Marsilio, 140, 216
Fiennes, Nathaniel, 330
Figgis, J. N., 250n.
Fletcher, Andrew, 356, 360–1
Florence, 4, 5–6, 10, 24, 87, 119, 126, 128, 134
　liberty of, 129–30, 148, 381, 383
　Medici and, 137–8, 139–42, 157–8
Florus, 314, 317
Foord, Archibald, 350
Forced Loan (1626), 291, 311, 321, 322
fortitude, 62–3, 64–5, 66, 131–2, 154, 203, 207
　representations of, 86–7, 88, 96
fortune, 136, 147, 159, 169, 171–2
Foucault, Michel, 413n.
Franco, Nicolò, 159
Franklin, Julian, 245–6
Frederick Barbarossa, Holy Roman Emperor, 11, 109
Frederick II, Holy Roman Emperor, 11
free state
　concept of, 6–9, 29–30, 205–6, 287, 289, 301, 315–16, 318, 379–82, 385–7, 395, 412
　England as, 286, 297
　Florence as, 128–30, 381
　Machiavelli on, 150–2, 153–4, 161–3, 176, 198–9
　Milton on, 297–300, 305–6
　Venice as, 127–8, 336–7, 381, 383
freedom, *see* free state; liberty
Froissart, Jean, 369, 370
Frugoni, Chiara, 72–3, 74–5, 83n., 106

Gadamer, Hans-Georg, 195
Garnett, George, 390n.

gaudium, 108, 112–14
　and glory, 110, 111
　and peace, 109–10, 111, 115
　see also dancing
Geertz, Clifford, 370n., 413n.
Genoa, 4, 10
Gerald of Wales, 11–12
Gerrard, Christine, 345n., 348n.
Gerson, Jean, 254–5, 257, 259
Geuss, Raymond, 166n., 405n.
Giannotti, Donato, 148
Gibbs, Benjamin, 189n., 190
Gibbs, Robert, 95n., 96n.
Giotto, 84, 100, 101, 105, 113–14
Girolami, Remigio de', 31
Glanville, John, MP, 288
Glasgow, University of, 257
glory and greatness
　of communities, 5, 7, 118, 127, 133, 139, 171, 201
　liberty as condition of, 27, 130, 150, 289–92, 293–4, 301–7, 358, 381
　light as symbol of, 106–7, 111, 115
　Machiavelli on, 143–4, 149–50, 151–3, 170, 174, 180–2
　of princes, 121–2, 123, 125–6, 136–7, 146
　Sallust on, 20, 23, 26, 27, 110, 130, 150, 306
Goldie, Mark, 356n.
Goodman, Christopher, 246
Gordon, Thomas, 357
Grafton, Anthony, 12n.
Gray, Hanna, 3n.
greatness, civic, *see* glory and greatness
Greenblatt, Stephen, 223n., 276n., 413n.
Greenstein, Jack, 96 and n., 97n., 106
Gregoire, Pierre, 396, 400, 401
Grenewey, Richard, 306, 313, 316, 322
Grimalde, Nicholas, 313, 315
Grosseteste, Robert, 42n., 73, 74
Grosseto, Andrea da, 107, 108 and n.
Guicciardini, Francesco, 92, 158
　Discorsi on Florence, 148, 375, 384
　Ricordi, 159, 376, 377
Gulliver, Lemuel, 284
Guy, John, 214n., 224n.

Haitsma Mulier, Eco, 210
Hall, Joseph, 280
Hampden, John, 323–4
Harding, Alan, 374n., 407n.
Harrington, James, 357, 362
　Aphorisms, 359
　Oceana, 160, 161, 196, 356, 358–9, 361
Hart, Jeffrey, 351, 352
Hayward, John, 397, 401
Hedley, Thomas, MP, 291, 292, 311, 320, 324

Hegel, G. F. W., 406
Helinandus of Froidmont, 11
Henri IV, king of France, 388
Henry IV, Holy Roman Emperor, 11
Herborn, Academy of, 388
Hercules, 123
Hermogenianus (jurist), 369
Hexter, J. H., 213n., 226n., 237
Heywood, John (author of *Gentleness and Nobility*), 225
Heywood, John (translator of Sallust), 289, 290, 314, 316
history, lessons of, 3–4, 120–1, 150, 173, 190, 249, 358–9, 363
Hoadly, Benjamin, 405
Hobbes, Thomas, 9, 160, 161, 188, 189, 266, 271, 274, 318, 406–9
  Behemoth, 319–20
  De Cive, 266, 368, 397, 410–11
  Elements of Law, 265, 285, 395, 397, 399, 402
  see also Leviathan
Holland, John, MP, 323
Holland, Philemon, 313–14, 317
Holles, Denzil, MP, 338
Holles, John, MP, 321
Holloway, Julia, 89n.
Holmes, Geoffrey, 351
Holy Roman Empire, 10–11, 14, 119–20, 379–80, 382
honestas, 217–19, 232, 274
Horace, 2, 132
Hoskins, John, 281–2
Hotham, John, 324
Hotman, François, 246, 373n., 388, 397, 411
Hugolinus (jurist), 17
Huguccio of Pisa, 17
humanism, 2–3, 4–5, 6–8, 9, 12
  and city-republics, 126–34, 148–59, 196, 372
  and princely government, 120–6, 134–42, 143–7, 374–9
Hume, David, 166
Humfrey, Lawrence, 377

Il Principe (Machiavelli) 5, 136
  fortune, 169
  glory and greatness, 143–4
  justice, 154–5
  lo stato, 143, 144, 374–5, 376–7, 378
  virtù, 144–7
imperium, 11, 13–16, 379, 382
Impositions, 290–1, 310–11, 320–1
independence, *see* free state; liberty
Irnerius of Bologna (jurist), 11, 15
Isneria, Andreas de (jurist), 382
Ivison, Duncan, 161n., 312

Jaucourt, Louis de, 408–9
John, king of England, 14
Jones, Philip, 119n.
Jones, William, 311
Jonson, Ben, 282
Julian, Roman emperor, 112
Julius II, pope, 255
just war, 123–4
justice, 25–7, 39–40, 62–4, 82–4, 131, 372
  and avoidance of harm, 124–5, 208
  and clemency, 124–5, 137, 146–7
  commutative, 73–6, 113
  distributive, 73–5, 113
  and lawgivers, 54–5, 71
  and liberality, 124, 137, 146
  Machiavelli on, 154–5, 207–8
  rectificatory, 52–3, 76
  representations of, 78–9, 82, 88, 95–6, 101, 104–5, 113–14
Justinian, Codex of, 2, 11, 38, 289, 370; *see also Digest* of Roman Law
Juvenal, 2, 132, 134

Kant, Immanuel, 166
Kelly, Joan, 1n., 125n.
Kempers, Bram, 97n., 98n., 101n.
Kennet, Basil, 407
Knolles, Richard, 395n., 401
Knox, John, 246, 247, 257
Kramnick, Isaac, 352
Kraye, Jill, 107n.
Kristeller, P. O., 18n., 92n., 225n.

Landino, Cristoforo, 140, 141, 224
Languet, Hubert, 388; *see also Vindiciae, Contra Tyrannos*
Latini, Brunetto, 19, 42; *see also Li Livres dou trésor*
law
  and lawgivers, 54–6, 71, 151, 176, 384
  as source of virtue, 156–7, 173–7, 179–85
  see also justice
League of Cambrai (1510), 255
Leiden, University of, 392
Leuchovius, Deborah, 100n., 101n.
Leviathan (Hobbes)
  liberty, 162, 187–9, 199, 205–6, 308, 312–13
  monarchy, 395, 397
  moral language, 265, 283–5
  persons, 390–1, 399, 402–4
  sovereigns, 284–5, 399–400
  the state, 368, 402–4, 411, 413
Lewkenor, Lewes, 385, 386, 413
Lex regia, 15–16, 398

Li Livres dou trésor (Latini)
  common good, 25, 47–8
  concord and discord, 23–4, 46, 50
  glory and greatness, 110, 111
  justice, 26, 51, 52–3, 55–6, 75–6, 372
  nobility, 132–3
  peace, 22
  self-government, 27–8, 57, 59–60, 67, 102, 382–3
  virtues, 61, 62, 64, 66–7, 84–91
Liber de Regimine Civitatum (Giovanni da Viterbo)
  on the church, 380
  common good, 25, 47
  concord and discord, 23, 25, 45, 46
  gaudium, 112, 115n.
  glory and greatness, 20–1, 26, 110
  justice, 26, 27, 51–2, 64
  peace, 44–5, 110
  self-government, 28, 58, 59–61
  status civitatis, 371, 372
  virtues, 55, 62, 64, 66
liberality, 124, 137, 146, 226, 227
liberties, fundamental, 287–8, 290, 291, 292–3, 309, 322–3
liberty, 7–9, 28–9, 151–4, 257, 259, 379–81
  Harrington on, 160–1, 196, 356, 358–9, 361
  Hobbes on, 161–2, 187–9, 199, 205–6, 308, 312–13
  Machiavelli on, 7, 150–1, 160–1, 170, 173–6, 177–84, 196–205, 206–10, 211–12, 356, 357–8, 361, 380
  as natural, 248, 298, 389–90, 397–8
  necessary for glory and greatness, 27, 130, 150, 289–92, 293–4, 301–7, 358, 381
  as 'negative', 186–8, 189–90, 192, 195–6, 198, 211–12
  Roman law on, 289, 290–1, 296, 310n., 313, 321
  Sallust on, 27, 130, 150, 163, 289–90, 306, 316
  and slavery, 289–97, 299–301, 313–18, 320–2, 324–5, 335–42, 359–62, 364, 389–90
  and virtue, 188–90, 192, 207–10, 210–11, 361–2
  see also liberties, fundamental
Libri, Matteo de', 19, 21, 22, 24, 26, 42, 50, 67, 110, 383
Littleton, Edward, MP, 322
Littleton, Thomas, 309–10, 312
Livy, 2, 130, 218, 291, 321, 322
  History, 289, 313–14, 317–18, 336, 337, 370
  Machiavelli's *Discorsi* on, 6, 142, 149, 168, 202, 204, 205

Locke, John
  Essay, 193, 264–5, 266
  Two Treatises, 251, 253, 319n., 324, 396, 405
Lodge, Thomas, 276
Lodi, 20
Lodi, Orfino da, 19, 41, 42, 43–4, 45, 55, 60, 111
Logan, George M., 214n., 221n., 242n., 243n.
Lombard, Peter, 256, 260
Long Parliament, 288, 293, 302, 323, 324
Lorenzetti, Ambrogio, 5, 39–40, 41, 93
  common good, 40–1, 76–7, 81–2, 99
  concord and discord, 69–71, 76, 95–6, 101–2
  gaudium (and dancing), 103–6, 108–14, 115–16
  glory and greatness, 110–11, 115
  justice, 72–6, 78, 95–6, 101
  and the *Nove*, 81, 94, 116–17
  peace, 68–9, 80, 96–8, 103
  self-government, 77–82, 99–103, 117
  virtues, 80–1, 82–8, 89–91, 93, 376
  tyranny, 69, 94, 102–3
  wisdom, 71–2, 96
Lothair (jurist), 11
Louis XII, king of France, 225–6
Lucca, 10
Ludlow, Edmund, 357, 360
Luther, Martin, 251, 252, 254
Lyly, John, 278

MacCallum, Gerald, 177n., 187
Machiavelli, Bernardo, 141, 142
Machiavelli, Niccolò, 8, 9, 92, 255, 362, 364, 412
  Istorie Fiorentine, 4, 126
  see also Discorsi; Il Principe
Mackie, J. L., 193–4
Macrobius, 61, 63, 64–5
Magdeburg, 252
Magna Carta, 288, 359
magnanimity, 64–7, 84, 96
magnificence, 64, 225, 226–7, 233–4, 240–2, 413
Maio, Giuniano, 135, 136, 137n.
Mair, John, 8, 256, 257–8, 260–1, 262
majesty, 136–7, 370, 412–13
Mamertinus, Claudius, 112
Manetti, Giannozzo, 134
manliness, ideal of, 123, 125–6
  questioned by Machiavelli, 144–5
Mansfield, Harvey, 351–2, 353
Mantua, 5, 118
Marnix, Philip, 246
Marsilius of Padua, 31, 39, 120, 122n., 124, 215n.
  Defensor Pacis, 30, 31, 35–7, 380

Marten, Henry, MP, 319, 329–30
Martini, Simone, 51, 79–80
Marx, Karl, 406
Mary, Queen of Scots, 396
Medici, Catherine de', 388
Medici, Cosimo de', 138, 142, 167, 376, 377
Medici, Lorenzo de', 138, 139, 141, 142
Medwall, Henry, 225
Melanchthon, Philipp, 251–2, 254
Memmi, Lippo, 52
Mendle, Michael, 329n., 330n., 335n.
Michels, Robert, 406
Milan, 4, 10, 20, 29, 111, 119
Militia Ordinance (1642) 294, 325–30, 333
Milton, John, 3, 281, 287, 412–13
   Areopagitica, 301, 302–3
   Commonplace Book, 288–9
   Defensio, 297, 300, 301–2, 304, 305
   Eikonoklastes, 297, 299–301, 303–4, 305
   History of Britain, 370
   Ready and Easy Way, 305–6, 387, 412
   Samson Agonistes, 306–7
   Tenure, 297–9, 300, 301, 303, 387
mixed constitutions, 32, 33–4, 57, 129–30, 329, 332–5, 360, 362–3, 365, 402
   Machiavelli on, 153–4, 156–7, 178–80, 203, 357–8
Modena, 119
Moerbeke, William of, 30, 32, 42
Molesworth, Robert, Viscount, 356–60, 362
monarchomachs, 246, 295, 297–8, 302, 379, 387–90, 391–4, 395–7, 399–400, 410
monarchy
   abolished in Britain, 286, 287, 297
   best form of government, 11–12, 32–3, 57, 94, 102–3, 139–42, 215–17, 245
   criticisms of, 27–8, 33–4, 35–7, 57, 131
   source of slavery, 304–7, 315–16, 319–20, 380–1
Montagnone, Geremia da, 42, 43, 45, 51
Montaigne, Michel de, 265
Montaperti, battle of, 79, 100
Montemagno, Buonaccorso da, 132, 224–5, 227
moral language, ambiguities of, 264–6, 276, 283–5
moral philosophy, study of, 3, 4–9, 42–3
Moralium Dogma Philosophorum, 43, 47, 50, 52, 61–4, 83n., 85–6, 98n.
More, Thomas, 213–14, 215, 217, 220, 222–4, 229, 236–7, 240, 241–4
   see also *Utopia*
Mornay, Philippe du Plessis, 246, 388
   see also *Vindiciae, Contra Tyrannos*

Morosini, Domenico, 128
Morpeth, Henry Howard, Viscount, 345, 346
Moyle, Walter, 356, 357, 360, 361
Mussato, Albertino, 2, 4, 22, 28, 29, 120

Nagel, Thomas, 166n.
Najemy, John, 19n., 143n.
Namier, L. B., 349, 350, 351, 353
Naples, kingdom of, 135, 136, 382
Nashe, Thomas, 276
necessity, 21, 254, 331–2
   Machiavelli on, 145, 147, 154–5, 173–4
Negative Voice, *see* prerogative, royal
Nevile, Christopher, MP, 321
Neville, Henry, 356, 357, 358
nobility
   and virtue, 7, 132–3, 134, 140, 224–5, 227–9, 231–2, 234, 242
   and wealth, 7, 133, 140, 225, 226–7, 228–9, 231, 232–4, 242
Nogarola, Isotta, 126
Norman, Diana, 106n.
North, Roger, MP, 292
Nove Signori (Siena), 58–9, 60, 67, 78, 81, 94, 101n., 116–17, 376
Nozick, Robert, 161

Oakley, Francis, 253n., 256n.
Observations (Henry Parker) 282, 334, 338, 339
   Charles I, 297, 335
   glory and greatness, 293–4
   liberty, 294, 335
   Negative Voice, 335–6
   right of resistance, 296, 297, 337
   salus populi, 335, 393
   slavery, 294, 296, 335, 336–7
   sovereignty of people, 295–6, 342
Ockham, William of, 254, 255, 257, 259
Oculus Pastoralis, 4, 19 and n., 41, 42
   common good, 25, 47, 376
   concord and discord, 22, 45
   glory and greatness, 20, 22, 25, 110, 111
   justice, 51, 72n.
   peace, 43, 110–11
   self-government, 58–9
   status civitatis, 371, 376
   tyranny, 94
Oldradus da Ponte (jurist), 382
Oppenheim, Felix, 187
optimus status reipublicae, 132, 215–20, 224, 371, 372–3
   Thomas More on, 213, 214, 229–30, 235–6, 240–4, 373

otium and *negotium*, 6–7, 97, 121, 131, 140–1, 216–20, 221–4, 228–31, 233
Ovid, 87

Padua, 2, 4, 10, 22, 29, 120
  see also Scrovegni, Cappella degli
Palmieri, Matteo, 134
paradiastole, 273–4; *see also* rhetorical redescription
Parent, William A., 192
Pareto, Vilfredo, 406
Paris, University of, 30, 31, 255–6, 257, 262
Parker, Henry, 298, 299, 301, 302, 303, 397
  Case of Shipmony, 293, 324
  see also Observations
Parliament, sovereignty of, 329–32, 335
Parma, 4, 5, 118
Partridge, Loren, 94n.
Paruta, Paolo, 158
patriotism, 348, 350, 351–2, 354–5, 365, 366
Patrizi, Francesco, 135, 139, 375, 383
Pavia, 20
peace, 5, 118
  humanists on, 127–8, 136–7, 139, 372–3
  pre-humanists on, 22–4, 43–5, 56, 61, 67, 80–1, 109–10, 115
  representations of, 68–9, 95, 96–8
  scholastics on, 31, 32–3, 119–20
Peacham, Henry, 268, 269, 270, 272, 273, 277
Peard, George, MP, 324
Peltonen, Markku, 311n., 312n.
people
  sovereignty of, 14, 16–17, 36–7, 245–6, 247–9, 255–62, 295–6, 298, 380, 386–7, 388–9, 390–4, 395, 405–6
  as *universitas*, 14–15, 16, 36–7, 258, 390, 391–2, 398–9, 410–11
  see also persons
Perrault, Guillaume, 43, 50–1, 52, 62, 63, 64, 83n., 85, 108
persons
  cities as, 100, 103, 403
  peoples as, 389–93, 398, 399–400, 409–10
  states as, 395, 400, 401–4, 408
Persons, Robert, 389, 393, 397, 401
Perugia, Raniero da, 18
Petition of Right (1628), 288, 311, 321, 322
Petrarch, 2, 130–1, 134–5, 216
  De Republica, 120, 122–5
  De Vita Solitaria, 6, 121
Pettit, Philip, 312n.
Petyt, William, 356
Phelips, Robert, 291
Philip Augustus, king of France, 14
Piacenza, 4, 5, 118
Pico della Mirandola, Giovanni, 141

Pisa, 4, 5, 10, 87, 118, 225
Pisano, Andrea, 84
Pisano, Giovanni, 87
Placentinus (jurist), 15
Plato, 140–1, 216, 219, 220–1, 235
  Laws, 127
  Timaeus, 103n.
Pliny, 87
Plumb, J. H., 344, 346
Plutarch, 169
Pocock, J. G. A., 12, 13n., 287n., 344n., 356n., 365n., 381n.
podestà, government by, 4–5, 10, 19, 29, 47, 58, 371
Ponet, John, 246, 385, 386–7, 412
Pont-à-Mousson, 396
Pontano, Giovanni, 135, 136–7
Popkin, Richard, 265n.
popular sovereignty, *see* people, sovereignty of
pre-humanists, on city government, 17–30, 41–56, 57–67, 109–11
  see also common good; peace
prerogative, royal
  as infringement of liberty, 288, 290–2, 292–4, 295–7, 309–12, 318–22
  of Negative Voice, 294, 297, 300–1, 325–6, 332, 334–42
Price, Russell, 200n., 210n.
princely government, theory of, *see* monarchy; *signori*
princes, and their state (*stato*, *status*), 9, 143, 369–72, 373–8, 382–5
  see also signori
principles, political, 344–5, 349, 365–7
  as legitimations, 354–6, 366–7
  as motives, 351–3, 366–7
  as rationalisations, 349–51, 356, 366
property, private, 227–8, 242–4
  abolition of, 235–6, 242, 244
prudence, 62–3, 65, 131, 154, 176, 202, 204–5, 207, 212
  representations of, 82–3, 84–5, 88, 96
Prudentius, 44–5, 95n., 108
Pseudo-Apuleius, 57n., 66n.
Ptolemy of Lucca, 30n., 31, 35, 36, 57
Pufendorf, Samuel, 407–8, 409
Pulteney, William, MP, 345, 346, 347
Puttenham, George, 268, 272, 273, 276–7, 279
Pye, Christopher, 413
Pym, John, MP, 326, 333

Quintilian, 269, 270, 271–2, 273, 275

Rabb, Theodore K., 319n.
Rand, William, 308

Ravenna, 5, 118
Ravenna, Giovanni da, 120, 121, 216, 236n.
Rawls, John, 161, 162, 178–9, 180, 182, 187
Reasons why this Kingdome ought to adhere to the Parliament, 339
religion
  and civic virtue, 156–7, 172–3, 180–4
  in *Utopia*, 237–40
Remonstrance in Defence of the Lords and Commons, 339–40
Renaissance, concept of, 1–2, 6, 9
representation
  of the people, 392
  of the self, 391
  of the state, 403–4, 405, 408, 409–10
republicanism
  in ancient Rome, 22, 27, 130, 260
  in England, 8, 196, 286
  in the Netherlands, 196, 246, 385, 388–9
  in Italy, 4–5, 10–11, 22–3, 118–19, 157–9, 196, 218, 379–85
  see also city-republics; Florence; free states; Venice
resistance, right of, 17, 245, 246–50, 260–2, 341, 342–3
  see also tyranny
rhetoric
  hostility to, 266–7
  study of, 2–3, 18
rhetorical redescription
  Aristotle on, 273
  and denigration of virtue, 275, 277–9, 280–1
  and extenuation of vice, 275, 276–7, 280, 281–2
  as form of amplification, 269–71
  Quintilian on, 271–3
Richard II, king of England, 369
rights, 8, 192, 196, 211–12, 245, 247–9, 258–62, 286–92, 322–5, 342–3
  see also resistance, right of; self-defence, right of
Rimini, 5, 24, 118
Rimini, Henry of, 31, 32, 34–5, 57, 63, 65n., 87n., 127
Rinuccini, Alamanno, 138, 383
Rinuccini, Cino, 134
Riva, Bonvesin della, 20, 29, 70, 111
Robey, David, 119n.
Rogerius (jurist), 15
Roman Law, 2, 3, 11, 13, 14–15, 17, 287–8; *see also Digest* of Roman Law; Justinian, Codex of
Rome, 2, 24, 111, 120
  Machiavelli on, 150–5, 165, 167–8, 172, 174–5, 179, 202–3, 208
  republic of, 22, 27, 130, 260

slavery of, under principate, 289, 304, 306, 316–17, 358, 360
Rome, Giles of, 31, 32, 57, 61n., 63, 94, 108n., 122, 133
Romulus, 151, 155
Rousseau, Jean-Jacques, 174, 188, 210, 412
Roy, Louis le, 315
Rubinstein, Nicolai, 12, 18n., 30n., 81, 99, 375n., 376n.
Rump Parliament, 286, 297

Sacchi, Bartolomeo (Platina), 132, 135, 136n., 137n., 214
Salisbury, John of, 11–12
Sallust, 2, 3, 4, 18, 42, 218, 314, 370, 379
  Bellum Iugurthinum 20, 23, 45, 69, 110
  see also Bellum Catilinae
Salmasius (Claude de Saumaise), 301, 304
salus populi, 295, 296, 316, 326–30, 332–3, 335
Salutati, Coluccio, 3, 29–30
San Gimignano, 52
Sandys, Edwin, MP, 311
Sandys, Samuel, MP, 345, 347
Sardo, Ranieri, 372, 376
Savile, Henry, 290, 306, 313
Savonarola, Girolamo, 142
Scala, Bartolomeo, 141–2, 217n.
scepticism, pyrrhonian, 265–6
Schmalkaldic League, 252
scholasticism, 3, 8, 40–1, 43–4, 57, 91–2
  and city-republics, 30–8, 57, 119–20
  and popular sovereignty, 255–62
  and the virtues, 63, 68–9, 73–4, 82–6
Scrovegni, Cappella degli (Padua), 72, 84, 96n., 100, 104–5, 113
Scudamore, John, MP, 321
Seigel, Jerrold, 3n.
Selden, John, 319
self-defence, right of, 251–2, 253–4, 259
self-government
  humanism and, 126–34, 148–59, 218–20, 223, 224, 382–7
  jurists on, 13–17
  Machiavelli on, 151, 162–3, 198–9, 381
  pre-humanists on, 4–5, 18–20, 27–30, 57–67, 102–3, 379–80, 382–3
  representations of, 77–82, 99–103, 117
  scholasticism and, 30–7, 127
Sellers, M. N. S., 312n.
Seneca, 2, 42, 46, 65, 66, 84, 114, 132, 134, 221, 229, 276, 371
  De Beneficiis, 96n., 109, 215n.
  De Clementia, 47
  Epistulae, 47, 55, 63, 65, 68, 109
  De Tranquillitate Animi, 111–12

servitude, *see* slavery
Severus, Septimius, Roman emperor, 145
Seymour, Francis, MP, 292, 321
Sforza, Caterina, 126
Shaftesbury, Anthony Ashley Cooper, Earl of, 356
Shakespeare, William, 326
Sherfield, Henry, MP, 322
Sherry, Richard, 269, 270, 271–2
Ship Money, 293, 323–4
Shippen, William, MP, 345, 346
Short Parliament (1640), 292, 322, 324
Sidney, Algernon, 356, 358, 360, 361, 362
Sidney, Philip, 277, 278
Siena, 4, 5, 10, 24
  church of San Francesco in, 85
  commune of, 77–80
  constitutions of, 41, 44, 46, 58, 60, 67
  Palazzo Pubblico in, 39, 52, 68, 81, 93, 116, 376
  representations of, 96–8, 100–2
  see also Nove Signori
Signa, Boncompagno da, 18
signori
  rise of, 5, 118, 120–1, 126, 134–5
  and theory of princely government, 120–6, 134–42, 143–7, 374–9
slavery, 7
  as cause of servility, 289–92, 293–4, 301–7
  dependence as, 289, 290–7, 299–301, 314–18, 320–2, 324, 335–41
  of England, 287, 290–2, 292–4, 297, 335–43
  and liberty, 289–97, 299–301, 313–18, 320–2, 324–5, 335–42, 359–62, 364, 389–90
  Machiavelli on, 162–3, 200–3
  of Rome under principate, 289, 304, 306, 316–17, 358, 360
  Roman law on, 289, 290–1, 296, 313, 321
  and villeinage, 309–12
Smalley, Beryl, 18n.
Smith, Thomas, 310
Somers, John, Baron Somers, 356
Sommerville, Johann, 287n., 312n.
Sorell, Tom, 265n.
Soto, Domingo de, 259n.
South, Robert, 282, 283
Southard, Edna, 79n.
sovereignty
  of Parliament, 329–32, 335
  of people, 14, 16–17, 36–7, 245–6, 247–9, 255–62, 295–6, 298, 380, 386–7, 388–9, 390–4, 395, 405–6
  of the state, 368–9, 379, 386, 395, 398–405, 407–10

Spagnoli, Cappella degli (Santa Maria Novella, Florence), 105
Spain, loss of liberty in, 363–4
Spinoza, Benedict (Baruch) de, 188, 196, 210
Spitz, Jean-Fabien, 190n.
Sprat, Thomas, 264, 266
St Andrews, University of, 257
Starkey, Thomas, 217, 218, 220, 236, 373, 377, 385
Starn, Randolph, 94n.
state
  concept of, 9, 164–5, 381–2, 393–4
  as a person, 395, 400, 401–4, 408
  sovereignty of, 368–9, 379, 386, 395, 398–405; 407–10
  state (*stato, status*) of princes, 9, 143, 369–72, 373–8, 382–5
Strangeways, John, MP, 321
studia humanitatis, *see* humanism
Suárez, Francisco, 250, 258, 259
Summa Theologiae (Aquinas) 30, 40
  common good, 77
  equity, 49
  justice, 73, 372
  monarchy, 32–3
  peace, 33, 44
  private property, 227
  virtues, 63, 64–5, 73, 82–3, 84–5, 87
  wealth, 226
  wisdom, 71
Sutherland, Lucy, 350
Swift, Jonathan, 284

Tacitus, 289, 293, 303, 320, 322, 357, 392
  Agricola, 306, 313
  Annals, 304, 306, 313, 316–17
  Germania, 313
  Historiae, 290, 313
Tarlati, Guido, 81
Tarr, Roger, 106
Taylor, Charles, 187–8, 189, 190
temperance, 62–3, 64, 65, 132, 154, 204–5, 207
  representations of, 85–6, 88, 91, 96
Thirnyng, William, 369
Thomas, Keith, 126n.
Tierney, Brian, 253n., 256n., 380n.
Tiptoft, John, Earl of Worcester, 224, 225
Toland, John, 357, 358, 359, 362
Toulouse, 396
translations
  of Aristotle, 30, 42, 52, 73, 274, 315
  of Bodin, 395, 401
  of Italian humanists, 132, 356, 385–6, 413
  of Roman historians, 303, 313–14, 317

of Plato, 127–8
of Pufendorf, 407
treason, 354, 411–12
Trebizond, George of, 127–8
Trenchard, John, 356, 357, 360, 361
Treviso, 118
tristitia, 107–8, 109, 112, 115–16
Tully, James, 161n., 319n.
Tuve, Rosemond, 43n., 65n., 98n.
Twelve Tables, Law of, 316, 326
tyranny, 102–3, 118–19, 257, 286, 299, 303–4, 315–16, 322, 360–1, 395–6
  representations of, 69–70, 94–6, 98
  see also resistance, right of
Tyrrell, James, 356, 359, 360

Ulpian (jurist), 49, 253–4, 370
universitas
  church as, 17
  people as, *see* people as *universitas*
Utopia (Thomas More)
  nobility, 132, 229–34
  optimus status reipublicae, 213–14, 217, 220, 229–30, 235–6, 241, 244
  otium and *negotium*, 221–3, 230–1
  private property, 235–6, 242–4
  self-government, 8
  Utopian religion, 237–40
  virtues, 231–2
  wealth, 231–3, 240

Valla, Lorenzo, 3
Vanni, Andrea, 91
Varro, 86
Venice, 5–6, 119, 134, 255, 260, 310, 321, 336–7
  constitution of, 34–5, 127–8, 138–9, 148–9, 158, 381, 386
  Machiavelli on, 152–3
Vergerio, Pier Paolo, 2, 6, 120, 127, 130, 131, 216
Vergerio, Pietro, 148
Verona, 5, 118
Vespasiano da Bisticci, 375, 376, 377
Vettori, Francesco, 376
Vettori, Paolo, 143
vices, the, 87, 107–9, 123–5, 222, 234–5
  Machiavelli on, 145–7, 152, 168
  as neighbours of virtues, 274–6
  representations of, 69–70, 94–5, 113–4
Vignano, Giovanni da, 19, 21, 27, 42, 50, 67, 112, 114, 119, 383
Villani, Giovanni, 372n., 374, 375
Vindication of the Parliament, 340–1, 342

Vindiciae, Contra Tyrannos, 246–7, 388, 389–94, 397
Virgil, 2, 87, 203
virtù, Machiavelli on, 144–7, 154–6, 163–4, 170, 171, 177–8, 201–5, 207–10, 361; *see also* virtues, the
virtues, the, 7, 61–7, 80–8, 122–6, 130–7, 140, 224–9, 231–2
  cardinal, 61–2, 80–1, 87–8, 115, 131–2, 207, 218
  denigration of, 277–9, 280–1
  law and, 156–7, 173–7, 179–85
  as neighbours of vices, 274–6
  theological, 61, 80–3, 96, 115
  of women, 125–6, 232
  see also fortitude; justice; liberality; magnanimity; nobility; prudence; temperance; *virtù*; *virtus*; wisdom
virtus, 22, 123–6, 128, 130–4, 136–7, 139–40, 144–5
  Cicero on, 62–3, 64, 83, 86, 114–15, 204–5, 218–19
  see also virtues
Viterbo, Giovanni da, 19, 41–2
  see also Liber de Regimine Civitatum
Vives, Ludovico, 240n.

Waley, Daniel, 10n.
Walpole, Robert, 344, 345–7, 350–2, 354, 362
Walzer, Michael, 246, 249, 253, 262
Wandesford, Christopher, MP, 281
Weinstein, W. L., 187
Wentworth, Thomas, MP, 320
Werdenhagen, Johann, 392
Wesembeeke, Jacob van, 246
Whichcote, Benjamin, 282
Whigham, Frank, 273n.
White, John, 106, 107
White, Lynn, 90, 91
Wilkins, John, 264, 266, 274, 284, 285
Wilson, Thomas, 268, 269, 270, 272, 276
wisdom, 54–5, 56, 202, 204, 267–8
  representations of, 71–2, 96, 113
Witt, Ronald G., 29n., 381n.
women, as rulers, 126
  virtues of, 125–6
Worsley, Benjamin, 308
Wotton, Henry, 281–2, 321
Wyatt, Thomas, 275–6, 277, 278–9
Wyndham, William, MP, 345, 346, 347

Xenophon, 123

Yonge, William, 354

Made in the USA
Monee, IL
28 April 2026

49136490R00272